HIGHLIGHTS
OF A
FIGHTING
HISTORY

Editorial Committee

HIGHLIGHTS
OF A
FIGHTING
HISTORY

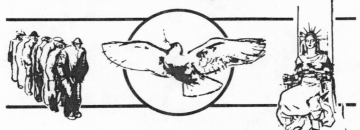

60 YEARS
OF THE
COMMUNIST
PARTY, USA

INTERNATIONAL PUBLISHERS

NEW YORK

Copyright Acknowledgments

The Academic Rebellion in the United States by Bettina Aptheker, Citadel Press, New Jersey, 1972. *The Big Strike* by Mike Quin, Olema Publishing Company, Olema, California, 1949. *Labor's Untold Story* by Richard O. Boyer and Herbert Morais, Banner Press, Illinois, 1955. "Lenin's Impact on the United States," *New World Review*, 1970. *Organize!* by Wyndham Mortimer, Copyright © 1971 by Irma Mortimer Stewart. Reprinted by permission of Beacon Press, Boston. "The SNYC" by Augusta Strong, *Freedomways*, 1st Quarter, 1964, Vol. 4, No. 1.

Library of Congress Cataloging in Publication Data
    Main entry under title:
    Highlights of a fighting history.

        Includes bibliographical references and index.
        1. Communist Party of the United States of America—
    History—Addresses, essays, lectures. 2. Communism—
    United States—1917-   —Addresses, essays, lectures.
    I. Bart, Philip Abraham, 1902-
    JK2391.C5H5   329'.82'009   79-14009
    ISBN 0-7178-0559-X
    ISBN 0-7178-0502-6 pbk.

1.
THE
FIRST
DECADE

2. THE GREAT DEPRESSION

3. CLASS STRUGGLE AND THE NEW DEAL

4. MASS INDUSTRIES ARE ORGANIZED

5. THE GREAT ANTI FASCIST WAR

6. LABOR'S POSTWAR FIGHTBACK

7. THE McCARTHY ERA

8. BLACK LIBERATION SPARKS THE SIXTIES

9.
VIETNAM
AND
THE
PEACE
UPSURGE

xi

10. THE PARTY RECORDS
NEW ADVANCES

ILLUSTRATIONS

Chapter Openings by Hugo Gellert

FOREWORD

The collection of writings that follows is history. However, it is not history that has been corrected, brought up-to-date or written with the aid of hindsight. It is the on-the-spot assessments, judgments and interpretations of events as they were unfolding. It is not history written by people who were watching the unfolding of events from the sidelines. *It is history recorded by people who were themselves makers of history.* It is history written in the heat of battle. This is not a full history of the Communist Party, USA. The articles are interesting and important flashbacks.

This is history at its very best because it is written from an honest partisan viewpoint. It is the working-class partisan viewpoint that gives it an objectivity that is not often found in books or articles on history. Because it is partisan, it comes closest to the truth.

Life is not an abstract balance of good and evil. To have meaning, what is just and what is unjust, what is progressive and what is reactionary, must be judged within the framework of the objective train of history. Because the train of human society has a progressive direction, all forces and events that propel it are just and progressive, and all forces and events that resist and retard its advance are reactionary and unjust. That is the objective truth of capitalism. The exploitation of the working class, from which the corporations extract their profits is—in human terms—evil, unjust and reactionary. And the struggles of the workers and the people against the monopolies and the exploitation are just and progressive. That is a basic, objective truth of our times.

To say that both the worker on the picket line and the corporation are equally responsible for the strike is not objectivity and therefore not the truth. To see a strike from the partisan viewpoint of the workers is both objective and the closest one can get to the truth, because it is the process of exploitation, the drive for corporate profits, that forces workers to strike. That is the objective truth of any strike. It is the basic objective truth about all struggles under capitalism.

That the articles in this book hold up in the light of experience is a test of their objectivity and truthfulness. When the same test is applied to most histories they will not measure up. The lack of objectivity and the untruths become exposed by time and experience.

Many books are being published about the history of the Communist Party, USA. Most of them are total fabrications. They were never intended to be the truth. Most are not histories of the Communist Party or the working-class revolutionary movements. They are histories based on anti-communism. They are not written to enlighten. They are calculated to misguide and misinform; they are written to be used for purposes of anti-Communist brainwashing.

Anti-communism was Hitler's biggest lie. Anti-communism is the biggest lie on the American scene today. It is the one lie that is spread without any apologies, hesitations or scruples. It is the one lie that is spread as a deliberate falsehood by a mass media that is fully aware they are spreading lies. There are historians, writers and educators who continue to dispense these Hitlerian falsehoods. Some, more liberal historians, use truth only as a thin veneer, as a sugar-coating to cover the anti-Communist poison they spread.

We do not object, and we are not concerned, when some write about our weaknesses and mistakes. In fact, we are the most vigilant and consistent critics of ourselves and our Party. However, we do object when writers misrepresent and distort our policies and our errors. We object most strongly to falsehoods and slander.

For some 50 years, the official policy of the FBI has been to demand from its agents falsehoods and slander about the Communist Party and its leading personnel. This is now revealed in the records of the FBI that have been made public. When agents sent in reports that were not derogatory enough they were rejected and returned with a demand for more slander, more distortions and lies. Some, who have resigned from the FBI, now admit that agents, knowing that Mr. Hoover wanted anti-Communist falsehoods and slander, sent in on a regular basis reports based on fabrications, with claims of accuracy and truth. This is a serious crime in itself.

But an even bigger crime is that for over 50 years the FBI has been spoon-feeding the press, radio, TV, and authors of hundreds of books and articles with these same fabrications about the Communist Party. These writers, the mass media and FBI agents knew they were lies. Only the readers did not, and still do not know. They are not aware of the sources or the fact that they are being fed total lies and distortions. It has been these reports of the FBI that have been the source material for most of the so-called histories of the Communist Party, USA.

The basic themes of big lie anti-communism the FBI expounds are that Marxism-Leninism is a foreign idea, that the Communist Party is related and connected to a foreign conspiracy and that socialism and communism are destructive of democratic and religious rights.

These false themes are calculated to arouse emotional feelings, and to appear as a challenge to one's patriotism, nationalism, religion and feelings about freedom and the rights of individuals. In their basic essence, these have been the falsehoods spread against an opposing class from the very inception of organized, human societies.

In our own history, one of the best examples is that the press and propagandists supporting the colonial rule of Great Britain accused Benjamin Franklin of being a foreign agent because he was against British rule.

These themes are not just ideas and concepts that the FBI circulates. They are the basic source material for most of the books and articles about the Communist Party, USA. Their aim is to cover up the fact that the Communist Party is a working-class revolutionary party, which has its roots in the economic and political landscape of the United States.

The Communist Party, USA is a working-class revolutionary party that fights on the side of the working class, the poor, the racially and nationally oppressed, women, youth, the elderly and, generally, all people who work. We are a party that believes socialism is not only the best of all solutions to the growing list of unsolved problems, but that socialism is an inevitable next step for civilization.

To acquire a deeper insight into historic events and historic turning points it is necessary to know something about the processes, the maturing of the forces, the changes in mass patterns of thought that give rise to and are involved in such events.

All historic moments and events are the products of such processes. These processes have their qualitative turning points when they give rise to something that is qualitatively new. Such is the chain of events that make history.

To understand historic turning points, to understand historic upheavals, one has to have a deeper knowledge of the dynamics of the process and the currents that prepared the forces that propelled the upheavals.

The birth of the Communist Party, USA was itself a product of such a qualitative turning point in the history of the United States. It was a product of a number of processes. The rising industrial development had given rise to a growing working class. The struggles for a decent standard of living gave the workers a class experience. The growing political understanding gave rise to political working-class movements, such as the Industrial Workers of the World (IWW), the old Socialist Party and many other groups and parties based on the concept of reforming capitalism, of making capitalism a livable system. However, after years of experience, this led many to conclude that capitalism was, at best, a dead-end street. They were forced to look for more basic solutions.

The revolutions in Europe, and especially the successful revolution that established the first working-class political and state power—the Soviet Union—had an electrifying effect on these processes and currents. The time had come, and the forces had matured, for the birth of a working-class revolutionary party that based its work on and was guided by the science of Marxism-Leninism.

The rise of the industrial mass production trade unions and the Congress of Industrial Organizations (CIO) was also a historic turning point. The CIO was not the brainchild of John L. Lewis. He did not organize or bring the CIO unions into being, which is the way most historians write the history of the trade union movement.

It is true that John L. Lewis and many others played an important role. However, before Lewis was able to make his contribution the processes that gave rise to industrial unions had to change the outlook and thought patterns of workers and even the outlook of John L. Lewis. He was a trade union leader long before he became involved with the CIO. It was the objective processes that brought about his involvement in the organization of the workers in the mass production industries.

A study of Lewis, Murray or Hillman would not give any real idea of why and how the CIO came into being. In fact, their contributions were made near the end of the process. Their roles were more like that of a midwife.

One of the processes that became a factor in the formation of the industrial unions and the CIO started in the struggles of the unemployed in the economic crisis years of the 1930s. For tens of millions of workers the struggles of the unemployed were a new experience. It was a militant movement of millions. It was a movement that was forced to fight in the political arena. The unemployed organizations were not divided into skilled and unskilled workers. The level of Black-white unity and the rejection of racism reached a new high. Because of the militant and political nature of the struggles there was a sharp rise in class conscious-ness. Mass thought patterns were changed. These mass struggles were largely influenced and led by leaders and members of the Communist Party, USA.

The lessons, the effects of this process flowed into and became a part of the turning point that resulted in the birth of the CIO.

For many years, before the CIO, there were small, militant, but very effective industrial unions in most of the basic industries. Because most of these unions had to function clandestinely their influence was always much greater than their membership. These were trade unions affiliated with the Trade Union Unity League (TUUL), led by such able and powerful Communist leaders as William Z. Foster. These unions led many militant strikes. Many of the strikes had to be conducted not only against the corporations, and the state and city police forces, but also against the policies of such conservative trade union leaders as Lewis, Murray, Hillman and others.

These were unions based on class struggle policies. These were unions organized along industrial lines. They took a stand against racism. In both membership and leadership, they were Black and white. They developed a higher level of political and class consciousness. Again, the Communists and Communist leaders made a major contribution in influencing these unions. This was another process that had a profound effect on the rise of the CIO. In most industries they provided the organizing cadre and know-how.

There was a third process in the pre-CIO days. There was a people's movement involving tens of millions of people in the struggle for world peace and against fascism. This left a deep imprint on the mass patterns of thought and on the social and political fabric of the United States. This movement was also influenced by the Communist Party, USA.

Then came a turning point in the economy. Industries began to hire workers. Tens of millions of workers who had been involved in the three historic processes not only went to work in the basic industries, but they took their political and organizational experiences with them. Thousands of members of the Communist Party, USA also went into the industries. It was these workers who had taken part in the struggles, who had learned from the mass struggles, whose class and political consciousness were at a higher level, who then became the initiating force for organizing the rank and file movements in the mass production industries. It was these militant rank and file movements in the mass production industries which not only gave birth to the industrial trade union movements, but also convinced and, yes, in a sense forced, John L. Lewis and many other conservative trade union leaders to become involved. They then set up the apparatus which became the organizing force of the CIO unions.

This truth about historic turning points and the processes that led up to them is important because similar processes are taking place today.

The millions who took part in the struggles aganst U.S. imperialist aggression against Vietnam, and the millions who took part in the civil rights marches and demonstrations against racism, are many of the same people who are initiating rank and file movements in the shops and in the trade union movement today.

To have a truthful and correct assessment of the contributions of the Communist Party, USA, it is necessary to know something about the contributions of the Party in influencing the mass movements that became the main foundation for the origin of the industrial trade unions in the mass production industries.

The period designated as "Roosevelt's New Deal" was also a historic turning point when a number of historic processes reached a new qualitative level.

A study of Franklin D. Roosevelt does not give one an understanding of the meaning of the dynamics of the forces that gave birth to that upheaval.

In the 1930s, capitalism in many countries, including the United States, faced a most serious crisis. How to respond to the critical questions of the crisis became a crucial matter. German monopoly capital took the path of making no concessions, the path of brutal oppression of the workers' and people's movements—fascism.

In his first four years, President Roosevelt and his Administration, and important sections of U.S. monopoly capital were maneuvering, refusing to respond to the problems of the people. But a number of developments forced a change in the outlook of the Roosevelt Administration, as well as in the ranks of sections of monopoly capital.

Among these developments, the most important one was the "change in the mood of the people." The struggles of the unemployed, the family farmers, large sections of the professionals and middle class reached a very high level. The process of radicalization took a big leap. The struggles took on more militant forms.

These upheavals helped to convince the dominant sections of monopoly capital that concessions, especially in the economic arena, were the better and more practical of the two directions. The New Deal measures were concessions that monopoly capital considered necessary to save capitalism. They were measures designed to stimulate markets, production and corporate profits. There was popular support for such measures because they also created jobs, housing and social security.

Here again, in order to understand and to have a correct evaluation of the contributions of the Communist Party, it is necessary to know something about the role of the Communists within the movements and the struggles of the people that helped to mold the forces of the mass currents that fought for the New Deal approach to the solution of the crisis.

Even a most casual examination of the last 60 years provides clear evidence that the Communist Party, USA has been an important factor in the struggles of the working class and the people. It is these contributions that the corporate propagandists, the mass media and the FBI try to distort and cover up.

The theme of the material in this volume is the class struggle in the United States. It stands as living proof that Karl Marx was right on the mark when he wrote: "The history of all hitherto existing societies is the history of class struggle." It is the theme running throughout this book because the class struggle has been and is the theme of life under capitalism.

The authors of the articles in this work have used the science of Marxism-Leninism to probe into the causes and effects of phenomena. The events are examined both in their separation, but also in the context of the objective and historic setting they are a part of.

There is an important lesson in this approach for all who want to influence the course of events—that tactics, slogans and programs to be meaningful, to be able to influence the course of historic events, must be moored and related to the objective processes that make history. Tactics and slogans that are not a reflection of the objective developments become abstract, powerless clichés. It is because of this approach and this understanding that the Communist Party, USA has been and is a part of the living organism of the class struggle. It is because the Communist Party, USA influences the historic processes and utilizes objective developments that it has influenced, and is influencing, the course of events.

GUS HALL
General Secretary, Communist Party, USA

PREFACE

Over one hundred and forty articles, speeches and reports to meetings and conventions make up this first-hand account of the Communist Party's participation in helping to shape the nation's developments over the past six decades. This is but a small part of the immense number of contributions which, but for lack of space, would have been included here. It is hoped this volume will stimulate further efforts to dig into the rich mine of material relating to the Marxist-Leninist movement in our country.

The material has been arranged chronologically wherever possible. But the object of preparing a meaningful collection of political writings was not always conducive to this form. In such instances the material is arranged according to theme as related to the particular period.

Corrections have been made of some typographical errors in the original publications. In a few instances small changes in language have been made to enhance clarity. Spelling, punctuation, and use of initials generally follow the original style. The word "Black" is used in editorial matter. Where "Negro" was used in original texts no change has been made.

Among the many persons who appear in this volume, either as authors or subjects or both, there are a few individuals who once played a positive role in the life of the Party but who later abandoned the movement or moved into anti-Communist by-ways. Fortunately they are only a few.

The editors wish to acknowledge the participation of Robert Phillipoff, who worked on the introductory material; Elmer Fehlhaber, who assisted in preparing chapter introductions; and Daniel Mason, who made valuable suggestions.

Dorothy Kahan prepared the manuscript and was helpful in other ways.

Of course, for any errors of omission or commission the editors take full responsibility.

HIGHLIGHTS
OF A
FIGHTING HISTORY

THE
FIRST
DECADE
1.

World War I (1914-1918), the first imperialist world war in history, changed the face of our planet. Old empires collapsed and new states emerged. Social and political storms shook every stratum of the U.S. population. The people were opposed to entering the war. President Woodrow Wilson was elected to a second term in 1916 under the slogan, "He kept us out of war." But six months later the United States was embroiled in the conflict. Opposition to the war was seen in the widespread strike wave during the two years in which the United States was involved. This occurred despite the efforts of the AFL bureaucracy to block militancy and win support for U.S. imperialist policy.

The war was a consequence of rivalry among the imperialist powers. The United States entered on the side of the Allies to emerge as the dominant power. A weakened Europe was left in ruins.

Revolutions swept the continent. Social Democracy, which had continuously pledged itself to oppose imperialist war, failed. The Second (Socialist) International and its constituent Socialist par-

3

ties, with the exception of the Bolshevik Party, collapsed. In Russia, czarism was overthrown, and the Marxist party, opponent of the war, under the leadership of V.I. Lenin, established the first socialist state in history. This event, which the American author and Communist, John Reed, described in Ten Days that Shook the World, *influenced the course of all humanity—and its effects were felt no less in the United States than elsewhere.*

The United States did not suffer the ravages of the war. It emerged as the most powerful imperialist nation. It used its economic advantage to resuscitate capitalist Europe which lay prostrate, and made its greatest contribution in helping the Krupps to rebuild the Ruhr, source of Germany's aggressive expansion.

A strike wave and other militant activities swept the country. A packinghouse strike (1918) and the Great Steel Strike (1919) were both organized by the AFL under the leadership of William Z. Foster. The Seattle general strike (1919) was also under left leadership.

Black sharecroppers emigrated North to enter the basic industrial plants and developed as a significant political force in the major cities. Black soldiers returning from France faced widespread lynch terror, and demonstrated a new militant resistance.

It was in these historic circumstances that the Communist Party (CP) came into being in September 1919.

The Socialist Party (SP), from which the CP derived, was formed in 1900. It was itself an outgrowth of socialist organizations which existed during the last quarter of the 19th century. From its inception the SP faced opposition to the opportunist policies of its leadership. When the United States entered the imperialist war, in 1917, the SP could not withstand the pressures of the new situation.

In April 1917, an emergency SP convention was held in St. Louis, Missouri. Charles E. Ruthenberg, an associate of the indomitable Eugene Victor Debs, was secretary of the Cleveland party organization. He emerged as the national leader of the Left, supported by Alfred Wagenknecht, Ohio state secretary. Both were in the Canton (Ohio) jail, for their anti-war activities, when they were visited by Debs. It was this visit, and a speech delivered

4

at Canton outside the jail, which led to Debs' ten-year sentence in the federal penitentiary in Atlanta, Georgia.

The young Communist Party faced formidable tasks in opposing the full force of government repression. Nationwide raids and police harassment were instigated by Attorney General A. Mitchell Palmer and the infamous J. Edgar Hoover. Foster described "the night of January 2, 1920, [when] the Department of Justice struck nationally in 70 cities, dragging workers from their homes, slugging them, and throwing them into crowded jails, often without proper food and toilet facilities. . . ." An estimated ten thousand were arrested and mass deportations took place.

Under these adverse conditions the Party began formulating its political program. Foremost among its objectives were: a) translating into life the concept of the vanguard party of the working class; and b) recognition of the Black people as an oppressed national minority whose struggle is central to social advance.

In mid-1921 the Party's position in the labor movement was reinforced when William Z. Foster, joined by Jack Johnstone, Joseph Manley, Sam Hammersmark and others, entered the Party. Among early Black trade unionists were Bill Herrin, organizer in the packinghouse drive (St. Paul, Minn.), Edward Doty, Cook County Plumbers Union, who organized a separate union when Blacks were denied membership in the AFL (he was later admitted into the AFL). These experienced trade union leaders helped strengthen the Party's base in the working class.

In 1922, soon after the formation of the Workers Party, the Communists began to establish themselves in the automobile industry. Edgar Owens, member of the Machinists Union in Chicago, an alternate member of the Party's Central Committee, was assigned to the Detroit organization. The independent Auto Workers Union was founded in 1893 as the Carriage and Wagon Workers International Union. It was an AFL affiliate for 25 years—until it was suspended for refusing to abandon its industrial form of organization.

Owens was invited to join the union's leadership and helped in halting its decline. A number of Communists joined the union and the Party began to give its attention to the auto industry. By March 1924, Owens called on all Party members in the industry to

5

join Local 127 of the union. The Party continued in leadership until the early 1930s. Phil Raymond, a Communist, was in charge of the organization drive. A number of Party members—among them John Schmies, Alfred Goetz, Phil Frankfeld and Phil Bart— participated in the drive and led strikes in the industry. The union's strength was confined to body shops, where the strikes it conducted won many concessions but failed to win union recognition.

A strategic section of the working class, whose influence helped shape the labor movement, was the coal miners organized in the United Mine Workers of America (UMWA). This chapter deals with a momentous struggle to save this great union. Among leading Communists involved were Tom Myerscough, secretary of District 5, one of the largest in the UMWA; Pat Toohey and Anthony Minerich, Young Communist League leaders; Frank Borich, Dan Slinger, Charles Gwynn and others.

The Communist Party and the Left also turned their attention to the one million textile workers, of whom only five percent were organized. In 1926 the Passaic, N.J., strike started. The formation of united front committees of textile workers gave a vital boost to the strike. The strike lasted 13 months and was principally led by experienced forces from the Party and the Trade Union Educational League (TUEL) such as William Weinstone, Charles Krumbein, Lena Davis, John Ballam, Alfred Wagenknecht and Elizabeth Gurley Flynn. A wage cut was rescinded and recognition of grievance committees was won.

In 1928, in New Bedford, Mass., the National Textile Workers Union, affiliated to the TUEL, led a strike of 26,000 workers against a wage cut in the cotton mills. The following year textile mills in Gastonia, N.C., were struck. Here fierce violence was unleashed against the strikers. Local government officials were augmented by vigilantes and the American Legion. A Communist, Ella May Wiggin—mother, union organizer, and songstress—was killed. Many others faced death and long jail terms when the death of Police Chief Aderholt resulted in mass arrests. Aderholt was killed when he led a raid by armed police and company guards against the strikers' camp. Of the 70 workers who were charged with murder, 15 were eventually convicted and sentenced to terms of 7 to 15 years.

The Communists were in the front line of battle. Foster said of these events: "The Passaic, New Bedford and Gastonia strikes represented new high levels of strike organization for the United States. . . . [These strikes] emphasized the role of . . . the Communist Party."

Although the AFL was at a low ebb and made no effort to organize the unorganized the TUEL, supported by the CP, initiated actions to resist the anti-union attacks, and made gains in some industries. It thereby won support from members in AFL unions. Thus in the Machinists Union elections in 1925, the Anderson progressive-left slate received 17,000 votes against 18,000 for the administration candidate, William H. Johnston. Morris Rosen, a New York carpenter and Communist, was credited with 9,014 votes, against 77,985 for William Hutcheson, a power in the top AFL bureaucracy. And this process continued in the needle trades, furriers and other trade unions. Ben Gold, Irving Potash, Dora Lifshitz and Joseph Boruchovitch were among the many who emerged as leaders of the rank and file.

No social issue requires greater analytical effort and attention than that of Black liberation. All other issues are closely tied to it. Racism, a deliberately fostered socio-ideological disease, permeates every facet of our society. It is engendered by the exploiting class because it divides the workers and yields superprofits. (See p. 422). The struggle for removal of this barrier is a prerequisite for progress. The history of the CP is one of constant review and attention to this question. It was Lenin's theoretical contribution on the national question which, for the first time, supplied the instrument for an understanding of the national question in general, as well as that of an oppressed national minority in particular.

The Party's Third (1923) and Fourth (1925) conventions adopted specific programs regarding the South, dealing with sharecroppers and tenant farmers. By 1930 the Party adopted a major resolution on Black liberation as a national question which, in the course of years, it developed and changed on the basis of further experience and struggle.

The Party was the only multi-racial organization invited in 1924 to the "All Race Congress or Sanhedrin" in Chicago. Following its daily sessions, organizations were invited to celebrate "Negro Progress Week." The first meeting was addressed by Communists Robert Minor and Lovett Fort–Whiteman. The Congress, which had only a short existence, was an important protest against lynching and anti-Black violence in all areas of the country.

The Party's defense of the democratic rights of all minorities also embraced the struggle against anti-Semitism. It was involved in this fight from its earliest days. The Party's historic position was aptly summarized by the late Hyman Lumer, editor of the Party organ "Jewish Affairs," when he wrote:

*"Like other forms of chauvinism and racism, anti-Semitism is an instrument of reaction, of the capitalist exploiters for sowing dissension among the people and dividing the working class. The struggle against anti-Semitism is part of the struggle for workingclass unity, for democracy, against the class forces of reaction in our society. It is part of the struggle against all forms of racial and national oppression." (*Zionism: Its Role in World Politics *by Hyman Lumer, International Publishers, 1973, pg 85.)*

Factional strife complicated the Party's formative period, as did sectarianism and insufficient ties to the working class. In due course it became evident that there was no principled political basis for continued factionalism. However, near the close of the decade, two groupings were still challenging the Party's Marxist position and its drive for unity. The factions represented opportunist influences, both right and ultra-left, corresponding respectively to the Bukharinite and Trotskyite groupings within the Communist International. Both groups lacked confidence in the concept of a Marxist party and sought to impose their sectarian ideas.

First the Trotskyites emerged in 1928, projecting a "leftist" position which could only lead to isolation from the working class. In face of objective difficulties they sought by "left" proposals and provocative acts to bypass the basic task of the Party to establish its roots in the labor movement and among the masses generally. When they refused to abide by the decisions of the Party the group, headed by James P. Cannon, was expelled.[1]

A right-wing group, led by Jay Lovestone, advocated class collaboration. The capitalist "prosperity" which accompanied the partial stabilization of the economy after a brief postwar crisis,

8

led the Lovestoneites to conclude that this country was immune from the operation of capitalist economic laws—that it operated under "exceptional" circumstances. (See p. 217).

While world capitalism was sinking into a depression that would last a decade, the Soviet Union completed its first five-year plan. Foster stated: "Between 1929 and 1933, when world capitalist production was cut almost half, that of the Soviet Union increased by 67 percent; the number of wage-earners jumped from 11,500,000 to 22,800,000; wages were doubled and unemployment became non-existent. . . ."

By eliminating destructive internal obstacles the Party was able to move into action on the problems facing millions of Americans. The response of Big Business, reformists, the labor bureaucracy, was to seek illusory palliatives. Their recommendations: the hungry share with the hungry, self-help, sale of apples, ad nauseam.

The Party, now united, responded quickly. Under its leadership Unemployment Councils were set up. Actions were initiated to gain immediate relief, stop evictions and halt shutting off of utilities essential for home. Independent movements, united in common action, emerged in all parts of the country. They reached the cities, hamlets and farm communities. Special attention was given to building Black and white unity. This was all part of a common struggle against the misery created in the wealthiest nation by monopoly domination.

The selections in this chapter deal with the first decade in the life of the Communist Party, USA.

□ ──────────────────────────────── □

THE SIGNIFICANCE OF THE COMMUNIST PARTY, USA

History of the Communist Party of the United States by William Z. Foster, International Publishers, 1952

The history of the Communist Party of the United States is the history of the vanguard party of the American working class. It is the story and analysis of the origin, growth, and development of a working class political party of a new type, called into existence by the epoch of imperialism, the last stage of capitalism, and by the emergence of a new social system—Socialism. It is the record of a Party which through its entire existence of more than three decades [in 1952], has loyally fought for the best interests of the American working class and its allies—the Negro people, the toiling farmers, the city middle classes—who are the great majority of the American people. . . .

The Party history is the record of the American class struggle, of which it is a vital part. It is the story, in general, of the growth of the working class; the abolition of slavery and emancipation of the Negro people; the building of the trade union and farmer movements; the numberless strikes and political struggles of the toiling masses; and the growing political alliance of workers, Negroes, farmers, and intellectuals. The Party is the crystallization of the best in all these rich democratic and revolutionary traditions of the people; it is the embodiment of the toilers' aspirations for freedom and a better life.

☐ ———————————————————————————————— ☐

THE FOUNDING OF THE COMMUNIST PARTY

"Formative Period of CPUSA" by William Weinstone, *Political Affairs*, September-October, 1969

[*William Weinstone (b. 1897) was a member of the Socialist Party and a founder of the Communist Party. For six decades he has held leading national posts and made significant contributions to the Party's theoretical work.*]

The Communist Party was born in Chicago on September 1, 1919. This is the commonly accepted date, although actually two Communist Parties came into being around that date—the Communist Labor Party on August 31 and the Communist Party on September 1. The formation of the two parties marks the beginning of the Communist Party in the United States. The Communist Party arose in two sections due to a split that occurred at the National Left-Wing Conference held several months before, not over principles but over tactics to be applied in regard to the Socialist Party Convention which was scheduled to be held at the end of August. . . .

William Z. Foster's *History of the Communist Party of the United*

States (International Publishers, 1952) gives a good and accurate account of the split in the Socialist Party and the formation and development of the Communist Party in this period. It is not necessary nor possible to detail them here. Since the book is out of print, it may be useful to summarize at least the highlights of the period in which the writer participated as a founding member of the Party. . . .

The war and the proletarian revolution in Russia, followed by revolutions on the continent, had a great impact on the workers in the U.S. Their fighting spirit rose, and though it did not reach the tumultuous heights of Europe, it was expressed in a vast strike movement. This included the militant three-month strike of 365,000 steel workers, led by William Z. Foster, the general strike in Seattle, the strike of copper miners in Butte, Montana, the 500,000 coal miners, and others. There was wide support for the Russian Revolution and strong opposition to the action of Wilson in sending American troops to Russia to help the counter-revolution. Discontent was high among the workers who were deeply disillusioned with the war. Soviet Russia had fully exposed the war's imperialist character.

The major immediate issue which led to a split within the Socialist Party was the acute discontent among the rank and file at the way the opportunist leadership had met the issue of the war. The Socialist Party leadership from the outset of the war in August, 1914, had opposed it, but chiefly on pacifist grounds. It exonerated the treacherous Socialist Party leaders of Europe who had betrayed the anti-war resolutions of the Second International and supported their imperialist governments. The Left wing of the SP, while not at first clearly differentiating itself from the official pacifist policy of the Party, began to sharpen up its anti-war stand. It increasingly demanded a strong working-class opposition. This grew, after the emergency convention of the Socialist Party, which was held in St. Louis in April, 1917, shortly after America's entrance into the war. . . .

It is true, Foster wrote, that Right and Left had united in a compromise resolution which produced great enthusiasm, "even the Left being more or less taken in by [Morris] Hillquit's anti-war demagogy." The Left made a serious mistake in not insisting on the inclusion of a condemnation of the treachery of the Social Democratic parties in Europe for supporting their governments in the imperialist war, and revealing that this social-chauvinism was the result of the whole line of opportunism followed by these parties for years.

However, there was soon disillusionment among the Left, wrote Foster, because "many of the party leaders who had voted for the [St.

11

Louis anti-war] resolution either failed to back it up in practice, or came out in support of the war." This also applied to a number of prominent trade union leaders who, while remaining in the Party, without censure or rebuke by the S.P. leadership, supported the Gompers war line. It applied to Meyer London, Socialist congressman from New York, who voted for the war appropriations in violation of the anti-war resolution. . . . Far from unity, Foster states, there were sharp divergencies and growing friction between Right and Left on the war issue.

Likewise, it is true that at first the S.P. leaders adopted tongue-in-cheek worded endorsements for the Bolshevik Revolution. Sentiment for the revolution was high in S.P. and working-class ranks. But in reality these leaders were hostile to the policies of the Bolsheviks, questioned the correctness of a proletarian revolution in Russia, and at the first favorable moment, showed their true position. . . .

On the question of affiliation to the Third [Communist] International, the Hillquit leadership maneuvered. It first tried to restore the Second International by electing delegates to the proposed Stockholm Conference in 1917 (which never assembled) and then supported the Berne Conference of the parties of the Second International in September, 1918, which was a failure. The Hillquit leadership proposed affiliation to the Third International under pressure of the Left Socialists who remained in the Party after the initial split. Hillquit took exception to a number of provisions in the 21 conditions of admission, and when the Communist International rejected his reservations, dropped the matter of affiliation entirely.

Opportunism in the world socialist movement, wrote Lenin in his famous articles in 1914-1917 on the collapse of the Second International, "is no chance occurrence, sin, slip, or treachery on the part of individuals, but a social product of an entire period of history." (*Collected Works,* Vol. 21, p. 247.) . . .

During this period, wrote Lenin, the Socialist parties built unions, made propaganda for socialism, conducted electoral activities and grew in size and influence. These were important achievements which Lenin and the Communists recognized at the time of the formation of the Communist International. But in the course of this period, the Socialist parties were joined by many petty-bourgeois elements. Also, there developed a stratum of trade union officials and of privileged workers who liked the idea of class collaboration. . . .

The Left wing carried on an intense campaign against the opportunism in the Socialist Party, seeking to change its policies and leadership. It took part in the referendum for a new national executive committee and swept the elections, winning 12 out of 15 seats and 4 out of 5 international delegates. The Hillquit leadership, determined to stay in power at all costs, refused to seat the newly elected committee, invalidated the elections and began a purge, expelling Left-led state organizations and language federations representing the overwhelming majority of the membership. By that arbitrary and bureaucratic expulsion the Right wing split the Socialist Party.

Soon thereafter the Left wing called the National Left-Wing Conference on June 21, 1919 in New York, which was attended by 94 delegates from 20 cities representing the bulk of the membership. . . .

The Left-Wing Manifesto which was adopted by the Conference condemned the whole political line of the SP leadership—root and branch. Foster wrote: "It accused Hillquit and Company of basing the Party program upon the petty bourgeoisie and skilled aristocracy of labor; of failing to support industrial unionism and the workers' economic struggles; of Gompersism [the class collaboration policies of Samuel Gompers, then head of the AFL]; of carrying on opportunist parliamentary policy; of sabotaging the struggle against the war; of opposing the Russian Revolution; of accepting a Wilsonian peace; of supporting the decayed Second International; and of generally carrying on a policy of reform which led not to socialism, but to the perpetuation of capitalism." (*History of the CPUSA,* p. 166.)

There was a serious omission in the Left-Wing Manifesto with regard to the Negro question. It failed to indict the segregation of Negro members in many Socialist Party branches in the South and the blatant chauvinism of many leaders, as well as the failure of the SP to take up a mass struggle against the severe oppression of the Negroes, particularly against the lynching campaign raging in the South.

The Left-Wing Manifesto not only made a thorough criticism of the opportunism of the SP leadership, but analyzed the basic issues at stake and outlined a policy of militant struggle in both the industrial and political fields. . . .

The Left-Wing Manifesto and the Communist programs were a long stride toward a Marxist-Leninist position. In its analysis of imperialism, the war, social democracy, the state, the nature of opportunism, the need for mass action as the decisive means to fight capitalism, etc., the Left wing surpassed the former Left wing oppositions.

The aim of the Left wing and the Communists in the USA in fighting for a revolutionary party—a party of a new type—was basically the same as that animating the revolutionary socialists throughout the world which joined together to form the Communist International in March, 1919.

13

[This] was the perspective and program arising from the new world situation and the historical period into which society had entered—the new era opened up by the proletarian revolution in which the working class takes the center of the stage, an era which marks the beginning of the transition from capitalism to socialism. It was around this outlook that the fight between the Right and Left in the U.S., between revolutionary socialism and opportunism, between Right wing social democracy and Communism took place. . . .

Sectarianism was expressed in the Left-Wing Manifesto and in the programs of the two parties in a dual-union line—that is, opposing in principle, work in the AFL and advocating the arbitrary setting up of competing unions. It was also expressed in the rejection of partial political demands and in the reduction of parliamentary action to merely agitating for socialism and for revolutionary formulas. The need of the workingclass for allies in the struggle for socialism was not recognized.

Furthermore, the Communist Labor Party did not mention the Negro question while the Communist Party gave, word for word, the DeLeon formula that "the racial oppression of the Negro is simply the expression of his economic bondage and oppression, each intensifying the other. This complicates the Negro problem but does not alter its proletarian character."

As Foster wrote, the political basis of the "Leftism" was a wrong estimate of the general political situation in the U.S. "Much of Europe then was in a revolutionary situation. Moreover, the revolution in Germany, had it not been betrayed by the Social Democrats, could have spread widely, thereby directly affecting the United States. It was therefore quite correct for the American Communist Parties to have a general socialist perspective. Their mistake was in conceiving this in an altogether too immediate sense and in a mechanical fashion. They failed to make a clear distinction between a Europe devastated by the war and the scene of active revolutionary struggle, and a capitalist America enriched by the war and by no means ready for socialism. This faulty analysis contributed directly to the young Communist parties' underestimation and neglect of the daily struggles of the workers for partial demands." (*Ibid,* pp. 173-174.)

The Party had not yet learned that, as Frederick Engels wrote: "Marxism is not a dogma, it is a guide to action." This mechanical, doctrinaire approach of applying general Marxist principles of social development without regard to the specific history and traditions of a country, and to the conditions and relationship of forces at the time, was to impede the Party's progress at various times later in its history. . . .

[But] Foster, in his review of Theodore Draper's book, *Roots of American Communism*, . . . effectively exposed the book's claim to being an authentic history of the Communist Party. . . . "The author strives to prove that the CPUSA is an artificially created Russian political instrument without any basic connections with the American working class and its struggles for economic and political betterment."

Foster refutes this on the basis of the Party's hard fight for the interests of the American workers, and for democratic rights in this period. He writes "that while the fledgling Communist Party in the U.S., as in other countries, was profoundly influenced by the combined effects of the Russian Revolution and the newly organized Communist International, especially it represented the historic Left wing of the Socialist movement in this country, reaching back for many decades and reacting to the conditions, struggles and aspirations of the American working class."

The Communists expressed the aspirations of the old Left for a class struggle policy but also reflected the latter's sectarianism.

It was sectarianism, tendencies to exaggerate differences, and doctrinairism on the part of a number of the Party leaders and some of the language federations, which accounted for the split in the Left wing. It was a mistake not to attend the Socialist Party Convention as many had proposed, even though the group, which later formed the Communist Labor Party, was summarily thrown out of the Convention by the police on the call of the SP leadership. It was important to attend, if only to expose the bureaucracy of the leadership and to clarify the program of the Left wing fully before the Socialist movement of the country and the delegates at the SP convention, many of whom hesitated between the Right and Left. It was an even worse error not to effect unity of the two parties, although negotiations took place between them.

The Communist parties proceeded to organize their ranks, enrolling the Left wing forces of the Socialist Party. They were joined also by forces from other organizations in the general process of realignment of revolutionary elements. Among them were some Socialist Labor Party leaders, a number of Negro leaders attached to Socialist journals and revolutionary organizations, young Socialist leaders, prominent women Socialists, and others. . . .

The Communists fought courageously in court for their principles and for democratic rights of free speech and assembly. They went on with their work of organization despite their virtual illegality. But the terror greatly reduced the membership of the parties. New strength came from the adherence of a group of former IWW members, headed by Big Bill Haywood, general secretary of the IWW, who joined in 1920. A considerable number of experienced trade unionists who had formed a Left trade union opposition in the AFL, headed by William Z. Foster, joined in 1921. . . .

C.E. Ruthenberg, general secretary of the CP, wrote in the April 25, 1920, issue of the *Communist* that to be a party of action, the CP must participate "in the everyday struggles of the workers and by such participation inject its principles and give a wider meaning, thus developing the Communist movement." It was ideologically an important step away from the narrow sectarianism of the year before. Ruthenberg and other leaders of the CP not only favored this outlook but, together with Alfred Wagenknecht, general secretary of the CLP, and others, undertook negotiations which led to the unity of the two parties and the formation of the United Communist Party in 1920. . . .

The Convention of the United Communist Party took a big step forward in rejecting the line of dual unionism and also in strengthening party structure by making the autonomous language federations, which had been virtually independent parties within the Party, subject to the general supervision and control of the Central Committee.

Full unity of all Communist groups was finally achieved a year later in May, 1921. In these efforts at unity, the Communist International, which saw no important differences between the Communist groups and pressed for a line of mass activities, helped at every stage.

A decisive weapon for overcoming sectarianism and putting the Communists in the United States and other countries more firmly on the road to becoming real Marxist vanguard parties, was the views of Lenin, and particularly his work *"Left-Wing" Communism—an Infantile Disorder.* It made a powerful impact upon the Communist leaders and members, enthusing and arousing them. It helped enormously to make the break with "Left" sectarianism and to recognize the need for closest contact with the masses in the Party's work.

Soon after, the United Communist Party resolutely took the path of breaking its isolation and taking up broad mass work. It established the Workers Party on December 21, 1921, as a "legal" means of carrying on wider public agitation and activity and thus reaching broader sections of the masses. This was done through an alliance with the Workers Council group [which was a second split-off from the Socialist Party] and many language groups which were not part of the Communist Party. Its membership was about 12,000 in 1921 and rose to about 16,000 in 1923 with the improvement in conditions of legality and the dissolution of the underground Communist Party. . . .

The Ruthenberg group was for restricting its [i.e., the "underground"

CP's] activities and eventually liquidating it as unnecessary. At the time of the struggle [over liquidation of the "underground" CP] for which a special convention was called in Bridgman, Michigan, in mid-August, Ruthenberg was general secretary of the Workers Party.

The vote on the question at the convention was evenly divided. When its deliberations were almost at a close, it was raided by the FBI. Seventeen delegates were arrested, including Ruthenberg. Forty more were later jailed, including Foster. Ruthenberg and Foster were tried under the Michigan criminal syndicalist law, Ruthenberg being convicted and Foster released because of a divided jury. He was not retried, nor were the others. Their cases were finally dropped in 1933.

The aim of the government in making the raid was not only to keep the Communist Party illegal and to restrict the activities of the newly formed Workers Party, but also to affect adversely the big strikes then in progress.

... The Party boldly and wisely seized on the new situation to achieve its desired goal of a complete public existence. On April 7, 1923 the Communist Party declared its full consolidation with the Workers Party. Thus the "underground" period of the Communist Party came to an end. The Workers Party changed its name to the Workers (Communist) Party in 1925 and to the Communist Party in 1930.

The Workers Party program was a big advance over the past programs. It contained both a maximum and minimum program, declaring that "the Workers Party will courageously defend the workers and wage an aggressive struggle for the abolition of capitalism." It gave a ringing endorsement to the Russian Revolution which, it stated, had ushered in "the era of Workers Republics." It demanded recognition of the Soviet government by the United States. But at its second convention, in December, 1922, the Workers Party recognized the need to go further— to replace the capitalist government by a "dictatorship of the proletariat". . . .

On the Negro question, it registered much progress over the past neglect. Discussing the "race problem" beginning with an analysis of the history of Negro oppression in the South, it stated that the "Workers Party will support Negroes in their struggle for liberation and will help them in their fight for economic, political and social equality." It would seek, it said, to end the policy of discrimination followed by organized labor. Its task, it said, would be to destroy together the barrier of race discrimination that has been used to keep apart black and white workers and to "weld them into a solid union of revolutionary forces for the overthrow of their common enemy."

Also, it decided to amalgamate all existing militant young workers' organizations and to launch the Young Workers League of America, which took place in May, 1922. The Young Communist League had been organized a month earlier, in April, 1922. In time, the Young Workers League merged with the YCL and assumed its name.

Central in the Party's activities was trade union work. The Communists gave full support to the Trade Union Educational League, formed earlier by William Z. Foster, which carried on a big campaign for industrial amalgamation of the unions, for recognition of Soviet Russia and for a labor party, winning widespread support for these demands. With its active militant participation in labor struggles, the TUEL, led by Communists but based upon a Left-progressive united front, quickly became an influence in labor's ranks. . . . It [the Communist Party] participated in electoral activities, putting up William Z. Foster for President in 1924. Thus, the Party embarked on a vigorous program of mass struggle.

☐ ── ☐

WORKING-CLASS UNITY

The Role of the Communists
in the Chicago Federation of Labor
by Phil Bart, New Outlook Publishers, New York, 1975

[*Philip Bart (b. 1902), active in the trade union movement, has held National and District posts in the leadership of the Young Communist League and Communist Party since the mid-1920s.*]

The closing of the second decade of the 20th Century and the opening of the third reverberated with sharp cracks in the world capitalist system. The Russian Socialist Revolution was a reality. Socialism was here to stay. Capitalism sought solutions in increased violence in the hope of stemming the growth of this new giant. . . . The Left faced the test of crystallizing greater unity against these new onslaughts.

The thrust of the attack was aimed at the trade unions; particular hostility was directed against the foreign born, and moves made to destroy the newly formed Communist Party. . . . One anti-labor sheet raved that efforts to establish militant trade unions were an attempt "to overthrow representative democracy and establish the Russian Soviet system." (Editorial, *Chicago Tribune,* June 2, 1919.) This was reinforced by poisonous racist propaganda, a terminal disease of capitalism.

The newly formed Communist Party became a constant and major target of the government. . . . When Attorney General A. Mitchell Palmer ordered [William J.] Burns to conduct raids on the foreign born, the dragnet caught some 10,000 victims [January 2, 1920]. . . . This act brought sharp protests from civil liberties groups, but hardly a ripple from trade unions.

The Bridgman, Michigan raid (August, 1922) on the Communist Party's national convention already reflected a new element which is important to record here. . . . It became evident that while the main target was the Communist Party, the rebound would hit the trade unions and, first of all, the progressive forces in their leadership. This was the opinion of the Chicago Federation of Labor, too. [The CF of L represented some 500,000 workers.]

The first to be hit was the Trade Union Educational League (TUEL) which was the national center of left forces in the labor movement. A raid on its offices . . . occurred during a TUEL conference. . . . Many delegates were beaten and arrested. The conference continued after the raiders left.

Prior to this assault, Foster was followed by state attorney's detectives. The procedure was not novel. The same frame-up methods used against Mooney and Billings were to be applied here. There had been a railroad wreck near Gary, Indiana and Foster was to be arrested and charged with sabotage. This, they figured, would make it possible with one blow, to destroy the left movement in the AF of L and simultaneously stymie the development of the new Marxist party. The plot was exposed and failed.

Since this phase of the Bridgman case received too little attention, I will quote extensively from the files of *The New Majority* (Organ of the CF of L) whose contributions were invaluable. Unlike the 1919 Palmer raids, the defense for the Bridgman victims found an immediate reaction in the labor movement. *The New Majority* saw a close tie between the court injunctions against trade unions and the raid on the CP. It associated its own cause with that of the TUEL and the CP. A mass meeting in Chicago addressed by Communist leaders William Z. Foster and C.E. Ruthenberg had as one of its speakers the editor of *The New Majority,* Robert M. Buck.

The CF of L took up the cudgels in this fight. Through the columns of its newspaper and at its meetings this question was under discussion. Here is the story which appeared in *The New Majority* two weeks after the raids: "In a desperate attempt to link recent railroad disasters with the activities of the Communist Party and the Trade Union Educational

19

League of which William Z. Foster is secretary and to turn the blame for wrecks away from the railroad officials who disregard the bad repair into which their equipment has fallen, the *Chicago Tribune* has commenced again the campaign of 'red raids.'" (September 2, 1922.)

The story continues: "Following the raid of Foster's office which occurred a week ago Sunday, exclusively conducted by the *Tribune* and detectives from State's Attorney Crowe's office, detectives trailed an alleged secret meeting of the Communist Party in Berrien County, Michigan, and arrested seventeen men. The prisoners were chained together like a pack of bears and led through the town of St. Joseph, where they are held on warrants under the Michigan criminal syndicalist law. Truckloads of so-called red literature were seized and the detectives are still busy scanning it in search of proof that Foster or the Communists are responsible for the wreck at Gary." (ibid.) The CF of L newspaper estimated that the police intended to turn the raid on the Communist Party into a "routine" frame-up of train wrecking.

It concludes: "The third act in the *Tribune's* stage play occurred last Sunday while the first national conference of the Trade Union Educational League was in session at the Scandinavian Labor Lyceum, Hirsch Boulevard. Headed by Detective Sergeant Laurence McDonough of war-time fame, a squad of assistants and police entered the convention hall. The conference adjourned while McDonough arrested thirteen men from among the delegates and visitors and immediately reconvened when the intruders with their prisoners had departed." (ibid.)

The lessons drawn by the CF of L weekly are worthy of the attention of every trade unionist today. In its issue of September 16, 1922, it editorialized: "The recent raids, however, in which more than a score of trade unionists were arrested in Michigan and Illinois, are felt throughout the entire country as a direct attack upon the labor movement as a whole, particularly upon the progressive trade union movement. Where in 1920 the red raids came and passed with hardly a protest from the unions and no concerted action on their part, the 1922 raids find unions all over the country aroused and ready to take action on behalf of the labor men now in jail or facing trial." It concludes that "Now more than ever, it is plain that the cause of the victims of Daugherty's raids is the concern of the labor movement and that an attack on 'reds' is a covert attack on unionism." (*The New Majority,* September 16, 1922.)

The widely expressed opinion that the series of raids on the CP "is the concern of the labor movement" was sound. It recognized that attacks on the CP are "a covert attack on unionism." This resulted from joint cooperation and experience in struggle.

☐ ── ☐

FORMATION OF THE MARXIST PARTY

"The Revolutionary Party" by C. E. Ruthenberg, *The Liberator*, February, 1924

[*Charles E. Ruthenberg (1882–1927) developed as a national leader of the Socialist Party in his native Cleveland, Ohio. World War I found him in leadership of the Left wing of the SP—and in prison as an opponent of the imperialist war. He was one of the founders of the Communist Party and was its first General Secretary until his death in 1927. He had the close cooperation of Alfred Wagenknecht, Ohio state secretary of the SP, who was also a founder of the CP and one of its leaders until his death in 1956.*]

From its Third National Convention, held at the beginning of 1924, the Workers Party emerges as a growing political force in the life of this country.

The task which the Communists of this country have set themselves is of Herculean proportions.

We have in the United States a social system more firmly rooted than anywhere else in the world. The industrial order upon which it rests has reached a development which is gigantic, and unrivaled elsewhere. The ruling class in this country possesses wealth and power which has not been equalled in human history. . . .

To this economic power, the tradition of the rights of property, the tradition of the capitalist system as the only possible method of production and distribution, the tradition of the government as a government of the people, add the organs for repression, laws and courts, police, the army and navy—and the picture of the strength of the existing social order is overpowering. . . .

Other organizations have set as their aim the creation of a new social order in the place of capitalism. It will, by contrast, throw some light on the principles and tactics of the Workers Party, if we first examine their principles.

The Socialist Party, which once had a hundred thousand members and polled a million votes for its presidential candidate, stated as its aim the establishment of a cooperative commonwealth. Its method of achieving this was theoretical propaganda about the beauties of the cooperative commonwealth, through which it hoped to educate a majority of the workers to an understanding of the need of the new social order and thus to win their support. To this theoretical propaganda it added a long list of abstract demands, the enactment of which were slowly to transform capitalism into the cooperative commonwealth.

The Socialist Labor Party, and its latest prototype, the Proletarian Party, both believe that they can educate the voters through abstract propaganda to an understanding of the necessity of replacing capitalism with socialism. Educate a majority in the theory of surplus value, educate a majority to an understanding of the beauties of the cooperative commonwealth and some fine day you will achieve it. To this conception the Socialist Labor Party added the idea of theoretically perfect industrial unions which were to aid in the achievement of the cooperative commonwealth.

The Workers Party, too, states its goal to the workers—the achievement of a new social order. It holds before the workers the ideal of Communism. It seeks to educate the advance guard in the basic principles of Marxian science. But these are the only points of similarity between its methods and those of the organizations referred to above. The Workers Party does not believe that a majority will be educated to an understanding of the theory of surplus value nor that they will be inspired to overthrow capitalism by the beauties of an abstractly presented cooperative commonwealth. Its methods of struggle are based upon quite a different conception.

"The history of all hitherto existing societies is the history of class struggles" wrote Marx in the *Communist Manifesto* of 1848. That is the key to the policies of the Workers Party, and of all Communist Parties.

In the capitalist United States the people are divided into economic classes with clashing economic interests. There is not only the main economic division of capitalist and proletarian, employer and employee, but there are the working farmers, the small shopkeepers, the professional groups, yes, even within the capitalist class there are economic groups with clashing economic interests. . . .

This does not mean only a campaign on the basic economic issue which sharply divides the interests of the capitalists and the workers—privately owned industry operated for profit-making purposes, versus socialized industry operated for service. The conflict between economic groups in capitalist society manifests itself in continuous struggles over immediate

22

questions. The workers fight for better wages and working conditions. They engage in struggles against restrictive laws, against injunctions, the use of the armed power of the government against them. The farmers fight against high railway rates, against the trustified marketing interests, against the banks which hold the mortgage on their land; they seek legislative action to improve their economic position.

These daily struggles are the starting point of the Communist struggle for the overthrow of capitalism. By entering into all of these struggles which grow out of the every day life of the exploited groups, by championing the cause of the exploited, by becoming their spokesmen, winning their confidence, the Communists establish their leadership of all those who suffer under the whip of capitalism. . . .

The sharp conflicts between the industrial workers and capitalists over wages, working conditions and during the recent years the right to organize, conflicts in which the government has appeared regularly as the agency of the capitalists fighting the workers, the farm crisis which has bankrupted millions of farmers, have developed a widespread movement for independent political action through a farmer-labor party. The Workers Party has been in the forefront of this movement. Through its aggressive campaign, through the struggle it waged at the farmer-labor convention, the Workers Party has greatly extended its influence among both industrial workers and farmers, and today it holds a position of leadership in the movement for a mass farmer-labor party which will fight the political battles of the industrial workers and exploited farmers.

In the trade unions the reverses of recent years have created a demand for more effective organization. The Workers Party stands before the organized workers as the exponent of amalgamation of the trade unions into industrial unions and a more militant leadership in their struggles. Representatives of hundreds of thousands of workers have voted in conventions in support of these proposals of the party, and these workers see in the Workers Party the leader in the struggle to create more effective fighting organizations upon the industrial field.

The capitalist government aims a blow at the whole working class in its proposal to register foreign-born workers and for selective immigration. These measures would create a class of coolie labor so tied down with restrictive legislation that it would be unable to offer resistance to the exploiters. The Workers Party, through the action of its second convention, reaffirmed by the third convention, takes up the cudgel in defense of the foreign-born workers and of the standard of living of the whole working class in its campaign for protection of foreign-born workers.

The working farmers of this country are facing a crisis which is deeper

23

than ever before in the history of this country. The [Communist Party] convention resolution analyzes the situation of the poorer farmers and raises the demand of a five-year moratorium for farmers and the ownership of the land by its users.

The Negro workers of this country are an especially exploited class. The Workers Party initiates a campaign against all forms of discrimination against the Negroes and will assist them in organizing their strength to make an end to these discriminations.

American "Irelands," "Egypts" and "Indias" are appearing as a result of the advance of American imperialism. The Workers Party sees in [those] . . . exploited by American imperialism in the West Indies, Central America, Hawaii and the Philippines its natural allies in the struggle against the centralized, imperialist capitalist government at Washington and it raises the slogans of independence for the victims of American imperialism and endeavors to rally the masses of this country in support of these slogans.

Soviet Russia is a sword thrust straight at the heart of capitalism throughout the world. Its flag is the inspiration and rallying point of the exploited everywhere in the world. The Workers Party takes up the fight in support of Soviet Russia in its struggles against imperialist attacks.

Thus there is being created a growing revolutionary force in American life. The capitalists hold in their hands a mighty power. But within the capitalist order are generated those forces which weaken and disintegrate that power through the process of the continuous class conflict which capitalism engenders. What is needed is the organization which can combine for the struggle against the capitalists all the forces of opposition which it creates. That organization is here—a Communist Party, the Workers Party of America.

☐ ─── ☐

THE YOUNG WORKERS LEAGUE IS FOUNDED

Manifesto, Program, Resolutions and Constitution
Young Workers League of America, adopted by the First
National Convention, May 13–15, 1922, New York City,
published by Young Workers League of America

[*The Young Communist League (YCL) was organized in April 1922, and the Young Workers League (YWL), subject of the present item, was launched a month later. The two organizations later merged, taking the name of Young Communist League (YCL). The YCL dissolved in 1943.*

24

The documents of this First Convention of the new youth organization contain a number of "leftist" formulations which were not uncommon in this period—not only in the youth league but in the Party as well. During the "formative years"—in the course of activity, experience and education—the "leftism" was largely corrected.]

The Young Workers League of America declares that the way out of the intolerable situation in which the workers find themselves today is to organize into a compact, centralized, militant organization to fight the battle of the workers both on the economic and political field.

The working class youth is confronted with problems of its own. For this reason a separate organization such as the YOUNG WORKERS LEAGUE is needed to unite all militant young workers of city and farm into one organization, striving to aid the young people in their fight against capitalism, to train and educate them to understand that the problems of the young workers of America are the problems of the young workers of the world. The struggle of the young workers, however, is not an isolated struggle. It is a part of the struggle of the working class as a whole. Only by concerted effort of all workers can their problems be solved.

The present system is doomed to destruction. In its efforts to reach and to alleviate the intolerable conditions of the proletarian youth of America, the YOUNG WORKERS LEAGUE is conscious of the fact that a struggle for immediate betterment can in no way be an end in itself and it emphatically seeks to point this out to the young workers. The aim of the YOUNG WORKERS LEAGUE is the abolition of capitalism by means of a REPUBLIC of Workers' Councils—a government functioning through the power of the proletariat to the exclusion of all other classes—as the first step toward the establishment of an International Classless society free from all political and economic slavery.

The YOUNG WORKERS LEAGUE is aware that the proletariat does not move on the basis of ideals [alone] but rather on the concrete facts of life. But the struggle for these concrete things leads to a conception of and a struggle for the ideal.

In its efforts to win to its side the masses of youthful toilers in this country, the YOUNG WORKERS LEAGUE seeks to reach them in the first instance by participating in the struggle of the working-class youth for a better chance to live, and therefore presents a working program, stressing the most vital issues that confront the youth. But in striving to attain these demands, the ultimate goal is neither overlooked nor abandoned. By participating in these struggles, we demonstrate to the workers the utter futility and hopelessness of REFORMING the present system, thereby showing the acute need for completely abolishing capitalism and instituting a WORKERS' REPUBLIC. It is primarily through action that the workers come to a realization of this fact.

□ ———————————————————————————————— □

THE "DAILY"

"Here is 'The Daily'!" *Daily Worker,* January 13, 1924

[*The first issue of the "Daily" was dated Sunday, January 13, 1924. It was the first Marxist English-language daily newspaper.*

John J. Ballam, previously New England organizer of the Textile Workers Union, became campaign manager in charge of the $100,000 fund drive. Its success demonstrated the determination of thousands of workers to establish a revolutionary working-class "Daily" in the United States.

Its first editor was J. Louis Engdhal, who was later associated in the campaign to free the "Scottsboro Boys." The paper was first published in Chicago. Three years later it moved to New York. Today the Daily Worker *is continued as the* Daily World. *It is the longest continued publication of a working-class daily in the history of the United States.*]

In the first issue of the *Weekly Worker,* Feb. 2, 1922, we wrote, "This, the first edition of *The Worker* is the advance agent of *'The Daily Worker.'"*

. . . Thus, from one advance position, we move forward to another next ahead. The Daily is here, and we turn a new page in the world story of labor's struggle. Another chapter begins for America's working class. The first English-language Communist Daily in the world has been realized. . . .

The Daily has already aroused its enemies. The labor lieutenants of the established order, joined with big business interests, the bankers, the merchant princes, the landlords and other profiteers, in a declaration of the National Civic Federation, seeking to prejudice the workers and farmers against it. . . .

But we have no fears. The bosses have declared The Daily their enemy, even before its first issue appeared. They know they have cause to fear The Daily. They know it will raise the standards of a real struggle against the few who rob and plunder the many and keep them in submission.

26

They know The Daily is a challenge to the continuance of their ruthless and bandit rule.

We have no fears because we know that the workers and farmers of the United States will rapidly rally in support of The Daily in increased numbers.

The Daily appears in Chicago but it is the expression of the oppressed workers and farmers of the whole nation. Its daily arrival in the shops, factories, mills and mines will be cheered by the workers because they will recognize in it their champion. It will be hailed by the agonizing tillers of the soil as their powerful weapon against bankers, landlords and the profiteers in the wealth they produce but do not enjoy.

The Daily fights for the organization of all labor and the strengthening of its ranks everywhere. It is for the organization of the unorganized and for amalgamation as two powerful weapons to prepare for the coming industrial depression and unemployment immediately ahead. . . .

□ ———————————————————————————————— □

HITCH-HIKING AT SIXTY-THREE

We are Many by Ella Reeve Bloor,
International Publishers, 1940

[*Few leaders in the socialist and labor movement have traversed the vast expanse of the United States and established closer ties with "common folk" than the noble, revolutionary woman Ella Reeve Bloor, known as Mother Bloor (1862-1951). Her activity in the socialist movement dates from the period when she "became a member of a group called 'The Social Democracy of America' organized by him [Eugene V. Debs] in 1897." She carried an honorary union card in the United Mine Workers of America and was honored by many trade unions throughout the country.*

When the Daily Worker *was established, it found in her one of its most ardent press builders. Her description of a hitch-hiking trip across the country at the age of 63 is an odyssey which, in her words, should inspire the youth.*]

I volunteered, in the summer of 1925, to hitch-hike across the country, from California to New York, having bundles of the paper sent me for distribution at each stop. I guaranteed that the Party would not have to pay anything for transportation, only for meals and lodging. I felt that if I could do this at my age (I was now 63) it might be an example to some of the younger comrades to save train fares for the Party.

My plan was accepted. A comrade drove me out to the edge of Berkeley, California, where I stood by the roadside carrying only a briefcase. On the side of it was painted "From Coast to Coast for the *Daily Worker.*" I must say I felt a little shaky and wondered what was ahead.

A man in a big car who gave me a lift to the Vallejo Ferry looked me over and asked, "Where are you bound?" "New York," I told him. He kept on staring and finally remarked: "Well, it takes all kinds of people to make the world, and I guess you are one of them."

I made Sacramento by 9 o'clock at night and got a room in a hotel. The next morning I got a ride from Sacramento to the foot of the Sierra Nevada mountains, the highest range in California. The mountain passes had only just been opened for travel, and there were still icy stretches of road. I saw a middle-aged man driving along, and learning that he was going over the Truckee Pass all the way to Reno, I got in. We climbed up and up into the high Sierra Nevadas, looking down thousands of feet to the tree tops below.

At Reno I went right to the post office and to my amazement found a card from my son Dick, whom I had left behind in Berkeley. it said, "I am at the Y.M.C.A. and have arranged a meeting for you there."

Understanding how much the success of this trip meant to me, he had taken a train ahead to Reno, knowing it to be a hard nut to crack. There was only a skeleton of a Party organization there. Some workers and farmers came to the meeting—a small group who had been consistent Socialists and later became Communists. I got some subscriptions to the *Daily Worker,* and later did some house to house canvassing, as I did everywhere.

The next morning, Dick said "good-bye" looking rather sad to leave his "little old mother" heading toward the lonely desert. I had been warned only to take a lift going the entire way across, and not to fall in with some prospector who might dump me in the middle of the desert. Luckily an agricultural agent came along who drove me to a nice little town where a comrade had arranged a meeting for me in a medicine show tent right on the edge of the desert. I got a number of subs there and travelled on across the Nevada desert, stopping wherever there was a little oasis and town, often having to wait nearly all day for a ride.

Barren and desolate, Nevada seemed all the lonelier because of the remnants of past grandeur in some of the deserted little mining towns, where fortunes had once been made over night from mines now abandoned, and where just a few stranded people remained.

At a little oasis near where "The Covered Wagon" had been filmed, the only place to stay was a cabin in the desert with a little restaurant attached, where a young couple lived—the man had tuberculosis. I waited there all that afternoon, and all night, but no car came by. Then, as they asked a high price for meals, I determined to start out into the desert the next morning, looking back for landmarks in order not to lose my way. After I had gone several miles, I came to a little house with children playing in the yard, and a forlorn looking woman leaning over the gate. She looked me all over. I must have appeared strange indeed to her—a white-haired woman in high boots and breeches, carrying a brief-case.

She asked me what I was doing. I told her, "I am going from coast to coast for a labor paper." And as she looked puzzled, I went on, "You see, I am working for the labor movement . . ."

"Oh," she interrupted, "don't do that. There is too much labor in the world already."

She was the wife of a smelter worker near Ely, Nevada, where it was impossible to bring up children because of the poisonous smelter fumes. So they had built this little place in the desert and her husband came to see her once in two or three months when he could get away.

I really felt scared when I left that little house behind. It was astonishing how far I could see when I looked into the broad expanse ahead of me—where an unbroken sea of gray sage and golden rabbit brush swept on for miles and miles to the foot of the next mountain range. I learned to love my trips across the deserts more than almost all the other experiences of my trips. But I love the Southern deserts best—there is something warm about the yellow Arizona desert soil, while the Nevada desert is lonesome and terrifying, for all its lovely colors.

At last a young man came along, driving an old Chevrolet. He cheerfully offered me a ride and told me that he had been all the way to California looking for a job as carpenter. Arriving in California, he found a telegram from his home town in Utah that a new courthouse was being built there and a job was waiting for him. So he had turned right around and was retracing his route. He drove me all day and that night I stopped at a hotel. The next morning he called for me and took me as far as his home town in Utah.

By a succession of such lifts, I reached Salt Lake City, where the comrades had arranged a nice meeting for me, and where I saw my capitalist brother whom I had not seen since the 1922 railroad strike. He was horrified that I was hitch-hiking. When I left his home, his wife drove me forty miles on my way. I got rides with all kinds of people, canvassing and holding meetings at every stop. I always tried, when possible, to ride with workers who stop for hitch-hikers more readily than people in swanky cars. At one point I got a lift in an old Model T Ford. I told the two men in it who, in their blue shirts, appeared to be railroad workers, that I was always especially glad to ride with workers. But I couldn't get them interested in what I was doing. After hearing a little of their conversation, I soon gathered that they were bootleggers and had a cargo aboard, and I made an excuse to get out at the next town.

Going to Rock Springs, Wyoming, after crossing the Continental Divide from Utah, we went through the Alkali Desert, where the air is heavy with the alkali dust that gets in your throat and it is impossible to get water fit to drink. Riding with a man and his daughter, I noticed that he did not seem to be able to judge distances well, nor to avoid bad spots in the road. We had some terrific bumps and several narrow escapes. When they left me, the daughter asked me: "Don't you think father drives very well, considering he only has one eye?"

At Rock Springs the next night we had a mass meeting of the miners at their union hall. I always got a warm welcome from the miners because I could show them my union card in the United Mine Workers of America. The following morning a Finnish comrade took me about thirty miles over the hills and mountains on my way to Colorado. There the Denver comrades had put up a *Daily Worker* booth at a big fair held by the Central Labor Council, and were eagerly awaiting me. I stood in front of the booth in my hitch-hiking costume, and sold many papers.

The rest of my route included stop-overs in Kansas City, Mo., Chicago, Dayton and other points in Ohio, then Pittsburgh and Philadelphia, winding up in New York.

I came back with a new knowledge of our country and its people, a new determination to work with all my strength so that this great and beautiful land of ours might one day belong to the people themselves. I had seen so many lonely and poor and dispossessed living bereft in the midst of untold riches. Coolidge "prosperity" was now in full swing, and many industries were booming. But new machinery and rationalization systems were filling the roads with people passing back and forth looking for jobs. On this trip I got to know the great, rich fellowship of the open road, and experienced the great kindness of people everywhere to hitch-hikers. I found thousands of people all over the country hungry for the message the *Daily Worker* brought them.

I arrived in New York on the day that the S.S. *Majestic,* with a load of scabs, was coming into port, during a marine workers' strike, and the

Party and the *Daily Worker* offices were humming with excitement. All the people who could be mustered were going down with banners to meet the ship when it came in. I joined the group leaving from the office, still wearing my hiking clothes. Morris Hillquit was arriving on that ship. We carried a banner greeting him: "Morris Hillquit, why did you come back on a scab ship?" The Socialists, there to meet him, were horrified when they saw our banners, and smuggled Hillquit out by a side door of the pier. The police came but did not arrest us because we just stood outside the dock entrance singing solidarity songs at the top of our lungs so the sailors would hear us. Many marine workers joined in this picketing.

After the demonstration, I went back and reported on my trip. The *Daily Worker* office was delighted with the large number of subscriptions I had secured on the road.

☐ ————————————————————————————— ☐

THE BLACK LIBERATION MOVEMENT AND THE COMMUNIST PARTY

**1. "Negro Race Movement Given Labor Vision thru the Constructive Role of Workers Party at Sanhedrin," *Daily Worker*, February 14, 1924
2. "The First Negro Workers' Congress" by Robert Minor, *Workers Monthly*, December 1925**

[*The Communist Party, from its beginning, devoted itself to Black liberation. It based itself on Karl Marx's historic dictum that "labor cannot emancipate itself in the white skin where in the black it is branded."*

Foster, in his History of the CPUSA *observed:*

" . . . the Communists quickly overcame the crass neglect and misunderstanding of the Negro question which had been such a marked weakness in the policies of the Socialist Labor and Socialist parties for the previous forty years . . ."

Among prominent Blacks at the Sanhedrin were W.E.B. DuBois, Monroe Trotter, Dr. Alain Leroy Locke and Mrs. Ida M. Wells-Barnett.

The Daily Worker, *which had begun publication just a month prior to the Sanhedrin, gave skillful coverage of the proceedings. It was the only daily in Chicago to report on the sessions.*

The Party gave major attention to the organization of the American

Negro Labor Congress (ANLC). A united front conference called by the Party, which convened in Chicago in October 1925, was a prelude to the Congress. It laid special emphasis on the organization of Black workers and farmers.

Lovett Fort-Whiteman was the national organizer. Delegates included a young Black woman, Correene Robinson, representing the Young Workers League of America.

The Congress summarized the struggles of Black peoples internationally against imperialist oppression and expressed its solidarity with the colonial and semi-colonial peoples.

Robert Minor (1884-1951) was born in San Antonio, Texas. He became the country's leading political cartoonist. He was a founder of the Communist Party and one of its most prominent and colorful leaders. He contributed his magnificent drawings to the Masses, Liberator *and* Daily Worker. *But, in the mid-1920s, he laid down his drawing instruments and dedicated himself to Party leadership activities.*

The following two items are extracts from the Daily Worker *and* Workers Monthly *as cited above.*]

1.

Growth of Workers Party influence among the Negroes is the certain result of the constructive work of its delegates at the big All Race Congress or Sanhedrin held here last week.

No one could follow the Sanhedrin without seeing that the only force fighting aggressively for the Negro race there was the force represented by the Workers Party delegates, the African Blood Brotherhood and several individual delegates from other organizations who rallied to the program.

The labor delegates insisted that the only hope of the oppressed Negro race was in lining up with the oppressed of other races; that the oppression of the Negro had an economic basis and was for the purpose of maintaining him as a voteless and unskilled worker in field and mill.

All Workers Party resolutions, incorporating their race program, had the unity of the Black worker with the white worker, as the solution of the race problem.

This was shown in their vigorous demand for the elimination of the color line in the unions; in their insistence that the Ku Klux Klan could only be fought effectively in cooperation with the foreign-born workers; in their demand that the same schools must be open to Blacks and whites because where the races were segregated the Negro always got less attention; in their solution of the residential segregation into "Black belts" by the remedy of having all housing let to first comers at stipulated prices—regardless of the applicant's color, and in other resolutions.

Ninety-eight per cent of the Negroes are workers or farmers, and when farmers are almost invariably tenant farmers, in many cases in peonage or debt slavery.

S.V. Phillips and Lovett Fort-Whiteman of the Workers Party made telling speeches and so did Otto E. Huiswood.

2.

For the first time in the history of the United States (or practically for the first time), an American Negro labor convention has been held. Never before, with the exception of the years just after the Civil War, has there been even a pretense of a big national congress of Negroes on the basis of their class character as workers.

The American Negro Labor Congress which met in Chicago the last week of October, was immediately recognized as a breaker of traditions. It created more excitement in the Negro press, I believe, than any other Negro convention that ever convened.

It must be said that organization, in the true sense of the word, is a new phenomenon among the Negro masses. And when we understand this, and when we see the reversal of the traditions and forms of the past, we get closer to the answer as to whether there was a mass character to the American Negro Labor Congress.

A hard-boiled organizer will have to say that there were only a very few thousand of organized Negro workers behind the delegates who sat in the American Negro Labor Congress. There was only a small handful who directly represented trade unions, and to anyone who appreciates the essence of this as a Negro Labor Congress, the matter is highly important. Undoubtedly, however, the significance of this weakness is mitigated by the fact that many Negro federal labor unions which wanted to send delegates and which were watching with earnest sympathy its results, were finally terrorized out of sending their delegates by the threat of the president of the American Federation of Labor, who implied that these unions would be deprived of their charters if they participated. (A considerable number of unions were represented indirectly through the delegates of "local councils" in which they participated.) . . .

However, none but the blindest of fools could say that this Negro Labor Congress has no large significance. Whether the movement has or does not have a mass character is a question which was not conclusively answered by this convention and which will be settled according to whether the young Negro leaders who have started it will now proceed to utilize the great beginnings which they have made. Unquestionably this convention resulted in forming a strong nucleus for a mass movement, and a nucleus which already has the beginnings of mass connections. The fact that it has succeeded in drawing together half a hundred young Negro leaders of exceptional ability—not "prominent persons," but young workingclass men and women with the gift and urge for organization and a clear goal, and having behind them at least a framework of mass organization—this fact will be ignored only by skeptics who know nothing of present day history.

But the "united front" principle did not stop there. The congress made the refreshing declaration in ringing terms that the Negro workers demand that all of organized labor espouse their cause. This takes concrete form in the plan to form "interracial labor committees" in every locality, to be composed of delegates elected by the "white" trade unions and those elected by Negro organizations, to meet jointly for the purpose of bringing the Negro workers into the trade unions, preventing discrimination, undercutting of wages, the use of one race against the other in strikes, etc., and for bringing about united action of all workers, black and white, against lynching and race riots. In this proposal there is a touch of reality that is nothing less than startling. If it is seriously taken up, it is full of potentialities for the future of the labor movement and of the Negro masses.

☐ ———————————————————————————————— ☐

THE LA FOLLETTE TICKET, 1924

"The Communists and the La Follette Movement, 1922–1924,"
History of the Communist Party of the United States by William Z. Foster, International Publishers, 1952

[*William Z. Foster (1881–1961) is widely regarded as the outstanding figure in the labor and Communist movements of the United States.*

He joined the Socialist Party in 1901 and left it in 1909 as a result of his syndicalist leanings. He then became a member of the Industrial Workers of the World (IWW) but left it in disagreement with its staunch dual-union philosophy. In 1912 he organized the Syndicalist League of North America which called upon the advanced industrial workers to work within the AFL unions.

A few years later, with the support of the leaders of the Chicago Federation of Labor, Foster directed a successful organizing campaign which brought hundreds of thousands of packinghouse workers into AFL unions.

He then turned his attention to a massive drive in the open-shop steel industry. In 1919 he led a great steel strike in which 350,000 workers took part.

He joined the Communist Party in 1921.

For the next forty years Foster played a leading role in the CPUSA and in the world Communist movement. He was the Party's candidate for U.S. president in 1924, 1928 and 1932 and was for many years the Party's National Chairman. He wrote hundreds of articles, scores of pamphlets and about a dozen books. His 600-page history of the Party appeared in 1952. The following are excerpts from a chapter of that book.]

The general resistance of the workers to the capitalist offensive in the years immediately following World War I crystallized in a big farmer-labor movement and culminated in the independent candidacy in 1924 of Senator Robert M. La Follette for the presidency of the United States. This was the biggest effort ever made, before or since, by the rank-and-file American workers and their class allies to set up an independent political organization in the face of official betrayal. The Workers Party, the Communist Party of the period, played a most important role in this significant development. . . .

In 1922, the Workers Party broke sharply with the thirty-year-old anti-labor party policy of the S.L.P. and the S.P. and took its place in the forefront of the growing struggle for a labor party. . . .

By 1922 the Workers Party had come to understand the vital importance of supporting the labor party as a break on the part of the workers with the two-party system and bourgeois political domination. This was a big stride away from sectarianism and into broad mass work. At its second convention, held in New York City in December 1922, the delegates therefore confirmed the earlier decision by the Central Executive Committee in May 1922, and declared: "The Workers Party favors the formation of a labor party—a working class political party, independent of and opposed to all capitalist political parties. It will make every effort to hasten the formation of such a party and to effect admittance to it as an autonomous section."[2] It added: "A real labor party cannot be formed without the labor unions and organizations of exploited farmers, tenant farmers and farm laborers must be included."[3]

The political situation at this time was propitious for the formation of a labor party. The workers in the United States, passing through the bitterest offensive of big capital, had carried out a whole series of fierce strikes. They had been largely disillusioned by Wilson's "liberalism" and of course, they had no use for Harding's brand of reaction. Besides, the Gompers leaders had been deeply discredited in the whole post-war struggle and they were little able to stem the strong tide for independent working-class political action. Also, for the first time in over 35 years, the Marxists, in the Workers Party and the T.U.E.L., were making a real fight for a labor party. Consequently, the workers turned sharply toward independent political action. . . .

The Workers Party and the T.U.E.L. meanwhile were actively pushing among the masses their agitation for a labor party. The T.U.E.L.'s national referendum on the labor party was a big success. All over the country unions voted favorably upon the T.U.E.L.'s proposition to establish a labor party forthwith. *The Labor Herald* reported that "the unions now on record in the League vote extend over 40 states and 47 international unions. In the thousands of locals in which the issue has been raised we have been informed of less than a dozen which failed to approve of a labor party."[4]

Meanwhile, definite working relations were developing nationally between the Workers Party and the Fitzpatrick-Nockels-Brown group. The ten years of cooperation between the Federation leaders and the Chicago T.U.E.L. militants, which had resulted in so many constructive national campaigns, was now developing finally into a united front between the Workers Party and the Farmer-Labor Party.

By mutual agreement of the two parties, a call was issued by the Farmer–Labor Party for a general convention to take place in Chicago, on July 3, 1923, of "all economic and political organizations favoring the organization of a Farmer-Labor Party." The W.P. and F.L.P. leading committees agreed upon the basis of representation, the construction and the number of the future party's leading committee and also upon certain resolutions to be proposed, including the recognition of Soviet Russia. They also agreed that if there were half a million workers represented at the convention, the new party should be formed. The W.P. and the F.L.P. shared the costs of the sending out of the convention call. On the agreed upon basis, invitations were extended nationally to all trade unions, local and state labor and farmer parties and the Socialist, Socialist Labor and Proletarian Parties, in addition to the two sponsoring parties.[5] The S.P. declined the invitation, but the general response was excellent. The movement grew in many directions.

As the July 3rd convention approached, however, the Fitzpatrick group began to waver and to grow visibly cool toward it. The A.F. of L. had cut off its subsidy to the Chicago Federation of Labor and many La Follette-inclined forces were trying to induce Fitzpatrick and his group to cut loose from the coming convention. The latter weakened under these pressures. Nevertheless, they went into the convention without openly repudiating their agreement with the Workers Party.

The convention of July 3, 1923, brought together an estimated 600,000 workers and farmers, represented by 650 delegates. Of these the Communists made up but a very small minority. The enthusiasm for the proposed federated party swept the gathering which was composed mostly of rank-and-filers. From the outset the Fitzpatrick group maneuvered against the convention's establishing a party. First they tried to reject the credentials of the Workers Party, but this move was defeated almost unanimously by the convention. Then they sought, through an out-of-town delegate, to transform the convention into simply a consultative conference. This move was countered by an amendment to form the new party, made by Joseph Manley, a Workers Party member representing Local 40 of the Structural Iron Workers Union, and supported by Ruthenberg.

Only on the night of the third and last day of the convention did the confused Fitzpatrick group bring in a definite proposition as to what they wanted done. They then proposed that all the organizations present should affiliate to the Farmer-Labor Party as autonomous units, except that the revolutionary elements, meaning the Workers Party, should be excluded. The F.L.P. proposal said "it would be suicide ... to bring into such affiliation any organization which advocates other than lawful means to bring about political changes"—strange charges indeed coming from the radical Fitzpatrick group, which had invited the W.P. to this convention and which only a few months before had voted to seat Ruthenberg and Foster at the C.P.P.A.[6] gathering in Cleveland. The Convention rejected the Fitzpatrick proposition with a roar and decided by a vote of about 500 to 40 to organize the Federated Farmer Labor Party, which was done.[7] As Fine says, the Fitzpatrick group wanted to bolt, "but they did not have enough of a following for that."[8] A representative group of workers and farmers were then elected as the Executive Committee. Joseph Manley was chosen secretary-treasurer, and the F.F.L.P. established its headquarters in Chicago.

The program of the F.F.L.P. proposed to "free the farm and industrial worker from the greedy exploitation of those who now rule this country and to win for them the right to life, liberty, and the pursuit of happiness which their exploiters deny them." The new party demanded "the nationalization of all public utilities and all social means of communication and transportation" and that these industries be operated democratically, eventually by the economic organizations of the workers and farmers. For labor the demands were the eight-hour day, the abolition of child labor, and a federal minimum wage. For veterans, the bonus. For all city and rural workers, the establishment of a general federal system of social insurance, covering sickness and other disabling causes. For the farmers, the demand that the land be assured to the users, as well as the issue and control of all money by the government, the payment of war debts by an excess profits tax, and a moratorium on all farm debts. The program made no specific demands for the Negro people.[9]

The organizations which voted to form the Federated Farmer Labor Party, on July 3rd represented approximately 600,000 members—some 50,000 miners, 10,000 machinists, 100,000 needle workers, 7,000 carpenters, 10,000 metal workers, the West Virginia Federation of Labor with 87,000 members, the A.F. of L. central bodies of Detroit, Buffalo, Minneapolis, and Butte, with 140,000, 40,000, 20,000 and 10,000 affiliated members. The farmer-labor parties of Washington, Ohio, California, Illinois, Wisconsin, and elsewhere added many additional thousands. But when it came later on to actually affiliating with the F.F.L.P., only some 155,000 did so, and these were mostly the more advanced organizations.[10] In short, the F.F.L.P. had failed to win the masses. The attraction of the C.P.P.A., plus the Fitzpatrick split—both with the help of the redbaiting capitalist press all over the country—succeeded in keeping the more conservative trade unions at the convention from joining up with the F.F.L.P. The latter organization gradually dwindled in strength.

Labor party sentiment continued strong, however, and a fresh attempt was made by the Workers Party to get such a party established on a broad basis. This new effort was organized in conjunction with the well-established Minnesota Farmer-Labor Party, with which the Workers Party had built up friendly relations. A general convention was held in St. Paul, Minnesota on June 17, 1924, for the purpose of setting up a national farmer-labor party. This convention assembled 542 delegates from 29 states, representing largely farmers. After adopting a program similar to that of the F.F.L.P., it elected as its executive secretary C.A. Hathaway, an influential Minnesota Communist machinist. The convention chose as its candidates in the approaching national elections, for president, Duncan McDonald, former U.M.W.A. head in Illinois, and for vice-president, William Bouck, chief of the Western Progressive Farmers League of Washington.

38

At the St. Paul convention, despite the overwhelming decision to form the new Farmer–Labor Party, there was much sentiment for La Follette, and proposals were carried for negotiations with the Conference for Progressive Political Action on the question of joint support for a La Follette ticket. The Workers Party, looking askance at La Follette as a petty-bourgeois reformist, declared to the St. Paul convention that "the only basis upon which the Workers Party will accept La Follette as the candidate is that he agree to run as a Farmer–Labor candidate, to accept the Party's platform and its central control over the electoral campaign and campaign funds."[11] La Follette rejected these terms. . . .

Most of the participants at that convention later mounted the C.P.P.A. bandwagon. Consequently, the Executive Committee of the Farmer–Labor Party deemed it the part of wisdom to withdraw its candidates, McDonald and Bouck, thereby dissolving the F.L.P. as a party. The Workers Party thereupon put up William Z. Foster, the leader of the 1919 steel strike, as its candidate for president. This was the first national Communist ticket, an event of prime historical importance in the life of the working class. The Party got on the ballot in 13 states, made a strong campaign, and polled for the national ticket, according to the unreliable official figures, some 33,316 votes.[12]

In the presidential elections the La Follette Progressive Independents polled 4,826,382 votes, or about 16.5 percent of the total vote cast. Undoubtedly, large numbers of votes were stolen from the La Follette column. La Follette's good election showing and the huge mass organizations behind the C.P.P.A. obviously provided a sufficient basis for a strong national party of workers and farmers; but this was the last thing wanted by the A.F. of L. and railroad union leaders, tied as they were to the two capitalist parties. Consequently, on February 21, 1925, they met in Chicago, and after rejecting proposals to form a labor party, informally dissolved the C.P.P.A. and went back to the old Gompers policy of "reward your friends and punish your enemies." . . .

It is clear that in this complicated fight for a labor party the young Workers Party, in its eagerness to help the working class to break out of the deadly two–party trap and to establish a labor party, made some serious errors. The most basic of these was to permit itself to become separated from the broad movement of workers and farmers gathered behind La Follette. Although the Party was barred from affiliating officially, nevertheless, through the mass organizations, it could have functioned as the left wing of the La Follette movement, even at the cost of a qualified endorsement of its candidates.

□ ———————————————————————————— □

AGAINST DUAL UNIONISM
FOR LABOR UNITY

"Needle Trades and the Left" by Rose Wortis,
The Labor Herald, May 1922

[*Despite the opposition of its top leadership, in an industry in which women were predominant, the needle trades produced a number of outstanding rank-and-file women leaders. Rose Wortis (1894-1958), a pioneer in the International Ladies Garment Workers Union, a Communist Party leader, participated in unifying the Left forces in the trade. At a time when strong sectarian tendencies existed in the trade unions she fought against dual unionism and stressed the importance of work in the AFL.*

The left wing, in cooperation with Communists, were a major factor in the International Ladies Garment Workers Union during the 1920s. They led a number of strikes which led to improved conditions in the industry. The right, under the control of the union's president, Morris Sigman, started a wave of expulsions. By 1925 the entire executive boards of the three big locals—2, 9 and 22, with about 35,000 members—were expelled. In 1932 David Dubinsky became president of the ILGWU, where he established a personal dictatorship that he maintained for the next four decades.]

The International Ladies Garment Workers Union, in common with the rest of the labor movement, has felt the evil effects of dual unionism. Although there has never been a dual union in the ladies' garment industry, yet the radicals there have been very much influenced by the teachings of the outside unions, and many spent years in a futile effort to organize a Textile Workers' branch of the I.W.W. which did not and could not perform the functions of a trade union. All that they accomplished by their efforts was to isolate themselves from the mass of the workers. . . . There were attempts made to remedy these conditions, for the radical workers instinctively felt the barrenness of their efforts; but these failed because the fallacy of dual unionism was not yet understood. . . . The International Ladies Garment Workers Union has faced many peculiar problems. (Although in existence but a few years, it has succeeded to a great extent in improving the conditions of the workers.) In order to evade the power of the union, the manufacturers began to transfer the industry to small towns, where it is more difficult for the

40

union to reach the workers. In the city, many of the large shops were disbanded and the industry handed over to contractors. A large number of the rank-and-file does not participate actively in the affairs of the organization as now constituted; in order to maintain the standards of the union it became necessary to mobilize the active elements and distribute them through the unorganized shops, so that the message of unionism could be spread from the inside. These problems of the unorganized and the out-of-town shops, among other difficulties, had become too serious to be handled by paid officials against whom workers have a distrust. Only by organizing the union on a basis that would enlist greater numbers into its activities could the union hope to maintain itself. ... At the elections just held, after a two months' campaign during which the official machine, in cooperation with the [right-wing Socialist] *Daily Forward* did their utmost to discredit the radicals, a complete victory was achieved in the largest local in the organization. They elected their full slate, executive board, managers, and delegates to the convention. The program upon which the fight was waged, as enunciated in the Shop Delegate League Bulletin, is as follows:

1. To bring about the reconstruction of the union along industrial lines.

2. To make the union a more militant and efficient organ of struggle by transferring power from union officials to the workers in the shops.

3. To abolish the sanctity of the collective agreement as a permanent institution.

4. To encourage solidarity of the labor forces of different industries, thereby strengthening the economic and social position of the working class.

□ ———————————————————————————————— □

CRISIS IN THE MINERS' UNION

1. "Miners Want a New Union" by Thomas Myerscough,
Labor Unity, **July 1928**
2. "Miners Surge Forward" by Pat Toohey,
Labor Unity, **March 1928**

[*The United Mine Workers of America (UMWA) is the oldest industrial union. In the late 1920s it had a membership of about half a million. By the end of the decade, under the class collaborationist policies and dictatorial leadership of John L. Lewis, it dropped down to 100,000. A disastrous stike in 1927-8 and the expulsion of a large part of the membership almost destroyed the union.*

The Communist Party and the TUEL worked consistently to preserve the union. In 1924 George Voyzey, a Communist miner from Illinois, ran against Lewis for president. Sixty-six thousand votes were counted for this "unknown" rank-and-filer and 136,000 for Lewis. Many miners claim that Voyzey had actually been elected.

The Left sponsored a Save-the-Union campaign, starting in 1925; its organ was The Coal Digger. *Tony Minerich, Tom Myerscough, Pat Toohey and hundreds of other Communists and progressives in the mine areas were active in this work. In September 1928, when the UMWA appeared to be near collapse, these forces joined in organizing the independent National Miners Union.*

Thomas Myerscough (1891-1971) was the secretary of District No. 5, one of the largest in the UMWA. He later became chairman of the National Miners Union.

He wrote this article for the TUEL journal, as did Pat Toohey. Since the Communists were opposed to dual unionism, the formation of the National Miners Union was seen as a temporary expedient. And so it proved to be. When John L. Lewis assumed a progressive role in the 1930s and the UMWA began to regain its health, the National Miners Union was dissolved and most of its members rejoined the UMWA.

Pat Toohey (1904-1978) was born to a miner's family. He was closely associated with Myerscough, and was elected secretary of the National Miners Union. In 1928 he was beaten by thugs in Pittsburgh and then charged with "inciting to riot." The famous attorney, Clarence Darrow, defended Toohey and John Brophy, a national UMWA leader. The charges were dropped.

Toohey was in the national leadership of the Young Communist League. Both he and Myerscough were members of the Communist Party.]

1.

The critical situation in the bituminous strike fields brought about by the ruinous policies of the John L. Lewis officialdom looms as a spectre in the eyes of the miners of America. Thousands of individuals and whole blocks of local unions are being expelled and their relief cut off because they demand that these policies be changed. Progressive miners everywhere are convinced that it would be a disastrous mistake to cling to the United Mine Workers of America any longer as the union of the miners.

Executive officers from newly reorganized districts and leaders of progressive movements in the unorganized field and other states where the rank and file has not yet taken over the local union machinery, have issued a call for a National Convention to extricate the miners from the death clutch of the Lewis machine, and build a new union. . . . [T]he call issued by . . . progressives for a convention [stated]:

"The U.M.W.A. was built by rank and file miners through a whole generation of struggle. Its history is full of heroic efforts of the miners to build it into a real union in the face of starvation, suffering, bloody assaults from company gunmen, organized attacks by the police, troops, injunctions and all-too-often betrayals by the union's official leaders. Nor were these struggles without success. With unbreakable solidarity and unconquerable fighting spirit, the miners slowly built up the union. . . ."

But since the reactionary Lewis clique took control . . . progress has stopped and the organization slowly disintegrated. Membership dwindled; four years ago it controlled 70% of bituminous coal mining, and today 20% still under union control is being filched away by the onslaught of the operators. . . .

Lewis' regime is characterized as the "worst that ever cursed any body of organized miners in the world's labor history." The policies which have practically turned the U.M.W.A. into a company union and which were responsible for the formation of the Save-the-Union Committee by rank and file miners to fight these policies, are specified one by one. . . .

Lewis' collaboration with the operators to drive 200,000 coal diggers out of the mining industry to swell the great army of unemployed which has already gone beyond the 4,000,000 mark, are sharply exposed. A six hour work day, five day week is the demand made by the rank and file to meet the heavy unemployment problem. A strong fighting union with an honest leadership rather than lickspittles of the bosses, and a Labor Party to drive out the corrupt politicians and substitute workers' representatives, are the demands of the progressives.

When Lewis took control of the union, it was among the most militant and progressive in the entire labor movement. The labor party, organization of all fields and the policy of one national agreement were supported by the rank and file representation at the first convention Lewis presided over when he assumed the presidency about ten years ago. As the years went by, and Lewis grasped the union machinery more firmly, these and other policies were flagrantly violated. The progressive spirit was choked. Conventions were packed, elections stolen, and the union was kept under his control by gangster methods. George Voyzey's votes in the

1924 election were stolen and then John Brophy's in 1926, and Lewis continued in office illegally. . . .

Finally, under the leadership of the progressive officialdom of District 5, Pennsylvania, representatives from all districts of the U.M.W.A. and the unorganized field were invited to a national conference in Pittsburgh June 12, which voted unanimously to call a National Convention to build a new miners' union.

2.

Profoundly convinced, after months of waiting for activity on the part of their officials that would lead to the winning of the great coal strike in Pennsylvania and Ohio, the miners have begun to organize themselves, the rank and file of the union, for action.

A series of left wing conferences, of which four have been held already, is crystallizing into organizational form the widespread sentiment, "Lewis Must Go!" and "The Strike Must Be Won!"

The last two conferences to be held, one in Illinois and one in the anthracite, demanded that the regional conferences be climaxed by a great national left wing conference, to mobilize the strength of the entire left wing for a fight to the finish against the employers who are bent on crushing the union from without, and the dark forces, the corrupt official machines which sap the vitality of the union from within.

The last regional conference was at Wilkes-Barre, Pennsylvania, Sunday, February 19, and was highly successful in spite of the conditions of terror which Cappellini[13] is trying to create, with characteristic Fascist methods.

Threats against prominent left wing leaders have been frequent, and when the members of Pittston locals elected an anti-Cappellini slate headed by Alex Campbell, gunmen supporting the machine ambushed and killed Thomas Lillis, one of the left wing officials. Their next move was to try to kill three members of the grievance committtee of Local 1703 (Pittston): Bonito, Moleski and Mendola, right in the union headquarters. In self defense, Bonito shot an administration gunman, Frank Agati, and has been arrested for murder. The anthracite conference voted unanimously to defend him, and the Save-the-Union committee is actively undertaking to save him from the frameup.

On the very day of the conference, Sam Grecio, another official of the left wing administration, at Pittston, was shot down with three bullets in his head while walking home with his wife. . . .

However, this terrorism did not prevent 150 delegates from 51 local unions from meeting, and making plans to combat not only the general evils against which the whole miners' union struggles, but some special difficulties in the anthracite.

The anthracite miners are tied down with a five year contract, including an arbitration agreement, made for them by the Lewis and Cappellini gang. Fifty percent of them are unemployed. The great evils are the speedup tactics of the bosses, the contractor system, the arbitration agreement, and the sell-out policy of the district officials. . . .

The Illinois conference took place absolutely in the open, in a big hall from which no one was barred. In addition to the delegates from left wing groups in the various locals, about 150 rank and file miners from the immediate vicinity were there. . . .

There were many speakers. Pat Toohey and Tony Minerich of the National Save-the-Union committee, Luke Coffee, Joe Angelo, John Watts, Freeman Thompson, and numerous others seized the opportunity to speak for the miners of their localities, and tell of the situation in its various aspects. The feeling of the conference was quite clear and correct. The miners have lost confidence in their official leaders; they will fight along left wing lines for a labor party, for organizing of the unorganized fields, for the six hour day and a five day week, for state relief for unemployed, for a tonnage rate on coal cutting and loading machines so that the machines will give part of their profit (taken out of the men's wages because of reduced crews in the mines) back to the miners. . . .

The question of machines, which are being introduced first into the southern fields, as the coal seam around Springfield is not so suitable to them, is one of the most serious. Mines with 600 men employed have cut down to 250 men when machines were installed, and still produce enough coal. The entry–driving machinery throws most men out of work. . . .

Another sore point with the miners of Illinois is the flagrant disregard of union rules intended for the safety of the men. The bosses not only fire and hire as they like, feeling sure that the Fishwick bureaucracy will not interfere on the side of men discriminated against, but they also force men to work in unsafe mines, mines filled with gas, without proper timbering, with the cars running too fast, etc. . . .

Sentiment is widespread among the men that the separate peace between the Illinois district and the operators was a mistake and treason to the rest of the miners; also that the operators having used them against Pennsylvania and Ohio, are trying now to break the Illinois union itself, as the wage negotiations have apparently fallen through, for the time being. . . .

In short, the miners know that the way to win a battle is to fight, and they are mobilizing their forces at last; they are on the march and their objective is a victory.

☐ ── ☐

EARLY YEARS IN AUTO ORGANIZATION

Labor and Automobiles by Robert W. Dunn,
International Publishers, 1929

[*Robert W. Dunn (1895–1977) was not a member of the working class but he placed at the disposal of that class all his considerable talents and unflagging energy.*

His name is principally associated with Labor Research Association (LRA) which he helped to found in 1927 and in which he worked to the end of his days, together with such notable collaborators as Anna Rochester, Grace Hutchins, Alexander Trachtenberg and Solon De Leon.

The book from which the following extract was taken is one of a series of volumes in the "Labor and Industry" series which were prepared by LRA and published by International Publishers.]

In the last few years the Workers (Communist) Party has turned its attention very determinedly to the organization of the unorganized. As a part of this program it has carried on energetic campaigns in Detroit much to the alarm of the employers' associations who have spent a good deal of money on "Red experts" to expose the movement. The Communists are relatively strong in some of the local unions, and such strength as they have among the working population of Detroit they have concentrated to a large extent on the auto industry. . . .

As in other American industries, the Party forms its own nuclei [clubs] also in the various automobile plants. They are chiefly engaged in preliminary educational work and elementary political propaganda. The Party has published the first agitation papers ever issued in the industry for the workers of particular companies or plants. Some of those published in Michigan are, *The Ford Worker, The Fisher Body Worker, The Dodge Worker, The Packard Worker, The Hudson Worker, The Chrysler Worker* and *The Buick Worker*. These little four-page papers, which range in circulation from 1,000 to 20,000 (Ford has the largest), carry about two pages of general news and editorials and two pages of shop reports, notes and letters,[14] with the purpose of relating the daily grievances of the workers to the broader issues of their lives and status under capitalism. The papers constantly urge the workers to join a union. Even the most conservative workers will buy these papers, sold for a penny at the gates of the plant by volunteers. . . .

The Party work among the automobile workers has always stressed the importance of organizing the women, the young workers and the foreign-born workers. . . .

To date, the efforts of the Workers Party have met with a considerable response, as shown by the circulation of the papers. However, the fear of discharge and spies has held the workers back from more active participation in organization activities. But the agitation is not decreased because at first it seems to meet with such little practical response. When the workers are organized in Detroit, and the other automobile centers, it will undoubtedly be with the aid of the most active elements of the working class, many of whom are Workers Party members.

□ ───────────────────────────────── □

THE SACCO AND VANZETTI FRAME-UP

The Rebel Girl: An Autobiography
by Elizabeth Gurley Flynn, International Publishers, 1973

[*The celebrated case of Nicola Sacco and Bartolomeo Vanzetti began with their arrest near Boston in 1920 and ended with their execution in 1927, after years of world-wide protest and struggle to save the lives of the two innocent men. Fifty years later the governor of Massachusetts decreed that they had not had a fair trial.*

At the beginning of this great struggle the Italian anarchists were the prime movers, and Gurley Flynn was then personally and politically linked to this group. She headed its Workers Defense League.

Soon the newly formed Workers Party moved into the struggle and, as William Z. Foster has written, "became the heart of the fight to save them. . . ."

Foster, who worked closely with Flynn during this period, says: "For the next seven years demonstrations, strikes, and protests against the legal lynching took place in many cities, with Communists everywhere playing a leading role. . . ." (History of the CPUSA, p. 209.)

Elizabeth Gurley Flynn (1890–1964) was one of the great women of the twentieth century. For nearly sixty years she was active in the most significant struggles of the working class. She joined the Communist Party in 1935 and was a member of the National Committee of the Party. She became National Chairperson of the CP in 1960.]

In April 1919 a bomb scare broke into the press. Some 30 mysterious packages, addressed to prominent people around the country, with a return address of Gimbel's [a New York department store] were allegedly picked up in the mail. By strange coincidence this happened on the eve of May Day. It was stated by the Department of Justice that they contained bombs. Again, in June 1919, a series of so-called bomb explosions took place in eight cities. The front porch of J. Mitchell Palmer's residence was damaged. No one was hurt. The whole thing was characterized as a frame-up by labor circles. It was a prologue to the Palmer raids. William J. Flynn was then in charge of the Bureau of Investigation, forerunner of the FBI. He claimed that a "pink leaflet" had been found near one of the spots under investigation, and in February 1920 arrested Roberto Elia, a Brooklyn printer, and Andrea Salsedo, a typesetter in the same shop.

These two men, although threatened with deportation by the Department of Justice, were not turned over to the Department of Labor, then in charge of deportation matters. Nor were they booked in any police court or placed in jail. They were private prisoners, practically incommunicado, held secretly and mysteriously in the office of the Department of Justice on the 14th floor of 15 Park Row [New York City], a most unusual procedure. Only their closest friends and families knew of their imprisonment and helplessly accepted it. They hired a lawyer with offices in the same building, who did nothing.

Salsedo had a group of anarchist comrades in Massachusetts who were troubled over his disappearance. Many of their group had been arrested and secretly deported as a result of the Palmer raids. They sent one of their number to New York City to investigate. His name was Bartolomeo Vanzetti. Italian workers from other places visiting New York City often came to the office of Carlo's [Tresca] paper at 208 East 12th St. I met a few, now and again, if I happened to know them personally. But I did not know of Vanzetti's visit; apparently it made little impression on the New York anarchists. . . .

What he found out about Salsedo shocked him very much. He felt that the lawyer that represented him was either scared or incompetent and decided they should raise funds to hire a better lawyer. They contacted Walter Nelles, a lawyer connected with the American Civil Liberties Union, who agreed to take the case. Salsedo's lawyer was later branded as a Department of Justice accomplice. Vanzetti had heard that Salsedo had been beaten and tortured by special agents there, especially one Francisco, that he had been threatened with death and was in a state of terror and collapse. Whether he jumped from the window or was pushed out, we will never know. Those who knew, never told. But early on the morning of May 3, 1920, his crushed body was found by passers-by on the street outside the building. The pavement was shattered by the force of his fall. Elia was quickly deported before his story could be told. But he left a sworn deposition telling of the torture of Salsedo, in which he stated: "I am afraid of the agents of the Department of Justice and I do not want this statement made public until I leave the country."

Vanzetti, on his return to Massachusetts, with others began to arrange protest meetings. One such meeting was scheduled for Brockton, Massachusetts, on May 5. Leaflets were distributed. They had many friends among the shoe workers there, but by now the Department of Justice was under severe criticism. Meetings on this ghastly death were not welcome to them. They had to be stopped. So on the very day of the meeting, two days after the Salsedo tragedy, Vanzetti and his comrade Sacco were arrested on a streetcar on their way to Brockton. For the next seven years a great point was made by the state about why these two radical foreign-born workers on their way to a meeting with other comrades of theirs, to protest the violence of a powerful government agency, *did not tell the*

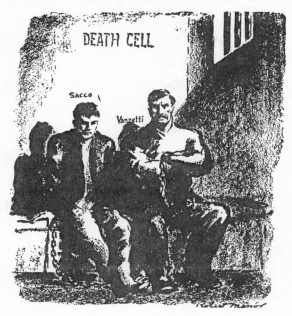

By Robert Minor, *Daily Worker* 1924

truth about where they were going and whom they were going to meet. It was very natural, especially in view of the fact that all the police asked them that night was, "Are you Reds?" They had every right to anticipate deportation proceedings, with possibly a similar fate to that of Salsedo added. Many of their closest comrades, including Luigi Galleani, the brilliant editor of their paper, *Cronaca Sovversiva,* in Barre, Vermont, had been victims of the Palmer raids.

Nothing much was said or done about the arrests of Sacco and Vanzetti by anyone at first. They were very humble and obscure foreign-born workers. A small Italian committee of close associates was set up in Boston. But soon they were to realize that this was a different matter—not a political charge but a criminal one. Sacco and Vanzetti were bundled into cars and taken around from one town to another, where they were put on exhibition. Strange people were brought in to look at them while the police queried insistently, "Are these the men?"—and insisted: "Sure, these are the guys all right!" They were told to put on certain caps, to crouch down, which was very confusing to Sacco and Vanzetti. Then, for the first time they were told they were accused of two murders and a robbery in nearby towns.

Vanzetti was tried and quickly convicted for an attempted robbery in Bridgewater, Massachusetts, on December 24, 1919. All that saved Sacco from this trial was a time-book record in the shoe factory that showed he was at work at that hour. Sacco and Vanzetti were jointly charged with the holdup of a $15,000 payroll in the yard of the Slater and Morrill Shoe Company at South Braintree, Massachusetts, on April 15, 1920, where the paymaster and guard had both been killed. The charge was first-degree murder. This was another Mooney case, in New England. But it took time for the American people to realize it.

□ ———————————————————————————————— □

THE GREAT ECONOMIC CRISIS

Editorial, "Wall Street Crash a Signal of Coming Struggle," *Daily Worker,* October 29, 1929

[*The great economic crisis of 1929–33 was the most catastrophic in the history of world capitalism. It was most severe in the United States where production fell by more than 50 percent and the official, conservative figures showed the rate of unemployment at 25 percent of the labor force.*

Acting true to their class blindness, the defenders of capitalism had been trumpeting glad tidings. On December 4, 1928, President Calvin Coolidge grandly proclaimed: "No Congress of the United States ever assembled, on surveying the state of the Union, has met with a more pleasing prospect than that which appears at the present time." And the captains of industry were no less optimistic.

Only the Communists, with the science of Marxism-Leninism as their guide, were able to penetrate beneath the glitter of surface appearances. The CP Central Committee, at two of its plenary sessions, observed the imminence of the growing crisis and predicted its onset. It dismissed the illusion of "organized capitalism" as a "dream dissipated by grim reality."

Excerpts from the Daily Worker *follow.*]

It can't happen now in America—but it did!

Only a few hours after [President] Herbert Hoover, the Pope of American business, had pledged his word that "the fundamental business of the country . . . is on a sound and prosperous basis"—and after J.P. Morgan, Charles E. Mitchell and other heads of the six biggest banking houses of the country had formed such a money pool as had never been heard of before anywhere in the world to prevent it—the Stock Exchange fell into a second crash, the biggest that has ever occurred since the panic that attended the beginning of the world war in 1914.

After the first crash of last Thursday, all the forces at the command of the kings of American finance were brought to bear to prevent this second crash of Monday. The money pool of the six biggest banks in the United States entered the market with a fund of one hundred million at their disposal and bought huge blocks of stock for the purpose of holding the price up—and yet the prices fell in avalanche after avalanche about their ears. Thursday's catastrophic fall in the market was followed by Monday's [October 29, 1929] still bigger collapse which wiped out unknown thousands of relatively small speculators and about five thousand millons of dollars of "values." The "best stocks in the world" were thrown on the market as "rank speculations."

For the second time in five days the gods of American finance are defeated in the effort to control the forces of the business "universe" over which they rule.

Hoover and the heads of the big money combines, in making public statements of reassurance, do not, of course, regard their own words to have as much to do with the real facts as with the "psychological necessities." In other words, the reassurances of the heads of the Wall Street oligarchy with its headquarters in Washington and New York, are false checks intended to prevent the little fellows from trying all at once to save themselves and thus driving the market down still further.

Capitalism cannot control the anarchy of the market which is inherent and inescapable in the system of capitalist production. The dream of Hoover, and of the social-democratic defender of the capitalist system, [Rudolf] Hilferding, which also attracts all opportunists even among those who try in quieter times to appear as Communists—the dream of "organized capitalism" which overcomes its inner contradictions and solves the problems of the internal market—this dream is dissipated by grim reality.

The working class of this and all other countries should give its attention to the events coming to light in the chaos of the capitalist market. Panic and business recession, with still more unemployment, and still sharper class struggle are ahead. As said by the Plenum of the Central Committee of the Communist Party:

"The coming of an economic crisis will immediately sharpen the contradictions inherent in American capitalism, will lead internationally in an accentuation of the general crisis of world capitalism, sharpen acutely the war danger, intensify the class struggle. . . . The efforts to overcome the crisis by throwing the burden upon the shoulders of the working class (wage cuts, unemployment, breaking down of living standards) will speed up the radicalization of the working class and lead to a perspective of big class battles."

But the naked fact is that this collapse in the stock market is a real tremor in the oncoming earthquake of economic crisis.

"Is the stabilization of American capitalism becoming stronger, or is it becoming more and more precarious, shaky and decayed?" This is a question which has been at issue for many months between the open and concealed defenders of capitalist class ideology, on the one side, and the spokesmen of the revolutionary Communist movement on the other.

□ ——————————————————————————————— □

2.
THE
GREAT
DEPRESSION

The great economic crisis (1929–1933) shattered the illusions created during the "prosperity period" of the previous seven years. The dreams of small investors were destroyed in the spectacular Wall Street collapse in October, 1929. After the crash millions were thrown out of work and hunger plagued the land.

Automobile production, an important economic indicator, which reached a high of 621,910 cars in April 1929, touched bottom with 119,950 by December. Similar declines were reported in other basic industries. Wage cuts prevailed and the AFL registered a marked decline in membership. At the bottom of the depression 17,000,000 people were jobless; but serious unemployment had actually preceded the devastating final quarter of 1929.

Anna Rochester, Marxist economist, noted that one-sixth of the population were chronically on the edge of destitution or already hopelessly submerged at the beginning of the crisis. The Black population was first to feel the economic seismic waves before they hit the rest of the country. The labor historian Philip Foner noted that Black workers felt the acuteness of the crisis four years earlier and added: "In the early months of 1929, with the economy supposedly flourishing as never before, 300,000 Negro industrial workers, about one-fifth of all Blacks employed in industry, had already been thrown out of work."[1] Such was the state of the Union.

Capitalism was incapable of cushioning the shock which fell heaviest on the wage worker. A trickle of charity was dispensed by private organizations, churches and individuals but starvation spread from coast to coast: the coal mines of Kentucky, the cotton fields of the South, the steel towns of the Midwest, the slums of urban centers. Soup kitchens and the shacks called Hoovervilles were characteristic of cities. The unemployed, especially youth, roamed the country in search of employment. The selling of apples on street corners, schemes to have an idle man employed by block neighbors to tidy up the area—none of these feeble devices brought relief. Henry Ford made the grand gesture of raising wages by $1 a day, only to cancel this shortly thereafter and turn to layoffs.

The trade union movement was numerically weak. William Green, president of the American Federation of Labor, and his associates pursued a class collaborationist policy which was opposed to the interests of not only the mass of workers but of other victims of the capitalist crisis as well. It was only the Communist Party, with leadership in the smaller left unions and in some AFL locals, that promoted organized struggle. The Party's experiences provided valuable training for a core of militants who were to make an invaluable contribution to the later drive for industrial unionism, especially in the CIO. Radicals, especially Communists, were targets for both management and the labor officialdom represented by Green. But it was becoming harder to belittle socialism. The Soviet Union, in contrast to the United States, had abolished unemployment. A planned economy in the interests of the working class was surpassing its five-year goals.

The Communist Party of the United States, even before the onset of the economic disaster, had come forward with a national program and in 1929 it joined with the Trade Union Unity League (TUUL) in a drive to organize the unorganized. The demand for unemployment insurance, opposed by William Green as a de-

meaning "dole," originated in 1930 and the Party led massive national and local demonstrations for jobs and relief for the hungry and homeless. The Central Committee of the Communist Party, following the unprecedented National Hunger March on December 7, 1931, to the nation's capital, appealed for a new round of protests against the government's callous rejection of the marcher's demands.

White and Black workers joined in the effort of the Communist Party for unemployment relief, in 1930, in Atlanta, Georgia. N.H. Powers and Joe Carr were charged with "insurrection" which carried the death penalty. As a consequence, a meeting of the American Negro Labor Congress was called in Atlanta to demand the release of the two. But before the meeting opened, four of the scheduled speakers were arrested and held on the same charges of "insurrection." The case became known as that of The Atlanta Six which included a young woman, Mary Dalton; a Black worker, Henry Storey; a young Black leader, Herbert Newton, whose premature death was hastened by picket line beatings and Ann Burlak, a veteran at 18 of organizing work by the National Textile Workers Union in New England, where she was known as "The Red Flame." Pressure and legal action eventually freed The Atlanta Six.

By early 1930 the southern headquarters of the Party was established in Birmingham with a largely Black membership in this steel center. In the same year the weekly Southern Worker began publication under semi-legal conditions with James Allen as editor.

In the early 1930s Louise Thompson was in Birmingham, Alabama, representing the International Workers Order, of which she was a national secretary. This brought her into confrontation with the prevailing anti-Black and anti-labor terror, and gave her a taste of a jim-crow jail. Louise Thompson participated in the first cultural delegation of Black artists to the Soviet Union in 1932—a delegation which included Langston Hughes, Loren Miller and others. The editor of The Crisis, organ of the NAACP, described her as "the leading colored woman in the Communist movement in this country."[2]

"Insurrection" was the basis for the indictment and death was *the pronounced sentence in the case of young Angelo Herndon of Atlanta whose "crime" was to protest the inhuman treatment of the unemployed. Organizing in the southland carried with it perils far more dangerous than in other parts of the country. Lynching, the denial of the vote, the peonage system were commonplace in the areas where sharecropping prevailed. The courage and skill required in putting together a resistance movement were personified by Black Communist leadership, as that displayed by Al Murphy and Hosea Hudson in unionization on farm and in factory.*

Another front of struggle which grew far beyond the expectations of its initiators, involved the veterans of World War I in a demand for what was popularly known as the Bonus.[3] The vehicle for action was the Workers Ex-Servicemen's League which had the support of the Communist Party and various left forces. A call was issued for a national march on Washington.

After the arrival of the veterans in Washington, President Hoover ordered General Douglas MacArthur to drive the marchers out of the capital. With the assistance of his aide, Dwight D. Eisenhower, the task was carried out with a brutality that shocked the nation. The heroes of the war were viewed by the government as the dregs of society. The embitterment of the public against President Hoover grew rapidly. In later years the Bonus, continually advocated by the Communist Party, became a reality. It had been vetoed by four presidents, but the last veto by Roosevelt was overridden by Congress, whose members bowed in 1936 to widespread public demand.

For the entire world the Scottsboro case threw a glaring spotlight on the injustices that were the lot of Black people in a land where government and society made a mockery of the constant claim of "equality." One of the most stirring accounts of that case was written by William Patterson in his autobiography, The Man Who Cried Genocide. *Patterson, who had joined the Party after the execution of Sacco and Vanzetti, was to become engaged for most of his life in struggles for civil liberties. (See also p. 81.)*

The farm community, operating in a declining economy, suffered a drastic drop in its gross income from 1929 to 1933 of over 55 percent. Farm struggles were not confined to sharecroppers. In the

East and Midwest opposition was rising against farm foreclosures. A device employed was the offering of a bid of one cent for a foreclosed farm and the turning back of the property to the original owner. These "penny sales" were reinforced by a mass turnout of neighbors who faced similar dispossession. In California agricultural workers, landless and migrant, were bitterly oppressed.

As early as 1925 the Communist Party took on an organizing task of extreme difficulty. The major effort was carried on by the Agricultural Workers Industrial Union, affiliated with the TUUL. Imperial Valley was the scene of some of the most militant actions in which workers of Japanese, Mexican and Filipino origin were mainly involved. Brutal repression was used against the union by the growers and the state. In 1930 a number of leaders, all members of the Communist Party, were convicted on the catch-all charge of "criminal syndicalism" and vicious sentences were meted out against them. Frank Spector wrote his account of the uphill organizing struggle and subsequent trial while he was imprisoned in San Quentin.

Towards the end of its first decade the CP made a significant contribution to solidarity with workers in the colonial countries, chiefly on the African continent. On the initiative of the Negro Workers Trade Union Committee, established by the Red International of Labor Unions (RILU), James W. Ford, a trade unionist with experience in the Chicago Federation of Labor, became secretary of the first International Conference of Negro Workers. He organized the conference in the port city of Hamburg, Germany, July 7–10, 1930, which was attended by representatives from the United States, Jamaica, the Gold Coast, South Africa and others. An international committee was established in which the United States was represented by Ford, Isaiah Hawkins (a Pennsylvania coal miner), and George Padmore. William L. Patterson collaborated closely with Ford.

Cuba, Nicaragua and other Latin American countries suffering from domination by exploitative US monopoly interests backed by armed force, were special concerns of the Party. The White House ordered an invasion of Nicaragua in 1926 to suppress a guerrilla uprising led by Augusto C. Sandino. In 1933 it sent warships into Cuban waters to insure continued US control of that island following the overthrow of the puppet regime of Gerardo Machado. The Anti-Imperialist League rallied mass support for the Nicaraguan and Cuban people with the declaration: "Let us push the struggle which is our struggle, demand the end to all intervention in Latin America." William Simons, a Communist, was the secretary of the League.

In this period the Party was striving to fulfill its obligations on both the national and international scene. Out of the mixture of victories and defeats came valuable lessons that led to greater achievements.

☐ ———————————————————————————— ☐

MOBILIZATION AGAINST HUNGER

"Unemployment Struggles of the Thirties" by Carl Winter,
***Political Affairs,* September-October, 1969**

[Carl Winter (b. 1906), editor of the Daily World, *was secretary of the Unemployed Councils of Greater New York for the years 1932 and 1933, and was one of the organizers of the National Hunger Marches. In the national unemployment movement Winter collaborated with Israel Amter (1881–1954), one of the most beloved individuals in the Communist and Left movements. Among Communists in its leadership were Henry Winston, Andrew Onda, Arnold Johnson, Claude Lightfoot and others.*

From its inception the Party worked to create a unified unemployed movement. There were three primary organizations: the largest was the Unemployed Councils under Communist leadership; the Workers Alliance, influenced by the Socialists; and the Unemployed Leagues, led by A.J. Muste, leader of a "leftist" group. At a unity convention on April 8, 1936, in the national capital, the three organizations established the Workers Alliance of America representing some 800,000 people. Arnold Johnson, prominent in later years in united front movements on behalf of the CP, was elected to the national board and served in its center in Washington.]

Never did the domestic spectre of Communism haunt the bankers, the industrialists and their representatives in Washington more than in the last months of 1929 and the early 30s. This was the period following the outbreak of the most deep-going economic crisis in the United States.

The sudden crash of the Wall Street Stock Exchange, in October 1929, gave a crushing blow to the self-serving promises of the ruling class that an unprecedented prosperity which it had long been enjoying would last forever. The long series of layoffs and cutbacks in working hours which had been held out to be merely temporary soon proved to be only the forerunners of mass unemployment.

The newly awakened self-doubt and fears among the ideologues of capital, however, were not the result merely of the mass misery and starvation which now became widespread. Unemployment, poverty and hunger were the constant companions of American capitalism, even in its more prosperous days. What now disturbed the ruling class was not only the tremors, which ran through its economic structure, but the rising tide of protest and resistance struggles on the part of its long–suffering victims.

At the outset, President Herbert Hoover attempted to reassure his class brothers and to pacify the people with repeated declarations that prosperity was "just around the corner." Organized charities and millionaire "philanthropists" tried to remove from public view the most glaring examples of human wreckage of the capitalist crisis by establishing free souplines and breadlines. Local Chambers of Commerce helped provide crates of apples for the unemployed to sell on street corners, in a desperate attempt to invoke the spirit of "self-help" and "free enterprise." And wherever the growing army of unemployed refused to be cajoled or slowly starved into silence, the ever–present police forces and jails were brought into service.

So it came about that shortly after its tenth birthday, the Communist Party of the U.S.A. was put to the test of giving leadership and direction to the wave of spontaneous mass struggles of the unemployed throughout the country. However, to equip itself for this task the Party first had to settle accounts with Right-opportunist forces within its own leadership who refused to assume the responsibilities of a vanguard party of the working class. Jay Lovestone, during his short tenure as national secretary of the Party had echoed such capitalist–apologist views as those later published in the Hoover report on Recent Economic Changes in the United States, making wildly optimistic predictions about a crisis–free future for "organized capitalism." But the majority of the Party, having wrestled with the complacent attitudes of this misleadership, and having rejected its theories of American exceptionalism and its forecasts of a Victorian Age for U.S. capitalism, was able quickly to rally for struggle against the effects of the crisis upon the lives of millions.

The removal of Lovestone from Party leadership by convention action in 1929, and his expulsion from the ranks together with his small band of incorrigible supporters, was accompanied by a new turn to the masses and serious efforts to organize for the solution of their most pressing problems. The Party was thus enabled early in 1930 to address itself to the American people through millions of leaflets, thousands of street corner meetings and appeals in the columns of the *Daily Worker* with the call, "Don't Starve, Fight!"

The first nationwide organized protest against the burdens of the economic crisis, being shouldered by the working people of the United States, was organized upon the initiative of the Communist Party. Together with the Left-led militant unions who constituted the Trade Union Unity League, the Party issued a call for simultaneous mass demonstrations on behalf of the unemployed to be held March 6, 1930, in the major cities of the country.

Huge outpourings of demonstrators responded in Cleveland, Milwaukee, San Francisco, Los Angeles, Seattle, Denver, Philadelphia and other cities; 50,000 turned out in Chicago and Pittsburgh; 100,000 took part in Detroit and 110,000 in New York City. It was estimated that one and a quarter million men and women joined in this first nationwide protest. The local police everywhere were taken by surprise. No one had expected such a show of strength and unanimity on the part of the victims of capitalism's operations, but everywhere the police and local authorities tried to wreak their vengeance at the end of each meeting or demonstration. Club-swinging police, on horseback and afoot, attacked the demonstrators in the hope that if unemployment could not be ended, at least protest against unemployment could. Leaders of the Communist Party who were in the forefront of these demonstrations were singled out for arrest, among them, William Z. Foster, Israel Amter, Robert Minor, [Harry Raymond] and others in New York City.

The answer of the Communists was to call upon the unemployed to organize their ranks for greater struggle, for defense of their rights and their daily needs.

The Trade Union Unity League meanwhile served to coordinate and give guidance to the mushrooming local committees among the unemployed. It called for a national conference in Chicago on July 4, 1930 to bring together their experiences and lay plans for future action. At that gathering 1,320 delegates were registered, representing unemployed groups across the country. They formed there an organization which was destined to play a historic role in defense of the very lives of the American people—the National Unemployed Councils.

From the very beginning, the Unemployed Councils drew into their ranks those workers most determined to combat the new calamity which had befallen them and their families with the sudden downturn of the national economy. Great numbers of Negro workers, in particular, joined the local struggles and played a leading part in the organized committees of the unemployed. Women played an active role, especially in the delegations which called upon local officials and charitable organizations, to demand emergency food and clothing for their children.

No federal system or legislation existed at this time to provide any form of social welfare or public assistance to those in need. The private charities, most of them denominational, were the chief known sources of what little aid was made available in the most extreme emergencies.

The employers took advantage of the growing desperation in the ranks of the working class to slash wages, in many instances 10 percent and 20 percent at a time. Hours of work and earnings were cut back in the name of "sharing the wealth," while speedup was enforced in an attempt to keep up output and profits. A major consequence, which overtook the employed as well as the jobless in every working class community, was a wave of evictions for delinquency in payment of rent.

One of the first big tasks undertaken by the Unemployed Councils was the organization of resistance to evictions. Squads of neighbors were organized to bar the way to the dispossessing officers. Whole neighborhoods were frequently mobilized to take part in this mutual assistance. Where superior police force prevailed it became common practice for the Unemployed Councils to lead volunteer squads in carrying the displaced furniture and belongings back into the home after the police had departed. Council organizers became adept in fashioning meter-jumps to restore disconnected electric service and gas.

Little wonder then that the ruling circles and their spokesmen soon raised the cry of "Communism" against the unemployed movement. The organized committees and councils were not only effectively uniting employed and unemployed, white and Black, but were challenging the sacred property rights of employers and landlords.

President Hoover offered, as his solution, a "stagger system" whereby more could be employed on a part-time basis with reduced earnings. William Green, President of the American Federation of Labor, pompously followed suit, calling for a 30-hour week with a corresponding cut in wages. The Communist Party countered with its widely publicized demand for the shorter workday and week without any reduction in earnings. The Government and the employers, it said, must shoulder the responsibility of providing either work or adequate financial relief. . . .

The number of unemployed grew to ten and twelve million; by 1933 it was estimated to have reached 17,000,000. The U.S. Department of Labor reported 200,000 children wandering across the country in search of food. City hospitals reported growing numbers of serious cases resulting from foraging for food in garbage heaps and hundreds of deaths from starvation. Yet the government provided no comprehensive figures assessing the actual number of unemployed or part-time workers. At the same time unsold stocks of foodstuffs on which high prices were maintained were regularly dumped at sea or burned in fields by profit-hungry corporations.

The spontaneous and isolated protests of the unemployed and the hungry now began to take organized and systematic shape. In one state after another mass marches converged upon the capital and demands for governmental assistance were presented to the legislatures. It was frequently reported in the press that mass street demonstrations and other gatherings of the unemployed were followed by their participants swarming into nearby restaurants, eating their fill, and then departing with advice to the cashier to "charge it to the mayor." . . .

Even in the rural towns the struggle against hunger was taken up in a collective manner. In the first days of 1931, an outraged capitalist press screamed that more than 500 farmers and their wives in the town of

"It means us!" By Clive Weed,
Daily Worker, 1926

England—near Little Rock, Arkansas—had stormed the business district demanding food for their families and threatening to take it if denied. Most of the farmers in this town of about 2,000 population came armed. An emergency businessmen's conference wired the Red Cross for help and received authorization to distribute the demanded food on its behalf. In the course of such struggles the United Farmers League grew side by side with the Unemployed Councils.

Aside from contributing the organizational skill and personnel for the crystallization of a centralized movement, the Communist Party supplied from its theoretical background and practical experience—drawing upon the history of the international movement as well—the central political focus for the struggle against the effects of the capitalist crisis.

Summarized in the most simple terms, the thrust of the Unemployed Councils, under Communist leadership and influence, was to place both the responsibility and the burden for relief for the suffering masses upon the government and the employers. Every speech, every article, every leaflet on behalf of the Unemployed Councils during this period emphasized, over and over again, the concept that a system of federal unemployment insurance must be established "at the expense of the employers and the government." The demand for federal unemployment insurance was first raised by the Communist Party and the Unemployed Councils. It was met by cries of indignation, not only on the part of avowed spokesmen for capital, but also by the class collaborationist officialdom of the A.F. of L. It was denounced as a "dole," beneath the dignity of American workers. . . .

Conferences of the unemployed, together with representatives from workers' organizations—including trade unions and newly-formed tenants' leagues—were held in many cities in the latter part of 1930 and 1931. Six hundred delegates met in New York City on December 19, 1930, and reconvened a New York Conference for Unemployment Relief on January 13. They decided to send a delegation to Washington with a massive list of signatures, demanding that Congress enact a bill providing Federal Unemployment Insurance. . . .

Taken up across the country was the campaign for enactment of "The Workers Unemployment Insurance Bill." Publicized as its major features were: 1) Unemployment insurance at the rate of $35 a week for each unemployed worker and $5 additional for each dependent; 2) creation of a National Unemployment Insurance Fund to be raised by (a) using all war funds for unemployment insurance, (b) a levy on all capital and property in excess of $25,000, (c) a tax on all incomes of $5,000 a year; 3) the Unemployment Insurance Fund thus created, to be administered by a

Workers' Commission elected solely by employed and unemployed workers. A Workers' National Campaign Committee for Unemployment Insurance was established to conduct the petition drive. . . .

Thus the first national hunger march was given its objective to demand federal unemployment insurance legislation from Congress. . . .

"The main demands of the millions of unemployed workers, whom the marchers will represent," stated the Call, "will be for unemployment insurance equal to full wages for the unemployed and part-time workers, for special winter relief in the amount of $150 for each unemployed worker and $50 for each dependent, for the 7-hour day without reduction in weekly earnings, for the initiation of a federal program of furnishing work to the workers at union wages, for the abolition of the brutal terror and discrimination against Negroes and deportation of foreign-born workers, demands of the ex-servicemen (who were organizing to demand an immediate federal bonus payment to veterans of World War I–CW) and poor farmers, etc. The marchers will demand that all war funds be applied to unemployment relief and be administered by the Unemployed Councils. They will demand the enactment of the Workers Unemployment Insurance Bill." . . .

The issuance of the Call for the first national hunger march to demand unemployment insurance legislation was quickly followed by police raids in many cities upon the headquarters of the Communist Party. Matthew Woll, Vice-President of the A.F. of L. and acting President of the National Civic Federation, initiated a letter to every Congressman from the latter reactionary organization denouncing the National Hunger March as a "Communist attack upon the government."

Four caravans of marchers converged upon Washington from New England, the Midwest, the Far West and the South. They came to the federal capital on December 6 and 7, 1931, by truck and automobile. They stopped in every city on their route, to hold meetings explaining their purpose and enlisting support. They carried banners including such slogans as "Employed workers—support the demands of the unemployed and part-time workers," "Unemployed workers—support the strikes of the employed against wage cuts," "Organize for the demands of the National Hunger March," "Build the Unemployed Councils."

A tired but enthusiastic band of 1,675 elected delegates from all parts of the United States finally marched up Capitol Hill. They attempted to present their demands at the door of the Senate Chamber, but were barred. When they appeared at the White House, President Hoover refused them admittance.

The official rebuff in Washington in no way slowed down the campaign for immediate relief for the unemployed and for unemployment insurance. Instead, the captains of the Hunger March organized within the shadow of the Capitol for the assembled delegates to redouble their efforts. The caravans retraced their trek across the country stopping again to hold report-back meetings in every city and to create new and larger committees and councils of the unemployed. . . .

At the beginning of December of that year 3,000 delegates came to the nation's capital, once again carrying the message of struggle for unemployed relief and insurance across the country. For days the marchers were blocked on New York Avenue, at the outskirts of the capital, by police barricades and heavily armed U.S. Marines. They bedded down in their trucks or on the concrete pavement of the highway for two nights while calls for support were wired to workers' organizations and unemployed committees around the nation. Protests from unions, fraternal organizations and indignant citizens finally lifted the blockade. The Second National Hunger March paraded through the streets of Washington and up Capitol Hill. This time, Vice-President Charles Curtis, as Chairman of the Senate, found himself compelled to meet the unemployed marchers' delegation and to receive its petition for enactment of the Workers Unemployment Insurance Bill. The Speaker of the House, Jack Garner, received the delegation as the representative of the lower body.

Such were the mass movements and the struggles which awakened the consciousness of the American people to their right to government and employer-financed welfare. But more important, they proved to the American people their capacity to win their just demands.

The first Unemployment Insurance Bill was introduced in the U.S. House of Representatives by Congressman Ernest Lundeen, Farmer Laborite of Minnesota, in response to the Unemployed Council movement. An A.F. of L. convention went on record for the first time in support of the principle of unemployment insurance. Committees for the enactment of the bill spread through local unions and other organizations in growing numbers of cities and towns. Some city governments and state legislatures began to establish public relief agencies and to dispense limited assistance in cash and in kind to the most needy. The first system of federal Social Security, including a national unemployment compensation law, was enacted early in the "New Deal" administration of President Franklin D. Roosevelt, in response to the years of mass struggle which immediately preceded it. . . .

None of the achievements of this epic period in the life of the American working class were either spontaneous or inevitable. They were the

hard–won products of careful planning, painstaking work, mass involvement and farsighted political guidance. In short, an advanced and
purposeful leadership was required to elevate and coordinate the elemental struggles which arose out of the plight of the masses. This role was
honorably fulfilled by the Communist Party.

□ ———————————————————————————————— □

THE BONUS MARCH

"Bloody Thursday," *Veterans on the March*
by Jack Douglas,
Workers Library Publishers, 1934

[*At a hearing before the House Ways and Means Committee in April,
1932, the Workers Ex-Servicemen's League (WESL) issued a call for a
national march on Washington. The WESL was a left-wing organization
of World War I veterans. At the Committee hearings the WESL was
represented by two Communists, James W. Ford and Samuel J. Stember.*

*The organization's chairman was Emanuel Levin, who had enlisted in
the Marine Corps in 1906 and was a veteran of many years' activity in the
CP. Other leaders were Harold Hickerson and Peter V. Cacchione.
(Cacchione later became New York City's first Communist councilman.)*

The following is an excerpt from the first chapter of Douglas' book.]

On the morning of Thursday, July 28, 1932, some twenty thousand
veterans were encamped in Washington, D.C. They had come to demand
money promised them as an adjustment of wartime pay for their services
in the World War fifteen years back.

These had been fifteen years of maladjustment, economic insecurity;
betrayal of the promises made them when they went to war, disillusion-
ments, privations and in hundreds of cases, actual starvation. The
increasing pressure of a crisis, which had begun three years before,
tumbled them out of what jobs and homes they had left and sent them
over the railroads and highways from every city and town in the nation to
Washington. Hundreds of women and children were among them.
Babies were carried in arms. A few of the women bore children after
arriving in Washington.

When they came they gathered sticks, boards, bricks, pieces of scrap
metal and loose sheets of tin and built themselves packing-box shacks.

Some moved into abandoned buildings about to be torn down. A few, remembering their experience in France, dug holes in the ground and lined them with whatever materials they could find.

During the ten weeks they remained every variety of threat and maneuver was tried to get them out of the city. Now the authorities had lost patience—some said, their heads. A series of conferences had been held in the high offices of the government the past few days. The veterans were to be driven out by force. Pressure was ordered.

In the next fourteen hours these thousands of ex-soldiers and the many wives and children who had come with them were pushed out of Washington by troops under the personal direction of Chief of Staff Douglas MacArthur and scattered pell-mell over the neighboring states of Maryland and Virginia. Their nondescript shelters were burned by the soldiers. Two men were killed by bullets of the Metropolitan police. Many were injured by thrown bricks and clubs. A man's ear was cut off by a cavalryman's saber. A woman's leg was laid open from knee to ankle. A boy's arm was pierced. Dozens of others were injured. Hundreds were gassed; many of them babies, two of which later died. Thousands were filled with horror, rage, fright. The citizenry who witnessed the rout were so infuriated that before the day was over they were throwing gas bombs back at the soldiers and police.

The Big Push began in the morning. The police department received an order from the Treasury to regain possession of a site on the south side of Pennsylvania Avenue, from Third to Four-And-A-Half Streets, which was being used by the veterans as a billeting place. This maneuver had been decided on by the authorities as a means of beginning a general evacuation. The veterans, arriving there some weeks before, had found two half-demolished buildings in a large brick and debris filled lot. One group cleaned the buildings and began to live in them. Most of the contingent encamped there made themselves huts of bricks and old lumber which they found lying about. Other shelters were thrown together in corners of the two blocks of park just south of the one fronting on Pennsylvania Avenue.

The wrecking contractor was told to put his men to work. He refused, claiming that should he do so, bloodshed was certain. The insurance company which carried his policies advised they would not cover any claims in case of injury if his men began to work before the site was entirely evacuated by the veterans. Police were sent to force the vets off the property.

A brick fight began. The police used their clubs. A number of minor injuries were received by both sides. A truce was soon called. A bit later a

By Robert Minor, *Daily Worker*, 1925

second battle started. The police tried to evacuate one of the still standing buildings. Veterans ran in to protect their living places. The police pulled guns. A veteran was shot through the heart. Another veteran was wounded and died after some days in a hospital. . . .

The newspaper men went to get Police Chief Glassford's statement. He gave his account of the shooting and said General MacArthur would soon be there with troops. He said: "I said to General MacArthur, 'There are women and children among them,' and General MacArthur answered, 'I know it'." Here Glassford smiled as if disowning in advance any responsibility for what was going to happen. He continued: "if conditions are propitious when we get through here, we're going over to clear out the camp at Anacostia."

One of the reporters asked, "To where do you intend to push the men?"

Glassford answered, "Right out into the streets. We'll still have them on our hands, but"—smiling sideways and making a gesture with his hands—"but not so all together." . . .

As I drifted about with the news and camera men, word came that the troops were arriving. We all thought they would come down the street south of Pennsylvania Avenue. No one thought they would actually come down the Avenue. We were waiting to see which way to run with our cameras to get arriving shots. Finally the cavalry were seen coming straight down Pennsylvania Avenue. I ran up to about Sixth Street with others to get my pictures. Got rows of horsemen, tanks and trucks carrying infantry. The cavalcade had come down the right half of the street. Now the cavalry and those behind them went through some maneuvers to take up completely the breadth of the street. They started into the battle zone, passed the Four-And-A-Half—Third Street block, some remaining just before and some just beyond the block. The police, getting ready to turn over the scene to the soldiers, gave their attention to the spectators and began to clear the north side of the block. They became tougher and pushed more roughly, becoming more rowdyish with the situation. The vets became more militant. They booed the soldiers inviting them to fight. . . .

An order was given. The block-long line advanced, infantry first, through and past the buildings, the cavalry following where they could; bayonets afoot, sabers in the air. The tanks went down Third Street and a batch of cavalry down Four-And-A-Half Street. Tear gas bombs were pitched ahead by the infantry. The vets had no chance. They retreated, trying to grab what they could of their possessions. Women and children were among them getting their full share of tear gas. Later it was reported that mustard gas also had been used.

Some of the attacking soldiers were detailed to remain behind to guard the ground already taken. Then the lines of attack formed again, this time with the cavalry leading because the two blocks south of the first group of billets were clear of buildings. More tear gas bombs were thrown, not only at the edge of the retreating crowd, but right into it as it retreated.

The attack moved according to plan. The troop commanders were trying to hurry it. The soldiers had not begun their push till late in the afternoon. There was only an hour or so of daylight left. The occupants of other Bonus Marcher camps were to be driven out as soon as this one was cleared. . . .

During the time of this retreat, some of the soldiers left behind at the billets set fire to the shacks and lean-tos of the vets. Fire engines were called to keep the fires from spreading. A fireman wanted to save the furniture in one of the shacks. One of the retreating ex-soldiers told me he heard a woman beg him to save it. The fireman played a stream of water over it till he was ordered to turn off the water and let it burn.

The feeling of a fight within a family pervaded the place. The vets kept taunting the soldiers that the marines had refused to come out against them. Some were calling the soldiers "Home Guards" and "Hoover's pets." (These troops were from Fort Myer and are popularly known as "The President's Regiments.")

The men who fifteen years before had marched down the Main Streets and Broadways of the nation and away to war to "save the world for democracy," were being sabered, bayonetted and gassed, driven out of the capital where they had come to petition their Congress, by the youngsters of the very next generation—almost their own children.

All the time the vets retreated they mocked and even propagandized in their favor the soldiers who followed with pointed bayonets only a few feet after them. It was the Military against the Citizenry; a scene of civil war. But the line of vets retreating backwards was for many moments as straight as that of the soldiers pressing them. One could see the same training in both lines—the retreating and the attacking. Only a bayonet-length separated them. Something ominous hung over the moving mass.

□ —————————————————————————————— □

COMMUNISTS IN THE SOUTH, 1930-31

Southern Worker, issued weekly
by the Communist Party, U.S.A., Birmingham, Alabama.
1. August 16, 1930; 2. August 30, 1930;
3. & 4. August 29, 1931

[*The first serious effort by the Communist Party to reach the South with its program was made in 1924, when William Z. Foster carried his campaign for U.S. President to a number of major southern cities.*

In 1929 the Communists led a drive to unionize the southern textile workers, which resulted in the great strike at Gastonia, North Carolina.

The Party began a vigorous drive in the Deep South in early 1930, organizing Black and white workers for unemployment relief in Atlanta. It established its district headquarters in Birmingham, the center of heavy industry. In August 1930, the first issues of the weekly Southern Worker *appeared, published at Birmingham and Chattanooga, under semi-legal conditions, with James Allen, author of a number of Marxist books, as editor. It appeared regularly for the next year and a half.*]

1.

August 16, 1930.

This is the first number of the *Southern Worker,* which is to be published regularly every week by the Communist Party of the U.S.A.

70

The *Southern Worker* is the Communist paper for the South.

It is being published because the southern workers and farmers need it and want it. The *Southern Worker* is the voice of the Negro and white workers and farmers of the South crying in united protest against the state of starvation, suffering and persecution to which they have been subjected by the white ruling class.

This is the first really workers' paper ever published below the Mason and Dixon line. It is the first Communist publication ever issued in the South. As such it will carry the Communist program to the white and Black workers and farmers, pointing out the path to struggle, offering the militant and understanding leadership of the Communist Party to the millions of southern toilers.

The *Southern Worker* is neither a "white" paper, nor a "Negro" paper. It is a paper of and for both the white and Black workers and farmers. It recognizes only one division, the bosses against the workers and the workers against the bosses. In this class struggle the *Southern Worker* stands always, without exception, unflinchingly, for the workers. It is a workers' paper.

2.

August 30, 1930

"Farmers Rally for Struggle at Election Meet"

Whitney, Ala. - Over 125 sharecroppers, tenant farmers and farm laborers attended the opening meeting of the Communist Party election campaign in the farming sections of Alabama last Saturday.

The meeting was held here in the heart of the cotton belt, some 40 miles north of Birmingham. The speakers were Seaton Worthy, Communist candidate for U.S. Senator from Alabama; Tom Johnson, District Communist organizer and Harry Jackson, organizer of the Trade Union Unity League. Roy Colley, a local farmer, was chairman.

The sharecroppers and tenant farmers, most of them working on big company plantations, face absolute ruin this year as the price of cotton reaches new low levels daily. Local farmers predicted the worst year in the history of cotton raising in the South.

3.

August 29, 1931

"Greetings from Y.C.L., District No. 17"

The District Council of the Young Communist League, District No. 17, extends revolutionary greetings to the *Southern Worker* on its first anniversary.

Not alone has the *Southern Worker* been a mass agitator but an organizer as well. In Camp Hill the *Southern Worker* was a tremendous aid in organizing the poor sharecroppers into the Sharecroppers' Union. Around the Scottsboro case the *Southern Worker* played a big part in building up the defense movement, the block committees. In Harlan, Ky., in Elizabethton, Tenn., the *Southern Worker* helped to organize the workers round the Communist Party and revolutionary unions.

Congratulations to our fearless little paper. This must be our resolve on the first anniversary of the *Southern Worker,* for all of us to buckle down to the job of increasing circulation, to spread it everywhere, to get workers to write for the *Southern Worker.*

To build the *Southern Worker* is to build the Communist Party and working class movement. Long live the *Southern Worker!*

4.

"Charlotte YCL Holds Meeting Against War"

Charlotte, N.C.—The Young Communist League held a meeting on the corner of Tenth and Alexander Streets. Eighty-six workers were present, most of whom were young workers.

The meeting was held in protest of boss wars. The speakers pointed out how the starvation and lynching system of the bosses helped them to force young workers to go out and fight in the next war.

The First Ward unit of the Young Communist League held a demonstration in protest of bosses' wars and in defense of the Soviet Union on International Youth Day at the corner of 6th and Alexander Streets.

□ ——————————————————————————————— □

THE ANGELO HERNDON CASE

"The Leaflet," *Let Me Live* by Angelo Herndon, Random House, 1937

[*In 1932, when he was nineteen years old, Angelo Herndon (b. 1913) was convicted of "insurrection" in Atlanta. This Black youth from Ohio first faced a sentence of death, which was later changed to 20 years in prison. After more than five years, most of it spent in Fulton Tower in Atlanta, during which his case traveled twice to the Supreme Court of the United States, he was freed. His mass and legal defense was conducted by the International Labor Defense.*

Herndon's lawyer was the young Georgia attorney, Benjamin J. Davis. Davis, who was educated in Morehouse, Amherst and Harvard, was recruited into the Communist Party by his young, working-class client.

Herndon's conviction of a capital offense grew out of his efforts to rally the unemployed of Atlanta for relief. The principal "evidence" against him was a leaflet which appears as an appendix in Let Me Live *and is reprinted below.]*

Workers of Atlanta!
Employed and Unemployed—Negro and White—Attention!
Men and Women of Atlanta

Thousands of us, together with our families, are at this time facing starvation and misery and are about to be thrown out of our houses because the miserable charity handout that some of us were getting has been stopped! Hundreds of thousands of dollars have been collected from workers in this city for relief for the unemployed and most of it has been squandered in high salaries for the heads of these relief agencies.

Mr. T.K. Glenn, president of the Community Chest, is reported to be getting a salary of $10,000 a year. Mr. Frank Neely, executive director of the Community Chest, told the County Commission Saturday that he gets $6,500 a year, while at the same time no worker, no matter how big his family, gets more than two dollars and a half to live on. If we count the salaries paid the secretaries and the investigators working in the thirty-eight relief stations in this city, it should not surprise us that the money for relief was used up and there is no more left to keep us from starvation. If we allow ourselves to starve while these fakers grow fat off our misery, it will be our own fault.

The bosses want us to starve peacefully and by this method save the money they have accumulated off our sweat and blood. We must force them to continue our relief and give more help. We must not allow them to stall any longer with fake promises. The city and county authorities from the money they have already collected from us in taxes, and by taking the incomes of the bankers and other rich capitalists, can take care of every unemployed family in Atlanta. We must make them do it.

At a meeting of the County Commissioners last Saturday, it was proposed by Walter S. McNeal, Jr., to have the police round up all unemployed workers and their families and ship them back to the farms and make them work for just board and no wages, while just a few months ago these hypocrites were talking about forced labor in Soviet Russia, a country where there is no starvation and where the workers rule! Are we going to let them force us into slavery?

73

At this meeting Mr. Hendrix said that there were no starving families in Atlanta, that if there is he has not seen any. Let's all of us, white and Negroes, together with our women-folk and children, go to his office in the county court house on Pryor and Hunter Streets, Thursday morning at 10 o'clock and show this faker that there is plenty of suffering in the city of Atlanta and demand that he give us immediate relief! Organize and fight for unemployment insurance at the expense of the government and the bosses! Demand immediate payment of the bonus to the ex-service-men. Don't forget Thursday morning at the county court house.

Issued by the Unemployed Committee of Atlanta,
P.O. Box 339

□ ──────────────────────────────────── □

ORGANIZING SOUTHERN SHARECROPPERS

Achievements and Tasks of Sharecroppers Union
(Speech of Comrade M. at the Extraordinary Conference
of the Communist Party, July 7–10, 1933),
Workers Library Publishers, 1933

[*The Sharecroppers Union was organized by Communists and went on to build a substantial base in Lowndes, Tallapoosa and Hinds counties in Alabama in face of murderous repression.*

Peonage and lynching were rampant when the Communist Party began its effort to organize the sharecroppers of the South. The Extraordinary Conference held in New York City (July 1933) heard this report by Comrade M. on the problems and achievements. It critically examined the work in this field. "Comrade M." was Al Murphy (1908-1978), a Black leader assigned to organize the Sharecroppers Union. Comrade Murphy was born in McRae, Georgia. He joined the CP in 1930. (See also p. 77.) The pseudonym was necessary to protect his ability to work and to avoid possible lynch-mob action.]

I want to explain the present condition and status of our organization in the Black Belt, the Sharecroppers Union and also explain some of the victories we have won. . . .

First I want to say comrades, next month will mark the first year of the existence of the Sharecroppers Union. During this period we have been able to organize between 2,000 and 3,000 members. Out of all of these

74

members we have not been able to organize one single white farmer and have been able to organize only five Party units, of 30 to 35 members.

Our union has accomplished something; new victories have been won. More victories could have been won with the tremendous possibilities which we have; but the reason we have not spread the union and have not built up a broader and stronger Party capable of leading the masses, the Negro sharecroppers and tenants, and also of mobilizing and leading the broad section of the white farmers, is because the Party is so small. And secondly, it is functioning in a sectarian line and manner. Thirdly, we have not developed local leadership.

What are some of the victories? We were able to force the landlords on three plantations to cancel all debts against the sharecroppers.

We have been able to force from the landlords not only immediate relief in the form of clothes and food, but we have also been able to get cash relief. For example, we had one comrade who wanted some clothes, food and money to buy medicine with. He went to the landlord and asked him for these things. The landlord refused. He came back to the union and asked us what he must do about it. With three or four other comrades we made up a committee consisting of about seven people who went to the office of the landlord who is a gin company operator and asked him for this relief. The landlord immediately saw that there was some organization behind it. At first he refused saying that he didn't have it, that he couldn't get it because he was in debt, but the second time they went to the landlord he immediately instructed the secretary of his firm to write out an order for whatever the cropper and his family wanted.

In addition to that, we have forced the landlord of two plantations to give the croppers the right to sell their own cotton. In the Black Belt the Negro sharecroppers in particular have not got the right to sell their own cotton. This is one of the main bases upon which the whole robbery system in the Black Belt is placed. For instance, a sharecropper who works on halves, makes ten bales of cotton. The landlord doesn't allow him to sell this cotton himself, but instead, the sharecropper is forced to turn the cotton and the receipts over into the hands of the landlord and then the landlord puts it in the warehouse; and the croppers are forced to pay for storage on cotton put in the warehouse. It remains there for months and months and the cropper cannot sell it; he has to wait until the landlord takes action. On two plantations we have absolutely destroyed these conditions. . . .

What do we see? During the trial of the sharecroppers,[4] the Negroes wanted to go to the courthouse despite the fact that they were threatened by the mobs and the sheriffs that if they were seen in the courthouse, they would be run off the farm. On the day the trial was to be held the roads were blocked. The deputy sheriffs came out with shot guns and blocked the roads to prevent the Negroes from coming to the courthouse. The group of Negroes walked up close to the sheriffs who told them to go back, that they were not going to go to the courthouse. Most of them turned around, not to go back home but to find another way to get to the courthouse; and they did. Some of them stood and argued with the sheriffs while the rest turned and walked across through the woods, through brooks, and went to the courthouse and left the sheriffs gabbing there with a few Party members.

What happened, comrades? The courthouse was packed with whites. Not a single Negro was in the courthouse on the first day of the trial and when the Negroes got to the courthouse the door was blocked and they couldn't get in. The attorney refused to go on with the trial until the Negroes were permitted to come into the courthouse and said he would call the trial an illegal one; and so the judge was forced to grant the Negroes permission to enter the courthouse. They were invited by sheriffs and the whites were driven outside and one whole side of the courthouse was given to the Negroes. The white fellows were angry about this. We watched them very closely. There were no hostile feelings against the Negroes, but against the sheriffs themselves, and since that time we have been able to win a few more white contacts who promised to come into the Sharecroppers Union as soon as they could find a way to come in. The reason this was not done was because we have not a white organizer in the Black Belt to work among the white farmers. . . .

We have come to the aid of a Negro tenant cropper and family, who were evicted from their home. Because a group of farmers formed themselves into a committee to put the furniture back into the house and the landlord was unable to find out who had put the things back, the tenant cropper was arrested and held incommunicado. No bail was set. No trial was held. . . . The tenant cropper was released and he is still living in the house . . . will live there tomorrow and will stay there.

☐ ─── ☐

A BLACK COMMUNIST IN THE DEEP SOUTH

"The Making of a Union Man and a Communist," Black Worker in the Deep South by Hosea Hudson, International Publishers, 1972

[*Hosea Hudson (b. 1898) was born in rural Georgia and spent his early life as a sharecropper. Forced off the land in the mid-twenties, he became an industrial worker and in 1942 became president of Birmingham Local No. 2815 of the United Steel Workers. He was active in the 1940s in a drive for the right to vote—almost twenty years before this campaign achieved its major goals. He was recruited into the Communist Party by Al Murphy (see previous item). He describes this step in the portion of his autobiography given below.*]

I was at a Communist meeting and though nothing sensational was happening, the idea was exciting. . . .

When he [Al Murphy] said that not everybody could be a member of the Party, I wondered if I could be—or who among that gathering of eight Black men from the shop could be. To be members, the man said, people had to be willing to sacrifice a part of their good times; they had to give the time they saved to activity and education among other workers who felt something was wrong with the setup but didn't know what to do about it.

I sat there wondering if I could fit in; then I looked at the other fellows and realized not one of them could read or write. I myself had to spell out every word before I knew what it was.

Al Murphy went on to say Communists spread the Party's message by distributing its leaflets and its newspaper. He said they would hold regular meetings, get to them on time and pay dues regularly. Then he added the Party would expel members who got drunk or were loose in their moral conduct or careless in handling finances.

After he had made all these points—very calm, quiet and convincing— he stopped. There wasn't much that anybody could fail to understand, and there weren't many questions. We all eight signed up, each paying 50 cents initiation fee and pledging 10 cents monthly dues, or more, based on our rate of pay. They elected me unit organizer.

In our brief meeting that night we agreed our main task would be among the workers in our shop. We'd pick out individual workers to make friends with and in this way we would be able we hoped, to build the organization in the Stockham plant.

As I've said, all of us molders were Black and because of this we were not recognized as molders by the Stockham Pipe and Fittings Company. It classed us as "machine-runners." In the late 1920s at Stockham's, when they'd be having photos taken of the machines, the big supers would order us, the Black molders, to get back from our molding machines. Then the little straw bosses would stand beside the machines as if they were running them. . . .

We had to be at the machine at 6:30 a.m., even though our time didn't start until seven o'clock. We had to work until three p.m., after which we had to clean our machines; and it would be nearly half-past three by the time we could leave. The 30 minutes we were supposed to have for lunch gave us time to gulp our food as best we could, sometimes as we were hurrying back to the machines.

We worked under these conditions, with the foremen cussing and rawhiding the men, until one cold day along about November.

We held our weekly unit meeting and reported on the conditions in the shop. A Party representative visited each meeting. This time he got started on a series of actions. "For the next meeting," he said, "sit down and write your complaints just like you are writing a letter—the best you can."

At the next meeting we had our letter telling what the foreman had said to us; how he cussed out John; how one man was doing two men's work and not getting paid for it and so on. We turned it over to the Party representative and he took it with him.

About two weeks later he brought it back—printed in the *Southern Worker,* weekly newspaper of the Communist Party, published in Chattanooga, Tennessee, with big headlines about conditions at the Stockham Pipe and Fittings Company plant. Our pride and excitement increased when we found out the letter also appeared in the *Sunday Worker,* published in New York. We read the papers as well as we could; we had never before been able to express our anger against these conditions like this and we were hopeful that the people in the communities would get so indignant that Stockham's would be compelled to do something about them. The Party representative gave us all extra copies to distribute among the people and one to put where the company stoolpigeon would get to it—actually we dropped it in his yard.

Another few days passed. Then one day the supers, worried-looking, came into the shop and said they didn't want anybody to leave for the bathhouse.

"We are going to have a meeting this evening. Nobody changes until after the meeting."

It was on the right-hand side of the shop, out in the open, in a broad space near a brick wall and the fence. Everybody was out there—Black molders and white machinists, the assistant super, the super himself and other supervisory personnel, including Mr. Nibley, the personnel director, who got up and said that he wanted to tell the men that "beginning tomorrow we don't want a man to put his hand on a machine before seven or he's fired. You-all will stop work at 2:45 and clean up your machine by three and be ready to go to the bathhouse."

He went over that again and again. "Times are getting hard," he said, "and we'll have to be cutting wages but I want to tell you men right now we don't want anybody to work more time than you-all supposed to. Stop for lunch when the whistle blows at 12. Be ready to start work when the 12:30 whistle blows. Stop work at 2:45, clean up your machines and be ready to get out of here by three o'clock."

I almost burst out laughing when he said, "If any foreman cusses at any man here, he won't have any more job here . . . and the same goes for you fellows"—meaning John Bedell, me, any number of other Black workers in the shop—in the same bag with the superintendents, assistant supers and straw bosses. Suppose one of those white guys did get fired for cussing us—and chances stood a thousand to one against it—he'd have another job before sundown. But let one of us get fired for "standing up" to or "talking back" to a white "bossman" and we might as well decide right then and there to get clean out of the state, because we'd be blackballed at every factory gate for hundreds of miles around.

Anyhow, when the meeting was over, the men all went out full of joy, and some of us said, "Them papers sure did stir things up!" and things like, "If they tell us to strike, I'm ready."

Black workers and white workers—all were openly talking about "this great victory," talking to anyone or everyone who would listen. And among the first talkers were the Communists. The Party put out leaflets calling on workers to organize, Blacks and whites together, for higher wages, job security, unemployment and social insurance for all unemployed. But the inexperienced Party leadership in the South didn't yet know how to guard itself or warn us in the shop unit to watch out for the traps our enemy set.

☐ ———————————————————————————— ☐

THE "YOKINEN TRIAL"

"Introduction" by James Allen to *Race Hatred on Trial,* Communist Party, 1931

[*While the Communist Party was moving ahead in many fields it simultaneously heightened the struggle against white chauvinism in its ranks. This resulted in a politically important event known as the Yokinen trial (1931). August Yokinen, a Party member, was a caretaker of the Finnish Workers Club in New York City. At a club social event he had refused entry to two Black workers.*

The trial was attended by 1,500 persons, including 211 elected delegates from 113 organizations. Alfred Wagenknecht, veteran leading Communist, presided. The jury consisted of seven Black and seven white people. Clarence Hathaway acted as prosecutor and Richard Moore, a Black leader in the ILD, was defense attorney.

The event received widespread attention and dramatically exposed the nature of racism. The proceedings of the "Yokinen trial" were published in a pamphlet for which James S. Allen (b. 1906) supplied this introduction. (See p. 70.)]

The trial of August Yokinen before 1,500 white and Negro workers in Harlem for acts clearly based on race prejudice was an event without example in the history of the American Labor movement. He was not tried before any court of American ruling-class "justice." He was tried by a court of workers. He was brought to trial by the Communist Party for conduct detrimental to the interests of the working class as a whole and for violation of the fundamental program of the Party.

It was a workers' jury which convicted him. And the workers throughout the country, who already understood the vicious anti-labor nature of race prejudice, together with those who were led to a clear understanding of it through this trial, acclaimed the verdict of "guilty" and approved of the tasks set for Yokinen to do before he could again apply for readmission to the Party.

The meaning of the guilt of Yokinen, the seriousness of the crime he committed against the working class is made clear in this pamphlet. Yokinen was guilty of upholding by his sentiments and his acts, the ideology of "white superiority" which serves as a ruling-class excuse for the acts of suppression and persecution of the Negro workers and farmers. He was guilty of permitting lynch law, in its less brutal but just as vicious form, take its course. In acting thus, he permitted himself to

80

become an instrument of the ruling class. For it is this wall of race prejudice by which the bosses in the factories, the landlords on the farm, keep the workers and farmers divided.

By this trial, the Communist Party has done two things. First, it has made clear the anti-working-class character of race prejudice. Second, it has shown that it will not tolerate any form of race prejudice within its own ranks and will fight tooth and nail to root it out of the working class as a whole.

Yokinen acknowledged his errors and pledged himself to carry on untiring activity against all forms of race prejudice. As a foreign-born worker he realized that he too was being divided off by the ruling class from the other white workers, in the same way as the workers were being divided on race lines. He really understood his crime.

So did the ruling class. While ruling-class justice has its Jim-Crow laws, aids in actual lynching parties, leaves lynchers go by unpunished, it reserves its prisons for fighters for working-class solidarity. After Yokinen had seen his errors before a working-class court and decided to energetically correct his mistakes by taking up an active fight for full Negro equality as a member of the League of Struggle for Negro Rights, the "laws" of the bosses jumped into action, arrested Yokinen and held him for deportation to Finland where prison or death awaits a Communist.

Yokinen now represents the very thing which he injured. He has now joined the struggle for full equality and for the unity of the workers. The ruling class answers with the threat of deportation. The workers' answer must be greater solidarity and greater fighting unity among the toilers of all colors and nationalities, against deportations, against all persecutions of the Negroes and against the capitalist system which maintains itself by such institutions.

□ ———————————————————————————————— □

SCOTTSBORO

"The Scottsboro Case," *The Man Who Cried Genocide*
by William L. Patterson, International Publishers, 1971

[In 1931 William L. Patterson (b. 1891) became National Secretary of the International Labor Defense (ILD). He was associated with the Scottsboro Case from its early stage and his energies were devoted to bringing it

to international attention. In 1949 he became National Executive Secretary of the Civil Rights Congress, successor organization to the ILD, and defended Willie McGee, the Martinsville Seven, the Trenton Six and numerous other victims of racist oppression, as well as working in the overall defense of civil rights.

In 1951, under his initiative, a petition signed by over 100 prominent Americans was presented to the United Nations. The famous document "We Charge Genocide—The Historic Petition to the United Nations for Relief from a Crime of the United States Government Against the Negro People" was submitted simultaneously to the UN General Assembly meeting in Paris and to the office of the Secretary General in New York City. Patterson presented it in Paris, France, while Paul Robeson led a delegation to the UN in New York.]

[The Scottsboro Case] had begun March 25, 1931, when nine Negro lads were dragged by a sheriff and his deputies from a 47-car freight train that was passing through Paint Rock, Alabama, on its way to Memphis. The train was crowded with youths, both white and Black, aimlessly wandering about. They were riding the freights in search of food and employment and they wandered about aimlessly in the train. There was a fight, and some white lads telegraphed ahead that they had been jumped and thrown off the train by "niggers." At Paint Rock, a sheriff and his armed posse boarded the train and began their search for the "niggers."

Two white girls dressed in overalls were taken out of a car; white and Black youths alike were arrested and charged with vagrancy. But the presence of the white girls added a new dimension to the arrest. The girls were first taken to the office of Dr. R.R. Bridges for physical examination. No bruises were found on their bodies, nor were they unduly nervous. A small amount of semen was found in the vagina of each of them but it was at least a day old.

The doctor gave his report to the sheriff and obviously it ruled out rape in the preceding 24 hours. But for the Alabama authorities that made no difference—they came up with a full-blown charge of rape. The nine Black lads stood accused.

The second day after the arrests the sheriff tried to get the girls to say they had been raped by the youths, and both refused. They were sent back to jail, but a southern sheriff can exert a lot of pressure, and on the following day Victoria Price, the older of the two women (who had a police record) caved in. Ruby Bates, the 17-year-old, an almost illiterate mill hand, still refused to corroborate the charge. But on the fourth day she, too, succumbed to the pressure. The Roman holiday could now be staged.

On March 31, 1931, 20 indictments were handed down by a grand jury, emphasizing the charge of rape and assault. The nine boys were immediately arraigned before the court in Scottsboro. All pleaded not guilty.

The first exposure of the infamous frame-up appeared April 2, 1931, in the pages of the *Daily Worker*, which called on the people to initiate mass protests and demonstrations to save nine innocent Black youths from legal lynching. On April 4, the *Southern Worker,* published in Chattanooga, Tenn., carried a first-hand report from Scottsboro by Helen Marcy describing the lynch spirit that had been aroused around the case. The trial began on April 7, with the outcome a foregone conclusion.

Thousands of people poured into Scottsboro—if there were "niggers" to be lynched, they wanted to see the show. A local brass band played "There'll Be a Hot Time in the Old Town Tonight" outside the courthouse while the all-white jury was being picked. The state militia was called out—ostensibly to protect the prisoners. Its attitude toward the lads, one of whom was bayoneted by a guardsman, was little different from that of the lynch mob. In short order, Charles Weems, 20, and Clarence Norris, 19, the two older lads, were declared guilty by the jury. On the same day, Haywood Patterson, 17, was the next victim. And on April 8, Ozzie Powell, 14, Eugene Williams, 13, Olin Montgomery, 17, Andy Wright, 18, and Willie Robertson, 17, were declared guilty. The hearing of Roy Wright, 14 years old, ran into "legal" difficulties. The prosecution had asked the jury to give him life imprisonment, but eleven jurors voted for death and it was declared a mistrial.

Stephen R. Roddy (a member of the Ku Klux Klan, it was said) had been retained by the Black Ministers Alliance in conjunction with the NAACP as a defense attorney. At the trial he said he was present only as an observer. But he had advised the boys to plead guilty so that he could try to get them off with life imprisonment. The court duly appointed another lawyer, Milo Moody, to act with Roddy as a defense counsel. His attitude was similar to that of the NAACP appointee and augured ill for the defendants.

Not one witness was called by counsel for the defense. The jury was not asked to acquit the defendants; indeed, there was no summation by the defense counsel in behalf of the boys. Nor was there any real cross-examination of the two women involved and neither of the lawyers consulted with the defendants until the day of the trial.

The day after the trial ended the ILD entered the case. George W. Chalmers of Chattanooga, armed with a battery of fellow-lawyers that included Joseph Brodsky and Irving Schwab of New York, interviewed the lads in their prison cells. After being retained formally Chalmers entered a motion for a new trial, stating that the boys were clearly innocent, that they had not had counsel of their own choosing and that they were the victims of a monstrous frame-up.

The very next day, April 11, the *Chattanooga Times* revealed inadvertently the true role of Roddy and Moody in the following statement: "That the Negro boys had a fair trial even the defense counsel fully admits. Stephen Roddy, chief defense counsel, declared: 'Judge Hawkins was most fair and impartial.'"

The sentence pronounced by this fair and impartial judge was death in the electric chair.

After I had become involved in the case, I began to examine all the available evidence as well as the alignment of the social forces arrayed against the youths. In reading the very first lines of the indictments, I read: "The People of the State of Alabama against—" and then the name of each defendant followed. The People of the State of Alabama, indeed! Almost half of the people of Alabama were Negroes, while those who were calling themselves by that name included the white sheriffs drunk with racism; the police who believed that their guns were synonymous with law and order; a press steeped in racism; landlords, bankers, businessmen and a racist white community. Both of the pathetic accusers were prostitutes. "They told me," Ruby Bates said later, "I must work with the police. What could I do?" . . .

But one thing was certain. The ILD had no intention of turning its back on the Scottsboro boys. It had neither the time nor the money to enter a fight with the NAACP. But it could not evade the ideological battle, for only thus could the government's role be exposed. If the NAACP leadership had been ready to go all out to save the youths, the ILD would have welcomed them as they would welcome the aid of any and every one who could help in the fight. We felt that the case was not primarily a legal matter; it was a political struggle of national and international import; the courts were being used as a shield to conceal the racist policy of government. Alabama knew nothing of justice for Black men and anyone who was seriously aiming at the freedom of the Scottsboro boys was inevitably labeled "Red". . . .

It was . . . impressive to read a letter to the *Daily Worker,* written April 19, [1932] from William Pickens, Field Secretary of the NAACP:

"I am writing from Kansas City, where I have just seen a copy of the *Daily Worker* for April 16th and noted the fight which the workers are making through the ILD to prevent the judicial massacre of Negro youth in Alabama. . . .

"In the present case the *Daily Worker* and the workers have moved, so far, more speedily and effectively than all other agencies put together. . . .

"This is one occasion for every Negro who has intelligence enough to read, to send aid to you and the ILD." (Alas, Mr. Pickens was later forced to recant by the NAACP leadership.)

The meaning of the fight to free the nine defendants was best expressed by Richard B. Moore, who had criss-crossed the country as a national board member of the ILD to bring the story of the boys to the American masses. In 1940, speaking in Washington, D.C., before a meeting of the National Conference of the ILD, Moore said:

"The Scottsboro Case is one of the historic landmarks in the struggle of the American people and of the progressive forces throughout the world for justice, civil rights and democracy. In the present period, the Scottsboro Case has represented a pivotal point around which labor and progressive forces have rallied not only to save the lives of nine boys who were framed . . . but also against the whole system of lynching terror and the special oppression and persecution of the Negro people. . . .

"Last year we came to a new development in the Scottsboro Case which shows more clearly than ever before the fascist nature of this case. Governor Graves (of Alabama) gave his pledged word to the Scottsboro Defense Committee and to leading Alabama citizens at a hearing to release the remaining Scottsboro boys. . . ."

Among the leaders of the NAACP, Henry Lee Moon was one who revealed that he recognized the international character and significance of the Communist defense. It was not however, until 1948, after the fierce heat of battle had subsided that in his book, *Balance of Power,* he said:

"It was during this period, in the spring of 1931, that nine colored lads, in age from thirteen to nineteen years, were arrested in Alabama and charged with the rape of two nondescript white girls. The defense of these boys was first undertaken by the NAACP. But the Communists, through the International Labor Defense, captured the defense of the imprisoned youths and conducted a vigorous, leather-lunged campaign that echoed and reechoed throughout the world. The Scottsboro boys were lifted from obscurity to a place among the immortals—with Mooney and Billings, Sacco and Vanzetti—fellow-victims of bias in American courts." . . .

"The Communists maintained that legal defense had to be supplemented by international propaganda; American consulates, legations and embassies were picketed and stoned in many parts of the world. Mass meetings of protest were held in the capitals of Europe and Latin America at which resolutions demanding the freedom of the Scottsboro boys were passed. Letters, telegrams and cablegrams poured in upon the President of the United States, the Governor of Alabama, the presiding judge and other state officials, demanding the immediate release of the boys."

And then Moon added: "This propaganda was effective in exposing the hypocrisy of American justice, but it did not gain the freedom of the boys." Nevertheless, when the NAACP left the case, the boys had been condemned to death. It was the fight waged by the ILD that saved their lives by refusing to be bound by the restraints of the narrow, legalistic arena. And it was the ILD that lifted the nine Negro lads from an ignoble grave "to a place among heroic figures." . . .

As Moon himself sums it up: "To the Communists . . . the whole campaign was much more than a defense of nine unfortunate lads. It was an attack on the system which had exploited them, fostered the poverty and ignorance in which they were reared, and finally victimized them by legal proceedings which were a mockery of justice." . . .

As the ILD increased its efforts to bring the true character of the case before the peoples of the world, it won ever more support. The flood of letters and petitions pouring in on the officials involved continued to mount; the people rose to defend their hard-won rights against the attack of their enemies.

After the trial, the convictions and sentencing, the ILD leadership was more than ever convinced that only world protests would save the condemned youth. Protests were called for from all parts of the world—and they came from such eminent men as Albert Einstein, Thomas Mann, Maxim Gorky, Theodore Dreiser, Waldo Frank and many others. The voice of the Scottsboro lynchers, *The Jackson County Sentinel,* declared that the mass movement to save the nine boys was "the most dangerous movement launched in the South in many years."

On May 1, 1934, the NAACP, over the signature of Walter White, issued a press release announcing that "The NAACP . . . had no connection whatsoever with the efforts of Communist groups or with the International Labor Defense in the case and that it would have no such connection."

In the June 13, 1934, issue of the *National Guardian,* a New York liberal weekly, this note appeared: "The National Equal Rights League invited the ILD and the NAACP to meet in conference in New York City this weekend with the League. Walter White, Secretary for the NAACP, declined on the ground that the Association had tried for a united defense and because, he claimed, 'the ILD was out for propaganda purposes and would never harmonize.'"

The ILD *was* out for propaganda—it was out for propaganda against racism and extra-legal lynching; propaganda against the racist policy of government; propaganda vital to the struggle for the lives of the intended victims; propaganda against the conspiracy to slaughter the boys as an act of terror calculated to quell the unrest of the Negro masses and to throw up a barrier to Negro-white unity. . . .

Thus, the Scottsboro Case had to be fought in such a manner as to save the lives of those innocent young men and at the same time expose the forces involved so clearly as to make a recurrence of Scottsboro difficult indeed.

It took seventeen years! It took all kinds of court maneuvers, all kinds of struggle outside the courts; it took tremendous sacrifices of time and energy by thousands of good people around the world—many of them Communists, many of them not Communists—to win that great battle. But at the end, not one boy was lynched. All were freed. And the South has not been quite the same ever since.

□ ─────────────────────────────────────── □

THE COMMUNIST PARTY AND AGRICULTURAL WORKERS

The Story of Imperial Valley by Frank Spector, ILD Pamphlet No. 3, International Labor Defense, (not dated)

[*As long ago as 1925, the Communist Party applied itself to the ever-difficult task of organizing the bitterly oppressed agricultural workers of southern California.*

The principal struggle was later carried on by the Agricultural Workers Industrial Union (TUUL). In 1930, a number of leaders, then members of the Communist Party, were convicted of "criminal syndicalism" and given prison terms of 3 to 42 years. While in prison, Frank Spector (b. 1895), a charter member of the CP and Los Angeles organizer of the ILD, wrote the pamphlet from which these excerpts are taken.]

On the heels of the field workers' strike [Imperial Valley, California, January 1930], a strike of white workers in the packing sheds broke out [in February]. Groaning under the terrible speed-up system, they refused to accept a drastic wage-cut. . . .

But the strike of the shed workers was short-lived. The bosses immediately planted among the unorganized workers self-appointed leaders, who with the aid of American Federation of Labor "organizers" tried to make it a "gentlemen's strike."

The misleaders called frequent meetings, "protected from the Reds" by the police. At these gatherings the white workers were filled with patriotic speeches by the "respectable" Chamber of Commerce officials and by the "well wishing" city and county politicians—all urging the strikers, as in the lettuce workers' strike, to have faith in the "fairness" of their bosses. The growers' agents, like the Mexican reformist leaders, used gangsters as well as police to prevent the Agricultural Workers Industrial League from addressing the workers. At one large meeting, however, the strikers compelled their fake leaders to give the floor to Danny Roxas, Secretary of the League. Greeting the strikers in the name of this union, he announced the walkout of 200 Filipino and Mexican field workers in sympathy with the striking shed workers. Roxas was greeted enthusiastically by the strikers. . . .

Owing to the failure of the strikers to carry on mass picketing the bosses were able to herd scabs in sufficient numbers to break the backbone of the strike. As in the case of the field workers, the shed workers returned to work under greatly worsened conditions.

Defeat failed to dampen the workers' militant spirit and their readiness to fight against increasing speed-up, further wage cuts and unemployment. With its militant class struggle program the A.W.I.L. was rapidly spreading its influence. At huge open-air meetings, in defiance of police terror, large numbers of Mexican and Filipino workers joined the revolutionary union. At these meetings the workers eagerly read the left wing labor press, *Labor Unity, Labor Defender, Daily Worker* and pamphlets in English and Spanish. The new organization was also rapidly enlisting the Negro, Hindu and native white workers.

The union flung its challenge to the bosses by opening its headquarters, guarded by the "Workers Defense Corps" against the attacks of the police and the American Legion fascists. Plans were made for a general strike to take place in the major season, in June and July, when cantaloupes are picked, packed and shipped. . . .

Orders were issued for the general mobilization of all reactionary forces, from the Federal Government down to the fascist gangster elements. A special representative of the Department of Justice arrived on the scene. Numerous gunmen were imported from Texas and Arizona to augment the sheriff's forces. Additional forces were deputized from among the local one-hundred-percenters. The Los Angeles Chamber of Commerce and the "Better America Federation" dispatched their highest paid, red-baiting elements to direct the onslaught upon the Valley toilers. No funds were spared in the task of crushing the workers' militancy.

A general call was issued by the Agricultural Workers Industrial League for a broad, rank-and-file conference, representative of the masses of ranch and shed workers, to unite the union and to adopt a definite program of strike action. In preparation for this important conference, numerous open-air and indoor mass meetings were held in Brawley, El Centro, Westmoreland, Calexico, Calipatria and other points and also at ranches. They were attended by thousands of workers whose enthusiasm increased with the approaching struggle.

One such preliminary meeting was held in El Centro on the night of April 14, [1930].

Over one hundred Mexican, Filipino, Negro and white workers gathered in a dingy workingclass hall in El Centro, the largest city of the Imperial Valley, in California. They had been called there by the Agricultural Workers Industrial Union to discuss their conditions and to prepare to participate, a week later, in a conference of delegates from ranches and sheds. The conference was to weld the ranks of the workers for the coming strike against inhuman exploitation, the contract system, speed-up, and unemployment.

One after another the workers stood up and spoke, each in his own tongue. They told of the starvation and sickness of their wives and children, of the constant wage cuts, and of the long hours of bitter toil under a scorching sun. Each one spoke of the readiness of the workers to fight under their union's militant guidance.

Suddenly the door burst open. Into the hall rushed a mob of policemen, deputy sheriffs and civilians—all armed with revolvers and sawed-off shotguns which they trained upon the assembled workers.

Out of this mob stepped Sheriff Gillette, the chief gunman of the Imperial Valley bosses. Ordering all workers to throw up their hands, he then directed a violent search of each worker, after which every one of the 108 were chained in groups. Then the mob, with a brutal display of force, threw them into huge trucks. The entire one hundred and eight were hauled into El Centro under heavy guard and thrown into the county jail there.

Two months passed. A number of the group, who were Mexican workers, were deported. A number were released.

Following that night of terror the Imperial Valley assumed the appearance of an armed camp. Everywhere, along the railroad tracks, packing sheds, bridges, warehouses, in the fields and on the ranches, before the houses of government officials, were placed guards, armed to the teeth. All the pool-rooms and halls, where workers gather, were closed. Newspapers told fantastic stories of "plots" to blow up bridges, sheds, railroads—"plots" to burn up crops, tear down vines and what not. This hysteria filled the "respectable citizenry" with bitter prejudice and hatred against the workers. Ministers in their churches and the one hundred percent patriotic organizations were frothing at the mouth, denouncing the Communist Party, the T.U.U.L., the I.L.D., and passing resolutions calling upon the "guardians of law and order" to make "short work" of the imprisoned leaders of the workers. Ugly threats to take the "law" into their own hands were uttered by the frenzied patriots. . . .

The Imperial Valley struggle was seized upon by the bosses in an attempt to strike a death-blow against the hated Communist Party and other militant workers' organizations. Through the criminal syndicalism law they hoped to force underground this militant leader of the California masses. Thirty-two defendants were charged with violating this law, among whom were many leading Communists throughout the state. Bail of $40,000, an unheard-of amount, was set on each of the arrested to insure their remaining in the bosses' clutches.

The International Labor Defense began a determined drive for the release of the workers and succeeded in forcing the reduction of the bail to $5,000 on each. Fearing the rising pressure of mass protests, the bosses changed their tactics. They dismissed the charges against the 32 workers and substituted grand jury indictments against 13 workers. Bail was set at $15,000 for each. The International Labor Defense again fought for the reduction of prohibitive bail, but the same judges, of the Appellate Court, who on the previous occasion were compelled to reduce the bail, now refused to do so.

The indictment returned by the Imperial County grand jury was drawn up on the testimony of three stool-pigeons: Sherman Barber, Charles Collum and Oscar Chormicle—all operatives of the scab-herding Bolling Detective Agency, in the employ of the growers. Notorious spies were employed to procure and manufacture the necessary evidence. Similar creatures were hired to worm their way into the new militant union and [manufacture] frame-up evidence.

Of the 13 indicted, 9 actually faced trial. Two were not found. Two were dismissed on the day of the trial, June 26, in Superior Judge Thompson's court. The trial, lasting 21 days, was conducted with a frenzy of prejudice and hatred, fanned by provocative reports of non-existent "plots." All attempts to organize protests under the leadership of the International Labor Defense were crushed by the police. . . .

The jury was composed entirely of ranchers and businessmen. Even without a pretense at deliberation, it returned a verdict of "guilty" on all counts against all the defendants. This, of course, was a foregone conclusion.

The most vicious sentences were meted out to Carl Sklar and Tetsuji Horiuchi, serving three to forty-two years in Folsom State Prison; Oscar Erickson, Lawrence Emery, Frank Spector and Danny Roxas, serving three to forty-two years in San Quentin Prison. Eduardo Herera and Braulio Orosco, both Mexican workers, were sentenced to two to twenty-eight years in San Quentin. Originally held for deportation, they were later ordered to jail.

Through the last strike movement the Imperial Valley workers have learned a number of valuable lessons which they will apply in the coming new struggles.

☐ ———————————————————————————— ☐

AN INTERNATIONAL CONFERENCE OF NEGRO WORKERS

"The First International Conference of Negro Workers,"
The Communists and the Struggle for Negro Liberation
by James W. Ford,
The Harlem Division of the Communist Party, circa 1930

[*James W. Ford (1894–1957) was an outstanding Black leader of the Communist Party. In July 1929 he and William L. Patterson participated in the Second World Congress of the League Against Imperialism at Frankfurt, Germany. When the First International Conference of Negro Workers was convened in Hamburg, he became its secretary. He maintained offices in the German port city, where he kept contact with and helped in the organization of African and Asian workers.*

Presented here are key excerpts of Ford's report to the Hamburg Conference.]

We are meeting at a time of acute crisis of capitalism that has reached throughout the world, most seriously affecting colonial lands. We have before us very big tasks. We must face the serious business of getting down to the problems that face the Negro workers and the Negro people under capitalist exploitation and oppression in the various parts of the world. We are gathered here at this conference for that purpose. [Hamburg, Germany, July 7–8, 1930]. This conference must make a broad political demonstration and broadcast to the widest possible masses of Negro toilers the results of our discussions. We must take up organizational questions relating to the economic situation and working conditions of the Negro workers—industrial and agricultural workers; we must discuss lynching, terrorism, police and soldier massacres, passlaws, and restrictions, racial discriminations, forced labor, the coming imperialist war and a number of other questions and problems. We will of course have to reach some decisions, but these decisions should not have to be of a binding character on the delegates here. We are here for no political controversies. We are of many political faiths here, to discuss openly and frankly the situation of the Negro workers as it actually is in the world today and to discuss and to study the effects of capitalist exploitation and imperialist oppression upon the Negro people—and I think we can all agree, despite what others may say, that the deplorable conditions of the Negroes grow out of the capitalist system of exploitation. We are here to discuss the role of the Negro workers in the international labor movement. It is under these conditions that I bring greetings to the representatives of the Negro workers—as well as to the fraternal representatives of the other races here—from the Provisional International Trade Union Committee of Negro Workers, that has convened this First International Conference of Negro Workers. In order to get down to these problems I would say that we must discuss the present world situation and the past which is also heavy upon the memory of the Negro toilers. What in general outline are the questions that we must take up? (1) Briefly, the economic and political situation through which the capitalist world has been passing during recent years. (2) The position and conditions of the Negro workers and the Negro people under capitalism—Negro oppression and the freedom of the Negro peoples. In discussing these questions we will naturally come to the significance and importance of workers. I assure you that the capitalists are looking with very great concern upon our efforts and the Negro workers expect much. . . .

The next steps are to organize the battles of the workers; we must here give consideration to all these questions. We must raise the signal of *Revolt*. We must point out how to organize to fight against class exploitation and race oppression; we must make it clear and declare that our struggles are a part of the international struggle against capitalism; we must organize our forces to this end, drawing from the experiences and lessons of our class brothers in China and India; in the capitalist countries and from the workers and peasants in the Soviet Union. We must give special attention to the question of the new imperialist war, especially being designed against the U.S.S.R. and the use that the capitalists intend to make of Negro soldiers in this war. Our conference

92

must give active leadership and support to the struggles of the Negro workers throughout the world and to do this we must indicate practical organizational steps and tasks. If we do this we will have gone a long way towards justifying our efforts and towards winning the Negro workers for the international class struggle against capitalism. Our battle cry must be: Down with Imperialism!

□ ———————————————————————————— □

FIGHTING U.S. IMPERIALISM IN LATIN AMERICA

"Hands off Cuba!" by William Simons,
Workers Library Publishers, New York, October 1933

[*U.S. imperialism in 1926 invaded Nicaragua to suppress the guerrilla uprising led by General Augusto C. Sandino, a coal miner. In 1933 it sent warships into Cuban waters to insure continued U.S. domination of Cuba, following the overthrow of the U.S. puppet regime of Gerardo Machado.*

The Anti-Imperialist League rallied mass support for the struggles of the Nicaraguan and Cuban peoples. It organized activities in many cities. The League declared: "Let us push the struggle which is our struggle, demand the end to all intervention in Latin America." William Simons, a Communist, was Secretary of the League.

On August 1, 1933, at an anti-war march and rally in Union Square, organized by the Communist Party, 23,000 workers demonstrated their support for the Cuban people in their struggle against U.S. intervention and Machado terror.

The anti-imperialist thrust of the Nicaraguan, Cuban and the other Latin American peoples was part of the upsurge which gripped the colonial and semi-colonial peoples of Africa and Asia during the post–World War I years, further spurred by the great economic crisis, 1929–33.

This is an excerpt from Simons' pamphlet.]

Thirty American warships are now in Cuban waters—the largest mobilization of the American fleet in the Caribbean since the Spanish–American war. . . . Do you . . . want this to happen? Are the American warships in Cuban waters and ports for your sake? The mass mobilization of American warships in Cuban waters is an act of war against our Cuban brothers and sisters. Are you in favor of such a war? . . .

No: It is not a question of protecting American lives. It is a question of protecting Wall Street property; of guaranteeing a Cuban Government that will do what the American Government and American bankers tell them to do.

We in the United States can help the struggle of the Cuban toilers for better conditions, by demanding for them from the Cuban Government their democratic rights of organizing and striking, for free speech, press and assembly.

[Our] first and foremost task is that of fighting for the right of the Cuban people to determine for themselves what government they shall have. We can help the Cuban people best by making demands upon "our own government," which is exploiting the Cuban masses.

What shall those demands be? First: The immediate withdrawal of American warships from Cuban ports and waters. Second: The surrender of the American naval base at Guantanamo. Third: The cancellation of the loans made by Wall Street banks to Machado and other Cuban presidents. Fourth: The abrogation of the Platt Amendment. Fifth: The abolition of the unequal "reciprocity" tariff treaty of 1903. . . .

Help the revolutionary masses in Cuba carry on the fight against the reactionary forces without the danger of American marines being landed to crush the rising revolutionary movement in Cuba. Help the sugar strikers get a dollar a day for eight hours work, without having their strike crushed by American marines. Help the exploited Cuban masses in their struggle for a free Cuba.

How can we help? By the biggest campaign of agitation through the country, reaching the entire working class, both industrial and agricultural workers, all workers' organizations, all trade unions and all mass benevolent organizations; by reaching all farmers and their organizations, all students and their organizations, all professional people, all the toilers whose class interests make them opposed to American intervention in Cuba.

□ ———————————————————————————————— □

CLASS STRUGGLE AND THE NEW DEAL

3.

A nation deluded by a "permanent prosperity" myth was told by the dour Herbert Hoover that the economic crash was a passing event. People should look forward to "prosperity around the corner," he said. Bourgeois economists, busy refuting Marxism, had observed nothing unusual when making their unrealistic forecasts. They were, as one said, "taken by surprise." Their class bias had blinded them to the true situation.

Marxists in this country and internationally had predicted the crisis and organized to defend the interests of the jobless. Herbert Hoover was in the White House when, in October 1929, the Central Committee of the Communist Party observed "the clear features of an oncoming crisis," and at its meeting in January 1930, stated: "We are dealing with the most far-reaching economic crisis in the history of capitalism, involving the whole world."

The crisis, further aggravated by Hitler's seizure of power (February 1933), increased the threat of fascism and war. As a result, still greater economic and political problems now burdened the peoples of all capitalist countries.

U.S. monopoly, swollen by huge profits, devised such schemes as "mutual help," private charity, shorter hours with less pay—a drastic decline in living standards as "remedial" measures. But a new, historic feature was introduced into the mass movement. A nation nurtured by the pap of "rugged individualism" began to reject this anachronism. The demand rose for social security—the government's responsibility to care for the unemployed, health, retirement. No such protections existed in this country. An issue long raised by the Party now became a popular slogan of action.

In this political atmosphere, Franklin D. Roosevelt took office on March 4, 1933. He established himself as a harbinger of great expectations. He was careful, however, to couch his promises in generalities; there was no flavor of radicalism in his oratory. Upon assuming office the new administration, backed by Congress, quickly secured the passage of a flood of measures in the period described as "The One Hundred Days." One of the president's staunchest admirers, the historian Samuel Eliot Morison, has described Roosevelt's various legislative acts as " . . . an opportunist, rule-of-thumb method of curing deep-seated ills," and added gratefully, "Probably [the New Deal] saved the capitalist system." That objective held by Roosevelt remained unamended throughout his entire political career.

Overall, public response to Roosevelt was favorable. For the first time in history there was recognition that the federal government should intervene to bolster the economy. Upon taking office the president moved promptly. On inauguration day there were huge demonstrations for jobs throughout the country.

The acute farm crisis was met with an act establishing the Agricultural Adjustment Administration (AAA). Farmers were paid for plowing under their cotton and the government bought six million pigs which it destroyed. The aim was to keep food and fiber prices from falling. Meanwhile millions went hungry and ill-clad.

Some of the major defects of this sheaf of legislation, first pointed out by the Party, became evident as time passed. Outstanding in the legislative flood was the National Industrial Recovery Act (NIRA) which called for the setting up of industrial codes covering prices and wages. The National Recovery Admin-

istration (NRA) was established to regulate the codes. It was totally dominated by monopoly capitalism. Opposition became so strong that Roosevelt appointed a Review Board, with the prominent liberal attorney, Clarence Darrow, as chairman, to monitor the NRA's performance. Darrow's group reported: "The NRA has given the sanction of government to self-governing combinations in the different industries. Inevitably this means control by the largest producers."

Section 7-A of the NIRA declared that employees "should have full freedom of association, self-organization and designation of representatives of their own choosing to negotiate the terms and conditions." But the administrators of the law proceeded to negate what was viewed by workers as the right to unionize. They collaborated with the employers in several ways. One was to refuse to accept any form of unionization; a second was the creation of company unions, and the third was by undercover dealing with AFL leaders, who promised subservient unions ruled by edict from on top.

But a Pandora's box for employers and government had been opened by Section 7-A. A massive union organizational drive flared out across the country. It stemmed in great part from intolerable working conditions. But within that upsurge were the guide and stimulus provided by the Communists, who drew on their previous years of effort that often fell short of goals but was rich with valuable lessons. A harvest of opportunity was now at hand, growing out of the sacrifices, courage and experiences of the past. From a posture that in the past had been of necessity defensive, the working class passed over to the offensive. It was to climax in the organization of the basic industries, with the industrial union replacing the craft union which had failed.

In 1934 the number of strikers reached nearly one and a half million and many of the stoppages resulted from the refusal of union recognition and the biased operation of the codes. Some strikes had a national character, such as those in textile, rubber and mining.

Not all of the AFL old guard failed to grasp the opening for rebuilding their forces. John L. Lewis of the United Mine Workers, Sidney Hillman of the Amalgamated Clothing Workers,

Charles P. Howard of the Typographical Union, and David Dubinsky of the Ladies Garment Workers, comprehended that they could raise the labor movement to a political and economic power never before realized. But it was down below at bench, lathe and production line where the battle was fought and won. The Party provided contact in innumerable shops where approach was difficult. Many of these conduits were made up of foreign-born workers, a part of the substantial number of immigrants in the basic industries. The International Workers Order, a Left workers' insurance society led by Communists, gave assistance through its various nationality sections.

Eventually Section 7–A and the entire NIRA were invalidated by the Supreme Court, but the strength of the labor movement had increased to such an extent that Congress felt compelled to adopt the National Labor Relations Act (NLRA), that set up a machinery for union recognition and collective bargaining. It was significant that this legislation arose out of Congress. Roosevelt at first played no influential part in securing its adoption—as Frances Perkins, labor secretary, pointed out.

*Ms. Perkins wrote in her biography: "It ought to be on record that the President did not take part in developing the National Labor Relations Act and, in fact, was hardly consulted about it. It was not a part of the President's program. It did not particularly appeal to him when it was described to him. All the credit for it belongs to [Senator Robert F.] Wagner." (*The Roosevelt I Knew *by Frances Perkins, Viking Press, 1946, p. 239.)*

Some other legislative enactments in "The One Hundred Days" illustrate the class intent of the authors. In the mish-mash of agrarian legislation there was a degree of relief from mortgage oppression, but the major government aid went to banks and large landholders. The consequence of the agrarian policy was the weakening of the family farm. Big capital, already controlling the market, moved to monopolize the production of foodstuff.

In both the NIRA and the agricultural acts no proposals were made to eliminate the discrimination against the South; the lower wage scales were maintained; Blacks and impoverished whites at best secured some subsistence, but in the case of the former, equal treatment was still denied. Attempts to enact an anti-lynching law were defeated by filibuster on the part of southern senators.

In the area of employment there were such creations as the Public Works Administration (PWA), the Works Progress Administration (WPA), the National Youth Administration (NYA), the Civilian Conservation Corps (CCC). With the exception of the PWA, which contracted with private employers, these were subsistence projects. Unemployment was reduced but the wages paid provided a thin diet. The accomplishments of these work forces were considerable and ranged from the creation of recreational areas and highway repair to the theater and arts. Despite these positive contributions, these agencies were the subject of growing attacks by Congressional voices prompted by big business who wanted an unemployed reserve to be used for strikebreaking. They also feared pressure for other concessions.

The example provided by labor in the extension of organizing and the taking of the offensive served to stimulate movement by other groups. And the Communist Party, which had been an integral force in the expansion of unionism, was to be found in the activity of these new fronts. One of special significance was the National Negro Congress,[1] formed in early 1936 and dedicated to enlarging and speeding up the campaign against discrimination. There was a broad representation in the Congress: educational, religious, fraternal and union, with the latter sending representatives from 83 organizations. A number of Communists were elected to the National Council.

The American Youth Congress came into being in 1934 and eventually reached some five million young people hitherto voiceless. Both the Young Communist League, with Gil Green as its representative, and the Young People's Socialist League were participants.

Other groups emerged: the American Student Union and the Southern Negro Youth Congress, which produced such notable leaders as Edward and Augusta Strong, Esther Cooper, James Jackson, Louis Burnham, and Henry Winston. Here again, there was the influence of the Party.

The Roosevelt administration established diplomatic relations with the Soviet Union in November, 1933. (From the early '20s the TUEL and the Party had conducted a campaign for recognition of Soviet Russia. This issue received wide support in the labor movement.)

*At the 1936 convention of the Communist Party the member-
ship was 41,000 as compared with 24,500 in 1934 and 14,000 in
1932. The Young Communist League exhibited a similar rate of
growth. The Socialist Party and the splinter groups that had been
expelled or broken off from the Communist Party declined in both
membership and activity. Many Socialists, lured by job opportunities offered by the Roosevelt administration, relinquished their
affiliation and surrendered to outright opportunism. Others
found a berth within conservative unions and acted as "red
hunters" for their superiors. The Socialist Party itself, which had
been torn by a factional invasion of Trotskyites, who were soon
expelled, watered down its already weak program and became
difficult to distinguish from somewhat left-leaning Democrats.*

*It was the Communist Party with its conscious dedication to the
interests of the working class and its commitment to the international fundamentals of Marxism-Leninism that stood before the
public as the recognized voice for socialism. And its vigorous and
unselfish participation in day-to-day struggles won it the trust of a
multitude far beyond its membership.*

☐ ——————————————————————— ☐

THE NEW DEAL AND THE TRADE UNION
UNITY LEAGUE

"The New Deal," *American Trade Unionism*
by William Z. Foster, International Publishers, 1947

[*The major piece of legislation of the early period of the New Deal was
the National Industrial Recovery Act (NIRA), which created the National Recovery Administration (NRA).*

*The item from which the following excerpts are taken was first
published in 1936.*]

The sum-up of the New Deal . . . was a greatly increased centralization of
the Federal government and its intensified intervention in economic life
along the following main lines: (a) pouring of government billions into
the banks, railroads, etc. to save them from threatening bankruptcy; (b)
raising of the price level through inflation (devaluation of the dollar,

100

immense bond issues, etc.), code price-fixing and organized restriction of agricultural and industrial production; (c) liquefying of billions of dollars of the banks that were frozen in unpayable mortgages on farms and homes by extension of payment periods on these mortgages; (d) "priming the industrial pump" and easing the workers' unrest by large government capital investments in public works; (e) tinkering up by law the worst breaks in the capitalist banking and credit systems, including supervision of the stock exchange, sale of foreign bonds, etc.; (f) intensified struggle for world markets—bigger navy, air fleet, army, new tariff agreements, etc.; (g) throwing a bone to the starving masses of unemployed and aged by allotting them a niggardly Federal relief and skeleton pensions; (h) granting of rights of the workers to organize into labor unions; (i) organized subsidies to farmers for reducing production.

By its heavy government spending and minor sops to the masses, the New Deal in substance was a shot in the arm, a doping of the economic system out of its deepening crisis. It was calculated to preserve the capitalist system by relieving somewhat the economic and mass pressure. The center of it, the National Recovery Act (N.R.A.), was contrived in Wall Street and was first enunciated by the U.S. Chamber of Commerce. Many capitalist theoreticians hailed it as the beginning of fascism. To call the New Deal socialistic or communistic is nonsense; it had nothing in common with either. . . .

The workers believed the promises of Roosevelt. . . . So, after the beginning of the New Deal and continuing all through 1933, 1934 and to a lesser extent, 1935, they developed a great surging mass organization and strike movement, one of the most tempestuous in the history of the American working class. It was a huge spontaneous outburst and explosion of proletarian wrath against the rapidly rising cost of living, long years of low wages, unemployment, inhuman speed-up and autocracy in industry. It also revealed a growing lack of faith in the capitalist system as a whole. The big strikes of 1919–22 were defensive actions of organized workers under employer attacks, but the 1933–35 upheaval was basically a militant and powerful counter-offensive of the unorganized masses. One of the most striking features of the whole movement was the solidarity of the unemployed with the strikers and their refusal to be strike-breakers. . . .

With the turn of 1934, the strike movement took on greater volume, the number of strikers for that year amounting to 1,353,608. But more important, the multiplying strikes were of a far greater militancy and a deeper political significance. This was because, early in the course of the New Deal, finance capital had made it clear that it was continuing its

By Lydia Gibson, *Weekly Worker,* 1923

traditional opposition to the unionization of the open shop basic industries and the government also soon showed that it would not insist upon
such unionization, despite its apparent sympathy towards trade unionism. . . .

As the New Deal codes developed, it became more and more clear,
therefore, that the government's policy especially in the unorganized
basic industries, despite its liberal phrases, led to company unionism,
starvation wages and long hours. Without fully realizing the implications
of this situation, large masses of workers nevertheless began to sense the
elementary truth—that if they were to secure the right of organization
and relief for their grievances under the New Deal, they would have to do
as the T.U.U.L. [Trade Union Unity League] was urging: write their own
codes on the picket lines. . . .

The strikes of 1934 to 1936 took on the most acute political character of
any in the history of the United States. Against the violent opposition of
the A.F. of L. leaders, the political mass strike, long a cardinal point in
the Communist Party's agitation, became an established weapon of the
American working class. The workers fought with splendid heroism and
solidarity in the face of the government, tricky union leaders and an
unprecedented use of troops, police, gunmen and vigilantes against
them. The great battles of Toledo, Milwaukee, Minneapolis, San Fran-

cisco [1934], Terre Haute (1935), Pekin (1936); the huge national 1934 textile strike, the national coal strike of 1935 and many other struggles of the period constitute one of the brightest pages in our labor history.

During the six years of their existence the T.U.U.L. unions developed a substantial resistance to the wage-cutting, starvation offensive of the employers. In the early and difficult Hoover years of the crisis, while the A.F. of L. was submitting unresistingly to the workers' wages being slashed, and was allowing the unemployed to be forced down into utter pauperism, the T.U.U.L. unions, supported militantly by the Communist Party, held aloft the banner of struggle. Their leadership of the unorganized into struggle was a decisive factor in winning a measure of relief for the starving jobless and their militant strikes not only placed a serious hindrance in the way of the wage–cutters, but also served as a powerful stimulus to the huge labor battles soon to occur under the New Deal. And when the big strike struggles developed in 1933-34, the T.U.U.L. was a real factor in furthering the organization and militancy of the workers.

□ ——————————————————————————————— □

WOMEN AND THE NEW DEAL

"Feminists and the Left Wing" by Grace Hutchins, *New Masses,* November 20, 1934

[New Masses, *which began as a monthly in 1926, started weekly publication at the end of 1933. Under such editors as Michael Gold, Joseph North and other prominent Communist and Left literary figures, it was a popular journal of art, literature, criticism and reportage for the next fifteen years. Grace Hutchins (1885-1969) was for many years associated with Robert Dunn and Anna Rochester in the operation of Labor Research Association. In addition to many newspaper and magazine articles, Grace Hutchins wrote* Labor *and* Silk *(International Publishers, 1929) and many pamphlets, such as* Youth in Industry *and* Women Who Work. *The following is a portion of Hutchins' article.*]

Special discrimination against women workers under the New Deal is recognized in a recent article by the National Woman's Party historian, Helena Hill Weed, under the title, "The New Deal That Women Want," in *Current History* for November, 1934. This article exposes the "marital status clause" No. 213 in the Economy Act of 1932, a clause that has now become a permanent piece of legislation. It has already resulted in the discharge of many efficient married women who had been a number of years in government service.

On this point, Left-Wing workers are in absolute agreement with all who oppose the discharge of married women workers wherever such action may occur. They have raised the slogan, "No discrimination against married women workers." In the workers' paper, *The Working Woman,*[2] writers have pointed out more vigorously than the National Woman's Party has ever done, that to take a job away from a woman who needs it and give it to another worker, either man or woman, is typical of the muddle, the inefficiency; the waste of human life that is capitalism.

From the very beginning of the National Recovery Administration, Left-Wing writers have called attention to the discrimination against women workers in the N.R.A. codes. With the official sanction of President Roosevelt, about one-quarter of the codes, at least 120 out of 465, have established a wage differential with rates lower for women workers than for men. These sex differentials are of three kinds, as shown in an analysis by the U.S. Women's Bureau: (1) codes which specify lower wage rates for the women than for men; (2) codes permitting lower rates for light, repetitive work in which so many women are engaged, but which so often require considerable skill and dexterity; (3) codes carrying the provision that persons paid below the code minimum in July, 1929, may continue to be so paid. This provision strikes largely at women and perpetuates the status of low-wage groups, whether women, foreign-born or Negroes.

☐ ─── ☐

THE NEW DEAL UPHOLDS
THE SOUTHERN STATUS QUO

"Class War in Alabama" by Jim Mallory,
Labor Unity, June 1934

[*Roosevelt's New Deal was not so new but that it accepted the old South of racial discrimination and, for all workers, the southern differential in wages and conditions.*

Jim Mallory, southern Party organizer, in Labor Unity *(monthly organ of the Trade Union Unity League) gives an account of the dimensions and depth of the conflict in the South.*]

A wave of strikes is sweeping Alabama like a prairie fire fanned by a high wind. Neither the pistols of the murderous company thugs, nor the rifles of the National Guardsmen, nor the menace of machine guns mounted along the roads to the mines—not even murder itself, the cold-blooded killing of six heroic strikers—has been able to smash the strikes or quell the determination of these southern workers. Coal miners, ore miners, steel workers, laundry and textile workers have within the short space of a few months, downed tools and fought not only against the bosses and their thugs, the police and the courts, but also against a union misleadership which tops all others in treachery.

Two burning needs, above all, have led the Alabama workers to go on with the struggle in spite of terror and in spite of treachery. The first of these needs is the right to organize . . . the second is equal wages with the workers in the North and West.

It is this second demand in particular that strikes at the very basis of southern economic relationships. The workers of the South have been forced to accept a standard of living lower than any other workingclass group in the country. . . .

The NRA and its heads have again and again given their official sanction to the lower wage scale for southern workers. The NRA codes decreed wages of from 10 to 50 percent lower for southern workers in various industries. . . .

The southern bosses and Chambers of Commerce say that costs of living are cheaper in the South. The fact is that the prices of food and clothing in any southern city are higher than the prices of the same grade of goods in a city of similar size in the North. An illuminating study of chain store prices undertaken recently by the *Southern Worker* proves that the dollar of the southern housewife will buy less food than the dollar of the housewife trading with the same firm in a northern city. Numerous reports by capitalist agencies prove conclusively that if the southern workers were to buy the same grade and quantity of food as the workers in the North, they would have to get more wages than northern workers.

What southern workers have is not a cheaper living cost but a lower living standard. Workers' tables in the South are laid with fatback in place of meat, with lard in place of butter, with greens, beans and other cheap articles of diet. Clothing and housing fall below the northern standard—low as the northern standard is. . . .

To keep the workers of the South from organizing, to keep them from fighting in a solid front against oppression and miserable conditions, the bosses have driven into their ranks the sharp wedge of race division. They forced the oppressed Negroes to accept slave conditions—and this acts as a weight dragging down the conditions of all the southern working class. Using white textile workers against Black, Black miner against white, the southern bosses have reaped a rich harvest in the form of a divided and weakened class of toilers and a lower standard of wages. . . .

Early in March [1934] began the first of the present series of strikes in Alabama's basic industries. More than 21,000 [coal mine] workers came out in this strike. In spite of the ruling of the Regional Labor Board of the NRA, in spite of the treacherous ruling of William Mitch, District [11] President of the Union [United Mine Workers], that the strike was "illegal," in spite of machine-guns, tear-gas bombs, airplanes and cavalry sent against the miners by the National Guard, the strike spread rapidly from mine to mine. . . .

Meanwhile, in Birmingham's swanky Thomas Jefferson Hotel, negotiations went on between the top union officials and the mine owners. On March 18, the strike was called off over the strong desire of the union locals. The determined struggle of the miners forced certain concessions; an end to the contracting system, the right to elect checkweighmen. Union recognition was limited to voluntary check-off. . . . Wages remained unchanged and it was later revealed that Mitch had arrived at a secret agreement with the operators to ask no wage increases during the life of the agreement. Worst of all, the agreement stipulated no strikes at least until April, 1935. The miners were given no opportunity to discuss this—the union locals were instructed to send delegates "to ratify" an agreement which had not been made public, much less discussed among the men. . . .

The position of the Negro miners remained the same after the strike. Not that the A.F. of L. refused altogether to organize Negro miners. They did not dare. Three years of struggle for the freedom of the Scottsboro Boys, the presence of several left-wing organizations (the Communist Party, the International Labor Defense, etc.), with a bold program of equal rights and conditions for Negroes—all this made it impossible for the A.F. of L. misleaders to refuse admission to the Negro miners. But never did the U.M.W. of A. officials raise the question of the right of Negro miners to the same pay as the whites or their right to hold anything but the lowest-paid and hardest jobs. Only the rank and file groups and the Communist Party raised boldly the demand: "Equal pay for equal work for white and Negro; right of the Negroes to any job."

In April a lengthy competitive struggle between two groups of industrialists came to a head. The mine owners of the North, fearing the competition of southern mines with the advantage of lower wage-scales, forced the NRA to order an end to the differential in the Alabama coal fields.

It is noteworthy that only in the coal mines—a highly competitive industry—did the NRA even for a moment consider putting an end to the differential. In every other industry—laundry, textile, lumber, shipping, leather—the NRA insisted on a lower wage-scale for the South. . . .

With the refusal of the Alabama mine owners to concede the higher pay-scale, 21,000 miners poured out of the mines. The captive mines of the great steel companies joined the movement. The four captive coal mines of the T.C.I. [Tennessee Coal and Iron Co.], (U.S. Steel), were shut down. This was the first strike since 1921 in this powerful steel company, which holds the economic and political life of Alabama in its grip. . . .

True to the prediction of the rank and file opposition groups and the Communist Party, the NRA agreed to "compromise" the wage-scale. Only 40 cents per hour increase was granted instead of $1.20. In an official statement, Roosevelt gave his permanent blessing to the double slavery of the southern workers. "On the question of southern differentials, the recovery act recognizes differentials. It is not our contention to produce any sudden or disruptive changes in an established economic relationship."

□ ———————————————————————————— □

THE ORIGIN OF UNEMPLOYMENT INSURANCE

1. *H.R. 7598—The Workers Unemployment and Social Insurance Bill,* Labor Fact Book No. II, 1934; ### 2. *The Social Security Act,* Labor Fact Book No. III, 1936

[*The present unemployment and social insurance laws had their roots in the campaign initiated by the Communist Party. The two most important groups to launch the drive for unemployment insurance were the National Unemployed Councils and the rank and file trade unionists organized by Louis Weinstock (b. 1904). Weinstock was elected—and ten times re-elected—Secretary Treasurer of District Council No. 9 of the Brotherhood of Painters, Decorators and Plasterers. He helped rid his union of racketeers. Under his initiative the AFL Committee for Unemployment Insurance was formed and he was elected as its secretary.*

This was a rank and file movement bitterly opposed by the AFL hierarchy and its president, William Green, who scorned unemployment insurance as a dole.

The committee was organized in January 1932 by a group of rank and file trade unionists. Despite sharp opposition by the AFL bureaucracy it won wide support and the endorsement of many AFL organizations. In an interview in the Daily Worker *(April 28, 1934), Weinstock described the initial steps taken by the committee: "Our first action was to circulate a referendum in the AFL unions to see if the workers in this body were for or against unemployment insurance." He added: "The great amount of endorsements we got for the Workers Insurance Bill in this referendum was a heavy blow to William Green and the Executive Council members who fought against any form of unemployment insurance."*

This popular movement led to the introduction of the Workers Unemployment Insurance Bill (H.R. 7598) by Representative Ernest Lundeen (F.-L., Minn.). The administration followed with a social insurance measure introduced by Senator Robert F. Wagner (D., N.Y.) which became law in August 1935.

When Roosevelt took office not only was there no minimum protection for the unemployed but social security was yet to be enacted. We publish extracts from the Lundeen bill and the Wagner Act, which became the first social security law in the nation's history.]

1.

The Workers' Unemployment and Social Insurance Bill was placed formally before the 73rd Congress, 2nd Session, as H.R. 7598, having been introduced by Representative Ernest Lundeen of Minnesota on February 2, 1934. It has the support of the Unemployed Councils, of several of the Unemployed Leagues, and up to March 1, 1934, had been endorsed by three state labor federations and by over 1,200 local unions affiliated with the American Federation of Labor. It is the only *federal* bill proposed for the purpose of paying workers and farmers insurance for loss of wages because of unemployment, part-time work, sickness, accident, old age or maternity. It is the only bill to propose that such insurance shall be administered by workers' commissions composed of rank and file members of workers' and farmers' organizations. It stipulates that funds for such insurance shall be provided at the expense of the government and of employers, and that no contribution shall be levied on the workers. The text in part reads:

The Secretary of Labor is hereby authorized and directed to provide for the immediate establishment of a system of unemployment and social insurance for the purpose of providing insurance for all workers and farmers unemployed through no fault of their own in amounts equal to average local wages. Such insurance shall be administered by workers and farmers and controlled by them under rules and regulations prescribed by the Secretary of Labor in conformity with the purposes and provisions of this Act, through unemployment insurance commissions composed of rank and file members of workers' and farmers' organizations. Funds for such insurance shall hereafter be provided at the expense of the Government and of employers, and it is the sense of Congress that funds to be raised by the Government shall be secured by taxing inheritance and gifts, and by taxing individual and corporation incomes of $5,000 per year and over. No tax or contribution in any form shall be levied on workers for the purposes of this Act. In no case shall the unemployment insurance be less than $10 per week plus $3 for each dependent. . . .

The benefits of this Act shall be extended to workers and farmers without discrimination because of age, sex, color, religious or political opinion, or affiliation, whether they be industrial, domestic, or professional workers, for all time lost. No worker shall be disqualified for the benefits of this Act because of refusal to work in place of strikers, at less than normal or trade-union rates, under unsafe or unsanitary conditions, or where hours are longer than the prevailing union standards at the particular trade and locality, or at any unreasonable distance from home.

2.

The Social Security act, sponsored by Senator Robert F. Wagner of New York to carry out President Roosevelt's "economic security" program, was passed by the 74th Congress in its first session and signed by the President, August 14, 1935. . . .

The act is in three main divisions: (1) federal old-age benefits for which workers must pay an income tax on wages received, and employers an excise tax on wages paid; (2) federal encouragement to states to enact compulsory state unemployment compensation laws; and (3) providing meager grants-in-aid to states from federal funds for old-age assistance, and for aid to the blind, to dependent and crippled children, for maternal and child health and public health. . . .

For the great majority of workers, averaging less than $100 a month in wages, old-age benefits will average less than $30 a month. Only if an individual has averaged $100 a month *steadily for 20 years* will he get as much as $32.50 in monthly benefits. These rates doom the great mass of workers over 65 years of age to a "living standard" of less than $1 a day.

A permanent income tax, ranging from 1% of a worker's wages during the first three years (1937–1939) up to 3% by 1949 and after, is established by this act. Those who still have jobs must pay one-half the cost of such old-age benefits as are to be paid. Employers, taxed for the other half, can pass on this tax to the workers and consumers by means of increased prices on commodities. . . .

As clearly stated in the Workers' Bill (declaration of policy), the costs of a social insurance system must be a primary charge on the national wealth and recognized as part of the federal government's budget, to be provided out of the national treasury. Any additional costs necessitated by the plan should be derived by suitable tax legislation, from high incomes, corporate surpluses and other accumulated wealth.

☐ ——————————————————————————— ☐

THE PROBLEM OF COMPANY UNIONS

"Our Tasks in Developing Activity Within the Company Unions" by B. K. Gebert, *The Communist,* January, 1936

[*The corporations' resistance to the workers' demands and militancy varied. On the one hand, there was stubborn resistance bulwarked by police repression. On the other hand, some of the corporations sought to divert the rising tide of organization into company unions—organized and paid for and directed by the corporations. Boleslaw K. Gebert (b. 1895), one of the leaders of the foreign nationalities' divisions of the International Workers Order and also a leader in the Communist Party, worked with Philip Murray, head of the Steel Workers Organizing Committee and later president of the CIO.*

The Party's leadership in the struggle against company unions, seeking to transform them into genuine trade unions, is the subject of this article.]

If we examine the development of the company unions, we find that their real growth dates with the introduction of the N.I.R.A. [National Industrial Recovery Act, 1933] and that they have developed primarily in the heavy mass production industries where the bulk of the workers were unorganized. Section 7a of the N.I.R.A. declares: " . . . that no employee and no one seeking employment shall be required as a condition of employment to join any company union or to refrain from joining, organizing or assisting a labor organization of his own choosing."

Yet even the survey of company unions made by the United States Department of Labor admits that 48 per cent of the workers in the 593 plants investigated automatically became members of company unions. Other workers are forced to become members of the company unions by means of pressure, intimidation and fear of losing their jobs.

The report further declares: " . . . By far the largest number of company unions are relatively young. Most of them were organized during the N.R.A. period of 1933 to 1935. During these years 377 company unions, or 63.5 per cent of the total number studied were established. These included 306,134 or 57.7 per cent of the total workers employed in the establishments covered that had company unions. . . ."

To date, two and a half million workers are chained in the company unions. When we consider that more workers in the basic industries (with the exception of mining) are in the company unions than in the genuine trade unions and when we note further that the entire trade union movement embraces only approximately four million workers, it becomes clear that the company unions constitute a great danger to the American labor movement. . . .

"Fellow workers----."
The Ruling Clawss
By A. Redfield,
Daily Worker, 1935

111

Company unions are not only promoted by the manufacturers, but are being financed by them. John Larkin, general chairman of the employees' representatives of the Weirton Steel Company, when he was asked at the hearings in Washington on the Wagner Labor Disputes Act, before the United States Senate Committee on Education and Labor, "How is your organization (company union) financed?", answered: "It is financed by $25 paid by the company per month for every representative that is elected." He further explained that all other expenses of the company unions have been paid directly by the corporation. To the question, "Why is it that the company pays all the expenses?", Mr. Larkin answered: "Well, to explain that, there are a lot of men that work in the various mills on laboring jobs and such as that, and it would be a crime to take money off a man making 40¢ or 42 & 1/2¢ an hour, working 40 hours a week to pay to any institution, would it not? Would it not be better to get somebody to finance a thing like that? If they had to pay into that institution it would be just robbing them."

In addition to the steel industry, company unions have made inroads in such industries as rubber, packing houses, auto, railroad and captive mines. The management of the company unions is in the hands of the same agents of the bosses who devise new methods of speed-up, blacklisting and spying on the workers. The United States Steel Corporation, for example, pays $75,000 a year salary to a vice-president, Arthur H. Young, whose special job is the so-called handling of labor relations. . . .

Our attitude toward the company unions is clear; it is one of uncompromising struggle for the destruction of company unionism. This does not mean, however, that we shall adopt a policy of smashing company unions. Such a policy would lead only to the isolation of the advanced section of the workers from the large majority of the workers in the basic industries who comprise the company unions. Therefore, the policy must be that of working within the company unions, with the general perspective of transforming the company unions into genuine trade union organizations. . . .

The most oppressed section of the workers in the basic industries is, unquestionably, the Negro workers who are jim-crowed and segregated in the company–controlled towns and forced to accept the worst jobs at lowest pay. They are the first to be fired and the last to be hired. The trade union movement must undertake the task not only of organizing Negro and white workers into the same local unions, but must develop the struggle for the equal rights of the Negro people. This of course, must be combined with the struggle of the unemployed. . . .

The task confronting the Communists is to give concrete daily guidance and leadership in such a movement. Here is where the role of the shop nuclei [clubs] of the Communist Party in the steel, rubber, auto, packing house and railroad industries can play a decisive role. The Communists in the plants can and must act in grouping around themselves all the advanced workers with the objective of developing systematic struggle within the company unions.

☐ ──────────────────────────────────── ☐

FROM WATERFRONT STRIKE
TO GENERAL STRIKE, 1934

1. "Solidarity on the Embarcadero,"
from *Labor's Untold Story* by Richard O. Boyer and
Herbert Morais, Cameron Associates, 1955;
2. *The Big Strike* by Mike Quin,
International Publishers, 1979 (new edition)

[The longshoremen on the West Coast struck when their modest demands were rejected by the employers. The combined terroristic measures of employers and government were directed against the waterfront workers. The labor movement in the area responded with a general strike that has become an epic in American labor history. Boyer and Morais have given a picture of this great struggle in their excellent history of the United States labor movement.

A weekly newspaper supporting the labor and Communist movements, the Western Worker, *was published in San Francisco. During the general strike in 1934, functioning under the most difficult conditions, it appeared twice weekly. In January 1938,* The Daily People's World *appeared, initiated by a broad-based movement of labor, progressives and Communists. It continued as a daily until early 1957 when it reverted to a weekly. Its present editor is Carl Bloice, a member of the Central Committee of the Communist Party.*

Mike Quin (1906–1947) was a writer of wide popularity among working-class readers. He was a regular contributor to the Western Worker, *the* Peoples World *and the* Daily Worker. *Quin possessed the talent for conveying the electricity of struggle which gripped the Pacific Coast as unionists and their allies threw back the offensive of the maritime employers, their political reinforcements and the assorted practitioners of violence. Quin's view of the general strike scene in San Francisco in*

113

1934 follows an excerpt from Boyer and Morais. (See also William Schneiderman, p. 119.)]

1.

San Francisco is a busy city of 600,000, its heart the waterfront, the chief source of its life. And yet the men who kept the city alive, who did its most important work, the longshoremen who loaded and unloaded the vessels that made the city prosperous with trade, the seamen who manned the ships, received in 1933 little more than $10 a week. To be precise, the average weekly wage of longshoremen was $10.45 while able seamen received $53 a month and ordinary seamen $36. . . .

And yet even more important was the fact that the maritime workers were voiceless serfs in an industrial autocracy, powerless employees of the shipping industry which received millions on millions of dollars, according to the Black Senatorial Investigation [Sen. Hugo Black], in subsidies from the federal government. A few seamen belonged to a corrupt, sell-out organization, the International Seamen's Union and still fewer to the militant Marine Workers Industrial Union (TUUL), but to all practical purposes they were unorganized. The longshoremen since 1919 had been dragooned into a creature of the shipping industry known as the Blue Book Union, an employers' organization, controlled by gangsters who forced the underpaid longshoremen to bribe them for jobs.

In 1933, under the impetus of NIRA and Section 7(a) as well as the spur of intolerable conditions, longshoremen in San Francisco and up and down the Pacific coast began flocking into the International Longshoremen's Association, AFL. Knowing something of Joseph P. Ryan,[3] its president, they were determined on rank and file control. One of their leaders was a sharp-featured, sharp-witted longshoreman by the name of Harry Bridges. A tough and rugged character, his assets were an impregnable honesty and a stout belief in the ability and right of the rank and file to govern themselves.

Although federal law made it mandatory that the shipping magnates negotiate in collective bargaining with any union that their employees chose, they unhesitatingly broke the law by refusing to so negotiate. Instead, in September, 1933, they discharged four rank and file leaders of the union. When the regional labor board ordered their reinstatement, the longshoremen surged into the ILA. . . .

After the employers had refused to negotiate or recognize the union over a period of months 12,000 longshoremen went on strike at 8 p.m. on May 9, 1934, in San Francisco, Seattle, Tacoma, Portland, San Pedro,

San Diego, Stockton, Bellingham, Aberdeen, Grays Harbor, Astoria and all other Pacific coast ports. The Marine Workers Industrial Union followed suit and by May 23 eight maritime unions and 35,000 workers were out on strike up and down the coast.

It was primarily unprecedented police brutality that turned the seamen's strike into a general strike of 127,900 San Francisco workers that in an instant transformed the city into a ghost town in which there was no movement. The police took their line from the Industrial Association, the combination of San Francisco's most powerful tycoons, organized in 1919 as a Law and Order Committee to break a waterfront strike and developing until it was the real ruler of San Francisco. . . .

The longshoremen had drawn up a list of demands, pay of $1 an hour, a six-hour day, a thirty-hour week, a union hiring hall, but officials of the Industrial Association declared there was no issue at stake but the suppression of a Red Revolt. Press, pulpit and radio combined with tireless unanimity to whip up hysteria against workers striving to better their lives. Not unusual was the first-page story of the [San Francisco] *Chronicle,* "Red Army Marching on City." The story read in part: "The reports stated the communist army planned the destruction of railroad and highway facilities to paralyze transportation and later, communication, while San Francisco and the Bay Area were made a focal point in a red struggle for control of government. . . ."

Bumbling Joseph P. Ryan, president of the International Longshoremen's Association, but in league with the gangsters of New York, was rushed from New York to quiet the strikers. Long known as an ardent fighter against Communism, he did his part as expected when unable to sell out the maritime workers. . . .

"A deafening roar went up from the pickets. Standing on the running board of a patrol car at the head of the caravan, Police Captain Thomas M. Hoertkorn flourished a revolver and shouted, 'The port is open!'

"With single accord the great mass of pickets surged forward. The Embarcadero became a vast tangle of fighting men. Bricks flew and clubs battered skulls. The police opened fire with revolvers and riot guns. Clouds of tear gas swept the picket lines and sent the men choking in defeat. Mounted police were dragged from their saddles and beaten to the pavement.

"The cobblestones of the Embarcadero were littered with fallen men; bright puddles of blood colored the gray expanse.

"Squads of police who looked like Martian monsters in their special helmets and gas masks led the way, flinging gas bombs ahead of them. . . ." [Cited from Mike Quin's *The Big Strike.*]

Fighting continued for four hours before a vast gallery of San Franciscans, perhaps half of the city watching it from the hills which loom above the waterfront. Two airplanes, packed with the curious, circled low over the bloody battle area. The battle was fierce but it was only the prelude to Bloody Thursday. The next day, after the initial attack of the police, was July 4 and by common consent there was a one-day truce before the battle resumed on Thursday, July 5. Quin writes:

"There were no preliminaries this time. They just took up where they left off. . . . Teeming thousands covered the hillsides. Many high school and college boys, unknown to their parents, had put on old clothes and gone down to fight with the union men. Hundreds of working men started for work, then changed their minds and went down to the picket lines." . . .

But the strikers and their thousands of sympathizers fought on with their bare hands against bullets and bombs. Their only weapons were bricks and stones. Hundreds were badly wounded. Two, Nick Bordoise and Howard Sperry, were killed. Sperry was a longshoreman; Bordoise was a culinary worker, a member of the Cooks' Union and of the Communist Party. . . .

The employers thought they had won; they had not. The strike was just beginning. . . .

The Painters Union, Local 1158, sent out a call for a general strike and it had scarcely been issued when the Machinists Union, Local 68, took up the demand. But first labor had to bury its dead. More than 35,000 workers walked behind the coffins. There were no police about as the stern-faced workers marched through the heart of the city. . . .

Now locals were meeting all over the city, one after another voting for a general strike. In the debates it was admitted that Communists were active in the struggle of the maritime workers. For that matter, it was said, they or other Marxists, had been active in every big strike since the railroad strike of 1877. Trade unionist after trade unionist declared that for the San Francisco labor movement to fall for the employers' red scare was to agree to its own division, to less pay, longer hours. On July 10 the Alameda Labor Council went on record for a general strike. On July 12 the powerful locals of the teamsters' union in San Francisco and Oakland issued a call for union solidarity; favored the general strike.

William Green sent telegrams forbidding the strike, but by July 15 some 160 local AFL unions, with a membership of 127,000 workers, had voted general strike effective the following day. . . .

But the force and violence of police and vigilantes moved not a wheel. The city was like a tomb all of July 16. Nothing moved on July 17. San

116

Francisco was a ghost on July 18. Yet on each of these days "the conservative wing" had succeeded in loosening the strike's grip. Restaurants were allowed to open on one day. It was extended to some trucking the next day. More exceptions were made the next. Rumors were spread that the strike was over. One of the biggest demonstrations in the history of American labor ended on July 19 when Deal, Vandeleur and Kidwell, conservative AFL officials, refusing a roll call vote, announced that the central labor body had ended the general strike by a standing vote of 191 to 174.

But the workers returned as if celebrating a victory. They put their hands to switch, throttle, wheel and assembly line and death became life. The maritime workers, rejecting all attempts to divide the eight unions out on strike, remained on their picket line but with an increased strength. No police assaulted their lines now. National Guardsmen stayed their distance. Labor had demonstrated its power and the tycoons of the Industrial Association fighting now among themselves did not want another taste of labor's unity.

On July 30 the 35,000 maritime workers went back to work. Within a matter of weeks the longshoremen had gained, as a direct result of the strike, the six-hour day, a thirty-hour week and time and a half for overtime. Wages were raised to a basis of ninety-five cents an hour; $1.40 for overtime. But above all they had won the basis for the union hiring hall, a method for democratic rotary hiring without which the union would have been powerless to protect its gains.

2.

The Communist Party numbered in its ranks mechanics, longshoremen, seamen, streetcar conductors, printers, laborers, store clerks, delivery boys, college students, stenographers, doctors, lawyers, school teachers, musicians, salesmen, housewives, members of the unemployed, newspaper reporters, bookkeepers and persons of every conceivable calling. Their influence reached almost everywhere. On the whole, it could be compared with a small plant having tremendous roots. When this vast apparatus swung into action behind the maritime workers it was able to rally enormous support not only in seaports but hundreds of miles inland. The members were not mere dues-paying adherents but active participants in the Party work, each one having his own duties and responsibilities. . . .

The most serious handicap the Communists experienced was the crippling of their newspaper, the *Western Worker*. On the eve of the raids they had announced they were increasing publication to twice weekly instead of once weekly. Shortly thereafter the editorial offices were wrecked; the composition shop where the paper was made up was set on fire and the commercial printer who usually ran it off on his presses was warned that if he did so again his plant would be demolished. The editors and writers were being hunted by the police and did not dare show their faces too prominently.

While Party representatives were scouring the city to find a printer who would run off the paper, a mimeographed edition was prepared and distributed. Every printer in town had been warned against accepting the job, and they were unable to find one who would take a chance on it.

Finally they located an old flat-bed printing press and a linotype in a remote part of town. The machinery was antiquated and had been out of commission for a long time. It was doubtful whether it could be put in shape again. Party mechanics set to work on it and after twenty-four hours of continuous work had it running at a low degree of efficiency.

Editors and writers set up makeshift offices in private homes and were pouring out the necessary copy. A score or more of men were ransacking the town for odds and ends of needed parts and type lead to feed the linotype. The old flat-bed press had no modern devices. They had to feed it by hand and peel it by hand and could print only one side of one sheet at a time. An enormous amount of hand labor was required. Nevertheless they succeeded in getting out the first twice-weekly edition on schedule and continued thereafter without interruption. Only one issue ever appeared in mimeograph form.

Once the paper was printed they faced another serious problem. The paper was legal in every respect, had second-class mailing privileges and once they could get it into the hands of the U.S. Post Office, delivery would be assured. The difficulty was to keep it from falling into the hands of local authorities. The post office where they had to deliver it was located right on the Embarcadero, which made the task still more hazardous. A careful study of the most favorable hour was made and a few men ran the gauntlet successfully in an old car.

While all this was going on a group of unidentified men were busy with hammers and nails in Hayward, one of the towns across the bay, erecting a scaffold in the public park opposite the City Hall. It had the customary thirteen steps leading up to it, a large knotted noose and a sign: "Reds Beware!" It was put up, the police said, during the night without their knowledge.

Since such a structure could be raised in the dark of night without attracting the police, it would be equally logical to suppose that thieves could dismantle the City Hall itself and make off with it without fear of detection.

Mayor McCracken of Oakland announced he had sworn in 3,000 citizen vigilantes. An additional 500 were mobilized in Berkeley and 500 more in Alameda.

Raids and arrests were continuing in full swing despite the fact that jails in most towns were already packed far beyond capacity. In Berkeley flying squadrons of vigilantes toured the city in cars, throwing bricks through windows of residences where suspected Communists were supposed to live. A note was attached to each brick:

"Members of a committee of Berkeley citizens organized for the purpose of purging the city of communists, bolsheviks, radicals, agitators and other anti-government groups, hereby notify you that you are known to be directly linked with this group that is trying to destroy our government. . . .

"We further warn you to leave this community immediately or drastic means will be taken." . . .

Permanent vigilante organizations were being formed in all towns and cities. Vehement demands were made that public libraries be "purged" of all allegedly Red books. Other patriots wanted to reorganize the public school system on a basis of rigid censorship to make certain that no Red ideas were lurking in the primers. Some urged the institution of concentration camps, either in Alaska or on the peninsula of Lower California, to which all Communists would be exiled. . . .

Meanwhile the Communist Party in all cities calmly moved back into their headquarters, swept out the broken glass, restocked their shelves with literature and resumed "business as usual." While the anti-Communist campaign was blazing at its highest, with newspapers printing such headlines as "Legion Asks Death Penalty for Reds," the Communists launched their state election campaign.

□ ———————————————————————————————— □

THE SHIPOWNERS RESUME THE OFFENSIVE

"The Pacific Coast Maritime Strike"
by William Schneiderman, *The Communist,* April, 1937

[*In the two years following the successful San Francisco General Strike (see also p. 113), the Pacific shipowners and their banking and corporate allies never accepted the fact that unionism was to endure. But they were frustrated by the constant emphasis on "closing ranks" in the unions, an essential task stressed by the Communists.*

119

William Schneiderman (b. 1905) was a prominent Communist leader in California during the events leading to the second major defeat for the West Coast employers. The Maritime Federation of the Pacific, to which Schneiderman refers, embraced seven West Coast unions: International Longshoremen's Association, Sailors' Union, Marine Firemen, Cooks & Stewards, Radio Operators, Marine Engineers, and Masters, Mates and Pilots.]

The Pacific Coast maritime strike [October 30, 1936, to February 4, 1937] came to an end in victory after ninety-nine days of unexampled solidarity, organization and discipline on the part of 40,000 seamen and longshoremen. The Maritime Federation of the Pacific, born out of the great 1934 strike, went through its greatest test of strength in a struggle which in many ways broke all precedents of previous strike struggles. The gains won by the maritime unions in 1934 were maintained only by a bitter and unrelenting struggle against repeated attempts of the employers to find an entering wedge with which to break the unity of the seamen and longshoremen, and the rank-and-file control of the unions.

The strike was only the climax of a long series of struggles in which the shipowners were girding themselves for a major offensive to smash the maritime unions, which was to begin with a coastwide lockout by the shipowners on last September 30 [1936], when the 1934 arbitration awards expired.

For this purpose the employers had gathered an enormous war chest, through a voluntary tax levied on their profits, with the intention of entering into a long and protracted struggle, a sort of endurance contest by which they hoped to starve the workers out and drive them back to work on the shipowners' terms. Because the role and influence of the Maritime Federation were having a far-reaching effect on ever-wider sections of the labor movement on the Pacific Coast . . . the Waterfront Employers' Association had the backing of powerful reactionary open-shop interests, such as the Industrial Association of San Francisco, the Merchants & Manufacturers' Association of Los Angeles, the Chamber of Commerce, and the big Eastern shipping interests.

A number of provocations were organized during 1935 and 1936 by the employers, directed mainly at the militant longshoremen of San Francisco, in an attempt to create a split between them and the rest of the Pacific Coast district of the I.L.A., which was under a reactionary district leadership until last summer. . . . In each case the employers were forced to retreat when they met a solid united front of the Maritime Federation. . . .

The shipowners prepared themselves, therefore, for their big offensive on September 30. All shippers stocked up great quantities of goods in warehouses well in advance. They attempted to mobilize all business interests behind them, frightening them with talk about the "I.L.A.'s march inland," pointing to the organizing drives among warehousemen, teamsters, and numerous other industries, influenced directly or indirectly by the Maritime Federation. They pointed to the "radical influences" beginning to make themselves felt in the San Francisco General Strike of 1934.

For the maritime unions, however, this was not merely a defensive struggle to maintain their unions and the gains they had made in 1934; it was turned into a counter-offensive by the unions, with far-reaching consequences on a national scale, which resulted not only in new and decisive gains for the Pacific Coast unions, but for the maritime unions on the Atlantic and Gulf Coasts as well. . . .

How did the employers expect to carry through their offensive against the unions? Their main strategy was to attempt to undermine the unity of the Maritime Federation, splitting away the longshoremen from the seamen, or vice versa. . . .

One of the great weaknesses of our work was among the Negroes. In San Pedro the I.L.A. progressives inherited from the former reactionary leadership a situation where the Negroes were practically excluded from working on the waterfront, with the exception of the Cotton Compress Local. The progressives made some attempts to fight against this policy of discrimination, but insufficiently. . . .

In San Francisco, due to a correct policy adopted by the I.L.A. against Negro discrimination since 1934, there was a better situation. A number of Negro workers were included on the leading committees of the strike. The National Negro Congress played an important role in winning the sympathy of the Negro population in the San Francisco Bay area for the strikers. . . .

The Communists in the union must take the lead in fighting against every form of discrimination toward Negroes, and must especially be vigilant to expose and fight against the undercover campaign of discrimination carried on by some reactionary elements in the I.L.A. The Party must also carry on patient work among the seamen to break down the prejudices and discrimination against the Filipinos, pointing out that unless this attitude is changed, the employers will take advantage of it to create a reserve of strike-breakers against the union.

The Maritime Worker, weekly organ of the Waterfront Section of the Party, and the *Western Worker* were indispensable weapons in the fight for maintaining the unity of the strikers and in clarifying questions of policy, as well as explaining the broader political aspects of the struggle. The *Western Worker* was distributed in thousands of copies, regularly, in the union halls and on the picket lines, and was as widely read and discussed by the strikers as was the *Voice of the Federation,* in spite of numerous attempts to bar it from the union halls.

The role and influence of the Party were reflected especially in the recruiting of over 300 new members to the Party from the strikers' ranks. (Nearly 2,000 new members were recruited into the Party throughout California during the approximate period of the strike.)

The Party organization as a whole reacted well to its tasks during the strike. Learning from the experiences of 1934, during the reign of terror and vigilante raids, the Party was prepared, if necessary, to continue its work under emergency conditions. Nearly every section and unit was in a position to issue its own leaflets if necessary, and to continue uninter-ruptedly its activity in the neighborhoods and factories. Open mass activity was carried on during the whole three-month period. . . .

The Party during the latter half of the strike organized more systematic political education for its new members, particularly among the seamen, in the form of new members' classes, unit discussions and the distribution of Party literature. But a great deal more of this could have been done. A big shortcoming was the weakness in Party recruiting and political education among longshoremen. . . .

The Communists are not out to "control" or "capture" the unions for some sinister purpose. Our aim is to fight for policies that will strengthen and unify the ranks of the workers in their immediate struggles for the advancement of their economic and political interests.

☐ ————————————————————————————————— ☐

SITDOWN IN THE RUBBER INDUSTRY

**"Akron Becomes a Union Town," from *Dangerous Scot,*
by John Williamson, International Publishers, 1969**

[*The rubber industry dominated the city of Akron, where its tire production plants were to become the scene of one of the most notable strikes in the labor history of the United States. Its success signaled the drive for industrial unionism in the open-shop basic factories.*

As early as 1926 the Party and the Young Workers League (YWL) sent

122

comrades to Akron to help organize the rubber workers and lay the foundation for the union. Phil Frankfeld (1907–1975), one of the YWL leaders, participated in this work.

A principal figure in the Communist leadership in Akron was John Williamson, the Ohio Party state secretary, who described the Akron events in his book, Dangerous Scot. *Williamson (1903–1974) was one of the national Party leaders who was sentenced under the Smith Act in 1949. After serving his sentence, he was deported to Great Britain in 1955 during the anti-Communist frenzy.*]

Even before the Fisher Body sit-down strike [which began December 10, 1936], the Party in Ohio had the rich experience of the sit-down strikes of the Akron rubber workers. . . .

The first real sit-down strike in America started in the Firestone plant in January, 1936. The men opposed a cut of 11 percent in the base rate of the truck-tire department, and the company had fired the union committeemen. Wanting to strike but fearful of losing their jobs, they recalled the story of a foreign-born union printer. They sent a committee to hear again his experience years ago in Sarajevo, Serbia, when the printers wanted to strike but knew the boss had a crew of scabs waiting to take their place. Said the printer, Alex Eigenmacht, "So we had an inside strike. We just sat around by our machines and, by God, nobody could come in and take our jobs and they couldn't arrest us either. We were on the job."

The committee asked, "Didn't the boss try to throw you out?" Alex replied, "He couldn't. He was afraid of hurting his expensive machinery if there was any fighting inside."

That night the Akron rubber workers did what no-one in the United States had ever done before: they initiated a sit-down strike. All hell broke loose when the bosses finally comprehended what was happening. . . . Inside, the union committee, among whom were members of our Party factory branch, occupied the foreman's office and issued union cards. After 53 hours the union members in Plant Two said if there was not an immediate settlement they, too, were going on a sit-down strike.

Firestone quickly settled. They reinstated the committeemen, agreed to pay the striking workers three hours pay for each day lost, and to open up negotiations on a new base rate. . . .

The union was back in business. Everything the Communists had said by word of mouth, in leaflets and at meetings was proving to be correct.

Within a month the critical showdown came. The largest of the Big Three, Goodyear, which had just reintroduced the eight-hour day [there were four shifts of six hours] in the entire plant except for the tire-building pits, became still bolder and announced a wage cut of 10 per cent.

At three A.M., February 14, 1937, the tire-builders in Goodyear Plant Two shut off the power and started a sit-down strike in protest against the layoff of 70 men, which they interpreted as the preparation for the introduction of the eight-hour day in their department also. This was the start of one of the greatest class battles in America's history, and the first major test of industrial organization as advocated by the C.I.O.

After rejecting a company ultimatum to go back to work, the sit-downers were fired. But they still were in the plant. The next day the local union leaders, guided by John House, the president, took the sit-downers out of the plant. The company had agreed to cancel the dismissals. But the men refused to return, because no provision was made to rehire the 70 men who had been laid off originally.

The entire factory was astir. The local union leaders, especially House, were not only inexperienced but afraid of responsibility. Thousands of men, union and non-union, were flocking into the big union hall. The Communist Party issued mimeographed leaflets calling for union action against the eight-hour day, wage-cuts and speedup, and distributed them widely.

In this charged atmosphere, Goodyear issued, as it had always done in the middle of February, its annual financial statement. This showed that the net profits for 1935 were five and a half million dollars, compared to four and a half million in 1934. The men were stung into action. . . .

Each of the next 32 days was action-packed. In the coldest winter in years, these workers, most of whom had never been on strike before, marched in snow on the picket lines that extended for 18 miles surrounding the Goodyear plant. By the third day all three plants were closed down.

Then the battle started. Courts issued injunctions, police and sheriff's deputies battled the strikers on the picket line, the company demanded the aid of the National Guard and refused to meet the union and a terrific newspaper and radio barrage was launched against the strikers.

In this situation our Party put all our experience at the disposal of the 14,000 strikers and the newly established trade union. We met with our own Party members and all other key forces in the strike apparatus and conferred with the local leaders of the Rubber Union, including some members of the international executive board. We had regular meetings with Wilmer Tate, the left-wing president of the Central Labor Union. . . .

We worked out a leaflet which dealt with what was happening in the plants—the eight-hour day, the speedup, wage-cuts—and the swollen company profits. We brought to the foreground the question of unity and the possibility of the workers responding with a general strike if violence and terror were used against the strikers. We called for total union organization and for union endorsement of the strike and then projected the following demands: The six-hour day; no layoffs; no wage-cuts; a wage increase of 10 per cent over the base rate; the end of speedup and a signed agreement. This leaflet was on the picket lines and in the Goodrich, Firestone and General factories by five o'clock that day.

House was still saying the strike was not union-endorsed and "just happened" and that the only issue was the reinstatement of the 70 discharged tire-builders. That night all the picket captains unanimously endorsed and adopted as their own all the demands in the Party leaflet. . . .

The picket captains met on the second day and again fulfilling the role of the absent leaders of the local's executive committee, decided that the work stoppage must be turned into a legal strike and that all strikers must be signed up in the union and given voting rights. Negotiations were to be opened with the company on the five demands. Picket lines were to be held solid, irrespective of injunctions, police or National Guard and efforts were to be made to win public opinion to the strikers.

Goodyear said it would never negotiate. Tension rose as the company appealed for court injunctions and armed intervention. The Central Labor Union voted full support and promised "to take all measures within our power to defeat" any injunctions. President Sherman Dalrymple of the International Rubber Union threatened "industrial paralysis affecting the entire city" if injunctions were issued. But the full court of six judges issued a sweeping injunction prohibiting mass picketing. Fortunately the police chief and the sheriff disagreed on shooting their way into the picket line. The company was still able to rally 2,500 workers against the strike and these men were used in every way. The strikers christened them "Red Apples," and that term became a permanent part of the rubber worker's vocabulary to describe company-minded men.

At this point John L. Lewis and the CIO moved in. The steps they advised—making the strike official and signing up everybody into the union—were carried out.

As the strike seesawed back and forth, a dangerous point was reached around the 14th day. The federal government sent in their so-called ace arbitrator, Edward McGrady. He was now an assistant secretary of labor, but had previously been an AFL organizer, which didn't endear him to the rubber workers. His technique was to promise the world to the strikers if they would just return to work and allow negotiations to take place. At one point, even some of the CIO people wavered on this issue. McGrady's proposals had become a delicate matter because the company had at first rejected them and the union leadership thought they would win public opinion if they accepted.

Again the picket captains were the decisive force. They made it clear to the leaders of the new union and the CIO officials that the strike would remain solid and they flatly rejected McGrady's scheme. . . .

The thing that had turned the tide was the information the Party had provided the picket captains and the workers about McGrady's sellouts at Industrial Rayon Co. in Cleveland and in Toledo. . . .

The Party leaders then met with all our comrades who were active in the strike. . . . After long discussions . . . it was decided that we could not advise an out-of-hand rejection of the company proposals, unsatisfactory as they were. We must prevent public opinion from being turned against the strikers. . . .

The picket captains endorsed these proposals. Then came the local union meeting with 4,000 inside and at least another thousand crowding around outside. . . .

Finally the committee arrived and reported on what the company said was their final offer. Silence greeted the report, till Bill Ricketts [head of the picket captains] got the floor and submitted a resolution indicating what was to be accepted and what amended. With great cheers, the meeting unanimously adopted Bill's motion.

The first newspaper headline was "Two Points of Peace Plan Accepted, Company Terms Partially Met." Later editions revealed the next moves of the enemy. The company broke off negotiations and declared the strikers had rejected their proposals in full. That night they organized a vigilante outfit called the "Akron Law and Order League." On its behalf, ex-Mayor Sparks went on the radio and called on all citizens "to gang up upon the out-of-town radical and Communist leaders." . . .

In the lynch atmosphere that was being created, it was decisive to maintain the unity of the strikers' ranks and the common front between ourselves and the CIO leaders. I made it my business to talk to Central Labor Union president Tate, CIO leaders John Owens, Leo Krzycki and Rose Pesotta and various leaders of the United Rubber Workers of America.

Tate went on the radio and answered Sparks. The union took the radio for nine continuous hours with National Secretary-Treasurer Frank Grillo in command, all through one night, interspersing announcements, news, music, warnings and speeches. These countermeasures subdued

126

the company hoodlums. The next day the company resumed negotiations with the union.

While the new negotiations were going on, two of our leading comrades who were picket captains argued for letting all the picket captains see and hear an official spokesman of the Communist Party. With great modesty, these two comrades, who had carried the burden for five weeks, pointed out that without Party leadership the strike would have been lost. It wasn't fair that the picket captains should get all the credit when actually the Party leadership was in great measure responsible. . . . By a big majority the invitation was extended.

☐ ——————————————————————————— ☐

THE COMMUNISTS IN THE GREAT FARM REVOLT

Farmers Unite Their Fight, Report of the Farmers' National Committee for Action by Lem Harris, Farmers National Committee for Action, Philadelphia, Pa., 1934

[*Harold Ware (writing under his pen name George Anstrom), summing up a year-long survey of American agriculture wrote: "Everywhere Big Business—the capitalists and their obedient government—has produced the ultimate absurdity: surplus and starvation."* (The American Farmer, *by George Anstrom, International Publishers, 1932).*

Harold Ware (1890-1935) was then directing the Party's farm activity. The Communist Party was reacting to the appalling situation of the farm population and to the farm revolt that was brewing. It had sent Erik Bert from the Daily Worker *staff to an obscure town in a treeless part of Montana called Plentywood. Bert edited the county-seat weekly paper, the* Producers News, *which was owned by a group of farmers. The paper became the official organ of the United Farmers League with membership scattered over Montana, the Dakotas and Minnesota.*

Mother Ella Reeve Bloor, a member of the Party's Central Committee, was sent to North Dakota and soon became State Organizer of the United Farmers League. She married Andrew Omholt, who had homesteaded in North Dakota. Omholt helped organize the radical Non-Partisan League and became District Organizer of the Communist Party.

When a farm strike broke out in the Iowa-Minnesota-Wisconsin area,

127

Mother Bloor drove into Sioux City, the center of strike activity, to direct the Party forces. Harold Ware,[4] her oldest son, joined her and they encouraged farmers who had come in from six states to endorse and participate in a national farmers' relief conference to be held in Washington in December 1932.

Lem Harris, who had worked with Ware on agriculture projects in the Soviet Union, was organizer of this conference.

The Farmers' Conference launched a militant newspaper, The Farmers National Weekly, with Rob Hall, and later Erik Bert, as its editor. The Conference also set up the Farmers' National Committee for Action with Lem Harris as its executive secretary. In November 1933, the Second Farmers' National Relief Conference was held, this time in Chicago.

Other Party farm actives included Clarence Hathaway and Clarence Sharp from Minnesota, Jasper Haaland from North Dakota and John Marshall from Ohio.

The following are excerpts from Lem Harris's report on 1933 farm struggles to the Chicago Conference.]

Fellow Farmers, Delegates from all over the country:

We have come here to unite upon a campaign of struggle for winning the most pressing demands affecting all working farmers. At the Washington Conference last year we started our national campaign against forced sales and evictions, for a moratorium on debts, an attack on the swollen profits of middlemen. . . .

Our record during the past year is a struggle to carry out the National Program of Action. In 1929, 123,000 farmers were foreclosed upon or evicted. In 1932, this number rose to 262,100 farms, or one out of every 24 farms. In 1933, the year after the Washington Conference, although farmers are in a worse condition, nevertheless the number of foreclosures and evictions dropped because we made it unhealthy to throw a family out of its home. . . .

In attacking the food trusts we need the cooperation of the city workers. We can report great numbers of food workers who have pledged solidarity with us.

The milk drivers of Philadelphia are organizing themselves and have invited our farmers to plan a joint strike of milk farmers and drivers in the Philadelphia milk shed. . . .

Strike is the weapon farmers have been using to force their demands upon the trusts.

We have seen farmers' strikes breaking out two times in Wisconsin, two times in New York and in Iowa and other parts of the country. We find farmers preparing for strike in Pennsylvania and Connecticut. We also find whenever a strike is planned the enemy makes the most prodigious efforts to get into control and keep it from making much headway. We find in New York, when the farmers came out on strike, that the Farm Bureau and Dairymen's League openly attacked the strike. The New York delegates report that the farmers of New York State are ready to go out on strike again when they get an organization going. . . . In order to win we must have leadership from the ranks of the farmers.

At every step of the way, as we get better organized, we encounter the enemy—the tools of finance capital. We find their courts, judges, sheriffs, legislators, governors and Congress lined up to enforce the ruin of the farmers and workers of the whole country. But we must realize that there are two kinds of enemies: 1. Those who carry bayonets and gas, who arrest, sentence and imprison our farmer leaders. 2. The false friends who get into positions of leadership and talk radically as they betray us.

One example covers the whole situation. In Pennsylvania, soon after the Washington Conference, farmers massed to stop a sale. It was the first time it had happened in that community.

When the sheriff, deputies and lawyer arrived they found children in the lane holding signs: "Save our home," and 300 farmers massed in the barnyard. The sheriff began by getting tough. "I want you fellows to know this farm is under the jurisdiction of the county. I'm its legal representative and I am in charge of this situation." A farmer who is in this hall right now stepped forward and said: "Wait a minute. This is a farm and this is a manure pile, Mr. Sheriff, and these are farmers and this is a farmers' community." . . . The lawyer . . . decided it is better to lose one client than to make enemies of all the people he had to see when he went for a walk on Sunday morning. He decided not to bid for the property. The mass power of the farmers was victorious.

One day later on, after many other sales had been stopped, 70 armed deputies were sent to the Pennsylvania village of Red Hill to force through the sale of a farm worked by John Lelko. Faced with this small army, the crowd of farmers refused to accept battle. They had a different plan. A girl speaker got up between the crowd of farmers and the line of deputies: "You have come out against us with arms. . . . We have another weapon. From now on this farm will be a scab farm. We are going to see to it that this owner suffers for this action. We are going to see to it that no new tenant comes on this farm because we are going to inform that tenant that this is a mighty unhealthy place for him and that nobody will neighbor with him and he will find it tough."

In Wisconsin, Iowa and New York this year, soldiers have been called out to stop the farmers from winning their just demands. But did you notice when they call out the militia, they used very young people—practically kids who did not know what it was all about—the ones least likely to turn against business men and to the farmers? Is that not true? (Answer from Iowa delegation: "Yes. They were high school kids. Many looked about sixteen.") . . .

The enemy has singled out various people, various good speakers and organizers and tried to victimize them, to terrify them and the rest of the farmers. I can tell you, in not one instance has the arrest done anything more than help build a larger and more powerful organization. I want to point here to John Rose, member of the State Committee of the Michigan Farmers League, who comes from prison. He was arrested at a sheriff's sale for helping save a farm. He was convicted and was just freed a couple of days ago. . . .

Rose of course is just one. There have been plenty of others. They usually pick the most successful organizers. Besides Rose, in Michigan they picked out Clyde Smith and George and John Casper. In Nebraska, Harry Lux, because he had a pair of lungs and vocal chords which were doing much good for the Holiday Association in that state. We have found that this is the opening gun as we widen this campaign. We must prepare for what is coming next. That is why we have organized a Farmers' National Defense Bureau. . . .

When the misleaders find they are losing support they bring in the "red scare." They start a cry: "Look out for the radicals, the reds." Fellow farmers, we most certainly are radical—present distress demands intelligent, radical action. We represent farmers of all views and political opinions.

At our wonderful united front convention in Lincoln, Nebraska, last February, the misleaders tried the red scare and failed. Crocker, the insurance man, and Parmenter, both officers of the National Holiday Association, testified before the Nebraska Senate Committee and broadcast to the state that the 350 farmer delegates assembled in Lincoln were just a bunch of reds. The result must have surprised Parmenter & Co. On the day following the broadcast, 3,500 more farmers came in to Lincoln to join their comrades in a march on the State Capitol. . . .

We are calling on the farmers of America, organized and unorganized, to join forces to win our demands. We are not building an organization but are a united front of all organizations and all exploited farmers.

We have a headquarters, a National Committee and a paper to help direct our national campaigns of struggle. In close cooperation with the

National Committee are the hundreds of organizers, speakers, etc., many of whom are sitting in this hall. Perhaps many who have not been out organizing will get vaccinated here at this convention and start some excitement when they go back home. . . .

[We must] get the farm women to participate. . . . I am mighty glad that we have more women delegates than last year. We are counting on them to get more women organized when they go back home. When a woman gets up at a sale and speaks it carries enormous weight. It is the voice of the people speaking.

You know that the farm youth have a job also. There are places, like in Pennsylvania, Wisconsin, Michigan, where the organized farm youth are used for all sorts of purposes. They help get the crowd when a sale is to be stopped. In Pennsylvania they have volunteered to be the Paul Reveres and scatter the strike bulletins throughout the milk shed.

□ ——————————————————————————— □

THE PARTY IN INDUSTRY AND COMMUNITY

1. "Actual Experiences in Building the Party in International Harvester Co." by a McCormick Worker, *Party Organizer*, September 1935; 2. "How the Meat Strike Started in Hamtramck," *Party Organizer*, September 1935

[*The* Party Organizer, *an internal publication of the organization, is indicative of the attention the Party devotes to problems in shops and in the community. It served as a forum for exchange of ideas and experiences on how to work best in reacting to issues facing workers on the job and the people in the community. Two articles are presented here, one dealing with activities of a Party club in a large Chicago plant and the other in an industrial community in Hamtramck, Michigan.*]

1.

When we came into the workers' homes, we talked very simply about the happenings in their departments, actual working conditions, worsening of the speedup system, etc. We always showed how these bad working conditions could be changed if we were organized and stuck together. We show them why the Communist Party is the only working-class political party that honestly fights for the workers' interests. Then we ask them to join this workers' party. In this way, in a short while, we had new units organized in International Harvester. . . .

The results of this work are plain to everyone. Already we can see the presence of the Party being felt by the workers in many ways. More than that, the foremen and the company feel the presence of the Party. For example: the foremen no longer bully the workers nor swear at them as they used to before we became active. The foremen seem to have shrunk from big arrogant cats into quiet humble mice. How did we do this? We organized a simultaneous agitation in all departments against the foremen's slave-driving bullying tactics. We exposed these foremen personally by name in the Party shop papers (McCormick Worker and Tractor Worker), calling them down on the carpet for their dirty work. When the papers come out with these exposures, some workers secretly place copies of the paper right on the foremen's desks, so that the foremen cannot but see their exposures. The foremen go up in steam when they read these exposures and although they are raging with anger they are afraid to attack anybody. Immediately the workers notice that the foremen go easier on them.

The presence of the Party was felt in other ways. At a so-called "safety" meeting of the company, held each week, the foremen announced to the workers that if they forget or lose their pass-checks, they must pay 25 cents and lose a day's wages. This fine really amounts to about five dollars. We at once put up this question in the unit meeting and started a broad campaign in all departments both through personal agitation and through the shop papers, demanding that the company do away with these scandalous regulations. How effective our Party campaign was can be seen by the fact that at the very next "safety" meeting held the following week, these regulations were withdrawn and the workers told that they could get new pass-checks without losing their day's wages.

2.

The Party Section Committee [of Hamtramck, Michigan] was aware of the high cost of necessary commodities of life and the sentiment of the people against it. Early in June when our Section Committee discussed the three-month plan of work we made it a point to fight against the high price of meat. It was decided to call a conference of all women's organizations to take up the question of meat, but the conference was delayed from one week to another. Finally the Section Committee assigned one comrade of the Section to attend the meeting of the working women of Hamtramck, to convince the women that action must be taken. . . .

Party and non-Party women were called to the Section Committee meeting and we planned with them the calling of a mass meeting. A committee of women comrades and non-Party members issued five thousand leaflets calling for a mass meeting on Friday, July 19, 1935, at the Polish Falcons Hall. The leaflets were issued in the name of the Provisional Women's Committee Against the High Cost of Living and were distributed by five women and six men who went from house to house knocking at the door explaining the purpose of the meeting and asking the people how they felt about the high cost of meat. The general opinion of the workers was that something must be done against the high cost of meat.

The housewives' response was very good, about 400 women attending; an announcement was also made through the Polish hour radio WMBC.

At this meeting twenty-five women volunteered to serve on the Committee of Action. Resolutions adopted to protest the high cost of meat were sent to President Roosevelt and Secretary of Agriculture, Mr. [Henry] Wallace, demanding action in order to reduce the cost of living. A resolution was also presented to Mayor Lewandowski and the Common Council of Hamtramck. . . . The City Council spoke favorably on the issue and decided to send resolutions to President Roosevelt and to the Michigan Congressmen, requesting that something be done in regards to the high cost of meat.

By William Gropper,
Daily Worker, 1939

In the discussion with our comrades to take strike action immediately, the Action Committee decided to call a larger mass meeting on July 28, and requested the Board of Education to grant them the school for this meeting. . . .

The meeting at the school was very successful; twelve hundred women attended. . . . Never before on any issue were we able to mobilize so many women into one meeting. A fighting spirit prevailed . . . at the meeting.

Women members of the Action Committee gave reports and proposed to strike the next day, Saturday, July 27. After discussion from the floor it was unanimously resolved to take strike action. The membership of the Action Committee was increased to sixty. Women who never spoke in public and did not think they were capable, became not only fine speakers but leaders of the strike. This strike involved about 75 per cent of the city's population of 48,000.

Four days after the strike women delegations visited small butchers asking them if they were willing to support them in the strike. Ninety-three butchers signed up and agreed to close their shops, thinking that the women would not be able to stage a successful strike. On Saturday, the day of the strike, all the butcher shops were open in the morning. Only when the militant women pickets stopped people from buying were the butchers forced to close. Over 80 per cent of the butcher shops were closed by evening, due to the militant picketing which kept all purchasers from the stores.

The first day of the strike was a tremendous success (even the bourgeois papers admitted this). After the first meat strike day in Hamtramck the movement spread all over Detroit. The Action Committee called upon the Detroit women to strike the following Friday and Saturday. First, action was taken in North Detroit, a district adjoining Hamtramck, where the militant picketing of Hamtramck housewives was duplicated and resulted in the closing of butcher shops. Additional communities in the suburbs—Dearborn, Lincoln Park, Delray and other districts of Detroit—took action at the same time. . . .

After the first day of the strike all the bourgeois papers attacked the strike as "communist led." Their purpose was to scare away new elements and break the strike. In this effort they were not successful. Our reply was that the strike was not only for Communists but for everybody who eats meat. Nobody is asked to state his political belief, whether Democrat, Socialist, Communist or Republican, or whether he goes to church or not, but we ask everybody who wants to support the meat strike to join our organization. We also said we have Communists in our ranks who are good fighters and we are glad to have them. These points were brought up at every meeting in a special *Strike Bulletin,* a two-page paper selling for a cent that went like wild fire and in special editions of the *Trybuna Robotnicza* (Polish workers' paper).

When the reactionary forces attacked the strikers as Reds, we called an open-air mass meeting and parade. Close to 2,000 people, mostly women, participated. Though the parade was to end at the City Hall, it continued right on through all the main streets of the city due to its great enthusiasm. A loudspeaker led the parade issuing slogans and calling on the small retail butchers for unity with Hamtramck women. . . .

Our Party members must pay due tribute to the splendid work of the women in this strike and particularly to the women Party members. They showed us how the job can be accomplished, that they know how to fight and are willing to fight.

□ —————————————————————————————— □

THE THREAT OF WAR AND FASCISM

1. "'Hands Off Ethiopia' is Demand of 100,000
in Harlem Rally"
by Cyril Briggs, the *Daily Worker,* August 5, 1935;
2. "Address Before the First International Congress
for Peace" by Cyril Phillip, in Brussels, Belgium, 1936
(from manuscript supplied by the author)

[*The Hitler-nazi takeover in Germany, 1933, presaged new aggression, a threat of world war. Imperialist rivalry continued, but a qualitatively new element was added which threatened the security of all humanity. Although imperialist powers courted Hitler's favor, they soon were engulfed in a war which endangered the existence of every European nation—and finally the whole world.*

In October 1935, the fascist brigand Benito Mussolini, who destroyed the Italian Republic, was emboldened to invade Ethiopia. The bombing of densely populated centers, a hallmark of fascist aggression, was used against the Ethiopian people.

The League of Nations, never decisive, now found itself paralyzed by refusing to meet the challenge of the aggressor. The Soviet Union, which had joined the League the previous year, appealed for collective action against the aggressor. Its representative, Maxim Litvinov, called for collective security as the only means to maintain peace. But this plea fell on the deaf ears of those who were devising schemes to divert the aggressors' attack eastward, against the Soviet Union.

The threat of war aroused the peace forces in the United States. A national conference was held in New York, September 29, 1933, which established the American League Against War and Fascism with Dr. Harry Ward as chairman. The Communist Party was affiliated to it. The League attracted wide support among tens of thousands throughout the country. It was a viable force in the national peace movement.

As Mussolini's threat loomed, the League supported a united front demonstration in Harlem in defense of Ethiopia. Cyril Briggs, Black editor, describes this action in the Daily Worker.

The Communist Parties responded to the threat by mobilizing their forces internationally. The 7th Congress of the Communist International (CI) heard a report from Georgi Dimitrov[5] calling for the most intensive action in creating the broadest united front to save peace and democratic institutions. The CI appealed to the Socialist International for common action.

As war clouds thickened, the First International Congress for Peace was held in Brussels, Belgium, September 3-6, 1936. Among its participants were the major trade union leaders from France and the Soviet Union—Leon Jouhaux and N. M. Shvernik. Parliamentary figures from Britain and the continent attended.

The United States delegation was represented by divergent views united in the single purpose of maintaining the peace. In the large delegation was a young Black Communist Party member, Cyril Phillip, who was elected by a united committee in his Harlem community.

The conference took place three months after the ravaging of Ethiopia, but this crucial question remained on its agenda. Phillip addressed himself principally to this question. We quote a part of his speech.]

1.

The streets of the Negro and Italian sections of Harlem resounded to thunderous shouts of "Hands Off Ethiopia! Down With War and Fascism!" on Saturday afternoon as 100,000 persons took part in a giant [city-wide] united front anti-war demonstration, sponsored by the Provisional Committee for the Defense of Ethiopia and the American League Against War and Fascism, with the active support of hundreds of other organizations including many Italian and Negro groups.

Thousands of workers cheered the marchers from windows and roofs of houses, while tens of thousands of other workers swarmed along on the sidewalk keeping step with 40,000 marchers in the parade as they swung along in serried ranks, with banners flying, bands playing and shouted protests against war and fascism and against Mussolini's projected attack on Ethiopia in particular.

It was the greatest parade Harlem has seen in many years. Its broad, united front character, involving Negro churches and organizations, pacifist groups, Italian and German anti-Fascists, Communist, Socialist and A.F. of L. workers, independent unions and workers' clubs, gave notice to the imperialist war-mongers of the determination of the American people to defend themselves against the horrors of another imperialist world slaughter.

The first contingent of the parade, made up mainly of Harlem organizations, started out at 1:45 p.m. from Lenox Avenue and 126th Street, marching South. It was headed by Italian and Negro leaders in the anti-Fascist, anti-war struggle and the Provisional Committee for the Defense of Ethiopia. Next in line was a uniformed body of the Brotherhood of Sleeping Car Porters, A.F. of L., with their band.

At 129th Street and Seventh Avenue it was joined by the second contingent, which had assembled at 120th Street and Second Avenue and paraded through the Italian section before turning west. The united parade then swept up Seventh Avenue and through 143rd Street to the square at 141st Street and Edgecombe and Bradhurst Avenues. As the head of the parade entered the square, it was greeted with cheers from several hundred workers who had already assembled around a huge platform erected for the occasion and equipped with loudspeakers. Negro workers crowded the windows of the houses adjoining the square and in many instances served iced water to the thirsty marchers from ground floor apartments.

2.

We can look with shame and disgust at the flagrant effrontery with which Italy treated and is still treating the covenant into which she entered with Ethiopia and other members of the League of Nations.

Millions of Ethiopians who are not yet under the domination of Italian aggression are facing total annihilation by Italy as was so cruelly done by her in Libya, the only difference being that the Ethiopians are subjected to a greater display of barbarism, bombing by incendiary and other bombs, with attendant increased suffering worse than the poor Libyans experienced. You can easily anticipate their feelings as the end of the rainy season approaches, when the unprecedented tortures to which they have been subjected will be let loose on an even larger scale. . . .

We who are gathered here today can do much to stop this butchery and torture. We can agitate among our fellow-citizens in the various countries and nations from which we came, to demand that our governments intercede even at this late day to stop this one-sided war.

Demand that the Ethiopians be permitted to continue their peaceful life. If our demands are not met, then it is our duty to initiate programs in our respective countries and nations to help that nation which is the object of such gross treaty violations, in which its independence and the existence of its inhabitants are in extreme danger. We should raise funds and send same directly to the defenders of that stricken country in order that by our example the whole world will see that we will support now, and in the future, any victim of aggression particularly when this victim has lived up to every letter of his treaty obligations. . . .

The crystallization of sentiment by the forces of peace throughout the world, will do much more than talk to forewarn politicians of the countries from which we came that they must support the machinery of the League for the preservation of treaties, or in other words, support contracts into which the parties concerned voluntarily entered.

Today in the hearts of all thinking people, particularly the minorities and oppressed groups, great fears have arisen concerning the weaknesses of the League of Nations in maintaining the sanctity of treaties.

We have listened with scorn and contempt to the many poorly fabricated excuses offered by some of the leading nations of the world as to why this vicious example of aggression was not arrested.

Already the world is aware that it was through the weakness displayed by the known instruments of peace in dealing with the Ethiopian question that fascism felt powerful enough to strike as viciously as is now being done in Spain. . . .

Peace is connected with the granting of democratic rights within the colonial possession to the same extent that it is operative within the confines of the home governments.

☐ ——————————————————————————— ☐

MASS INDUSTRIES ARE ORGANIZED

4.

When the Roosevelt administration entered its second term, a vigorous organizing movement and widespread strike struggles were under way. The right to organize had been established and the main target was the organization of the mass production industries. The demand for unionization could not be held off.

Those who controlled the American Federation of Labor realized that if the workers now knocking on their door were rejected they would turn elsewhere. The radical Trade Union Unity League had already shown that workers in steel, coal, textile and other fields were ready for industrial forms of organization. Despite this, the conservative officials of the AFL made it plain that in the basic industries they intended to divide the workers among the existing craft unions. AFL president William Green and his close associates planned also to bypass democratic procedure by appointing key officers rather than electing them. Green and his cronies were particularly hostile to the shop steward system. They denounced this as a device favored by the Communists and other radicals—and this was certainly true.

139

But there was a split in the top echelon of the AFL. Some among them realized that the time for industrial unions had come. Outstanding in this group was John L. Lewis, president of the United Mineworkers of America (UMW). Under the leadership of Lewis, the Committee for Industrial Organization (CIO) was formed within the AFL. Its goal was the organization of basic industries into industrial unions. From the outset the CIO drew a response which showed the mass appeal of the industrial—as opposed to the craft—form of unionism.

The answer from the AFL was to expel the original ten international unions involved. In 1938 a permanent national labor organization was formed, called the Congress of Industrial Organizations (CIO). This was a step of landmark importance in the history of the U.S. labor movement.

A considerable number of new workers in many industries were white and of southern origin. Their hiring was deliberate, for management believed they would be less susceptible to unionism. The contrary proved true and they were among the staunchest supporters of a new tactic of labor in the United States—the sit-down.

In most of the major walkouts and sit-downs, members of the Communist Party played a key role. Often they provided the principal leadership. This was especially true in the General Motors sit-down strike which preceded the conflict at the mills of Little Steel. The contribution of Communist leadership in the two industries was exemplified by two talented organizers. In auto there was Wyndham Mortimer, former coal miner who earlier had organized the White Motor Co. in Cleveland and was then sent to Michigan. In steel there was Gus Hall, whose original roots had been in northern Minnesota in the iron mines of the Mesaba range. Hall was one of some 60 Communists who had been appointed to the organizing staff of the Steel Workers Organizing Committee (SWOC) by Philip Murray, a UMW official who had been placed in charge of the campaign to organize steel. Hall became the leader of the Little Steel strike in Warren, Ohio. In later years he became the General Secretary of the Communist Party.

Murray was quick to pick up other Communist assistance.

Benjamin L. Carreathers, Pittsburgh Black Communist and an organizer for the SWOC, led in staging a national conference of Black organizations supporting the steel drive. Boleslaw "Bill" Gebert organized a conference of foreign-born workers whose enlistment in the union was of key importance.

In the organization of these two industries there was a difference of significant import. The United Auto Workers was organized by auto workers under the direction of democratically chosen auto workers. In steel, Philip Murray from the UMW became the president of the United Steel Workers and staffed the key positions with miners and others who committed their loyalty to him. It was a repetition of the dictatorial structure long employed by Lewis to shackle the rank and file in the UMW.

Lewis was able, without a strike, to come to contract terms with the huge United States Steel Corporation. But it was a different story with Little Steel and its spokesman, Tom Girdler, who pledged himself to break the strike and retain the open shop. Employer-provoked violence spread at the plants of Republic, Bethlehem, Inland and Youngstown, and in Chicago in the Memorial Day Massacre (1937) 10 pickets were murdered and more than 100 wounded by police. It was a setback for the union, but a determined effort followed, which culminated in a contract.

The forward movement in the basic industries spurred workers in other occupations to fight for their rights in determining their conditions of work. There were 5,000 strikes in 1937, involving two million workers. Many employers came to terms without a strike. Strike-breaking was reduced because of the growing appreciation of the community of interest between employed and unemployed. While the Workers Alliance supported the strikes, CIO unions and some AFL locals pressed for higher relief standards and government projects for the unemployed. Both were entering the field of political protest. Already the Senate had bowed to their pressure with the passage of the Fair Labor Standards Act, which led to the establishment of the 40-hour week with a minimum wage in interstate commerce.

Labor had reached a new plateau. This was mainly due to the victory in the basic industries, an objective long sought by the Party and achieved in the face of seemingly insurmountable obstacles.

Now new methods of counterattack were used by the monopolists, such as the enlistment of conservative Congressional figures from both parties and especially the Democrats from the South, where the poll tax and illegalities prevented Blacks and many poor whites from voting. The American Liberty League, founded in 1934 with a membership that constituted a roll call of the most powerful business and banking interests, included influential Democrats such as Alfred E. Smith and John J. Raskob. A.B. Magil and Henry Stevens wrote that the Liberty League "marked the first large-scale attempt to set up a reactionary bipartisan political coalition. . . . The American Liberty League was the first organized national expression of the regrouping of political forces that [was] aligning reactionaries of both Democratic and Republican parties. . . ."[1] James A. Farley, chairman of the National Democratic Committee, had close relationships with the reactionary circle as did Joseph P. Kennedy, father of the future president. Kennedy, named Ambassador to Great Britain, worked diligently in London to support a hands-off policy with regard to fascist aggression.

It was by no means accidental that there emerged, in the center of the auto industry in Michigan, a well-financed terrorist organization, the Black Legion, with the bigotry of the Ku Klux Klan and heavy emphasis on mayhem and murder directed against union activists in Michigan and Ohio. Another group committed to storm trooper violence was the Christian Front, launched in Detroit by the radio priest, Charles E. Coughlin. Originally a supporter of Roosevelt, Coughlin switched to bitter opposition interlaced with anti-Semitism, denunciation of the CIO as Communist and, eventually, to outright support of fascism.

In the same period a left-center coalition without national structure was springing up in various areas. This included Labor's Non-Partisan League (LNPL), the American Labor Party (New York), the Epic Movement (California), the Minnesota Farmer-Labor Party, the Washington Commonwealth Federation and others. The elements for a formidable pro-labor, anti-war combination were appearing, but the pace toward coalescence lagged behind the needs of the day. Republican gains were scored in the Congressional elections of 1938; stagnation was setting in with a *severe decline in production. The economic recovery, which began after Roosevelt came to office, was largely erased.*

The Washington Pension Union (WPU) was a unique organization founded on August 31, 1937, and formally dissolved 24 years later. Among the founders of the WPU were three Communists: Henry (Heinie) Huff, Lenus Westman, and William (Bill) Pennock.

The political spectrum of the state of Washington was well represented both at the top and at the grass-roots levels of the WPU, but it was the input of the Communist leaders that was indispensable in establishing it as a social and service organization for the elderly. Its finest achievement was the campaign for a state old-age pension, which became law in 1941. Washington thus became the only state to pay a pension to its elderly. This was before the federal old-age benefit program actually became effective.

Outstanding was the work of the young Communist William Pennock who, at the age 22, dedicated himself to activity with the elderly and led the work of the pension union to expand the frontiers of social security. He led in this work for over 12 years. McCarthyite harassment caused the dissolution of the organization.

The sabotage of the AFL leadership extended from the economic to the political area. When the CIO pushed the building of Labor's Non-Partisan League, Green and Co. forbade their affiliates to participate in it. Yet the Second National Convention of LNPL (Washington, March 1937) was attended by 600 delegates representing 3,500,000 workers in the AFL, CIO and Railroad Brotherhoods.

On the issue of peace and war both the AFL and the CIO opposed Hitler and Mussolini. But there was a gulf between them on this stand. The CIO stood for collective security and the quarantine of the aggressor; the AFL leadership in essence rejected any concrete steps to throw back fascism.

In the years of Roosevelt's first term and into the second, the European scene steadily became more ominous. As in 1914, Germany coveted territorial revisions and looked beyond the European continent to riches held by other imperialist powers. With the advent of nazism in 1933, the danger to world peace increased.

143

There was, however, a major difference between 1914 and the 1930s. In 1914 there was a capitalist Tsarist Russia; now there was a Soviet Union, which on the day of its birth had raised the banner of peace, which was applauded around the globe.

In 1934 the USSR entered the League of Nations, where its representative, Maxim Litvinov, put forward the concept of collective security to check aggression by Germany, Italy and Japan, all of whom had withdrawn from the League. This Soviet approach was reinforced in 1935 at the Seventh Congress of the Communist International by Georgi Dimitrov, who proposed a broad people's front to throw back the fascist offensive and thereby avert a second worldwide war.[2]

But the capitalist powers, supported by the Social Democrats, remained disdainful of the invitation to unity. This included the Roosevelt administration, for while the president spoke for a "quarantine of the aggressor," he did not follow up this appeal with efforts to form an alliance against Hitler's aggressions.

Year by year, day by day, the three Axis powers moved to fulfill their ambitions. Early in the '30s Japan invaded Manchuria. Hitler took power in 1933 and marched into the Rhineland. Italy invaded Ethiopia. Alarmed, Roosevelt told Congress that the aggressors had "reverted to the old belief in the law of the sword or to the fantastic conception that they, and they alone, are chosen to fulfill a mission and that all the others in the world must and shall learn from them and be subject to them."

In the summer of 1936 democratic Spain was plunged into civil war by General Francisco Franco, a traitor to his country and an admirer of Hitler and Mussolini. The two dictators gave massive support—planes, munitions and tens of thousands of troops to reinforce mercenaries from North Africa. Had the outcome been left to the Spanish people, Franco would have been defeated. The distant Soviet Union was the sole government extending aid to the Spanish republic. Solidarity did come from the International Brigades, which consisted of volunteers. Among these was the heroic Abraham Lincoln Battalion from the United States, of whom more than half were Communists, including YCLers. Approximately 1,500 members of the Battalion, half of its total roster, are buried in Spanish soil. When the survivors returned home they were persecuted by such agencies as the Federal Bureau of Investigation. Though the government professed to be anti-fascist, it hounded those who had offered their lives in behalf of democracy.

The Congressional act that contributed to the defeat of the Spanish Republic was the mislabeled "Neutrality Act," placing an embargo on shipments of arms for use by "either side." In practice this cut off the legal government of Spain from weapons while the flow continued unchecked from Germany and Italy. The Congressional legislation signaled a green light to the aggressors in their plans for the future.

Austria was gobbled up by Germany, and Hitler proceeded with plans to absorb Czechoslovakia. This presented no problems for the Third Reich. The British Prime Minister, Neville Chamberlain, a Tory, and Edouard Daladier, Premier of France, a Radical Socialist, capped a series of retreats with the signing of the infamous Munich Pact on September 29, 1938. Thus these two "statesmen" destroyed an independent state in Central Europe. The guilt of those who paved the road to Munich was not confined to the contemptible politicians of Great Britain and France. The United States shared in the betrayal. Constant appeasement of fascism had been based on the illusion that Hitler would satisfy his expansionist aims at the expense of the Soviet Union and let the West escape from nazi aggression.

Commenting on the Munich sell-out, Secretary of State Cordell Hull said in a statement to the press: "As to immediate peace results, it is unnecessary to say that they afford a universal sense of relief" and added, "I am not undertaking to pass upon the merits of the differences to which the Four-Power Pact signed at Munich on yesterday related. . . ."[3] A true estimate was recorded later by the historian D. F. Fleming, who wrote: " . . . the Munich conference was decisive for a long period. In this global sphere the exclusion of Russia from Munich was the fact of towering importance. For five years the Soviet government had tried to work with the western democracies through the League of Nations to stop the fascist aggressors. At every step their cooperation had been rejected in favor of appeasing the aggressors."[4]

It was this repeated refusal of cooperation that led the Soviet

Union to consider its own security in the event of an outbreak of a European war. That possibility became more likely as Poland now became a target of intimidation by Hitler. The Polish semi-fascist government spurned any military help from the Soviet Union to oppose invasion. The socialist state, at great sacrifice, had converted itself from the backwardness of old Russia to an industrial power which was exempt from the economic crisis wracking the capitalist world. The successes of socialism drove its enemies into ever more aggressive tactics. The logic of this situation led the Soviet Union to the signing of a mutual non-aggression pact with Germany, on August 23, 1939. By this step the Soviet Union delayed the eventual aggression against her. It was also a rebuff to those in the West who professed to be seeking guarantees of peace while provoking Hitler's aggression against the USSR.

The war which began on September 1, 1939, when German tanks and troops crossed the border into Poland, proved to be the most devastating war in history.

□ ———————————————————————————————— □

THE COMMUNIST PARTY—ITS LONG HISTORY IN STEEL

"Thirty Years of Struggle for a Steelworker's Union and a Working Class Ideology"
by Gus Hall, *Political Affairs*, September, 1949

[*Writing in jail during the first Smith Act trial of Communist Party leaders, Gus Hall recounted earlier efforts to organize the steel industry. William Z. Foster, drawing the lessons of the 1919 strike, wrote of the steelworkers: "... while they are recovering from the effects of their great struggle ... it will not be long before they have another big movement underway."[5] After many heroic struggles, U.S. Steel, the leader in the industry, was forced to sign a union contract in March 1937.*

The Steel Workers Organizing Committee (SWOC) then concentrated on organizing "Little Steel"—which included such giants as Republic, Bethlehem and Weirton. This part of the organizing drive proved to be especially tough. It caused the loss of many lives, but it too ended in victory. Gus Hall, a founder of the steel union, was chairman of the strike

146

committee during the 1937 strike in Little Steel in Warren, Ohio.[6] Hall was born in 1910 on the Mesabi iron ore range in Minnesota into a family of miners and steelworkers. He worked in the Youngstown and Mahoning Valley steel mills in the 1930s.]

This year marks the 30th anniversary of two major landmarks in American labor history. It is 30 years since the founding of the Communist Party, U.S.A. and 30 years since the first successful organizing campaign of the steelworkers and the Great Steel Strike of 1919.

It is not an accident that these two anniversaries coincide. For it was the same working class which had attained a new maturity thirty years ago, that gave birth to the Communist Party and to the epic struggles of the steelworkers. Many of the same individuals took part in both of these historic events. Our beloved Comrade Foster was the initiator, leader and organizer of the campaign to organize the steelworkers and of the history-making strike that followed. Shortly following the strike and the founding meetings of our Party, Comrade Foster, in 1921, led a group of militantly progressive trade union leaders and members into this newly-founded Marxist-Leninist Party of the working class—Jack Johnstone, "Scotty" Williams and many others. It was the blending of the experiences of the American working class, embodied in these outstanding trade union leaders, with the science of Marxism-Leninism that laid a firm foundation for the Communist Party of the United States of America. . . .

[Foster wrote:] "For the tense situation existing the unions are themselves in no small part to blame. Many of them sharply draw the color line, thus feeding the flames of race hatred. This discriminatory practice is in direct conflict with the fundamental need which demands that all the workers be organized without regard to sex, race, creed, politics or nationality. It injured Labor's cause greatly. Company agents harp upon it continually to prevent Negroes from joining even the organizations willing to take them in. This was the case in the steel campaign. . . . Such a condition cannot be allowed to persist. But to relieve it the unions will have to meet the issue honestly and broadmindedly. They must open their ranks to Negroes, make an earnest effort to organize them and then give them a square deal when they do join. Nothing short of this will accomplish the desired result."[7]

The essence of Foster's study of the Great Steel Strike is that only industrial unionism based on nationwide, simultaneous organization in all plants, companies and areas and on the organization of unskilled and semi-skilled, as well as skilled workers, Negro and white, can do the necessary job of organizing the steelworkers in the United States and leading them in militant struggles for their needs and interests.

In conclusion, Foster showed that the steel strike was not a "lost" struggle. Writing even before the ultimate concessions granted by the steel corporations a few months later as a result of the strike, he showed the whole working class the significance of struggles like the Great Steel Strike:

"No strike is ever wholly lost. . . . An unresisting working class would soon find itself on a rice diet. But the steel strike has done more than serve merely as a warning that the limit of exploitation has been reached; it has given the steelworkers a confidence in their ability to organize and to fight effectively, which will eventually inspire them on to victory. This precious result alone is well worth all the hardships the strike cost them."[8]

History has fully confirmed these far-sighted words of Comrade Foster. The "theory" of the "invincibility" of the monopolies against unionism was destroyed forever. . . . The working class was now more confident of its own united power, more conscious of itself as an exploited class struggling for a better life. It gained a deeper understanding of the class struggle.

The Great Steel Strike, moreover, was not without material success. One of the direct results of the strike was the abolition of the 12-hour day for the steelworkers. The winning of the shorter working day was, however, accompanied by an increase in speedup and the mechanization of the industry. The unorganized steelworkers were not able to put up an effective fight against these developments. The years that followed were years of inhuman speedup, of a rising rate of exploitation and of growing intimidation of the steelworkers by the open-shop employers. . . .

In 1929 the economic crisis struck its devastating blow. The unorganized workers in the mass-production industries were helpless victims of the thirties. The giant monopolies maintained their high profits at the expense of the workers who suffered indescribable misery. The majority of the steelworkers were laid off for long periods of time. Already by 1929 the wages of steelworkers were down 50 per cent from 1927. In 1933 the U.S. Steel Corporation announced that it had no full-time steelworkers on its payroll.

The steelworkers were deserted by the misleaders of labor—but not by the Communist Party. In the absence of a steelworkers' union, the clubs and individual members of the Communist Party organized and led many limited struggles. The CP shop papers in many cases exposed and stimulated struggles on various grievances with many local victories. Considering the continued reign of terror, this pioneering was the work of heroes.

In 1929, the newly-founded Communist-led Trade Union Unity League organized the Steel and Metal Workers' Industrial League. Comrade Foster was on the job as ever. It was not the original purpose of the League to go into competition with the A.A. [Amalgamated Association of Iron, Steel and Tin Workers, AFL], but the League did take a forthright stand against the class-collaboration policies of the A.A. It carried on an educational campaign for militantly progressive class-struggle unionism. The steelworkers responded very readily but the A.A. officials, as was to be expected, did not. The A.A. leadership reacted violently against the whole idea of fighting for the interests of the steelworkers. . . .

[I]n 1932 the League reorganized itself into the Steel and Metal Workers Industrial Union. From the day of its birth, this militant union was engaged in one struggle after another. The S.M.W.I.U., quickly made a name for itself especially in departmental struggles. The long list of militant strikes it conducted includes Republic Steel in Warren and Youngstown, Ohio; Empire Steel in Mansfield, Ohio; many actions were organized in Western Pennsylvania and in the region of Gary, Indiana. During its short life-span of two years, this small union left its mark in all the important steel centers, its education of the workers in policies of class struggle reaching numbers many times its membership. . . .

Unemployed Councils mushroomed in the steel communities and soon grew into the largest organization of steelworkers in the country. They organized the largest body of steelworkers in active struggle since the 1919 strike. . . .

When the economic crisis began to recede somewhat, the workers who went back to work showed a strong determination to organize new unions. A new wave of militancy was sweeping the working class. The great strike struggles of the early and middle thirties propelled masses of unskilled and semi-skilled workers, Negro and white, most of whom had never before been union members, toward the organized labor movement. The membership of the trade unions began to grow.

In order further to unite the ranks of the workers and build the unions, the Communist and Left-led T.U.U.L. industrial unions decided to send their members into the other existing unions, most of which are still headed by reformists and reactionary Social Democrats. The original formation of the T.U.U.L. in 1929 and of its affiliated industrial unions, had been made necessary by the outright betrayal of the trade unions and the interests of the workers in the twenties by the reactionary, bureaucratic leaders; the refusal of these leaders to organize the millions of unorganized; and the terrorist and mass-expulsion practices of these labor misleaders against the Communist and Left-progressive forces. By 1935 these policies had become bankrupt. The rank-and-file was in a mood for unity and struggle and was eager to merge with the militantly-led T.U.U.L. unions which had amply proved their mettle in struggle.

The S.M.W.I.U. decided to disband and join forces with the members of the A.A. This was like an injection of vitamins for the membership of the A.A. In spite of the actual resistance of its leadership, the union began to grow.

By 1935 the working class had not only shown its determination to organize trade unions, but also expressed in no uncertain terms, its desire to organize industrial unions. The lesson had finally hit home. Ever since 1901, William Z. Foster and other militant trade unionists had been hammering away for industrial unionism; and ever since its birth, our Party had been teaching the workers the need for industrial unionism.

The growing rank-and-file sentiment for industrial unionism that had now become a demand resulted in the organization of the Committee for Industrial Organization by the A.F. of L. The committee did not break with the notorious class-collaborationist policies of the A.F. of L. officialdom, but it did see the need for the industrial form of organization. Step by step, growing rank-and-file pressure forced the Committee to move from mere education for industrial unionism within the A.F. of L. to outright industrial organization. The expulsion of the unions embraced by the committee brought the issue to a head.

While the C.I.O. officials were still hesitating, a rank-and-file movement of steelworkers grew under the leadership of Communists and other progressives. Rank-and-file committees sprang up in most of the large steel centers, organizing and leading many struggles and carrying on an educational campaign for progressive unionism. This rank-and-file movement also published a weekly newspaper in Youngstown, Ohio, edited by Charles McCarthy and Joe Dallet. The rank-and-file movement of the steelworkers sent dozens of delegations to press the C.I.O. leaders to initiate an organizing campaign in the steel industry. Thousands of steelworkers signed pledge cards and petitions to the same end, promising full support for such a campaign. It was only after this campaign of the rank-and-file that the C.I.O. leaders in 1936 set up the Steelworkers' Organizing Committee (S.W.O.C.).[9]

It is a matter of record that the only working class organizations which had continued to provide genuine leadership to the steelworkers since 1920 were the Communist Party, the Communist-led Unemployed Councils, rank-and-file committees and the Steel and Metal Workers' Industrial Union (S.M.W.I.U.). The work of these organizations had also been supplemented in the thirties by the Communist and Left-progressive-led organizations of the nationality groups and the National Negro Congress. Our Party was already engaged in mobilizing capable forces for the campaign long before the S.W.O.C. had established its offices or staff. It was inevitable therefore, that the various district directors of the S.W.O.C. established close working relations with the local leaders of the Communist Party. Many leading Communists went on the staff of the S.W.O.C. Almost without exception the first union contact in the steel mills, the organizing core, proved to be a club of the Communist Party or individual Party members, an ex-member of the S.M.W.I.U., a reader of the *Daily Worker,* a member of the National Negro Congress or a member or supporter of one of the Left-progressive-led nationality organizations. Many of these activities had also been the spark for the union in 1919 and 1930.

But the Communist contribution to the campaign did not end here. Before the drive started Comrade Foster wrote two pamphlets addressed to the steelworkers: *Unionizing Steel* and *Organizing Methods in the Steel Industry.* These pamphlets[10] reflected the rich, accumulated experiences of the working class in general and of the steelworkers in particular. They immediately became the guide for the work of all Communists in the steel industry and especially for those of us who were on the organizing staff. Through us, the ideas and policies put forward by Comrade Foster were passed on to the whole staff.

Comrade Foster also gave personal leadership to the drive. He spent many days and nights in meetings with those directly involved in the campaign. He met with Communists and non-Communists in the staff and leadership of the S.W.O.C. In addition, the names of Jack Stachel, Jack Johnstone, Pat Cush, John Williamson, Joe Dallet, Al Balint, John Steuben, George Powers, Ben Careathers, Dave Doran, Bob Burke, Abe Lewis and many other leading Communists are known to steelworkers for their effective leadership during this period. The Young Communist League, as part of its work in helping to organize the steelworkers in 1936, published a popular pamphlet called, *Get Wise—Organize* [by Dave Doran]. The *Daily Worker, The Communist* and the nationality group newspapers were outstanding mobilizers and educators throughout the organizing drive.

The steel organizing drive broke all records. The campaign broke through a veritable "iron curtain" of corporation spy systems, intimidation and terror. In a few months, 2,000 new members were joining the union daily. Whole departments of plants and groups of workers joined simultaneously.

The campaign very closely followed the proposals made by Foster in his pamphlets. The very heart of these proposals is guaranteeing full rank-and-file participation. On the basis of his experience Comrade Foster recommended use of the "chain system" in which each union member signs up another member; the "list system" by which unionists provide lists of potential recruits to the staff for home visiting; the system of "key men" in each department; and the system of voluntary and part-time organizers. By using these techniques, the full-time staff became the center of a whole network of rank-and-file organization and activity.

The U.S. Steel Corporation recognized the new mood of militancy which swept the masses of steelworkers. U.S. Steel did not give up the struggle against the steelworkers when it signed a union contract in March of 1937; it decided merely to change its tactics. The House of Morgan, the real boss of U.S. Steel, decided to try to make of the new steel union another A.A.

□ ——————————————————————————————————————— □

THE "LITTLE STEEL" STRIKE

1. *Labor Fact Book No. IV.,* **Labor Research Association, International Publishers, 1938;**
2. *Chicago's Memorial Day Massacre* **by George Robbins, New Masses, June 15, 1937;**
3. *The Legend of Joe Cook—Union and Community Crusader* **by George Powers. Printed and distributed on behalf of the United Steel Workers of America, 1973**

[*The recognition of the Steel Workers Organizing Committee (SWOC) by the U.S. Steel Corporation (Big Steel) did not lead immediately to the capitulation of Little Steel. That came only after hard struggle and the only major strike in the SWOC drive. It was here, Gus Hall notes, that the Party gave its main efforts.*

In the organization drive, the SWOC made full use of the skills, honesty and dedication of Communists. (Most of them were later fired when the Steel Union started its "anti-red drive.") Among them was Joe Weber, first District Director of SWOC in the Gary–South Chicago area.

In the three brief items which follow, Labor Fact Book No. IV *gives a summary of the violent and ultimately successful course of the 1937 struggles of Little Steel in 1937.*

George Robbins then describes in greater detail the massacre at Republic Steel which took place on Memorial Day that year. It was the most bloody battle, but it was not the only one which took place to establish the union in Little Steel.

In the third item we learn of Joe Cook (1890–1965), a man totally devoted to his union, dedicated to his neighbors and their problems, and honored by the Communist Party, which elected this Black steel worker to its Central Committee. He faced a situation in relation to his Party membership similar to that of Wyndham Mortimer in the UAW. The tribute of Len De Caux to Mortimer (see p. 158) holds true for this outstanding steelworker as well.

George Powers, a steelworker, knew Cook well. (Both were members of District 31, USW.) Powers wrote a series of biographical sketches depicting the life of Joe Cook.]

1.

Following refusals to negotiate, more than 70,000 men in seven states struck the plants of Republic, Inland and Youngstown Sheet and Tube companies on May 26, 1937, and were joined by Bethlehem Steel Corp. workers in Johnstown, Pa., and also by the miners employed by several of the companies. Republic alone attempted to continue operations and police attacked picket lines near its South Chicago plant for three successive days, injuring 20 men on May 28. Two days later occurred the "Memorial Day Massacre," when 200 heavily armed police attacked a picket parade, resulting in ten deaths. . . .

In Youngstown, Sheriff Ralph Elser led 50 deputies in an attack on strikers July 7 and several A.F. of L. unions voted for a city-wide general strike if pickets' blood were shed. Police fired tear-gas shells point-blank into a picket line of women and children, shooting and gassing strikers who rushed to protect them, on July 25. Two were killed and 27 wounded. Governor [Martin L.] Davey, elected with labor support, first followed the lead of Governor [George] Earle of Pennsylvania in declaring martial law to prevent plant openings in Youngstown. A few days later however, Davey turned against the strikers, suddenly ordering troops to escort strike-breakers into the mills. He took similar action in Canton and Warren on June 30. . . .

On June 12, over 10,000 workers at Bethlehem's Cambria plant in Johnstown [Pennsylvania] joined the strike, following by 24 hours the 350 who had struck on the company's railroad subsidiary. About 6,000 miners later walked out bringing the strikers' total to 90,000.

By the end of June, with "repeaters" being used to swell back-to-work figures, with bomb plot frame-ups and coercion of strikers, the companies proclaimed the strike broken. The union claimed 72,400 were still out when on July 1 a "truce" agreement sent Inland's 13,000 employees back to work. The second break in the ranks of "Little Steel" came on July 11, when Youngstown Sheet and Tube, employing 23,000, settled by signing a statement to the Indiana governor acceptable to the union. It embodied collective bargaining, wage-rate, time-and-a-half for overtime and 40-hour week provisions.

2.

A midsummer sun, hot and blistering, hung over Chicago on Memorial Day. People deserted their homes, crowded public parks and beaches; motored to the Indiana sand dunes. You felt the holiday spirit as you filed out of the narrow, crowded street car on Avenue O in South Chicago and strolled across the prairie land to strike headquarters with workers in shirt sleeves and summer garments.

Thousands of men, women and children were congregated at the south end of the dance resort, waiting for the speakers to ascend the improvised platform. A long line of strikers filed into Sam's place [formerly a dine-and-dance resort, now used as headquarters by the strikers of Republic Steel], where members of the Women's Steel Auxiliary had set up a food kitchen. Joe Weber, field representative of the Steel Workers Organizing Committee and chairman of the meeting, announced that the gathering had assembled to protest police interference with peaceful picketing at the Republic plant, six blocks away from strike headquarters. He reviewed the events that led up to the meeting.

More than 25,000 workers, native Americans, Negro and white, Slavs and Mexicans, had walked out on strike in the Chicago area on May 26 when Republic Steel, Youngstown Sheet and Tube and Inland Steel refused to sign a collective bargaining contract with the S.W.O.C. Several hundred scabs remained in the Republic plant, but the other two companies stopped almost all operations. Under a pre-strike agreement a small number of men wearing special badges were permitted entrance into the two mills so as to keep Chicago supplied with gas. Violence at the Republic plant had flared up the first day of the walkout. Chicago police, commanded by Captain James Mooney, had roughed up a mass picket line, arrested forty strikers including John Riffe, field director of the S.W.O.C.

The Chicago chapter of the National Lawyers Guild wired a sharp protest to President Roosevelt, charging the Chicago police with violence against the strikers, preventing peaceful picketing and illegal and discriminatory arrests of strikers and sympathizers. The *Chicago Tribune* lauded the police for preserving "life and property, the business with which it is entrusted by the community." . . .

Swarthy Leo Krzycki, regional director of the S.W.O.C., stood before the microphone on the improvised platform at Sam's place and said: "Violence against peaceful picketing must stop. Republic Steel must abide by the Wagner Act. We don't want fascism in America."

At the close of the meeting men and women fell into a marching line on Green Bay Avenue. There was a good deal of laughter and camaraderie; several strikers joked with news photographers. Marchers held up a forest of placards: "Republic Steel shall sign a union contract," "Win with the C.I.O." Some of the women took their children on the line. . . .

[D]eep into the prairie they marched. You could see the blue-coated policemen, five hundred of them, their badges glistening in the sun. When the marchers came within two blocks of the Republic gates the police closed ranks; halted the picket line with menacing clubs. One cop whipped his revolver out, fingered it gingerly and slid it back into its holster. Police captains and picket leaders exchanged words. A group of cops began to prod the strikers' front line and when the workers refused to move, the police billies began to swing relentlessly.

"Hold your ranks," strikers shouted to each other. "We've got the right to peaceful picketing."

Tear-gas grenades sailed into the crowd, enveloping the strikers in a thick, yellowish-blue cloud. The marchers quickly retreated, coughing and sputtering, and scattered in all directions on the rough and swampy prairie land. There was a crackle of pistol shots followed by a rapid volley of gunfire. The bullets danced in the field like grasshoppers. . . .

The field was strewn with dead and wounded. Police swept over the prairie, pummeling half-conscious men and women, hauling them into patrol wagons. Half a dozen private cars from strike headquarters, red-cross signs on windshields, raced into the prairie to carry away the injured. Five hospitals in the South Chicago area were taxed beyond capacity. Dr. Nickamin, staff physician of the South Side Hospital said, "The wounded looked as if they had come from a virtual massacre." The most seriously wounded were taken by police to the Bridewell Hospital, attached to the criminal jail, at least thirty miles from the scene of the shooting. Two of the wounded pickets bled to death in the patrol wagon for lack of attention. Scores of the injured were treated in Sam's place, converted into a hospital by the Women's Auxiliary. . . .

More than one hundred people were wounded in the massacre. Three

155

strikers were killed on the spot, one was clubbed to death, three more succumbed to their wounds within the week. The seventy-five persons who were jailed were booked forty-eight hours later and charged with conspiracy to commit an illegal act, which carries a maximum sentence of five years and a $2,000 fine.

Police officials and the *Chicago Tribune* were quick to place blame for the massacre on the C.I.O. leaders and the Communist Party. The speed with which the Cook County Communist Party issued a mimeographed leaflet condemning the shooting was cited by a police captain as evidence that "they knew in advance the workers were going to be led into attacking the police and they encouraged the attack." When it was discovered that one of the slain marchers, a cook in the pickets' soup-kitchen, was a Communist, the *Tribune* unearthed the "Red" scare.

Defending the murdered worker, the local Communist Party replied: "Comrade Rothmund was a worker, a member of the bakers' union, a citizen of Chicago and far more valuable than Colonel McCormick of the *Chicago Tribune,* or Tom Girdler, the parasite "exploiter of steel workers and other tax dodgers who live off the sweat and blood of Chicago men, women and children." . . .

3.

It has been only eight years since Joe died, but already it seems that his life story was buried with him. Like Joe Hill (the legendary labor organizer who was murdered by the copper bosses in 1916), Joe Cook's life story is a legacy which must never die. His dreams, ideals and his struggles to improve working conditions must be remembered wherever people are fighting injustice and oppression. . . .

I first met Brother Cook at a Labor conference in the mid–1930s when I lived in Pennsylvania. In the late 1940s I moved to South Chicago where I worked in the mill for twenty-three years. It was during much of this period that I maintained a close friendship with Joe Cook, the first Black local union president [of Local 1029, United Steel Workers of America] . . . It is indeed a credit to the membership and the able president of Local 1029, Brother Dannie Payne, that they have memorialized the contributions of Joe Cook, by naming the local union after him.

Few people . . . are aware of the constructive work performed during those depression years by talented writers, artists, skilled craftsmen and laborers who worked on federally-funded projects. Fine stage plays were created and presented; excellent books were written and published about labor, the poor and Black people in our country.

Many public buildings were constructed by W.P.A. (Works Progress

Administration) workers where none had previously existed. In the 1930s South Chicago was in need of a public library, particularly one that could meet the needs of workers' children. This became the active concern of a number of community and laboring folks in the area. The port agent for the National Maritime Union, Horace Peterson of the South Chicago Labor Council, Joe Cook and a few others went to see Alderman Rowan and pressed him to back the campaign to build a branch library in South Chicago.

Joe Cook was outstanding in this effort. He helped circulate petitions among residents. Resolutions to support this campaign were passed in union locals, churches and fraternal groups. The united effort paid off. By 1940, federal funds were appropriated and a brand new library was built.... Aside from its cultural and educational value the building of the library provided employment at union wages for many unemployed craftsmen and laborers.

This victory was to Joe Cook only the beginning of a whole series of projects providing interesting educational services to the community. Unlike some labor leaders who often get bogged down in union routines, shop grievances, sub-district meetings, etc., Joe seemed to manage his time so that he was available whenever his services were needed. The community felt Joe was a man who could always be counted on to lend a hand. He always had creative ideas and solutions for the problems of the people in his neighborhood.

Mrs. Evelyn M. Stanley, chief librarian for many years at the South Chicago Library (now retired) remembers Joe Cook well. "He was an excellent person," says Mrs. Stanley. "During the early 1940s he helped organize the South Chicago Community Forum and he kept it alive for more than a dozen years. Mr. Cook was most helpful in providing a variety of appropriate topics and interesting speakers. Needless to say, he encouraged union people to attend these sessions.

"Mr. Cook invariably chaired the annual February meeting of the Forum, when the lectures were dedicated to some phase of Black history and culture. It was his suggestion to encourage students from the South Chicago public schools to write competitive essays dealing with the heritage of Black Americans. This able and dedicated steel union leader was certainly ahead of his time. He seemed firmly convinced that unionism, community and educational services go hand-in-hand."

☐ ——————————————————————————————————— ☐

BREAKTHROUGH AT GENERAL MOTORS

"The Great General Motors Sit-Down," *Organize!*
by Wyndham Mortimer, Beacon Press, Boston, 1972

[*The 1930s were a time of great struggles for the organization of the unorganized in basic industries. None was greater than the 1936-37 sit-down strike in General Motors' Fisher Body plant in Flint, Michigan.*

William Z. Foster, who gave close attention to the historic break-through in the mass production industries, wrote in his History of the CPUSA: *"The main stroke in organizing the auto industry nationally . . . was the big G. M. sit-down strike of January 1937. After this resounding victory, it was only a question of gathering in the mass of auto workers now thoroughly ready for organization."*

He stressed the Party's contribution by noting that "Nearly all of the seven members of the strike committee in the key Fisher Body No. 1 plant were Communists, and their leader, Walter Moore, was the Party section organizer in Flint. The Communist Party in Michigan, of which W. W. Weinstone was the district organizer, gave everything it had to the strike, and not without success."

Len De Caux, editor of the CIO News *and publicity director of the CIO, pays a well-deserved tribute to the leader of the strike, Wyndham Mortimer. In his autobiography,* Labor Radical *(Beacon Press, 1970), De Caux says:*

"American Communists had to dodge so many penalties, and were so lied about, that specific answers could long cause individuals to be hurt. Perhaps future historians—after anti-communism has been factually damned even at its American source—may delve into the role of actual Communists in the great 1936-37 upsurge and cite many names, not to 'expose' but to honor."

Wyndham Mortimer (1884-1966) was one of those not to be exposed but to be honored. He was a member of the Communist Party; he was the leader of the Flint sit-down strike.]

On December 29, 1936, the General Motors Corporation secretly began to remove important dies from Fisher #1 [body plant in Flint, Michigan]. The purpose was to get them out of this union "hotbed." One of the workers on the night shift, John Ananich, called [Robert] Travis and said, "They are going to move the dies out, Bob!" Travis[11], who was quick to make decisions, told Ananich to get some of the other union men and to stop the dies from being moved. Travis then called . . . Hazel Simon, and told her to put the flicker on. The flicker was a two-hundred-watt bulb over the union hall across the street from the plant. When it was on it meant that something of importance was happening, so at lunchtime the workers came streaming across the street to the union hall.

The meeting was short and to the point. Travis told them that the dies meant their jobs, and if they permitted the dies to be taken away, many of them would be unemployed. The workers decided to strike the plant, and to sit in and protect their jobs. It was a crucial decision, since if the workers went home over the weekend, and New Year's day following, they would be leaving their jobs unprotected and the dies could be moved without opposition. The workers went directly from the meeting and took over the plant. . . . Thus began the historic forty-four-day sit-down strike, on December 30, 1936. . . .

I had no illusions about the struggle we were in. It was certain that so powerful an enemy as General Motors, supported by every open-shop employer in America, would use every weapon at its command including the courts, the police, the newspapers, the radio, and demagogues like Father Coughlin, who joined Frank Norris, the howling Baptist from Fort Worth, in denouncing the union and its leadership as Reds.

The sit-downers in Fisher #1 immediately began to organize the strike. They held an election. Walter Moore, a Communist, was elected Mayor, with a council of ten. Mayor Moore appointed a Chief of Police, whose duty it was to maintain order. The strikers' police chief immediately asked the company police to leave. They complied and the entire Fisher #1 plant was now controlled by the strikers. A Sanitary Engineer was appointed to see that everything was kept clean and orderly. It is a widely accepted fact that the factory was kept cleaner and more orderly than it ever was before.

A restaurant owner near the union hall turned over his kitchen and all the equipment to the strikers for the duration. The union employed a professional cook, Max Gazen, from the Detroit cooks' union. Each day a detail of strikers was sent to help in the kitchen, to serve as bus boys, to wash dishes, and to prepare the food. The strike was conducted like a well-run household. Liquor was banned from the plant and every precaution was taken to prevent disruptive elements from causing trouble. The sit-down strike aroused immediate and worldwide attention. Every news agency and publication of consequence had reporters stationed in Flint and Detroit. Many stories went over the wires about this remarkably effective strike.

The strike was less than a week old when Judge Edward D. Black, of

By William Gropper,
New Masses, 1938

the Detroit Circuit Court, issued an injunction ordering the strikers to vacate the plants. Brilliant work by attorneys Maurice Sugar and Lee Pressman revealed the fact that Judge Black was a heavy owner of General Motors stock, over $200,000 worth, in fact. Under a Michigan law prohibiting any judge with a financial interest in any case from sitting on it, Judge Black's injunction was null and void. . . .

On January 25, General Motors went into the court of Judge Paul V. Gadola, asking for a mandatory injunction which, if issued, would compel immediate evacuation of the plants. Keep in mind the fact that the Supreme Court of Michigan had previously ruled that there was no such thing as peaceful picketing, thereby outlawing picketing as a weapon in labor's hands. This injunction then, if granted, would leave the union legally defenseless and unable to prevent the corporation from reopening its plants. . . .

The union's answer to Judge Gadola's injunction and the back-to-work movement begun by GM was a sit-down strike in plant #4 of Chevrolet. This was the engine assembly department, and while the entire General Motors empire would still be paralyzed by the strikes in Fisher #1 and Fisher–Cleveland, this strike in plant #4 demonstrated the

160

union's ability to spread the strike wherever necessary. It was the chief factor that caused General Motors to reply favorably to a letter from Governor Murphy requesting a meeting between the company and the union. . . .

Negotiations began February 3, 1937, in Judge George Murphy's court. Judge Murphy was the brother of the Governor, Frank Murphy. As I have said, the representatives of General Motors refused to enter the same room with the union representatives, claiming that it would constitute "recognition of the union." They demanded, too, that Governor Murphy enforce the injunction issued by Judge Gadola, by the use of the National Guard, if necessary. . . .

Murphy's position was that, since at long last the corporation and the union were in communication with each other, nothing would be gained by enforcement of the injunction. Only bitterness would result and the war between GM and its workers would be prolonged indefinitely. Since the three corporation representatives refused to enter the same room with us, it was necessary that Murphy be a go-between, meeting first with one group, then with the other. He carried messages between us for several days. . . .

After several days of negotiations by remote control, with John L. Lewis, [Lee] Pressman, and me in one room of Judge [George] Murphy's court, and the representatives of General Motors and the Du Ponts in another, [Governor Frank] Murphy came to us very much worried. It was about 1:00 p.m. and the Governor said, "They have not removed their hats or coats. They are demanding that the strikers vacate their plants. They told me you have a half-hour to decide, and if you do not comply, they are leaving."

"They will not leave, Governor, they wouldn't dare," Lewis replied. The half-hour passed and they were still there. An hour passed, and they did not leave. Lewis then said, "Governor, invite them in here, and let us talk to them man-to-man."

The Governor conveyed this invitation to come, and after a short period, they came in. . . .

John L. Lewis was a tower of strength. He knew, as did we all, that to get these men's signatures on a contract with the union meant an enormous victory for the CIO and a shattering defeat for the open shop. The Du Pont–General Motors combine was the fortress that dominated the entire automotive industry, and we were at last face-to-face with the men whose decisions were final.

Governor Murphy withdrew and left us alone with these men for the first time. The three representatives of Du Pont-General Motors were now face-to-face with the representatives of their workers. It was an experience they did not enjoy and would not have endured had not grim necessity demanded it. We entered into serious discussions with them on the issues involved and made it crystal clear that the resumption of work depended entirely on their entering into a contract with the UAW–CIO. . . .

It was embodied in a one-page document. . . .

It was signed by John L. Lewis for the CIO, myself for the UAW, and Lee Pressman as the Union's attorney.

☐ ─────────────────────────────────────── ☐

ANTI-UNION TERRORISM

"The Roots of the Black Legion," *The Black Legion Rides* by George Morris, Workers Library Publishers, 1936

[*The corporations' resources of repression included not only local and state police and the militia, but the organization of violence and murder within the trade union movement. One of the most vicious of these enterprises was the Black Legion in Michigan, spawned by the auto companies as an attempt to prevent the unionization of their plants. George Morris (b. 1902), from whose pamphlet the following excerpt was taken, has been writing on labor since the early thirties, especially for the* Daily Worker, Western Worker, People's World *and* Daily World.]

Where are the roots of the Black Legion?

The Black Legion began its activities some time in 1932, though members of the organization trace their history to some years earlier. It appears that there was a split in the Klu Klux Klan of Michigan, Ohio and Indiana. The Klans in these states were at one time among the strongest in the country. A strong base for the Klan was the mass migration of southerners to the North, especially to the automobile centers.

Whatever the direct cause might have been for the development of the rift in the K.K.K., it was about the end of 1932 that the Michigan manufacturers took advantage of the opposition to the Grand Dragons to bring into existence the Black Legion. The new organization was to be an "up-to-date" outfit conforming to the requirements of the northern manufacturers. The white robes were dyed black and a strictly disciplined military structure was set up. The old program of race hatred and religious intolerance was retained, but now the main emphasis was to be on the anti-labor, or as they termed it, the anti-Communist aspect of the program. The Black Legion promised to be a "real" night-riding organization and to promote more aggressive terror action.

The "new line" in night-riding was introduced in 1932-33, shortly after the Briggs strike (January, 1933) and the historic Ford Hunger March (March, 1932). This march marked a turn in the development of the workingclass movement of Michigan—the country's foremost open-shop region. It marked the shattering of the Ford illusion.

All the strength of the Ford and Detroit police was thrown against the marchers who were on their way to "King Henry" to ask for bread or jobs. A shower of bullets was poured into the mass of workers. Five were killed and scores were wounded. This aroused unprecedented mass indignation among the workers and people generally. The workers resisted the reign of terror that followed. This swing upward climaxed in a May Day [1932] demonstration of over 50,000 in Detroit.

Coupled with this there began a rapid influx of automobile workers into the newly-created federal unions of the A.F. of L.[12] This was stimulated by the promise of collective bargaining in the just-introduced N.R.A. In such traditional open-shop cities as Flint, 11,000 workers flocked to the unions. Similarly they joined in Pontiac, Detroit and other places. Strikes of auto workers occurred more frequently. The manufacturers were seriously worried. Michigan labor was at last raising its head.

The Black Legion was one of the means that the manufacturers advanced to counter the sweep towards unionism. It was designed to be a network of strike-breaking terror bands, spies and killers of active union workers. From then on their instructions were to come not from a Grand Dragon in Georgia but from the northern kings of industry—General Motors, Ford, Chrysler, Du Pont. . . .

The poison fruits of the Black Legion blossomed forth first in Michigan because that region furnished the most fertile ground for it. The state is traditionally open-shop. The workers had as yet learned little of the power of solidarity and had little influence on the political life of the state. Most of the auto cities are like huge company towns. Industrial spies hound the workers at every turn. Civil rights are unceremoniously violated. The impotency of craft unions in such a highly organized mass production industry as automobile put unionism in a bad light to many workers. Michigan was "a prosperity paradise" during the Coolidge–Hoover dynasty. It was in such a field that Hearst's *Detroit Times,* and those newspapers that are almost down to its level, and

163

Father Charles Coughlin planted their poisonous seeds—the seeds of Red-baiting and false Americanism.

The Black Legion was not the first organization of its kind to rise in the United States. But it was developed further than any of its predecessors to play its evil role. For at least three years without interruption it trained its terror bands. With the financial and political backing of the industrialists and brigades of morons and sadists for an active core, the organization laid a foundation for itself. Its roots already began to stretch out to parts outside of Michigan. They spread easiest in those regions where the workers were unorganized and where the Liberty League–Hearst Republican combination enjoyed strongest support.

□ ———————————————————————————————— □

COMMUNISTS AND HARLEM TRANSPORT WORKERS

"Development of Work in the Harlem Section" by James W. Ford and Louis Sass, *The Communist,* April 1935

[*The item which follows is a brief selection from a long and full report on the work of the Harlem Section of the Communist Party. It deals principally with the Section's industrial concentration on helping to build a union in the shops of the IRT (a part of the subway system in New York City).*

Similar work was being carried on simultaneously by Communist clubs in other parts of the city. Shop papers such as Red Shuttle *and* Red Dynamo *were issued. The* Daily Worker *played a vital part in the organization drives during this period.*

The activities of Communists, inside and outside of the transit system, helped immeasurably in the organization—and recognition—of the Transport Workers Union (CIO). The work in Harlem at the key 148th Street shop and at two power plants was a major contribution to the successful unionization drive. Before the union became "legal" however, extreme caution was necessary to protect the jobs of those involved in the organizing work. Hence the references such as "X shop" and "Y power plant" in this article.]

At the time of the [8th] Convention [April 1934], we had five shop clubs. We have at the present time eighteen shop clubs. However, only a few of these clubs are in basic industry. We could speak of each shop club separately and give examples as to their good work as well as to their shortcomings. However, we will single out only a few which have done very valuable work in basic industry.

We have at the present time two shop clubs in the I.R.T. [Interborough Rapid Transit] system and one metal club, one C.W.A. [Civil Works Administration] club, two food, one laundry, five hospital and four H.R.B. [Home Relief Bureau] and also two [public] school clubs involving industrial workers.

I want to single out the I.R.T club at the X shop. Our concentration club of carefully selected new members has succeeded in organizing this club first with three members and it has grown since to seven members. The union membership in this shop is about 350, directly the result of the club and the concentration organization. This concentration club and the shop club were instrumental in creating organization at the Y power house and the Z power house of the I.R.T. which are outside of our Section's territory. The concentration club and the shop club, and the [trade union] organization at the X shop, according to the comrades of the union, form the backbone of the union organization. We succeeded in defeating the new agreement at the company union meeting. . . . We have a shop paper now and we distribute the *Daily Worker* regularly. Our other club in the I.R.T., in the A———— Department, is not in as favorable position as the X shop. Lately however, it carried on a successful struggle to reinstate laid-off men. . . .

We have thirty street clubs [community clubs]. In the past year we have been engaged in putting through the group system with some success. On several occasions the group system has been most effective in mobilization. Our clubs, however, are yet weak. We have not been able to digest the tremendous influx of new members. We must increase our educational activities in the clubs, through the Harlem School as well as through special functionary training schools. Our main weakness is the Club Bureau [i.e., club executive committee]. We have systematic meetings of club organizers and meetings of other club functionaries. However, the tempo of improvement is extremely slow. The task in connection with the club must be, first of all, more attention by every member of the Section Committee to his particular club, from which most of our Section Committee members and other leading comrades are unfortunately disconnected.

□ ———————————————————————————————— □

THE GLORY AND TRAGEDY OF SPAIN

1. "In Madrid" by Robert Minor,
Daily Worker, January 27, 1937;
2. "Americans Defend the Spanish Republic"
by Joseph North, *Political Affairs,* September-October 1969;
3. "In the Spirit of Dave Doran"
by Gil Green, *Young Communist Review,* July 1938;
4. "A Negro Nurse in Republican Spain,"
The Negro Committee to Aid Spain with the North
American Committee Medical Bureau to Aid
Spanish Democracy, New York, (not dated)

[*On February 16, 1936, the Popular Front won an overwhelming electoral victory in the Spanish Republic. On July 18 General Francisco Franco began a rebellion against the government. He was supported by nazi Germany, fascist Italy and by the "non-intervention policy" of the leading capitalist powers.*

Robert Minor (1884–1952) left New York in December 1936 for Spain, where he was correspondent for the Daily Worker *and for other labor newspapers and for progressive magazines. Joseph North (1902–1976) followed Minor in that assignment and spent sixteen months reporting on the Spanish War.*

A fraternal tie was developed between democratic Spain and the democratic movement in the United States in the struggle against Franco fascism.]

1.

Madrid, January 27, 1937

Madrid is now the center of the world and everybody knows it. Here the fascist forces, on an international scale, are staking their claim for the conquest of Europe.

Here is where the question of war and peace—the question of whether we shall have an immediate Second World War—is being desperately fought out; because Spain is staked out as an essential foothold of the Third Reich of Hitler, to ensure the success of the military venture against European democracy. Already Germany's infiltration into Spain and into Spanish Morocco through Melilla, with perhaps rather small but powerfully equipped military units, has gone far toward the strategic arrangement which the German general staff considers necessary for the Second World War. If Hitler wins Spain the Second World War is prepared.

The sight of a fleet of bombing planes over a city is a frightful thing. I saw 19 big German Junkers, shining in the sunlight, high above the city, going straight for their objective. What objective? They were seeking out the working-class sections of Madrid. In the working-class sections, large crowds gather in long lines, about five abreast, waiting for certain essential food supplies. The German planes specialized in aiming tremendous aerial bombs at these crowds. It is a policy of frightfulness, a policy of trying to terrorize and break the spirit of the civilian population and, first of all, of the working class.

This kind of warfare is not aimed at any immediate military objective. No soldiers are killed. It is a studied policy of killing civilians.

2.

In Spain, reaction had mobilized to regain power after King Alfonso, the Bourbon, was dethroned in 1931. In 1934 thousands of Asturian coal miners were massacred. Evidence exists that Nazi Berlin was already sounding out individuals among the reactionaries of Spain.

Undoubtedly fascist Germany represented the greatest menace to the world. . . .

In 1935 the Communist International met in Moscow at the Seventh World Congress. There it developed the famous policy of the anti-fascist people's front. Instances of the urgent need for that policy were indicated by developments in France and Spain. Major sectors of the populace were alarmed by the peril of fascist domination. The Popular Front was conceived as a combination of all democratic strata—workers, farmers, intellectuals, small merchants, Communists, Socialists, Catholics and others—all who were willing to stand side by side against fascism and war. . . .

[O]n February 16, 1936, the Spanish People's Front triumphed in the elections. The Left got 268 members in the parliamentary Cortes as against 205 for the reactionaries.

As always, the moneyed classes refused to abide by democratic verdicts. So, on July 17, 1936, Franco led a revolt in Morocco, aided by Hitler and Mussolini money, military guidance and force.

The social democratic prime minister of Spain, Largo Caballero, confused and vacillating, failed to react with vigor; the revolt gained ground rapidly.

Who alive today can forget the role of the Communists everywhere—and here in the United States. We sounded the alarm from the very first moment and mobilized all lovers of freedom and peace. . . .

From the first day the *Worker* warned its readers of Spain's enemies here at home; they were the people's enemies everywhere. Two days after the fascists struck the leading *Worker* editorial was bannered: "Hearst Raises Cry for Support of Fascist Terrorists in Spain." . . .

The presence of our boys convinced the Spanish Republicans that our people, at grass roots, did not oppose them; that the arms embargo was the fault of monopoly power. They understood that. They saw our 3,500 boys come, get a few days of military training and rush into crucial battles. They saw hundreds of Black Americans among the volunteers; they saw some of the finest men America had produced die trying to halt fascism. . . .

Spain held against the torrent of steel for three long years. The Spanish Communists played the decisive part in the resistance. Its policy of unabating support for the Popular Front, its stellar performance on the battlefront and the defense of Madrid from the outset, brought its ranks from less than 30,000 when the war started, to over 300,000 at its end.

Our Party established the warmest fraternal ties with the Spanish Party. Our leaders were frequently sent by our membership to speak to the people and the troops—and did so. We were central among the many U.S. forces helping to create moral and political support for Spain. Our members in the trade unions, in the political and cultural fields, stimulated the sending of delegations to go to the Spanish fronts. Many went to Spain; not only writers like Dorothy Parker, Lillian Hellman, young Jim Lardner (who enlisted), and many others, but more significantly, trade unionists from the newly-formed CIO came to see their members who had volunteered and fought in the ranks.

I remember meeting such heroic figures in Spain as Paul Robeson, who sang to the troops at the front. Films were made that reached millions at home, like "Spanish Earth," with script by Hemingway and camera work by the eminent movie man, Joris Ivens of Holland.

Our comrades were among the leading figures on the weekly cultural magazine *New Masses* that played an honorable part in mustering support for the Republic. Hemingway appeared in *New Masses'* pages, Vincent Sheean, Dorothy Parker, Lillian Hellman, Dr. J.B.S. Haldane, Franz Boaz, Sir Stafford Cripps, Martin Anderson Nexo, Erskine Caldwell, Albert Maltz, Norman Rosten, Millen Brand and innumerable others of the arts and sciences, here and abroad, all came together in our pages for the cause of Spain.

Inspiring work was done by medical volunteers, headed by the great Dr. Edward K. Barsky, top-flight figures like Dr. Leo Eloesser of San Francisco and other physicians. Nurses volunteered who did their noble work at the front as well. Who can forget the ardent work of such an organization as the North American Committee to Aid Spanish Democracy? . . .

Millions became convinced we were right. Despite the unalterable opposition of the Catholic hierarchy to the Republican cause, Gallup showed that more than half of the lay Catholics polled, favored the Popular Front government.

3.

Dave is gone. For those who knew him this seems impossible to believe. One never associated Dave with death—only with life. His sparkling eyes, his swinging gait, his ringing laughter, his buoyant spirit; all seemed to radiate the eternal rhythm of youth in the melody of life.

Dave came to us in 1930. Even this was characteristic of him. This was a year of growing mass unemployment, of starvation and wage-cuts. It was a year of Hoover and Hamilton Fish, of clubs and bullets for the hungry and prison sentences for the militant. It was a year of struggle. That is why Dave came to us, for he gravitated towards struggle like steel to a magnet. His heart beat with a passionate love for the working class and all oppressed peoples and with a deep hatred for those who profited by exploiting them. His mind stirred with thoughts of a new and better world. By analyzing his own experiences as a worker, by reading and study, he became a young Communist in thought and action. . . .

When the workers in the basic industries of this country began their great organizing drive, Dave was one of the first to enter the Western Pennsylvania steel and coal regions. He came to build the trade unions and to lead the work of the YCL. As a member of the new steel union, he was known and loved by tens of thousands of workers throughout the industrial heart of America. His last assignment in the United States was that of Trade Union Director for the National Council of the Young Communist League. . . .

In Spain, Dave joined the Washington–Lincoln boys of the International Brigades. He joined as a private. As a soldier in the ranks, his sterling qualities of political leadership and personal bravery combined to make him the outstanding leader of the Brigade. As his comrades-in-arms have since stated in tribute to him: "He was first to advance, last to retreat." He was an example of a true Communist leader.

Our League, our Party, the American working class, have lost a young

Communist of unusual ability. We who were closely associated with him have lost one of our dearest comrades and friends. Dave is gone, but the cause for which he fought and died lives on in each one of us.

4.

When Salaria [Kee] went to Spain hundreds of Negro men had already recognized Spain's fight for liberty and freedom as part of their own struggles. Oliver Law, Walter Garland, Douglas Roach, Milton Herndon were on the Jarama front. The brigade had been one hundred and twenty days in the trenches. Oliver Law was commanding. They say it was his turn for a leave. He had come over with the first American volunteers to Spain and had not had a day's leave. He was delighted at the thought of a Negro nurse coming and prepared to welcome her. But, the story goes, from months in the trenches his clothes were in rags. He had no shoes and his underwear showed through rents in his trousers.

He was in excellent spirits. He called the Negro chaps together and suggested that they draw straws, the one drawing the shortest should go in his stead. Douglas Roach drew that one. The others watched him eagerly as he dressed himself for the occasion. Doug's wardrobe was in good shape despite months in the trenches. He had an amazing technique for successful foraging. He would have loaned the outfit to Law but Doug was short and Law inches taller.

Later Salaria had Doug as a patient. He came to Villa Paz with a deep shrapnel wound in his shoulder. Recovery was never complete. He was furloughed home and died some months later. She nursed Lieutenant Garland when he was wounded a second time. This was in the same battle in which Oliver Law was killed. Garland was twice a patient at Villa Paz. Salaria describes him:

"Garland could never be convinced that he was wounded and not fit for the front lines. Every morning he would ask, 'Will the doctor send me back to my brigade? Those boys need me.' One day planes flew low over the hospital continuously. At supper check-up Garland was missing. About ten o'clock next morning the Brigade headquarters telephoned our Commandant to know if we were missing any patients. Two Americans, an Englishman and a Frenchman had reported for duty. It was Garland and his companions. Anti-fascist fighters never felt they were unfit for action as long as they could walk." . . .

So many tragedies she shared with the Spanish people! Her face became a familiar one in Spanish papers and movie houses. (She appeared in two movies in this country—"Heart of Spain," and "Return to Life.") Several times the Republican Government dispatches cited her for courage and efficiency.

170

More and more Spain's cause seemed to her the cause of minority groups throughout the world. . . .

"Negro men have given up their lives there," she says, "as courageously as any heroes of any age. Surely Negro people will just as willingly give of their means to relieve the suffering of a people attacked by the enemy of all racial minorities—fascism—and its most aggressive exponents—Italy and Germany."

□ ——————————————————————————————— □

APPEASEMENT IN ACTION

The Munich Betrayal by Harry Gannes,
Workers Library Publishers, 1938

[*In November 1937, Lord Halifax, one of Prime Minister Neville Chamberlain's closest associates, went to Germany to negotiate with Hitler. Halifax told Hitler that Britain would place no obstacles in the way of fascist expansion in Eastern Europe.*

Thus encouraged, the nazis occupied Austria in March 1938, and started preparations for the occupation of Czechoslovakia. Concession after concession at Czechoslovakia's expense extracted by Chamberlain and Premier Edouard Daladier of France were not enough for the nazis. On September 29 and 30, 1938, Chamberlain and Daladier held a conference with Hitler and Mussolini, in Munich, which doomed Czechoslovakia. As a result of the Munich deal, Czechoslovakia was open for complete occupation by the nazis, an event that happened six months later.

The Munich agreement was the most abysmal example of the foreign policy of capitalist nations in the period between the two world wars. United States foreign policy under Franklin Delano Roosevelt basically supported Britain and France.

Daily Worker foreign editor Harry Gannes (1901–1941) discusses the implications of the Munich surrender in this excerpt.]

Far more alarming to the American people than the war hysteria aroused by the Nazi tyrants against Czechoslovakia should be the crimes committed against world peace and democracy by the Four-Power combination at Munich, September 30, 1938.

Humanity is today faced with the gravest menace to peace and liberty since the fascist scourge first plagued and threatened the world.

The American people, stirred as never before by world affairs, have every reason to be deeply disturbed by the peril of the Four-Power conspirators. . . .

Looming over all democratic peoples now is an enormous peril to their liberties, vaster dangers to their livelihood and trade unions and a more acute menace to peace.

Look back at the horrible record. The fascist path to war is lined with such "appeasements"—realized and attempted—as Manchuria, Ethiopia, Spain, Austria, China and now Czechoslovakia.

Let it never be forgotten that from his rise to power Hitler received invaluable assistance from the British Tories. They assisted him to build armaments in the feverish Nazi campaign to blackmail, bluff and threaten the world.

The course of the Chamberlains and Daladiers was made easier by the role of certain Labor Party chiefs in Great Britain and certain Social Democratic leaders in other parts of the world. These aides of the Chamberlains and Daladiers fought against the solidarity of labor. They resisted the anti-fascist, anti-war unity of the democratic peoples. By trying to keep labor impotent and the people disunited they permitted the Chamberlains and Daladiers to act with impunity.

Trotsky and all his agents, faithful to their alliance with fascism against the Soviet Union, sprang to the support of the Chamberlain and Daladier attacks on the anti-fascist forces of the People's Front. A typical example of Trotskyite approach to the Chamberlain betrayals was the "Left" speech of the Independent Labor Party leader of parliament, James Maxton, which concluded with complete endorsement of the Chamberlain betrayal.

Arch-betrayer Chamberlain, referring to the typical Trotskyite "Leftist" support to the fascists and their abettors, approvingly said: "No one could listen, without being moved, to Mr. Maxton."

The fascist warmakers, enemies of world peace and democracy, bitterest foes of human civilization, culture and progress, were enabled through treachery to extend their conquests. The Nazi war machine was enabled to roll over great portions of Czechoslovakia.

When the peace forces of the world were so overwhelmingly superior in every way, fascism was enabled to snatch victory from the very jaws of certain defeat. When it appeared positive that fascism could be held at bay by an aroused democratic and peace-loving world, Hitler was handed one of his greatest triumphs. . . .

How did it come about that the fascist dictatorships which were facing economic calamity and active popular discontent were able to achieve such gains?

The reason that Hitler won at Munich, the reason that fascism was given such impetus, was not that it had became stronger between May and September when it plotted world war; on the contrary. The whole fascist war-breeding triangle had grown weaker during that period.

But the ruling cliques of the big democracies, Great Britain and France, the Chamberlains and Daladiers and their kind in other countries, had become more cowardly, more traitorous to their national interests in order to preserve their own narrow class interests from an aroused people struggling for democracy, peace and progress.

The road to the Munich betrayal was paved by the policy of concessions and appeasement of the fascist aggressors.

Why did the Chamberlains and Daladiers barter away their national interests? Why did they betray Czechoslovakia to Hitler?

The class represented by Chamberlain in Great Britain, particularly, was fearful of the progressive upswing of the people. The Daladiers, too, were won over to betray the people of France. The heads of the French Cabinet, under the promptings of the financiers of London and the 200 rich families dominating the banking and industrial life of France, joined in bringing to fruition the long-schemed treachery to democracy and world peace.

The reactionary ruling circles of Great Britain and France abhorred the growing struggle of democracy against fascism. They dreaded the People's Front of France and similar movements throughout the world. Their class hatred against the land of socialism, the Soviet Union, grew fiercer as the popular upsurge against fascism grew stronger.

□ ———————————————————————————————— □

BUILDING THE DEMOCRATIC FRONT

Building the Democratic Front, Report to
the Tenth Convention, CPUSA, by Earl Browder,
Workers Library Publishers, 1938

[*The landslide victory of Franklin D. Roosevelt in the 1936 elections confirmed the wide support for the administration. Although compelled to clash with the "economic royalists" (to use his words), he maintained a vacillating relation with the trade unions, Blacks and all minority groups, and the popular mass movements.*

The Party gave qualified support to Roosevelt. This was basically sound. But Earl Browder, the Party's general secretary, interpreted this to mean greater reliance on and uncritical support to the administration. This was a compromising, opportunist stand. It took the form of apologizing for Roosevelt instead of a critical, working-class position.

His analysis reflecting this trend included:

1. A characterization of the 1937–38 economic crisis as a "sit-down of capital." The use of economic sabotage by monopoly interests cannot be dismissed. But this was not the situation. The sharp economic decline indicated a "normal" cyclical crisis of United States capitalism. Although brief, its effects were acute. It was estimated that approximately thirty per cent of the work force was unemployed in the Spring of 1938. Responsibility had to be placed on the administration and the dominant monopoly interests. But Browder sought to make the administration blameless.

2. In dealing with the South, Browder gave promise of a "New South." Some changes took place, but they were far from a "break-up [of] its solid reactionary character." The administration adapted to southern reaction, which was part of its political structure. It continued the unequal wage differential. The undemocratic and racist poll tax system was maintained. (It was not eliminated until January 1964.) This opportunism led to the liquidation of the Party in the South.

How was Browder able to impose his opportunist position without serious challenge? The liberal New Deal program contained vital measures to cushion the people's hardships in the most severe crisis of US capitalism. It was also the means to save the capitalist system and was so recognized by many of its proponents. The New Deal reached into every facet of the people's lives. Its ideologues sought to shape the country's political development.

President Franklin D. Roosevelt's program was ameliorative. Following the crass and criminal neglect by the Hoover administration, the New Deal won wide support and held an ideological grip on the people, especially the working class. The Communist Party was not exempt from these social pressures. While correctly supporting reform measures, it was essential for the Party to expose the limitations inherent in a capitalist state.

But Browder yielded to liberal ideological pressures. He conceded, step by step, to the totality of the New Deal. This encouraged the dulling of class consciousness and capitulating to the top labor bureaucracy. This could only lead to the alienation of Communists and their allies in the trade union movement.

These opportunist paths led Browder to the eventual rejection of

174

revolutionary theory. The Party as a whole, however, strove for a correct policy. Learning from experience in struggle, it succeeded finally in eradicating Browderism and reestablishing itself on the principles of Marxism-Leninism. This subject is dealt with in Chapter 5.]

At our Ninth National Convention [June 1936] two years ago, we sounded the alarm against the danger of the reactionary forces, moving toward fascism, which were attempting to seize control of our country. We raised the central slogan, "Progress against reaction, democracy against fascism."

We identified the main enemy gathered around the banner of the Republican Party. We warned the masses who rallied to President Roosevelt that the standard of his party, the Democratic Party, sheltered many sinister forces which stood close to the Liberty League economic royalists who manipulate the Republican Party, which were equally enemies of democracy and the people. We declared the necessity of a new political alignment to meet the issues of the American and world crisis—an alignment of the people against the economic royalists. We called for the fullest possible use of the 1936 elections to defeat the reactionaries and build the united front of the people for democracy and peace.

Two years full of rich experiences have passed since then. The people have learned through advances and setbacks, through victories and defeats. From these experiences we emerge strengthened by a deeper understanding of our tasks, by broader organization of our forces and occupying stronger positions from which to advance. Our difficulties have increased but so have our capacities to overcome them. Let us review briefly the main items of our political ledger of the past two years, on both sides, advances and setbacks, victories and defeats.

In 1936, the people won a brilliant victory over the reactionary camp in the overwhelming electoral successes of Roosevelt and the New Deal—but the reactionary camp had smuggled into Congress, under cover of formal adherence to Roosevelt, a sufficient minority which, united with the Republicans, was able to sabotage and defeat the main program for which the people voted in the elections.

In 1936 and since, the workers have broken through the capitalist strongholds of the "open shop," the basic and trustified industries, have established a strong industrial union movement, have more than doubled the numerical strength of the trade unions and begun to build independent political organizations—but the reactionary forces have been able to split the labor movement into competing centers engaged in fratricidal struggle.

175

The workers, farmers and middle classes were able to establish new measures of protection of their incomes and living standards and thus ward off to some extent the miseries of a new economic collapse—but the economic royalists still retained such powers and the Roosevelt administration proceeded with such hesitation that a "sit-down strike of capital," with the slogan of "lack of confidence" in democracy, was able to plunge into a new economic crisis of unprecedented severity and swiftness of development.

The progressive movement has been able brilliantly to penetrate into the territory of the old "Solid South," break up its solidly reactionary character, arouse the mass democratic movement and already show the promise of a "New South"—but the reactionary camp still controls most of the main positions in the South, which they are trying to unite with the northern reaction of the Republican Party.

Finally the camp of progress and democracy has awakened to the realities of the world about us, emerged from its dreams of "isolation" in a world threatened with fascism and war and found expression for its awakened conscience in Roosevelt's call to "quarantine the war-makers"—but the everyday practical policy in Washington continues along the reactionary line giving aid and comfort to the bandit governments in their aggressions and to Chamberlain's policy of surrender to and complicity with them.

We can sum up the main results of the past two years as follows: The camp of the people, of progress and democracy, has won some important battles and positions, has become conscious of its own existence, of its enemies, of its own potential forces and of the main direction of the program which alone can fulfill its tasks and bring victory to the people; it has begun the first steps in the organization of its forces. The camp of reaction, of the economic royalists, has suffered some serious defeats; it is feverishly calling its reserves into action, uniting all its many armies under a single command and preparing a desperate general attack, all along the line, against the living standards and democratic rights of the people. It follows a strategic line for division of the democratic camp and the defeat of its separate sections through concentration of the united forces of reaction, point by point, against a divided democracy. . . .

The attacks of monopoly capital against the living standards of the masses have forced the people to organize more and more for self-protection and to hammer out new measures to that end. Thus the forces of democracy are more and more organizing themselves and tending to unite in a common front. For several years we have witnessed how this struggle has cut through all the old political party structure which governed America since the Civil War and now recasts American political life into the mold of two quite new political camps. We are now approaching the climax of this national political realignment.

Of central importance is the deepening struggle of progressives against reactionaries within the Democratic Party. Already we foresaw this and adjusted our policy to facilitate it at our Ninth Convention two years ago. . . .

The New Deal wing of the Democratic Party, created under the leadership of President Roosevelt, is supported by a great following, largely unorganized, of workers, farmers and city middle classes. It is with but few exceptions under the leadership and control of a party apparatus composed of professional politicians drawn from the middle classes and representing primarily middle class interests and aspirations. It responds to the interests and desires of the workers and farmers to the extent that, first, it finds this necessary to draw to it the support of the unorganized masses, and, second, that the workers and farmers are independently organized, vocal and clear in their demands. With all its weaknesses and inadequacies, its hesitations and confusions, this New Deal wing under the Roosevelt leadership is an essential part of the developing democratic front against monopoly capital. Its role is not played out by the splitting away of the Right-wing Democrats to fuse with the Republicans. On the contrary, only with this split does the New Deal wing enter into its full development. It furnishes today the broadest framework, albeit a precarious and incomplete one, for the gathering of the full forces of the democratic front of the majority of the people in the 1938 elections. . . .

These broadest and largely unorganized progressive masses are stimulated and drawn into closer collaboration by the growing independent political organizations of the masses—of workers, farmers, middle classes, Negroes, etc.—whereby the people are entering the political arena as a conscious organized force. These independent organizations are chiefly on a national scale, Labor's Non-Partisan League, based upon and reflecting the growth of the trade unions, both the A.F. of L. (witness Green's efforts recently to draw them out of it) and of the C.I.O., the great group of industrial unions that have arisen largely since our Ninth Convention; on a state scale, the American Labor Party of New York, the Farmer–Labor Party of Minnesota, the Progressive Party of Wisconsin, the Commonwealth Federations of Washington and Oregon, etc. and representative special groups on a national scale; the National Negro Congress, the American Youth Congress, the American League for Peace and Democracy and similar organizations. These independent political organizations of the people are the most dynamic, the most advanced and the most solid and reliable sectors of the growing democratic front.

The building and strengthening of the democratic front, to defeat the forces of reaction, fascism and war, requires the simultaneous building of the independent political organizations of the workers and the uniting with them of the farmers and middle classes, as the means to preserve the unity of the majority which moved against monopoly capital and reaction in the 1936 elections and the strengthening of that majority in order to guarantee at all costs the defeat of the reactionary forces.

□ ———————————————————————————————— □

THE GREAT ANTI FASCIST WAR

5.

Once the armies of nazi Germany smashed through the frontiers of Poland on September 1, 1939, war engulfed the European continent with astounding rapidity. Great Britain and France, their "diplomacy" in ruins, declared war two days later. But their spineless cringing, which had led to the Munich capitulation, now made avowals of their support for isolated Poland a meaningless pledge. And Poland's general staff had made its plans in expectations of a war toward the East, not invasion from the West.

The Soviet Union was resolutely determined to protect its own borders. In 1938 and again in 1939 the Japanese had launched formidable probing thrusts along the Manchurian border. These forays were utterly routed by the Red Army and convinced the Japanese military clique that their best prospect for expansion was in the Pacific rather than the Siberian land mass. And when Hitler marched into Poland, the Soviet Union occupied the eastern portion of that country where the Polish government had collapsed. It thus constructed a defense against the penetration of nazi troops to the Soviet border.

Still another protective step was taken by the Soviet Union on the frontier with Finland, where the armies of Baron General Carl Von Mannerheim were being reinforced with the obvious objective of menacing Leningrad a short distance away. The Soviet government, well aware of Mannerheim's strong sympathy with the aggressive designs of Germany, insisted that territorial revisions be made to remove Leningrad from danger—a proposal that was flatly rejected. War between them followed.

The reaction of the capitalist powers to the Finnish events was one of incredible frenzy. The governments of France and Great Britain conducted a propaganda campaign for intervention and 50,000 Allied troops were earmarked for an invasion in the Black Sea area. In the United States Herbert Hoover collected aid for Finland. The League of Nations, with its record of procrastination and evasion with respect to Japan, Germany and Italy, promptly and illegally expelled the Soviet Union. To the embarrassment of the western powers, Finland joined the nazis in the war.

For a time, a period known as the "phony war" prevailed. The western front remained quiet. But on April 9, 1940, Denmark and Norway were invaded by Germany and in early May a blitzkreig attack by the nazis overran Luxembourg, the Netherlands and Belgium and drove deep into France, which capitulated on June 22.

Public sentiment in the United States, from the day war clouds appeared over Europe, was overwhelmingly in favor of non-participation. Gallup polls recorded that as high as 96 percent were in opposition to the nation's involvement. This sentiment found expression in the slogan "The Yanks are Not Coming" initiated by the Communist Party with wide support in the labor movement and other mass organizations. In the fall of 1940 the American Peace Mobilization was organized in Chicago, with 6,000 delegates attending from groups with a membership of about twelve million. There was a broad spectrum of representation in the new peace force, which opened a vigorous campaign in many cities from the East coast to the West.

The position of the Communist Party was well publicized. In 1939 the Party had declared that "the war that has broken out in Europe is the Second Imperialist War." But within the context of that war the Communist Party resolutely supported the resistance and liberation movements. These national struggles in Europe were always betrayed by the capitalists, whose "patriotism" was superseded by their unremitting drive for superprofits and by their transnational interests.

The domestic opposition to the entry of the United States into the conflict included, however, elements closely linked with the nazi viewpoint. Heavily financed by wealthy industrialists, the public stance of these pseudo-peace proponents avoided, as a rule, open approval of the barbarity of fascism. Drawing upon the deep-seated recognition that this war, like World War I, was at bottom a fraud upon the people, the propaganda appealed to "isolationism" without touching upon the class interests involved. The America First Committee spearheaded this approach, with an assortment of millionaires that included Robert M. McCormick of the Chicago Tribune, *Henry Ford, Edward Rickenbacker, the steel magnate E.P. Weir and Hugh S. Johnson, who had been Roosevelt's choice to administer the National Recovery Act. Norman Thomas, the Socialist, spoke at one of its rallies in New York City as did Charles A. Lindbergh of aviation fame, who had been attracted to the "orderly" and "efficient" new society of Adolf Hitler. There were sympathetic voices in the Senate, one of them Robert A. Taft of Ohio, who was coming to the conclusion that "victory for communism would be far more dangerous to the United States than a victory for fascism."*

Roosevelt, while taking into account heavy public sentiment against sending troops abroad, worked energetically, often secretly, toward involvement. In this he was supported by the Committee to Defend America by Aiding the Allies headed by William Allen White, an influential Kansas editor.

The motives propelling the interventionists were mixed. For example: there were those who wanted Great Britain, France and the Netherlands to survive but looked beyond the war for the United States to step into the shattered colonial empires and bring them within the exploitative influence of Wall Street. There was also a budding neocolonialist outlook that was to be pressed vigorously at the termination of hostilities by such persons as Henry Luce, with his extensive publishing empire, who foresaw an "American Century."

The presidential campaign in 1940 resulted in a gain for intervention. Neither of the major parties put forward a candidate committed in full to participation in the conflict. Wendell Willkie, a wealthy utilities lawyer, obtained the Republican nomination over the opposition of the "isolationists" but had no difference of substance with Roosevelt on foreign policy.

President Roosevelt turned to making peace with long-time critics in powerful financial circles. Plans for domestic reform were shelved. Even before the election, under cover of a "national emergency," he gave support to a series of undemocratic acts in which the Communist Party was the chief target. Severe repressive legislation was enacted. The Smith Act (June 1940) provided extreme penalties against those allegedly "teaching and advocating the overthrow of the United States government by force and violence." It compelled the fingerprinting and registering of 3,600,000 non-citizen foreign-born. (The notorious prosecution and jailing of Communist leaders, which began with indictments handed down in July 1948, was based on this act.)

The Voorhis Act[1] (October 1940) deprived Communists of the right to international affiliation, a right which was enjoyed by political, labor and other institutions for generations. Voorhis was a member of the Dies Committee.

It was in these circumstances that an event occurred which shaped the future course of the war. June 22, 1941—the invasion of the Soviet Union by Germany—brought a qualitative change in the character of the war. The elements leading to that transformation had long been present. It was impossible for the Allied powers to rally behind a cause so besmirched and devoid of consideration for working masses. Now history—and Hitler's fatal misjudgment—had provided them with a resolute ally of major proportions and a force that would give meaning to the struggle. It was an ally whose earlier advice, if heeded, would have averted the cruel slaughter and enslavement of untold millions.

The Communist Party of the United States responded by a pledge of full support to the transformed war. Now the continuing episodes of retreat, betrayal and collaboration were checked. The cost of victory would be beyond measurement but a meaningful victory was now possible.

182

The Communist Party of the United States made an immediate declaration pledging "its loyalty, its devoted labor and the last drop of its blood in support of our country in the greatest of all crises that ever threatened its existence." That pledge was honored to the hilt. Fifteen thousand Communists were in the armed forces. It was a striking exhibition of patriotism in contrast to the attitude of employers, who enjoyed lush profits and even threatened non-cooperation if their greed went unsatisfied.

In the drive for national unity to support the war, the Communist Party placed major emphasis on winning the "battle for production." Labor gave a no-strike pledge and was obliged to accept a wage formula keyed to a 15% cost of living increase which fell far short of the actual increase. The overall real income of workers did rise, but this was because of heavy overtime, beefing-up of premium shifts and other such circumstances. The war finally ended the massive unemployment which had lasted a dozen years.

In the midst of war, racism did not disappear. It required the most intense struggle to compel government and corporations to open job opportunities for Black workers. A militant movement for a Fair Employment Practices Committee (FEPC) was initiated by A. Philip Randolph. It found wide endorsement; it had the full support of the Communist Party. The Party, though handicapped by Browder's revisionist practices, did not yield on its basic policy of fighting for Black and white unity.

The Party supported the "no-strike" pledge of labor but this did not halt its battle against racist oppression. Local 22 of the United Cannery, Agricultural, Packing and Allied Workers (UCAPAW) in Winston Salem, N.C., had a number of Communists in its leadership. Among them was Moranda Smith, noted trade union leader. UCAPAW struck R.J. Reynolds in June 1943 when a Negro worker died because the "foreman refused [him] permission to see a doctor." When the strike was over "the first concession was payment of $1,250,000 in retroactive pay for low-paid Negro workers. . . ." (Philip Foner: Organized Labor and the Black Worker 1619–1973, *International Publishers, 1976, p. 262.)*

As a result of the mass movement and threat of a march on Washington, Roosevelt issued Executive Order 8802 on June 25,

1941, which curbed some discriminatory practices. But "the last to be hired" had no future guarantee against being "the first to be fired."

On the battlefronts a critical issue arose—the opening of a Second Front by Great Britain and the United States to force the Germans to divide their forces and thus speed the day of victory. This was not to the taste of Churchill, who anguished over the increased prestige of the Soviet Union with its skill of turning defense into counter-offensive wherein the names of Stalingrad, Moscow and Leningrad evoked worldwide admiration. In the United States there were those, such as Senator Harry Truman of Missouri, who favored a war of exhaustion between the USSR and Germany. This position found little public support.

The Communist Party helped rally the people for the Second Front. Mass gatherings were promoted throughout the country, with 60,000 persons meeting in New York City to demand this step. Roosevelt was not as reluctant as Churchill to implement the Second Front but he agreed with the Prime Minister to delay it until 1943. Publicly, he issued a joint statement with Molotov, the Soviet foreign minister, that "complete agreement was reached with regard to the urgent tasks of the creation of a second front in Europe in 1942." What materialized, however, was the invasion of Africa and Italy. The Second Front was delayed until June 1944— by that time the Soviet armies were rapidly advancing to the West.[2]

On many occasions Earl Browder had displayed opportunism relating to the New Deal program. However, in the course of the war Browder began to project a revisionist program embracing every phase of Party activity. This led to the dissolution of the Party in 1944 and its replacement with the Communist Political Association. (This subject is dealt with more extensively in items at the end of this chapter.)

As the war was coming to a close and the role of US imperialism was further revealed, uneasiness and questioning arose in the Party. William Z. Foster's opposition had been suppressed by Browder with the warning that it threatened the "unity" of the organization. Foster wrote: "The threatening domestic and international situation produced increasing doubts . . . [which] were reflected in the Political Committee."

Thus the Party, with a record of magnificent achievement in the defeat of fascism, moved into the tumultuous postwar era.

The 79th Congress (1945-47) sharpened its axe against the labor movement even before the war ended. A host of bills were introduced, including an attempt to eliminate the National Labor Relations Board. In 13 states "right to work" measures were put into the hopper. Wage "stabilization" instituted during the war, it was hoped, would be continued. But the 1945 strikes were a harbinger of what was to come.

The Party, having removed the opportunist shackles, was now prepared to make a major contribution to labor's struggles.

□ ——————————————————————————————— □

WORLD WAR BEGINS

"The Communist Position on the War" by
William Z. Foster, *History of the Communist Party, USA*,
International Publishers, 1952

[*William Z. Foster was Chairman of the Communist Party when his* History of the Communist Party, USA *was published in 1952. Like his eleven comrades on the Party's political committee he was indicted under the Smith Act in 1948. When the* History *was published the eleven others were either in jail or were political refugees.*

Foster's case was severed from the others because government medical specialists acknowledged that he was physically unable to stand the rigors of a long trial. (The trial lasted ten months.)

In the period from February 1951 to February 1955, William Z. Foster published five volumes of class-struggle history.

The brief item below summarizes the Party's initial estimate of the earliest stage of World War II.]

On September 19, 1939, the National Committee of the Communist Party issued a statement on the war.[3] It said: "The war that has broken out in Europe is the Second Imperialist War. The ruling capitalists and land-lord classes of all the belligerent countries are equally guilty for this war. This war, therefore, cannot be supported by the workers. It is not a war against fascism, not a war to protect small nations from aggression, not a war with any of the character of a just war, not a war that workers can or should support. It is a war between rival imperialisms for world domination." The Party called for "maximum support to China and to all oppressed peoples in their struggles against fascism, for freedom and national independence." It urged the forging of "the Democratic Alliance of the workers, toiling farmers and middle classes against the economic royalists and imperialist warmakers." It would fight to "protect and improve living standards, democratic liberties and the right to organize and strike." It called for support of "the peace policy of the Soviet Union—the land of Socialist democracy, progress, peace and national liberation." The central slogan was, "Keep America Out of the Imperialist War." . . .

The Communist policy was not of isolationism or neutrality, but of dynamic struggle to defend the rights of the conquered peoples, to prevent the spread of the war and to bring the war to the quickest possible democratic conclusion. It was along this general line that the CPUSA conducted its fight in the first phase of the war, between September 1939 and June 1941.

□ ———————————————————————————————— □

COMMUNIST YOUTH COMBAT DISCRIMINATION

Old Jim Crow Has Got to Go! by Henry Winston, New Age Publishers, 1941

[*While employment was increasing because of the impending world war, Blacks were still shut out of major industries. Breakthroughs began when the United States joined the war and corporations were searching for workers.*

When the war began, the Red Cross persisted in blood segregation until forced by public opinion to reverse its policy. In the army itself segregation was practiced. There was one all-Black infantry unit in Italy and also an all-Black air group.

Henry Winston (b. 1911) is now National Chairman of the Communist Party. Born in Mississippi, he is the grandson of a slave. At the time he wrote this pamphlet he was National Administrative Secretary of the Young Communist League and a member of the National Committee of the Communist Party.]

You and I—walked the streets of Harlem, South Side Chicago, Bedford-

Stuyvesant, the Filmore area of San Francisco—in fact, every city where Negro youth live; ten years ago, five years ago, one year ago.

You and I—were jobless. We were in search of a way to earn a living. We were looking for a job. There were a million of us—Negro men and women in every section of the country. We were not alone. Many of the great factories were then closed. The giant steel mills of Pittsburgh and Youngstown, the mines of West Virginia and Ohio, the longshore, metal, garment and laundry industries of New York, the packing industry of Chicago—all were laying men off by the thousands. We were an army of job-seeking youth. We sought in vain. . . .

Things are a little different now.

The blast furnaces of the great steel mills are roaring and working at top capacity. The aviation industry is being expanded and transformed along mass production lines, employing thousands of workers. American industry is experiencing a "boom" to meet a war situation and to prepare for America's participation in this war.

Yes, it is true that you and I are not among those thousands that have been called to work—even though the factories are now open. . . . There appear to be no jobs for Negro youth whether industry is shut down or opened up. . . .

The Glenn L. Martin airplane plant in Baltimore now employs some 18,000 workers and plans to employ an additional 10,000, but refuses to hire Negro workers. In the Chicago area the U.S. Arsenal refuses to hire Negro die-casters. According to the report of the Illinois State Commission on the conditions of the urban colored population, in over sixty Chicago firms which have received national defense contracts totalling over $35,000,000, less than one-tenth of 1 per cent of their employees are Negroes. The Los Angeles Council of the National Negro Congress made a survey of the airplane industry in southern California last summer. It found only one Negro employed out of a total of from 40,000 to 60,000 workers.

The job prospect for young Negro women is even more restricted. The white collar job is limited to the Jim-Crow community. Jobs as clerical workers, stenographers, secretaries, cashiers, telephone operators, tellers and statisticians in the industrial plants and public utilities are closed to them. The jobs that are obtainable in the community are very few. Jobs in private industry are almost exclusively limited to laundry, canners, food and to some extent meatpacking and needle. The average Negro girl in search of employment must turn to domestic and agricultural work. . . .

This discrimination against Negro workers is a fixed policy of the trusts and corporations. Confirmation—brutal and frank—of this fact is to be seen in the case of Vultee Aircraft. The Executive Secretary of the National Negro Congress in Los Angeles, Robert S. Robinson, protesting this discriminatory policy, received the following reply from Gerald Tuttle, industrial relations manager of Vultee Aircraft:

"I regret to say that it is not the policy of this company to employ people other than those of the Caucasian race. Consequently, we are not in a position to offer your people employment at this time."

Joint action by locals of the C.I.O., the A.F. of L. and the National Negro Congress succeeded in forcing the management of Douglas Aircraft to reverse this policy of discrimination and hire Negro workers. . . .

As I have indicated before, the discrimination that exists on the job is also apparent in the Vocational Training Program. During the past ten years more than 200,000 Negro youth have graduated from mechanical and trade schools, the majority of whom are unemployed and many registered with the State Employment Service, not to speak of those who have been thrown out of industry. A survey made of many northern cities indicates that discrimination is quite evident. In Hartford, Connecticut, it was found that not one Negro was receiving training; in Kansas City, no provision for training Negro youth was contemplated as announced by the Board of Education. In Boston, only two Negroes were receiving training under the Vocational Training Program.

Another difficulty which confronts Negro youth is the fact that after being trained it is the efficiency experts, personnel managers and foremen who do the hiring of youth from the training schools. The labor and progressive movement must reject this entire policy. They must demand equal opportunities for Negro youth in training under the program and fight for the employment of Negro youth without discrimination. It is encouraging to see that many of the locals of the C.I.O. are beginning to take up this fight in an energetic manner. It must become a uniform fight embracing the entire labor and progressive movement.

On October 9 an ominous statement was issued from the White House through the President's secretary, Stephen Early:

"The policy of the War Department is not to intermingle colored and white personnel in the same regimental organization. This policy has proven satisfactory over a long period of years and to make changes would produce situations destructive to morale and detrimental to preparations for national defense. For similar reasons the War Department does not contemplate assigning colored reserve officers other than those of the medical corps and chaplains to existing Negro combat units of the regular army." . . .

Can you see any difference between this enunciation which comes from the White House and that of Jefferson Davis, Chief Justice Taney, [Senators] Tom Heflin [and Theodore G.] Bilbo or the Ku Klux Klan? The only difference is that Roosevelt speaks in the name of "national defense" while those dark forces of yesterday spoke of defending "white civilization." They really mean national offense. How dare the President of the United States speak in the name of "civilization," "democracy," "freedom," "culture," and "world order"! What can better expose this entire setup than the reactionary attitude of the Administration toward one-tenth of America's citizenry?

As the fight for equality develops among Negro youth, increasing numbers of white youth join the fight. They are beginning to take it as their very own. Negro youth do not fight alone. They are locking hands with white youth as expressed in the recent Town Meeting held in Washington, sponsored by the American Youth Congress, which represented some 4,000,000 organized youth in the country. Protesting this discrimination, the Youth Congress organized delegations of Negro and white who lobbied in Washington, reaching most of the Senators and Representatives. Two hundred youth with placards picketed the War Department demanding that "Old Jim-Crow has got to go!" This picket line was led by white young southerners from the heart of the "solid South." . . .

Now we must agree that by the united efforts of the young Negro Americans on the basis of the program of the Young Communist League, it is possible to improve our position today. But you and I are not merely interested in easing our present hardships. We wish to solve our problem in a more permanent and lasting manner. The Young Communist League offers a program which leads in that direction. The dream of Negro youth for freedom, equality and opportunity is an objective realizable only in a Socialist America.

□ ——————————————————————————— □

NAZI ARMIES INVADE USSR

"Support the USSR in its Fight Against Nazi War!"
Statement of the Communist Party, USA, June 22, 1941,
The Communist, **July 1941**

[*The Nazi attack on the Soviet Union was the climax of the appeasement policy with which the western powers had encouraged Nazi aggression. When the attack came it caused the loss of 20 million lives, vast devastation of the land and industry. But it ended in the defeat of nazism. It was on the soil of the first socialist state that the German fascist war-machine was destroyed.*[4]]

The armed assault by German fascism and its satellites against the Soviet Union is an unprovoked criminal attack upon the greatest champion of peace, freedom and national independence—the land of socialism. This military aggression by the fascist rulers of Germany is also an attack upon the people of Germany. It is an attack likewise upon the peoples of the United States and of the entire world.

With the fullest support of all its people, the Soviet Government is now waging a struggle not only in defense of its socialist land but also in defense of the most vital interests of the peoples in all countries. It is waging a just struggle for the cause of the freedom of all nations and peoples.

Since its inception the Soviet Union has consistently and courageously fought for peace among the nations, for preventing war and checking aggression. When the Munich conspirators secured the upper hand in the ruling circles of the capitalist countries they destroyed existing possibilities for collective security, thereby making the second imperialist world war inevitable. The Soviet Union adopted and pursued a consistent policy of neutrality toward both sides in the imperialist war, a policy based upon rendering aid to those nations that were waging a just struggle for national independence and liberty. It aids the Chinese people as it aided the Spanish Republic. It liberated the peoples of the Western Ukraine, White Russia, Bessarabia and the Baltic states. It fought against the extension and prolongation of the war. Thus it served the best interests of the working class and peoples of the entire world.

The reactionaries and imperialists of both sides have opposed and conspired against the peace and neutrality of the Soviet Union. They sought to drag the Soviet Union into the imperialist war.

By Fred Ellis, *Daily Worker,* 1945

Now the rulers of fascist Germany, in their desperate struggle with their imperialist rivals in England and the United States and in mortal fear of the oppressed masses in Germany and in all the countries ravaged and enslaved by Germany, have seen fit to lay their criminal hands upon the Soviet Union.

Hitler is calling upon his friends and supporters in all the capitalist countries to join hands in war against the Soviet Union, in war against the working people and oppressed masses throughout the world. The rulers of fascist Germany are dangling before the imperialists of all countries, especially in England and the United States, the vision of a new Munich, a new conspiracy to redivide the world at the expense of the peoples of all nations, to crush the Soviet Union, to exterminate democracy in Europe and to strengthen reaction throughout the world. This was the message [Rudolf] Hess brought to England. The friends of fascism in the United States and England are reaching out for this reactionary vision. The Scripps-Howard press, just before the attack of Hitler began, cynically declared, "That's one war we could really favor. . . ." This is likewise the position of the Social-Democratic lickspittles of big capital, who have long been demanding war against the Soviet Union.

The American people—the workers, toiling farmers, the Negro mas-

191

ses, the middle classes—all those who hate fascism and oppression and cherish peace and liberty, see in the cause of the Soviet Union and its peoples the cause of all advanced and progressive mankind. They should defeat every attempt at a new Munich conspiracy. They should strive for active friendship and fraternal solidarity with the peoples of the Soviet Union.

Down with the criminal war of German fascism against the Soviet Union!

For full support and cooperation with the Soviet Union in its struggle against Hitlerism!

Against all those reactionaries of every stripe who seek in any manner to aid Hitler's attack against the Soviet Union!

For a people's peace based upon the liberation and independence of all nations!

William Z. Foster, Chairman
Robert Minor, Acting Secretary[5]
Communist Party, U.S.A.

□ ———————————————————————————————— □

RESTORING THE RIGHT TO VOTE

"The New Stage in the Fight to Abolish the Poll-Tax," by Theodore R. Bassett, *The Communist,* May 1943

[*The poll tax, widespread in the southern states, was designed to deny the vote to Blacks. But it did more than that. Many impoverished whites were unable to pay the tax accumulations of years and thereby could not qualify as electors.*

Theodore R. Bassett (b. 1901) has been an outstanding Black leader of the Communist Party since the 1930s. He is prominent as a pamphleteer and as a writer for various publications, including the Daily Worker *and* Daily World. *In this war-time piece he emphasized the contradiction of the poll tax to the democratic goals of the war.*]

Passage of H.R. 7, the Marcantonio Anti–Poll Tax Bill, is the vital concern of the entire American people because the speedy wiping out of the poll-tax in this session of Congress is a win-the-war necessity. Repeal of the poll-tax will strengthen national unity, will enhance America's power in the United Nations and will contribute to speeding the destruction of the Hitler Axis.[6]

At the very moment when Congress should have been taking steps to carry out the people's will for prosecution of the war, at the very moment when the glorious offensive of the Red Army presented the U.S.A. and Great Britain with the opportunity of speeding up the destruction of Hitler Germany through the opening of the large-scale military offensive in Western Europe, the defeatist forces put over in Congress a first-rate victory for Hitler. The House endorsed the poll-tax Congressman Martin Dies, 302–94. [By this vote it decided to continue the life of the Dies Un-American Committee, whose continuance was to do irreparable harm to civil rights for years to come.]

The Congressional poll-taxers are doing their utmost to carry out the "divide and conquer" tactics of Hitler. Particularly notorious in this regard is the racist Representative John Rankin of Mississippi, arch Negro-baiter, anti-Semite and Soviet-hater.

Further, the disfranchisement of 10,000,000 Americans through the poll-tax weakens United Nations' unity and brings into question among the darker peoples of India, China and Latin America the sincerity of America's and the United Nations' aims. . . .

The Communist Party has played an important part in the development of the 1943 campaign for the repeal of the poll-tax. It has consistently argued and fought for the abolition of the white supremacy poll-tax system.

□ ——————————————————————————— □

WOMEN IN WAR PRODUCTION

Women in the War by Elizabeth Gurley Flynn, Workers Library Publishers, 1942

[*Between 1940 and 1944 the female labor force increased by 29 percent. But the influx of women into the nation's mills and factories did not come automatically. Barriers of discrimination had to be overcome. Progressive trade unions played an outstanding role in mobilizing women in industry.*

Elizabeth Gurley Flynn (1890–1964), prominent Communist leader, describes the problems facing women entering major war plants. On the contention that women will not be able to handle certain heavy jobs, she wrote: "Any job, except some very heavy types of physical labor, can be undertaken by women." And she added: "With mechanical assistance most of these can be handled too."]

193

Today it is . . . useful and . . . heroic to make arms for our fighting forces and our brave allies. Our main tasks are on the home front. Eighteen people are required at work to keep one fighter on the field, at sea, or in the air. Woman's work is manifold today. It includes industry, civilian defense, politics, the labor unions, and as trained auxiliaries to the armed forces. . . .

Our armed forces are expected to reach ten million in 1943. They are drawn mainly out of production. Their needs take precedence. They must be fed, clothed, shod, trained, transported, given tanks, guns, airplanes, bullets, bombs, jeeps, ships, parachutes and a myriad of other essentials. Civilian needs must also be adequately met to keep our home-front forces healthy and efficient. It is estimated that fifty-eight million workers will be required in 1943. War Chief Paul McNutt announces that eighteen million must be women or five million more than are employed today. One out of six able-bodied women, over eighteen years old, will be in war jobs within the next year. . . .

War emergency accelerates the entry of women into industry . . . there were ten million women employed in 1930, two and a half million more than in 1920. Many more will remain in industry after this war than were there before, especially in new industries. . . .

A lively interest in the mobilization of women is sweeping the country. It is not only a recognition of their importance but a campaign to stimulate larger numbers to enter plants. The "soldierettes" of the home front are interviewed, featured on the fashion pages of newspapers and magazines in their snappy uniforms, are the heroines of movies. The glamour girl of today, the woman in the news, is the working woman. Every day brings a thrilling account of a new difficult or delicate job mastered by a woman; every such accomplishment lays low some ancient superstition about women. They are not afraid of heat, electricity, noise, lights, gas, smells, high, dark or dangerous places. They do not worry about their appearance. "Feminine vanity" does not balk at dirty faces, greasy hands, hair plastered down under a protective cap, severely tailored uniforms, shoes conditioned for safety and a lunch box instead of a fancy purse. Our women measure up to the stern requirements of modern industry. . . .

[I]n reply to a questionnaire sent out by *Modern Industry* to 1,000 plant executives, 74 per cent reported present or contemplated employment of women. It is encouraging, too, to hear that their experience condemns "all-women" departments. Men and women working side by side is more satisfactory, once men overcome their fear of women as rivals. . . .

Recent trade union conventions have either not discussed the requirements of these millions of new women workers or disposed of them with the customary general resolutions, a hangover of their past bad practices. . . .

That there were less women delegates (21) at the recent convention of the United Auto Workers than at the previous one is deplorable. . . .

To summarize—the vital needs of American women workers to help win the war are as follows:

1. Equal opportunity to work for all women (Negro and white) at all occupations.

2. Adequate training for jobs, under government and union supervision.

3. Equal pay for equal work.

4. Safe and sanitary shop conditions.

5. Equal membership, protection by and participation in labor unions.

6. Child care centers, with federal funds and supervision.

□ ———————————————————————————————— □

CONQUEST OF THE FORD EMPIRE

Brother Bill McKie: Building the Union at Ford
by Phillip Bonosky, International Publishers, 1953

[*Ford Motor Co. did not knuckle under until June, 1941, when it was forced to sign a contract with the United Auto Workers (UAW). Ford had been the last major stronghold of open-shop resistance in the auto industry.*

A strike was called on April 1, 1941. Ten days later it ended with an agreement to negotiate with the union grievance committees, return the strikers to work and to hold an NLRB election within forty-five days to determine the collective bargaining agent—an election overwhelmingly won by the UAW.

[William] Bill McKie, Communist, was a leader of the strike. William Z. Foster, in a foreword to Bonosky's biography said: " . . . Bill McKie is the fine fighting stuff that Communists are made of. The whole logic of his life—his long fight for unionization and better conditions for the workers and his unconquerable perspective for ultimate socialism, brought him inevitably into the ranks of the Communist Party, the true party of the working class and of the democratic masses of the American people."]

195

Slowly he walked through the gate, on down the stone pavement, his heart skipping a quick beat; on past the huge machines throbbing again, smelling again that strange mixture of sweat, grease and iron, hearing again that undercurrent rhythm of machine-and-men, his eyes focusing slowly on the faces as he passed by.

"There goes old Bill McKie!" he dimly heard someone cry.

"There goes old Bill!"

They stopped to shake his hand, to grip him in an embrace of pride and love and so pass him down the long corridor of smiles and welcoming hands. "Here comes Bill McKie!" they said and the word passed along the line, going ahead so that they were already smiling as he came into view.

His hair was gray, his body was leaner, the blue eyes a little milder than before, his walk slightly less springy. He was sixty-three years old. He was going to work.

He was going to work again after seven years on the outside, often hungry, making never more than $20 or $25 a week top, organizing these very men. David, he had wrestled with Goliath and found many Davids everywhere; and Goliath lay wounded, if not dead.

He was old Bill McKie back to work as an expert sheet-metal man. He came back as that and as a Communist. "There goes Bill McKie!" they echoed up and down the plant. "He beat Ford!" And as they touched him passing by they knew they were touching themselves in this Communist. And so they handed him, smile by smile, down the pathways of victory through the shop.

He too had stood in Cadillac Square when 80,000 throats had roared a great victory shout that burst off the stone buildings of Detroit. . . .

The negotiating committee had brought back a terrific contract from the meeting with the Ford officials. On May 21, they had gone to the polls and 58,000 of them had voted for the CIO—the crushing, overwhelming answer to goons, Service Men and speed-up.

[Harry] Bennett and the Ford board of directors had bowed; and when the committee entered the room to start negotiations they found Bennett more than willing to meet them halfway. Old Man Ford had told Bennett to give them enough rope to hang themselves. So not only did he concede the union demands; he went them one better. He himself volunteered a union shop and the check-off. Wily Ford had said of the check-off: "That will make us their bankers, won't it? Then they can't get along without us. They'll need us just as bad as we need them." By the "they" he meant the leaders of the union, on whom he was already casting a calculating eye.

Bennett granted the union's request that the company enter into collective bargaining in good faith; that overtime be paid for Sundays and holidays and time over 40 hours; that the Service Department be put into uniform; and that men discharged for union activity be rehired.

That last meant 400 of them—and it meant Bill.

It meant Bill, but Bennett wasn't reconciled yet to having Bill back. Bill waited until July and then the slip he received through the NLRB sent him, a sixty-three-year-old man, to the foundry!

"No," he said. "I won't go to the foundry—I'll go back to the department I was fired from; the tin shop."

They allowed him finally to go there and an hour later his shop foreman, Jack Lewis, came up to him and said: "Bill, you're to go down to the employment office." He looked oddly at Bill and added sheepishly: "Seems there was some mistake—you were hired before your time."

"What do you mean?" Bill cried, "I was first fired!"

He took his story to Percy Llewellyn, who brought it up in the union meetings. Again in September he was back but again for only an hour. Now he went to Pat Rice who told him: "If they don't let you in tomorrow, we'll carry you in!"

But there was no obstacle the next day. They crowded around him to shake his hand. They wanted to tell him how much they had missed him on the inside, though they knew he was busy on the outside. They wanted Bill there—as the ultimate proof that Ford was beaten and his simplest and most powerful enemy, the Communist Bill McKie, had won out. His victory was their victory. His defeat was theirs; they knew that. Life itself had taught them this profound lesson. . . .

For Bill McKie was living proof of what a Communist really was. He had shown with his life what Communism meant. It meant complete devotion to the workers. "If my life could be of any help to the workers," Bill said simply, but with his life backing it, "I would give it up without any regret." . . .

They elected him to the National Negotiating Committee to meet with the Ford Motor Company. The company negotiating team was headed by John Bugas, the ex-FBI agent. "As a Communist," said this FBI man and also Walter Reuther and Company, "you take orders from Moscow."

This is how Bill took "orders."

It was a hot July night. The union committee was meeting in a hotel room with Bugas and the company committee. They were not getting very far. In a room across the hall the Ford Motor Company was supplying food and drinks to the negotiators.

The negotiations dragged on past midnight and into the small hours of the morning. Bill decided to get something to eat.

"Plenty in the room across the hall," one of the Ford men said.

"Nothing doing," Bill snapped. "I'll order my own from the hotel clerk."

And he did.

The next day, Mark Belltaire, newspaper correspondent, wrote up the incident in his column in the *Detroit Free Press.* He said that Bill McKie, a well-known Communist, had bought his own refreshments while sitting at a negotiating conference with Ford representatives. "McKie," remarked the columnist, "said he did not want the Ford Motor Company's food or drinks. He preferred to pay for his own." The press, for once, was correct.

Where did Bill get his "orders" to act like that? From Moscow?

The reporter shouldn't have been surprised. Any honest worker would have acted the same.

□ ── □

THE STRUGGLE FOR THE SECOND FRONT

"The Second Front and the Winter of 1942-43"
by Eugene Dennis, *The Communist,* November 1942

[*While the Soviet Union was carrying the brunt of the fighting on the Eastern Front, Hitler's forces faced little military opposition in the West. The underground in France, Belgium and other European countries was increasingly effective in holding down Hitler's forces. The Communist parties were a vital part of the underground and suffered heavy losses. The agreement to open a second front was continuously delayed. The historian D.F. Fleming wrote:*

*"Molotov was assured that we were preparing for a second front and that we expected to open it in 1942. He was permitted to write a sentence in the communique issued on June 11, 1942, which said: 'In the course of the conversations full understanding was reached with regards to the urgent tasks of creating a Second Front in Europe in 1942.'" (*The Cold War and its Origins—1917-1950, *Vol. I, p. 149). But two years were to pass before the United States and Britain met this commitment.*

A popular movement developed in which the Communist Party played a significant part. A rally on July 22, 1942, at Madison Square Park in New York City was attended by some 60,000 trade unionists and by members of civic, fraternal, veterans, community and church organiza-

tions. Two hundred and fifty trade unions affiliated to the Greater New York Industrial Union Council, CIO, gave it support. Similar actions occurred throughout the country.

Eugene Dennis (1905–1961) joined the Communist Party in 1926. He became a national secretary of the Party in 1938 and was elected General Secretary in 1946. In 1947 he was sentenced to one year in prison for challenging the House Committee on Un-American Activities. With ten fellow members of the Party's national committee he was sentenced to five years under the Smith Act in 1949.]

The second winter of fateful fighting on the Soviet-German front, the decisive front of the people's war for national liberation, is now approaching. The conditions have been created, especially by the epic struggle of the Red Army, for the anti-Hitler coalition to make this the last year of the Hitlerites.

Will this take place? Will Hitler be destroyed as speedily as objective conditions make possible? Will victory over Hitlerism, which was possible in 1942, finally be fought for by all the Allies and won early in 1943? Will the winter of 1942–43 witness effective coalition warfare, a concerted offensive of the United Nations against Hitler Germany which can smash the Nazis? Will the mighty resistance, the developing counterattacks and the pending counter-offensive of the Soviet Union against the Nazi invaders be buttressed by an Anglo–American invasion of the continent from the West in the last quarter of 1942?

These questions are on the minds of everyone, friend and foe of fascism alike. These questions dominate the thoughts and outlook of every resolute anti-fascist and haunt the Brown Shirts. Especially do they permeate the thinking of every American patriot, of every enemy of Hitler's Axis who girds to make 1943, the fourth year of the war against the Hitlerites, the last year of the war, the year to rid the world of Nazi fascism. [Germany capitulated on May 7, 1945.]

Much time and many opportunities have been lost already. . . . This has given the Nazis and their satellites unnecessary breathing space and advantages. It let the chances for victory over Hitler in 1942 slip by. Consequently this has accentuated the military dangers and jeopardized the national interests and safety of all the United Nations and in the first place, of England and America. For despite the heavy blows which the Red Army has inflicted upon the Nazi war machine, the Nazi advances in the Don, Volga and Caucasus regions, during the summer and autumn fighting, have multiplied manyfold the dangers to the Middle East, to England itself as well as to the Americas.

Because of this the realization is growing in the United States and Britain that to delay further the opening of the Western Front against Hitler Germany—the heart and core of the Axis—means to needlessly prolong the war; it means not only to handicap the glorious struggle of the U.S.S.R., but likewise it means to gamble with the very national existence of the British and American peoples and with the common fate of the United Nations.

This is why the mass movement for the Second Front now is national in scope and continues to develop and expand. This is why the C.I.O. and influential circles of the A.F. of L. and why wider sections of labor—the backbone and driving force of the strategy of the offensive—are intensifying their independent activity in support of the most rapid fulfillment of the Roosevelt-Churchill-Molotov agreement for creating a Second Front in Europe this year.

By Fred Ellis,
Daily Worker, 1945

THE COMMUNIST PARTY ON
BLACK LIBERATION AND THE WAR

"Letter to Editor" by Benjamin J. Davis,
New York Age, published July 11, 1942

[*During the war the charge was made that the Communist Party discarded its fundamental position in the struggle for Black liberation "for the duration." The editor of the* New York Age, *leading Harlem weekly, discussed this question in an editorial entitled "Communism and the Negro," which appeared June 27, 1942. Ben Davis (1903–1964), Harlem leader and an outstanding figure in the Communist Party, replied to it. (Davis was then publisher of the* Daily Worker.) *A portion of the letter follows.*]

June 29, 1942

To the Editor of the *New York Age:*

It is apparent from the editorial in your issue of June 27, entitled "Communism and the Negro," that your paper is under great misapprehension. This editorial quite fairly credits the Communists and the *Daily Worker* with a great fight for the Negroes' cause before the present war, but makes a gross error in assuming that we have ceased to do so now. The *Daily Worker,* the Communist Party and other clear-headed, win-the-war forces, are fighting for full Negro equality now as before and we consider it even more necessary now in order to secure our country's victory over Hitler. . . .

For some time there has been a whispering campaign under way among the Negro people with reference to the *Daily Worker* and the Communist Party, responsibility for which campaign does not lie upon the Negro people. This campaign is aimed not alone against the Communists and the *Daily Worker,* but it is also inimical to the best interests of the Negro people and of the nation's war effort. It claims falsely and fantastically that since the *Daily Worker* and the Communist Party support the war they believe "now's the time to keep silent" about Negro rights. This is so patently and notoriously untrue that we are surprised to see the *New York Age* taken in by it, especially to the extent of innocently using the very same words of the whisperers. . . .

The Negro people cannot be true to their own best interests without supporting the war.

The slaveowners' Fuehrer, Jeff Davis of 1861, is today reincarnated in

Berlin—his name is Adolf Hitler. The lynchers, Ku Kluxers, the Rankins, the jim-crow poll-taxers, the defeatists and fifth columnists—are serving Hitler today as the Copperheads served Jeff Davis against Lincoln in 1861. The Negro people will fight the Jeff Davises of Berlin today as they fought the Jeff Davises of Montgomery, Alabama, in 1861.

Jeff Davis' slave-market stench, in 1861, extended into the North and poisoned the Union forces with a brutal attitude toward the Negro, a hatred of Abolitionists that seriously impeded the war. In order that the people could be united to crush the "Adolf Hitler" of 1861, it was necessary to combat these brutalities and weaknesses in the northern forces. But the war had to go on, even while the injustices still continued in the North. Also now the stench of Hitlerism must be removed from our American life in order to strengthen national unity for victory over Hitler—and this is not in contradiction to our demand that the war must go on. No enemy voice must side-track us from that necessity.

There are those who say this is a "white man's war," as many of the followers of Garrison said of the Civil War. In reply permit us to quote Frederick Douglass, the noblest Negro leader and the one who saw clearer and further than any other man—even Lincoln—and who proved himself to be one of the greatest statesmen of our country's history:

"There are weak and cowardly men in all nations. We have them amongst us. They tell you this is a 'white man's war'; that you 'will be no better off after than before the war'; that the getting of you into the army is to 'sacrifice you on the first opportunity.' Believe them not; cowards themselves, they do not wish to have their cowardice shamed by your brave example. Leave them to their timidity or to whatever motive may hold them back." (*Life and Times of Frederick Douglass: An Autobiography.* Pathway Press, 1941, p. 374.)

We do not believe the *Age* is or intends to be in the category which Douglass criticized.

The last paragraph of your editorial states:

"The Negro can less afford to keep silent at this time than at any time in his history. For the record shows that we only get what we are willing to fight and die for. At the same time we are fighting to repel an invading foe, we must insist that our neighbors here at home realize and recognize us as and give us all the rights and privileges of Americans too."

With this statement the *Daily Worker* agrees 100 per cent. We make at all times all of the demands for equality of the Negro. As you truly say, we have made these demands and fought for them in the past. But the peculiarity of the present situation is that the granting of these demands is absolutely necessary now in order to strengthen our country's war effort. We can and must win these demands now, where we could not win them before. We never could before, but we can now wipe out the jim-crow system. These demands are not demands against the war, but for the war at the same time that they are for the Negro. We demand the wiping out of the ugly stain of "racial" persecution, of Hitlerism in America, as a necessary strengthening of our country so that we can wipe Hitlerism off the face of the whole earth.

There is evidence too voluminous to quote here to prove this in the records and deeds of both the *Daily Worker* and the Communist Party—and in the experiences of the Negro people. How is it possible for the *Age* to contend that the *Daily Worker* counsels "silence" on Negro rights since June 22, 1941, when on the same page of the *Worker* of June 14, 1942, containing an article by the writer which you attack, there were articles castigating jim-crow in the armed forces and in industry? How can your editorial contend that the *Daily Worker* counsels "silence" on Negro rights since June 22, 1941 (or since Pearl Harbor), when the *Daily Worker* has been and is campaigning against the poll-tax, lynching, discrimination, segregation and when these campaigns are seen in virtually every edition of the paper regularly. Evidently the *Age* editorial writer did not understand our contention that the fight for Negro rights must be intensified for the very reason that we are at war and want the strongest national unity to win that war.

While the *Daily Worker* agrees with the *Age* that "Negroes can less afford to keep silent than ever"—something must be said in addition. Not alone can the Negroes ill afford to be silent. No Americans—white or Black, capitalist or worker, Jew or Gentile, Catholic or Protestant—can afford to be silent about the jim-crow evils which shamefully exist against Negroes. For these evils, always unjust, now impair winning the war and must be eliminated without delay. Without the full integration of the Negro into war industries, into the governing councils of the nation, into the armed forces—as free and equal citizens—victory is endangered.

In view of all this, it is even more ridiculous for the *Age* editorial to claim that the *Daily Worker* has the same position as [publisher] Roy Howard's flunkey, Westbrook Pegler. We don't believe the *Age* editor would on second thought insist upon this contention. No Negro in the country, no matter how misinformed he may be with reference to the *Daily Worker* or the Communists, would seriously think our position is anything like Mr. Howard's little pro-fascist Negro-and-Red-baiter. In fact, the editor of the *New York Age* sent a statement to the *Daily Worker* at the writer's request, denouncing Pegler's attack upon the Negro press; and the statement was printed in the *Worker* of May 17.

As "evidence" that the *Daily Worker* has the same position as Roy Howard's underling, the *Age* editorial cited an open letter by the writer to A. Philip Randolph published in the *Worker* of June 14. But the *Age's* case collapses when it strangely fails to print a single quotation from this open letter. Among other things this letter stated:

"The *Daily Worker* emphasizes today that because our country is defending its very national existence, it is imperative that jim-crowism be eliminated from our armed forces and civilian life. The integration of Negro citizens into the war effort on a basis of full equality is vital to national unity and victory." . . .

The abolition of slavery came as a war necessity even before the Civil War was triumphantly won. Does the *Age* object to the opportunities now being opened to Negroes—although entirely too slowly—because these opportunities are necessary to our winning the war in which we Negroes have as much—or more at stake than any other minority American group? Does the *Age* wish to hold up the progress of the Negro until full citizenship comes as a result of some overnight utopian philanthropy—handed down on a silver platter in a dream world? Does the *Age* wish to sit with folded hands until Hitler wins and nothing is attainable—until American minorities are drenched in their own blood as in occupied Europe?

Douglass said of the far too inadequate Emancipation Proclamation:

"For my own part, I took the Proclamation first and last, for a little more than it purported and saw in its spirit a life and power far beyond its letter. It was in my estimation, an immense gain to have the war for the Union committed to the extinction of slavery, even from a military necessity. It is not a bad thing to have individuals or nations do right, though they do so from selfish motives." (*Life and Times of Frederick Douglass,* p. 390.)

President Roosevelt has appointed the historic Fair Employment Practices Committee, the unions are learning the necessity of unity with the Negro people for equality and the Negro people are making gains in the very prosecution of this war, even though these gains must especially be speeded by our national government, by labor and by the Negro press and people. These things are done to win the war. Are they any the less beneficial to the Negro people?

Yours truly,
Ben Davis, Jr.

PAUL ROBESON SPEAKS

**"American Negroes in the War." Speech by Paul Robeson
at the Twelfth Annual Herald-Tribune Forum,
New York Herald-Tribune, November 21, 1943**

[*The forums of the now defunct* New York Herald-Tribune *were addressed by prominent figures. President Franklin Delano Roosevelt and General de Gaulle presented papers to the forum which Paul Robeson also addressed.*

A debate was underway as to whether Black Americans subjected to a whole system of racial and national oppression should support the war against Hitler and his axis partners, Mussolini and Hirohito.

Robeson, who was chairman of the Council on African Affairs, noted that the great majority of the peoples of Africa were being kept on the sidelines of the war. He sharply criticized those who argued that the fight for Black equality endangered the fight to defeat the axis powers.

Here are portions of Robeson's speech.]

World War II has been repeatedly and eloquently described as a war in the interest of the common man, the little man—a people's war of liberation. Americans who have not known through personal experience the meaning of fascist oppression may be prone to think of such characterizations of the war as only fine rhetorical and idealistic expressions.

But the Chinese, the Ethiopians, the Russians, and all the peoples of Europe upon whom the axis forces have heaped murder and destruction know full well what it is they are fighting for. *They* understood—in their hearts and in every conscious moment of their existence—what a people's war of liberation means.

Other peoples however, besides the direct victims of axis aggression, also have a genuine awareness of the democratic significance of the present conflict. Their awareness is born of their yearning for freedom from an oppression which has pre-dated fascism and their confidence that they have a stake in the victory of the forces of democracy.

The American Negro has such an outlook. It dates from the fascist invasion of Ethiopia in 1935. Since then, the parallel between his own interests and those of oppressed peoples abroad has been impressed upon him daily as he struggles against the forces which bar him from full citizenship, from full participation in American life.

The disseminators and supporters of racial discrimination and antagonism are to the Negro, and are *in fact,* first cousins if not brothers of the Nazis. They speak the same language of the "Master Race" and practice, or attempt to practice, the same tyranny over minority peoples.

There are three things in American life which today arouse the bitterest resentment among Black Americans and at the same time represent the greatest handicap upon his full participation in the national war effort. First is their economic insecurity which they know to be the result of continuing discrimination in employment even now, coupled with other forms of economic exploitation and social discrimination in urban communities such as Harlem.

Second is the segregation and inferior status assigned to Negroes in the armed forces and their complete exclusion from most of the women's auxiliary services. Added to this are the insults and acts of physical violence nurtured by the segregation policy, which have been inflicted upon them in many of the camps and camp communities, even in areas which before the coming of the army camps had been free from racial prejudice. . . .

Third is the poll-tax system of the South, which operates to maintain undemocratic elements in places of authority not only below the Mason Dixon line but in our national life as a whole.

Some progress has been made in righting these wrongs. The most positive action has been in the accomplishments of the President's Committee on Fair Employment Practice. . . . But these gains are pitifully small indeed when measured against the loss of manpower, the lowered morale, the interracial friction and national disunity which characterize America at war.

And yet there are some who deplore the Negro's present-day struggle for democracy and equality as *endangering* national unity and our war effort. They point to the trouble (so they say) that the FEPC has stirred up in the South and to the disgraceful race riots—insurrections or pogroms would be more accurate—in Detroit and other industrial centers which resulted (so they say) from Negro militancy.

Such people are looking at the world upside down or hind-parts forward. They believe the wagon is pushing the horse. They are the people who believe Hitler's lie that nazism and fascism were and are necessary in order to save the world from Communism.

Today's militant protest of the Negro people, as illustrated in the recent election of a Negro Communist [Benjamin J. Davis.] to New effort—acceptable candidates rather than party labels—this militant protest

206

represents the development of a clearer understanding among Negroes of their goals, their allies and their enemies. Negroes know that their rights can only be achieved in an America which has realized *all* of its democratic ideals. . . .

The great majority of these peoples, especially in Africa, are on the sidelines of the war. They have not been mobilized to any appreciable extent by their colonial administrators in either the military or production services. Their participation *now* in the United Nations' war effort—just as in the case of the American Negro—is the measure of the kind of victory and the kind of peace that is in store for them.

Let me read to you something that a Negro leader in South Africa recently said: "I know like anybody else that although we are fighting for Democracy, we do not enjoy democratic rule in this country, but I look with hope to the influence that will be exerted by America and Russia towards our rights, as I think that if the Allies win, a new order of government will be brought about."

Those words represent the thought of millions of colonial peoples throughout the world.

A few days ago, Americans honored the Soviet Union on the occasion of the 10th anniversary of the establishment of friendly diplomatic relations between that great nation and ours. We honored the heroic fight which the people of that nation have made against Hitler's erstwhile invincible legions. Two years ago, many Americans, like Hitler, expected the Soviet Union to crumble under the treacherous blitz attack. Now Americans are beginning to know something of the great power of the Russian people—a power born of unity, of legally-enforced equality, of opportunity for all the many millions within its wide borders, regardless of race, creed, nationality or sex. No other nation on earth has achieved such a thing. And no other nation has stated with such explicitness its war aims: "abolition of racial exclusiveness; equality of nations and integrity of their territories; the right of every nation to arrange its affairs as it wishes."

The United States and Great Britain must learn from their Soviet ally the true meaning and application of democracy to minority and colonial peoples. Upon these three great powers rests the primary responsibility, accepted by them jointly in the recent Moscow Conference decisions, of turning military victory into enduring peace and security for all peoples. America and Britain must prove to the world that they are in truth waging a people's war of liberation, or they must face the shame and scorn of the world.

□ ———————————————————————— □

THE YCL IN WORLD WAR II

An Appeal to American Youth
by the National Committee, Young Communist League,
USA, October 1941

[*The nazi armies, having marched through Europe, were ravaging the western areas of the Soviet Union. An appeal by Soviet youth found a ready response from the Young Communist League. The League fortified its pledge by intensifying action at home and greater efforts at the front.*

Communists and young progressives who were veterans of the Spanish anti-fascist war contributed their valuable experience. Capt. Herman Boettcher (who had faced deportation to nazi Germany as a "premature anti-fascist"), was awarded the Distinguished Service Cross (DSC). He won his commission in action and was killed in battle in the Philippines. Sgt. Robert Thompson, national Party leader, won commendation for valor in New Guinea and also was decorated with the DSC. Hank Forbes, who had been Party secretary in western Pennsylvania and lower Manhattan, died on the beaches of Anzio in Italy.]

The freedom-loving youth of the United States have expressed unbounded admiration for the heroic struggle of the Red Army against the Nazi hordes.

American youth knows that this tremendous front stretching from the Arctic ocean to the Black sea is the dam which holds back the Nazi armies from overwhelming all peoples and all nations in the dark night of Hitlerism.

On Sunday, September 28 [1941], the youth of the Soviet Union spoke to the young people of every land, on every continent. They broadcast by radio, a call to youth from an anti-Nazi meeting held in Moscow. The participants were young military heroes, men and women, pilots, tankists, nurses, together with distinguished young artists, film stars, composers, writers and exemplary workers from the factories and fields of the Soviet land.

The meeting also broadcast greetings that were received from the youth of other countries. These greetings were from organizations and individuals of all political affiliations and every religious belief.

From this anti-Nazi meeting in Moscow came a stirring appeal to the youth of the whole world to march forward to victory over Hitler.

American youth! Let us reply to this powerful appeal by strengthening in every way our own fight to give all aid to Britain and the Soviet Union.

Pass the second Lend-Lease Bill! Extend its provisions to include the Soviet Union![7]

Repeal the Neutrality Act!

Collect money for medical supplies to the brave Red Army! Send gifts and packages to the heroic fighters of the Red Army!

Full economic, political and military collaboration between the United States, Great Britain and the Soviet Union in the fight to destroy Hitler and Hitlerism.

☐ ——————————————————————————————————— ☐

ELECTORAL VICTORY IN NEW YORK

PETE—The Story of Peter V. Cacchione
by Simon W. Gerson, International Publishers, 1976

[*The election of Peter V. Cacchione (1897-1947) to the New York City Council was not one of those freakish upsets that occasionally occur in politics. Cacchione ran as a Communist and was proud of his affiliation.*

It was not Communists alone who brought about his victory. Cacchione possessed the talent to identify himself with the people's aspirations and they accepted him as their champion.

Here is a section of the Cacchione story as told by Simon W. Gerson[8] (b. 1909), a long-time veteran of Communist electoral and legislative activity.]

If Pete was ill at ease at his first council session in January, 1942, there was no outward sign of it. Immaculate and smiling, he greeted his council colleagues warmly, recognizing them mostly by voice, since his vision was already badly dimmed. The man whose first night in New York was spent in a municipal flophouse was now an elected official of the great city and, in fact, something of a celebrity, the first to win city office as "an avowed Communist," to use the *New York Times'* arch phrase.

There was an undercurrent of tension in the ancient oak-paneled chamber as news photographers snapped pictures endlessly and reporters waited hopefully for some explosive copy. [Hugh] Quinn's[9] threat to bar Pete had fizzled out—the cagey Democratic council leaders had effectively throttled the Queens loudmouth—but would there be some fireworks anyway? Pete waited calmly; and back in the visitors' seats,

Dorothy,[10] a new corsage on her dress and surrounded by a delegation of Pete's supporters, beamed. . . .

He had already rented an office and anteroom at 26 Court Street in downtown Brooklyn, a location easily accessible from all parts of the borough. Office workers and a legislative assistant, Don Schoolman, were chosen, the latter a young man who could drive Pete to meetings as well as help on bills, resolutions and research.

"And now," said Pete as the cheerful group returned to his Brooklyn office after the council session, "we thank everybody who helped. We'll send out thank-you letters to the 30,000 people who signed my nominating petitions and invite them and their neighbors to come to the office with any problems." It was done, a host of volunteers sitting up nights addressing envelopes. Peculiar, some people thought. One newspaper reported it as a "singular" action. And further, Pete insisted, he was going to account regularly to his constituents. He would increase the frequency of his *Daily Worker* column and make a weekly radio report. WHOM, a commercial radio station with a large ethnic listening audience, particularly among Italian-Americans, was selected.

Only after these matters were cleared away did Pete begin to concentrate on his legislative activity. His priorities were clear: first, strengthen his links with the people and then, and only then, would his parliamentary activities have meaning. He was not of that school of politicians who do things *for* the people; he did things *with* the people. He never swerved from his conviction that his chief job as an elected official was to help organize the people in struggle. There was no Chinese wall between Pete's resolutions in the City Council and his activity in the street. They were one.

Pete was hardly naive about his committee assignments or, in fact, the political weight of the Council. He knew that within the city government, the Mayor and the Board of Estimate were dominant (and that behind them was the "permanent government," the bankers, insurance trusts, real-estate sharks and other huge corporate interests who effectively controlled the city) and that the City Council had very little real clout. He knew that on the basic question of the power of the purse, the Council was virtually impotent, since the Mayor drew up the budget and the Council had only the power to cut. The council members were in fact fiscal eunuchs.

Nonetheless, Pete, with his superb head for figures, would have liked to be on the Council Finance Committee where he could at least have a crack at the all-important city budget. He understood that the huge eight-pound city budget, virtually incomprehensible to most New Yorkers, was in fact a class document indicating the actual direction of city policy. He knew, for instance, that a hefty percentage of the budget annually went to pay interest and principal to the bankers to whom the city had been in hock for lo! these many years. As Pete anticipated, the Council bosses kept him far from the Finance Committee and instead put him on Buildings, Codification and Parks and Playgrounds, relatively innocuous committees which met rarely and performed only a few perfunctory chores. In his second and third terms he was on Buildings & Housing, Civil Employees, Veterans and Parks committees into which he introduced some important resolutions.

Assigned to toothless committees, Pete quickly saw that to advance issues of importance to working people he would have to put forward his own legislation. At the same time he was determined to work together with those in the Council, particularly the Laborites, Councilman [Adam Clayton] Powell[11] and the independents, with whom it was possible to find common ground.

But what about his very first proposals, his maiden resolutions? These should dramatize his central campaign slogan, "Unity Against Hitler," particularly now that the United States was directly involved in the anti-Axis war. (The Japanese attack on Pearl Harbor took place exactly a month before Pete's first council session). . . .

And so it was. At the Council's third session the clerk read aloud: "By Mr. Cacchione, a resolution. . . ." The members perked up. What was the Communist going to propose?

It turned out to be a resolution to petition the State Legislature to adopt Assemblyman Stephen Jarema's bill for free transportation on municipal facilities for soldiers, sailors and marines in uniform. Cacchione resolution No. 2 was a companion measure calling on the Mayor "to use his good offices to request all privately owned transit facilities under franchise of the City of New York to provide free transportation of soldiers, sailors and marines in uniform."

Immediate consideration? Hell, no. Council vice-chairman Joseph Sharkey, leader of the Democratic majority and thus the boss of the Council, promptly objected, and the Cacchione resolutions were referred to committee, there to gather dust. But some of the Democrats were uncomfortable. Why hadn't the flag-waving Tammany crowd thought of this simple courtesy to low-paid servicemen? Army privates were then getting $30 a month; free fares while on leave in the Big Apple would have been helpful. The usually voluble Quinn was silent. Pete had stolen a march on the ultrapatriots with his modest resolution.

Later, Pete confounded his foes in the Council by displaying an intimate knowledge of city finances. He didn't just "leave it to the experts." Unlike most of the Council members, Pete dug through the complicated budget messages and the maze of figures. He spotted Albany's usual robbery of the city and introduced a resolution calling on the state to pass legislation granting New York City a larger share of state tax receipts and increasing the city's power to tax utilities and financial institutions. After Governor Thomas E. Dewey announced an anticipated $70 million state surplus, Pete organized a vigorous fight for a special session of the State Legislature.

Significantly, a bitter floor fight took place on the issue, with the Democratic machine members coming to the aid of Republican Gov. Dewey and the minority—Laborites, Independents and two out of three Republicans—voting with Pete.

□ ———————————————————————————— □

BLACK AND WHITE UNITE
BEHIND BEN DAVIS

"The 'Impossible' Candidate,"
from *Communist Councilman from Harlem,*
by Benjamin J. Davis, International Publishers, 1969

[*A coalition embracing the American Labor Party, Democratic and Fusion Parties broke the all-white composition of the New York City Council in 1941 with the election of Adam Clayton Powell, Jr.*

For the 1943 election, the County Committee of the Communist Party named Benjamin J. Davis, Jr. as its Manhattan councilmanic candidate. Davis, a lawyer and graduate of Harvard Law School, had been drawn to the movement through his defense of Angelo Herndon (see p. 72). He was elected with more than 43,000 votes in a borough where there were about 6,000 members of the Communist Party.

These are extracts from a book he wrote while a Smith Act prisoner.]

When, in 1943, my candidacy for the New York City Council on the Communist ticket was announced, the press was unanimous in declaring my election impossible. For entirely different reasons, some of my friends joined them. The difficulties were considered insurmountable....

But the impossible happened. I was elected. The opposition and its two-party machine were shocked and dismayed. They had already had to swallow the bitter pill of the election of Peter V. Cacchione, Brooklyn Communist leader, in 1941, and they had hoped to get rid of him in 1943. Instead, they were now faced with two Communists in the city council. . . .

A part of the campaign against me was that I would never get elected because I had two strikes against me. I was a Negro and a Communist. An amusing incident as to this "deadly" combination occurred when I called my father the night I was elected. He thought it was a gag and wouldn't believe me. I finally gave up—I knew how stubborn father could be, especially when he had predicted another outcome.

The next morning I got a call from him. Excited and happy, he exclaimed: "Son, I guess you were right. I see there's a headline in the paper here which says 'Black Red elected in New York. White Yankees vote for him.'" . . .

Far from considering it a handicap to be a Negro and a Communist simultaneously, I considered it a double weapon against the ruling class. An American Negro has a background of 300 years of oppression in this country, and great indeed is the Negro's anger. When that same Negro is a Communist, he is equipped with a science—Marxism-Leninism— which alone can help realize his 300-year aspiration for freedom and equality.

In 1943, the only Negro member of the city council was Adam Clayton Powell, Jr., who had been elected as the first Negro member in 1941. He had been elected pretty much as an independent, securing designations from the City Fusion Party, the American Labor Party and the Democratic Party. He was the symbol of the progressive people's coalition in the city. This was the dramatic start of Powell's political power as an independent, when he first proclaimed his motto: "I will wear no man's collar." He was swept into office in 1941 on the crest of a wave of demands by the Negro people and their supporters for representation in the city legislature. . . .

As the chief executive functionary of the Harlem Communist Party, I had a deep concern in having the community retain the seat held in trust, as it were, by Councilman Powell. I had heard that he did not intend to run for re-election, but, putting no stock in rumors, I decided to have a personal talk with him. We had a long discussion, a friendly one, but not successful, on the question of the city council. He said, in effect, that he had already announced his candidacy for congress in 1942. The new congressional district which made it possible to elect a Negro representative from Harlem had been carved out in 1941, and Powell was determined to be the first Negro congressman from that district. . . .

Our Harlem Communist Party surveyed the situation, consulted with

Negro and labor leaders. My own conversations with various Negro spokesmen demonstrated that all felt that the place in the council must not be lost. They felt that the failure of the two major parties to designate a candidate of the community's choice should be exposed during the campaign. Our Party had nominated a candidate, Carl Brodsky, well known in labor and progressive circles. He offered to withdraw in my favor and to permit the Party to substitute my name for his as candidate on the Communist ticket. . . .

Carl Brodsky was truly a representative of the Jewish people. In withdrawing in my favor, under circumstances in which the Jewish people needed a representative in the City Council, he demonstrated the close bonds of cooperation that could exist between the Jewish and Negro people. His action was a warm, human and generous symbol of recognition on the part of progressive Jewish workers of their own profound stake in the cause of Negro liberation. . . .

It was my duty and responsibility, as well as my privilege, to explain to the voters why I was running on that ticket, what the Communist Party stood for and why I was a member. If I couldn't trust the people, why should they trust me? I did not believe in hiding "the light of Marxism-Leninism" under a bushel. It was necessary to point out that though I had backers of other parties in my corner, I nevertheless was a Communist whose program went much farther than the present election campaign; that I believe in socialism and would ever strive for its triumph at home.

My campaign spread like wildfire. Overnight the non-partisan committee for my election leaped from about 50 to approximately 2,000—a real cross-section of ministers, doctors, lawyers, businessmen, trade unionists, social leaders, women, youth, foreign-born, native-born, workers, artists—indeed, people from every conceivable stratum of life. . . .

The campaign was becoming irresistible; the smell of victory was in the air. Councilman Powell was now ready to take his stand. He issued a statement declaring that I was the "worthy successor" to his seat in the city council, and called upon his supporters and friends to vote for me. . . .

The large vote I received from the Puerto Rican community was indispensable to my victory. During the campaign two things struck me with great force: First, that the Puerto Rican community in lower Harlem, victimized by discrimination, had no representation whatever at any level of government; second, that I could not speak Spanish. I resolved to do something to help correct both these conditions. . . .

When election day came, the trade unionists took over all our poll-watching assignments—most outstanding were the organized seamen, the furriers (CIO) and the food workers (AFL). Church women prepared hot coffee and sandwiches at various assembly spots on election day. Many elderly Negroes voted for the first time in their lives. . . .

From the first day of the count, I was leading the field. Radio commentators blasted out that this was the upset of the election. Actually, they were counting those districts which included Harlem. But after the first two or three days, my vote began to level off as the count reached other parts of the city. I remained among the first three, however, and five were to be elected. It seemed that my election was assured. But then the stealing began in earnest. The votes for me began to disappear from my table, and the closest Tammany candidates began to congregate around my table, seeking to create an incident. We appealed to Mayor La Guardia, to the Honest Ballot Association, to every clean-government group. Statements were issued informing the public of the conspiracy to count me out.

On the fourth day Pete Cacchione, his own election in Brooklyn now assured, brought his entire staff over to the Manhattan court to assist me. Soon after he arrived, I discovered that some of my Harlem districts were missing and hadn't been counted. One of the ablest of our party election workers demanded a halt to the count and demanded the right to search for the missing votes. He dug through the huge pile, district by district, and found not only the missing votes we knew of but also some unknown ones. In all, 1,500 votes had been stacked away, stolen right before our eyes. How perilous this was could be seen in the fact that I won by a little over 2,000 votes. It was a dramatic moment. . . .

In this campaign for the City Council, as well as in my subsequent campaigns in 1945 and 1947, the dominant note was its people's character. By this I mean that my platform, which was based upon the major issues facing the electorate, was shaped in such a manner as to facilitate the coming together of the largest sector of the people in defense and extension of their all-round welfare. Republican and Democratic voters rallied to my support no less than independents. It was the difference between a narrow partisan campaign designed to reach primarily those who agreed with my Marxist socialist views, and a people's non-partisan campaign designed to reach those who could unite on immediate issues such as housing, equality, police violence and civil liberties, irrespective of their party affiliation or long-range political perspective. The latter was especially adapted to Harlem, characterized by the all-people's character of the movement against the jim-crow ghetto system.

My electoral victory rested upon years of conscientious and consistent work of the Communist Party in Harlem in the struggles of the Negro people. Many gave their lives or served in prison, victims of police brutality, frame-ups or what have you. Progress seems slow and then, all at once, when conditions are ready, it takes a big leap forward. . . . It is always toward the qualitative leap forward that the Communist works, for it is only in this way that socialism can be established.

☐ ———————————————————————————————— ☐

THE STRUGGLE AGAINST BROWDERISM

1. "The Struggle Against Revisionism"
by William Z. Foster. Report to the Special Convention
of the Communist Political Association, July 26-28, 1945.
Marxism-Leninism vs. Revisionism,
New Century Publishers, 1946;
2. "Some Aspects of Our Policies and Tasks"
by Eugene Dennis. Report to the National Committee,
C.P.A., June 18-20, 1945. *On the Struggle Against
Revisionism,* Communist Party, U.S.A., 1946;
3. "On the Dissolution of the Communist Party of the
U.S.A." by Jacques Duclos.
Reprinted in the *Daily Worker,* May 24, 1945,
from the April 1945 issue of *Cahiers du Communisme;*
4. "The Present Situation and the Next Tasks."
Resolution adopted at the National Convention of the
CPUSA, adopted July 28, 1945. *On the Struggle Against
Revisionism,* Communist Party, U.S.A., 1946.

[*The opportunist tendencies of Earl Browder matured as the struggle against fascism and war developed. Increasingly he saw the struggle as devoid of class antagonisms. In the course of the war this view began to be systematized into a revisionist program which discarded the ideology of Marxism-Leninism. Beginning correctly from the need of unity of divergent classes to defeat nazi aggression, he erroneously conceived the end of class conflict with the close of the war.*

On the international scene he anticipated an end to imperialism with the victory of the allies. The imperialists, he concluded, would "wisely" help develop the colonies as independent states. On the domestic scene he predicted an increase in production for the benefit of the people. Racism, he implied, was a problem that was practically solved.

Under these circumstances he saw no need for the Communist Party, and proposed instead a Communist Political Association (CPA). This would be an educational sect which would not be in conflict with the capitalist system. It would eliminate the revolutionary working class forces and dispense with the need for a vanguard party to create a socialist society.

This political degeneration, which sought to impose a revisionist line on the Party, created great concern, as indicated in the documents printed here. Browder also sought to export as universal his brand of opportunism. This is why Jacques Duclos, a leader of the French Communist Party, responded so sharply.

All this triggered a national convention, called in July 1945, a year after the formation of the CPA. The national convention was preceded by state conventions. The most intensive discussion was organized in the Party. Every avenue for discussion was made available to the membership—newspapers, magazines, and special discussion bulletins. The outcome was near unanimity. The convention reconstituted the Communist Party.

Browder refused to accept the decisions of the organization. He proceeded to stall, while planning to establish his own sect. This intention was later revealed by one of his ideological supporters, George Charney, in his autobiography.

Browder was expelled by a unanimous vote of the National Committee in February 1946. He had promised to abide by the decisions of the convention, but he continued his factional activity and published literature attacking the Party.

The direction in which Browder had been moving was revealed conclusively some years later in lectures he delivered at Rutgers University (1957) and at the New School for Social Research (1958). Here he clearly rejected socialism and again verified his reliance on the "intelligence" of the capitalist class.

The following words in particular expose Browder's views: "Above all America has nothing to copy from the political and social methods of the Soviet Union, because that would mean going backwards. We have already achieved a higher level than they, and our own experience shows that we achieved it through expanding democracy," [emphasis Ed.] (Earl Browder, Marx and America, Duell, Sloan and Pearce, 1958.)

These ideas are a classic restatement of the bankrupt components of "American exceptionalism," a body of doctrine that was ejected from the Party in 1929 together with its advocate, Jay Lovestone.

We publish here parts of the report to the Central Committee which

217

*convened the Special Convention. Foster's report to the CPA takes note
"of an impending change of Party policy." The report by Dennis is
devoted to the tasks of the Party. The article by Jacques Duclos is
reprinted from* Cahiers du Communisme, *theoretical journal of the
Communist Party of France. It notes that among right elements in the
French Party, the "political association" idea was attractive and this led
to a request by French Communists for further clarity on the question.
Duclos rejects Browder's thesis and is steadfast in support of a Marxist-
Leninist Party. The final document is the resolution adopted by the
convention.*]

1.

Browder's line is a rejection of the Marxian principles of the class
struggle. Comrade Browder denies the class struggle by sowing illusions
among the workers of a long postwar period of harmonious class
relations with generous-minded employers; by asserting that class relations no longer have any meaning except as they are expressed either for
or against Teheran; by substituting for Marxian class principles such
idealistic abstractions as the "moral sense," "enlightenment," "pro-
gressivism," and "true class interests" of the big monopolists, as determining factors in establishing their class relations with the workers.
Browder's theories of class collaboration and the harmony of interest
between capital and labor are cut from the same opportunistic cloth as
those of Bernstein, Legien and Gompers,[12] except that his ideas are more
shamelessly bourgeois than anything ever produced by those notorious
revisionists of the past.

Browder's line is a rejection of the Marxian concept of the progressive
and revolutionary initiative of the working class and with it, the vanguard role of the Communist Party. The very foundation of Marxism–Leninism is that the working class, with the Communist Party at its
head, leads the democratic masses of the people in the amelioration of
their conditions under capitalism and also in the eventual establishment
of Socialism. But Comrade Browder has thrown this whole conception
overboard. His books *Victory—and After* and especially *Teheran: Our
Path in War and Peace,* present the thesis of a progressive capitalist class,
particularly American finance capital, leading the peoples of this country
and the world to the achievement of the great objectives of the Moscow,
Teheran, Yalta and San Francisco Conferences and the building of a
peaceful, democratic and prosperous society. Browder sees labor and the
democratic forces, including the Communist Party, playing only a
secondary, non-decisive role in the present-day world.

Browder's line is a rejection of the Leninist theory of imperialism as the final stage of capitalism. Comrade Browder, in his books and speeches, paints a utopian picture of a world capitalist system, not moribund, but vigorous and progressive, especially in its American section—a world capitalist system about to enter into a period of unprecedented expansion. It is a denial of the general crisis of the capitalist system. Browder believes that under the leadership of his "enlightened" American monopolists, the imperialist ruling classes in this and other capitalist countries will peacefully and spontaneously compose their differences with each other, with the U.S.S.R., with the liberated countries of Europe, and with the colonial and semi-colonial countries, without mass struggle. This is the bourgeois liberal notion that the epoch of imperialism is past. It conflicts fundamentally with the Leninist theory of imperialism as the last stage of a decadent capitalist system. . . .

Our Party discussion has made it clear that Comrade Browder's revisionism has exerted a weakening effect upon our wartime policy. Many of our comrades still believe that Browder's policy was necessary during the war. It was not. It was definitely a detriment in our war work, as I have shown in detail in my article in *The Worker* of June 19 [1945]. And not a few believe that Browder worked out our policy of all-out support of the war, of strengthening the United Nations coalition, of the fight for the Second Front, of maximum war production, of the no-strike pledge, etc. But this is not true. Browder was in Atlanta when this correct general war policy was developed and he had nothing whatever to do with its formulation. Almost as soon as he was released from prison, however, he began to undermine our correct policy with his enervating revisionism. He did not succeed, however, in completely destroying our otherwise correct wartime policy. Despite his revisionism, our Party may well be proud of its record during the war. The full destructive force of Browder's revisionism would have been felt, however, if we had attempted to extend his policies over into the postwar period. . . .

There were, indeed, many signs of impending change of Party policy. The end of the war against Germany, the death of Roosevelt, the imperialist raid upon the San Francisco conference of the United Nations, the obvious preparations of the N.A.M. [National Association of Manufacturers] for a postwar drive against organized labor, the development of many strikes, etc., were awakening concern among our leaders in the National Board: Comrades [Eugene] Dennis, [Gilbert] Green, [Robert] Thompson, [John] Williamson and other leading members[13] were either beginning to express directly opposing views to Comrade Browder's, or were raising questions that he found it increasingly difficult, on the basis of his distortions of Teheran, to answer.

2.

Generally speaking, I have not been among those who considered that the objectives of Teheran and Crimea would be fulfilled automatically and without the most active intervention of the masses. I have not been one of those who minimized the resolute struggle which must be waged against pro-fascist reaction, or who underestimated the independent role and activity of labor and the people.

Yet it is a fact that I have held and fostered certain opportunist illusions regarding the post-war role of the anti-axis sections of monopoly capital. And in so doing I participated in and contributed toward the main errors which our national leadership has committed. Besides, on such specific questions as liquidating the C.P.A. in the South,[14] as well as in incorrectly estimating the significance of the Labor–Management Charter, I bear a particular responsibility. . . .

The point is, that neither American nor British imperialism will be weakened, nor their reactionary conflicts and aims thwarted, by Browder's appeal to their "intelligence" and "true" class interests; nor by his fantastic blueprints designed to soften their antagonisms, to divide up peacefully the world market, or to arrive at arrangements whereby Downing Street would voluntarily liberate the British Empire. American, just as British imperialism, will be weakened and curbed, particularly when the American working class and people, by their unity and struggle, weaken and undermine the position of the most reactionary and aggressive forces of finance capital and establish closer and firmer unity of action with the freedom-loving peoples of all lands. . . .

Moreover, we of the National Board cannot agree with Browder's fatalistic position and his arbitrarily chosen alternatives of the future course of world development. For instance, we do believe that if the imperialist bourgeoisie of the U.S. and Britain reneged on Crimea and were to force a rupture in American–Soviet–British relations—that this would engender new aggressions, great suffering, damage and untold hardship for the world and not least of all for the American people. This is why everything must be done to preserve and strengthen the unity of the Big Three.

Yet we cannot agree that the only alternative to Browder's concept of the Grand Alliance is chaos, anarchy and the end of civilization. Browder has not yet drawn all the necessary conclusions from this war of national liberation in which there has emerged a stronger and a more influential Soviet Union, a new and democratic Europe and a stronger world labor movement. These historic developments certainly are an indispensable part of the world of reality; they are an essential basis and an organic part of the anti-Hitlerite coalition—a part and basis which has already created an entirely new relationship of world forces, irrevocably strengthening the cause of world democracy and national freedom.

3.

Many readers of *Cahiers du Communisme* have asked us for clarification on the dissolution of the Communist Party of the USA and the creation of the Communist Political Association. . . .

The reasons for dissolution of the Communist Party in the USA and for the "new course" in the activity of American Communists are set forth in official documents of the Party and in a certain number of speeches of its former secretary, Earl Browder.

In his speech devoted to the results of the Teheran Conference and the political situation in the United States, delivered December 12, 1943, in Bridgeport [Connecticut] and published in the *Communist* magazine in January 1944, Earl Browder for the first time discussed the necessity of changing the course of the CPUSA.

The Teheran Conference[15] served as Browder's point of departure from which to develop his conceptions favorable to a change of course of the American CP. However, while justly stressing the importance of the Teheran Conference for victory in the war against fascist Germany, Earl Browder drew from the Conference decisions erroneous conclusions in nowise flowing from a Marxist analysis of the situation. . . .

Earl Browder declared in effect, that at Teheran capitalism and socialism had begun to find the means of peaceful co-existence and collaboration in the framework of one and the same world; he added that the Teheran accords regarding common policy similarly presupposed common efforts with a view of reducing to a minimum or completely suppressing methods of struggle and opposition of force to force in the solution of internal problems of each country.

To put the Teheran policy into practice, Earl Browder considers that it is necessary to reconstruct the entire political and social life of the U.S. . . .

Such are the facts. Such are the elements of understanding which permit passing judgement on the dissolution of the American Communist Party. French Communists will not fail to examine in the light of Marxist-Leninist critique the arguments developed to justify the dissolution of the American Communist Party. One can be sure that, like the Communists of the Union of South Africa and of Australia, the French Communists will not approve the policy followed by Browder for it has swerved dangerously from the victorious Marxist-Leninist doctrine whose rigorously scientific application could lead to but one conclusion, not to dissolve the American Communist Party, but to work to strengthen it under the banner of stubborn struggle to defeat Hitler Germany and destroy everywhere the extensions of fascism. . . .

We too, in France, are resolute partisans of national unity and we show that in our daily activity; but our anxiety for unity does not make us lose sight for a single moment of the necessity of arraying ourselves against the men of the trusts.

Everyone understands that the Communist Party of the United States wants to work to achieve unity in their country. But it is less understandable that they envisage the solution of the problem of national unity with the good will of the men of the trusts, and under quasi-idyllic conditions as if the capitalist regime had been able to change its nature by some unknown miracle.

In truth, nothing justifies the dissolution of the American Communist Party, in our opinion. Browder's analysis of capitalism in the United States is not distinguished by a judicious application of Marxism-Leninism. The predictions regarding a sort of disappearance of class contradictions in the United States correspond in nowise to a Marxist-Leninist understanding of the situation. . . .

And it is clear that if Comrade Earl Browder had seen, as a Marxist-Leninist, this important aspect of the problems facing liberty-loving peoples in this moment in their history, he would have arrived at a conclusion quite other than the dissolution of the Communist Party of the United States.

4.

The military defeat of Nazi Germany is a great historic victory for world democracy; for all mankind. This epochal triumph was brought about by the concerted action of the Anglo–Soviet–American coalition—by the decisive blows of the Red Army, by the American–British offensives and by the heroic struggle of the resistance movements. This victory opens the way for the complete destruction of fascism in Europe and weakens the forces of reaction and fascism everywhere. It has already brought forth a new anti-fascist unity of the peoples in Europe marked by the formation in a number of countries of democratic governments representative of the will of the people and by the labor-progressive election victory in Great Britain.

The crushing of Hitler Germany has also created the conditions for the complete defeat and destruction of fascist Japanese imperialism. The winning of complete victory in this just war of national liberation is the first prerequisite for obtaining peace and security in the Far East, for the democratic unification of China as a free and independent nation and for the attainment of national independence by the peoples of Indonesia, Indochina, Burma, Korea, Formosa, the Philippines and India. The smashing of fascist-militarist Japan is likewise essential to help guarantee the efforts of the United Nations to build a durable peace.

All these crucial objectives are of vital importance to the national interests of the American people; to the struggle for the complete destruction of fascism everywhere. Now with the defeat of Nazi Germany and the axis, the possibility of realizing an enduring peace and of making new democratic advances and social progress has been opened up for the peoples by the weakening of reaction and fascism on a world scale and the consequent strengthening of the worldwide democratic forces.

However, a sharp and sustained struggle must still be conducted to realize these possibilities. This is so because the economic and social roots of fascism in Europe have not yet been fully destroyed. This is so because the extremely powerful reactionary forces in the United States and England, which are centered in the trusts and cartels, are striving to reconstruct liberated Europe on a reactionary basis. Moreover, this is so because the most aggressive circles of American imperialism are endeavoring to secure for themselves political and economic domination in the world.

The dominant sections of American finance capital supported the war against Nazi Germany, not because of hatred for fascism or a desire to liberate suffering Europe from the heel of Nazi despotism, but because it recognized in Hitler Germany a dangerous imperialist rival determined to rule the world. From the very inception of the struggle against fascism, American finance capital feared the democratic consequences of defeating Hitler Germany. . . .

Only when these policies proved to be bankrupt, meeting growing opposition from the ranks of the people, from the millions of patriotic Americans fighting in our heroic armed forces and working in war production. Only when it became obvious that the Soviet Union was emerging from the war stronger and more influential than ever, precisely because of its valiant and triumphant all-out war against nazism, did American capital reluctantly and belatedly move toward the establishment of a concerted military strategy and closer unity among the Big Three. . . .

On the home front the big trusts and monopolies are blocking the development of a satisfactory program to meet the human needs of reconversion, of the problems of economic dislocations and severe unemployment, which is beginning to take place and will become more acute after the defeat of Japan. Reactionary forces—especially the NAM and their representatives in government and Congress—are beginning a new open-shop drive to smash the trade unions. They also endeavor to rob the Negro people of their war-time gains. They are trying to prevent the adoption of governmental measures which must be enacted at once if our country is to avoid the most acute consequences of the trying reconversion period and the cyclical economic crisis which is bound to arise after the war. Likewise, they are vigorously preparing to win a reactionary victory in the crucial 1946 elections.

Already the reactionaries are using the increased cutbacks to lower wages and living standards and to provoke strikes in war industry. They are obstructing the enactment of necessary emergency measures for federal and state unemployment insurance. They are sponsoring vicious anti-labor legislation, such as the new Ball–Burton–Hatch labor relations bill and are blocking the passage of the FEPC [Fair Employment Practices Committee] and anti-poll-tax bills. They are trying to scuttle effective price and rent control and to exempt the wealthy and the big corporations from essential tax legislation. They are endeavoring to place the entire cost of the war and the difficulties of reconversion upon the shoulders of the working people. . . .

To forge [the] democratic coalition most effectively and to enable it to exercise decisive influence upon the affairs of the nation, it is essential that the working class—especially the progressive labor movement and the Communists—strengthen its independent role and activities and display far greater political and organizing initiative. It is imperative that maximum unity of action be developed among the C.I.O., the A.F. of L. and the Railroad Brotherhoods, and that their full participation in the new World Federation of Trade Unions be achieved. It is necessary to rally and imbue the membership and lower officials of the A.F. of L. with confidence in their ability to fight against and defeat the reactionary policies and leadership typified by the Greens, Wolls, Hutchesons and Dubinskys. . . .

The American Communist movement confidently faces the future. We are proud of our consistent and heroic struggle against reaction and fascism over the years. We draw strength from and are particularly proud of our efforts to promote victory over Nazi barbarism and Japanese imperialism.

☐ ———————————————————————————————— ☐

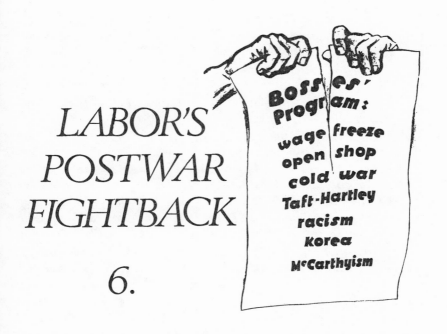

LABOR'S POSTWAR FIGHTBACK

Bosses' Program:
wage freeze
open shop
cold war
Taft-Hartley
racism
Korea
McCarthyism

6.

The end of the most barbaric war in history also ended the colonial empires of Great Britain, France, Holland and Japan: movements for national liberation barred the restoration of the old system. Imperialism had suffered a severe weakening of its structure. The United States, having emerged as the dominant imperialist power, flexed its muscles, ready to fill the void left by the weakened colonial empires.

Simultaneously, socialist states arose on the ruins of archaic-feudal and fascist regimes in eastern and central Europe and in Asia. A world system of socialist states was now a reality. The Soviet Union, having led in the defeat of nazism, rebuilt its widespread shattered industrial areas with phenomenal speed. Here was the opportunity for the United States and the USSR to lead in the creation of a world at peace. But United States cold warriors were in no mood for such an eventuality.

Furthermore, the United States aimed to dictate its policies to west European states. In the April 1948 Italian elections it rushed aid in an effort to stave off a leftward move of the electorate. It *mobilized Italian-Americans, trade unions and fraternal organizations to correspond with their families and friends, urging them to vote for the Christian Democratic Party. More significantly, it sent the Seventh Fleet to the Mediterranean. Three years later, with less vigor, it sought to intervene in the French elections. These were brazen interventions by the United States in the domestic affairs of its allies.*

As the war ended, workers at home were in no mood to continue the wartime economic restrictions. They would not endure the wage freeze and the end of price controls. The new year opened with strikes embracing nearly every major industry in the country. In 1946 there were 5,000 strikes involving 4,600,000 workers in a record surge of action. Steel, coal, automobile, railroad and electrical were involved, and the government under Truman struck back with aid to the employers. Despite a court fine of $3,500,000 against the United Mine Workers, a 59-day walkout won the union a Welfare and Retirement Fund, a pace-setting advance which other unions sought to emulate. Truman, who posed as a friend of labor, further revealed the falsity of this label when he threatened to use the army against the railroad workers.

Early in 1946, more than 300,000 packinghouse workers took to the picket lines. Ten days later the government seized the plants but the union refused to knuckle under. A month passed until the government ordered a 16-cent an hour increase for the union, a hike of 20 percent. Central to this victory was the growth of Black and white unity. No other industry with the exception of lumber, tobacco and personal services employed more Blacks than meatpacking. The Communist Party had been the leading factor in knitting together this solid alignment against the packing corporations.[1]

While previous postwar periods were marked by rising unemployment and business stagnation, the four years after World War II saw national production increasing from 215 to 259 billion dollars. Corporation profits during the war and after had no restrictions comparable to the wage freeze. When President Roosevelt had proposed, during the war, that personal income be limited to $25,000 annually, the high-salaried executives retorted by threatening non-cooperation in production. And between 1945 and 1949, corporate profits before taxes leaped 47 percent, or over three times as much as wages and salaries. In 1946 alone corporate profits before taxes increased 25 percent over the previous year. In 1947 profits in the iron and steel industry almost doubled over the previous year—$1.1 billion to $1.9 billion. In the automobile and parts industry the 1947 profit figure was $1.9 billion, 10 times greater than in 1946.[2]

A large portion of returning veterans were absorbed into the work force; others elected to make use of federally financed educational courses. Wages were forced upward, but the gains in compensation were offset by a 70 percent jump in the cost of living which resulted from the lifting by Congress of price controls.

For US industry to proceed with its design for global expansion, it was vital that the trade unions be pushed back to the state that existed before the emergence of the powerful CIO. The fraternal alliance between the CIO and unions in other countries could flower into formidable opposition to the expansionist aims of US financial circles. This required subverting the CIO leadership, shackling the unions through restrictive laws and promoting anti-red hysteria. The first step in this direction, as the monopolists saw it, was the suppression of the Communist Party.

The opening salvo fired against the labor movement was the enactment of the Taft-Hartley Act. The closed shop was enmeshed in a maze of legalistic obstructions written into the law. Union contributions for political action were forbidden and union leaders were required to take a non-communist oath if they were to obtain the services of the National Labor Relations Board in elections to select union representation. This latter provision, together with the Marshall Plan, proved to be a lever for division within the CIO and for the weakening of its militant character.

President Philip Murray of the CIO had been nurtured in the family of John L. Lewis' bureaucratic machine which controlled the mineworkers' union and denied participation by the rank and file. It was necessary for Murray to hide his autocratic practices and adopt a progressive posture in the drive for industrial unionism. In 1946 he declared: "We ask no man his national origin, his religion or his beliefs.... Our union has not been and will not be an instrument of repression. . . . As a democratic institution we

227

engage in no purges, no witch-hunts. . . ." And in 1947 Murray said that all affiliated unions had autonomy and that the national body was without the power to expel.

All these fine-sounding words were erased when at the 1949 CIO convention Murray and a majority of the leadership combined to expel the 450,000 members of the United Electrical, Radio and Machine Workers, followed shortly thereafter by the expulsion of 10 other unions. It was significant that the burden of the accusations by Murray and his associates was the refusal of the eleven unions to endorse positions that were part and parcel of US imperialism's projects abroad. To draw support from the AFL leadership for Truman's break with the wartime alliance was, however, a simpler matter.

On April 23, 1945, less than two weeks after he succeeded Franklin Delano Roosevelt as president, Harry S. Truman gave a preview of the cold war style that was to mark his entire term in office. He received the Soviet foreign minister, V.M. Molotov, who was en route to the April 25 founding session of the United Nations in San Francisco, and treated him with extreme rudeness. Less than a year later Truman invited Winston Churchill to speak at Fulton, Missouri, where the former prime minister called for a US–Great Britain alliance against the Soviet Union. It was a war-inciting harangue giving backing to the president's constant endeavor to persuade the public that "the Russians are coming," a phrase that has become a stock false alarm sounded by every succeeding administration to justify more billions for the Pentagon. Churchill's speech also did spadework to pave the way for the North Atlantic Treaty Organization (NATO) in 1949, which drew in western Europe, the United States, and Canada to form an aggressive military bloc.

In 1947, with the granting of financial and military assistance to Greece and Turkey, there evolved the Truman Doctrine, whereby, under the cloak of "combatting communism," the United States intervened to smother the Greek revolutionary forces and to wipe out any democratic or left movement. (See also p. 252.) With this step Washington replaced Great Britain, which could no longer finance its self-appointed police rule in the Mediterranean; from the Suez Canal to Gibraltar, its waters were considered by the US

Navy as "our lake." The Truman Doctrine was enunciated by George Kennan, a State Department expert on the Soviet Union in these words: "... the main element of any United States policy toward the Soviet Union must be that of a long-term patient but firm and vigilant containment of Russian expansive tendencies..." Kennan in later years, faced with the hard facts of history, was to repudiate his "containment" proposal on the grounds that he had been misunderstood.

The AFL rushed to endorse the plan by Secretary of State George C. Marshall whereby billions were to be poured into Europe for three principal reasons: to gain a dominating economic and political control, to rearm Europe with hostility toward the Soviet Union and the new socialist states, and to curb Communist and Left influences among the electorate and in particular the trade unions.

It was harder to persuade the CIO to sing in concert with the AFL officialdom, but Murray brought Marshall to the 1947 convention to push his scheme under the label of benevolence. By 1948 the Marshall Plan and the cold war program gained approval. Thus monopoly influence was succeeding in drawing a large part of the trade union leadership into the role of accomplices in the expansionist design of imperialism. This was accompanied by the weakening of class unity and the blunting of struggles for improvements in wages and working conditions.

Typical of the misleaders of labor was James B. Carey, a protégé of Murray and national secretary of the CIO, who said: "In the last war we joined with the Communists to fight the fascists. In another war we will join with the fascists to defeat the Communists." Anti-Semites and fugitives from justice who were wanted for trial for war crimes were protected and given sanctuary in the United States. Brutal dictators who cried out against socialism or communism were rewarded with support that enabled them to stamp out any vestige of democracy.

Congress was diligently serving its masters with a ferocious and many-sided assault on the Communist Party. While the Communists were designated as the "enemy," there came a flood of legislative proposals of such wide construction that they would make null and void the Bill of Rights whenever the government decided

229

on prosecution of protesters, petitioners or any advocates of change. The FBI began the accumulation of names of "subversives" which ran into the millions.

Even before the war—1938—a Committee on Un-American Activities had been established by the House, and it spent millions of dollars in harassment of Left and liberal activists. The Committee laid traps for contempt of Congress convictions when it was unable to find "cooperative" witnesses for its reactionary conspiracies.[3] Contempt citations were brought against those unwilling to finger associates and friends.

In the feverish war-inciting atmosphere, new anti-democratic laws were passed, and existing repressive legislation was brought out for use. Under these circumstances sentiment for a peace ticket in the 1948 elections began to materialize.

Former vice-president Henry A. Wallace—who had been denied renomination in 1944 by President Roosevelt in favor of Truman—became the nominee of the newly-formed Progressive Party. He drew the support of the Communist Party, a small part of labor's rank and file, and a section of the middle class and intellectuals. The leadership of the AFL supported Truman and denounced the peace stand of Wallace, the keystone of his platform.

Lacking a substantial base in labor, short on financing, targeted by red-baiters and denied publicity by the press, Wallace's vote was below expectation; but he did give the electorate a choice. Truman won an upset victory. To some degree this was due to the last minute defection of Wallace supporters who dreaded the prospect of the arch-reactionary Dewey as president. They were deceived by Truman, who put on the pretense of a peace advocate even to the extent of appearing to share some of Wallace's ideas.

□ ——————————————————————————— □

THE POSTWAR STRIKE WAVE

"Lessons of the Strike Struggles" by Jack Stachel,
Political Affairs, March 1946

[*The postwar strike wave, in which workers tried to make up for the years of the wage freeze—and catch up with rampant inflation—was covered in numerous articles in the Communists' daily and periodical press as indicated in the selections which follow.*

In the steel industry alone, 750,000 workers walked out. Art Shields, who has been a reporter for the Daily Worker *and* Daily World *for over fifty years, covered the steel strike for his paper. The steel mills, he found, were shut from coast to coast. Writing from Pittsburgh, the national center of the Steelworkers Union, he reported that the "entire steel industry from Baltimore to San Francisco went down at the same moment." (*Daily Worker, *January 21, 1946.) The only exception was the Kaiser plant at Fontana, California, which reached an agreement with the union. This was the response of the working class to monopoly's offensive.*

Jack Stachel (1900–1965) came into the Party in its early years from the youth movement. He assumed the leadership of the TUUL in 1932, when William Z. Foster fell ill. In 1948 he was one of the 12 members of the National Board of the Communist Party arrested under the Smith Act. At that time he was national educational secretary of the Party. He was sentenced to five years in prison and fined $10,000 for conspiring to "teach and advocate" the philosophical and economic theories of Marx, Engels and Lenin.]

At no time in the history of the United States have so many workers been on strike at the same time as at the beginning of this year. . . . The workers involved included entire industries, as in the case of the steel and the packinghouse workers, the majority of the workers employed by the giant electrical manufacturing corporations, all employees of General Motors, and the farm equipment workers. Outstanding local strikes during this period included A.F. of L. machinists, the Western Union employees in New York, the Western Electric workers in New Jersey, the A.F. of L. tugboatmen in New York, and numerous strikes of the A.F. of L., C.I.O., and independent union workers in diverse industries in all parts of the country. . . . Prior to this high point in the wage and strike movement, other workers had already gained a rise in wages either through strikes, as in the case of the oil workers and the New York longshoremen, or through direct collective bargaining negotiations, as in the case of the men's clothing workers, textile workers, leather workers, etc.

Thus it can be said that the wage movement in the immediate postwar period, not only became nationwide, but actually embraced the majority of the organized workers. And while the C.I.O. unions were in the forefront of both the wage and strike struggles, the wage demands and the strikes embraced large sections of the A.F. of L. workers, the independent unions, and in some cases unorganized workers as well. An outstanding feature of these struggles is the large number of utility workers and white collar workers, largely unorganized, or organized into independent unions, which entered the struggle for the first time. . . .

The breadth, depth, and momentum of the wage and strike movements, the solidarity and resoluteness of the strikers, and the strong solidarity of all workers with the strikers are due, not only to the growing maturity of the labor movement, but also to the serious drop in take-home pay resulting from a cut in the hours of employment, abolition of premium pay, downgrading, etc. The C.I.O. proved conclusively that during the war the basic wage rates had increased only 16 per cent, while the increase in the cost of living amounted to a minimum of 45 per cent. With workers going back to a 40-hour week at the mere basic rates, and with the cost of living threatened even further as price control was increasingly being undermined, it was inevitable that the workers, now organized 14-million-strong into their trade unions, would not accept this deterioration of their living standards. Another factor playing a role in the development of this struggle was the growing realization that the monopolists were out to weaken and undermine the trade unions preparatory to a more frontal attack both on the living standards of the workers and the trade unions, once they succeeded in weakening the unions.

The more progressive of the labor organizations were fully aware of the relationship of the struggle for full employment to the struggle for wage increases. The mass layoffs following V-J Day, involving many millions and hitting hardest at the Negro and women workers, resulted in a renewed demand on the part of the workers for the passage of the Murray Full Employment Bill [introduced by Sen. James E. Murray (D.-Mont.) in the 79th Congress, January 1945], for the raising of unemployment benefits uniformly throughout the country to a maximum of $25 a week for 26 weeks, and for a permanent Fair Employment Practices Committee [FEPC]. Big business, on the other hand, bent

232

upon reducing the workers' living standards, anxious for a large reserve army of unemployed, seeking to promote division between the white and Negro workers—all for the purpose of taking the offensive against the workers and the trade unions—unloosed the most vicious campaign against these legislative proposals. Thus far, in this fight, the labor and people's movement has been unable to rally its forces to the maximum extent. With the growing wage and strike struggles there has even been a weakening of this fight and an insufficient realization of the interrelationship of the struggle on these questions with those of the wage demands and the defense of the trade unions. The full employment bill has in fact been turned into almost its opposite. The increased unemployment compensation bill has been pigeonholed, and the FEPC legislation has again been shelved through the shameful filibuster of the poll-tax Senators in connivance with the reactionary Republicans and the passive acquiescence of the Truman Administration.

The relationship of the legislative struggle to that on the picket lines is now being brought home to the workers by the attempt to force through Congress vicious anti-labor legislation for curbing unions, while the courts are being used in increasing cases in an attempt to lay the basis for breaking the strikes through the infamous injunctions. What is also being brought home to all the common people, is the fact that the workers' struggle for wages, for the protection of their unions, and for progressive legislation, is a people's fight, that the struggle carried on by the trade unions is in reality a struggle in behalf of all the common people against the conspiracy of the trusts.

This conspiracy represents an assault upon the great mass of the people. Able to pay more than the full $2-a-day wage increase demanded by most of the workers, the trusts refused to pay unless they received price increases which would not only cover this increase but be much in excess of it. At the same time, the monopolists, by putting forward their so-called company security demands, coupled their fight for price increases with an attempt to rob the unions of the protection they had gained for the workers in the form of union security. This demand on their part is, in substance, an effort to do away with the closed shop, maintenance of membership clauses, etc., and in fact lays the basis for the return of the open shop and unrestricted company dictatorship over the workers' right to work and their working conditions.

But not all the plans of Big Business, in its assault on the workers' living standards and the trade unions, have materialized. One of their most important aims was to utilize the returning war veterans against labor, as they had done with much success after the First World War....

The returning veterans have quickly learned the true facts and can now see for themselves the responsibility of the arrogant and profit-soaked trusts for the present strikes. They can see that in these attacks on the labor movement there is also an attack against their own living standards and against their families. The result is that the returning veterans are almost everywhere among the most active strikers and in many cases are among the leading forces on the picket lines, in the strike committee, and in other phases of the activity in winning the workers' demands. The veterans could play an even greater role if the unions would in all cases realize the great contribution they have to make and take measures to bring about their full support and activity. . . .

Despite the failure of a number of trade unions to take up the fight for the Negroes' right to work and the generally insufficient struggle on the part of the unions against the mass layoffs of Negro workers following V–J Day, the Negro workers are, in the present strike struggles, displaying the same militancy and maturity that they have already displayed in the course of a number of years in the economic and political struggles of labor and the people as a whole. With the great strike of the packinghouse workers as the outstanding example, Negro workers are to be found in the forefront of the struggle everywhere. These same workers who, in the period following the First World War, were brought North by the capitalists in an attempt to crush the workers' struggle, are today among the most progressive and militant trade unionists. At this point it must be stated, however, that most of the trade unions, including some of the more progressive, have not yet drawn the Negro workers to any large degree into the leading bodies of the unions, and that this narrow and dangerous course is also reflected in the setting up of the strike machinery. In addition, the labor movement cannot continue to neglect the necessary fight for the right of the Negro workers to all jobs without discrimination.

The strike struggles have everywhere exposed all the strong and weak sides of the labor movement. These gigantic strikes showed for the first time that those unions that had made good advances in building progressive and democratic organizations, had prepared the workers ideologically, had brought about a greater participation of the membership in the inner life of the unions, and had taken up the fight against anti-Negro discrimination, were able to develop the maximum strike activity, involvement in mass picketing, etc. . . .

The Communists are almost everywhere playing an important role in helping to forge victory for the striking workers, a victory in which the future of the whole labor movement and of all progressive America is involved. Those Communists belonging to unions directly involved in the strike struggles are, as was to be expected, in the forefront of the struggle on the picket lines, in helping to unify the workers, in relief activity, in the mobilization of mass support to their unions. In those areas and industries where the Communists are more numerous among the workers, or even if few in numbers have established themselves among the workers on the basis of their union activity, it is almost universally true that the strike struggles are better organized and a greater section of the workers is being involved. In such cases, mass picketing is more quickly developed and company provocations more easily met. . . .

The Communist organizations have made some efforts to bring *The Worker,* the *Daily Worker,* and the left and progressive foreign language press to the strikers. While the actual number of papers sold or distributed is small in comparison with the number of workers involved in the strike struggles, these papers are having, in many cases, a significant influence on the strikes because they reach key workers active in the strike struggles, and influence the thinking of many others. One of the great contributions made by the Communists and the Communist press is the exposure of the provocative activities of the counter-revolutionary Trotskyites who, camouflaging themselves in the mantle of militancy, are trying to disrupt the unity of the workers and the strategy of the C.I.O. led by Murray.

Without being boastful or self-satisfied, the Communists of the United States, under the leadership of Comrade Foster, can be proud of the contributions they are making to labor's victory. They are able to do this only because they have corrected, in time, the situation which existed in the Communist movement until last May. Had Browderism continued to dominate our movement, the Communists would today be isolated from these great struggles. . . .

In the struggle to forge a broad anti-fascist people's coalition in the struggle for peace, for greater economic security, and for the defense and extension of the people's democratic liberties, our Party will grow in numbers and maturity. It will help the workers understand the nature of the struggle and the ultimate solution of the pressing problems of today. It will, by always being part of the broadest movement of the people, and yet never forgetting its principles and its independent role, make the greatest contributions to the struggles of today and educate and prepare the people in the struggle for socialism.

THE COLD WAR BEGINS

The Menace of a New World War by **William Z. Foster,**
New Century Publishers, 1946

[*A speech made by Sir Winston Churchill at Fulton, Missouri, on March
5, 1946, is recognized as one of the opening salvos of the cold war.*

*In fact, the cold war began very hot indeed on August 6, 1945.[4] On that
day the first of two monstrous atomic bombs was dropped on Japan by
the United States. Japan was already offering peace proposals via the
USSR. The Soviet Union entered the war against Japan, as previously
agreed among the allies, on August 9. The imminent defeat of Japan
without heavy US losses was a foregone conclusion.*

*Thus the great anti-fascist wartime alliance against the axis powers
began to deteriorate even before the end of World War II. Truman was
present on the platform when Churchill, with the president's approval,
made his aggressive anti-Soviet "Iron Curtain" speech at Fulton.*

*The outstanding historian D.F. Fleming characterized Churchill's
Fulton speech as a "... world crusade to smash world communism in the
name of Anglo-Saxon democracy. In print, Churchill's battlecry became
the bible of every warmonger in the world."[5]*

*Two days after the Churchill speech, the Communist Party rallied
15,000 people to a meeting at Union Square in New York City, on March
7, 1946. They heard Foster make a slashing attack against US foreign
policy. Portions of his speech appear below.*]

We are gathered together in historic Union Square at a grave moment in
world history. The imperialists in the United States and Great Britain are
trying to stampede the peoples into another world war. This constitutes a
deadly national danger, one which must be faced boldly. World War II is
still on officially; our soldiers are not yet back from the battlefields. Yet
the reactionaries are already trying to launch World War III. It used to be
that they would let a generation elapse between world wars, but now, like
chain cigarette smokers, they light one war from the other.

Winston Churchill's speech yesterday in Fulton, Mo., was a call for a
general capitalist war against the Soviet Union. Make no mistake about
that being what he was driving at. His proposed Anglo-American
military alliance, directed against the U.S.S.R. and the colonial peoples,
is an up-to-date version of Hitler's anti-Comintern Axis. His speech was
built around the Red bogey and the whole business stank of fascism. It

was the voice of Churchill but the hand of Hitler. Such an anti-Soviet tirade is not to be wondered at, coming from a man who only a few years ago was full of praise for Mussolini and who declared that if he were an Italian he would be a fascist.

The war that Churchill wants would necessarily be a war against democracy all over the world. It would be aimed not only to overthrow the first Socialist Republic, but especially to smash the colonial liberation movements in Britain's sphere in the Middle and Far East, to undermine the new democracies in Europe and to curb the workers in Great Britain, the United States and other countries. The people of this country and the world won't stand for such an imperialist war and they will give Churchill a resounding "No!" that will ring around the world.

How could it be that the diehard old Tory Churchill, driven out of office by his own people, could dare to make such a war-mongering speech in the United States? For this outrage our government is heavily responsible. Churchill's speech was fully in line with the American Government's get-tough-with-Russia policy and it fits right in with similar speeches made a few days earlier by Secretary of State Byrnes and Senator Vandenberg. President Truman himself bears direct responsibility because he deliberately staged Churchill's speech and he gave it his virtual endorsement beforehand. In taking such action, together with many others of his foreign policies, President Truman violated the peace mandate given to President Roosevelt and himself by the American people in the last elections.

The British Labor Government is no less responsible for the war-provoking speech of Churchill. It also is following a get-tough-with-Russia policy in the American pattern. Foreign Secretary Bevin's violent Soviet-baiting prepared the way for Churchill. This hard-boiled Tory never would have ventured to make the firebrand speech he did had he not received direct encouragement from the course being followed by the Attlee [Labor Party] Government. . . .

Churchill in his speech poured out insults upon the Communists of the world, challenging their spirit of democracy and patriotism. What a contemptible ingrate! Has he forgotten so soon that had it not been for the Communist-led Soviet Union and its gallant Red Army, his country and the rest of the world would now be under the boot of fascist conquerors? And as for the patriotism of the Communists, we may be sure of one thing, that everywhere they will do their utmost to save their peoples from being plunged into the imperialist bloodbath that Churchill and his fellow British and American monopolists are preparing for them. The Communists will not fail in this high patriotic duty.

Churchill's speech—with Byrnes' and Vandenberg's—will sharpen political tensions all over the world; it will deepen the already dangerous division among the Big Three powers; it will bring good cheer to the remnants of fascism in Germany, Japan and elsewhere; it will be meat and drink to Soviet-baiters and all reactionaries throughout the world; it will extend more than a ray of hope to the Goerings, Hesses and Ribbentrops in the prisoners' dock at Nuremburg; it will hearten reaction in Turkey, Iran and China and make more difficult a friendly settlement of the differences between these countries and the U.S.S.R.; it will bring grist to the anti-Soviet crusade of the Vatican; it will give renewed vigor to the predatory monopolists of the United States—all of which reactionary ends are precisely what Churchill wants to accomplish. . . .

The cold fact is that the great monopolists of the United States, who are now dictating our foreign policy, are aiming at establishing American imperialist domination over the rest of the world, with the British Empire serving as a sort of junior partner. It is this imperialist drive by the US, abetted by the British, that is the root cause of the present split among the Big Three powers.

The United States, coming out of the war with its cities undamaged, with its industries enormously expanded, with tremendous armed forces, with fabulous gold supplies, with the atom bomb under its control—is far and away the richest and most powerful capitalist country in the world. The great monopolists want to cash in on this superior American strength in the midst of a starving war-devastated world. They believe that now is the time to begin to realize the "American Century" of Henry Luce. Hence, all over the world, with the aid of President Truman, they are carrying on policies of aggression and expansion that are threatening the peace of the nations.

□ ———————————————————————————— □

COLD WAR IN THE CIO

"Expulsions and Union Wrecking,"
American Labor—Which Way?
by George Morris, New Century Publishers, 1961

[*After the great strike wave of 1946, big business launched an offensive against the unions with the full cooperation of the government. The principal weapon was the Taft-Hartley Law of 1947. One of its most sinister and disruptive features was a requirement that all union officials must sign affidavits certifying that they were not Communists. A number of provisions negated the gains made by labor in the struggles which culminated in passage of the Wagner Act of 1935.*

The right-wing labor bureaucracy made its accommodation to these anti-democratic government strictures in the hope that it could operate without interference. It failed in this effort. This is an excerpt from the Morris pamphlet.]

The climax of the drive to tie the unions to the cold war chariot came in the fall of 1949 when the convention of the CIO expelled 10 unions with a million members for alleged "Communist" domination. The basic charge against these unions was their refusal to endorse the Marshall Plan (of aid to countries on condition of forming an alliance against the Soviet Union) and their refusal to endorse the candidacy of Harry Truman for the presidency in 1948. That action was the consequence of four years of the most intense anti-Communist hysteria ever whipped up in unions. The House Committee on Un-American Activities called each of the unions on the target list before its hearings, for "exposures" of their "red" influences. The newspapers and radio commentators made the most of those hearings for screaming headlines. The government meanwhile brought out its Smith Act indictments against the leaders of the Communist Party and enacted the McCarran anti-Communist law. This was clearly timed to fan the hysteria and throw fear into those who hesitated to conform to cold-war policy.

Having succumbed to the pressure, the CIO leaders quickly made up for their hesitations. In place of the expelled 500,000 member United Electrical, Radio and Machine Workers [UE] the CIO chartered another union under the presidency of James B. Carey (IUE). With the aid of immense finances, the government and even the clergy in many areas, a drive was launched to destroy the UE and file for bargaining elections in all the major plants under that union's contracts. . . .

The same wrecking operation was followed, or attempted, against the other expelled unions. Certain of those unions were almost wiped out. It should be further borne in mind that some months after the expulsions the Korea war broke out [1950]. The union-busters, happy to see the trade union leaders do their work, raised the cry that the smashing of the expelled unions was a "wartime urgency." To cap this period, after the war came the disgraceful McCarthyism era.

Every tactic, including strikebreaking, was considered "justified" against the expelled unions. In that period the reactionary forces invented the term "political picket line" to apply to strikes of the expelled unions. In view of what these unions had to go through for more than a decade, it is almost a miracle that a sizable section of them has survived.

Another heavy price paid for conformance to the cold war was CIO withdrawal from the World Federation of Trade Unions its leaders had helped to form five years earlier. The CIO leaders joined those of the AFL to cooperate with the State Department's move for the formation of a new organization, the International Confederation of Free Trade Unions. The first step in that direction was a European conference of the U.S. "labor attachés" in the Marshall Plan machinery of each of the 16 countries getting the funds. Thus also was inaugurated the junior partnership of the CIO leaders to the even more conservative AFL leaders. The cold war was the basis for that "unity."

How did the top union leaders sell the cold war program to their organizations? They relied principally on the widespread view that the cold war would be permanent and a hot war with the socialist countries was sure to come. They encouraged a belief that by jumping on the cold war bandwagon, the unions could gain a "respectability" and escape the harsh effects of the Taft-Hartley or other anti-union laws. They claimed that expulsion of left-led unions and a purge of unions of "communism" would clear the way for "easy" organization of the South. To Negro trade unionists, they held out the prospect of speedier progress for civil rights if the cold warriors were helped to influence the colored peoples in Asia, Africa and Latin America. Elimination of "communism" was also held out as a way to prevent enactment of new anti-labor laws. . . .

The most decisive factor to figure in the cold war perspective of the top trade union leaders was undoubtedly the skyrocketing military budget and the widely held view that a permanent high level military economy was a guarantee of permanent prosperity. They played on such illusions to build a ground for support of the policy of "peace through strength" and "preventive war" advocated by the most rabid cold-warriors.

The sad results of the program envisioned by the top leaders of America's unions are today plain for all to see. . . .

The heaviest price the trade unions paid for following the cold war course of their leaders . . . was the loss of much of the spirit of militancy, dedication and drive-ahead that had been built up through the hungry and fighting thirties. Much of the anti-fascist conscience of that period, too, faded. And coinciding with that process has been the mass retirement on Social Security in recent years of the main body of the fighting veterans of the thirties—those who waged the struggles of the unemployed of the thirties—who engaged in the strike sitdowns, who crusaded in the mass volunteer organizing drives in auto, steel, electrical, waterfront, textile and other of the newly-organized fields. The McCarthyism hysteria and its effect inside many unions also reduced rank-and-file participation in union life, in voluntary activity and initiative. . . .

The situation is far from one-sided, however. The inherent class spirit of the American working class remains in force and has repeatedly broken through the false facade of class collaboration the top trade union leaders often display.

□ —————————————————————————————— □

TELLING OFF THE "UN-AMERICANS"

"Ben Gold Raps Red-Baiters,"
Daily Worker, September 17, 1948

[*The attempt of the Un-American Activities Committee to use its hearings to discredit the International Fur and Leather Workers Union (CIO) backfired when its then president, Ben Gold, used the occasion to expose the violent employer-gangster alliance in the industry. Morris Langer, manager of the Newark, N.J. local, had been killed by hired gangsters. Other fur workers were beaten and maimed. Lepke and Gurrah, two notorious gangsters, were finally convicted on the courageous testimony offered by Irving Potash, a Communist leader of the fur union. The union was exemplary in its democratic procedure and in its gains for the workers.*

Speaking against the cold war at the Eleventh Constitutional Convention of the CIO in 1949, Gold declared that "when I came into this union I was not hiding that I was a member of the Party. . . ."

Here's how the Daily Worker *reported his 1948 confrontation with the Un-Americans.*]

Communists are the most conscious supporters of democracy and the most loyal and devoted Americans in the United States, Ben Gold, CIO Fur and Leather Workers Union President, today told the two-man House subcommittee investigating "Communist influences" in the fur industry.

In a heated exchange with Rep. Wingate Lucas (D., Tex.), Gold declared that the Communists will "fight to the death any fascist conspiracy to overthrow our democratically-elected government in our country."

The exchange climaxed a three-hour duel between Gold, Lucas and

241

the subcommittee chairman, Rep. Max Schwabe (R., Mo.). The two committee members repeatedly stopped Gold in his attempt to refute the charges made against the union by fur bosses.

Ignoring objection of the two impatient congressmen, Gold related the story of "gang rule" in the fur industry before right-wing and left-wing unionists consolidated their efforts to organize the industry.

"The worst kind of racket was organized by the employers and gunmen," Gold charged in the morning session. He said Lepke and Gurrah, the two notorious gangsters directing the racket in the industry, were convicted and sentenced largely on the testimony offered in open court by Sam Burt and Irving Potash,[6] two union leaders.

"And it's high time it became public knowledge that there was an effort made to put me on the payroll of the employers," Gold revealed. He said the offer was made to him by the late Sam Samuels, then president of the Fur Manufacturers Association.

He outlined the methods used by the manufacturers to break the union and maintain the split engendered between the right and left-wing furriers, by the bosses.

"Were these men promoting violence, Communists?" Schwabe asked, interrupting Gold. Gold flared up.

"No, these men were gunmen. Communists don't believe in force and violence. The Communists fought against the use of force and violence."

Later Gold enlarged on this statement when Schwabe asked him the same question.

"No one in our union used force and violence. If he did he'd be expelled. . . ." he said vigorously.

"No, we don't operate any spy rings in our union. Every worker has a right to talk about any kind of political belief he wants to," Gold explained.

After the hearing, Gold declared:

"Congress has opened up a new phase of undemocratic and un-American activities aimed at destroying the rights of the people. The investigations of trade unions have been undertaken under false pretense. Their real purpose is to intimidate labor, to slander the trade unions and destroy their effectiveness in the political and economic life of the nation.

"They are a continuation of the Taft-Hartley slave labor law. Further, they are aimed at every trade unionist who exercises his democratic right to support Wallace and the Progressive party which, in this critical period, is the hope of the nation for peace, progress and prosperity."

□ ── □

MUNDT-NIXON STOPPED

"7,500 Lobby in Capitol," *The Worker,* June 6, 1948

[*The Mundt-Nixon Bill was first trotted out in 1948 by Congressmen Karl Mundt and Richard Nixon of subsequent Watergate infamy. It passed the House on May 19, 1948, but could not be brought to a vote in the Senate because of mass opposition. The Communist Party helped initiate the most intense nationwide campaign for its defeat. It was the forerunner of the infamous McCarran Act which was passed in 1950. (See p. 277.)*]

Washington—Members of the U.S. Senate were reluctantly learning last week that the American people do not want any part of the Mundt–Nixon Police State Bill.

Attempts of Senate Judiciary Chairman Alexander Wiley (R-Wis) to narrow hearings on the bill to three days flopped in face of mounting protests from every state in the union and after a fourth day of hearings, 6,000 persons were still demanding to be heard.

Wiley's committee, bombarded by fresh protests, called an executive session to decide whether or not to hear the vast number of witnesses seeking to testify against the bill.

The committee heard Henry Wallace, Third Party presidential candidate, denounce the bill and ask why the Senate has enacted no legislation to curb the "real perpetrators of force and violence—the lynchers." He said the New Party would refuse to register if the Bill became law.

Paul Robeson, noted singer and actor, appeared at another session and lashed the so-called anti-Communist legislation, stating he would refuse to obey it. Robeson and Joseph Kehoe, CIO leader, were threatened with contempt citations by irate committee members when they refused to state whether they were or were not members of the Communist Party.

Communists are carrying on "a magnificent struggle for civil rights," Robeson told the committee. "I have many dear friends who are Communists and who are doing a magnificent job."

William Z. Foster, chairman of the Communist Party, told the committee the Mundt Bill "embodies the philosphy of our Axis enemies of World War II." He warned the committee against trying to place a curb on persons demanding to be heard against the bill. He charged the few days allotted by the Senate for hearings "are not enough for a bill which establishes a fascist state in America." . . .

As the demands to be heard mounted and delegations continued to pour into the capital, a special committee to coordinate activities of organizations fighting the Mundt Bill was set up. Jerry J. O'Connell, former Democratic Congressman from Montana, was elected chairman of the committee.

The committee coordinated work of two giant delegations that arrived here Wednesday.

Rep. Vito Marcantonio, who was among the first witnesses to testify against the Mundt legislation, urged all persons desiring to be heard by the Senators to send telegrams to all members of the Senate Judiciary Committee and not just to Chairman Wiley.

□ ———————————————————————————— □

HISTORY AS A WEAPON OF STRUGGLE

"Negro History: Arsenal for Liberation"
by Herbert Aptheker, *New Masses,* February 11, 1947

[The writing of history is a tool of the class in power. The glorious history of the American working class, the Black people and all of the oppressed has been distorted to suit the needs of the exploiting class. Frederick Engels, while preparing material for a "History of Ireland," observed that "the bourgeoisie turns everything into a commodity, hence also the writing of history. It is part of its being, of its condition for existence, to falsify all goods: it falsified the writing of history. . . ." (Karl Marx and Frederick Engels, Ireland and the Irish Question, *Progress Publishers, Moscow, 1971). History is part of ideological big business.*

Herbert Aptheker (b. 1915), Marxist historian, has made valuable contributions to the study of American history in general, and to the Black liberation movement in particular, over the past forty years. He has been editor of Masses and Mainstream, Political Affairs, *and* Jewish Affairs. *He is a member of the Central Committee of the CPUSA. Since the founding of the American Institute for Marxist Studies (AIMS) in 1964 he has been the Institute's director and editor of its popular newsletter.*

Dr. Aptheker is the author of numerous books, pamphlets and articles. Like a number of other Communist and progressive historians he has had to function largely outside collegiate confines—as did such scholars as Dr. Alphaeus Hunton and Elizabeth Lawson and many others. (Alphaeus Hunton is the author of Decision in Africa, *International Publishers, 1960. In a Foreword to the book, W.E.B. Du Bois wrote: "I know of no one today who has a more thorough knowledge and understanding of that continent." Elizabeth Lawson was a prolific pamphleteer who wrote extensively on American history.)*

In the article, abridged, the author sharply condemns those "historians" who have turned their profession into a defense of oppression. At the same time he affirms history's value as a liberating force.]

The United States announced its entry into the world of nations with a flaming manifesto of revolution, with the battlecry of "liberty or death," and while the words were being uttered, the brains of the rebels were seared by knowledge of the fact that twenty percent of their country's population was in chains! Atop the dome of this Republic's Capitol stands a heroic bronze female figure symbolizing the Goddess of Liberty. It was cast, shortly before the Civil War, by Negro slaves!

Our historiography mirrors, quite naturally, this schizophrenia. The writing and teaching of history are crafts peculiarly sensitive to the demands of the status quo, for here there are no allusions and there can be no abstractionists. One is, by definition, dealing with the people's past, and the dullest must see that the present is made up of the past, while a moment before the present was itself the future.

Fighters for the Negro people's liberation, understanding this, have been attempting for generations to rescue their past from oblivion and vilification. This is true of the Abolitionists, white men such as Joshua Coffin, John Brown and Wendell Phillips, and particularly Negroes, like William C. Nell, Martin Delany, James McCune Smith, William Wells Brown and Frederick Douglass; and it is true of the post–Civil War epoch. During the latter period Negro writers have again been outstanding in this regard. To be mentioned are such people as Joseph T. Wilson, George W. Williams, Daniel Murray and John W. Cromwell, while in our own day excellently-trained historians like Charles H. Wesley, L.D. Reddick, Luther P. Jackson, Lorenzo G. Greene, W. Sherman Savage, John H. Franklin, Alrutheus A. Taylor, Eric Williams, Horace M. Bond, James H. Johnston and, of course, the two Grand Old Men of the crusade whose works span two generations and who remain more prolific than any others—W.E.B. Du Bois and Carter G. Woodson— have been doing an invaluable job of spadework and pioneering.

Whites, too, particularly those who understand the indivisibility of human freedom, and even a handful of academicians, have joined in the effort to present, in realistic terms, the American Negro's past. Back in

1903 Professor James S. Bassett of Trinity College (now Duke University) was nearly fired for daring to suggest that the historical treatment of the Negro might need some revision. Starting over twenty years ago there began to appear the monumental source collections edited by Elizabeth Donnan (on the slave trade, in four volumes) and Helen T. Catterall (on judicial decisions, in five volumes) which, if only read and used, would help demolish the myth of Negro docility. Some fifteen years ago, Frederic Bancroft wrote an excellent study of the domestic slave-trading business, tearing up a segment of the moonlight-and-molasses nonsense, but only a relatively unknown Baltimore publisher would issue his work.

Six years ago the American Council of Learned Societies took its first hesitating steps towards the organization of a Council on Negro Studies, while at about the same time the American Historical Association devoted one session of a yearly meeting—the only one in sixty years!—to a consideration of the history of one-tenth of the American people. . . .

Having said all this, we have said much, and yet it remains true that the enemy still dominates the field. It remains true that Negro historiography, as a whole, is characterized by the two great sins of omission and distortion. . . .

Two of the outstanding living professors of American history, Henry S. Commager and Allan Nevins, edit a massive work supposed to present *The Heritage of America,* and the Negro is practically absent. Professor Dwight L. Dumond of the University of Michigan writes a book labeled *The Anti-Slavery Origins of the Civil War* in which he finds space to mention obscure white Abolitionists like Augustus Wattles and Calvin Waterbury; but not a single Negro—neither Douglass nor Tubman nor Ruggles, nor Ward, nor Garnet, nor Purvis, nor Truth—is so much as mentioned.

Probably even more common is distortion. One who has any regard whatsoever for truth stands aghast when he sees such statements as this, for example, appearing in W. E. Woodward's *Meet General Grant* (a Literary Guild selection, by the way): "The American negroes are the only people in the history of the world, so far as I know, that ever became free without any effort of their own. It [the Civil War] was not their business. They had not started the war nor ended it. They twanged banjos around the railroad stations, sang melodious spirituals, and believed that some Yankee would soon come along and give each of them forty acres of land and a mule." And what is one to say when a work like Myrdal's *An American Dilemma,* that is filled with dozens of demonstrably erroneous assertions of historical fact, including the remark that the Negro people were enfranchised "without their asking for it," is rapturously received by almost all experts and reviewers and when such egregious errors are not pointed out even by the handful of critical commentators. . . .

Such purblindness will persist so long as the outstanding professional historians insist upon dismissing scholars like Dr. Woodson and Dr. Du Bois as "propagandists and special pleaders," to quote the characterization offered me some years ago by a distinguished Columbia University professor. And it will persist so long as these historians do not realize that the Negro's past runs through the warp and woof of the fabric of America, that his history must be understood not only because it is the history of some fourteen million American citizens, but also because American life cannot be understood without knowing their history.

The study of the Negro's record is not an act of benevolence: it is an act of science.

Actually, of course, men like Woodson and Du Bois are "propagandists" only because their convictions are contrary to the dominant ideology, and "special pleaders" only because that for which they plead is disagreeable. This truth was enunciated with significant naiveté by Prof. Ellis Paxson Oberholtzer, an outstanding authority on nineteenth century America who, in 1903, explained to Dr. Du Bois that, in conducting the biographical series that he was then editing he was assigning the biographies of southern leaders like Jefferson Davis to "Southern writers as a guarantee of greater impartiality!" Again, in 1907, when Dr. Du Bois asked *McClure's Magazine* if they would publish a reply to several vicious anti-Negro pieces that had appeared therein, he was originally turned down on the ground that the magazine wished to avoid controversial articles! . . .

Why do omission and distortion characterize the treatment of the Negro's history? Very simply put, it is because of the super-exploitation of the Negro people, and because denying them an inspiring past worthy of study and emulation weakens them and their allies in the present-day efforts for equality and freedom.

How like men of straw would Americans be without Valley Forge and Gettysburg, without Jefferson, Paine, Lincoln, Altgeld and Debs! Without a past a people is castrated and impotent. As the embryo is nurtured within the womb and, with sufficient development, emerges in a cataclysmic act as a functioning human being, so history is the people's womb. From their history a people may gain sustenance, guidance, courage, dignity, maturity.

Specifically, let the Negro people know and let all other Americans know that in the unspeakable days of chattel slavery the American Negro fought like an enraged tiger for his freedom, that the Underground Railroad was his creation, that the Abolitionist movement's pioneers were Negroes, that that movement's greatest source of strength throughout its life was the Negro people, that in America's War for Independence Negroes by the thousands were vital participants, that the Navy which defied Britain in the War of 1812 was about one-fifth Negro, that 200,000 Negroes fought in Lincoln's Army and another 30,000 in his Navy, while still another quarter of a million labored for the Union, and that in the Civil War the Negroes suffered the greatest proportionate loss of any of the participants—let these things be understood and the ancient canard which holds that the Negro people, unique in history, were given their freedom would be seen for what it is—a colossal hoax and lie. The Negro people earned their freedom by fighting for it, and by so doing helped mightily to preserve this nation for all its inhabitants.

And let all Americans know of the Negro's militant efforts, long antedating the Civil War and continuing to this minute, for the right to vote and be elected to office, for equal educational opportunities, for labor solidarity, for decent jobs, for good homes, for political independence from the parties of the exploiters and their lackeys, for unity among all the dispossessed—Negro and white—let all this really be known and understood, and then decent white people might well be proud to grasp the outstretched hands of their Negro brethren with respect and with devotion.

The position of the Negro has ever been the touchstone, the acid test of American democracy. This is why the Negro is the first enemy, the original recipient of the blows, of reaction. The thorns upon the Negro's head have drawn blood from America's body. America's strange fruit has embittered the mouths of all its inhabitants.

He who knows the history of the Negro people will face the future with supreme confidence. For this history proves that, let the despoilers of humanity do what they will, the integrity, the aspirations and the struggles of the mass of mankind continue and endure.

Of the Negro people it may be said more truly than of any other people that they have had nothing to lose, in fighting for a better world, but their chains. This has forged with their hearts and brains a yearning for peace and security, a knowledge of the necessity for unity, and a contempt for the oppressor and the traitor which constitute a revolutionary potential of the utmost significance.

It is a duty and a necessity to resurrect and to treasure the precious heritage that the Negro people have bestowed upon America. This can serve as a weapon of incalculable power in our present critical period when each man and each woman must stand up and be counted.

□ ———————————————————————————————— □

MARITIME WORKERS IN POSTWAR USA

1. *Report of the National Secretary to the Sixth Convention of the National Maritime Union,* by Ferdinand C. Smith, National Secretary, September 1947;
2. "Women in NMU," *New York Herald Tribune,* May 25, 1946

[*The Communist Party's contributions in helping to build and strength-en the National Maritime Union (NMU) are an outstanding example of unity in action of a revolutionary working-class party and a militant trade union.*

Al Lannon, a leader of the Communist Party, was a founder of the union.[7] *Another Party member, Ferdinand C. Smith, became its first National Secretary, the highest elected post held by a Black worker in any union in the country.*

The first item below gives excerpts from Smith's report to the Sixth National Convention of the NMU in September 1947. It does not pretend to present the position of his Party. It depicts the united will of the NMU, of which the Communists were a part.

Ferdinand Smith's report is followed by an interview with NMU member Anne L. Conroy which appeared in the New York Herald-Tribune. *Ms. Conroy was elected in 1946 to the post of union patrolman. She received the second highest vote among the five chosen and was the only woman to fill this position—a remarkable achievement in the male-dominated maritime industry.*

When NMU head Joe Curran and others in the top labor bureaucracy went on their redbaiting binge, many Communists and left-minded workers, among them Conroy and her husband—Frank Novich, a seaman and ship's delegate since 1929—were expelled from the union. They were members of the Communist Party. Anne L. Conroy died in 1970.]

1.

The Sixth Constitutional Convention of the National Maritime Union comes at a critical time in the life of our country. No convention of the NMU has been faced with such urgent and varied problems as now confront us.

Our first convention in 1937 symbolized the successful struggle of the rank-and-file seamen to free themselves from the tyrannical yoke of the misleaders of the old International Seamen's Union. . . .

Our 1943 convention, held in New York in the middle of the war, dedicated itself to an all-out struggle for the defeat of world fascism and for strengthening the unity of the United Nations. The Officers' Report to that convention took note of the long struggle carried on by NMU members as "premature anti-fascists," when fighting fascism wasn't popular; of our struggles against the Japanese militarist invasion of China, against Mussolini's ruthless attack on Ethiopia, against the nazi-fascist attack on the Spanish Republic. . . .

[Smith proceeds to deal with] American workers [who] must mobilize to secure adoption of measures which will delay and shorten the coming depression and divert the burden from their backs. In this respect the situation differs greatly from that of 1929. In the twenties the A.F.L. misleaders called upon workers to increase their productivity; to speed up. This was the false panacea advocated by the labor bureaucrats then and advocated by some today. It weakened the unions and left them impotent in the face of economic crisis. The oldtimers in the industry remember the crisis in shipping after the last war and the general crisis of 1931–33, when wages were lousy and 50 men fought for every job in a dog-eat-dog competition. . . .

On August 22, 1947, the National Labor Relations Act went out of existence and was replaced by the Taft-Hartley Law. From that day forward, the NLRB, at one time an agency which aided workers in their fight for organization and collective bargaining rights, became an openly anti-union agency, to be avoided by all honest unions. The law established, as a condition of utilization of the services of the new board, execution of the so-called anti-Communist affidavits.

The affidavits are an insult to American Labor. They are a flagrant attempt by Big Business to dictate who shall lead the American trade union movement. . . . The slave-labor law is aimed equally at the newest and oldest member of our union, at the most active and the most passive, at the Communists and non-Communists alike. We cannot afford to capitulate to the anti-labor bill by recognizing this or any other provision. . . .

When we talk of labor unity we must discuss various levels. First and foremost is the re-establishment of unity within our own union. Then comes the all-important job of re-establishing close working relationships with all other maritime unions, seafaring and shoreside, with the objective of realizing the national maritime federation of which we all have dreamed for many years and of opening the way towards formation of a real national industrial union in marine.

The third level with which we must concern ourselves is labor unity of CIO, AFL and other groups. Lastly, we must think in terms of our relationship with the world labor movement and particularly of the great World Federation of Trade Unions. . . .

I am sure that this Convention will wish again to take note of the historic role of the National Negro Congress. Ever since the establishment of the CIO, the Congress has cooperated with organized labor, particularly the CIO, in inducing Negro workers to become trade unionists. The Congress was instrumental in rallying the Negro automobile workers in support of CIO against Ford and other anti-union employers in the difficult days of that union. Even in our case, we, at one time, used the services of the secretary of the National Negro Congress in our organizing drive on the rivers. . . .

You will recall that the Negro Labor Victory Committee, organized by Charles Collins and myself, was the organization primarily responsible for the mobilization of the Negro people in support of the war effort. We hope that the Council will render the same kind of services in peacetime in rallying the Negro people in support of the trade unions' fight against the Taft-Hartley Law, against oppressive minority legislation, and for the maintenance and defense of American democracy. . . .

It is only a little over two years since President Truman signed the Charter of the United Nations, which pledged respect for the rights of all peoples, supporting the desires of colonial peoples for independence. Where are those rights today in Greece, Indonesia, China, Palestine?

The most concrete revelation of Truman foreign policy is encompassed in the Truman Plan proposed in March, 1947, and the more recent Marshall Plan. These plans are of particular concern to seamen, who, above and beyond their general obligations as citizens to influence foreign policy, are directly involved in the execution of any foreign policy. To a large extent, the prosecution of foreign policy depends upon the merchant vessels manned by members of the NMU and other seafaring unions. Because seamen visit all of the ports of the world, they know at first hand what problems exist in various countries. And because they man American ships, they are often forced to transport cargoes for the aid of economic, political or military aggression.

The recent recommendation of the National Office that our members refuse to haul war materials for the use of the Dutch in Indonesia or for the use of the British in Palestine is only a small step in the right direction. Let us not forget that our ships are carrying munitions to Chiang Kai-shek, and are still carrying cargoes to ports of Franco Spain. . . .

The sharpest expression of the new, monopoly-dictated foreign policy of the Truman–Republican coalition was revealed in the President's March 12, 1947, message to Congress.

Stripped of its camouflage and zigzag paint job, the Truman Doctrine is a bold attempt to intensify American imperialist exploitation of the world's resources. Military intervention is definitely considered a weapon if political and economic intervention do not yield desired results. Its political objective is to dictate the form of government and economy under which all peoples shall live and to grant or withhold loans for food and relief as a means of enforcing this objective.

In his message to Congress asking a "loan" with no conditions as to repayment, of $450 million to Greece and Turkey, Truman charged that the "very existence of the Greek state is today threatened by the terrorist activities of several thousand armed men, led by Communists, who defy the Government's authority," and pleaded for funds and authority to build war machines for the tyrannical governments of Greece and Turkey.

Within 24 hours, Henry Wallace lashed out at the Truman Plan in a nationwide radio address. Wallace called for aid to all needy nations and declared that it was "not a Greek crisis that we face," but an American crisis. He castigated Turkey's role during the war, saying that she "fought against us in the first World War and in this war refused to help the United Nations." . . .

The [Women's] Auxiliary's work in the period since the 1945 Convention can best be evaluated in the light of its established purpose and role in relation to the Union. Because a high percentage of the Union's membership are now men with families, the role of the Auxiliary in bringing the program of the Union to the families and acting as liaison to the community is increasingly important.

During the latter part of 1945, activities were centered around those issues of interest to the seamen and the communities, such as rent and price control, child care, the Murray–Wagner–Dingell Health Bill, the GI Bill and unemployment insurance for seamen. . . .

Because of the long, bitter years just past, Auxiliary members understand the need to continue and intensify the fight against all forms of fascism, whether at home or abroad. The Auxiliary supported the demand to break relations with Franco Spain, picketed the Consulate and participated in street corner meetings on this issue. They protested the Hitler-like action of the British Government against the Jews and continue to demand that the gates of Palestine be opened to these victims of fascism. They protested vigorously the wanton shooting down of the Indonesians by the British and Dutch and condemned the use of

252

American lend-lease weapons for this purpose. They participated in the campaign to bring our boys home and to halt American intervention in the Chinese civil war. They condemned the Truman Doctrine of aid to the reactionary fascist-like governments of Greece and Turkey. They protested the fact that food has been and is being used by our Government as a political weapon over the heads of the peoples of Europe, and the interference of our Government in the internal affairs of the peoples of Europe, while at the same time we support reactionary governments and yet claim that we cannot interfere in the affairs of fascist Franco Spain.

2.

Barred during the war from holding jobs on ocean ships, women are returning to sea in increasing numbers. A survey yesterday showed that already 175 women were employed in several types of shipboard work. It also showed that at least another 2,000 women would like to be so employed.

Miss Anne L. Conroy, recently appointed [elected] women's patrolman of the National Maritime Union, reported that women are filling jobs as nurses, attendants, stewardesses, waitresses and telephone operators, salad makers and matrons. American women, unlike the Russians, are not permitted to become deck or engine room seamen or to try for posts as ships officers.

With a peak of 250 jobs available to women on all passenger ships, Miss Conroy said there is no difficulty in filling them from hundreds of applications arriving weekly from all over the United States. Steamship lines report the same conditions. Women are not employed on freighters. . . .

Miss Conroy said that women receive the same rates of pay aboard ships as men holding similar posts. She said it amounted to a little more than $150 a month, but that tips boosted it to about $200.

□ ——————————————————————————— □

THE SOUTHERN NEGRO YOUTH CONGRESS

"Southern Youth's Proud Heritage" by Augusta Strong, *Freedomways,* First Quarter, 1964, Vol. 4, No. 1

[*The Southern Negro Youth Congress (SNYC) made an indelible mark on the struggle for Black liberation, democracy and progress in the nation's Southland. For more than a decade (1937–49), SNYC waged a militant struggle against lynching, peonage, police brutality, the segregated school system and job discrimination, and for the right to vote.*

The SNYC understood the significance of the culture of Black Americans in their aspirations for freedom. It established people's theaters and held annual art shows. More than 1,000 delegates attended the seventh conference entitled "A Southern Youth Legislature" held in Columbia, South Carolina, in October 1946. Among them were Paul Robeson, Dr. W.E.B. Du Bois and other prominent national Black leaders.

The SNYC, which was directly spurred by the National Negro Congress, was affiliated to and played an important role in the American Youth Congress. It sprang out of the ground which had been broken by the Communist Party in the fight to organize the sharecroppers, to win relief and jobs for the unemployed and to free Angelo Herndon and the nine Scottsboro youths.

Communist youth helped spark the formation of this representative united front movement. Among its leading participants were: Henry Winston, James E. Jackson, Edward Strong, Louis Burnham, Esther Cooper Jackson, Mildred McAdory and Henry Mayfield.

Below we reprint, in part, a first-hand summary account of the SNYC by Augusta Strong North (1915–1976), member of the Young Communist League and the Communist Party. She was associated with the SNYC from its inception and held important posts, including the editorship of Cavalcade, *the Congress newspaper.*]

Over 500 delegates came to Richmond, Virginia in February 1937 for the unprecedented assembly of southern youth, who had come in response to an appeal to cast off their chains and continue the tradition of struggle against second-class citizenship of previous generations North and South.

There were students and young school teachers, sharecroppers from Alabama, steel workers, domestic workers, writers, artists, young professionals, civil service workers, the unemployed, from the prairies of Texas to the shores of Virginia. One-fifth came from religious groups; another fifth from campuses . . . a significant sixteen were from trade unions; a handful from the farms and sixty-six "adult observers" were present. . . .

Dr. Mordecai Johnson, dean of Negro intellectuals and an inspired orator, spoke for the many socially-conscious southern leaders who would support this militant movement during the next decade, when he appealed to the young people to forgo conformity. "Deliver yourselves from the hypnotic influences of the world as it is," he said. He urged them to believe that: " . . . the most thrilling adventure in this world is the adventure to be had by having something to do with the changing of the old world, against which I am protesting, into the new world which I see possible." . . .

The most spectacular achievement of the Congress during its first year was the organization of 5,000 tobacco workers of the city of Richmond into their first labor union. . . . As a result of the efforts of the Young Congress workers, the workers were able to almost double their yearly wages.[8]

Volunteer organizers, none over 22 years old, helped organize other locals of the union, later, in Durham, Raleigh and Winston-Salem. Classes to teach the workers reading and writing and elementary civics, to encourage an interest in voting were formed. At the same time, in some areas, efforts were made to form unions among women domestic workers.

By another year and the convening of a second conference, the Congress had established itself . . . in more than twenty communities. A youth leadership training seminar had been held. In accordance with their decision to penetrate the South, young people had traveled into North Carolina, Alabama, Tennessee and Virginia reaching thousands of people with the message of uniting for economic betterment and civic rights.

Here the young people who had a year before supported and endorsed the anti-lynching campaign of the NAACP, outlined an immediate and practical program of their own for the right to vote and for the abolition of poll-tax disfranchisement. . . .

By another year the Congress had penetrated further South. It moved to Chattanooga where church, school and civic organizations awaited the Congress with welcome arms . . . a school holiday was declared . . . statements of welcome came from the mayor of Chattanooga, from the federal government's National Youth Administration and from the Congress of Industrial Organizations (CIO). The mayor came out to greet the conference and public school classes in colored schools were suspended half a day to allow students to attend the opening session. . . .

A handful of trade unionists attended the Chattanooga conference, representative of the small segment of organized industrial workers in the South—young miners and steelworkers from Alabama and a few from the newly organized tobacco unions. But the main problem the youth faced was not labor organization, but unemployment . . . and then as now, admission was sought to the apprenticeship training programs of the American Federation of Labor. Equal opportunities in federally aided projects was asked. The inclusion of domestic workers in a social security program and "equal opportunity for Negro workers in all federal projects, to set an example for private industry" were also set as goals.

The Congress took positive steps on job security and unemployment, convinced from their success with the tobacco workers that gains could be made in this direction. It established a labor committee, recommended the building of local job clinics to probe employment possibilities in each community where there was a council; communicated with the AFL protesting the exclusion of Negroes from vocational training and pledged aid to the labor unions beginning to organize in the South. . . .

Both AFL and CIO unions were helpful to the young movement, especially since the youth councils tried to spread a labor consciousness among the workers of every community they entered. The CIO's Steelworkers and Packinghouse Union, the John L. Lewis United Mine Workers in Alabama and West Virginia, in the Carolinas the Tobacco Workers, in the seacoast towns the National Maritime Union, participated in the councils and materially aided them.

The Congress in turn, from its earliest days, organized Labor Youth Clubs to acquaint more people with the ideals of trade unions; provided educational and cultural programs in union halls for their members, taught classes in history, current events, parliamentary procedure and even in reading and writing. On a larger scale, a successful labor school was organized in New Orleans for longshoremen, stevedores and maritime workers in trade unionism . . . several hundred workers eagerly filled the classes, held twice weekly at night for a period of two months and the labor movement cooperated in planning the curriculum and in bringing in students. . . . The next year the city of Birmingham was awakened to the first effort of Negroes to unite for social action in its history. There were 650 delegates—again students and tenant farmers, miners, factory workers, young people from the churches, businessmen, clergy, teachers, the jobless. Not all were young—for now and to the end of its days, the Congress attracted to its ranks adult community leaders who found both leadership and willing aides among the young people . . . but all were hopeful of changing the pattern of the South . . . and all were way ahead of the temper of the times. . . .

With councils now functioning in all the southern states; with a four-point program of Citizenship, Education, Jobs and Health, setting up permanent headquarters in the state of Alabama, home of Scottsboro, where the rights of Negroes had been most denied, in 1939 the youth movement touched "home base." . . .

In setting the goals of freedom, equality, opportunity, the young people also accepted the responsibility of rallying and developing the cultural resources that lay within the Negro community. . . .

The Negro Community Theatre, the first such development in Richmond, Virginia and the People's Community Theatre in New Orleans, Youth Congress ventures, were non-profit in nature, designed to entertain, raise the cultural level of participants and audience, to advance social ideas. An annual art exhibit was held each year, usually in conjunction with a conference, where young southern artists were invited to show their work—an opportunity that otherwise was almost non-existent.

For several months, a group of young people calling themselves "The Caravan Puppeteers" made their own puppets and built a portable stage which they transported in an aged car, touring the rural areas with plays they had written on the same social themes with which the youth councils were concerned. In the late '40s an Association of Young Writers and Artists was launched, an affiliate which aimed to further mutual concern for the arts and to aid the social goals of the Youth Congress.

In 1940, following a conference in New Orleans, a large-scale assault upon the poll-tax was determined upon. A national campaign was considered to make Americans conscious of the 19 million southerners, 4 million of them Negroes, who were denied the vote in the South by the poll-tax, white primaries and numerous voting restrictions. . . . In several cities, the right-to-vote movement was dramatized—in New Orleans in a mock election held in a public park and in a class in registration procedures—in other cities mass meetings were held, and in Birmingham, an interracial conference. In Alabama, locals of the United Mine Workers, social clubs, church groups, took part in the campaign. . . .

Only a short time later, the nation was at war . . . and in the fifth year of its existence, the organization addressed itself to the question of the contributions of Negro youth to winning the war and continuing a campaign for the democratic procedures which would release the full potential of the Negro. At Tuskegee, a program was advanced to obtain jobs for Negroes in defense industries, for training young Negro women for service, for ending jimcrow policies in the Army, Navy and Air Force. . . .

The Youth Congress led a drive for defense training opportunities for Negroes in the city of Birmingham, center of southern industrial activity. Thousands of signatures were collected of those who wanted to take defense training, cases of discrimination documented and the year-old Executive Order 8802 barring bias in job training invoked with appeals to Washington by resolution and delegations. As part of the dramatic campaign, an FEPC hearing was held for the first time in the city; prominent members of the Negro community formed a citywide committee on jobs and job training for Negroes. The climax came when the Bechtel-McCone-Parsons Corporation put into operation a huge aircraft plant and more than 10,000 Negroes stood outside the plant on hiring day in response to the Youth Congress call. Both points were won—training and jobs numbering in the thousands for men and women who had formerly looked forward only to menial labor. . . .

The leadership of the national office gave special help in the formation of rural youth councils; self-help projects of quilting and basketry, products sold outside the area, helped these groups establish educational and recreational programs for the youth in their areas and to raise money for civil rights activities. Groups such as these carried on many campaigns incidental to their work, as when for example, they secured the freedom of Nora Wilson, a 16-year-old Alabama country girl, sentenced to years at hard labor for the alleged theft of six ears of corn from a field. Rural councils aided the formation of sharecroppers' and farmers' unions—and often embraced whole families, parents as well as young people.

The Fairfield, Alabama youth council opened a youth center and set up a library; the Birmingham council waged a successful campaign for the first swimming pool in the city for the use of Negroes; the Tuskegee council presented Paul Robeson for the first time in the deep South, in a non-segregated concert. . . .

With the close of the war and the securing of victory, the problems of returning servicemen were taken up by the youth councils. In Alabama, a statewide veterans organization was formed to work for improvements in the GI Bill of Rights and to insure their equal application to Negroes. Wide publicity here and in other states was given to the failure of the Veterans' Administration to curb the rampant discrimination practiced against Negroes in the apprenticeship training programs. They called for federal prosecution of the mob leaders who instigated violence against returned servicemen in Columbia, Tennessee and in other communities. They invited white servicemen to join their Negro brothers in a victory for democracy at home.

Again the Congress turned to a major drive for the ballot as the main instrument for achieving full citizenship status in the South. An "oust Bilbo"[9] movement gained impetus in Mississippi, with the youth councils aiming for a total of 100,000 signatures on petitions to remove one of the most hated racists ever to sit in the U.S. Senate and for the first time,

3,000 Negro voters registered for the Democratic primary in that state . . . numbers of them stimulated by the youth councils' campaigns.

The Congress called a "Southern Youth Legislature" to meet in Columbia, South Carolina in October 1946, to reassess the position of Negro youth in the South and to plan further strategy for the vote . . . and to demonstrate in a dramatic way "the will of our youth to gain possession of the ballot and to wield this weapon of democracy with skill and courage; to secure for ourselves and our people all the rights and opportunities of an equal and unfettered citizenship."

Almost a thousand young people responded. Besides the voting issue, they asked the enactment of an FEPC law, adequate and equal housing and an end to "white supremacy customs and practices" in all forms.

This was the most significant of the conferences, the most spectacular, the one which showed most clearly the role of the movement. . . .

Abroad, it was known and respected in the international field, through exchange visitors and delegations sent to youth conferences in Europe, Mexico, Canada and Cuba. . . .

The SNYC was both non-partisan and non-sectarian—for most young southerners to whom the ballot was denied, political expression was not possible, but Republicans and Marxists, devout Catholic youth and Protestant church leaders, graduate students and domestic workers with only a few years schooling merged into a unified organization—even stretching a fraternal hand to white youth to attend their meetings, where possible as observers—and to organize themselves, a movement they spurred and initiated into the League of Young Southerners. The latter organization flourished for a while but never had far-reaching influence. . . .

The movement which had lived twelve glorious years came to an end with the emergence of McCarthyism which scattered the northern supporters and progressive and trade union allies of the young people, and gave new strength to the native southern reactionaries like "Bull" Connor.[10] Naked terror broke up the Congress. That was in 1949. But what the movement began, the seed it planted, did not fall on barren ground. What has happened since, in the last several years especially, is ample testimony. For example: "Bull" Connor is gone from office and the Negro Freedom Movement is waxing ever stronger.

Moreover, as the young people who had initiated the movement had grown older, added responsibilities came their way. . . . Further, the problems the movement had tackled originally as youth, had burgeoned into problems for the entire South. The anti–poll tax campaign for instance, had become a national question. Equality in education was heading to the point where it was to become the nation's number one issue. And similarly the other planks of the movement: jobs and equal opportunity in all phases of American life. For a dozen years the South had carried the baton in this fateful race; they had influenced the perspective of a generation of southerners. Now they handed the baton on to the Negro people as a whole.

☐ ─── ☐

THE 1948 ELECTIONS

1. "The Meaning of Truman's Election,"
The *Daily Worker,* November 4, 1948;
2. "Resolution on the Situation Growing out
of the Presidential Election (Final Text),"
National Committee CPUSA, *Political Affairs,* July 1953

[*The 1948 elections took place in a cold war atmosphere incited by Truman. The two-party objective was to avoid a debate on the foreign policy issue. The formation of the Progressive Party and the nomination of Henry Wallace (former vice-president) as its presidential candidate shattered this maneuver. Peace became the central issue in the campaign.*

During the campaign and subsequently, the country was bombarded with a barrage of anti-communism to divert it from the central issue.[11]

The Daily Worker, *in a front-page editorial entitled: "The Meaning of Truman's Election," exposed the attempt at a "rigged" election which failed.*

In 1953, the Party in a further examination, published in Political Affairs, *concluded that without a substantial base in the labor movement, it is impossible to establish a popular mass party in the United States.*

Excerpts from both articles appear below.]

1.

The election results which have returned President Truman to the White House, and which gave the boot to the notorious 80th Congress dominated by the GOP, prove that the Left-sounding speeches which Truman copied from Roosevelt and Henry Wallace found a profound response among the electorate. . . .

They voted for Truman because he took advantage of their vivid fear that Dewey spelled Hooverism, naked reaction and another 1929 crash.

Truman got their support by echoing their own conviction that the 80th Congress, which wrecked price control, was the "worst in the nation's history." Truman won support when he announced—even though he did not carry out—the Vinson peace mission to Moscow while Dewey was talking ominously of the "showdown" which spelled atomic war. Truman and Dewey carefully cooperated in keeping out of the election the basic problems of foreign policy. But Dewey hailed the Taft-Hartley Law and praised the 80th Congress. The voters heard Truman echo their own belief that the GOP "spy scares" were a "red herring" to divert attention from the profiteers. They agreed with him even though Truman's appointees are enforcing the Taft-Hartley Law with a vengeance, and he himself helped kill price control and launched the "loyalty" witch-hunts and frameup trials against the Communist Party.

In short, Truman won the election by a hypocritical copying of the speeches of Franklin Roosevelt and by imitating as much as he dared the charges of the Progressive Party and Henry Wallace whose campaign forced into the elections the vital issues which neither of the candidates of the old parties had intended to discuss.

The Congressional vote and the state votes show what the voters want. They kicked out the red-baiters John McDowell and Richard Vail, members of the Un-American Committee. They re-elected the fighter for peace, Marcantonio, and gave the Communist candidate in Brooklyn, Simon W. Gerson, the biggest vote for a Communist recorded in that borough. They kicked out labor-hating Senator Ball in Minnesota and did the same for the reactionary puppet of the *Chicago Tribune,* Senator Brooks. . . .

The returns, therefore, are a crushing defeat for the naked, open extreme right-wing forces of reaction whom the people rejected in a manner which, however, still keeps them within the Wall Street–controlled two-party system. The vote shows an enormous democratic upsurge which remains locked within the two-party system for the reason that the illusion still persists that the Democratic Party can be the vehicle of the genuine liberal-labor forces. . . .

The vote for Wallace, it must be admitted, fell below not only the unrealistic quotas assigned to him by certain forces, but even below what his most sober supporters, including this paper, had expected. This fact does not in any sense negate the enormous effect which the Wallace platform had on forcing the issues into the open. . . .

The Communist Party played no small part in breaking through the two-party plan to stage an election in which not even the pretense of debate would have been permitted. The Communist Party did not cease

261

for a moment its warning that the Truman–Dewey foreign policy spells disaster for the nation, that behind this bi-partisan policy lurks the menace of fascism and imperialist war. There can be no question but that this courageous and patriotic service to the country made it impossible for this election to proceed in the rigged manner originally planned for it by the financial bosses of the bi-partisan war program.

2.

In the 1948 elections we were confronted with the task of finding the broadest united-front electoral vehicle for bringing sharply before the American people the question of peace. From this arose the need for our Party to help stimulate the formation of a united-front peace ticket and even the formation of a united-front party machinery to campaign for that ticket.

However, the mistake our Party made was to confuse this task with the historic task of forming a new mass party of the people. As a consequence, there existed the wrong estimate that the formation of the Progressive Party represented something more than the simple emergence of an important fighting force for peace; that it represented in fact, the emergence of a great mass people's party.

This estimate erroneously ignored the fact that in mid-twentieth century America there could not emerge a great new mass party as against the two parties of Wall Street until the labor movement, at least its decisive sections, had broken from the two-party system, particularly the Democratic Party. This arose in no small measure from an over-estimation of the radicalization of the masses and an under-estimation of the deep-seated influence of the labor reformists on the organized working class.

This mistake also arose in large measure from a Right-opportunist exaggeration of the role which liberal bourgeois forces (around Wallace) could play in bringing about a basic political realignment in the ranks of the working class and its allies.

It has been increasingly clear that the formation of a broad and mass people's party in the United States, which will represent an historic and necessary advance on the part of labor and its allies, must arise out of the basic mass trade union and people's organizations. Movement in this direction will be facilitated in the degree that every effort is made to stimulate independent political action and resistance against the attacks and policies of reaction.

THE McCARTHY ERA

7.

The start of the new decade found the United States engaged in a new aggression—the Korean war. At home widespread reaction prevailed. It was the period known for the infamy of McCarthyism.

*On June 25, 1950, the invasion of North Korea began. On June 28 a jam-packed meeting was held under the auspices of the Civil Rights Congress at Madison Square Garden in New York. One of those who addressed the meeting was Gus Hall, then National Secretary of the Communist Party. Hall discarded his prepared speech and delivered one which began: "Tonight, Americans of every creed and color, every walk of life, every political belief are drawn close together by a common fear of war, and a common desire for peace. The cold war has run its course. Yesterday, President Truman announced that the United States has launched an undeclared shooting war against all the peoples of Asia and the Pacific." (*Hands off Korea and Formosa *by Gus Hall, New Century Publishers, 1950).*

Within five days U.S. troops were in Korea. President Harry

263

Truman called it a "police action." But before this "action" was over, 33,000 US forces had lost their lives. The loss of Korean lives, military and civilian, was beyond calculation. The land was ravaged. The war threatened Asia again with atomic warfare and it was reported that germ warfare was used.[1]

To promote and conduct this war, the country was subjected to an unprecedented assault on its democratic rights. Opposition was crushed through "legal" and extra-legal means. In this atmosphere McCarthyism flourished.

The infamous term "McCarthyism" was derived from the name of Joseph R. McCarthy, a small town judge with a shady record who projected himself out of the obscurity of Appleton, Wisconsin. Trading on a spurious war record, he won a surprise victory in 1946 over Robert M. La Follette to become the junior US senator from Wisconsin.

McCarthy was hardly noticed in the Senate until 1950 when he told a meeting of a Republican women's club that he possessed a list (never produced) of a large number of "known Communists" who were then employed by the State Department.

Over the next several years he repeatedly made similar sweeping charges about "subversives" in government—always without proof or evidence. He thereby helped generate a chilling atmosphere of intimidation and stimulated unrestrained red-baiting and witch-hunting. In this he had help from the Nixons, McCarrans and many others of that sort.

Some thought at first that McCarthy represented the lunatic fringe of the ultra-right, but it soon became apparent that he represented the interests of the most reactionary group of monopoly capital. McCarthy supported Gen. Dwight D. Eisenhower for president (though the former's extremism later brought about a rift between them). He worked closely with Robert Kennedy, the future Attorney General. Most people would agree with W.E.B. Du Bois, who warned in his Autobiography *that the "democratic right of freedom of thought and speech must be preserved [from the McCarthys] or America was dead." (International Publishers, 1968, p. 388.)*

The unrestrained bulldozing by McCarthy alarmed growing numbers of people, among them old-line conservatives. In the

Wisconsin village called Sauk City, a Republican, Leroy Gore, editor of the Sauk-Prairie Star, *initiated a movement with the popular slogan: "Joe Must Go." The object was to recall the rampaging senator and hold new elections. The campaign had wide support, but anti-communism was a defect of the movement and as Gore acknowledged, the movement was unable to attract workers.*

Throughout this oppressive period the Party operated under great difficulties. It nevertheless directed its efforts toward attracting workers to the anti-McCarthyite movement. For example: in Milwaukee, a worker and local Party secretary, Mort Altman, took charge of this campaign. He states: "We were constantly tailed, threatened by the police and FBI. We printed a four-page leaflet in 20,000 copies and distributed them to all important shop gates and working-class neighborhoods. We tried very hard to get labor support and did get some, but late in the campaign." The Party laid its stress on reaching the strategic forces in the major industrial areas.

Black leaders and movements were a major target because reaction found here its greatest challenge and resistance. Constituencies of various views united in a common effort to defend democratic rights. The heroic acts of these Black men and women added a brilliant page to the historic struggle for civil rights.

The National Negro Labor Council (NNLC), established in Cincinnati, Ohio, October 27–28, 1951, received the support of the Party. It had a strong base in the United Auto Workers Union in Detroit. It immediately found itself under sharp attack not only by governmental bodies, but the UAW leadership as well. Ford Local 600 of the UAW had five of its leaders removed by Reuther and was placed under an administrator. Among those removed were pioneers who helped build the union, David Moore and Nelson Davis, both Communists. Davis was widely known for gaining hundreds of readers for the Daily Worker *among his fellow workers.*

The most criminal repressive act was the railroading of Ethel and Julius Rosenberg to the electric chair for having "conspired to commit espionage." This frame-up was condemned by millions of Americans, with worldwide support. The Party helped develop the great movement to save the doomed couple. Henry Winston, speaking in Union Square, June 19, 1978, on the occasion of the 25th anniversary of their execution, recalled that "a leading member of our Central Committee, William L. Patterson, Mr. Civil Rights, the man who wrote We Charge Genocide, *led 3,000 people to Sing Sing, even at the eleventh hour, to prevent this act of political murder and to continue the legal and mass struggle for the Rosenbergs' freedom."[2]*

Foreign born have been a target of persecution since the founding of the nation. Many men and women who had made outstanding contributions to the labor movement, to revolutionary and progressive advance, were exiled. They had spent most of their lives here. Many had families born in the United States. The list of such victims is a long one. Among them are Irving Potash, Ferdinand Smith, John and Mae Williamson, Claudia Jones, Beatrice Johnson, John and Evelyn Vafiades, Emil and Grace Gardos, John and Ann Peters, George Siskind, Dora Lifshitz, Charles and Micky Doyle, James and Eula Papandreu and Anthony and Nell Cattonar.

The government and its chief political policeman, J. Edgar Hoover, FBI chief, sought to entangle the Party solely in legal defense and thereby to prevent it from conducting its normal activities. This had an effect on its work, but the plot failed. The organization remained involved in numerous activites.

*The central task was the continued struggle for peace. The Party helped initiate a broad united-front movement. In its resolution adopted by the 15th Convention of the CPUSA (1950) it demanded the withdrawal of American troops from Korea, hands off China and the banning of the atom bomb, and opposed the fascization and rearming of Germany and Japan. (*Political Affairs, *January 1951.) Foster writes in his history of the Party: "One of the most significant of the many mass protest meetings against the Korean War was that of August 2, 1950, in Union Square, New York, which was brutally dispersed by police violence."*

In the peace movement, Party and Labor Youth League members played a large part in the collection of 2,500,000 signatures on the Stockholm Peace Pledge.

At the same time, the Party did not neglect the workers in basic industries—firstly, in the steel plants. This effort would contribute later to the crystallization of a militant movement in steel mills. The Party began reconstituting its organization in the South and assigned one of its outstanding Black leaders, James Jackson, to this work.

The anti-Red hysteria did not stop the Communist Party from putting forth its own candidates in the 1952 elections. Well-known Communist leaders were nominated on independent party tickets such as the Freedom Party and the Peoples Rights Party. Among them were Benjamin J. Davis, the imprisoned Black leader, and Simon W. Gerson, who had been acquitted in the second Smith Act trial in New York City. In Massachusetts, Otis Hood ran on the Independent ticket.

December 2, 1954, the US Senate, by a vote of 67 to 22, condemned Senator McCarthy. His fascist-like antics also covered shady deals, as investigation revealed. "The published [Senate] report of this investigation included . . . McCarthy's financial transactions and activities for such special interest groups as the real estate, sugar and China lobbies." (Labor Fact Book No. 12, 1955.)

The discrediting and final elimination of McCarthy was not achieved merely by an act of Congress. Congress was cowed by him; and the media either surrendered or kept silent while elementary democratic rights were being extinguished. His defeat was a tribute to the inherent democratic spirit of the American people. The Communist Party helped put an end to his threat. McCarthy is gone but the menace of McCarthyism persists. Only constant vigilance and struggle can thwart it.

This period was, as Gus Hall characterized it, "the stormiest in our history." They were "storms [which] have already rocked our nation." The Party rode out these storms with added knowledge and experience to meet new storms ahead.

□ ———————————————————————————————— □

AGAINST U.S. IMPERIALIST AGGRESSION

"Peace Can Be Won,"
Report to the 15th National Convention
of the Communist Party, USA by Gus Hall,
New Century Publishers, 1951

[*The 15th National Convention of the CPUSA was held from December 28 to 31, 1950, with the main report presented by Gus Hall, National Secretary. Eugene Dennis, General Secretary, was serving a term in the Atlanta Penitentiary for "contempt of Congress." Six months after the convention the elected Party leadership was either in jail or hunted as political refugees.*

The spirit of the convention was expressed in a letter by Chairman William Z. Foster, who was unable to attend because of ill health. He wrote that "we face the situation calmly, clear-headedly and unafraid, amidst all the capitalist storms of frenzy, despair and desperation. The future belongs to the people, with the Communists at their head."

Extracts from the report of Gus Hall to the 15th Convention follow.]

The two-and-a-half years since our 14th National Convention have been the stormiest in our history. These mid-century storms have already rocked our nation. All signs point to rougher weather ahead for our people and our class. Our Party has been lashed by the winds of pro-fascist reaction, but it has not been veered from its course.

Future historians will properly note the two-sided character of this period. This has been a time of brutal, murderous aggression by the profit-greedy, war-mad Wall Street monopolists. These same two-and-a-half years have been marked also by the people's defense of peace, democracy and economic security. The period has seen a growing resistance of the working class to the attacks on its living standards and an upsurge of militant struggle by the Negro people against the intensified violence, brutality and white chauvinism of the ruling class.

Since our 1948 Convention, our country has been pushed dangerously down the road toward fascist rule and atomic world war. In the words of the Wall Street magazine, *Business Week,* "The defense program is over. The new plans are for a war program."

American imperialism has moved from the stage of war preparations and war talk to open military aggression against the peoples of Vietnam, Indochina and the Philippines.

Another center of war provocation—perhaps the most crucial and dangerous—is now developing in western Europe. The Brussels Conference was a war conference, to set the stage for new war provocations aimed directly at the Soviet Union. It sped the plans to arm the Atlantic Pact countries and especially to base U.S.-directed military aggressions on a rebuilt Nazi army in western Germany. These plans have been further advanced by the appointment of General Eisenhower, whom Wall Street regards as the man best able to whip together and command the aggressive military forces being readied for attack. U.S. rejection of the Soviet Union's proposals for a Four-Power Conference to work out a peaceful solution of the German and other European problems further emphasizes the need to alert the American people to the dangers arising out of these imperialist war preparations and provocations.

Wall Street's diplomatic errand boys are scurrying around the globe arranging hurried conferences to prepare provocations for new wars: for more Koreas. Truman flies to see MacArthur, Attlee flies to confer with Truman, Acheson rushes off to Brussels. The bipartisan atom-maniacs are in a constant hustle and bustle, dashing from one meeting to another to plot history's most terrible crime against humanity—an atomic war of worldwide dimensions.[3]

Barely six months have passed since American imperialism entered this new stage in its drive to enslave the world. But already thousands of American boys lie dead in graves half a world away from home. Tens of thousands more have been maimed and crippled for life. The Houses of Morgan, Rockefeller, Du Pont and Ford, demand free raw materials, more oil, iron ore, tin—more *"lebensraum"* for their foreign investments, more slave labor from which to squeeze super-profits. Their ruthless aggression has brought mass murder, pillage, rape and destruction to Korean homes and families—grief and fear to the families and homes of America.

Under the direct command of General MacArthur, villages and cities are bombed and burned to the ground in Korea. Dozens of Lidices lie in ruins. Tens, yes, hundreds of thousands of men and women are dead. Innocent children, countless still unborn have been robbed of life by bombs, tanks, jet planes and shells made in the U.S.A.

Every day this criminal war is permitted to continue adds to the already huge casualty lists. As long as the U.S. imperialists continue their crimes of aggression, the peoples of Asia will give their lives in heroic defense of their liberties, their national independence, their homes and world peace.

Meanwhile, mid-century America has acquired a "new look"—the

269

look of militarization. Our youth is becoming a generation in uniform, to be trained as a generation of killers. The standing army is fast being expanded to full wartime proportions. The draft is being revised to get World War II veterans and the older men. Our schools, from kindergarten to college, are taking on a military bearing and atmosphere. Little children are forced to line up in military fashion and answer "yes, sir" and "no, sir" to their "superior officers." Drills are becoming an important part of the curriculum. Our parks and streets assume a martial air as bomb shelters and air-raid sirens are readied.

With cold-blooded brutality the warmongers are conspiring to accustom the public to the idea of atomic warfare. We need to find a stronger and more accurate word than warmongering to describe the fiendish, cannibalistic demands for dropping the A-bomb, inspired by President Truman's off-the-cuff atomic threat. Every effort is made to divert the people's discussions from proposals for outlawing atomic weapons to secondary questions. Americans are being conditioned to take for granted the use of atomic bombs by our government. That is why big discussions are organized around such questions as who should have the authority to order the dropping of the first atom bomb; when and under what conditions should the holocaust begin; what kind of defense measures should our cities adopt against atomic destruction; and other such questions. Our Party has the urgent task of bringing this discussion back to the key question—how to straitjacket the Wall Street war criminals and prevent them from plunging our country and the world into the horrors of an atomic war. We must not permit the American people to slip, by degrees, into acceptance of the idea of atomic war.

Despite the speed with which events have been moving these past two-and-a-half years, the imperialists are not satisfied with the progress of their war drive. They demand a bigger army and navy, a bigger air force. They call for faster stockpiling of A-bombs and the production of H-bombs. They push speedup for more production of death–dealing weapons. They demand bigger and bigger sacrifices from the working class, the Negro people, the poor farmers. They insist on wage cuts and wage freezes, on price boosts and unrestricted profits. They are determined to shift an ever heavier share of the tax burden on the low income groups. They fan the fire of war hysteria, speed the destruction of the Constitution and its Bill of Rights, hasten the development toward fascism. They are hell-bent to choke off all talk of peace.

These demands for accelerating the feverish tempo of the war drive explain President Truman's National Emergency Decree. The proclamation of this fake "national emergency" is a confession that the war camp has been unable to win mass support for its imperialist ambitions through demagogy and deception. So the President has taken to himself unprecedented dictatorial powers. He has decreed more war production, more advanced mobilization, more regimentation for all-out war. . . .

The organization of a full war economy is the dominant trend and is swiftly gathering momentum in our country's economic life. This fact must get basic consideration in all our thinking about questions of economics and economic development.

The years 1947 and 1948 were years of expanding peacetime production accompanied by a steady growth of the elements of a war economy and of war-stimulated inflation. They were also years in which a new economic crisis was maturing in the surroundings of a rapidly deepening general crisis of the world capitalist system. Consequently, an economic decline began in October 1948, which marked the beginning of a new economic crisis. But its rate of development was being retarded by the armament program and most particularly by the inflationary forces resulting from the general war preparations. The cumulative effect of these developments, together with the temporary upswing in the production of autos and housing, by the end of 1949, was to halt the decline and to bring about a rise of "boom" proportions in a number of industries (steel, motor vehicles, airplanes, housing), while others continued to lag.

In search of an imperialist way out of the developing crisis of American capitalist economy, Wall Street began shifting more rapidly to the building up of a war economy. Driving for world domination, American imperialism passed over to direct acts of aggression—in Korea and China—and intensified the preparations for an attack on the Soviet Union. This had the effect of making the building of a war economy the dominant economic trend, which modified and distorted the course and forms of the economic crisis which began in the fall of 1948. The expanding war economy is bound to sharpen the inner contradictions and accelerate the process toward an economic crisis or toward all-out war.

□ ── □

THE FICTITIOUS FOE

The Enemy Forgotten by Gilbert Green,
International Publishers, 1956

[*"Before the steel doors of political bigotry clang behind me, I am filing my own political brief before the highest court in the land—the court of public opinion . . . "* says Gil Green in a prefatory note to The Enemy Forgotten.

Green was convicted in the first trial of eleven Communist leaders. (Gus Hall, Henry Winston, Gil Green and Robert Thompson became political refugees in July 1951. They were found guilty of "contempt of court" and additional years were added to their sentences.)

Here the author examines some aspects of anti-communist and anti-Soviet policies.]

Despite the re-evaluation which many liberals have begun there is a grave danger that this will be so half-hearted, so devoid of a probing search for the truth, that it will accomplish little. We particularly have in mind the current practice of a number of liberals who, beginning to see the grave danger of extreme reaction, think they are meeting this threat by placing their stress upon what they call the "external threat of Communism" as opposed to McCarthy's emphasis on the "internal threat."

One such liberal is James A. Wechsler. After his appearance before the McCarthy Committee in 1953, Wechsler wrote a book, *The Age of Suspicion,* in which he describes the "quiet horror" of this experience and correctly observes that the battle against McCarthyism—with or without the man—"is far from over." But he is far from correct in his advice as to how this battle is to be won. It will not be won, he warns "by men who are so distracted by the McCarthy danger that they dismiss the external challenge of Soviet imperialism." He accuses McCarthy of distorting reality "by picturing the bedraggled communists as far more menacing than the massive Soviet power and by identifying with the communists all those who reject McCarthy's intolerant version of history."

We shall skip over the fact that this book was written as another one of those "I done it" confessionals of ex-Communists. It is unfortunate that Wechsler felt called upon to distort and discredit the account of his best years of youthful idealism and courage merely so that no one could call his anti-Communist conversion anything but complete. The age of suspicion is also, for some, the age of contrition. Nor shall we discuss who it is that is "bedraggled," the Communists who fight with honor for convictions and principles, or those who trample upon their own liberal heritage. We also want to make it plain that we make a distinction between ex-Communists and even anti-Communists who are conscious tools of McCarthyism, and those like Wechsler who desire to fight McCarthyism and do fight it in their own way.

The Communist dispute with Wechsler, over and above ideological differences, is that he fails to comprehend how McCarthyism came into being and how it can be defeated so decisively that it never threatens the nation again. His major difference with McCarthy, despite what he says, is not whether the Communists represent more of a domestic than an external threat. If that were the main difference, we would be compelled to conclude that little indeed separates them. For no one in his right mind, not even those who have been taken in by the lie that Communists believe in or advocate force and violence, really believes that America is in imminent peril of revolution. Yet the fear of Communism has reached such frenzied peaks that countries like France and Italy, with millions of Communists or Communist followers, look upon the anti-Communist hysteria in the United States with amazement.

There is only one explanation for this—the insidious drive to build up the hoax of a Soviet war threat to America. It is precisely this unreasoned fear of an "external threat," built up by those who profit from it, that has made possible the unreasoned fear of a domestic one. For if America is really menaced by "massive Soviet power" and confronted with the danger of Soviet aggression, then by McCarthyite logic, every Communist and Communist sympathizer is also dangerous. Thus, by stressing the "external" threat, Wechsler is not fighting but feeding the fires of extreme reaction.

Whatever one may say of McCarthy and the cabal of demagogues associated with him, no one can deny them consistency. For them, "A" cannot be separated from "B," any more than "B" from "C," and so on to the end. If it is true that the Soviet Union menaces us, then anything and everything is justified in the nation's defense. It is likewise true that if the Communists are the agents of this foreign foe, then they, even if relatively small in numbers are a fifth column and highly dangerous. Moverover, if it is also true that the Communists are diabolical plotters and prepared to employ any and all means toward their end, then it may also be true that even Wechsler's renunciation of Communism is a fraud, perpetrated in behalf of this conspiracy against America. And if there is the slightest chance of that, then McCarthy is serving his country by challenging Wechsler's sincerity and that of all self-confessed ex-Communists. Furthermore, if these things be true, McCarthy is also correct in viewing with suspicion every former sympathizer and friend of the Soviet Union no matter how they since recant. Depraved indeed must such persons be to have sympathized with a cause which they now claim to be so ignoble, with a power which they now describe as so devoid of all human decency. It also follows from this that those who oppose McCarthy's methods, while protesting agreement with his motives, are totally wrong for they are hedging on doing what is necessary to defend the nation from so deadly a peril. And is it also inconsistent, with all this that such people should not be trusted, being open to the suspicion of hidden reservations and sympathies with the Soviet Union?

This is the deadly logic of the Big Lie. Of such is made the Procrustean bed in which all must be stretched out or cut down to size once the original fraudulent premise is accepted. And there is no escape from it. For in the words of Shakespeare, "in the night, imagining some fear, how easy is a bush supposed to be a bear!"

The change in political climate which began in 1954 and continued through 1955, was made possible only because the unreal fear of Soviet aggression has subsided. With the end of the Korean and Indochinese wars there has taken place a significant reduction in world tensions. Were this not true McCarthyism would still be on the ascendant. That is why the continued practice of some liberals to sprinkle liberally every speech, editorial, article or statement with references to the "Soviet threat" is so dangerous. It adds to the war tension and actual danger of war. It thereby contributes to spreading McCarthy's "intolerant version of history."

Those who really believe that the Soviet Union is an aggressor power seeking world domination should ask themselves one simple question: Why is it that the United States, which is separated from the Soviet Union by two mighty oceans and five thousand miles, frequently gives the appearance of being distilled almost to jelly with fear, while countries ever so much closer to the Soviet Union are in no such state of nerves? Or, to put the same question another way: Why is it that the anti–Communist hysteria of our time is a product bearing a "Made in USA" label and exported to the four corners of the earth at great cost to the American people? Why is it accepted by other nations rather reluctantly, at best, even though it is handed out free with an extra door prize thrown in for good measure?[4] . . .

When Europe and Asia faced real threats to peace and freedom the situation was quite different. It was the common people of the world who then were most fully aroused to the great danger stemming from fascist aggression. It was however, the statesmen and public leaders of the western capitalist democracies who closed their eyes to this menace and only saw it in its real light when they themselves were directly periled. Even under the liberal Roosevelt, the United States refused to come to the assistance of the beleaguered Spanish Republic and continued shipping scrap iron to Japan. But today, it is precisely the common people, those who always do the fighting and dying for freedom, who fear Wall Street's intentions the most and the Soviet Union's the least. It is the western capitalist statesmen today, and first of all America's, who insist upon keeping the cauldron of war tension ever boiling.

□ ———————————————————————————————— □

FASCIST-STYLE TERROR AT PEEKSKILL

**"Joint Statement by the National Committee and
New York State Committee of the Communist Party,"
The Worker, September 11, 1949**

[*Paul Robeson, world-renowned people's artist and leader, was scheduled to sing at a concert near Peekskill, New York, on August 27, 1949, as on several occasions in previous years. But this time Robeson was prevented from singing. Using "Nazi-like" methods, a fascistic "anti-Semitic" and "anti-Negro" mob drove away the audience, the liberal magazine the* Nation *reported (September 10, 1949).*

Paul Robeson vowed he would return. On September 4 he came back. Thousands of people were present to hear him and to defend his right to be heard. However, as the audience left the grounds after the concert, they were attacked by a vicious mob which was protected by the police. Over 200 men, women and children were injured, many seriously. Rocks were thrown through car and bus windows; cars were overturned and smashed. Police openly fraternized with the rioters; terrorism spread over the whole area.

Here follows part of the statement of the Communist Party.]

There was no difficulty in seeing at Peekskill who it was that stood for peace, democracy and civil rights, and who it was that stood for mass hysteria, fascist degeneracy, for lynch–terror against the Negro people, for anti–Semitism, for force and violence.

There was no difficulty in observing what was so evident in Germany as Nazism began to rise, namely, that without the collusion and cooperation of the state and its police force, the mobsters and hoodlums would never have dared to attack.

Peekskill demonstrated, once again, that the cry against Communism and Communists is but the stepping stone and the opening wedge to destroy the rights of all Americans, to unleash terror against all of the people.

Let the trade union leaders and workers who failed to participate in this great people's demonstration and failed to raise their voice in protest against the vicious assault upon this peaceful meeting ask the ghosts of thousands of German trade unionists whether the fight for civil liberties, for the rights of the Negro people, against red-baiting and anti-Semitism, is their fight or not.

To the working people of America, to American youth and women, to the Negro people and to the vast multitudes of Americans of various national groups and origins, Peekskill must become a symbol and a clarion call. There the people saw fascism. There ominous warning was given of the lengths to which the American ruling class is willing to go in its efforts to stifle every protest, to crush every democratic voice.

But in Peekskill 25,000 Americans demonstrated by their courage, resourcefulness and discipline that democracy can be preserved, that the voice of democratic Americans can be heard, that the battle for peace can be won.

To Americans for whom democracy is more than an empty gesture or a hypocritical phrase, we call for the creation of a mighty and powerful unity to smash the fascist offensive. To Americans, regardless of political beliefs, regardless of religion or nationality, we call for the welding of a firm and unshakeable bond to defeat the lynch spirit that is inspired by those who would destroy the people. Fight back the attacks upon the Negro people and all other minority groups. Resolve that Peekskill and every other American city and town shall be host to democratic and progressive opinion and action and not to fascist violence.

□ ———————————————————————————————— □

SMITH ACT AND McCARRAN ACT

1. *In Defense of Your Freedom* by Eugene Dennis,
New Century Publishers, 1949;
2. "An Open Letter to the American People,"
Statement by the National Committee,
Communist Party, U.S.A., *The Worker,* June 25, 1961

[*Disguised as a measure against aliens (which would be sufficient to condemn it), the Smith Act actually sought to restrict the democratic rights of those who, in its interpretation, "may advocate by any method the overthrow or destruction of any government in the United States . . . by force or violence. . . ."*

Dr. Herbert Aptheker, in his book Dare We Be Free?, *points out that Zechariah Chafee, Jr., Harvard Law School's—and the nation's—leading authority on the law of civil rights and liberties, failed at the time of its passage to note that the Smith Act's "other purposes" were most important. Chafee wrote: "Not until months later did I for one realize that the statute contains the most drastic restrictions on freedom of speech ever enacted in the United States during peace."*

All twelve members of the Political Bureau of the CPUSA were indicted in 1948. They were: William Z. Foster, Eugene Dennis, Henry Winston, John Williamson, Jacob Stachel, Robert G. Thompson, Benjamin J. Davis, John Gates, Irving Potash, Gilbert Green, Carl Winter and Gus Hall.

Foster, then Chairman of the Party, was severed from the case because of illness. Eugene Dennis, General Secretary of the Party (the case became known as the Dennis Case) acted as his own counsel at the trial at Foley Square before Judge Harold R. Medina. The 11 defendants were convicted and all served heavy sentences.

In 1953, Elizabeth Gurley Flynn was convicted under the Smith Act, together with 12 other of her associates. All those convicted were sent to prison. Smith Act trials took place throughout the country and scores of Communists were convicted.

The "Internal Security Act," known as the McCarran Act, was passed by Congress, September 23, 1950. It was the most sweeping thought control measure ever enacted and was designed to repeal the Bill of Rights.

The law required the registration of officers and members of all "Communist Action" organizations and placed them under the control of the Subversive Activities Control Board. The law's application was not limited to the Communist Party. It also included officers and members of "Communist Front" organizations and thereby provided an almost unlimited catch-all. Under the "Communist Control Act of 1954" a third category, "Communist Infiltrated" organizations, was added along with a provision which prohibited members of "Communist organizations" from holding office or employment in labor unions.

To register under these two Acts would amount to an admission of criminal guilt and would immediately expose the registrants to prosecution under the Smith Act with its drastic penalties. But failure to register was also punishable by as much as $10,000 in fines and five-year prison terms for each day of continued refusal to register.

Another section provided that in the case of "a declaration of war," of "invasion" or of "insurrections," the authorities could throw into concentration camps (without trial) all whom the Subversive Activities Control Board declared "subversive." Such camps were immediately constructed and for many years were kept ready to receive their victims. The Act also barred members of "Communist organizations" that had been ordered to register from holding any non-elective job with the federal government and prohibited members of such organizations from applying for or using passports.

The McCarran Act required, among other things, that the Communist Party register itself with the Subversive Activities Control Board. The Party refused to do so and, for eleven years, by legal action and mass struggle, it persisted in this refusal. Finally in the winter of 1961-62, the Party and two of its officers, Gus Hall and Benjamin J. Davis, were indicted. Hall and Davis were arrested in March 1962. In December 1962, the Party was found guilty and sentenced to pay fines of $120,000.

(In May 1966, the case against Gus Hall was dropped. Ben Davis died August 22, 1964. The case against the Party itself was effectively nullified in March 1967 by a US Court of Appeals decision.)

Counsel for the Party during all phases of the long struggle was John J. Abt (b. 1904). In 1933 Abt went to Washington to work for the Agricultural Adjustment Administration. Later he was employed as counsel for the WPA and for the Securities and Exchange Commission.

Perhaps his most outstanding achievements during the period (1933-38) were made as chief counsel to the Senate Committee on Civil Liberties (known as the La Follette Committee). Here he helped expose the naked warfare being carried on by the monopoly corporations in their efforts to stem the tide of industrial unionism. He was instrumental in bringing out the truth regarding the Memorial Day Massacre of May 1938. (See Jerold S. Auerbach, Labor and Liberty, *Bobbs-Merrill, 1966).*

278

After leaving government employment he became counsel to the Amalgamated Clothing Workers and in 1944, was "lent" to the CIO Political Action Committee (PAC) as assistant and legal adviser to its chairman, Sidney Hillman. (See Matthew Josephson, Sidney Hillman, Doubleday, 1952).

Now, as for many years past, John Abt is general counsel for the Communist Party.

After the decision of the Supreme Court ordering the Party to register, the Party issued its response.]

1.

Members of the Jury:

As millions of people have come to realize, this is a historic trial. This is so because it involves eleven Communist leaders. This is so because it also involves the political principles and the inalienable rights of an American working-class party which bases its theory and program on scientific socialism. This is so because this trial involves the First Amendment to the United States Constitution, the rights of freedom of speech, press and assembly—and therefore involves the democratic liberties and future of all Americans.

We defendants contend, and have proved, that our trial is in fact, a most extraordinary trial, a political trial, a thought-control trial.

The prosecution has tried to try the untriable, as the evidence and testimony prove. While contending that this is just an "ordinary criminal case," it has nonetheless put before a court and a jury a whole body of mind-readers and crystal-gazers. They presumed to tell the jury what we Communist leaders would do, would teach, would advocate—if and when.

The prosecution could not bring us Communist leaders to trial for anything we have done, taught or advocated—individually or collectively. Yet it did not dare say frankly that it seeks to convict us for our political beliefs or for alleged hidden "dangerous thoughts." . . .

The prosecution says we defendants reconstituted the Communist Party as a working-class political party, basing itself on the principles of Marxism-Leninism.

This event took place in the broad light of day, three years before the indictment of July 20, 1948, was put together in the dark of the moon. The reconstitution of the Communist Party was front-page news in every newspaper and grist to the mill of every editor, columnist and radio commentator. The Communist Party documents setting forth the details, aims and purposes of this political event were public documents, widely circulated in June and July 1945, and thereafter.

What do these documents show to be the true facts concerning the reconstitution of the Communist Party? . . .

[They show] that we defendants, led by Foster, had been waging a struggle against Browder's incorrect and revisionist policies and his false estimate of the postwar world for a whole year before Jacques Duclos' important and wise article put the French Communists on guard against Browder's anti-Marxist influence. This protracted inner–Party conflict had nothing at all to do with any question of the advocacy of force and violence. Browder and his adherents held that sections of American monopoly would guarantee world peace and would lead the bandwagon of social progress after the war and that the working class could hitch on behind with not a care in the world.

In 1945, we defendants, as well as Foster, differed fundamentally with Browder. We understood that monopoly does not change its spots. We held then, as we hold today, that monopoly was and is reactionary and that only by joint action to curb the economic royalists could the workers and common people prevent the rise of fascism in our country, defend their living standards, achieve a stable peace and march forward along the road of social progress.

The record shows that our aim and the purpose in reconstituting the Communist Party was to enable it to become a more influential and effective working-class force in this postwar struggle to save our people from the force and violence of monopoly reaction, lynching and atomic war. It was to equip our Party to perform its role as the Marxist vanguard of the working class, leading the people's fight for peace, democracy and socialism.

The prosecution does not claim that we defendants organized a new political party or adopted a new set of principles in 1945. All it claims is that we went "back to the old Communist Party."

What "old" Communist Party? Even the prosecution cannot deny it means the Communist Party founded in September 1919. This was the same Communist Party which had been on the American scene, teaching and advocating the principles of Marxism-Leninism, lo, these many years. . . .

Probably most of you jurors never saw a real live Communist before you came to Foley Square. Perhaps you were surprised to find descendants of Daniel Boone and John and Priscilla Alden sharing leadership in our ranks with descendants of heroic Negro slaves. You must also have noted that just about half of these witnesses were World War II veterans. The record shows that there are 15,000 such veterans in our relatively small Communist Party. Many of them, including four of the defendants, hold leading posts in our Party.

By Fred Ellis, *Daily Worker,* 1948

It cannot have escaped your notice that men and women, Negro and white, of all national and religious origins and occupations—most of them workers and trade unionists—find their way to our Communist Party on the basis of their own experience and socialist convictions. . . .

One need not be either a Communist, or a Communist sympathizer, or a progressive, or a trade unionist, to recognize the difference between people with good or evil intent. One need not understand a single Marxist principle, or agree with a single word ever written by Lenin, to recognize the real conspiracy symbolized by the prosecution and its false witnesses; or to know that the defendants and the defense witnesses are men and women who are dedicated to serving the interests of the American people—Negro and white, and seek to promote peace and democratic advance.

2.

Fellow Americans:

Your constitutional rights, your security and welfare have been placed in mortal danger by decisions of a one-vote majority in the Supreme Court in two so-called anti-Communist cases on June 5, 1961.

By a 5 to 4 vote (including Justice Tom Clark, who should have disqualified himself as the Attorney General who first indicted Communist leaders in 1948 under the Smith Act) the Court has now imperiled the rights of all Americans.

For the first time in America's history, voluntary associations are made subject to licensing by the Federal government and activity on behalf of a legal political party is to be treated as a crime. This is the meaning of the registration requirements of the McCarran Act of 1950, both of which were upheld by the Supreme Court majority.

As a result:

• The Communist Party of the U.S.A. is ordered to register as an "action organization" described in the law as an agent of a foreign power promoting a conspiracy based on espionage, sabotage, terrorism and other heinous crimes. As such it is required to list publicly its officers and members.

• Persons described as "active" Communists can be jailed on testimony it was their "intent" to bring about the forcible overthrow of the government.

Under the McCarran Act a body of appointed government officials, the Subversive Activities Control Board, is given the right to decide who may or may not voluntarily associate themselves in any organization. The Board may decide this moreover, purely on the basis of the legislative "findings" of guilt in the Act itself. The accused is denied the right to trial.

At the same time these laws make it possible to attach the false designation of "action organization" or "front" to political parties, peace groups, labor unions, Negro organizations and a wide variety of civic bodies. After that, their members are deprived of many rights. They become subject to criminal prosecution unless they accede to public self-denunciation as traitors to their country or join the anti-Communist witchhunt.

Failure to comply with the registration order carries the fantastic penalty of a five-year prison sentence and a $10,000 fine for each day of such a failure.

In Hitler Germany a special group, the Jews, were singled out and compelled to wear a yellow arm band with the Star of David. In the U.S. today—unless the McCarran and Smith Acts are nullified—organizations which refuse to conform to the views of the powers-that-be are likewise to be compelled to bear a government-designed brand.

Under the labeling provision of the McCarran Act, even the Declaration of Independence or the Bible—if distributed by a group branded by the S.A.C.B. as a "Communist action" organization—would be required to bear on their covers a label designating them as Communist propaganda; nor is organized labor immune. More than once, unions have been branded by courts as conspiracies seeking illegal ends. Today they are shackled by the Taft–Hartley and Landrum–Griffin Acts which subject them to close government control. From here it is not a long step to their inclusion in a "Communist front" dragnet.

Once labeled, an organization's members become liable by that very act to prosecution under the individual membership clause of the Smith Act—a built-in unconstitutional self-incrimination device. Clearly, the Communist Party cannot go along with such un-American practices, any more than can militant trade unions or the embattled southern chapters of the National Association for the Advancement of Colored People, when faced with like demands.

The Court majority's disregard of traditional constitutional rights rests basically on two stale fraudulent arguments: that the Communists are foreign agents and that they advocate the forceful overthrow of our government.

The "foreign agent" canard has been used by reaction throughout our history to divide popular movements and discredit dissenters. Thomas Jefferson and his followers were labeled "Jacobins," agents of the French Revolution. Sen. Robert LaFollette and other loyal Americans were assailed as "pro-German" because they opposed our entrance into World War I; and have not our Catholic fellow-Americans, in and out of public life, been slanderously hounded as loyal to a foreign power, the Vatican?

Yet the truth is that in the entire 42-year history of the Communist Party not a single member has been convicted or even indicted as a foreign agent or for engaging in sabotage or treason. Nor has a single member ever been convicted of an act of force directed against our government. . . .

The McCarran Act was jammed through Congress on September 30, 1950 in the Korean War hysteria over the veto of President Truman. In his veto message President Truman warned:

" . . . these (registration) provisions are not merely ineffective and unworkable. They represent a clear and present danger to our institutions."

The Communist Party will defend its right to a legal existence under the Constitution and the Bill of Rights as a legitimate current in American political life, a movement that can trace its existence back a full century into our history, from the Communists who supported Lincoln and the Union, through the old Socialist Party. . . .

We have a profound confidence in the American people. We are proud of those in the American tradition—abolitionists, trade unionists, liberals, Negro leaders—who contributed so much to the democratic struggle and never flinched before threats of prosecution, jail or terror. Today's Freedom Riders are in that great tradition. . . .

It is not for ourselves alone that we speak. For we know full well that reactionary laws like the McCarran and Smith Acts have an evil purpose and a relentless logic and that in nation after nation the destruction of the democratic rights of all began with the attack "only" on the Communists. Inevitably the assault spread and sought to destroy all who stood for peace, economic security and democratic rights—the trade unions, the Socialists, the Jews, the liberals.

That is why we say to all our fellow-Americans, irrespective of political faith: the bell tolls not for the Communists alone, but for the hard-won rights of all Americans. All must act together to save American constitutional liberties.

National Committee
Communist Party, U.S.A.

□ ——————————————————————————————— □

IN DEFENSE OF BLACK LEADERSHIP

"Let Us Unite in Militant Defense of Negro Leadership!"
Statement issued by the National Committee
to Defend Negro Leadership, 1952

[*During the postwar repression Black leaders on a wide political spectrum were singled out for attack. The formation of the National Committee was in response to this move to stifle protest. Among the members of the committee were such outstanding leaders of the Black people as Bishop C. Alleyne, Bishop R.C. Ransom, Mrs. Mary Church Terrell, Reverend Charles A. Hill, Esther Cooper Jackson, James W. Ford and others.*

The leaders take note in this statement that all who seek changes "in the many Jim Crow laws" face the threat of the Smith Act.

The substance of their statement follows.]

Things have reached such a state in our country that almost any Negro leader who dares to fight hard for Negro rights is headed for trouble with the law, with "public opinion," or with hoodlum assassins.

Hundreds of our most devoted and militant leaders are now being pilloried in the daily press, or barred from speaking in public halls, or arrested and beaten by the police for alleged "disorderly conduct" or some other trumped-up charge. They are being prosecuted in the courts, or "investigated" by the Un-American Activities Committee, or hounded by the Federal Bureau of Investigation. Some have been forced to leave the country; others are barred from travel abroad; and more than a few have been murdered with impunity by hate–crazed enemies of Negro freedom.

No matter whether these leaders are Communists, non-Communist or anti-Communist, the "explanation" is most always the same. They are labeled "subversive" or "communistic," or "undesirable aliens," or "dangerous troublemakers."

Negro leaders active in the Communist Party are singled out for special persecution; but the attacks extend far beyond the Communists.

Benjamin J. Davis, Jr., member of the National Committee of the Communist Party and twice elected to the City Council of New York, is confined in a federal prison in Terre Haute, Indiana, and denied even the right to correspond with his friends. . . .

Mr. Davis, long a powerful fighter for Negro rights on many fronts, was convicted for alleged violation of the Smith Act. His "crime" was "conspiracy to teach and advocate" the theoretical principles of the Communist Party. Mr. [Harry] Moore, militant leader in the Negro's fight for the right to vote and for decent schools, was killed by the bomb of unknown assassins. Ku Klux Klan leader William Hendrix "explained" that the N.A.A.C.P. leader got "involved in a communistic crowd." . . .

• To be charged by the Un-American Activities Committee with associating with so-called "subversive organizations" leads to the barring from a New Jersey high school of one of the most eminent educators and civic leaders of the United States, Dr. Mary McLeod Bethune.

• To write and speak for Negro rights and for peace brings prosecution as a "foreign agent" and denial of passport rights to one of the greatest scholars this country ever produced, the 84-year-old Dr. W.E.B. Du Bois.

• To argue vigorously in Federal Court against conviction of his clients, Communist leaders indicted under the Smith Act, brings a "contempt" citation and six months in prison to an outstanding Detroit attorney, George W. Crockett, Jr.[5]

• To fight against segregated schools brings arrests for N.A.A.C.P. President Dr. W.A. Fingal and other leaders in Cairo, Illinois, and threats of death to Mrs. J.J. Hannibal, in Kingston, North Carolina.

• To lead the fight for the lives of Willie McGee, the "Martinsville Seven," the "Trenton Six" and other victims of Jim Crow frame-ups brings two trials for alleged "contempt of Congress" for the Executive Secretary of the Civil Rights Congress, William L. Patterson—the charge growing out of a hearing at which Georgia's Representative [Henderson] Lanham called the C.R.C. leader a "G-d damned black s.o.b.," and tried to attack him physically.

• To support a Negro veteran moving into a lily-white neighborhood in Cicero, Illinois, brings mob destruction of the apartment house and police arrests for N.A.A.C.P. attorney George Leighton and other leaders—for "conspiracy to lower property values!"

• To become an active leader of the Progressive Party brings discharge from his position to a professor of philosophy at the University of Minnesota, Dr. Forrest O. Wiggins.

• To fight hard for Negro rights, African freedom and peace brings public abuse, barring from concert halls and denial of the right to travel abroad to the great people's artist, Paul Robeson.

These are just a few examples of the mounting drive against hundreds of Negro leaders who defy the Jim Crow policies of our country and fight hard for the full citizenship rights of our people. There will be many hundreds more unless we put a stop—RIGHT NOW—to this unjust persecution of Negro leadership.

These growing attacks against Negro leaders are really directed against Negro citizens as a whole. They are designed to frighten off our leaders and curb the mounting struggles of the masses of our people against the rising tide of "white supremacy" during these years of war hysteria— especially since our country has been waging war against the colored peoples of China and Korea, and helping imperialist governments suppress the liberation struggles of other colored peoples in Asia and Africa.

For every Negro leader attacked there are thousands of rank and file Negro citizens beaten or killed by the police, "lynched" in the courts on frame-up charges, bombed in their homes, denied the right to vote, and forced into poverty by increasing job discrimination. Moreover, it is no accident that those Negro leaders singled out for attack are precisely the ones who fought hardest to establish the dignity and full citizenship of the masses of our people.

We here declare to all enemies of Negro freedom—whether they be outlaw hoodlums or officials of Government: Sirs, your efforts will fail! The Negro people will keep on fighting for their rights, ever more powerfully, until the very last vestige of Jim Crow oppression has been wiped off the face of our land!

The drive now under way against militant Negro leadership is greatly strengthened by a whole series of executive and legislative measures designed to silence all serious opposition from any quarter to basic foreign and domestic policies of the Federal Government.

The democratic rights of Negroes and all other Americans are being seriously undermined by the so-called "Loyalty Oath" purges of Federal employees and public school teachers; the curbing of trade union rights under the Taft–Hartley Act and other measures; the exercise of thought-control and the building of concentration camps under the McCarran Act; the wholesale round-up and deportation of aliens; the new restrictions on West Indians coming to this country under the McCarran–Walter Act; and especially the prosecution of Communist leaders for alleged violation of the Smith Act. . . .

The Smith Act poses a very special threat to Negro citizens. We have got to "teach and advocate" changes in the many Jim Crow laws and practices of federal, state and local governmental agencies. Thus we always run the risk that some paid "informer" will appear in court to testify that our intent, despite our words and deeds to the contrary, is to "overthrow the Government by force and violence."

This is why two eminent Negro attorneys—Richard E. Westbrooks and Earl B. Dickerson, of Chicago—urged the Supreme Court to reconsider its decision upholding the conviction of the Communist leaders under the Smith Act. They argued: "In the first place, advocacy of fundamental changes in government so as to extend democratic protection to the Negro people might well be equated, under the broad terms of the Court's decision, with advocacy of the violent overthrow of the Government. . . . The inevitable effect of the decision is to undermine, if not destroy, effective protest with regard to government practices and policies inimical to the welfare of Negroes."

Six Negro leaders of the Communist Party have already been victimized by the Smith Act. Henry Winston, National Organization Secretary, was convicted along with Benjamin J. Davis, Jr. and nine other members of the National Committee. Claudia Jones, Secretary of the National Women's Commission, and Pettis Perry, Secretary of the National Negro Commission, are now on trial in New York. . . .

The warning of Attorneys Westbrooks and Dickerson is tragically confirmed by the increasing number of unwarranted attacks against Negro leaders during this period of Smith Act prosecutions. Our "right of protest" is, indeed, being undermined; and without this right the Negro people have no hope of winning full citizenship.

The spokesmen of our Government proclaim their fervent desire to "extend democracy" everywhere throughout the world. Let them direct a little more of their democratic fervor toward the defense and extension of democracy here at home!

□ ———————————————————————————————— □

THE PERSECUTION OF ETHEL AND JULIUS ROSENBERG

"Statement of the National Committee of the Communist Party," signed by William Z. Foster, Pettis Perry and Elizabeth Gurley Flynn, *Daily Worker*, June 23, 1953.

[*Shortly before sunset on Friday, June 19, 1953, Ethel and Julius Rosenberg were executed at Sing Sing prison, Ossining, New York. Their deaths constituted the most brutal of the criminal governmental actions in the period of the cold war and aroused millions throughout the world in demonstrations of protest.*

Julius Rosenberg was arrested in July 1950, about a month after the outbreak of the Korean war. He was charged with having conspired to commit "espionage." In August his wife, Ethel, and Morton Sobell were also arrested and the three were charged with being instrumental in conveying the "secret" of the atom bomb to the Soviet Union. After a three-week trial, marked by fabricated and contradictory testimony, the Rosenbergs were sentenced to death and Sobell to 30 years in prison. Sobell was imprisoned from the time he was seized on August 18, 1950 to his release January 14, 1969. With court appeals exhausted, demands for clemency flooded the offices of two presidents. Truman left office without acting and Eisenhower refused to stop the execution.

The evidence that the federal government had arranged the murder of these two martyrs is continually growing with the passage of time. It testifies to the most heinous crime ever perpetrated in U.S. history.

The Communist Party, functioning under severe, semi-legal conditions, with much of its leadership in jail or indicted, participated actively in the campaign to save the Rosenbergs. Presented below are parts of a statement issued by the National Committee of the Communist Party following the executions.]

The Rosenberg case became the focus of the entire world's hatred of Washington's war policies, of the hatred and resistance to the effort to

McCarthyize America in the image of the swastika. Though foully murdered by the Eisenhower-Brownell-J. Edgar Hoover forces, in an atmosphere of McCarthyism, the Rosenbergs succeeded in unmasking the plot before the eyes of literally the majority of mankind. Though dead, they live on, growing more powerful every minute as the world camp of peace and democracy refuses to let their murderers get away with their conspiracy.

Around the defense of the heroic Rosenbergs there arose a wide popular movement which was gaining momentum rapidly. So much so that the Eisenhower administration hurried with obscene speed to get the execution over with before the people's movement against the murder would become irresistible. Americans in every walk of life were roused to protest the death penalty, including thousands of ministers and rabbis, leading atomic scientists, and others.

The final clemency train to Washington brought 15,000 to the White House, the biggest demonstration in the capital in this generation. The outpouring at the Rosenberg funeral was a grief-stricken but militant and angry demonstration of tens of thousands, determined to fight back.

In this historic battle for the preservation of democracy in the United States, it is a tragic fact that the organized labor movement was deceived by the colossal frame-up propaganda in this case; that it fell victim to the stupid and criminal myth that there existed an "atom bomb secret" which the Soviet Union had to "steal," and that this explains the terrible danger of atomic war under which our country lives today. Yet, this crude myth was debunked completely by the nation's leading scientists, and the Soviet Union offered time and time again to enter into a pact with our country to outlaw the atom bomb under a strong system of U.N. controls and inspection. . . .

There must be no more Rosenberg frameups! There must be a halt to the Hitlerization of America by the Eisenhower-Brownell-J. Edgar Hoover forces working hand in glove with the swastika-minded McCarthy and his goons. . . .

The task is now for us Americans not to falter in the face of this challenge, but to take inspiration from the courage of these two patriotic Americans who would not give the Jew-haters and the war-plotters what they wanted. It is up to us now to see the lessons of the Rosenberg case and to act on them!

The truth about the "whys and wherefores" of the frame-up must be brought to the labor movement, which should be shown that behind the Rosenberg frameup stood the worst enemies of all labor; that if the Rosenbergs could be framed "as spies," then any labor leader or militant

289

worker can be framed by the same forces on trumped-up charges of any kind. The Rosenberg case—like the Sacco-Vanzetti and Mooney and later cases—is a labor case. . . .

We bow our heads in tribute to two immortal American patriots, Ethel and Julius Rosenberg. The American people vow that those who murdered them and tried to murder America's heritage shall not succeed; but shall meet the threat of fascism with a new national resistance worthy of our great traditions.

□ ——————————————————————————————— □

REACTION ATTACKS THE FOREIGN BORN

The Deportation Terror, Abner Green,
New Century Publishers, 1950

[*The foreign born have always been a special target of reactionaries— from the Alien and Sedition laws of 1798 to the present-day hue and cry about "illegal aliens." Inevitably the oppressive atmosphere of the McCarthy period generated new assaults on the rights of the foreign born.*

The Smith Act, which is the legislation notorious for its use against Communist Party leaders, was passed in 1940 ostensibly as an alien registration act. Its provisions were made even more stringent in 1952 by the Walter-McCarran Act.

The American Committee for Protection of Foreign Born was organized in 1932 as an agency to assist non-citizens and naturalized citizens with problems arising as a result of their foreign birth.

Abner Green (1913-1959) who wrote the pamphlet from which we quote below, had been Executive Secretary of the Committee for seventeen years when he died in September 1959 at age 46. He was one of four trustees of the Civil Rights Congress Bail Fund who were sent to jail in 1951 for refusing to give the names of contributors to the Fund when ordered to do so by a prying Federal judge.

Two outstanding women distinguished themselves among the many persons who are remembered for their dedicated work in the Foreign Born committee. They were Carol King, its general counsel, and Harriet Baron, administrative secretary. Together with Abner Green they devoted many years to a tireless defense of foreign-born victims of ruling-class injustice.]

290

Three million non-citizens in the United States already live in an atmosphere of regimentation.

They have all been fingerprinted.

Every detail of their personal lives is on file with the F.B.I.

They cannot move from one address to another without notifying the Justice Department.

Their activities are under the constant surveillance of the F.B.I. and the Immigration and Naturalization Service.

They can be—and are—called in by immigration officials and subjected to hours of searching, questioning and examination.

They are warned by Justice Department officials to discontinue membership and activity in organizations which do not have the support or approval of the F.B.I.

They are threatened with denials of citizenship, deportation, imprisonment, loss of their jobs if they do not conform with the instructions of Justice Department officials.

The Justice Department wants to dictate to 3,000,000 citizens what they shall think, what they can read, whom they may see, erecting a legal and political concentration camp around the minds of the non-citizen population.

Our democracy will not long survive under these restrictions. Citizens will find their rights equally restricted and endangered once thought-control is imposed on non-citizens. . . .

The Justice Department is using the non-citizen as a guinea pig in an attempt to establish dangerous and undemocratic principles.

Arrests of non-citizens are accompanied by false and misleading statements to the press.

Most metropolitan newspapers need no encouragement to use their news columns for alien-baiting and provoking hysteria against the non-citizen.

Deportation arrests secure front-page spreads and banner headlines, with the aim of inflaming the public's mind against so-called dangerous alien Reds.

It is clearly the belief of the Justice Department that the American people will not come to the defense of the rights of non-citizens if non-citizens can be made a sufficiently unpopular minority. . . .

In the course of its deportation drive, the Justice Department has repeatedly attempted to use deportation to weaken and destroy trade unions.

Of the 135 non-citizens arrested to date, 41 are active members and leaders of trade unions. . . .

Just as his union was entering negotiations with employers in March, 1948, Irving Potash, leader of the Furriers Joint Council of New York, was arrested in deportation proceedings.

This pattern of using the deportation laws to interfere with the legitimate activities of American trade unionists is carried out by the Justice Department in every section of the country.

The recent attack on the union of Alaska Cannery Workers, in Seattle, is one more example of the anti-labor bias of Justice Department officials.

The Alaska Cannery Workers Union, F.T.A.-C.I.O., Local 7, has raised its members' wages from $25 a month in 1934 to $250 a month in 1949. Throughout the years the Associated Farmers of California and the Alaska Salmon Industry have tried unsuccessfully to destroy this union.

All other efforts failing, finally in 1949, the Justice Department moved in, and during September arrested for deportation to the Philippine Islands the three leaders of this union: Ernesto Mangaoang, business agent; Chris Mensalvos, educational director; and Ponce Torres, dispatcher.[6]

Then there is the unrelenting drive against Harry Bridges—a history of 15 years of persecution because of his progressive and militant leadership of longshoremen and warehousemen on the West Coast. . . .

The deportation drive and the hysteria against the foreign born are an essential part of the concentrated drive on the rights of all minorities in the United States and the general assault on the liberties of the American people.

□ ── □

RACISM—PATTERN FOR GENOCIDE

We Charge Genocide: The Historic Petition to the United Nations for Relief from a Crime of the United States Government Against the Negro People,
William L. Patterson, ed., Civil Rights Congress, 1951

[*The presentation of* We Charge Genocide *to the United Nations was a bold and dramatic step taken by representatives of the Black people, with the support of white progressive forces. In December 1951, William L. Patterson (b. 1891) appeared at the 5th Session of the General Assembly in Paris, while Paul Robeson led a delegation to the Office of the*

Secretary General in New York City. Thus the petition was presented in Europe and in the United States simultaneously.

The document cites a history of crimes against an oppressed people. The evidence refers principally to events from 1945 to 1950. The list has grown considerably since then.

The 1951 printing of We Charge Genocide *was followed by several more editions presenting additional evidence.*

The historic challenge raised by William L. Patterson more than a quarter of a century ago remains. In the preface to a new edition published in 1970, (International Publishers), the noted actor and playright Ossie Davis writes: "We Charge Genocide—not only of the past but of the future. And we swear: it must not, it shall not, it will not happen to our people."

Here is the introduction to this historic document.]

Out of the inhuman Black ghettos of American cities, out of the cotton plantations of the South, comes this record of mass slayings on the basis of race, of lives deliberately warped and distorted by the willful creation of conditions making for premature death, poverty and disease. It is a record that calls aloud for condemnation, for an end to these terrible injustices that constitute a daily and ever-increasing violation of the United Nations Convention on the Prevention and Punishment of the Crime of Genocide.

It is sometimes incorrectly thought that genocide means the complete and definitive destruction of a race or people. The Genocide Convention however, adopted by the General Assembly of the United Nations on December 9, 1948, defines genocide as any killings on the basis of race, or, in its specific words, as "killing members of the group." Any intent to destroy, in whole or in part, a national, racial, ethnic, or religious group is genocide, according to the Convention. Thus, the Convention states, "causing serious bodily or mental harm to members of the group" is genocide, as well as "killing members of the group."

We maintain, therefore, that the oppressed Negro citizens of the United States, segregated, discriminated against and long the target of violence, suffer from genocide as the result of the consistent, conscious, unified policies of every branch of government.

The Civil Rights Congress has prepared and submits this petition to the General Assembly of the United Nations on behalf of the Negro people in the interest of peace and democracy, charging the Government of the United States of America with violation of the Charter of the United Nations and the Convention on the Prevention and Punishment of the Crime of Genocide.

We believe that in issuing this document we are discharging an historic responsibility to the American people, as well as rendering a service of inestimable value to progressive mankind. We speak of the American people because millions of white Americans in the ranks of labor and the middle class, and particularly those who live in the southern states and are often contemptuously called poor whites, are themselves suffering to an ever greater degree from the consequences of the Jim Crow segregation policy of government in its relations with Negro citizens. We speak of progressive mankind because a policy of discrimination at home must inevitably create racist commodities for export abroad—must inevitably tend toward war.

We have not dealt here with the cruel and inhuman policy of this government toward the people of Puerto Rico. Impoverished and reduced to a semi-literate state through the wanton exploitation and oppression by gigantic American concerns, through the merciless frame-up and imprisonment of hundreds of its sons and daughters, this colony of the rulers of the United States reveals in all its stark nakedness the moral bankruptcy of this government and those who control its home and foreign policies.[7]

History has shown that the racist theory of government of the U.S.A. is not the private affair of Americans, but the concern of mankind everywhere.

It is our hope and we fervently believe that it was the hope and aspiration of every Black American whose voice was silenced forever through premature death at the hands of racist-minded hooligans or Klan terrorists, that the truth recorded here will be made known to the world; that it will speak with a tongue of fire loosing an unquenchable moral crusade, the universal response to which will sound the death knell of all racist theories.

We have scrupulously kept within the purview of the Convention on the Prevention and Punishment of the Crime of Genocide which is held to embrace those "acts committed with intent to destroy in whole or in part a national, ethnical, racial or religious group as such."

We particularly pray for the most careful reading of this material by those who have always regarded genocide as a term to be used only where the acts of terror evinced an intent to destroy a whole nation. We further submit that this Convention on Genocide is by virtue of our avowed acceptance of the Covenant of the United Nations, an inseparable part of the law of the United States of America.

According to international law, and according to our own law, the Genocide Convention, as well as the provisions of the United Nations

Charter, supersedes, negates and displaces all discriminatory racist law on the books of the United States and the several states.

The Hitler crimes, of awful magnitude, beginning as they did against the heroic Jewish people, finally drenched the world in blood and left a record of maimed and tortured bodies and devastated areas such as mankind had never seen before. Justice Robert H. Jackson, who now sits upon the United States Supreme Court bench, described this holocaust to the world in the powerful language with which he opened the Nuremberg trials of the Nazi leaders. Every word he voiced against the monstrous Nazi beast applies with equal weight, we believe, to those who are guilty of the crimes herein set forth.

Here we present the documented crimes of federal, state and municipal governments in the United States of America, the dominant nation in the United Nations, against 15,000,000 of its own nationals—the Negro people of the United States. These crimes are of the gravest concern to mankind. The General Assembly of the United Nations, by reason of the United Nations Charter and the Genocide Convention, itself is invested with power to receive this indictment and act on it.

The proof of this fact is its action upon the similar complaint of the Government of India against South Africa.

We call upon the United Nations to act and to call the Government of the United States to account. . . .

The Civil Rights Congress is a defender of constitutional liberties, human rights and of peace. It is the implacable enemy of every creed, philosophy, social system or way of life that denied democratic rights or one iota of human dignity to any human being because of color, creed, nationality or political belief.

We ask all men and women of good will to unite to realize the objectives set forth in the summary and prayer concluding this petition. We believe that this program can go far toward ending the threat of a third world war. We believe it can contribute to the establishment of a people's democracy on a universal scale.

But may we add as a final note that the Negro people desire equality of opportunity in this land where their contributions to the economic, political and social developments have been of splendid proportions and in quality second to none. They will accept nothing less, and continued efforts to force them into the category of second-class citizens through force and violence, through segregation, racist law and an institutionalized oppression, can only end in disaster for those responsible.

Respectfully submitted by the Civil Rights Congress as a service to the peoples of the world, and particularly to the lovers of peace and democracy in the United States of America.

William L. Patterson
National Executive Secretary, Civil Rights Congress

□ ─── □

YOUTH FIGHT RACISM

"The Murder of Emmett Till,"
New Challenge, November, 1955

[*The launching of a new Marxist youth organization challenged the myth that the youth had become a "silent generation."*

On May 28, 1949, the Labor Youth League (LYL) was established in Chicago. It revived the tradition of the Young Communist League. In 1950 the League was engaged in the campaign against the Korean war. It collected over half a million signatures for the Stockholm peace pledge. On November 24, 1950, it helped organize 5,000 youth in an anti-war demonstration. In the summer of 1951, one of its young Black leaders, Roosevelt Ward, was sentenced to three years imprisonment on a trumped-up draft evasion charge.

The Subversive Activities Control Board (SACB) in a drive to liqui- date militant organizations, subpoenaed League leaders to appear before it in 1953. In 1955 the SACB ordered the League to register as an alleged "Communist front." The League never complied. Some years later the LYL disbanded.

The Labor Youth League came into being at the beginning of the McCarthy period. Throughout its stormy existence it was subject to harassment by the McCarthys, the McCarrans and the HUACs. Never- theless it did not lose its fighting spirit or its ability to respond to issues. This was shown, for example, in 1955, when it reacted to the brutal murder of young Emmett Till in a special issue of its organ New Challenge.]

On August 20, 1955, a 14-year-old Negro schoolboy from Chicago went with his cousin to visit his great-uncle in Sumner, Mississippi. His name was Emmett Louis Till.

Barely two weeks later, Emmett Till was dead, brutally murdered for supposedly "whistling" at a white woman. Half-brothers J.W. Milam and Roy Bryant, who admitted kidnapping Emmett, were indicted for the murder.

Their trial lasted 5 days. The jury—which had no Negroes, no women, no young people—"deliberated" for an hour and a few minutes and returned the expected "not guilty" verdict.

What did Americans say about Emmett Till's murder? Why did it really happen? What can be done about it?"

Emmett "Bo" Till was a popular 8th-grader at the McCosh School in Chicago.

But school opened without him this fall, for "Bo" had become the latest in an endless line of lynch-victims reaching from the defeat of Reconstruction in the 1870s.

Chicago, especially the 800,000 strong Negro community, has become boiling mad, first at the bestial crime and then at the arrogant acquittal of the lynchers.

Demands for action quickly followed the gigantic funeral demonstration of nearly a quarter-million who viewed "Bo's" battered body. A triple overflow crowd of 10,000 jammed one of the South Side's largest churches to hear leaders of the National Association for the Advancement of Colored People, of the Steel Union, of the Packinghouse Workers, demand Federal intervention and passage of Federal anti-lynch legislation.

Organized youth have also spoken out.

A Youth Memorial to Emmett Till was called by the Chicago NAACP Youth Council September 30. Fully 40 percent of those who turned out were white young people. The meeting launched a campaign for 25,000 signatures to a giant 5-foot-square telegram to the President demanding that he "denounce . . . this hideous crime" and "instruct the Attorney General to take Federal action." They voted their support to adult proposals for a March on Washington.

And they urged a similar march on City Hall to demand that Mayor Daley end Chicago's "Mississippi" at Trumbull Park Homes. . . .

They realize that racist violence anywhere encourages violence everywhere.

Terror in the South: Behind the murder of Emmett Till lies a campaign of terror against southern Negroes—and whites. Its aim—to halt the growing movement to apply the Supreme Court no–school–segregation decision.[8]

Race hatred was whipped to a fever pitch following the widely–hailed high court ruling. Southern governors and congressmen openly called for flouting it. They were afraid—afraid of the new militancy and

297

courage of southern Negroes. And they were afraid of the new, but little-publicized, democratic feelings of many whites.

Example: a meeting this summer of 375 college students from 9 southeastern states at the Methodist Assembly Center, Lake Junalaska, North Carolina, unanimously adopted a resolution pledging support to the Supreme Court decision. They also called for an end to rules barring Negroes from swimming at the center.

Young white southerners especially have been saying, "If it was left to us school segregation would end tomorrow." (This was why young people were kept off the Till murder jury!)

According to a dispatch from Orangeburg, South Carolina, in the "Pittsburgh Courier" of Sept. 17, war has been declared on Negroes signing petitions for desegregation:

"Public officials from the mayor of the city to the sheriff of the county are all mobilized in a campaign of terror, economic pressure and widespread firings. Enlisted in the campaign to subvert the U.S. Supreme Court's anti-bias decision are representatives of the New York Life Insurance Company, Standard Oil, Coca Cola, Shell Oil and Ford Motors." . . .

"The murder of Emmett Till must be the beginning of the end of segregation and lynching!"

This is what people are saying in memorial meetings and protest rallies throughout the U.S.

But so far, the administration in Washington hasn't said a word about the murder of Emmett Till and this is an administration which doesn't spare words when it claims a violation of freedom—thousands of miles from our shores!

Clearly, the unpunished murder of Emmett Till and the force and violence used against would-be Negro voters in Mississippi show a plot to subvert the Constitution.

First, therefore, the federal government must declare that there is a breakdown of law and order in Mississippi.

All the power that resides in Washington must be used to investigate and to guarantee justice in the murders of Emmett Till, Lamar Smith and Rev. George Lee and to guarantee Negroes the right to vote, in accordance with the 15th Amendment to the Constitution.

If Mississippi persists in refusing to allow Negroes their vote, then Congress has the duty under the 14th Amendment to cut down that state's representation to Congress.

The next session of Congress, opening in January, also has the opportunity to pass laws making lynching a federal offense, doing away with the poll-tax and guaranteeing equal employment rights for all. . . . Congress can also halt federal grants to any state which tries to evade the Supreme Court anti-segregation decision.

Through our individual letters and telegrams, through our organizations and unions, young Americans can influence the White House, Congress and both political parties to at once move into action—to wipe out the shame of Mississippi and to protect democracy and freedom right here at home—for all of us!

□ ——————————————————————————— □

PEACE STRUGGLE IN MILWAUKEE

**1. "Peace Appeal of Milwaukee
Labor Peace Committee, 1950"
2. "Only 20 to Blame at Nash, Says Webb,"
Milwaukee Journal, July 27, 1950**

[*At the start of the Korean war a national hysteria was let loose to crush all opposition. The war started right after the huge Stockholm peace petition campaign in which more than two million signatures were collected in the United States. The hysteria was abetted by the top labor bureaucracy to stifle peace sentiment in the labor movement. Mob violence was instigated in a number of plants.*

Vigilantes operated unhampered in many plants throughout the country. At Nash Motors in Milwaukee, Roy M. Webb, a Communist and a pioneer in organizing the plant, was attacked by a gang of vigilantes. This resulted in his hospitalization with a broken back. It was a reprisal for the circulation of a peace petition which was sponsored by a group of rank-and-file workers.

In Los Angeles, on July 20, 1950, four peace activists, members of Chrysler Local 230, United Auto Workers, were severely beaten by a local goon squad led by a railroad detective employed by the Santa Fe Railroad. Days later, on July 31, at the General Motors plant in Linden, N.J. two workers were attacked for passing out leaflets.

But the overwhelming sentiment of the people was for peace, not war. The same state in which Roy Webb was assaulted became the scene of a "grassroots revolt" with "embattled farmers in western Wisconsin massing in revolt against what they called too drastic draft regulations," reported the St. Paul Pioneer Press *(May 16, 1952). And Roy Webb was elected shop steward at the Nash plant!*]

1.

Milwaukee Labor Peace Committee—Milwaukee, Wis.

July 20, 1950

TO: Trygve Lie
    Dean Acheson, Sec'y of State
    Wisconsin Congressmen and Senators:

Gentlemen:

We, the undersigned trade unionists of Wisconsin are deeply concerned for fear that the Korean war might grow into a worldwide atomic war which would kill and cripple millions of Americans and people of other countries.

The best way to prevent this is to bring an end to hostilities in Korea as soon as possible by withdrawing all American troops and weapons from Korea immediately, and giving full freedom to the Korean people to decide their own destinies free from all outside interference.

We agree with the *Wisconsin CIO News* editorial of July 7, 1950, when it says: "As in China and the Philippines, the United States has repeated the same mistake in Korea. . . . In our hurry to find somebody to take hold in Korea, we took hold of the wrong friends."

We oppose any support by the U.S. Government to the South Korean Government of Syngman Rhee, which has imprisoned and killed tens of thousands of trade unionists and political opponents in the past five years.

We oppose the use of the atomic bomb against the Korean people. In 1925, the United States took the lead in proposing the outlawing of poison gas in warfare. We urge now that the U.S. Government take the lead in bringing about the outlawing of the atomic bomb by all nations and declaring that government which first uses it, to be an enemy of mankind.

We support the Stockholm World Peace Appeal and call on all other trade unionists of Wisconsin to sign that appeal and to circulate it in the interests of peace in the world.

[The following are the original sponsors of the petition:]
Robert Berberich, Vice Pres. Lodge 191-B. of R.T.; Edmund V. Bobrowicz, Int'l Rep.—Fur and Leather Workers; John Chaplock, Member—Local 75—UAW-CIO; Harold Christoffel, Former Pres. Allis Chalmers Union—UAW-CIO; Emil Churchich, Steward—Local 75—UAW-CIO; James De Witt, Int'l Rep.—UE-FE; Alfred Hirsch, Former Editor, *Wisconsin CIO News;* Joseph Horton, Member AFL

Linoleum Layers Union; William Landrum, Member AFL Laborers #113; Perry Love, Member CIO Steelworkers Union; Charley Moore, Executive Board Member Local 47—IFLWU; Matt Pirkir, Member Hosiery Workers Union; George Sommers, Member Brewery Workers #9—Delegate to Milwaukee CIO Council; Roy M. Webb, Member— Local 75—UAW-CIO; all these are from Milwaukee and Robert Buse, Greendale, Former Pres. Allis Chalmers Union—UAW-CIO; Albert Ruppel, Sheboygan, Member UE-FE; and Ewald Schultz, Former Secretary USA-CIO-1343.

2.

Roy M. Webb claimed Wednesday through his attorney that "no more than 20" Nash Motors workers are responsible for the disturbances at the plant.

Webb is one of eight men forced off the job Friday and Monday by fellow workers who suspected them of pro-Communist leanings. Webb was thrown out of the plant and his back was broken Tuesday when he attempted to go to work in his regular department.

Two of the other seven were Webb's sons, Roy B. and Clyde.

Webb's attorney, M. Michael Essin, state chairman of the People's Progressive Party, asked Dist. Atty. William J. McCauley to issue John Doe warrants for four men who actually threw Webb out of the plant while 300 others watched. . . .

Essin claimed the company's insistence that it does not know who the four men are is "ridiculous" because, according to Webb, some company officials witnessed the incident.

☐ ———————————————————————————— ☐

STICKING TO BASICS

"Foreword," *Steel Labor's Road,*
Published by the Communist Party, USA, 1953

[*In the year 1953 the Communist Party was being harassed by the McCarthyites, the House Un-American Activities Committee, the McCarran Act, the Taft-Hartley Act, the Smith Act and the FBI. Before the decade was over, the Internal Revenue Service would join the pack, all seeking to destroy the Party.*

But the Party continued to drive for its major objectives. Industrial concentration has been a prime activity of the Party since its early days—

and no area of concentration was ever considered more important than steel, where the establishment of Left-Center unity remains so important. With Steel Labor's Road *the Party reached the steel workers, inspiring them with their own history, pointing to problems while acknowledging that "we claim no monopoly on solutions."*

Here is the text of the opening pages.]

This book is dedicated to the more than one and a half million steel-workers of our country, over one million of whom are organized in a mighty union, the United Steelworkers of America (CIO).

The steelworkers and their union are one of the strongest sections of the working class of the United States. They are destined, by virtue of their strength and decisive position in the economy, to play a leading role in moving our country forward to a new day of peace, prosperity, democracy and social progress.

Sixteen years ago, in March 1937, the great open-shop fortress of the industry, U.S. Steel, was forced to sign a contract with the Steel Workers' Organizing Committee. Two months later, on May 26th, the plants of "Little Steel" were struck when the corporations, led by Republic Steel, decided to prevent the union from becoming established. Tom Girdler, ex-police thug turned corporation president, sounded the battle-cry: "I would rather go to the farm and pick apples than sign a union contract." After four months of bitter struggle, followed by court fights and NLRB elections, the corporations signed a contract. But Girdler didn't go apple-picking; he stayed around to pick up new millions in profits. The more than 50-year long struggle to unionize steel had been won.

The historic 1892 five-month long strike at the Homestead–Carnegie plant and most especially the great 1919 organizing drive and steel strike led by William Z. Foster, were the dress rehearsals for the victorious organizing drive of the thirties.

As a result of the 1919 strike, the 12-hour day was abolished and the workers learned, even though their effort to establish the union was temporarily smashed, that the steel trust was not "invincible," that it could be licked and compelled to deal with the steelworkers.

For 16 years following the 1919 strike, the Communist Party, led by William Z. Foster, its National Chairman, labored long and tirelessly to bring unionism to the steelworkers. Guided by Foster's tremendous experience (summed up in such writings as *The Great Steel Strike and Its Lessons, Unionizing Steel, Organizing Methods in the Steel Industry, What Means a Strike in Steel?*, etc.) the Communists made valuable contributions to organizing the industry.

302

Important and decisive as was the role of the Communists in founding and building the union and the CIO, the Communists make no claim to being solely responsible for this great achievement.

The fact is that credit must be shared by many forces of differing viewpoints: Those AFL unions which advocated the industrial form of organization; the mighty United Mine Workers Union under the leadership of John L. Lewis, which provided the drive, the resources and many skilled leaders, such as Philip Murray and others and the Communists.

This coalition of differing trends which merged their efforts in a common great goal produced the powerful CIO. The American labor movement knows no times in its past history which were more glorious than when this great coalition existed. Never before had the working class made such great gains as in the days of that coalition.

So long as the coalition was maintained, the CIO was on the upgrade, growing in strength and prestige and building up a superb record of improved working and living conditions for its members from year to year. That coalition—and its momentum for a time even after it was smashed—succeeded in raising the average steel wage from $.66 an hour to over $1.86 an hour.

At the peak of its power, the CIO had over 6 million members. That was when the coalition was at its strongest. Then came the break-up of the coalition.

The Big Business interests unleashed their anti-Communist offensive, McCarthyism was let loose on an unsuspecting public and there were those in the CIO who joined the chorus of anti-Communist hysteria. Eleven unions were expelled from the CIO as "Communist-dominated," war was declared on Communist and militant workers in the remaining CIO unions; the CIO membership dropped to around 4 million members.

Big Business always hated the CIO. It always dreamed of destroying it. The Taft-Hartley Law, the present efforts to ban industry-wide bargaining (which is a source of strength for the CIO and especially the steel union), and new anti-labor legislation, are aimed at the destruction of the unions. You can imagine the joy in Wall Street when the financial tycoons saw the break-up of the grand coalition within the CIO instead of an even stronger unity against ruling class attacks.

The weakening of the CIO was only the first step. Big Business had a purpose in mind in bringing about the break in CIO unity. Its aim was to bring about an attack on wages, working and living conditions as the means of vastly increasing its already swollen profits. That attack is now unfolding.

Today new problems face the steelworkers and their families, along with all American workers, small farmers and the Negro people.

Wage increases are eaten up by price and tax increases; speed-up runs rampant through the mills; the Taft–Hartley axe and other anti-democratic laws hang over the unions; the unions themselves and all the gains won by the working class face the threat of destruction; the fires of war rage in various parts of the world, menacing all with the danger of a third world war, in preparation for which three and a half million young Americans are already in uniform.

The open taking over of the government by Big Business, with its billion dollar cabinet, has served to aggravate the whole situation and matters will not be long in coming to a head. The whole labor movement is coming to an important turning point.

It is the fervent hope of every forward-looking American that the labor movement will be able to not only weather the storm, but will be able to provide that leadership which will help guide our country past the shoals and rocks of war and fascism and into the safe harbor of peace, democracy and social progress.

How can the mighty steelworkers' union best defend the interests of its members and the working class today? Can a new and great coalition of united labor strength be forged in the American labor movement? How? What is at the bottom of our difficulties and why? What can be done to overcome these difficulties?

These are some of the questions for which steelworkers demand an answer; for which they must have answers.

We claim no monopoly on the answers. There are many answers, offered by many "authorities." The steelworkers themselves are the best judge of what are the right answers.

We offer this book as a contribution to the thinking of steelworkers. We are confident that workers need but the opportunity to weigh matters for themselves provided they get all the facts in order to determine what is the best course to follow.

□ ——————————————————————————————————— □

A COMMUNIST PROGRAM FOR THE SOUTH

**The Southern People's Common Program for Democracy,
Prosperity and Peace, issued by the Southern Regional
Committee of the Communist Party, U.S.A., 1953**

[*The work of the Communist Party in the South was seriously disrupted
during the last few years of Earl Browder's administration as general
secretary of the Party. It was essentially replaced by non-Party forms.
After July 1945, when the Party restored its Marxist-Leninist character,
the task of rebuilding the Party in the South had to be undertaken, a
process which, given the circumstances, was to take many years.*

*It hardly needs to be reiterated that the Party was under sharp and
varied attack during the 1950s and had to spend much of its energies and
resources in defending itself and its democratic allies. Nevertheless it did
not permit itself to be diverted from its major political responsibilities.*

*One of its outstanding efforts during the difficult years of this period
was the preparation and distribution of "The Southern People's Common Program." This well-printed and attractively illustrated document
of 24 pages offered "Ten points to rally round for united struggle—for
real Democracy in Government—for Equality in Rights and Privileges
for ALL! For Neighborly Relations in a World at Peace!"*

*Virginia-born James E. Jackson, prominent national Party leader,
drafted the program and coordinated the distribution of 100,000 copies.
This was accomplished in a single day, using a number of widely
separated post offices to avoid disruption of the mailing by anti-Black
gangs inside and out of the government. Following are summary sections
of the Program.*]

We southerners live in a part of America that is very rich in the bounties
of nature. Its farmland is blessed with the most favorable climate. There
is plentiful pasturage and timberland upon our good earth. Beneath the
southern soil are great deposits of oil, coal, ore, sulphur, nitrates and
many other mineral riches. We have excellent harbors and our rivers are
among the country's finest.

Yet, we who live in this future garden-spot of our country have the
lowest incomes in the United States. Our education is the poorest. Our
housing is the worst. Our health facilities don't begin to meet the needs of
our citizens.

Just as we southern people are less well-off than the people of all other sections of the country, we are also the victims of the worst tyranny. We have fewer democratic rights than our countrymen living in states outside of our southern region. . . .

If we, the plain people of the South are to save our lives, our liberty—if we are to secure our future, we must stand together, work together, establish firm bonds of unity for a common program for peace, progress and democracy. . . .

Such a program of united action, such an approach on the part of the southern people to meet the challenge of the threatening crisis is not without historical precedent. It is in keeping with the glorious traditions bequeathed us in the thoughts and deeds of past generations of southern men and women. The democratic aspirations of the plain people of the South today date back to some of the thoughts of Thomas Jefferson of Virginia and some of the works and ideas of Andrew Jackson of Tennessee. Our generation of southern men and women take pride in the history of our struggle for real democracy. We draw strength from the heroic endeavors of the Radical Republican regimes of the decade following the Civil War. We take pride in the valiant battles and noble dreams of Populists and Alliance men of the turn of the last century. We associate ourselves with and would further extend the significant beginnings toward a New Deal for the Common Man—so auspiciously begun during the Roosevelt decade of the late 30s and so shamelessly betrayed by his successor. The New Deal concept was born of the united political aspirations of labor, the farmers, the Negro people and local businessmen. It was the concerted action of the plain people which wrested significant concessions and reform promises from the privileged and wealthy rulers of the country. . . .

To insure the success of this broad popular front of the southern people for democracy, progress and peace, it shall be necessary for the organized workers (white and Negro) to become the most conscientious, determined and tireless class component. It is the organized workers who must supply initiative and eventually leadership for the whole movement. The best road forward for the southern workers lies in taking the lead in this struggle of the vast majority of the southern people for genuine democratic reforms, for economic advancement and peace. Victory will create the conditions for the southern workers—in league with their class throughout the country—to undertake their historic march toward that next stage of mankind's progress—Socialism.

For the popular movement of the southern people to accomplish lasting victories, it must include Negroes in its ranks and leadership. It must seek unity of action and alliance with the Negro Liberation

Movement on a number of specific common issues and mutual objectives. . . .

The Communist Party puts forward this Common Program as a minimum and practical basis for unity and struggle of the greatest number of southern people for democracy, progress and peace in their region of our country. The Communist Party declares its unreserved and unequivocal allegiance to this program. It adopts it as its own immediate, minimum demands and pledges its cooperation with all organizations which unselfishly work for the realization of the Common Program or any part of it. . . .

The Communist Party will work for greater cooperation and united action of the trade unions. It will resolutely combat the prejudices of white supremacy which operate to divide the workers along the color line and sap their strength. It will work for the organization of the unorganized workers and working farmers. It will work to expose the false ideas of the bosses and their agents in the ranks of the workers. It will strive always to raise the consciousness of the workers to their own class needs and their political responsibility to themselves and the whole people.

The Communist Party underscores the fact that the Common Program is not a program for the establishment of socialism in the South. This is a program around which the vast majority of the southern people—white and Negro—workers, farmers and city middle classes, can work together regardless of their beliefs concerning the future of capitalist society. The central goal of this movement is to eliminate antidemocratic, feudal and autocratic political and economic relations, laws, institutions and practices from the South. The program aims to bring the local and state governments into line with the best intentions of the U.S. Constitution and its Bill of Rights. . . .

The Communist Party teaches that a permanent solution of the problems of the workers, poor farmers, Negro people—all the oppressed and exploited—can be achieved only by a government established and led by the working class and its allies, that is, a socialist government. Socialism is a social system under which there is no exploitation of man by man, no poverty or unemployment. Under Socialism, the aim of production is not to secure profits for a handful of capitalists. Production is geared to secure the maximum satisfaction of the constantly growing material and cultural requirements of the whole of society.

The Communist Party can adopt and support the Common Program as the guide for its activity because it recognizes that the fight for democratic reforms is in the interest of the workers and all the oppressed sections of the population. The struggle for these partial democratic reforms is thoroughly consistent with the fundamental beliefs of the Marxist-Leninist science of social progress. Only democratic achievements as envisaged in the Common Program will make it possible for the working class to consolidate its forces, consummate its alliance with all other exploited classes and fully establish its leadership and authority in the eyes of the people. The Communist Party declares that the fight for the Common Program is the necessary road for the working class to take now in order to continue on its march toward its ultimate goal of Socialism and Communism. . . .

The Communist Party urges all thinking people of the South to study the Common Program carefully, to join discussions, debates and to criticize it. The Communist Party places its program before all of the people's organizations—trade unions, political clubs, fraternal societies, civic clubs, etc.—throughout the South for discussion. The Communist Party urges these organizations to express themselves publicly upon the program and to adopt it—in whole or in part—for their program. The Communist Party calls upon democratic minded, forward looking leaders in all walks of life—and particularly trade union leaders—to initiate local and Southwide coalition movements for united action for one or all of the ten objectives of the Common Program.

Southern men and women—Negro and white!

Workers, farmers, youth, professionals and small business people!

UNITE BEHIND A COMMON PROGRAM!

- for Real Democracy in Government!
- for Equality in Rights and Privileges for ALL!
- for Neighborly Relations in a World at Peace!

□ ———————————————————————————————————— □

FIGHTING BUREAUCRACY

What it Means to be a Communist by Henry Winston,
New Century Publishers, N.Y., 1951

[*Trade union democracy is basic to the functioning of the labor movement. It gives the rank and file the means to participate in shaping policy and developing its activities. But bureaucracy in the top leadership serves as a barrier to its full realization. Communists in union leadership fought against bureaucracy, as the pages of this volume show. But some have succumbed to this pernicious practice.*

308

Henry Winston, National Chairperson of the Communist Party, directs his attention to this crucial question. He discusses the standards and values of Communists who are entrusted with leading posts in a trade union. He is uniquely qualified to deal with this subject.

His contributions reach into all fields of Party and public life. He is widely known for his attention to questions of Party organization and his talent in developing Party leadership. He does not view this in a narrow, partisan manner. He is the sworn enemy of bureaucracy and opportunism, twin evils of the hierarchy in the trade unions.

Winston's history personifies the noblest qualities of leadership. Convicted in the first Smith Act trial, he was confined to Terre Haute prison where he was criminally neglected while suffering from a brain tumor. He was finally rushed to a US Public Health Hospital where, following surgery, he lost his eyesight. In an interview with the press he charged: "Had officials and governmental authorities, even as late as 1959, heeded my complaints, I might not be blind today." As a result of popular pressure, President John F. Kennedy issued a presidential order which gave him his freedom when he left the hospital, Friday, June 30, 1961.

His words, after release, will remain an inspiration to all who fight oppression. He said: "I return from prison with the unshaken conviction that the people of our great land, Negro and white, need a Communist Party fighting for the unity of the people for peace, democracy, security and socialism. I take my place in it again with deep pride. My sight is gone but my vision remains."

Below he examines the weaknesses of some Communists who fell into bureaucratic ways. In his report to the 15th Convention, he calls for the eradication of undemocratic methods. Characteristically he insists on maintaining the highest standards for Communists who are entrusted to positions of leadership.]

The training of cadres requires a struggle against Right-opportunist and "Left"-sectarian tendencies. Under the pressure of enemy blows, there will be casualties, and we should not be taken by surprise. But lying at the bottom of such casualties are bourgeois influences which have captured those individuals and shaken their confidence in the working class.

Let me give you an example of one such individual, as reported by one comrade whom we will call John Daniels.

He is a man who reads Lenin and considers himself a man of principle—a Communist in the true sense. In the days of open-shop terror, he started out as a worker, a rank-and-file Communist. He had to build his union through "underground" groups of workers, starting from scratch in an unorganized field. The trust he worked for was merciless. It maintained a company union and tolerated no independent organization. After many struggles in the early '30's, finally in '36 and '37, with the upsurge of labor in this country, his union arrived. It gained recognition, broke the company union, established itself. Naturally, he found himself in the top leadership of the union.

Times were such that many less experienced and conscientious than he were able to build unions because the masses were clamoring for organization. Numerous were the Communists who had built union organization in shop after shop, during that period. Yet he began to attribute the success of his union to his own genius. Less and less he came to depend on his Party club. He merely took it for granted that in every department where there was a Party member the interests of the union would be well cared for.

Then, little by little, he began to see the Party club in a new light. He found he could do without the Party members very nicely. Every now and then he needed them when he had to win an election. But otherwise, the club was pretty much of a nuisance. In the old days, he had looked at his comrades and had seen great courage under the most difficult conditions, absolute dependability, native wisdom, self-sacrifice and devotion. He now saw different traits among them. They seemed inarticulate, had little finesse, sometimes didn't agree with him and gave their first loyalty to the defense of the workers' interests. When he wanted advice now, he could get it from "better brains." He believed that to a large extent the Party relied on him for a correct policy in the union. He did not see the need for a mass Party in the industry, because, said he, the union leadership is more capable, more effective in bringing the policies of the Party to the workers.

In the union he made smart moves. He had a good lawyer. He got gains for the workers without much difficulty and with little struggle. Sometimes, it was not even necessary to mobilize the workers in action to back up the negotiations. The brief was filed, the arguments were made around the table. Things were going fine. He was in the mainstream—not only in the labor movement, but generally. Mrs. Roosevelt invited him to lunch with her now and then. And life was good. There were problems, difficulties, but if he was on the ball and shrewd enough, he could maneuver.

He naturally began to lose Communist perspective. He began to get flabby. Suddenly—boom! The bourgeoisie launched a ferocious drive against the labor movement. Somehow, the smart negotiations no longer worked. They didn't produce. He could get practically nothing from the companies except through a real fight. The reactionary drive, supported by Social-Democracy and other company agents, began to make inroads among the membership. A new alignment took place in the labor movement. Left-Center unity was broken. And he not only had to face the attacks of the trusts, but also the C.I.O. leadership—the Murrays and Reuthers. The A.C.T.U. [Association of Catholic Trade Unionists] began to play a role and challenge his leadership. He had to deliver the bacon if he was to retain the leadership of the union.

In the meantime, the old militancy of the union has been dulled. The Party organization has been weakened. The old type of union organizer who built the union when the going was tough has been retrained into a Philadelphia lawyer or has been changed altogether. Now our man faces a difficult problem. What to do?

Mind you, this guy is not merely trying to hold on to his job—at least, not consciously. He is really very much worried about the danger of his own and the Party's isolation from the masses. He must avoid that at all costs. In the early days he knew that workers got nothing without a fight. Though he faced the powerful trust and a company union, though he looked at the workers and saw inertia, disunity and backwardness, yet he knew that "there was gold in them thar hills."

His whole life and work in those early days was based on the fact that he relied on the workers. He called on them to overcome their disunity. He aroused their courage, called for self-sacrifice, knew that eventually it would be forthcoming. He had unbounded faith in eventual victory. In fact, that was what gave him the courage to withstand poverty and starvation, police clubs and injunctions. He was not afraid of any isolation because he considered an attack on him by a labor faker as the greatest tribute. He built his cadres from among the workers. And as long as he had the respect of the workers, he felt he was anything but isolated.

Now, in a new situation, he found a great deal of fat around his political mid-section. Now, all he sees is the ignorance of the workers, their disunity, their reluctance to lose their jobs. They don't understand. And he doesn't feel he can make them understand. Yet, they expect him to get something for them. He is convinced they are not going to fight. Above all, he sees the power of the enemy. He can see no way of breaking that power to force even the slightest concession. The only way to get concessions is through some deal. But that is no longer easy, either. One way is to join the Murrays and Careys and then life will be much easier.

But he is a "man with a conscience." He hates a rat. He therefore sees no way out, has no perspective, and loses his bearings completely. He begins to rationalize.

After all, Socialism is clearly not on the order of the day. So what is wrong with leaving the future to the future and dealing today with the problems of today, giving honest, conscientious leadership to the workers on economic issues and leaving political questions to the Party?

And what is this honest, conscientious leadership? It turns out to be: Get anything you can that the company is willing to give. Get anything you can get without a fight and with no politics. Well, perhaps that will include support to the Marshall Plan, the U.S. invasion of Korea, and support for anything Murray orders you to support—because refusal to accept any part of C.I.O. policy means bringing politics into the union. . . .

I cite this example because there have been others who deserted the struggle in the past two years. And the lesson to be drawn is the need for a merciless struggle for Communist methods and practices and against every manifestation of opportunism—a merciless struggle to enhance the strength of the workers in the industries, involving them democratically in the struggle of their unions, inspiring them, fighting to create confidence in the working class, not only on the economic front, but in the general democratic struggle. And all this will, at the same time, make it more difficult for the workers to be taken in by charlatans.

This example is important for us because it raises many serious questions in the fight for a correct cadre policy. Chief among them is the need to guarantee that the closest ties are maintained between leadership and membership, and with the mass of the workers. When these ties are broken, then it is impossible to continue in the position of leadership. For the job of leadership is not alone to guide and direct the work of others—it is also necessary to learn from others—to learn from the members and the workers. Separation from the membership, from the workers, can result only in bureaucracy, in placing oneself above the Party, above the interests of the workers.

Secondly, it is necessary to show the utmost vigilance in noting and checking the corrupting influences of our present-day society on the thinking and living habits of some comrades, to expose these influences in the interest of the comrade himself, but primarily in the interest of the Party as a whole.

Thirdly, it is necessary to eliminate all self-complacency, cliquish and "family circle" atmosphere in relationships between Communists, especially rooting out all elements of false praise and flattery. For, as one wise comrade put it, flattery corrupts not only the flattered but the flatterer as well. Of course, we must continue to guard against any annihilating type of criticism which undermines the confidence and

312

abilities of our cadres, which creates subjective personal reactions hindering their growth and development.

Fourthly, it is necessary to apply criticism and self-criticism in the molding of Party cadres. Criticism and self-criticism are not to be applied on occasions—on holidays—so to speak. They must be applied daily, as indispensable weapons in the examination of the work of our Party and the individual cadres, with the aim of isolating our errors and weaknesses, and helping comrades overcome their weaknesses and mistakes at the time the mistakes are committed. Only by learning the lessons from mistakes can our Party cadres develop Communist methods, habits, and qualities of leadership.

Finally, only those leaders can withstand the pressures of enemy ideology, can relentlessly fight against opportunism in practice, who constantly strive to master Marxism-Leninism—the great liberating science of the working class, which alone gives us the confidence in the inevitable victory of the working class, headed by its Communist vanguard. Those who see only backwardness, immobility and disunity in the working class, are bound to ignore the essential truth that it is the working class that possesses all the necessary qualities to bring about the transformation of society, and build Socialism.

□ ——————————————————————————————— □

8.

BLACK LIBERATION SPARKS THE SIXTIES

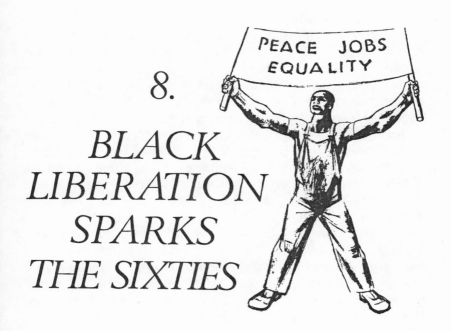

Post–world war revolutionary impacts continued to effect the break-up of colonial empires and forced readjustments in imperialist positions. The United States adopted neo-colonial forms, while seeking to plug up the dikes against the flood of national independence movements. Although it remained powerful, it was no longer the sole dominating force. A new factor emerged in the final decades of the twentieth century. A system of socialist states now existed and former colonies joined the family of independent states.

US imperialism would not reconcile itself to the existence of new socialist states, either in Europe or elsewhere. It sought to exploit weak points, encouraging disaffected elements in some countries. Hungary was one of them. There, playing upon dissatisfaction with anti-democratic tendencies in sections of the leadership, an uprising was instigated by Washington-backed forces seeking a return to capitalism.

The Marxist historian Herbert Aptheker wrote critically that *"In Hungary, while the anti-democratic aberrations appeared in aggravated form, there also appeared strong efforts at change. These efforts had secured notable successes by 1956."* (The Truth About Hungary, *Mainstream Publishers, 1957.) But, the author reveals, "The armed uprising [had] actually moved 'too far to the Right too fast' even for some officials of the American Embassy in Budapest. . . ." They were embarrassed that "By November 3, [1956] the Cardinal [Mindszenty] was publicly calling for the return of all lands to the Church, the return of education into the Church's hands, the destruction of socialism and in fact, a return to all the splendid 'freedoms' identified with the name of Admiral Horthy."* (American Foreign Policy and the Cold War *by Herbert Aptheker, New Century Publishers, 1962.) These were the "freedom fighters" Washington was defending.*

Closer to home was the successful Cuban revolution in 1959. This was in the "backyard" of US imperialism, which considered the Caribbean and all Latin America its private domain. In a hemisphere rich in natural resources millions live in abject poverty. Now the Cuban people served as an inspiration for basic social change. Consequently in less than two years the US broke diplomatic relations, created a trade embargo and followed with direct counter-revolutionary actions. Every means, including attempted assassination of Fidel Castro, was mustered to overthrow the popular government.

President John F. Kennedy admitted responsibility for the CIA collecting a group of emigré adventurers and riffraff to launch an invasion of the first socialist republic in the western hemisphere. The Bay of Pigs turned into a military and political fiasco. But this adventure, followed by the "missile crisis," caused a confrontation between the United States and the Soviet Union. For a brief moment the world seemed at the brink of a nuclear holocaust. The Soviet Union was not seeking a confrontation with the United States and mutual concessions defused the explosive situation. An agreement between the two countries resolved this dangerous affair, and the easing of tensions reaffirmed that peaceful solutions are the only barrier to atomic devastation (see p. 356).

In the first two years of the Eisenhower administration the government's harassment of the left was a continuation of the policies inaugurated by Truman. After the decline of the charlatan

316

McCarthy, a revulsion against witch-hunting brought a partial decline in the frenzy of prosecution. Still, the federal authorities pressed for convictions under the McCarran Act, and on March 28, 1956, raiders from the Internal Revenue Service (IRS) seized the property and padlocked the office of the Daily Worker *in New York. The preposterous claim was made of failure to pay taxes on "profits"—something that had never been realized from a publication that relied on its supporters to make up the annual deficit. Simultaneously the National Office of the Communist Party and a number of District Offices were padlocked by the IRS on the charge that the Party had not paid taxes. This was absurd in view of the Party's chronic fiscal deficit. Besides, and more significant, political parties are exempt from taxation. But this was of no concern to the government. These attempts were eventually defeated.*

The student youth of the 1950s have been called the "silent generation." It would be more accurate to say that they were silenced. On the broadest scale, university administrations fostered intimidation of faculty and students and penalized those who ventured outside cold-war guidelines in their pursuit of "academic freedom." Radical political expression emerged dramatically at the University of California, Berkeley, in 1964. An attempt by university authorities to bar student political activity and social-action support from the school's premises led to the organization of the Free Speech Movement. The protest movement rapidly escalated into a protracted struggle which received nationwide prominence and spread to other university communities.

The stirring on college campuses took on added importance, for it developed a link with the growing and militant Freedom Movement in which Black youth were a strong force. The Prayer Pilgrimage in 1957, arising primarily in the South, was a massive demonstration of the Black people. This dynamic movement reached a new plateau at the gathering of 200,000 people on August 28, 1963, under the leadership of the Rev. Martin Luther King, Jr. (see p. 320).

Throughout its history, in periods of advance or in moments of great difficulty, the Party maintained its ties with the aspirations

317

and struggles of the Black liberation movements. It gave special attention to winning the white community, especially white workers, for Black-white unity. It was a son of the South's Black people, the National Chairman of the Communist Party, Henry Winston, who stressed that Birmingham, base of the steel industry, would spark the new struggles in the South.

In 1955 the CIO and AFL merged to form the AFL-CIO with George Meany as president. The United Mine Workers was not affiliated with the merged organization and in 1957 the AFL-CIO expelled the International Brotherhood of Teamsters on the grounds of "unethical conduct." Thus two of the most powerful unions were outside the united body.

The reunification of the CIO and AFL failed to produce advances for the working class. Unions had been pushing for years for a shorter work week and had achieved a 5-day, 40-hour week when Roosevelt was in office. The Korean War brought an inordinate amount of overtime with premium pay. Originally the objective of premium pay for overtime was to force employers to hire additional help as well as to cut laboring time to a reasonable week in the interests of health and recreation. But the leadership of the AFL and CIO viewed overtime solely as an earnings increase. In consequence there was a softening of the drive for higher hourly rates. Contracts made acceptance of overtime mandatory. Thus in times of production slumps the drop in take-home pay was severe.

The gulf between the leadership and the rank and file grew. The rights of Blacks and women to equal treatment with white males were more and more ignored. Where labor, especially during the rise of the CIO, developed as a force for social change as well as a champion for improved wages and shop conditions, it now declined to a passive auxiliary of the Democratic party.

The "Conversations" of a group of local UAW officials (see p. 358) reflected more than their personal, defeatist moods. They unwittingly reflected the sentiments of the rank and file in search of the militancy which Communists and left forces had contributed.

Moments of rapid social development and change present a test of consistency of principle and decisiveness in action. At such times any tendencies to vacillation and yielding of principles are

318

sharply exposed. It was in the mid '50s, during serious difficulties in some socialist countries in Eastern Europe, that vacillation and disorientation affected many liberals, and also some members of the Communist Party. John Gates, then editor of the Daily Worker, *became the leader of a factional group that rejected the basic principles of the Party and called for its liquidation. His perfidy was hailed by the capitalist press, and won him support by the right wing in the trade union movement.*

The Party was weakened by this internal struggle although as later shown the organization remained basically sound. When attempts to resolve differences failed, Gates and his associates left the Party, mostly in 1958, some of them assuming positions in Right-led organizations.

Several articles in the present chapter illustrate the basic soundness of the Party's health. Nowhere is this shown better than by the Party's activity on the electoral front. One example is the experience of the organization in southern California.

The Communist Party had always faced electoral law obstructions in its efforts to be on the ballot. This basic right has been curbed through devious state laws. The Party recognized in the '60s that it had not pursued vigorously enough its right to the ballot. However, in southern California, where the Los Angeles Party had not participated in a ballot-box contest for fourteen years, the Communists put forward William C. Taylor for the County Board of Supervisors in the 1964 elections. He received an impressive 34,516 votes and the campaign generated a determination to revive electoral participation and beat back the attempt to deny citizenship rights to the Party.

The years 1955–1965, the approximate span of the present chapter, were a singularly complex political period. Its complexity was exacerbated by the situation in Vietnam, which was just beginning to develop in 1955 after the 1954 defeat of the French at Dienbienphu. By the end of 1965 the United States had intervened deeply into the political and military situation and in the following decade this intervention led to one of the greatest defeats ever suffered by the forces of U.S. imperialism.

□ —————————————————————————————— □

THE FREEDOM MOVEMENT

"The Pilgrimage to Washington" by Benjamin J. Davis, *Political Affairs*, July 1957

[*From the end of 1955 to the day in 1968 when he was killed by a racist's bullet, Dr. Martin Luther King, Jr. (1929-1968) was the most prominent and effective leader of the Black people. In 1957 he became president of the newly formed Southern Christian Leadership Conference (SCLC) and developed a policy of non-violent but massive confrontation as a tactic suited to the time and to the place—the mid-sixties deep South. A dramatic high point of his work was the March on Washington in August 1963, which brought 200,000 protesters to the nation's capital. Moving ever closer to an appreciation of the progressive role of the working class, he was in Memphis in April 1968 to help a strike of city workers, mostly Black, when he was assassinated.*

Following Dr. King's death an editorial in Political Affairs *said: "A true monument to Martin Luther King demands a new commitment to the fight against racism . . . a ceaseless, unremitting struggle by all who cherish democracy and social progress, and first of all by those in the growing Left and Communist ranks."*

Throughout the period of 1955-65 there were numerous activities, primarily in the South. The Birmingham Bus Boycott, sparked by Mrs. Rosa Parks' refusal to give up her bus seat, was historic. School actions embraced students from primary schools to universities. The movements against lynching and for the right to vote were accelerated.

The Communist Party participated in a number of these actions. Rep. Adam Clayton Powell, speaking from his own experiences in Harlem, wrote: "There is no group in America, including the Christian church, that practices racial brotherhood one-tenth as much as the Communist Party." (Cited in Organized Labor and the Black Worker—1619-1973, *by Philip S. Foner, from* Marching Blacks *by Adam Clayton Powell, Jr., p. 69).*

An estimate of the May 1957 Prayer Pilgrimage is excerpted here.]

The Prayer Pilgrimage of May 17 was a magnificent and historic protest demonstration, representing a new high level of the Negro people's movement. . . .

Under the slogan, "to arouse the conscience of the nation," the Pilgrimage put forward five main objectives: to demonstrate Negro unity; to provide a means for northerners to aid southern "freedom fighters"; to protest the persecution of the NAACP; to protest violence against Freedom Fighters; and to urge passage of pending civil rights legislation. Whatever the diversity of opinion on various matters, the Negro people, thanks to the influence of the two million Negro trade unionists and their advanced white supporters, were in unison on these demands. . . .

Among the participants were adherents of all political parties, featured by a cross-section of the Negro people in particular. The atmosphere was charged with militancy from both speakers and audience. Southern Negro ministers declared with electric response from the audience, "We are ready to lay down our lives for freedom." At the same time, these expressions of militancy and determination took place within the framework of non-violent resistance and non-cooperation, which constitute the new form of Negro people's struggle now taking place in deep southern urban centers.

Not since the Civil War has there ever been such a powerful, massive demonstration of the Negro people for first-class citizenship; nor has there been in modern America a similar mobilization from any other section of the population, not excluding labor, in its own direct interest. As for the Negroes attending from the South, scores of them put their homes, their children, their jobs and their lives on the line to be present. The Negro workers played a tremendous role in this regard. . . .

The behavior of Eisenhower and his whole General Motors cabinet is thus far disgraceful and contemptible. The President refuses to speak out against the lynch terror, bombings and racist defiance of the law of the land; he makes no attempt to place the executive branch of the government behind the Supreme Court decisions; and he flatly refused to fight even for his own watered-down civil rights bills. . . .

Such an example by the President of the United States denotes a corrupt standard of public morality which cannot but have its corroding effects upon the fibre of American society and life. It is no wonder that the ideas and examples of socialism are having an increasing appeal to Negro and white Americans no less than to workers and other peoples in the so-called "free world." When, in 1956, the Soviet leaders self-critically made public the Stalin revelations, our pious Secretary of State Dulles pointed a self-righteous finger at the socialist countries. But what has he to say of the still continuing 300 years of capitalist crimes against Negro Americans and against the colonial peoples?

The fight for the full citizenship of the Negroes in the deep South and for the democratization of that blighted area intersects the whole pattern of American life and, for the most part, is determinative of the social progress and future of the nation. . . .

A number of lessons can be drawn from this Pilgrimage which will have a profound effect upon the Negro people's movement as it continues the struggle to end racist violence, and to realize its objectives of human dignity and full citizenship. The richness of the event is bound to stimulate the widest discussion, enhancing the possibility of even more united and effective mass actions and struggles.

First of all, the Pilgrimage arose out of the will to struggle and initiative of the masses of the Negro people in the South to end segregation and achieve their full constitutional rights. Secondly, the leadership of the movement now comes out of the South itself, with the Pilgrimage being an adoption of a new form of struggle developed in the South, highlighted by the technique of mass boycotts. There was certainly more than prayer at the event, though prayer was the main form of its summons. Undoubtedly this form lent itself more readily to continuance of the struggles by the Negroes under the difficult conditions of the deep South, conditions under which active mass support from white labor, farmers and masses in the South is almost negligible. Besides, the political content of this movement in the South is so meaningful, militant and revolutionary that the [Senator] Eastland racists try to suppress it, notwithstanding its religious character.

Thirdly, the movement evinced on both sides of the platform a high degree of solidarity with the colonial liberation movements of Asia and Africa. The presence of a number of U.S. Negro leaders in Africa at the birth of Ghana, whose Prime Minister, Nkrumah, denounces both imperialism and capitalism and advocates a "socialistic society" for the Negro nation, was of considerable importance. The heavy hand of American imperialism in Puerto Rico, in Haiti, in the Caribbean, and in Latin and South America is of the same cloth and will eventually be seen as such.

Fourthly, the readiness of the Negro people for independent political action was apparent in the enthusiastic response to the proposal of Rep. A. Clayton Powell for a "third force" in political life. Both the Democratic and Republican Parties were scathed for their failures on civil rights, and the Republican–Dixiecrat alliance in Congress indicted. With the advent of the Roosevelt New Deal, the Negro voters demonstrated that they were no longer in the vest pocket of the G.O.P.; now they are demonstrating that they are not in the vest pocket of the Democratic Party.

Fifthly, the Negro people in the North, and the labor movement in particular, have a profoundly important role to play in supporting the Negro liberation movement in the South, in the use of the ballot, and in organizing the unorganized in the South. The Dixiecrat flunkeys of the northern monopolies are the source of racist poison throughout the nation, and, at the same time, are mainly responsible for the anti-union right-to-work laws which frustrate trade union organization and weaken the whole labor movement. Sen. McClellan is the common enemy of both the Negro and labor.

Sixth, the Rev. Martin Luther King placed as the most urgent and basic demand of the Negro people in the South—the demand which underlies those put forward by the Pilgrimage and then some—the right to vote. The realization of such a demand would spell the end of the Eastlands and Talmadges, and the election of officials pledged to uphold constitutional freedom, and the extension of democracy in the South for both Negroes and whites. In an exceedingly thoughtful address, the Rev. King brought forth a number of interesting new ideological approaches which bear serious examination.

Although the shortcomings of the event are secondary to its tremendous positive significance, it obviously faces many serious problems. It is regrettable that the role of white workers was not dramatically symbolized by the participation of leading white trade union speakers. The failure of Meany or Reuther, for example, to be present, was noticeable.

However, the most dangerous weakness—in the sense that it goes to the core of the Negro–labor alliance—was the scant presence of white workers and popular forces, due largely to failure of trade union leaders to really back the effort. Many unions undoubtedly sent delegates representing many thousands of white workers in locals; but this was a mass demonstration involving maximum individual participation as well as indirect representation.

One would understand that the repeated calls of the Pilgrimage leaders, certainly on the Eastern seaboard, for interracial participation, was a direct invitation to the white allies of the Negro people to be present. For full strength and effectiveness, the struggle for Negro rights must be interracial. The question requires further examination, since the strength of the Negro–labor alliance, which has shown disturbing strains recently, is based essentially on the initiative of the white workers in the struggle for Negro rights, on the political as well as on the economic front. . . .

Various speakers registered themselves as opponents of Communism. But this is the sort of competition that Communists welcome in free, open market of ideas. It remained for [A. Philip] Randolph to introduce red-baiting with false characterizations of "disruption and infiltration" against the Communist Party. Not only are such characterizations slanderous and untrue; they are old hat and don't meet the strong, wise desire of the Negro people for unity irrespective of political or any other label as long as one is fighting for the universal cause of human dignity. . . .

Communists are among those most conscious of the fact that the white workers and popular masses should see the struggle for Negro rights as in their own self-interest, and simultaneously, that the Negro people's movement needs white allies and should combat all go-it-alone tendencies. Communists, no less than any other Americans, Negro and white, or any other partisans of human dignity, fight for the indivisibility of the struggles for freedom. Conscious participants in the upward struggles of peoples and societies, Communists move with confidence in the triumph of socialism and have no need of mechanical putsches or captures of movements and organizations. Those are the anti-democratic methods of fascist reaction and imperialism.

The most active contradiction within American society today is the struggle for the full citizenship of the Negro people—for civil rights—against the system of national oppression and jim-crow imposed upon Negro people. It is a struggle that takes place on many fronts—economic, social, political and legislative—the core of which is in the South, where the right to vote is the next big crusade of the freedom fighters, actively supported by labor and democratic forces all over the country. The whole future of the nation depends upon the sharpening and quick resolution of this struggle in a democratic manner; and on the immediate agenda is civil rights legislation in Congress.

☐ ———————————————————————— ☐

CAMPUS REBELLION

1. "Introduction" by Angela Davis to
The Academic Rebellion in the United States
by Bettina Aptheker, Citadel Press, 1972;
2. "Party Membership Announced" by Bettina Aptheker,
Daily Californian (Berkeley), November 9, 1965

[*On the broadest scale, during the 1950s, school and university administrations fostered intimidation of faculty and students and penalized those who ventured outside of Cold War guidelines in their pursuit of "academic freedom."*[1]

Professor Angela Davis (b.1943), a national leader of the Communist Party, whose trial in 1972 attracted the widest attention, is an internationally renowned figure in the civil rights movement. In her introduction to Bettina Aptheker's book she analyzes the "roots of the modern campus protests. . . ." Davis points to the close tie of the student movement with the great upsurge of the period.

Bettina Aptheker relates developments in the Free Speech Movement (FSM) of which she was a leader. The West Coast movement took on national significance. In the November 1965 general student elections at Berkeley, she received the highest number of votes. During the election campaign she made public her membership in the Communist Party.]

1.

[T]he roots of the modern campus protests may be found in the sit-in demonstrations of Black students in the South—specifically, the first sit-ins in Greensboro, North Carolina in 1960. Indeed, the impetus for the Free Speech Movement came from civil rights demonstrations conducted in the San Francisco Bay Area in the Spring of 1964. At that time, students—especially from the Berkeley campus—participated in sit-in actions directed against the hotel industry in San Francisco because of their discriminatory hiring practices. In order to prevent such activities from continuing, the Regents of the University of California instituted a ban on all on-campus forms of political activity. This edict precipitated four months of rebellion during the Fall of 1964, a rebellion for which Bettina Aptheker emerged as a leading spokeswoman.

During the era of the Civil Rights struggle, students—Black and white—left the campus for the wider community. The second half of the sixties saw new offensives emerging from the campus community and specifically directed against the schools themselves. The groundwork for a new political consciousness on the campuses was forged.

The creation of Black and Brown student organizations marked a period of attack upon the racist foundations of the university. Mounting pressure was exerted on higher educational institutions in order to force them to respond to demands for knowledge arising out of the ghettos and barrios. These demands not only called for traditional modes of knowledge but, more significantly, for modes of knowledge which would assist in the development of a militant Black and Brown Liberation Movement. My own experiences at the University of California at San Diego, where Chicano and Black sisters and brothers struggled over a long period of time to establish the Lumumba-Zapata College confirm this view of the intrinsic ties between Black and Brown students and their oppressed communities.

325

Not only have Black and Brown student struggles reflected community needs and demands; the communities themselves have responded to the demands of Black and Brown students and faculty. During the strike of the Third World Liberation Front at San Francisco State College commencing in November, 1968, the Black, Brown and Asian communities expressed their solidarity with their embattled sisters and brothers by their physical presence on the campus. Prominent leaders from these communities came repeatedly to San Francisco State College and many were arrested. . . .

Dr. Carleton Goodlett, publisher of the largest Black newspaper in San Francisco, led an "illegal" rally on the campus, proclaiming that "The Black Community is not going to permit Black students to be isolated on this campus."[2] A Black sociologist on the campus informed the press that:

"The Black students have captured the imagination of the entire Black community and we have no choice but to support them. . . . From now on, the governor, the trustee, Mayor [Joseph] Alioto [of San Francisco] and [S.I.] Hayakawa [then President of San Francisco State College] will be arrayed against not only militant students and discontended faculty but against the aroused Black community as well."[3]

This interrelationship between the academic revolt and the movement has had a profound impact on the academic revolt. The radical, indeed revolutionary potential of Black Studies—and of Third World Studies in general—entails a new history, a new sociology, a new political science and ultimately even a new perspective for the natural sciences. All this incorporates the experiences of racially and nationally oppressed people which were hitherto unknown to the white intelligentsia in the United States. It has forced many white scholars to develop a new consciousness, however limited, of Black and Brown history and culture and their impact on the history of the United States and the lives of American people. . . . The white students and academics developed a consciousness of the war in Indochina and as that protest swept campus after campus, the anti-imperialist consciousness, inherent in the Black and Brown experiences penetrated the ranks of the white rebels. It should be recalled that very early in its own development during the Civil Rights era, the Student Non-Violent Coordinating Committee aggressively opposed the war in Vietnam and made this opposition an integral element of their program for fighting racism in the United States.

The emergence of an anti-imperialist consciousness among the intelligentsia is immediately attributable to the combination of their moral outrage against the war and the new Black consciousness, the new Brown

326

consciousness engulfing their institutions. As the anti-war movement and the movement against racism and repression mingled and converged, the white component was forced to deal more concretely and more realistically with the nature of American society—and with the concrete needs of nationally oppressed communities and the working class as a whole. Consequently, the late sixties saw a new awareness in the student and academic movement and the consolidation of a conscious Marxist component.

Bettina Aptheker seeks to demonstrate that this new consciousness, derived from the interpenetration of social movements, was reinforced by the new social conditions prevailing in the university and the new relationship of the university to the society as a whole.

As a Marxist, Aptheker situates the campus movement within the broader political movements in the United States, while seeking to uncover its specific features and its potential as a distinct thrust originating with students and professors. This new thrust, she contends, is unprecedented, both in its politics and in its immediate and long-range objectives. Students and intellectuals in general have participated in virtually every revolutionary struggle history has witnessed. And in the United States, political movements have generally reverberated onto the campuses. However, the movement climaxed by the 1970 nationwide campus strike against the war in Indochina and racial oppression and repression had qualitatively different foundations and has projected qualitatively different goals. The key to Aptheker's analysis is that she detects behind this movement not only a developing political consciousness among the intelligentsia, but more important, changing trends in the concrete existence of this group.

2.

There has been speculation for some time as to whether or not I am a Communist. Due to the attempt to outlaw the Communist Party it has been difficult to answer that question. I have, however, always affirmed that I am a Marxist and a socialist and have never hesitated to express my views.

I wish however, to take this occasion to go further. I have been for a number of years, I am now, and I propose to remain a member of the Communist Party of the United States. . . .

As a student, as an American and as a Communist I have participated in common struggles for democratic liberties, for civil rights and for peace. I did so because I believed them to be virtuous struggles commensurate with socialist aspirations. I am a member of the Communist Party

327

because, as I see it, that Party upholds principles which combine a particularly enlightened view of society with a sense of humanity and peace not to be found elsewhere. As a Communist I believe in the fullest expansion of the democratic liberties of the American people. I believe in an end to poverty; an end to racism; an end to unemployment; an end to U.S. intervention in Vietnam and the Dominican Republic. The revolutionary Marxist outlook as developed in the Party's approach and program is profoundly relevant to the fundamental questions facing the American people today. . . .

It is time to challenge the assumption that there is an international Communist conspiracy; that Communists are agents of a foreign power; that Communists are traitors; that Communists are by definition "evil" and must be exterminated. Anti-Communism has served as the fundamental objective of American domestic and foreign policy, certainly since 1946. In the Holy name of anti-Communism this government has conducted witchhunts and executed and imprisoned its victims. It has waged war, overthrown governments (by force and violence), intervened in the internal affairs of other nations and is daily committing unspeakable atrocities in Vietnam.

It is time to affirm the right to be a Communist; the right of Communists to speak and act; and the right of the American people to listen and think for themselves.

□ ———————————————————————————— □

COMMUNIST SPEAKERS ON
THE COLLEGE CAMPUS

"Talks With Students" by Gus Hall,
Political Affairs, April 1962

[During the 1950s Communist speakers were essentially banned from the campuses of U.S. colleges.

Benjamin J. Davis, Jr., who was then Chairman of the New York State Communist Party, was invited to speak at a forum to be held on October 16, 1958, on the campus of City College in New York. But on October 1 The New York Times *carried a small item under the heading: "Red Denied Rostrum." James S. Peace, associate dean of students at the college, denied Davis permission to speak.*

The Communists did not accept their exclusion from the campuses as final. But it was early in 1961 before Ben Davis returned to City College as the first Communist to speak there in a long time.

A major breakthrough was made by Gus Hall in February of 1962 when he undertook a tour of campuses on the West Coast, particularly in the Pacific Northwest. Between February 10 and 15, Hall spoke to 19,000 persons on five campuses.

This was followed by appearances before American students by Ben Davis, Gus Hall, James E. Jackson and other Communists touring the "campus circuit" in the early sixties. They can be credited with helping to change the picture of political apathy amongst the student bodies and to stimulate the kind of campus response which played such an important role in the subsequent civil rights struggles and the opposition to the Vietnam war.

Gus Hall reported on his West Coast speaking tour at a meeting in New York City on February 26, 1962. Below we give portions of his talk.]

It would be a mistake to view my experiences as a personal, successful speaking tour. We must ask ourselves: What is the cause for this upsurge? What answers do those who are part of it seek? . . .

The historic factors that are behind this development were already evident at my meeting at Cornell two months ago. They were evident in the actions of the students of the city colleges of New York in demanding the right to hear Ben Davis. They were present in the Freedom Rides and Sit-ins. We should actually be the last ones to be surprised at the development, because the fact is that even as early as and even earlier than the 17th Convention of the Communist Party, 26 months ago, we foresaw many of these developments as indicated in its resolution. Obviously many of us didn't fully grasp what was said, else we would have participated more actively in these developments.

What we are witnessing are mass waves, often erupting into turbulent movements which are reflections of the new realities of the new epoch.

What we are seeing are the reactions and movements of the first generation that is molded in the image of the epoch. This is fundamental and must be grasped to understand what is taking place.

Any individual, party or group who does not understand the fundamental nature of the new factors that make for this new epoch, cannot understand the new mass reactions that reflect the new realities in these movements. And if one does not understand the deep and fundamental nature of these new factors, such an individual becomes an observer. Such a party becomes a sect and ceases to be a political factor in life. It is necessary to understand what forces are at work in order to help the

329

people achieve the proper answers to the questions that disturb them. And to understand, it is necessary to be part of all the movements to which their needs are giving birth.

It would be a big mistake to view my experiences on the West Coast as a personal achievement. They were the result of the work of many progressives and above all the reflection of the good, democratic sense of the people, especially young people on the West Coast. It's a part of a stubborn struggle for democratic rights that's going on in our country and in which millions of people are involved. It had to face and overcome powerful opposition of big-money, reactionary, ultra-Right forces.

In those few weeks, it was estimated that the ultra-Right forces put out approximately half a million pieces of literature specifically directed to stop Gus Hall. Some of it was vile, real gutter type of literature.

"Stop Gus Hall" Conferences were called by the ultra-Right a week or two before my appearance. There were many threats, including bomb threats. I was hung twice, in effigy, it is true. Once in Portland and once in Los Angeles. Big corporations actually spent millions of dollars. For instance: the Boeing Corporation in Seattle spent millions to promote the war-mongering ultra-Right and to gag all voices for peace and democracy including the Communists. . . .

There are some rather abstract ideas concerning the role workers are playing in this fight for democratic rights and peace. Many students work during the summer and many come from working-class parents. Workers took part in this struggle although not always through trade union channels. Because of the reactionary position of some leaders of the AFL–CIO, taking part is not easy. But in spite of that they did participate in this struggle. In Washington and Oregon, six central labor bodies went officially on record against the ultra-Right at the height of the campaign to prevent me from speaking. So that even in official channels, the struggle for democratic rights is growing.

The faculty and the college administration are in most cases truly standing up for democratic rights. Arthur Flemming, President of the University of Oregon, who was in the Eisenhower Cabinet, said that any university which does not permit a Communist to speak very shortly will be a second-rate institution.

Leaders of Negro organizations are playing a very prominent role in this development.

Many newspapers, especially in the cities where monopolies do not completely control the press, spoke out for my right to speak.

There were "open end" types of discussion on radio and T.V. where I appeared.

330

Leaders of the YMCA's and YWCA's, especially the student branch, stood up under great pressure, including threats to cut off financial contributions.

The President of the Washington Publishers Association, a conservative Republican, supported the right of Communists to speak.

Leaders of the ACLU, the Quakers, progressive people behind the *National Guardian,* liberals of all kinds joined this movement. At the University of Oregon where I spoke to 12,000, they built a speaker's platform in the middle of the football field. The committee told me later that I drew a thousand more than usually attend a football game. . . .

The realities of the 30s were the depression and the rise of fascism. Compared to present complex problems they were relatively simple.

You can't speak to this generation in the same way as in the 30s. This generation won't accept agitation as the answer. They want serious discussion. I would say that is why freedom of speech is so vital a need. It's a weapon they feel they must preserve in order to be able to thrash out the very complicated problems they face.

There is a very deep feeling that if you can preserve the right of Communists to speak, then you can preserve the right of all to speak. That's true.

But it's more than just a fight for the right of Communists to speak. The fact is that they want to hear a Communist speak.

My recent experiences have given me new confidence in the people of the United States, especially this wonderful new young generation. It has strengthened my sense of oneness with these people in motion. Too often in the past we tended to evaluate the weaknesses of our people in the abstract. We must evaluate them against the odds that are thrown against them. These odds are tremendous. There was never a people that faced such a barrage of propaganda for so many years at such a cost. Billions of dollars have been spent to confuse and distort their view of the real problem, the real enemies they face.

I think if we take these odds against our people into account, we will have a more positive estimate of our people and a far greater confidence in their determination to preserve our democracy and peace.

We have spoken of the need to break through the wall of isolation. We said that years ago. I think now we must say more, yes, the enemy works to isolate us, but mainly we isolate ourselves. That's the main obstacle. We have to break an ideological wall that we have built between ourselves and the people.

□ ———————————————————————————— □

331

THE GHETTO: A SYSTEM OF OPPRESSION

1. *Ghetto Rebellion to Black Liberation*
by Claude M. Lightfoot, International Publishers, 1968
2. "Storm Over Los Angeles" by William C. Taylor,
Political Affairs, October, 1965

[*Events in Watts, in the summer of 1965, are fervently described in an editorial in* The Worker *by its editor, James E. Jackson. He condemns the cold-blooded murder in which of "29 people who died in the four days of wrath, 26 were NEGROES." He notes that of "676 persons hospitalized for injuries . . . 640 were Negroes. Negroes arrested in the Watts area of Los Angeles were jammed into every available space in the city jails—of the 2,157 people who were arrested in the area all were Negroes." The editor continues: "This was an elemental scream of outrage from a violated people entombed in a prison house of social deprivation and economic impoverishment." It was an event which was duplicated in a number of cities during this period.*

The outbreaks were also a reflection of the deep discontent of Black America with infringement of the right to vote and hold office, particularly in the South. Writing in Political Affairs *(September 1951), Pettis Perry, an outstanding leader and secretary of the Black Liberation Commission, stated that the movement for "Negro representation must be approached . . . as a major step to extend democracy in the United States. . . ." He concluded "there can be no rounded approach to Negro representation without the most serious efforts" to win the universal right to elect and be elected to every level of government.*

The drive for Black representation took a step forward in the '60s and into the present. A number of civic and citizens' committees were established in several areas. They stressed the election of Blacks to leading positions in government. These movements took varied forms and contributed to the election of mayors in Los Angeles, Cleveland, Detroit, Newark and Washington, D.C., Gary, Indiana had elected a mayor previously, and a number of southern cities, including Atlanta, Georgia, followed.

Claude M. Lightfoot was born in Arkansas in 1910. He has spent most of his adult years in Chicago, where he is a prominent political figure. Lightfoot was one of the victims of the Smith Act persecution, and is a member of the Communist Party's Central Committee. The chapter from his book excerpted below deals with the super-exploitation of the

Black ghetto, which greatly contributed toward igniting the rebellions in cities across the country during the '60s.

William C. Taylor, then Chairperson of the L.A. Party's Black Liberation Commission, was a participant in the civic committee in Los Angeles, previously in Washington, D.C., contributes this estimate of events in Watts.]

1.

There are many reasons for the present situation. First and foremost is the nature of the times in which we live. This is the most revolutionary period in history. What people were forced to accept for centuries is no longer acceptable in any corner of this globe. The black ghetto is no exception. Its protest movements have been influenced greatly by world-wide trends, especially the African revolution. Like others, the Negro senses objective possibilities of challenging the present situation and winning victories that would have been unthinkable a few decades ago. An assessment of today's ghetto must take into account this new mood, which is not satisfied with minor concessions but demands fundamental changes. . . .

[Michael] Harrington (*The Other America,* Penguin, 1963) was among the first in the recent period to rediscover deep pockets of poverty in America, of which the black ghetto represents the worst. He did not forecast the eruptions that came later. Nonetheless, he discharged a great social responsibility by laying bare the material out of which revolt could grow. Dr. James B. Conant, the former President of Harvard University, in his *Slums and Suburbs* (New York, 1964), predicted violent revolt unless the evils were remedied. He described the state of affairs as follows: "In a slum area of 125,000 people, mostly Negro, a sampling of the youth population showed that roughly 70 per cent of the boys and girls aged sixteen to twenty-one were out of school and unemployed. When one considers that the total population in this district is equal to that of a good-sized independent city, the magnitude of the problem is appalling and the challenge to our society clear" (p. 34). He concluded: "We are allowing social dynamite to accumulate in our large cities" (p. 126).

A considerable segment of black youth to whom work experience is unknown is a new central feature of the ghetto. However, it is *not* only the youth; it is a problem of all the Negro people. Those who have some affluence, as well as the poor, are affected. There are few Negroes, if any, who can escape the problems of being black.

Historically, the Negro ghetto was created for the purpose of super-exploitation. In this regard a whole superstructure has been erected. The problem facing the Negro in the ghetto is primarily a matter of money. It involves unemployment and underemployment, discrimination in hiring and on the job, segregated housing, schools of poor quality, high rents, price-gouging merchandising and exploitation by outside business interests who take all they can out of the community and put nothing back into it. Through these and other devices, it is estimated, over $32 billion a year is taken from the Negro worker over and above the profits that are extracted from his exploitation as a worker. . . .

Negroes also suffer greatly from underemployment. Into this category fall workers who are employed, but who are often not as well off as people on relief. During the postwar years the big corporations, in their efforts to prevent strikes, made concessions which went mainly to those in the skilled and semi-skilled categories. The mass of unskilled production workers did not receive comparable wage increases. This contributed to increasing the numbers in the category of the underemployed.

But the greatest gap in wage scales is that between organized and unorganized workers. It is among the tens of millions of workers in unorganized establishments, who have no means of protecting themselves against profit-hungry employers and whose levels have consequently remained at the lowest levels, that we find a high percentage of Negro workers. Here, poverty is at its worst.

Recent figures issued by the Bureau of Labor Statistics show that nearly 37 per cent of all Negroes employed receive less than $3,000 a year, compared to 16 per cent of whites. This means that more than one out of three employed Negroes receives wages below the "poverty" level.

The Chicago chapter of the Negro-American Labor Council recently made a study of this problem, and it issued a white paper entitled, *The Other Chicago: The City's Employed Poor* (March 1965). This study reveals that some hundreds of thousands in the Chicago area earned less than $3,000 a year in take-home pay. They were employed in a variety of industries including apparel, merchandising, laundry and cleaning services, hospitals and other health services, amusement and recreation, and miscellaneous business and repair services. The paper concludes: "Thus, in the Greater Chicago area at least 515,000 are working poor. Of these, at least 400,000 live in the city of Chicago, the overwhelming part in the slums and ghettos." This situation is typical of Negro communities. . . .

During the past 15 years, the Negro communities in almost all metropolitan areas of the country have expanded considerably. Generally, however, this expansion has resulted in the extension of the ghetto, rather than its abolition. This has happened despite open-occupancy laws and Supreme Court rulings outlawing restrictive convenants. . . .

[A] survey by Mobilization for Youth helps explain much of what took place in the upheavals in the Negro ghettos from Watts in California to Detroit in Michigan. To condemn the looting and the burning down of business establishments leads one to fight symptoms rather than causes. To paraphrase the words of Frederick Douglass, what is needed is not a shower of criticism of the victims but a thunderstorm to eradicate the evils which produced this condition.

Not long ago I had occasion to walk through the devastated areas of Watts, the West Side of Chicago and the Hough area of Cleveland. I was struck by the common pattern which characterized these eruptions. I saw instances where certain merchants—black and white—were left untouched while other places were destroyed or looted. The Negro masses struck, in any given block, mainly at those places that were guilty of the kind of price gouging uncovered by Mobilization for Youth in Manhattan [New York City]. . . .

Thus, many layers of exploitation are revealed in the ghetto. They arise on the base of the super-exploitation of the Negro by capitalism, creating the basic inequality that results in lower standards of living and the evils of the slums. The loan sharks, the swindling ghetto businessmen, the peddler of inferior goods, the slumlord, the parasitic real estate operators prey on the Afro-American victims of the capitalist extra-exploitation. . . .

Aside from the economic problems, the ghetto suffers from poor quality education, inadequate health facilities, and other numerous disadvantages that make life most miserable.

The miracle is that Negroes have not blasted everything in their path; for we are forced to live in subhuman conditions. From these conditions the black revolution is born.

2.

Recent events in South Los Angeles, publicized as the Watts riot, have highlighted the need for some examination and re-examination of the fight for Negro freedom and dignity. They have sharply focused the eyes of all on the Negro's demand for full equality, decent jobs and housing, and end to de facto segregation, not only in schools, but in the purchase of food, clothing and other necessities of life, and to be treated by county, city and federal officials, and particularly the police forces, as citizens of this—our United States.

All of these demands were contained in the resentment that exploded during the week of August 11 to 17, 1965. To see the Watts explosion only as a riot with looting, burning and destruction featured by anarchy is wrong. . . . The rebellion was not prepared, nor was it led by any group. The press, radio, television, together with the police, through dissemination of untruths and half truths, tried to project the impression that it was a race riot. . . .

The spontaneous action developed out of a long, constant struggle for all the issues mentioned. It had its roots in widespread chronic unemployment, which is even worse in the Green Meadows area and the locale of the beginning of the explosion. Unemployment in this area runs as high as six or seven times that of the average of the city and county of Los Angeles. Thirty-four per cent of the adults are unemployed, and sixty per cent of the total population is on relief. . . .

The greater part of the community in revolt is located in the 21st Congressional District, represented by [Augustus] "Gus" Hawkins. His attempts to hasten the war on poverty in this district were stymied by the Mayor and the City Council, who were attempting to use the war on poverty to further their own political ambitions. . . .

The elected white representatives of the area are Kenneth Hahn, against whom I ran a little over a year ago in an attempt to change the lily-white composition of the Los Angeles County Board of Supervisors [see p. 317] and John Gibson, a member of the City Council who has been very weak. It is important to note that although Gibson and Hahn are elected officials from the deprived areas of South Los Angeles, they both have been part of the machine—playing footsie with the mayor in sabotaging the funds for the war on poverty. They have been strong supporters of Chief of Police Parker, Los Angeles County Sheriff Pitchess and their policies, which result in law enforcement by discrimination. . . .

The policies of the Parker-led police department, backed by Mayor Yorty, represent somewhat the same enforcement of law in the Negro community of Los Angeles as is found in the Negro communities of Alabama, Mississippi, etc. The use of chauvinist epithets to and about Negroes is common among policemen. Raids on Negro homes are conducted without warrant, at the whim of the police, and fear of savage reprisals prevents the people from making official complaints. . . .

While the uprising was spontaneous and unorganized, this did not prevent its participants from focusing their wrath on those white merchants who were notorious for their anti-Negro policies and robbery of the community. It must be recognized, however, that that wrath was also directed at some businesses owned by Negroes, Japanese and Mexican-Americans, while some white-owned businesses were protected by the community on the ground that their owners were "decent white people."

The white communications media has deliberately sought to conceal the fact that the cry "Get Whitey" was aimed not at all whites, but at unscrupulous white merchants, the white police and those sensation-seeking white outsiders who visited the embattled ghetto to enjoy the sight of Negroes being shot down and whipped into subjection. . . .

[A new realignment is beginning to appear in the Negro community.] Congressman Hawkins played no small role in fighting for the concessions to guarantee that the war on poverty get off the ground quickly. Billy Mills and Gilbert Lindsay, while Thomas Bradley was out of the country, stood alone in the City Council in placing demands for investigation and in opposition to a move in the City Council to whitewash Parker by a vote of commendation. . . .

The immediate and most pressing issue now is the freedom and defense of those arrested in the upsurge. . . . At this writing, from two to three hundred children between eight and sixteen years of age still remain in the jail called Juvenile Hall. Excessive bail is demanded for all, whether old or young, with or without records. . . .

Since August, many more are being arrested and their possessions

Angela Davis Freed. By Bill Andrews, *Daily World,* 1972

taken from them. The police have been conducting house-to-house searches in the South Los Angeles area for so-called "loot" taken from burned-out businesses. Thus, a family which has a new television set, new furniture, etc. and which is unable to immediately produce evidence of its purchase is arrested, the furniture confiscated, and a new criminal record is in the making. . . .

The Party has played some role in the struggle for the demands of the people. During the curfew period, it mobilized the Left for relief in food and necessities in the first days. The *People's World* and *The Worker* carried full coverage of the events. Thousands of copies of the *People's World* were distributed in the community and were well received; many community centers not only accepted the paper, but helped to distribute it.

The experience of the Left was mobilized in the defense and helped the United Civil Rights Committee, the American Civil Liberties Union, the Southside Defense Committee, etc., in approaches to the problems of bail and defense.

And finally, the Party played no small role in initiating activity in the white communities to understand and to see clearly the events of August. Despite the red-baiting of Yorty and Parker, the Communist Party developed supporting actions.

What are the conclusions that can be arrived at?

This upsurge was not motivated by any one issue, but developed out of the feeling of being "fed up" with unemployment, double standards in employment and income, police brutality, welfare insults and inhuman attitudes, double standards in the price and quality of food, furniture and other commodities, social worker and do–good approaches of whites and from professional and middle-class Negroes.

The upsurge has resulted in a growing respect for the Negro and a deepening of the understanding of the fight of the Negro. Many are beginning to see that this fight is not a simple civil rights struggle, but a struggle for full economic, political and social equality. The fact that the "burning and looting" was not just a wild riot is shown by the fact that homes were not burned by design in the sixty–square–mile area. Ire was vented only against those places that had been cheating the people, whether owned by Negro, Japanese, white, etc.

There has developed a strong and growing unity in the Negro community. The vast majority of the Negro population felt as though they were participants, even though the active participants were relatively few in number. (About 200,000 people live in the area.)

The organizations of the Negro community have been maturing.

Recently organized, the Watts Labor Community Council—composed of representatives from United Auto Workers, Laborers and Hodcarriers, Packinghouse Workers, Building Service Employees, Laundry Workers, County Employees and Social Workers Unions—has played a role in pressuring the Central Labor Union to act in the interests of the community.

The youth of the Watts–Green Meadows area have organized into a movement called SLANT (Self-Leadership for all Nationalities), and are ready to play a role in winning some of the demands of the community. New leadership has already begun to play a role and especially is this true of Negro women.

Many committees, official and unofficial, are investigating and conducting hearings on the August revolt. In most cases, there is an attempt to whitewash the police. However, this was prevented by Councilman Thomas Bradley in a Committee of the City Council which is probing the situation. Through probing for the facts and the searching questions, the open chauvinism of Parker was further exposed and the Committee is continuing its investigations. . . .

Within the Negro community, there has developed a higher and stronger level of unity than ever before. This development has grown out of the recognition by the Negro middle-class of their responsibilities in relation to the aspirations of the poor and the working Negro people.

□ ————————————————————————————— □

PUBLISHING SCIENTIFIC SOCIALISM IN THE U.S.

1. Preface by Alexander Trachtenberg,
Letters to Americans **by Karl Marx and Frederick Engels,**
International Publishers, 1953;
2. *Lenin's Impact on the United States,*
edited by Daniel Mason and Jessica Smith,
New World Review Publications, 1970

[*Karl Marx and Frederick Engels kept up a constant correspondence with their associates in the United States. These ties were started with the arrival of Joseph Weydemeyer in the United States in 1851. At the same time Marx began writing for Charles Anderson Dana, an abolitionist and managing editor of the* New York Daily Tribune. *Marx was European correspondent for the* Tribune *for over 10 years.*

Alexander Trachtenberg (1884–1966) acquired extensive knowledge of the publishing field, first in the Socialist Party, later in the Communist Party. He founded International Publishers in 1924, and applied his scholarship to the verification of authentic texts and engaged the cooperation of leading publishing houses abroad. Besides the classic writings of Marxism–Leninism, he published works by American and foreign authors on political economy, history, philosophy and literature. He also published works by Black authors and members of other minorities, concerning the liberation movements. Trachtenberg was the first to introduce V.I. Lenin's writings to U.S. readers on a mass scale.

One of the extraordinary features of all the Smith Act trials was the use of books and pamphlets as the principal "evidence" to convict the defendants of their "conspiracy to teach and advocate." Trachtenberg was in the position of being the publisher of most of this unprecedented "evidence."

The second of the two items printed below is taken from the foreword of a book which was prepared to honor the centenary of the birth of V.I. Lenin. The book's contents first appeared as the Winter 1970 issue of New World Review.

Jessica Smith (b. 1895), who was then editor of that magazine, has been associated with the cause of friendly relations between the Soviet Union and the United States for well over half a century. Daniel Mason (b. 1905), Marxist writer and editor for several decades, is on the editorial board of Political Affairs. *Both Mason and Smith worked closely with the late Alexander Trachtenberg.]*

1.

The letters in this volume have been selected from the voluminous correspondence of Karl Marx and Frederick Engels with Americans. Most of the letters [are addressed] to Americans of German origin, who came to play an important role in the labor and socialist movement of the United States. Covering a half century, from 1848 to 1895, the correspondence deals with many events and themes of great historic interest and with the views and activities of numerous personalities in Europe and the United States.

Marx and Engels have scarcely a peer as letter writers, either in the encyclopedic range of their interests, the sheer volume of their correspondence, or the influence they exerted through this medium. . . .

In the mid-century, when the correspondence begins, the United States was a haven not only for European capital seeking profitable investment, but also for immigrants fleeing religious and political persecution and mainly seeking better economic opportunities. The stream of German, Scandinavian, Irish, English and other European immigrants provided the labor force and most often the skilled workers for nascent industry, soon to be spurred to rapid development by the Civil War. Many joined the stream of settlers from the East to the free lands toward the West. In the fifties the country was already reaching a level of capitalist development which made possible the overthrow of the slave system, the last major obstacle to the unification of the country and capture of the home market. This was followed toward the end of the century by the emergence of the United States as a great industrial power, ready to embark fully upon the imperialist stage. . . .

The chief correspondents of Marx and Engels on this side of the Atlantic played an important role in the American socialist and labor movement. From the fifties on, German–American workers were active participants in the struggle of the Negro people to free themselves from bondage and their organizations in New York, Boston, Chicago and elsewhere were in many cases the precursors of the first nationwide trade unions of the American workers as a whole. German–American followers of Marx organized the pioneer socialist groups and became the core of the First International in America and subsequently of the Socialist Labor Party.

Joseph Weydemeyer and Friedrich A. Sorge[4] were the outstanding socialist leaders, the former during the fifties and sixties and the latter in the period following the Civil War. Marx and Engels were thus in direct touch with the most active socialist forces then at work in the United States. Through these letters and in their numerous articles in the *New York Tribune,* which cover the same period as the correspondence with Weydemeyer, as well as in other publications, Marx and Engels made their influence felt during the formative period of the labor and socialist movement in the United States.

2.

In the nineteenth and twentieth centuries mankind thrust onto the stage of history two men who have dominated this decisive period. These two were Karl Marx and Vladimir Ilyich Lenin. Many have marched across the stage of history in this period: statesmen, politicians, generals, scientists, capitalists. Many among them have created misery in war and peace, enslaved peoples, destroyed nations. Among those who have played a positive role, none has had a permanent effect on society to equal that of Marx and Lenin.

Lenin carried forward and multiplied the theoretical legacy of his great teachers, Marx and Engels, relating their work to the new historical conditions. . . .

Frightened by the tremendous influence of Marx and Lenin on the world's working people, capitalism has sought in every way to belittle and slander them. Its scholars and journalists have tried to picture Marx and Lenin as beasts; they have attempted to separate the two from their work by emphasizing their "frailties" as human beings; they have tried to divide Marx and Lenin into younger and older periods; they have aimed their biggest guns at the theories of Marx and Lenin. . . .

[Yet] Leonard Schapiro, that foremost "Kremlinologist," had to admit that "Lenin's personal impact on events both in his own country and in the world outside may well have been greater than that of any other individual in this century." (*Lenin: A Reappraisal,* Praeger, New York, 1967.)

The interplay between Lenin and the United States was very extensive. Lenin had learned the English language early in his career and became an avid student of US economics, politics, education and social life. But he did not limit himself to study. He sought out contacts among the American people and became a firm sympathizer with the struggles of the US working class and of the Black people to achieve liberation. . . .

The earliest meeting of Lenin with an American of which we have any knowledge is the one in 1905 with Arthur Bullard, a journalist. . . .

There is evidence in the Lenin archives in Moscow that would indicate that many other American workers had heard of Lenin and his activities before 1917. On December 1, 1913, the editorial board of *Appeal to Reason,* the biggest Socialist newspaper ever published in the United States, sent Lenin "16 two-page leaflets and eight 32-page pamphlets [which] comprise our list of publications to date." A working-class club in New York City, on March 30, 1914, sent "the sum of 1437 kronen and 90 heller ($292.61), which is a contribution from the Workmen's Circle to the Russian Social-Democratic Party (Bolshevik)" to Lenin, then in exile in Cracow, Poland. Late in 1915, the Socialist Propaganda League, a left-wing group in Boston, sent Lenin a copy of its manifesto. Unfortunately, the records of other manifestations of this sort have been lost.

But it was after the October Revolution in 1917, and the successful birth of the Soviet Union, that Lenin's influence upon the American working class really began to grow. Even before that, during the earlier years of World War I, Lenin and his Russian Bolshevik Party had become known in Socialist circles in the United States because of their persistent struggle to win the international socialist movement for the struggle against that imperialist war. Left-wing groups in the US Socialist Party fought for that position in their party. Recognizing that the most significant way to influence their fellow-workers was through the printed word, the Socialist propaganda league of Boston late in 1916 started a paper called *The Internationalist.* In April, 1917, this was absorbed by the *New York International,* published in New York City. In mid-1917, *The Class Struggle,* a bi-monthly magazine, was started in New York City. Both of these journals played an important role in bringing Lenin to the American working class. (*The Class Struggle,* in its December, 1917 issue, published a section of Lenin's *State and Revolution.*) . . .

One of these publications that was not printed by local workers' groups was *The Soviets at Work,* a pamphlet that was issued by the Rand School in New York City, the central educational institution of the Socialist Party. This was a reprint of a report written by Lenin, entitled "The Immediate Tasks of the Soviet Government," which was first published in *Pravda,* April 28, 1918. The response to this Rand School pamphlet reveals how eagerly US workers were seeking a new way out of their misery and how quick they were to respond to Lenin.

One indication of the widespread impact of the pamphlet was what happened in Seattle in 1918–1919. A copy found its way to the Northwest metropolis and was reprinted in the *Seattle Union Record,* the official organ of the local central body of the American Federation of Labor. Because of the demand of the workers on the West Coast for this Lenin work, the Seattle labor movement republished it as a pamphlet. Twenty thousand copies were printed and were soon in the hands of workers up and down the Pacific coast. As Harvey O'Connor writes in his book, *Revolution in Seattle,* "the extraordinary influence of this pamphlet was to be felt in subsequent events in Seattle as workers pondered the problems of 'management' in a workers' state."

Those early publications of Lenin's writings by local workers' groups were a dominant influence in changing the entire course of workingclass struggle and workingclass politics in the United States. They focused the attention of the labor unionists on the need for organization of the masses of workers in industry, which finally transformed the weak craft-unionist AFL into the powerful AFL-CIO. And they confronted the more advanced elements in the working class with the realization that they needed a new form of organization through which to conduct their political struggles. This resulted in the formation of the US Communist Party which became the dominant force in left-wing political activity. . . .

Lenin was a serious student of the problems of the Black people in the United States and the relation of their struggles for liberation to the emancipation of the American working class. His position on this question was epitomized in an essay, "Imperialism and the Split in Socialism" published in *Sbornik Sotsial-Demokrata,* December 1916 (*Collected Works,* Vol. 23).

Lenin's influence upon the Black Liberation movement was almost immediate as soon as the Blacks became aware of him, as is evidenced in such incidents as the call upon the US Socialist Party in 1918 by leading Black Socialists to follow the road of Lenin and fight for the freedom of the Black people to achieve socialism in the US; by the cable of the Garveyite movement, the biggest mass movement of the Black people in the early 1920s, on Lenin's death, expressing the "deep sorrow" of "four hundred million Negroes of the world" and declaring that "to us Lenin was one of the world's greatest benefactors"; by the eloquent recollection, published in *A Long Way From Home,* of Claude McKay, the noted Black poet:

> And often now my nerves throb with the thrill
> When, in that gilded place, I felt and saw
> The simple voice and presence of Lenin.

Lenin's impact upon US youth is reflected today in the espousal of Leninism, however confusedly in some respects, by such advanced sections of the young people as the Black Panthers, the Young Lords and the Students for a Democratic Society. . . .

Of special significance today as our country is engaged in an invasion of Vietnam, it should be noted that Lenin led the first victorious resistance to a war of intervention and blockade by the United States and other imperialists in 1918–1922 in their attempt to destroy the new socialist state. In the resistance to that war of intervention, many sections of the American people, in Congress, among the churches, in the organized labor movement, among the Black people, played an important role in reversing the intervention policy of Washington.

Above all else, Lenin sought peaceful coexistence with the United States from the very birth of the USSR in 1917. He abhorred any imperialist war in which workers would have to die. In April, 1914, when World War I was in the making, he was interviewed by Alfred Maykosen, a Polish journalist, who asked him: "Would you welcome a conflict?" Lenin replied:

"Certainly not. Why should I want a conflict? I am doing—and will do—everything I can, everything within my power, to prevent mobilization and war. I do not want to see millions of workers killing each other to pay for capitalist madness. There can be no two opinions on that score.

"It is one thing objectively to predict a war and, should it break out, take maximum advantage of the situation. But to want war—that is quite another thing." (*Vladimir Ilyich Lenin. A Biography,* Progress Publishers, Moscow, 1965, pp. 193–4.) . . .

The impact of Lenin on the United States can be measured above all in the statement by Eugene V. Debs, the great workingclass leader, when he heard of Lenin's death in January, 1924:

"I regard Lenin as the greatest thinker. . . . He towered head and shoulders above every other statesman in Europe . . . He has carried two bullets fired into his body by an assassin, and at the same time has been forced to bear a burden of official responsibility and care greater than any other man's in the world. His place in history is certain. He will go down in history as one of the greatest statesmen, a towering personality, a heroic soul and in the loftiest sense a champion of the rights and liberties of the common people."

In 1845, Marx concluded his *Theses on Feuerbach* with this challenge: "The philosophers have interpreted the world in various ways; the point, however, is to change it."

Lenin accepted that challenge. He changed the world!

□ ———————————————————————————— □

UNITY OF THE COMMUNIST PARTY

**On Uniting and Strengthening the Party
and its Mass Base by the National Committee, CPUSA.
(A resolution adopted by a majority vote,
February 14–16, 1958), Political Affairs, March 1958**

[*Those who control the means of exploitation also dominate the ideological field. The exploiters do not use only naked oppression; they seek also to win ideological acceptance of their system. To this end they utilize every means at their command. Their objective is to undermine class consciousness and to propagate class collaboration. The penetration of capitalist ideology into the workers' camp is therefore of serious concern to its vanguard, the Communist Party.*

*This phenomenon is not easily detected. Often it takes the form of expediency and the rejection of mass action. It takes sharpest form in times of crisis. Gus Hall observed that "often unnoticed, it eats at the revolutionary fabric of a working-class movement, and is not noticed until there is a critical moment." (*Imperialism Today, *p. 322.) The constant fight for Marxist-Leninist principles is not a pedantic exercise, but a necessary part of class struggle.*

Aggressive imperialist acts are often hidden under a smokescreen of "defense of democracy" and "human rights." In the '50s the CIA covertly instigated counter-revolutions. It toppled the democratically elected government in Iran (1953). Later (in 1961) it engineered the murder of Patrice Lumumba in the Congo. During this period some socialist countries experienced acute internal problems.[5] *Fishing in troubled waters, the CIA aided by native renegades sought in the 1950s to undermine the new postwar socialist states and to destroy confidence in a system based on complete economic, social and political freedom.*

The 20th Congress of the Communist Party of the Soviet Union in 1956 acknowledged serious mistakes in the socialist democratic processes under Joseph Stalin. These grave errors were exposed and corrected, and since then great progress in the democratic process has been achieved as registered by the adoption of the new Soviet Constitution in 1977.

Of course there have been mistakes and reverses in the course of the sixty years of the history of the Soviet Union. Lenin in 1921 wrote: "We do not forget for a moment that we have committed and are committing numerous mistakes and are suffering numerous reverses. How can reverses and mistakes be avoided in a matter so new in the history of the world as the building of an unprecedented type [*Lenin's emphasis*] *of state edifice!" (V.I. Lenin,* Collected Works, *Vol. 33, pp. 54-55, Progress Publishers, Moscow, 1965).*

Since history does not move in a straight line, mistakes and reverses will occur and have occurred. But it would be a misreading of history to consider these the significant experience of the past 60 years. What is really significant is that the Soviet Union has opened up a road which the majority of mankind has begun to follow: the transition from capitalism to socialism.

Despite incredible difficulties—such as capitalist encirclement and tremendous sacrifices, including the loss of twenty million people—the Soviet Union crushed Hitler fascism and thereby saved civilization. It freed the nazi-occupied countries from imperialist domination, initiated the formation of a powerful system of socialist states and stands today, notwithstanding all the slanders and lies of imperialism and its lackeys, as the most democratic country in the world, as the foremost fighter for peace, human rights and social progress.

Some persons in the leadership levels of the CPUSA had been moving to the right even before the 20th Congress. They had been yielding to the combined pressures of government repression and the illusions of the "affluent society." Now they went further in that direction. With leaders of the right-wing group dominant on the Daily Worker, *they were able to*

346

disorient many of the paper's readers and managed to use the paper as an instrument for their anti-Sovietism and opportunism. They threatened the unity of the Party and challenged its right to exist. A serious loss of supporters led to suspension of the cherished Daily in January 1958 (see p. 380). When John Gates left the Party with a group of his allies, the conservative New York Herald-Tribune *hailed this prodigal's return with an editorial entitled: "Welcome Home."*

Before this the group had questioned the need for a party of socialism. They resurrected the Browder formula that had been repudiated a decade earlier. Following a long period of discussion within the Party they came to the 16th Convention (February 1957) with the dreary thesis "that the transformation of our Party into a political action association is necessary and desirable...." (Proceedings, 16th National Convention Communist Party, U.S.A., 1957).

Their idyllic view of the future was unrelated to the real world. They preached that with increasing productivity, a reduction in working hours was inevitable. But concessions are never inevitable. Every concession won is at the expense of sacrifice and struggle. Their utopian picture omitted this detail. There was no gain for the workers in their proposals—but it did land Gates a job with the bureaucracy of the International Ladies Garment Workers Union.

A major challenge was developed by the right-wing group regarding the question of international solidarity, a fundamental principle whose rejection leads to national chauvinism.

The opportunists, who were ready to give up a Marxist–Leninist party in the United States, found international ties an embarrassment. They were especially desirous of disassociating themselves from solidarity with the Soviet Union and the community of socialist states. The CPUSA, however, continues its participation in international meetings which are of ever-increasing value. (See address by Gus Hall in Ch. 9.)]

Since the 16th National Convention, the Party has been subjected to numerous attacks, difficulties and desertions. It has weathered these and remains very much alive and active. And during this period it has made constructive contributions in certain fields of mass work.

Nonetheless, the Party finds itself on the whole still in the critical state into which it has been plunged for some time—a situation for which the entire National Committee bears a collective responsibility. For the most part, the Party has been unsuccessful in breaking out of its isolation. Basic ideological differences continue to exist within the Party, and the

Party leadership itself is sharply divided, and therefore largely immobilized. . . .

To fulfill our Party's responsibility to our people and country in this year of challenge, to unite and strengthen the Party and to extend its political influence and mass ties, the National Committee considers that the following things should be done:

a) First and foremost, it is essential to insure that our Party participate ever more effectively in the vital struggles of today, that it make the many political, ideological and organizational contributions of which it is fully capable. . . .

b) [T]he 16th national convention established a generally sound orientation on the main questions confronting us. Among these are the crucial fight for peaceful coexistence; the building of an anti-monopoly coalition; the exceptional role of the Negro liberation movement and of the national task of democratizing the South; the fight for labor unity and independent political action by labor and its allies; the indispensable role of the Communist Party; the establishment of broad united front relations on the most vital mass issues with other democratic elements and organizations, including with diverse pro-socialist groupings; the promotion of proletarian internationalism; the vital importance of the fight against sectarianism and dogmatism, as well as the urgent necessity of combatting Right-opportunism and revisionism; and the charting of a peaceful, constitutional American road to socialism.

c) Particularly noteworthy is the stress of the national convention that "our chief task is to strengthen, rebuild and consolidate the Communist Party and overcome its isolation." And the convention clearly defined the essential features of the Party, reaffirming that it must be a working-class party based on the principles of scientific socialism, of Marxism-Leninism, applying and developing these in accord with the traditions and class struggle in our country.

The convention emphasized the indispensable vanguard role of a Marxist working-class party of socialism, and the necessity of striving as such to win mass influence and leadership for our Party. It declared that the Party, guided by the principles of Marxism-Leninism, is motivated by both the highest patriotism toward our own country and the great concept of proletarian internationalism.

It defined the Party as a party of action—not a debating society—in which the minority must be subordinated to the majority once a decision is taken. At the same time, it took steps to combat bureaucracy, reinforcing inner-Party democracy to assure the fullest contribution of all members in the making and execution of policy, while prohibiting all factions and anti-Party groupings and practices. . . .

d) In estimating the twin evils of Left-sectarianism and Right-opportunism, the convention correctly declared that our errors of the past period were chiefly of a Left-sectarian character. It pointed out that sectarianism and dogmatism have been a historic weakness of our movement, against which a decisive struggle must be waged—a struggle that will necessarily be a protracted one. But the convention also pointed out that both Left-sectarianism and Right-opportunism have objective roots in the capitalist society in which we live and that both must be fought at all times, with emphasis on that which at a given moment constitutes the greater danger. . . .

But the National Committee also recognizes that there are other issues which presently serve as sources of differences and division within the Party. One has been the controversy in the national leadership over the recently issued Declaration of the Twelve Communist and Workers Parties[6] of the socialist countries.

This is a document of far-reaching, historic importance. Together with the 64 Party Manifesto on Peace, it serves to unite all peace forces in a successful struggle to avert war and promote peaceful coexistence. It reinforces the unity both of the socialist countries and of the international working-class and Marxist movements. It is a major Marxist-Leninist contribution to the fight for world peace, democracy, national freedom and socialism. Communists, socialists and progressives everywhere should study it and learn from it, Americans no less than others. . . .

Finally, a most serious threat to Party unity is the destructive effect of factionalism. To defend and reinforce unity, it is necessary at all costs to eradicate all factional activities and groupings in our ranks.

e) To help end the present impasse and virtual paralysis within the national leadership of the Party, it is necessary to strengthen this leadership in a number of ways. . . .

Our Party has suffered severe blows during the past years. The forces of monopolist reaction have dedicated themselves to nothing short of its utter destruction. But they have not succeeded in this, nor will they ever succeed, notwithstanding those in our ranks who become disoriented and desert or betray the Party. For our Party grows out of the class struggle and the needs and socialist aspirations of the American working class; hence there will always be devoted working-class adherents of Marxism who will, under the most difficult of circumstances, keep it alive and flourishing.

□ ——————————————————————————————— □

ARMS AND THE ECONOMY

"The Economic Role of Armaments Expenditures" by Hyman Lumer, from *A Symposium: Disarmament and the American Economy,* edited by Herbert Aptheker, New Century Publishers, 1960

[*United States' foreign policy, since the end of World War II, is feeding the insatiable appetites of its huge monopolies. A vast apparatus spreads the ideas that this position is not only essential for the nation's "defense" but is of economic benefit to the people. Although this argument is becoming more threadbare, it requires an exposure of its contentions.*

On January 30, 1960, the Faculty of Social Science held a Conference on Disarmament in New York City. In a collection of eight papers presented to the meeting, the editor, Herbert Aptheker, wrote in the Foreword that "the smash-up of the projected Summit Meeting [7] *to have been held in Paris in May, 1960, offers additional urgency to the subject of this volume."*

Hyman Lumer (1909-1976), then the associate editor of Political Affairs *and a participant at the conference, was formerly head of the biology department at Fenn College (Cleveland). He served as Educational Director of the Ohio-Kentucky District of the United Electrical, Radio and Machine Workers Union. In the 1950s he was imprisoned under the infamous anti-communist section of the Taft-Hartley Act. He was the National Educational Director of the Communist Party for a number of years.*

He is the author of a number of books on economics and wrote extensively on the Jewish question and on Zionism. The Lumer report, slightly abridged, examines the crucial issue of disarmament and the struggle for peace.]

We live in what has been termed a permanent war economy. Since World War II, large-scale military budgets have become a prominent ongoing aspect of the American economic picture. Moreover, they have come to be widely viewed as a necessary prop to the economy—as a means of warding off crisis and assuring a high level of employment.

The average American draws such conclusions chiefly from the empirical observation that when local industries receive more military orders more men are hired and business improves. Economists, however, have given them a more sophisticated rationale, based on the central doctrine of J.M. Keynes, namely that the government, through large-scale spending (and particularly deficit spending), can regulate the economy and keep it on an even keel, and can assure full employment at all times.

This theory had its inception in the thirties, at the time when the New Deal "pump-priming" program was being put into effect as a means of combatting the depression. As we know, this program met with indifferent success, and the large army of unemployed was finally absorbed only after the outbreak of World War II. . . .

[But] the relative prosperity of the postwar years lent further credence to such ideas and gave birth to the belief in many circles that a regulated economy and a "welfare state" had been substantially achieved—a "welfare state," be it noted, whose foundation is the expenditure on armaments of 10 per cent of the national product and well over half the federal budget.

Such has come to be the most widely accepted view of things. The reality, however, is somewhat different. To be sure, the production of armaments may have a stimulating effect on the economy. But it is temporary and limited, and arms budgets are not at all the economic regulator which the Keynesians consider them to be. Their actual effects are, of course, rather complex, and we can undertake here only to outline them briefly.

First of all, an armaments program means the diversion by the government of a share of the nation's purchasing power, or real wealth, from other purposes to this one. The government may do so by taxation, by borrowing from the existing money supply or by credit inflation that is, by creating new money. But whichever of these methods is employed, the net result is the same: part of the nation's economic resources is taken by the government, and civilian purchasing power is accordingly diminished, whether through taxation or inflation. In this sense, armaments do not represent a net addition to the national output, but only a shifting from one form of production to another.

In a capitalist economy, however, the full utilization of resources for civilian purposes does not always take place. Capitalism generates overproduction, excess productive capacity and accumulation of capital which cannot readily be profitably invested. Under these circumstances, by providing an outlet for such capital, military spending may stimulate investment for a time. "It brings about a shifting of capital investments to war goods industries, entailing large expenditures for conversion to war production together with the investment of additional capital to expand the productive facilities in these industries. . . . In this way, the decline in capital investments is temporarily arrested. For a time, at least, there is rising production and employment in the expanding arms industries." (Hyman Lumer, *War Economy and Crisis,* International Publishers, 1954, pp. 144-145.)

But the stimulus is only temporary, wearing off as the facilities required to maintain the given level of arms production are completed. A jump in military expenditures may also give rise to a spurt in production of consumer goods and raw materials in anticipation of possible shortages. This occurred, for example, at the start of the Korean war. Such spurts, however, prove to be even more short-lived, particularly since there is in the end no corresponding spurt in consumer demand.

The most striking feature of arms production is its utter wastefulness. Economically, it is a means of systematically destroying a part of the national wealth, for armaments are neither capital goods nor consumer goods and have no utility other than to be consumed in wartime. Failing this, they speedily become obsolete and are scrapped to make way for fresh stocks of arms.

However, what is destroyed must be paid for. The money used to pay capitalists to produce arms represents, as we have indicated, a share of the national purchasing power appropriated by the government for that purpose. If this were taken from the capitalists themselves, they would lose more than they gain in profits from military production, and would have no interest in pursuing such a course. But the fact is that it is the working people who bear the lion's share of the costs. It is they, as the official statistics show, who have been paying a steadily increasing share of the rising tax burden. It is they who suffer most from the inflation and rising prices which are the result of military budgets.

On the other hand, it is the makers of the arms who gain. The rate of profit on military contracts is, as a rule, considerably higher than that to be obtained in civilian production. Such contracts offer not only a guaranteed market but all sorts of opportunities for padding of figures and other forms of graft and corruption, especially in connection with the experimental and pilot operations which are such a large part of peacetime military budgets. In many instances, moreover, the productive facilities have been built at government expense and turned over to private corporations which extract profits from their operation without themselves having invested one penny in them.

The net effect of an arms economy, therefore, is not to expand the total market, but to siphon purchasing power from the hands of the working people to the profit of the capitalists in the armaments and related industries. This impoverishment may at times be obscured by other factors. As the French Marxist economist Henri Claude points out, it "can be partially concealed when the militarization of the economy coincides with the upward swing of the cycle, that is, parallel with a real expansion of the capitalist market caused by ,arge-scale renewal of fixed capital." ("Whither Does Militarization of the Economy Lead?" *World Marxist Review,* December, 1959.)

Nevertheless, it manifests itself, even under such conditions in the form of partial crises of overproduction—in the "crisis within a boom" phenomenon which occurred, for example, in 1950-52 during the Korean war. Here, in the face of an over-all upswing involving a big jump in arms outlays, there took place simultaneously a sharp drop in output of many consumer goods, especially consumer durables. Thus, between June, 1950, and June, 1952, the Federal Reserve Board index of production of major consumer durable goods (1947-49 = 100) fell from 163 to 108, or by more than one-third. The result was declining employment in these industries, culminating in a wave of layoffs late in 1951.

The impoverishment of the people as a consequence of the militarization of the economy is evident also in the growing shortages of schools, hospitals, low-cost housing and other vital social needs. These needs the forty-odd billions a year now being spent on arms would more than suffice to fill, even after a substantial tax cut. Finally, it should be noted that in the face of these huge military outlays, we have experienced three postwar economic slumps as well as a rising level of unemployment in the intervening boom periods. . . .

Furthermore, since the effects are temporary and limited, they can be prolonged only by further increases in military spending. Such a course of action, if persisted in, leads in the end to all-out militarization of the economy, accompanied by extreme impoverishment of the masses of working people. This is exactly what happened in Hitler Germany in the thirties; by 1939 the average German worker was putting in twelve to fourteen hours a day turning out arms for Hitler's Wehrmacht, and at the same time suffering severe shortages of all the necessities of life.

In addition, since military expenditures can be justified only on the grounds that they are needed for war, such a course of action is possible only under conditions of mounting war hysteria—as an accompaniment of an aggressive foreign policy leading ultimately to all-out war. This, too, was the final outcome of the Nazi "prosperity" built on guns and tanks.

Such, in brief, are the principal features of an arms economy.

Of course, not all of these features are peculiar to this form of government spending; certainly, whatever economic stimulus may be

353

provided by spending for military purposes may equally be achieved by spending for other purposes. Yet in practice, military expenditures have far exceeded any others. Indeed, they are today greater than all other government outlays combined. Nor is this accidental, for in the capitalist economy of today they offer certain unique advantages from the view-point of the big monopolies, aside from their relationship to an aggres-sive, warlike foreign policy. . . .

[Thus] the scope of government spending for purposes other than military is sharply restricted by this jealous regard for the prerogatives of private enterprise. While big business may not oppose expenditures for such things as new post offices, it fiercely resists any outlays which encroach in the slightest degree on its own sacred domain. This hostility is discussed as an obstacle to Keynesian fiscal policy in an article by two American economists, who write:

"This resistance appears even in minor cases such as prison industries and housing activities of universities, and in intensified form in connec-tion with public ownership of power facilities, public housing, public health services, etc. Government spending thus tends to be restricted to those relatively limited projects which are traditionally governmental or which are not likely to be commercially profitable. . . . As a result, expenditure for defense remains about the only large form of outlay which can be substantially increased without taint of infringement on private enterprise." (Howard R. Bowen and Gerald M. Meier, "Institu-tional Aspects of Economic Fluctuations," in: K.K. Kurihara, ed., *Post Keynesian Economics,* Rutgers University Press, 1954, pp. 164-165.)

Since the production of armaments can be justified only on the grounds that they are necessary to meet a threat of war, the easing of world tensions and the growing demands for disarmament to which it gives rise progressively diminish the basis for continuation of large-scale military outlays. These developments do not, however, lessen the need of monopoly capital to rely upon the economic resources of the state to prop up its profits. For this reason, as well as others, big business will on the whole strenuously resist any serious reduction of armaments. At the same time, as it is increasingly compelled to adapt itself to new conditions beyond its control, it will seek out other, even though less satisfactory, state-monopoly capitalist measures to meet its needs.

But if an arms economy best serves the monopolies as a means of enhancing their profits at the expense of the working people, then by the same token the best interests of the people will be served by disarmament and the use of the immense sums thereby released for their own benefit—to reduce their taxes and to provide the schools, hospitals, housing, health protection, improved social security and other social services which are today so badly needed. Such measures, moreover, will create far more jobs than does the production of armaments. However, even if the funds now wasted on arms would become available, it does not by any means follow that they will automatically be used for the people's welfare. . . . The economic benefits of disarmament for the working people will materialize, therefore, only if they are energetically fought for. . . .

[T]he economic significance of disarmament must be seen in terms of the class struggle. The working class is compelled at all times and under all conditions to wage a struggle in defense of its living standards—a struggle over the division between the capitalist class and itself of the product of its labor. A growing part of this struggle is the conflict over the disposition of the financial resources of the state. More and more, the working class and its allies are compelled to battle in the political arena over such questions as who shall pay the costs of government spending and who shall receive its benefits. These questions are involved in the fight for disarmament itself.

The economic advantage of disarmament lies in the fact that it offers conditions vastly more favorable to the workers in their struggles. If war economy strengthens the forces of reaction, disarmament strengthens those of progress. If war economy squanders the nation's resources and perverts its scientific and technical potentials to turn out instruments of destruction, disarmament frees them to be used for providing the means for a better life for all. It opens the door to imposing social and economic advances by the American people, advances which will realize at least in some degree the enormous promise held forth by the new developments in science and technology, and which are blocked by the present huge military expenditures. Hence disarmament is something to be welcomed from the economic point of view and not, as is still all too often the case, something to be feared.

We have confined ourselves here chiefly to the economic aspects of armament and disarmament. We have not dealt with the more fundamental question of peace or war, of existence or annihilation. For disarmament means living in a world freed from the gnawing fear of nuclear destruction—a world at peace. That this is most fervently to be desired, certainly no one can question.

□ ———————————————————————————— □

THE CUBAN MISSILE CRISIS

"Fellow Americans: There is Still Time to Prevent War,"
Editorial, *The Worker*, October 28, 1962

[*Three months after President John F. Kennedy took office, Cuban emigré forces, trained and led by CIA agents, landed at the Bay of Pigs in an attempt to overthrow the government of Fidel Castro. The attempt ended in total failure.*

The Bay of Pigs, CIA plans to assassinate Castro, illegal overflights of Cuba by U-2 planes, subversion, sabotage—all were elements in the US effort to reverse the Cuban people's revolution.

U.S. intelligence learned in October 1962 that the Soviet Union was furnishing Cuba with missiles with which to defend herself in the face of the obvious designs against her.[8] The US response to this information provoked the "Cuban missile crisis," a confrontation between the United States and the Soviet Union of the gravest kind. Curtis LeMay, a hawk of hawks, the Chief of Staff of the Air Force, urged the president to commence a military attack but Kennedy opted for a naval blockage of Cuba. The world spent fearful, sleepless nights until the situation was defused with an agreement by the USSR to remove the missiles in return for a pledge by the United States not to attack Cuba.

Fear of an imminent nuclear war pervaded the country. New York City headquarters of the United Nations was the scene of the most intense activity. SANE (National Committee for a Sane Nuclear Policy) in an advertisement in the New York Times *(October 28) asked the president: "If it is so wrong for the Soviet Union to set up a nuclear base in Cuba, so close to our shores, then why is it right to have nuclear bases (and to have them for many years) in Turkey, which is directly on the Soviet border?"*

The Worker *carried a full-page editorial containing a 5-point program for immediate action. Ten thousand people who had been mobilized to demand a peaceful solution of the situation at United Nations Plaza turned the occasion into a victory celebration when they learned that the crisis was ended. The* Worker *on October 30 carried the banner: "Glad to Be Alive, Say 10 Thousand in Front of UN."*]

In our country, almost any child the age of the President's daughter, Caroline, can tell you that the most fundamental ethic of religious faith is TO DO UNTO OTHERS AS YOU WOULD HAVE THEM DO UNTO YOU. Caroline knows this but has her Daddy irrevocably turned his back upon this simple but profound teaching? That is the question that agonizes the nation today and causes the whole world the deepest anxiety.

The proclamation of a unilateral aggressive course and naval blockade of Cuba and threat of imminent invasion, which President Kennedy put his signature on last Thursday, could become a death warrant for world peace and the life of our own nation. It is an act that leads to war.

No thoughtful person can believe the charge that the litle island country of Cuba with a total population less than that of New York City, is such a threat to our mighty country that it calls for drastic war moves that carry the world to the brink of nuclear holocaust. It is not Cuba that is the urgent threat to the peace and safety of our country but Washington's policy of armed adventurism against Cuba.

Differences with Cuba can await negotiation and settlement at the conference table, but the menace of war, embraced in the foolhardy naval blockade cannot wait. It must be called off NOW!

THE PROCLAMATION must be recalled by the will of the American people and the massive manifestation of world public opinion.

Each American who has a patriotic concern for his country's safety and honor, everyone who has a sane regard for his own life and the lives and treasures of the world's peoples MUST NOW SPEAK UP and make their voices heard in WASHINGTON.

• Demand that President Kennedy withdraw the ring of warships, planes and armed forces around Cuba and order their return to their stations in the U.S.

• Demand that President Kennedy recàll and nullify all orders which would interupt the normal traffic on the trade routes of Cuba.

• Demand that President Kennedy respect and utilize the good offices of the United Nations to enter into immediate negotiations with the governments of Cuba and the Soviet Union for the sensible and peaceful settlement of all matters under dispute.

Indeed it has never been more necessary than it is this day that President Kennedy and our Government should in this matter Do Unto Others As We Would Have Them Do Unto Us, for is it not perfectly plain that if our government arrogates to itself the right to stop other countries' ships on the high seas headed for Cuba, other countries could stop, search or sink our ships bound for ports of nearby countries which are hostile to them?

We cannot go ahead committing this criminal folly in respect to Cuba. Would we want the Soviet Union to stop, search or sink our ships headed for Turkish ports? Would we want China to stop, search or sink our ships en route to Japan or Okinawa? Would we want Cuba to stop, search or sink our ships carrying arms to Panama, Nicaragua or Honduras?

One week ago the President himself denounced the ultra-Right politicians such as Senators [Homer] Capehart and [Barry] Goldwater as "those self-appointed generals and admirals who want to send someone else's sons to war and consistently voted against the instruments of peace."

He stated that American intelligence reports revealed only defensive arms buildup in Cuba.

What then has produced this sudden about-face?

Is this the work of the same CIA-Pentagon war-lovers who, behind the back of former President Eisenhower, in May, 1960, plotted the U-2 flight over the Soviet Union which wrecked the scheduled peace talks?

Is not this "intelligence finding" a hoax, a fraud designed to trigger the blowing up of the peace hopes of civilization, or unleashing war by the U.S. on Cuba, the Soviet Union and the world?

Citizens, the situation is grave; the hour is late, but there is yet time to act. Even the sightless can sense that Captain Kennedy is heading our ship of state into the path of a hurricane. Our country and vast areas of the world can be shattered on the rocks of the nuclear war that looms ahead. There is still time to signal the man at the helm to change course. . . .

Fellow Americans! Call upon President Kennedy to refrain from any further measures which shatter the peace of Cuba, such as we would not want Cuba or others to do unto US!

☐ ———————————————————————————— ☐

COMMUNISTS AND LABOR: SOME SECOND THOUGHTS

Labor Looks at Labor. Some Members of the United Auto Workers Undertake a Self-Examination. Center for the Study of Democratic Institutions, Santa Barbara, California, 1963

[*As Chapter 4 described, the Communists played a leading role in the founding of the United Auto Workers union. The union subsequently came under the anti-communist, right-wing, social-democratic leadership of Walter Reuther and his associates. With the help of the*

CIO's unbridled attack on the Left, plus the punitive measures of the Taft–Hartley law, plus the prevailing anti-Red hysteria of the 1950's, the Communists and the Left were formally excluded from UAW leadership.

In September 1963, at the Center for the Study of Democratic Institutions, a principal activity of the Fund for the Republic, there was held one of a series of what the Center calls "Conversations." Essentially it was a roundtable discussion, led by W.H. Ferry, vice-president (in 1963) of the Center, and Paul Jacobs (the only union official named), who was staff director of the Center's Study of the Trade Union. Ferry had been publicity director for the Political Action Committee of the CIO, and Jacobs was a UAW official on the West Coast.

The other participants in the "Conversation" were a group of UAW leaders. Judging from the published account, there were about ten such men present. They are referred to in the published text not by their names but as "UAW #1," "UAW #2," etc. One can only surmise why, at a meeting to study "democratic institutions," these persons found it necessary to remain anonymous.

The "Conversation" discussed the state of labor unionism. (They acknowledged the mistake in "kicking the Communists out." A number of unions today are considering resolutions to rescind the anti-communist clause from their constitutions. Others have already removed this anti-labor clause.) In September 1963 that appeared rather bleak to some of the participants. In an introductory note to the published text they claim "the trade unions are consistently declining in power . . . we may be witnessing the beginning of the end of the trade union movement." This gloomy view of some labor officials did not represent the opinion of millions of organized workers.

The leaders' lack of confidence in the trade union movement does not coincide with the thinking and activity of the Left, let alone that of the Communist Party. While the labor movement faces serious problems, as some participants stressed, the solution rests with the growing rank-and-file movement and resistance to domination by class-collaborationist leadership.

The observation of the UAW #10 that, "Maybe what I am saying is that we ought to have a labor party" and the point raised by UAW #5 that we must place events "into a broad international context" suggest some of the positive content of this sober colloquy by this group of trade union officials.

The quotes below show that, though Communists had been expelled from UAW leadership, the Party was an uninvited presence at the conference table in Santa Barbara where this "Conversation" took place.]

Jacobs: I suggest that the basic fault is one of the things that you indicated, the drive to conform. I submit that we made a great mistake when we kicked the Communists out of the CIO—and, as you know, I was one of those who fought most belligerently to throw them out. I think now that the way the UAW leadership behaved toward its minority was a mistake. We ran scared. That's really why we kicked out the opposition. And when we did it, we really threw the baby out with the bath, because we set up a pattern of conformity. We set up a pattern of refusing to break with traditional ways of thinking. We weren't willing to run the risks of having the Communist Party guys inside the CIO and inside our own unions. We should have been willing to run that risk because when we gave in we became part of the general movement of "acceptability." [One may be justified in questioning what "risk" was involved in having "the Communist guys inside!"—Ed.]

That is why, for example, you can't dignify what goes on at a UAW convention today by calling it "debate." Policy questions are not being debated at UAW conventions. What is being argued about is administrative jazz and union legislative problems. There are no arguments about foreign policy questions or even about domestic policy questions. . . .

UAW #5: They say that there is much joy in heaven for a sinner who repenteth and I couldn't help having that run through my mind when Jacobs mentioned the purge of the left-wing in the trade union movement. I have felt this for a long time. My background, while left, has been one of opposition to the Communist Party in the trade union movement. However, I did not go along with the idea of expelling these people. If we grant the hypothesis that they had to be removed from the scene, it seemed to me to be incumbent upon the victorious forces to put something in there to fill the vacuum that was created. This was never done. I say, this is still incumbent upon them. . . .

These were the people who were carrying the ideological ball at that time. Now we are in a time when we go to a trade union educational class and we talk about which wing of the Democratic Party we are going to support. This carries no spark back to the plant. They can get this kind of information out of the *Los Angeles Times*. There is nothing here to capture the imagination of the young people who are going to take our place. . . .

The labor movement today, certainly as evidenced by the disputes between such people as Meany and Reuther, is certainly not a homogeneous grouping of any kind. There are as many different trends of opinion in the trade union movement as there are in this room. I personally am not content with just simple trade union collective bargaining goals. I think we have to go beyond that. I think we should have learned, through a couple of generations now, that when we just stick to simple trade union goals, we run head-on into the institution that we talk about here as the establishment. What are we here for? To maintain a docile labor force by seeing that people get enough in the way of wages and fringe benefits and finally go to the grave well-fed and content? Life consists of more than that.

We determined some time ago that the old idea that the unions ought to stay out of politics had to be discarded. But what kind of politics did the unions get into? It seems to me we are sort of playing a game of company unionism in that area.

I believe our role has to be more independent, to seek out some social goals that are not on the horizon of either the Republican or the Democratic Party. In some other countries, the trade union movement has already moved toward more independent political action. I believe the very reason the movement has been declining in America is that we have not been more aggressively independent, politically speaking.

UAW #10: The number one political problem, I think, is that the things you win at the bargaining table can be taken away from you in the halls of the legislature. I am of the opinion that one of the new things we will have to take on is a more concerted effort in the legislatures to bring about some changes in the things we feel are hindering the labor movement. . . .

I firmly believe that to change this trend and to get the younger people more active and more favorably inclined toward the labor union, we must take people from the ranks of labor to carry our battles into the federal and state legislatures. Until that is done, the labor movement as we know it today will regress further and further. Maybe what I am saying is that we ought to have a labor party. . . .

UAW #5: For example, is there a correlation between the rise of the right wing in American society and the attendant decline of the labor movement? I think there is. Secondly, are we proceeding on the assumption that the economic system is inevitably healthy and that it is going to continue that way? If so, we look at it one way; if not, then there might be a "radicalization" of a sort. Thirdly, in the international context, is an increase in the militancy of the American trade union movement likely at a time when it is necessary for us to be taking certain defensive or even aggressive steps against an ideology that has come to be identified to a certain degree with the trade union movement? By that I mean the rise of socialism around the world, while at the same time the United States remains one of the last strongholds of laissez-faire capitalism.

When we examine the questions that have arisen here today, I believe they must be put into a broad international context if we ever hope to reach the right answers.

□ ———————————————————————————— □

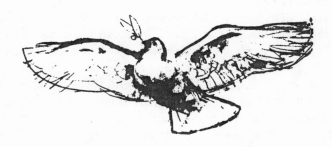

9.

VIETNAM AND THE PEACE UPSURGE

No event in recent history left such lasting effect on US foreign policy as did the intervention in Vietnam. The invasion of Indochina was started by President Kennedy, expanded by Presidents Johnson and Nixon and ended in the early days of President Ford. It resulted in a jolting blow to US interventionist hopes. It was a watershed in foreign policy. No longer did people accept the maxim that debate and action end at the nation's shores. They questioned the policy and forced a change.

In the midst of war, they questioned the reasons for the war. To the demand for greater support, they intensified their opposition. The American people, who had demonstrated their support for an anti-Nazi war, now could not stomach aggression against small underdeveloped countries, fighting for their independence.

A united front in varied forms crystallized. The peace movement was unquestionably unique in its development and composition. Though only the Communist Party fully grasped the anti-imperialist content of the struggle (see Betty Gannett, p. 366), there were pacifists arm-in-arm with class-conscious radicals;

students constituted a large sector as universities became the seat of peace activities; youth, generally, were the dynamic contingent of this movement. The Black liberation movement, tempered in the bitter struggle for civil rights, developed a magnetic voice in the person of Dr. Martin Luther King, Jr.

Sinister Wall Street cliques sought to instigate a "hard hat" pro-war group among building-trades workers. The move spread to several industrial communities, but failed in its purpose. Gus Hall, himself a "hard hat"[1] steel worker, warned that this campaign was a time bomb, dangerous to the working class. Organized labor peace action played no small part in winning trade union support for the peace movement. (See George Meyers p. 369).

When this protracted aggressive war came to a crashing end in Saigon in April 1975, Henry Winston and Gus Hall, speaking for the Central Committee of the Communist Party, declared: "'The victory won by the Vietnamese people against the most powerful of the world's imperialist powers and their satellite puppets was made possible by the unreserved sacrifices and determined solidarity rendered by the Democratic Republic of Vietnam.

"This is also a victory for the majority of the American people who opposed a criminal, genocidal, brutal war waged by U.S. imperialism.'

*"They noted that the Communist Party was always initiator and forerunner in the struggle for ending that aggression by US imperialism against the Vietnam people. Its vanguard resistance to the war of US imperialism against Vietnam upheld the country's honor and was in the highest national interest, even as it was in the finest traditions of working-class internationalism." (*Daily World, *May 1, 1975).*

The restoration of the Party's channels to the rank and file of labor was carried out with slow but determined steps. An important victory along this road was scored in the Archie Brown case (see p. 379). The prosecution and harassment of the Party lessened in accordance with the inability of the government to sustain its frenzied anti-communist propaganda. The war was producing an inflationary spiral that had the effect of wage cuts. In contrast was the rise in monopoly profits and the growth of unabashed corrup-

tion in government and business. Tax loopholes for the rich were widened; the lower the income the heavier the tax burden. The shadows of Watergate were gathering.

The return of the Daily Worker *in the form of the* Daily World *gave the movement an expanded voice. Again, after a prolonged absence, the Party was returning to the electoral field. The McCarran Act was nullified.*

In 1968 the Communist Party, which had not been on a presidential ballot since 1940, returned to the field. An editorial in Political Affairs *commented (January 1969):*

"The Communist Party, for the first time in 28 years, put forward its own presidential ticket, headed by the outstanding Negro woman leader Charlene Mitchell and its National Youth Director Michael Zagarell. The onerous requirements to place a minority party on the ballot in most states made it a foregone conclusion that, except for isolated instances, the candidates would call for a write-in vote. . . ." The experience gained in this campaign was applied with vastly increased effect in the campaigns of 1972 and 1976. In 1964, in a regional election in southern California, the Communist leader, William Taylor, had demonstrated the effectiveness and political value of serious election activity (see p. 319).

The candidacies of Senators Eugene McCarthy and George McGovern for US president, while unsuccessful, nevertheless stimulated dissident sentiment amongst the people. It was McCarthy's favorable showing in an early New Hampshire primary that led President Johnson to decide not to seek re-election.

The glow of Vietnam's victory brightened the prospects of eliminating colonial oppression and creating a community of totally independent nations on all continents. But imperialism will not yield readily, but seeks new forms of exploitation and divisiveness. Aid to the further development of a conscious anti-imperialist movement remains a key objective of the Communist Party.

In the Middle East, Israel and its Zionist aggressive policies are allied with other reactionary states. They continue to oppose independence for the Palestinians and the resolutions of acute problems in the region.

A condition of detente whereby tensions would be eased, firstly, between the United States and the Soviet Union, remains to be resolved. This would contribute to the elimination of the threat of nuclear war and advance world peace.

The burden of military appropriations continues to grow. Thus the struggles for economic needs are more and more associated with the move for peace. This subject will be dealt with in the following chapter.

□ ──────────────────────────────────── □

THE U.S. INTERVENES IN VIETNAM

End the War in Vietnam by Betty Gannett, New Outlook Publishers, 1965

[*The war in Vietnam was the longest war in U.S. history and involved the administrations of five successive presidents.*

The Associated Press Almanac wrote in 1960, "Insurgent activity against the [U.S. puppet] Diem regime increases as does U.S. aid." At the time this pamphlet was written the Almanac noted, "The United States commit[s] its 23,000 advisers to combat. . . . American casualties mount as the United States increasingly takes the major military role from the South Vietnamese." Thus the American people were drawn into an adventure which finally came to an end in an ignominious defeat of U.S. imperialism.

Betty Gannett (1906–1970) was an outstanding woman leader of the Party. She was prominent as an organizer, educator, administrator and writer. She served a term in Alderson prison as a Smith Act victim in the 50s. At the time she wrote this pamphlet she was executive editor of Political Affairs. *A section of the pamphlet appears below.*]

It is difficult for most Americans, because our country was born in revolution against British colonial rule, to entertain the idea that the United States would interfere in the internal affairs of another country. Despite claims to anti-colonialism, the United States became directly involved in Indochina before World War II ended. As far back as 1950, it agreed to supply money and arms to the French imperialists in their desperate attempt to reinstitute their colonial rule over this peninsula.

The countries now known as South Vietnam, North Vietnam, Laos and Cambodia once comprised French Indochina. For more than 80 years, ever since 1858, French colonialism brutally dominated this area, kept the peoples in virtual bondage, plundered the natural wealth. Numerous rebellions of the people were drowned in blood. . . .

In the early months of 1954 the French army faced disaster in the battle of Dienbienphu, that stronghold collapsing after a 55-day dramatic siege by the Vietminh. The French had been fought to a standstill. But Secretary of State Dulles was bent on keeping the French fighting. He unfolded the banner of anti-Communism. He promised them American troops, the deployment of the Seventh Fleet, and atomic bombs. Frenzied efforts were made to "internationalize" the conflict by attempting to draw in our European and Asian allies.

While Dulles had the support of the Nixons, Knowlands, McCarthys, the people in the country refused to buy the package he was selling— neither would America's allies. Senator Ed Johnson (D., Colo.), speaking out for a vast chorus of opposition, challenged the White House (April 26, 1954):

"At what point, and to what degree, has this war, which every record shows to have been a war for freedom and independence against imperialism, at what point did it suddenly become a war of Communist aggression? . . . .

"Asia is in revolution—revolution against colonialism."

Fortunately, the conflict did not spread; the atomic bombs were not dropped; the troops were not dispatched—and peace negotiations were begun in Geneva, Switzerland. On July 21, 1954, after three months of meetings, the final agreements were adopted. The war which had lasted eight tragic years was at an end. Vietnam, Cambodia and Laos were declared independent and sovereign states.

Up to the very end, John Foster Dulles and his emissaries tried to prevent a peaceful resolution of the war at the Geneva Conference. In fact, Dulles demonstratively stalked out of the conference to flaunt his disagreement. The United States refused to sign the agreements and "convinced" the government in South Vietnam to follow suit. The ink on the agreements was hardly dry when the United States embarked on its unilateral course to violate them.

In September 1954, the United States formed the Southeast Asia Treaty Organization (SEATO) as an aggressive military alliance to provide a cover, if necessary, for interventionist designs. C.L. Sulzberger points out (*N. Y. Times,* June 3, 1964) that Dulles admitted that the principal purpose of SEATO "was to provide our President legal authority to intervene in Indochina."

And intervene we did, without delay. The people of South Vietnam had little to say in the choice of their government. Ngo Dinh Diem, the despot violently overthrown in 1963, was Washington's choice to replace the French puppet, Bao Dai. Sam Castan, senior *Look* editor, put it squarely (January 28, 1964): "Secretary of State John Foster Dulles picked him. Senator Mike Mansfield endorsed him. Francis Cardinal Spellman praised him. Vice-President Richard Nixon liked him and President Dwight D. Eisenhower OK'd him."

To clothe this despot in an aura of legality, elections were held, and Ngo Dinh Diem stepped forth as the people's choice. But, as every objective observer has pointed out, the elections were not only rigged but accompanied by a reign of terror and intimidation to silence any and all opposition.

These elections had another ulterior motive—to circumvent the provisions of the Geneva Agreements for the holding of a general election in July, 1956, to peacefully reunify the country. At the time of Geneva a temporary military demarcation line had been established which divided Vietnam in two: the Vietminh to regroup above the 17th Parallel, the French and the Bao Dai forces in the south. But the 17th Parallel was explicitly a temporary demarcation line which "should not in any way be interpreted as constituting a political or territorial boundary."

The aim of the United States and its puppet regime in Saigon was to bring about a permanent division of the country. They had no intentions of holding the 1956 general elections. What is more, Diem's unpopularity and Ho Chi Minh's great prestige made clear what the outcome of a national election would be. A pretext had to be found. It was. Diem declared that circumstances in North Vietnam did not assure a democratic election. The elections to democratically reunify the country were never held.

With the bypassing of the general elections, the course was set to seal off South Vietnam from North Vietnam, and under the guise of combatting Communism, to foist upon the country a fascist military dictatorship that ran roughshod over the aspirations of the South Vietnamese people.

□ —————————————————————————— □

LABOR AND THE VIETNAM WAR

"Labor Speaks Out for Peace" by George Meyers, *Political Affairs,* January, 1968

[*The deliberate concealing of anti-war sentiment combined with the media's effort to disclose every hawkish phrase of George Meany, created a distorted view of labor's attitude to the war in Vietnam. The object was to create the impression that only a handful of Left supporters represented peace sentiment. Actions such as the "hard hat demonstrations" were deliberately instigated with the intent of showing that peace sentiment is out of harmony with the trade union movement.*

In November 1967, a National Labor Leadership Assembly met in Chicago with the purpose of strengthening labor's opposition to the Vietnam war. The response was beyond the expectation of its organizers. It attracted a representative group of nationally prominent leaders and a large number of trade union leaders on a local and shop level.

George Meyers (b. 1912), Labor Secretary of the Communist Party and former president of the Maryland CIO, assesses this significant event.]

"This conference—a united expression of varied branches of labor—reaffirms that the trade union movement is part of forward–looking America; that no matter what the formal resolutions of higher bodies may state, the troubled conscience of the working people cannot be stilled. This conference speaks for millions. You here today will long be remembered as those who had the courage to speak out and the wisdom to be right."

These words of Dr. Martin Luther King, Jr. to the National Labor Leadership Assembly for Peace, held in Chicago on November 11–12, are an apt summation of the historic significance of this gathering. For the first time in the United States, a broadly based section of organized labor met to condemn the war policies of the government in the midst of war.

The Assembly leaders had expected a maximum of 350 delegates. Instead, over 550 trade union leaders arrived from 38 states including Hawaii, to tax facilities at the University of Chicago's Center for Continuing Education. They came from more than 60 national and international unions. Some were delegates sponsored by local, state and national bodies; others came as individuals. In addition to local union officers, there were over 60 top union leaders, including 30 international vice-presidents, in attendance. Two original sponsors of the Assembly,

Frank Rosenblum, secretary-treasurer of the Amalgamated Clothing Workers, and Emil Mazey, who holds the same office in the United Auto Workers, were speakers. Another sponsor, Patrick Gorman, head of the Amalgamated Meat Cutters, sent regrets that he was unable to attend due to a death in the family. UAW Director of International Affairs Victor Reuther, was active in the Assembly and one of the main labor speakers. Cleveland Robinson, president of the Negro American Labor Council, was a delegate from District 65 of the Retail, Wholesale and Department Store Employees and led one of the panels.

From the independent unions, the International Longshoremen's Union (ILWU) delegation was led by its president, Harry Bridges. James Matles, Secretary-Treasurer of the United Electrical Workers (UE), led a similar delegation. Several Teamsters Union leaders, including Larry Steinberg, former administrative assistant to James Hoffa, and Jake McCarthy, editor of the *Missouri Teamster* were also present. A Canadian trade union group was officially represented, as were the Negro American Labor Council and several trade union peace committees.

Eleven high-ranking peace advocates from outside the labor movement were active participants in the Assembly. Outstanding was Dr. King who spoke at the banquet, chaired by Russell Leach, president of the Wayne County (Detroit) AFL-CIO Council and one of its official delegates. UAW's Emil Mazey and U.S. Senator Vance Hartke (Dem-Ind.) were the other banquet speakers.

At the opening session, Professor John Kenneth Galbraith sharply condemned the war while proposing a series of U.S. occupied enclaves in Vietnam as steps toward peace. He was followed by Socialist leader Norman Thomas, who shattered the enclave theory so thoroughly in a devastating attack on U.S. policies that it was barely mentioned during the next two days. Representative John Conyers, Jr. (Dem.-Mich.), Rear Admiral Arnold L. True (retired), Dr. Robert F. Brown and Professor Seymour Melman were among the other non-labor participants. Senator Eugene J. McCarthy (Dem.-Minn.) addressed the final session of the delegates. While he lived up to his reputation as a "mild dove," the fact that he was considering bucking President Johnson in a number of Democratic Presidential primaries gave added significance to his presence and was widely noted by the press. . . .

While the overflow attendance and the top-level caliber of non-labor participants were important to the success of the conference, what made it historic was the high degree of trade union unity achieved around the central question of ending the war in Vietnam. The policy of non-exclusion, implicit at the Assembly's conception, was strengthened as it developed and took concrete form at Chicago, where a variety of AFL–CIO and independent union officers acted as panel leaders, participated in floor discussion and also helped work out the Statement of Policy that received unanimous acceptance.

The spontaneous ovation given Harry Bridges when he rose to speak from the floor was recognition not only of the personal fight Bridges has made over the years, but of the meaning of his presence as an expression of trade union unity. While no official note was taken, the unity achieved was greeted from all quarters. More than one prominent AFL–CIO unionist saw good portents of future trade union unity of action and as a UE leader put it, "Two years ago I would have crossed the street to keep from saying hello to some of these [AFL–CIO] guys, and now I'm happy to be here with them."

Among AFL–CIO unions the UAW was well represented, as were the Amalgamated Clothing Workers, the Amalgamated Meat Cutters, the Packinghouse Workers, the American Federation of Teachers, the State, County and Municipal Workers and many others. New York City's Hospital Workers Local 1199 and District 65, both had substantial delegations. There is no question that United Steelworkers' president I.W. Abel's recent shift to support of the war was responsible for a drastic cut in that union's representation. Most USW delegates came from the former Mine, Mill and Smelter Workers section. While steel union officers were theoretically free to attend as individuals, at least several district directors sent out the word to "stay away."

In response to a letter of inquiry, Jay Lovestone, AFL–CIO president Meany's "Secretary of the Cold War," stated that it was "not the practice of the AFL–CIO to send representatives to participate in bodies organized by others where policy decisions are made; we do this inside the AFL–CIO." (This was revealed by Victor Reuther as he questioned AFL–CIO participation in the reactionary American Institute for Free Labor Development, a tri-partite body made up of AFL–CIO leaders, government representatives and reactionary businessmen.)

While there was substantial participation of Negroes in the work of the Assembly, both from the labor movement and through the presence of Dr. King, Congressman Conyers and Professor Brown, less than 10 per cent of the delegates were Black. Discrimination against Negroes at union leadership level, even among the Left and center forces from which the majority of delegates came, again found reflection in Chicago. While a number were elected to the larger Continuations Committee, an earlier error which left out Negro trade union leaders in the detailed planning of the Assembly appears to have been compounded by the failure to name a

Negro to the operational leadership elected to further the work of that body. This serious weakness will have to be quickly corrected if the Assembly is to develop its maximum potential. There is certainly no lack of talented Negro trade union leaders, as their participation in the Chicago gathering well proved.

The number of women trade unionists present was small, though higher than in most union gatherings. Women delegates were active participants in the Assembly and expressed some of the more advanced peace concepts. Considering the high average age of present trade union leadership in the United States, the delegates represented a relatively youthful age level, with many in their late thirties and early forties. A number of young delegates held a caucus after adjournment which decided to press for participation of young radical intellectuals in the trade union movement. However, no plans were made to involve young workers as such directly in the fight for peace, even though they make up a substantial section of such unions as steel and auto.

The Assembly tied the tremendous wave of strikes, the ghetto rebellions and the other economic struggles which have engulfed the country to the organized drive to end the war in Vietnam. The relationship of the war to the struggles for Negro freedom, against the deterioration of living standards, and against the attacks on the right to strike and on democratic rights generally, was emphasized in the remarks of many speakers, both from the platform and from the floor. They were the principal topics of three of the six panel discussions. The Statement of Policy, which was unanimously adopted, ended with these words: "American labor must play its part in bringing this savage war to a swift and just conclusion, so that we may devote our wealth and energies to the struggle against poverty, disease, hunger and bigotry." . . .

The conference successfully carried out its primary purpose of providing the possibilities for a real challenge to the war in Vietnam from within the ranks of organized labor. And in doing so, it brought a significant section of organized labor in the United States into harmony with labor throughout the world. Not only the trade unions in the socialist countries and under WFTU [World Federation of Trade Unions] leadership, but also those of a host of other countries—literally thousands of unions in all parts of the world—have condemned this war of U.S. imperialism in one way or another, increasingly isolating the AFL–CIO leadership abroad.

In the process of fulfilling its purpose, the conference demonstrated the ability to build trade union unity around a specific issue. It is significant that except for a gratuitous condemnation of "Communist, fascist and military dictatorships" by Emil Mazey, there was a total absence of red-baiting. Several speakers attacked anti-Communism for the harm it had done to the labor movement and there were frequent warnings of the need to guard against efforts to reimpose a reign of McCarthyism in the name of "supporting our boys in Vietnam." The beginnings of the re-emergence of a Left in the trade union movement were also evident, and the possibilities for rebuilding the sort of Left-center coalition that had made the CIO such a vital force for progress in past years.

In the effort to bring organized labor to its rightful place in the fight for peace, the Chicago conference was truly a milestone.

□ ——————————————————————————————— □

THE FORT HOOD THREE

The Fort Hood Three: The Case of the Three G.I.'s
Who Said "No" to the War in Vietnam,
Fort Hood Three Defense Committee,
New York, 1966 (pamphlet)

[*Tens of thousands of young Americans refused to serve in Vietnam. Their action contributed to the rejection of a policy which its perpetrators would like us to forget.*

Three young soldiers who were previously unknown to each other refused to ship out to Vietnam. They became known as the "Fort Hood Three." They were Pfc. James Johnson, now city editor of the Daily World, *Pvt. Dennis Mora, from the Du Bois Club, a Marxist youth organization, and Pvt. David Samas. In addition, Donald Lockman, Philadelphia, honorary national chairman of the Du Bois Clubs of America, was court-martialed and sentenced to 2½ years in Leavenworth Penitentiary for refusing to go to Vietnam.*

On September 6-9, 1966, they were court martialed. Johnson and Samas received the maximum sentence—five years at hard labor. Mora was sentenced to three years.]

Joint Statement by Fort Hood Three
The following statement was read to over 40 cameramen, reporters and anti-war fighters at a press conference in New York on June 30th. The statement was prepared jointly and read by Pvt. Dennis Mora.

We are Pfc. James Johnson, Pvt. David Samas and Pvt. Dennis Mora, three soldiers formerly stationed at Fort Hood, Texas, in the same company of the 142 Signal Battalion, 2nd Armored Division. We have received orders to report on the 13th of July at Oakland Army Terminal in California for final processing and shipment to Vietnam.

We have decided to take a stand against this war which we consider immoral, illegal and unjust. We are initiating today, through our attorneys, Stanley Faulkner of New York and Mrs. Selma Samois of Washington, D.C., an action in the courts to enjoin the Secretary of Defense and the Secretary of the Army from sending us to Vietnam. We intend to report as ordered to the Oakland Army Terminal, but under no circumstances will we board ship for Vietnam. We are prepared to face Court Martial if necessary.

We represent in our backgrounds a cross section of the Army and of America. James Johnson is a Negro. David Samas is of Lithuanian and Italian parents; Dennis Mora is a Puerto Rican. We speak as American soldiers.

We have been in the army long enough to know that we are not the only G.I.'s who feel as we do. Large numbers of men in the service either do not understand this war or are against it.

When we entered the army, Vietnam was for us only a newspaper box score of G.I.'s and Viet Cong* killed or wounded. We were all against it in one way or another, but we were willing to "go along with the program," believing that we would not be sent to Vietnam. . . .

But later on Vietnam became a fact of life when someone you knew wondered how he could break the news to his girl, wife or family that he was being sent there. After he solved that problem, he had to find a reason that would satisfy him. The reasons were many—"Somebody's got to do it," "When your number's up, your number's up," "The pay is good," and "You've got to stop them someplace" were phrases heard in the barracks and mess hall and used by soldiers to encourage each other to accept the war as their own. Besides, what could be done about it anyway? Orders are orders.

As we saw more and more of this, the war became the one thing we talked about most and the one point we all agreed upon. No one wanted to go and more than that, there was no reason for anyone to go.

The Viet Cong obviously had the moral and physical support of most of the peasantry who were fighting for their independence. We were told

---

*The word Viet Cong was encouraged by the army brass, but was rejected by peace forces as derogatory. The three young heroes who were isolated by the army should not be faulted for using it.

that you couldn't tell them apart—that they looked like any other skinny peasant.

Our man or our men in Saigon has and have always been brutal dictators, since Diem first violated the 1954 Geneva promise of free elections in 1956.

The Buddhist and military revolt in all the major cities proves that the people of the cities also want an end to Ky and U.S. support for him. . . .

No one used the word "winning" anymore because in Vietnam it has no meaning. Our officers just talk about five and ten more years of war with at least one half million of our boys thrown into the grinder. We have been told that many times we may face a Vietnamese woman or child and that we will have to kill them. We will never go there—to do that—for Ky!

We know that Negroes and Puerto Ricans are being drafted and end up in the worst of the fighting all out of proportion to their numbers in the population; and we have first hand knowledge that these are the ones who have been deprived of decent education and jobs at home.

The three of us, while stationed together, talked a lot and found we thought alike on one over-riding issue—the war in Vietnam must be stopped. It was all talk and we had no intentions of getting into trouble by making waves at that stage.

Once back in Texas we were told that we were on levy to Vietnam. All we had discussed and thought about now was real. It was time for us to quit talking and decide. Go to Vietnam and ignore the truth or stand and fight for what we know is right.

We have made our decision. We will not be a part of this unjust, immoral and illegal war. We want no part of a war of extermination. We oppose the criminal waste of American lives and resources. We refuse to go to Vietnam!

□ ——————————————————————————— □

U.S. YOUTH DELEGATION IN VIETNAM

Liberation vs. Vietnamization by Michael Zagarell,
Tony Monteiro and Jay Schaffner,
Young Workers Liberation League, 1970 [pamphlet]

[*Soon after the founding of the Young Workers Liberation League in February, 1970, the newly established organization was invited by the Ho Chi Minh Working Youth Union to visit their country. Both organiza-*

tions are affiliates of the World Federation of Democratic Youth. The delegation had an opportunity to visit areas destroyed by US bombings and exchange experiences with Vietnamese youth.

In the introduction to their report, Jarvis Tyner, who was then National Chairman of the League, observed: "The delegation also contributed information about the growing peace movement in the US among young workers, the struggle for a united front against war, racism and repression and the problem in building Black-white unity. In this way the YWLL representatives brought for the first time to Vietnam first-hand experiences of young workers in the fight against US imperialism."

This part of their report is entitled, "The Youth are Decisive."]

Among the youth the "Three Ready" Movement has grown rapidly. In Thanh Hoa province, for example, 98 per cent of the youth have joined it. The Three Ready Movement means: get ready to go to the front, get ready to go anywhere the Fatherland needs you, get ready to increase work and study.

In the Three Ready Movement, the youth join shock brigades of young volunteers for the most dangerous jobs. For example, young shock brigade workers go into the rice fields and defuse time bombs, or volunteer to work in factories constantly under bombardment. In the shock brigades, youth train militarily in their spare time. Since so many youth have joined these brigades, North Vietnam has no need for military conscription. Instead, when soldiers are needed, they send a request to the local brigades. Then, only the best trained are chosen by the youth themselves. Thus Vietnam has far more volunteer soldiers than needed. Further, all youth enter the military already trained and ready to go to the front.

Most of the youth we met were waiting until they were thirty years old before getting married. We also met some young couples who had volunteered to go to the front together. In some families both father and son have gone to the front.

In Hanoi, we met a young woman member of the shock brigades. She was about twenty years old and was very embarrassed about being singled out from her comrades. But finally her story was told to us:

Though U.S. planes bombed everything moving on the highways, they failed to stop the Vietnamese. So the planes concentrated on bombing focal points, like highway intersections, every 5 minutes. But the youth brigades moved in immediately under the slogan, "Even if the enemy attacks us, we repair our roads," within the five minutes between the

By Ollie Harrington,
Daily World, 1971

bombings; they quickly repaired the highway and helped the trucks pass over the crossroads before the next bomb fell. Then the U.S. began dropping time bombs set to go off in between bombings. This young woman volunteered to stand out near the road and count the bombs that fell and those that exploded. She then ran out and marked the unexploded time bombs, while another group of youth would defuse them. When they judged that a bomb would not go off in the next five minutes, they would stand on the bomb to prove to the truck driver that it was safe to pass.

The young people we spoke to stressed that the U.S. changed their tactics many times. Each time they did, some of the youth died. But each time they learned a little more and were able to defeat the U.S. efforts.

In Thanh Hoa we traveled to the site of the most difficult and heroic battle, the one which spelled defeat for the U.S. In learning about the Battle of Hamrong Bridge, the focal point of the fighting in Thanh Hoa province, we learned why the Vietnamese have complete confidence in their impending victory.

Hamrong Bridge connects two sections of the highway that runs from North to South Vietnam. Over the bridge, food and supplies traveled to the Vietnamese brothers in the South. It was therefore a prime goal of the U.S. to destroy this bridge and to do so, they brought in their top pilots

377

and dropped enough bombs to fill the entire river. To defend the bridge, all the people in the surrounding area were organized. Children gathered plants to camouflage guns. Monks cooked rice for the soldiers. Young men were in the anti-aircraft units. Young women fought in the women's militia units.

On the first day, April 3, 1965, 47 U.S. planes were shot down; by the end of the battle which lasted for 3 years, 99 planes were destroyed. But the Hamrong Bridge continued to stand, carrying supplies to the front. The bridge of course, was hit many times, but each time brave mechanics went out over the river to repair it. Hamrong Bridge is a monument to the Vietnamese people and shows that U.S. imperialism, despite its military strength, can no longer have its own way when it confronts the power of the people of Vietnam and the world. Throughout the world, there are many bridges, longer, more graceful, but none stands more proudly than the Hamrong Bridge. . . .

The young people play a decisive role in the defense of Vietnam, but not all the fighting is done by young people. For example: while in Thanh Hoa we learned about the old people's militia unit. All over 65 years of age, they volunteered for anti-aircraft work. As a result of their hard labors and long hours of practice they succeeded in shooting down two U.S. planes. For this achievement they were specially rewarded by the government and received a personal letter of congratulations from Ho Chi Minh. In his congratulations he said: "The older you become the more courageous become your minds."

Such heroes, of course, are found not only in Thanh Hoa province, but in every province and village across Vietnam.

When we first arrived in Vietnam, we were surprised to see almost no soldiers. By the time we left we fully understood that there were soldiers all around us, millions of them. They were armed, trained and ready to fight at any time. The whole population of Vietnam is part of a great people's army.

ANTI-COMMUNIST LABOR LAW ENDED

"High Court Kills 'Red' Clause in Labor Law,"
The Worker, June 13, 1965

[*To all the restrictions placed by the Taft-Hartley Law in 1947 against the functioning of the organized labor movement, the Landrum-Griffin Law, passed in 1959, added some more. Among its provisions, all designed to hamstring the labor unions, was one which barred Communists from holding union office. This replaced a similar, but less categorical, provision of Taft-Hartley.*

Archie Brown (b. 1911), prominent California Communist and popular member of Local 10 of the International Longshoremen's and Warehousemen's Union, was an elected member of the executive board of his local union. He was convicted of violating the federal law and sentenced to six months in prison. He, his union and civil liberties defenders fought the conviction in the courts.

In June 1964 the U.S. Appeals Court ruled Brown's conviction unconstitutional. This ruling was upheld in June 1965 by the U.S. Supreme Court. It was an important victory for democratic rights—and it was won without official support from the AFL-CIO.]

After 19 years of the ban on the right of Communists to hold union office, the U.S. Supreme Court got around in a five to four decision, to declaring such laws unconstitutional and bills of attainder.

The decision . . . was specifically in the case of Archie Brown, member of the executive board of Local 10, International Longshoremen's and Warehousemen's Union, San Francisco. The Supreme Court rejected the government's appeal against a district court's decision in favor of Brown.

Brown was sentenced to six months in 1962 for violating a provision in the Landrum-Griffin Law that makes it a crime for a member of the Communist Party to accept office in a labor union. The ILWU joined in Brown's defense, supported by the American Civil Liberties Union. When the Ninth District Court reversed the lower court, the Department of Justice appealed to the Supreme Court.

"This decision goes a long way to restoring the basic democratic right of the members of unions to elect their own leaders. It wipes out a reactionary McCarthyite attack on trade unionism," said Gus Hall, leading spokesman for the Communist Party when the news came of the high court's decision. "Communist trade unionists have a long and

379

honorable record of serving their unions honestly and militantly in many leading positions. Union members can again elect Communists without fear of punishment whenever they are convinced it best serves their own self-interests. This is a victory for democracy."

Brown's was the first case of its kind tested since the Landrum–Griffin Law was enacted in 1959. But it was basically the first decisive victory in a 19-year effort to eliminate the ban on the right of Communists in unions. The ban was first enacted in 1946 in a provision of the Taft-Hartley Act that all officers of a trade union, from the local unit upward, must submit affidavits to the Department of Labor, declaring they are not Communists or in any way related to organizations that allegedly aim to overthrow the government by "force and violence." Filing of false affidavits was punishable by up to five years in prison, $10,000 fine or both. If any of the unions failed to file such non-Communist affidavits for ALL its officers, its rights under the National Labor Relations Board were forfeited. That meant it had no right to have the union's name on the ballot in bargaining elections or file complaints with the NLRB.

In effect, that law turned the majority of unions into agencies for eliminating Communists from union office for fear of losing rights— often life or death rights—for their union under NLRB rules. The law also turned the Taft-Hartley files into a witch-hunt checklist of some half million union officers, and at times use of false witnesses to charge some progressive labor leaders with signing "false" affidavits. . . .

The Supreme Court's decision knocks out the anti-Communist provision of the Landrum-Griffin Law and thereby, for the first time in 19 years, clears the labor law of a ban on Communists. Justice Earl Warren, who handed up the opinion backed by the court's majority of its more consistent liberals, said the law as applied against Archie Brown "plainly constitutes a bill of attainder."

☐ ─── ☐

THE "DAILY" IS BACK

**1. "Here We Are," editorial, *Daily World,* July 16, 1968;
2. "A New Paper With a 46-Year History,"
The Worker, June 25, 1968**

[*When the* Daily Worker *ceased publication in January 1958 it was exactly thirty-four years old. The high hopes with which it had been launched in 1924 had been more than realized. The "Daily" had taken hold and had become one of the best known papers—though not the most widely read—in the country.*

But the punishing circumstances under which the Communist Party functioned in the 1950s, climaxed by the anti-Party factional struggle, finally caused the paper to succumb.

It continued, however, as the weekly Worker *and in 1961 became a bi-weekly. In July 1968, the irrepressible "Daily" was back again as the* Daily World.

In the following items the Daily World *makes its bow and the* Worker *prepares to bow out.*]

1.

Today the *Daily World* begins regular publication as America's only English-language daily newspaper dedicated to peace, democracy and socialism.

We hope to fuse professional know-how with passionate partisanship to the working people and all the oppressed, avoiding the sin of dullness and achieving the goal of clarity.

Ours is a unique enterprise, a reader-supported newspaper in a communication world dominated by monopoly. But we are profoundly confident that great forces are at work that will nurture this newspaper; the men and women, young and old, Black and white, actively engaged in today's fierce upsurge for peace, equality and economic betterment. Together with them we shall march to a better America in a world of peace and plenty and brotherhood.

2.

[*The Worker* had previously printed a chronology of the paper's 46-year history and listed a number of the major struggles in which it was involved:]

The Worker, proud bearer of the best in American radical journalism, is about to help bring forth a new lusty fighter in the great workingclass tradition—the *Daily World. . . .*

Roots of the new paper go deep into American labor and radical history. Its predecessor papers include *The Worker* and the *Daily Worker,* and less directly a number of other journals reflecting Socialist, trade union and Negro freedom currents.

Chronologically, the story goes back more than 46 years:

● Feb. 2, 1922. Appearance of the weekly *Worker,* which announced that it was "the advance agent of the *Daily Worker.*"

● Jan. 13, 1924. First issue of the *Daily Worker.* The Daily existed exactly 34 years, making it the longest–lived radical daily newspaper in U.S. history.

- Jan. 19, 1958. Appearance of *The Worker* as a weekly.
- Sept. 28, 1961. Publication of the first Midweek issue of *The Worker*.
- July 4, 1968. Preview issue of the *Daily World*.

Various papers helped to shape the currents that merged into the *Daily Worker* and its successor paper.

Among those were the famous *Appeal to Reason,* born in 1895, a national weekly with an especially heavy circulation in the Midwest; the *Ohio Socialist,* a Left-Wing Socialist newspaper which gave way in November 1919 to the *Toiler.*

Part of the general background of the Marxist publications was formed by many Negro weeklies of the post–World War I era and the traditions of the Abolitionist press of the mid-19th century. [*The Messenger,* 1917, a socialist paper, included Negro pioneer Communists. *The Crusader, The Challenge* and *The Emancipator* also appeared during this period.]

At every stage of the struggle, *The Worker* and its predecessor papers focused on the struggles of the working class and its allies. The very first issue of the *Daily Worker* stressed the fight to organize the unorganized workers, the formation of industrial unions, building of a Labor Party, extension of diplomatic and trade relations with the Soviet Union and education of the American workers for socialism.

Down the years, *The Worker* and its journalistic forbears fought racism, fascism and war. The *Daily Worker* fought vigorously for freedom of the Scottsboro Boys and helped to turn that frame-up into an internationally acclaimed victory over the lynch system in the 30s.

Similarly, the *Daily Worker* fought to warn the nation against the menace of fascism. It resolutely backed the Spanish Loyalist government against General Franco's fascist revolt, warning that this was the opening of World War II. When the war broke out, the *Daily Worker* sought to unite the nation to defeat Hitlerism and maintain the Grand Alliance with the Soviet Union to extirpate fascism.

In the cold war era, the *Daily Worker* battled against the whole foreign and domestic policy being erected upon the hoax of anti-Communism.

☐ ── ☐

U.S. ASIAN LABOR

"A Brief History of U.S. Asian Labor" by Karl G. Yoneda
Political Affairs, September, 1976

[*Immigrants from Asian countries have long been victims of racism, discriminatory practices and persecution. They are often relegated to jobs in low-paying industries. Among the two million Asians are Chinese, Japanese, Filipinos and people from other areas of the Pacific.*

Karl G. Yoneda (b. 1906), whose article, in abridged form, appears here, is the head of the Asian Commission of the CP in northern California.]

Contributions made by Asians to help enrich this country must be made known along with those of Blacks, Chicanos, Puerto Ricans, U.S. Indians and other peoples. Asians helped build the sugar, pineapple, longshore and shipping industries in Hawaii; the mine, railroad, agriculture, fishing, fish cannery and sawmill industries on the mainland, especially in the western states. However, these facts, along with those of the incarceration of over 110,000 people of Japanese ancestry into U.S. style concentration camps during World War II, are glossed over in history books.

And as with other ethnic minorities, Asian workers have suffered brutal exploitation, racial discrimination and special repressive measures. During that history, deportation for daring to speak out has not been uncommon and mob violence has been encouraged by monopoly capital lackeys, including beating, jailing and even lynching. . . .

[But] . . . new pages of labor history were begun in 1937 when the International Longshoremen's and Warehousemen's Union (ILWU) came to the Hawaiian Islands to organize sugar, pineapple and longshore workers without discrimination as to race, color or creed. The strike for better working conditions went into a lapse during World War II, but immediately thereafter, in 1946, a strike was successful. The plantation owners failed in their plan to use 6,000 Filipino new arrivals as scabs, for the workers had signed up with the union before coming ashore. The 157-day longshoremen's 1949 strike ended in another ILWU victory in spite of the barrage of pressure of the Big Five corporations and of U.S. government officials, including President Truman. These forces wanted to destroy the union because its multiracial membership had faith in unionism, plus the support of other unions and communities.

The Big Five corporations, gloomy over growing ILWU strength, raised the cry of "Communist." This resulted in the 1951 arrest, under the Smith Act, of seven activists as leaders of the Hawaiian Communist Party, including Hawaii ILWU Director Jack Hall and four Hawaiian Japanese—K. Ariyoshi, C. Fujimoto, Eileen Fujimoto and J. Kimoto. All were convicted and sentenced to five years, except Eileen Fujimoto, who received a three-year prison term. An appeal to the Federal District Court resulted in the verdicts being reversed. . . .

In 1925, Japanese, mostly Communists, simultaneously organized the Japanese Workers Clubs in New York and San Francisco and the Los Angeles Japanese Labor Association. The latter published a monthly, *Class Struggle,* as well as initiating the Agricultural Workers Organizing Committee of Southern California which conducted many strikes among Japanese, Filipino and Mexican workers until 1929, when it merged with the Agricultural Workers Industrial Union–Trade Union Unity League (AWIU–TUUL.)

The AFL San Francisco Central Labor Council invited the independent Chinese Laundry Workers Union in 1929 to report on its victorious one-week Bay Area strike. This is the first known participation of Chinese in an official delegated AFL meeting.

Asian workers, under Communist leadership, took active part in the 1930s unemployed movement, establishing National Unemployed Council Japanese branches in Los Angeles, San Francisco and Seattle, as well as a San Francisco Chinese branch. In Los Angeles, during the 1930–31 unemployed demonstrations, many workers were brutally beaten and jailed by the notorious Hynes' Red Squad—among those arrested were E. Yamaguchi and Karl Hama (Yoneda), farm worker organizers. The former faced deportation, the latter served a 90-day jail term for "disturbing the peace."

In 1930 when T. Horiuchi, Japanese, Danny Roxas, Filipino and eight other AWIU organizers (all CP members), attempted to organize in Imperial Valley 7,000 Mexican, 1,000 Japanese and several hundred Filipino farm workers they were arrested, tried and sent to prison under the Criminal Syndicalism Act. After serving two and a half years in Folsom, Horiuchi was ordered deported. The International Labor Defense (ILD) and its Japanese branches helped in the trial and appeal.

The foregoing California activities resulted in deportation orders in 1932 against fifteen additional Japanese, one Chinese and an Indian as undesirable aliens—Communists. After all appeals failed, the ILD obtained voluntary departure to the Soviet Union, because they faced imprisonment or even death upon return to their home countries.

384

But the work of organizing the unorganized workers continued, particularly in California. More than fifteen AWIU strikes were recorded in 1933, with some 35,000 Mexican, Filipino, Japanese, Black, white, Korean and other participants and over 100 strike leaders—including five Japanese and a Korean—arrested. Four strikers were killed and scores wounded and arrested in the San Joaquin Valley cotton pickers' strike, involving 18,000 workers. The AWIU Japanese Section, ILD Japanese branches and the Chinese Workers Club were among those that raised money for defense and strike relief. . . .

During the 1934 Pacific Coast maritime strike, which developed into the San Francisco general strike, truckloads of farm products were donated by Stockton, Sacramento and Los Angeles AWIU Japanese sections. The Chinese Vanguard and Japanese *Rodo Shimbun* (Labor News–CP organ) issued leaflets urging readers "Not To Scab!" City police and vigilantes raided the Japanese Workers Club and the Chinese Workers Center, smashing furniture and destroying many books. Two Japanese at the Workers Club were arrested and served 30 days in jail on "vagrancy" charges.

For the first time Asians ran for public office on the mainland in 1934. Karl Hama, *Rodo Shimbun* editor, ran on the CP ticket for the San Francisco 22nd Assembly seat—a workingclass district composed of whites, Blacks, Filipinos and Japanese—receiving 1,017 votes and Republican C. Arai, Alaska Japanese labor contractors' attorney, got only 320 votes for a Seattle Assembly seat. . . .

The largest integrated union of that period was the San Francisco AFL Alaska Cannery Workers Union (ACWU) Local 20185, formed in late 1935 with 2,000 Mexican, Spanish, Chinese, Filipino, Puerto Rican, Japanese, Black, white and other members. When the union switched affiliation to the Congress of Industrial Organizations (CIO) in 1937, K. Yoneda, Nisei; B. Fee, Chinese; S. Caballero, Filipino; and F. Fukuda, Nisei, were elected 1st, 2nd, 3rd vice presidents and recording secretary respectively. A similar union was the Seattle-based CIO Cannery and Farm Laborers Union Local 7, organized in 1937 with a membership of 4,000 Filipino, Japanese and other Alaska cannery workers. Officers were: President I.R. Cabatit, Secretary T. Rodrigo, Filipinos and Vice President G. Taki, Nisei. Both these locals broke down the almost half a century semi-slave conditions which prevailed under the labor contractor system in the seasonal Alaska salmon canning industry, winning the union shop, higher pay, etc. . . .

In 1938 the CIO launched a large organizing drive among California farm and cannery workers. Organizers Mary Imada and Karl Yoneda signed up several hundred Terminal Island and Monterey Japanese women cannery workers.

The San Francisco Chinese Ladies Garment Workers Union Local 134, ILGWU–AFL, 1938 strike against the National Dollar Stores was an important milestone. After thirteen weeks on the bricks, a union contract was signed, but the workers were double-crossed by owner Joe Shoong, who sold the garment factory section of his holdings, thus eliminating the union. . . .

After subjugating Manchuria in 1931, Japan declared war against China on July 7, 1937. Tokyo dispatches repeatedly stated "Japan was fighting Chinese communist bandits," while its fascist Axis partners— Germany and Italy—carried on violent aggressions in Europe and Ethiopia.

The December 7, 1941 attack by Japan's armed forces shocked and enraged the American people, including Japanese Americans. The Communist Party immediately denounced it as "the culminating outrage of Axis aggression aimed at the domination of the entire world. The fate of every nation and every people has been thrown into the arena for determination by military means. . . . The Communist Party pledges its loyalty, its devoted labor . . . in support of our country in this greatest of all crises that ever threatened its existence." (*The Communist,* December 1941.) Nisei [Persons of Japanese descent born in the US] Communists and supporters immediately wired President Roosevelt: "We stand ready to join the ranks of fighting forces under your command to defeat the vicious military fascists of Japan."

Led by the Hearst and McClatchy press, Native Sons and Daughters, American Legion and others who had sparked passage of the 1924 Japanese Exclusion Act, the "yellow peril" forces crawled out of the woodwork. They whipped up such frenzied racist hatred against those of Japanese ancestry that posters "Jap Hunting License Sold Here—Open Season Now No Limit" and an illustrated article in *Life*'s December 22, 1941 issue "How to Tell Japs from the Chinese" appeared. Similar statements and articles were everyday occurrences in all media and government circles. Racist hysteria and vigilantism prevailed over decency and common sense.

Many Asians began wearing "I Am Chinese" or "Korean American" buttons. Significantly, CWMAA [Chinese Workers Mutual Aid Association] members refused to wear them on the basis "there were many pro-China, anti-Axis activists among persons of Japanese ancestry and our solidarity has to be shown them."

After President Roosevelt signed Executive Order 9066 on February

19, 1942, General J. L. DeWitt, without trial or hearing, began the removal from the West Coast of more than 110,000 men, women and children—citizen and non-citizen alike—of Japanese descent into ten U.S. style concentration camps.

In Hawaii, where the attack occurred, no mass evacuation took place. Why? Because there Japanese made up over a third of the population, held many elective offices and had become a major source of labor. Martial law was imposed to guarantee economic stability.

The question then is asked, "Why didn't West Coast Japanese Americans fight the evacuation order?" Here only a very small number of religious and other organizations such as the California CIO, through its then secretary Lou Goldblatt, spoke in opposition to the plight facing them. Also, it should be remembered, Japanese workers on the mainland were mostly unorganized and not a major economic factor. . . .

Nisei Communists were among Manzanar enlistees—the first from behind barbed wire—in November 1942, for military intelligence service in the Pacific. Nearly 30,000 Nisei and Issei (Japan born) men and women served with the US armed forces, OWI [Office of War Information] and OSS [Office of Strategic Service] in European and all Pacific theaters.

Also to be noted is that 1,500 Seattle CIO Cannery Workers and Farm Laborers Union Local 7 members volunteered for the all-US Army Filipino Battalion to help avenge Bataan. Other Asians worked in defense and farm industries; many joined their respective unions. . . .

In the 60s, great impact was made upon young US Asians by the Freedom Marches, Berkeley UC Free Speech Movement, Delano grape pickers' strike and other related events.

Asians, along with other instructors, students and employees were on the picket line during the 1968-69 strike at San Francisco State College. S.I. Hayakawa, its then president, emerged as a strikebreaker despised by students and labor, but remains the idol of reactionaries, including Japanese bankers and Nisei growers. Some of the latter formed the Nisei Farmers League in 1971, whose main purpose is to hamper the United Farm Workers of America (UFW).

The evacuation experience, although only briefly covered here, remains a shameful period in U.S. history. Since 1969 hundreds have participated in annual pilgrimages to Manzanar, former camp site near the base of Mt. Whitney. The California State Department of Parks and Recreation in 1973 designated Manzanar as a historical landmark and after much struggle agreed to "MAY THE INJUSTICES AND HUMILIATION SUFFERED HERE AS A RESULT OF HYSTERIA,

RACISM AND ECONOMIC EXPLOITATION NEVER EMERGE AGAIN" as part of the official plaque text. Pilgrimages to Tule Lake in northern California began in 1974; to Poston, Arizona and Topaz, Utah in 1975.

Two million people of Asian and Pacific Islander ancestries are now in the U.S. They face the same problems, including racism, as the Blacks, Chicanos, Puerto Ricans, U.S. Indians and other people of color. . . .

Asians with limited visas are caught up in U.S. Immigration Department bureaucracy which makes them less resistant to exploitation, thus less apt to take part in workers' struggles. They are among the scapegoats in the midst of the economic crisis in this country. It is necessary to extend protection to all foreign-born workers entwined in anti-alien drives.

In 1975 the arrival of 150,000 Southeast Asians—the majority Vietnamese—presented additional problems, as they are being used as scabs to undermine wages and working conditions and in counter-revolutionary activites.

As can be seen, Asians are of different national origins, and have different cultures and traditions. Yet as Asians and Pacific Islanders, they face identical problems of racism, exploitation and oppression at the hands of the U.S. ruling class. . . .

Because the Party suspended its Nisei members for the duration of WW II and failed to speak out against the evacuation, so-called revolutionaries and some Asians have used this to attack the Party. They ignore that the 1959 and 1972 CP National Conventions "publicly repudiated past errors, reflecting the grave inroads of racism in our ranks, one of the most serious of those errors being our failure to mount a struggle against the racist incarceration in 1942 of more than 110,000 Japanese in the U.S. concentration camps." (From 20th Convention CPUSA resolution on "Asians in U.S.").

Asians take great pride in the historic overthrow of imperialism by the Chinese people as well as the heroic Vietnamese victory over U.S. imperialism and the liberation struggles of the peoples of other Southeast Asia areas, the Philippines, etc. Maoists seek to exploit this natural pride. Some have been won to the anti-Communist, anti-Soviet positions of the Maoist-oriented groupings, influenced by their pseudo-revolutionary, ultra-leftist terminology, Therefore, Maoism's reactionary character—its support of the Chile junta and its collaboration with South African racists in opposition to liberation of Angola—and the sectarian splitting Maoist tactics need to be constantly exposed as anti-internationalist and anti-working class.

388

Four years ago Communist Party Chairperson Henry Winston wrote: "Maoism is a rejection of Marxism-Leninism. It is, at the same time, rejection of proletarian internationalism which in our country, means the unity of Black, white, Chicano, Puerto Rican, Indian and Asian workers, to achieve the maximum solidarity of the class."

One of the major elements of U.S. imperialist policy, since the rape of the Philippines, the Boxer Rebellion, down through the Hiroshima–Nagasaki atomic atrocities, the assault on Korea and Southeast Asia, has been the efforts to control Far Eastern nations by maintaining Asian military bases. The U.S. working-class struggle to overcome the divisive effects of racism toward the peoples of Asia, the U.S. Asians and all racially oppressed peoples in the U.S. is an essential prelude for the unity of all anti-monopoly and anti-imperialist forces.

□ ——————————————————————————————— □

COMMUNISM AND CULTURE

"No Wall Between Politics and Culture" by Joseph North, *Political Affairs*, August, 1966

[*Struggle for a people's progressive culture has always been a part of the Communist Party's activity.*

John Reed (1887-1920), a founder of the Party, is one of those whose names are associated with the cultural tradition of the CP and of the people's movements with which it has been identified. Reed was a poet and a journalist. In books like Ten Days that Shook the World *and* Insurgent Mexico *he raised journalism to the level of art.*

Reed, born to affluence in a mansion in Portland, Oregon, chose not to identify himself with his own moribund class but rather with the vital socialist future. He died of typhus in Moscow in 1920 and his ashes are interred in the Kremlin Wall.

Mike Gold (1893-1967) was another pioneering Communist writer and editor. His background was as different from John Reed's as it could possibly be. He was a product of the poverty of a New York Jewish ghetto. As an editor of New Masses *he was the encourager of young, working-class talent and the scourge of decadent middle-class authors. Over a span of 33 years he wrote thousands of pithy columns for the* Daily Worker *and other working-class publications.*

Joseph North, the gifted son of working-class parents, first turned to

389

bourgeois journalism, but soon abandoned a conventionally successful career to develop into one of the great writers and editors of the Communist movement.

One could call a long roll of others who, like the three we have mentioned, made contributions not only to our country's literature but to its music, graphic arts and performing arts. Some were in the Party; others were sympathetic to many of its goals and ideas. Ollie Harrington, Hugo Gellert, Anton Refregier carry on this tradition. Rockwell Kent, Fred Ellis, Robert Minor and Art Young helped to create it. W.E.B. Du Bois was a unique part of it. Eugene Gordon, Richard Wright, Langston Hughes and Jesus Colon helped shape it.

Of course, Paul Robeson, the People's Artist, towered above his contemporaries in the performing arts. V.J. Jerome, John Howard Lawson and Sidney Finkelstein were critics and creators. And having mentioned Lawson, who can forget the Hollywood Ten?

Meridel Le Seuer, Philip Bonosky and Lloyd Brown continue to contribute to progress with their pens. But we are conscious of all the many others who should be enumerated, besides the representative few above.

In a foreword to his book, Karl Marx' "Capital" in Lithographs *(Long and Smith, New York, 1934), Hugo Gellert said: "The heroism of the American revolutionary vanguard, the dogged struggles of the workers and farmers . . . are the source of a new vigorous art movement in America worthy of the tradition of John Reed. . . ."*

In the remarks which follow, Joseph North reminded delegates to the June 1966 (18th) convention of the CPUSA of the place of culture in the totality of the Communist movement. Here is an abbreviated text.]

[I]n a letter written by Walt Whitman, who would probably have been a delegate here or at least have carried an observer's card if he lived today, Walt said: "The trouble is writers are too literary, too damn literary. There has grown up, Swinburne, I think an apostle of it, the doctrine . . . Art for Art's sake. Think of it, Art for Art's sake! Let a man really accept that, let that really be his ruling and he is lost. Instead of regarding literature as an instrument in the service of something larger than itself, in the service of humanity, it looks upon itself as an end, as a fact to be finally worshipped and adored. To me that is a horrible blasphemy."

With some amendments against over-simplification, I believe Walt's injunction can stand. And as Pablo Neruda said at the P.E.N.[2] Congress the other day, "If some people would call me a propagandist, and they do, let it be. I will accept the description." Yes, he is a propagandist, this poet of universal fame and veneration. I believe he is supplying us with a clue. I want to cite two more witnesses. They confirm the concept that there can be no ultimate wall between politics and culture. I want first to quote a man who perhaps put best what Emerson, Whittier, Thoreau, Whitman and other giants of our Golden Age of Literature felt. I am quoting a foreigner who was nonetheless close to their viewpoint—or theirs to his. His name was Tolstoy. He said: "Belief in the triumph of good vitalizes a race; enlightened optimism fosters in man a constructive purpose and frees him from fears that fetter his thoughts." . . .

How welcome is an optimistic viewpoint at a time when pessimism reigns over the domains of American letters! In much of it we wade through marshes and swamps. We are given pictures of the world of existence, as a vast wasteland, and Americans, mankind, as waste grass that sprouts for a day and then is gone.

I hold with that paragraph in the Draft Party Program which says, on page 15, speaking of television (and it can go for virtually every other form of our national culture):

"Monopoly contaminates the air waves. Profit is the governor of the sights and sounds disseminated through these principal channels for shaping the intellectual attitudes and moral values of society. Corruption of public taste is fostered for immediate commercial returns. But such corruption also reflects deeper causes and serves broader ends. Insensate violence, reduction of human emotions and relations to animal levels, are brutalizing cultural conditioners for the shameful role of world policeman and nuclear triggerman. The demeaning of the human personality, the emphasis on the irrational, the flight from reality—all cultivate a sense of futility and irrelevancy of ordinary man in shaping the world he inhabits. Thereby they reinforce the image of monopoly as all-powerful and indestructible."

. . . [M]ost of our American world of letters today is anti-human. The literary men of the Establishment see corruption, ugliness, horror everywhere they turn. Most of it they see in the soul of the human being himself. Gone in our Establishment literature is the brooding humanism of Nathaniel Hawthorne, of Herman Melville, or the social daring of Jack London, Frank Norris, Theodore Dreiser, the titanic laughter of Mark Twain, the continual sweep of Thomas Wolfe, the elemental sorrows of Ernest Hemingway, the Gothic dimension of Faulkner. Gone is the hero from our contemporary literature. Our anti-novel, anti-life literature is of course, anti-hero. We must cut man down to the size of, well, say who, Richard Nixon? . . .

"The Family Romance of Freudian Mythology" as literary historian

Maxwell Geismar describes it, speaking of Saul Bellow's number one best-seller *Herzog*, or Norman Mailer's number one best-seller *The American Dream*, or John Updike's latest number one best-seller—well, this "new literary psychology," Geismar says, is "a convenient escape from the crucial issues of world history. Alas for Asia, alas for Africa, alas for South America, such continents exist not in this constrained embrace of thwarted child and hostile parents, any more than American society does." He describes this as a kind of "do-it-yourself brain-washing which marks our fashionable literature today."

Now what is wrong with most of our present-day writers is not their lack of talent. Many have that; talent is not as rare as diamonds. Rather, they lack knowledge, experience, contact with reality, with life's struggles, they fail to see how they themselves have been brainwashed. Take one of the titans of our modern literature, Faulkner. He saw, brilliantly, the phosphorescent decay of our aristocratic South, the end of the Magnolia era. But he could not envisage one single Medgar Evers.³ Although he lived nearby, he could not dream up that heroic little seamstress, Rosa Parks of Montgomery, who refused to go to the back of the bus and marked the boundary of a new period. Though he lived in their midst, all his life in Oxford, Mississippi, Faulkner could not imagine an entire heroic generation of Negro youth who faced the fang of police dog, the torture of electric prod, the bludgeon of the southern constable and continues to face them in the irresistible crusade for freedom. For Faulkner was not color-blind; he was blinded by color. His prejudice hobbled his genius. So, great a writer as the world deems him, he failed as prophet. This is in large part true of so many of our present and past generation of writers and artists. I believe that Sidney Finkelstein, in his latest book *Existentialism and Alienation in American Literature* had many thoughtful and sage, as well as provocative insights on this crucial question. It is published by that valiant publishing house, International Publishers.

The truth is, as everybody in this room knows, that we have heroes in America. This continent is rich in resources and it does not fail us when we come to the greatest capital of all, the human resource. Yet where is the literature that captures their existence, the vision, the epic, simple everyday heroism of the anonymous. The Establishment wants to rob us of them, for heroes are our most precious possession. Hence, we must ask today, as Mike Gold asked Thornton Wilder thirty years ago, is this the literature to describe America? We can, with equal and perhaps greater justice, ask it again today. Yes, who has caught Medgar Evers in a novel, a poem, an opera, a symphony? Who has described the giant Henry

Winston blinded by his jailers as surely as though they had forced a branding iron into his eyesockets, yet who willed himself to live, to triumph over them, to retain his vision though they had robbed him of his sight, and who continues his titan labors for the freedom and peace of the American community—a human lighthouse. What I say of him goes in great measure for a whole generation of Communist leaders, and one of the suggestions I make for the final draft of this inspiring Program is that it lose its over-modesty on this score.... Let us find a way to tell the truth about this generation of Communist leaders, for I assure you, you will not find it elsewhere—not as yet. The truth as I have seen it, men maligned, imprisoned, forever under the threat of prison, ever at the borderline of poverty, yet they stood, they stand. Get that to the youth, for they yearn for heroes. They are weary of the Establishment image.

And our literature must tell them of the anonymous heroes of labor, say, the nearly six thousand members of the National Maritime Union who went down on the freighters bringing the stuff to Europe during World War II (John Howard Lawson caught that in his film, "Action in the North Atlantic"). But one swallow does not make a summer, one film is not enough for the imperishable epics of labor, like that of Republic Steel and the many similar that built the unions, or the epics of the starving Americans who marched and counter-marched and forced the Establishment to relinquish the few dollars for some degree of social and unemployment insurance and all the rest you know so well.

We had the beginnings of such a literature in the work of the splendid writer who has gone from our ranks this past year. Philip Stevenson, in his novels about the miners of New Mexico. Mike Gold's *Jews Without Money* is a classic, as is Conroy's, *The Disinherited.* I see Meridel Le Sueur in this auditorium and I await her next inspiring works; I saw Philip Bonosky; I remember the work of Lloyd Brown and his *Iron City;* of Alvah Bessie, whose pen matches the rifle he carried against Franco; Barbara Giles and her early book, *The Burning Bush.* Strong is the poetry of Walter Lowenfels. These writers began something. . . . They show the heroism of the common man. They show that we can have nothing to do with fascism, with slavery; we can triumph over the corruption of the human spirit. . . .

It has not been written down. But I see the beginnings. I know that I differ with most of the American writers I met at the P.E.N. Congress last week, in that I foresee a renaissance of American letters greater than ever in our history. It can already be found in the new poetry, the new independent film and theater, the budding satire. It is already coming from among the young who have been down to Mississippi. We have begun to see it in the works of young Negro poets and writers and playwrights. We see it in the Southern Freedom Theater which gives masterpieces in the heart of Eastland territory. We saw it in the tragically brief life of Lorraine Hansberry and I wish we would pay especial tribute to the heroic spirit here, for she would have been among us were she living today. We see it in the work of John Killen, in *Youngblood;* in the stories of Alice Childress; in the works of Gwendolyn Brooks; in the essays and other books of James Baldwin; yes, one can look toward the Negro young writers to spark the Renaissance that is surely coming. And the young white writers shall join just as many did, in life, in the past several years, as Schwerner and Goodman joined Chaney.

Under P.E.N. auspices Pablo Neruda gave a reading of his poems at the 92nd Street YMWHA. The place was jammed to the rafters. Never have I seen such enthusiasm for a writer. North American poets crowded forward after the readings to kiss the hands of the Chilean writer. (How different reality is at those grass roots, for in the waters of Latin America the gunboats of the Establishment roam, cannon at the ready.) Now this Chilean poet, it should be said to anybody who may not yet know it, is what is known as a card-carrying Communist for a generation and is proudly so. His dues are paid up in every conceivable way. His poetry has ringed the world in innumerable translations. Its worth has shattered political barriers. This is the poet about whom Shelley wrote when he said that the poet is the natural legislator of mankind. Neruda was elected to the Senate of his country in a constituency, let me remind West Virginia here, where miners made up the majority. Miners elected a poet. Incidentally it is happening in our country too. Julian Bond, the poet[4] whose verse appeared in the last issue of *American Dialog,* is a case in point. He will get his seat in Legislature as Pablo Neruda got his place in the heart of the world, of which he is a governor. No, the tide is turning; it has already turned even if it will take some awhile to realize that. But they will. Pablo Neruda wrote, "Let the Railsplitter Awake." The sons and daughters of that railsplitter are awake and they are marching, Pablo, and many of them are in this room.

□ ——————————————————————————— □

COMMUNISTS AND INTERNATIONALISM

"Toward Unity Against World Imperialism" by Gus Hall, *Speech at the World Conference of Communist and Workers' Parties, Moscow, June 5–17, 1969,* New Outlook Publishers, 1969

[*Seventy-five Communist and Workers' Parties met in Moscow from June 5 to 17, 1969. They discussed the major political and social issues of our day. In a document to which all subscribed they recognized that the present situation "demands united action of Communists and all other anti-imperialist forces . . . for broader offensive against imperialism, against the forces of reaction and war."*

Gus Hall, head of the CPUSA delegation, addressed the conference on June 12. As one who came from the most powerful imperialist nation he recalled "the continuing, irreversible shift in the balance of forces between imperialism and anti-imperialism. There is a changing scene between the countries of imperialism, reflecting the laws of uneven development of capitalism . . ." He therefore stressed the need ". . . to take note of these changes, because they are also reflected in the changing and shifting battle plans of imperialism."

The proceedings of the meeting were published by Peace and Socialism Publishers, the institution which also prints the monthly magazine, World Marxist Review. *This publication is a product of many parties, a number of whose representatives are on its editorial body, while others attend its regular bi-annual conferences. The magazine reaches 145 countries.*

A section of Gus Hall's address appears below.]

In an earlier period the acid of opportunism, unseen and unnoticed, weakened the ideological fibers within the revolutionary movement, and at a crucial moment in history it finally destroyed powerful working-class parties of socialism. The acid had done its harm. It is of great importance that the crisis brought on by opportunism came in the struggle against imperialism. When the test came the professed internationalism of the different working-class parties vanished. The unity between parties first was diluted to a formal unity. But very quickly even the formal ties became obstacles. World class ties between parties became an embarrassment. . . .

The leaders of the socialist parties very quickly made new discoveries.

Very quickly, they decided Marx was wrong. There were no laws of capitalism that applied universally. There were no worldwide concepts of the class struggle. In each country they discovered fundamental national peculiarities that overshadowed international similarities.

The class struggle became purely a people's struggle. Class concepts became "national" concepts. No party condemned internationalism, they just put it on the shelf "for the duration."

Many of the parties became large mass parties. This was good. But what was *not* good, was that they became broad popular parties by going along with popular concepts of nationalism and classlessness. They became mass parties by giving up their advanced working-class positions. They ceased to be revolutionary parties and became mass reformist parties.

Only Lenin saw the nature of the acid. Only Lenin took up the struggle before it reached the crisis stage. Only Lenin saw its creeping insidious nature.

Much has happened since then. Much has changed. The ideological fiber of the Communist parties is stronger. But the need to be on guard against the acid of opportunism has not lessened. The acid is the same. It still eats at the fibers of internationalism, It still erodes class concepts. It feeds on and itself feeds nationalism. It still leads to an accommodation to the pressures of the enemy. It still leads toward reformism. In its "Left" cloak it still leads to petty-bourgeois radicalism, to dogmatism.

The relationship of forces is different—the pressures are different—the influences of opportunism are different. But as long as there is a struggle between the two classes there will be a need for a struggle against opportunism. In the absence of such a struggle the pressures of opportunism keep mounting.

There are two opposite approaches to the question of relationships between internationalism and national interests. Whenever there are momentary differences between one's class international responsibility and some specific national interests, opportunism will in all cases lead to the discounting of internationalism. Opportunism leads to an emphasis on difference and on seeming contradiction by its emphasis on nationalism. A working-class revolutionary concept will lead to a search for the points of unity. Opportunism will seek to widen the points of difference. A revolutionary concept leads to the elimination of the differences. The struggle for concepts of internationalism is a struggle against opportunism.

Theories of disunity are also not new in the history of the revolutionary movement. They appear in exact ratio to opposition to working-class internationalism.

In the parties of the Second International, internationalism was never actually condemned. It was simply dispensed with, as an obstacle to inner class unity. Their scuttling of internationalism was also covered by numerous theories of disunity.

We are for the rejection of all theories of disunity.

We rejected the theory that constant splitting is as natural for the revolutionary movement as it is in nature. It is an open theory of disunity. It is a disguise for nationalism. It is also a distortion of the dialectics of nature.

It is also one thing to take note of and examine differences and momentary contradictions within the world socialist sector. But it is another matter to use this as the basis for a theory of disunity that in essence says "that's how things are and that is how it will be," that we must therefore accept this as a fact of reality, and that any attempt to find a path of unity is only an illusion. . . .

We reject all theories that efforts to bring about working-class unity in fact only bring disunity.

We also reject the concept that silence can disperse ideological differences and thus create the basis for unity. U.S. imperialism has never for a moment given up its drive to chip away at the unity of the socialist world. For it, the focus of the class struggle on the world scale is the Soviet Union. For it, the Soviet Union is the political and military power base of the world's working class. It views the Soviet Union as the main roadblock to its plans of world conquest. This has been and remains the pivot of its imperialist policies.

Thus its main ideological attack is on the Soviet Union. U.S. capitalism is ready to make significant short range concessions to any group, party or state, if these concessions fit into the tactical or strategic plans of U.S. imperialism against the Soviet Union, into its plans of dividing the socialist sector and the other forces of anti-imperialism.

For example, for years there has been a well-organized, high-power political group, composed of some of the most reactionary imperialist forces and called the "China Lobby." It has been the organizational and ideological center for the U.S. policies of aggression in the Far East. This most reactionary force has now undertaken the drive, both in the open and behind the scenes, to bring about a working relationship between the U.S. and the People's Republic of China. This is a well-financed drive, supported by some of the most aggressive monopoly circles in the heartland of world imperialism. Needless to say, these forces are not interested in U.S.–Chinese friendship. Their main interests are not even trade with Communist China. Their aim is to use the split in the socialist

397

world. Their aim is to try to use the People's Republic of China in their anti-Soviet plans. Their aim is to open the doors of China for political penetration. One cannot blame China for what U.S. imperialism does, but one cannot ignore policies that lead imperialism to conclude that it can use them.

The use of such negative policies is not necessarily a matter of agreements or contracts with imperialism. The same end is accomplished by giving the massive imperialist networks the material with which to vilify and slander the Soviet Union, socialism and the Communist parties of the world. The imperialist network is much more anxious to spread slander coming from such a source than slander from its own barn of ideological fabricators. They are fully aware of the credibility gap of a Morgan, a Nixon, or a Rockefeller.

U.S. imperialism has a specific, worked-out plan of action for every socialist country—for every newly liberated country—for every political party throughout the world.

What the progressive forces of the world must understand is that no world power has ever had an active policy of penetration, of subversion, of corruption, of buying off, of terror and murder on such massive scale as is the case with U.S. imperialism.

The policy is worldwide but the pivot around which these plans revolve is the plan against the Soviet Union.

Any accommodation to the ideological pressures that arise from this reality weakens the forces of anti-imperialism. No amount of ideological tiptoeing or sidestepping is going to change this hard rock of reality. Any attempt by one socialist country or one Communist party to gain favors by being silent or by any other form of accommodation can only lead to capitulation and defeat.

It is true that the Soviet Union does not ask for nor does it need the kind of defense it did as the first young socialist Republic. But even then the significance of the worldwide campaign was far more than the defense of the Soviet Union *per se*. It was an important ideological campaign. In fact this was its central purpose.

For this same reason the statement by some people concerning Soviet self-sufficiency, while correct, cannot be a cover for not taking up the challenge of the anti-Soviet campaign. Such silence, for whatever reason, has political and ideological consequences—not in the Soviet Union, but for the masses in the rest of the world. Herein lies the importance of replying to the slander no matter where it comes from. Anti-Sovietism is a form of anti-communism. It is a special ideological instrument in the imperialist drive to create dissension in the socialist world, to mislead the anti-imperialist movement.

398

No one wants to condemn or to "read out" any other Communist party. The best possible of all solutions would be for all Communist and Marxist parties to be here in this comradely and democratic discussion. This is the only path to greater unity. However, no one can honestly say that every possible effort has not been made to bring this about, I am sure we are of one mind in our determination to continue to work to bring about such a collective dialogue between all parties.

But let us not forget—there is a long history to the efforts of most Communist parties in trying to find a basis for a dialogue with the present leading group in the leadership of the Communist Party of China. In this history there have been periods of private exchanges, periods of public discussions, periods of no public or private retorts, to the vituperative and slanderous attacks from Peking. But as we know it has all fallen on deaf ears. Silence in the face of injustice, silence in the presence of slanders and falsehoods, silence in the knowledge of a military attack is acquiescence, is support for the slanders, the falsehoods and the attacks. Whether one inwardly means to acquiesce or not, is not important. It is the effects of such silence that count. The imperialist network spreads such silence as support for the slanders. Silence in the face of the slanders and acts of provocation by the Maoist group is itself opportunism.

The main content of the Maoist ideological attack is anti-Soviet. It is directed against the other socialist countries and the world Communist movement, but it is sharply focused against the Soviet Union. This, as we all know, is the main focus of U.S. imperialism's attack also. How are we, then, to separate these attacks? They cannot be separated in content, in their viciousness, in their scope and persistence.

Where then is the logic in a position of some parties remaining silent in the face of every possible kind of slander, and of vilification that has no limits? Remaining silent when there is proof of military attacks and provocations is acquiescence. But on the other hand, as soon as there is even the most responsible and measured reply to the slanders and attacks, then the silence of these parties ends and the response to these slanders, is called slander and abuse—these *responses* are called divisive. During this Conference the Mao group has said: "The Soviet Union and its socialist satellites are a fascist prison camp of peoples." How can partisans of socialism, partisans of the working class, remain silent? Must not one weigh the effects of such silence? Do not masses have a right to draw the conclusion that such silence is, in fact, acquiescence? Whether they have such a right or not, they do draw such conclusions.

Under these circumstances those who remain silent and those who dig into the pile of slander and falsehoods, in search of a word or two from which they can construct some far-fetched positive connotation, may do so. But they must also accept the responsibility for what conclusions the millions draw from such positions, from such silence. That responsibility cannot be escaped.

What should concern all, of course, is the slanders and the attacks, but what is of even greater concern is the consistent direction of the Maoist policy.

It is not a policy of confrontation with the forces of imperialism anywhere. The policy moves in the direction of a sharper confrontation with the forces of socialism and anti-imperialism everywhere. Neither the ideological nor the military confrontation moves in the direction of confrontation with imperialism—anywhere.

The point is not to read the Communist Party of China out. The real question is how to reverse the present direction of the Maoist policy and to bring the Chinese people and nation back into the stream of anti-imperialism, and in the world Communist and socialist movements.

We are in full agreement with the draft document in its emphasis on the centrality of the struggle against U.S. imperialism. This a worldwide struggle.

In the other imperialist countries, however, this struggle will be most effective if it relates to the struggle against the imperialism of one's own country. Communists can never be in the position of supporting the replacement of one imperialist domination by another—especially if the replacement is the imperialism of one's own country. A revolutionary party cannot evade or soften the struggle against one's own imperialism in the name of the struggle against world imperialism.

This can also be a form of opportunism.

□ ———————————————————————————————— □

A POLITICAL STRIKE OF COAL MINERS

"The Black Lung Victory" by Art Shields, *Political Affairs*, April, 1969

[*The Black Lung strike of West Virginia miners in 1969 not only won compensation for coal dust victims for the first time, but it also started the democratic upsurge in the United Mine Workers Union that brought the overthrow of the corrupt (William Anthony) "Tony" Boyle admin-istration.*

The strike was successful because it united the coal miners and progressive scientists with the community. In covering the strike Art Shields had the active support of Genne Kuhn of Wheeling, West Virginia, a miner's daughter who has been fighting on the miners' side all her life. Art Shields (b. 1888), veteran labor and Communist correspondent, reaches into his six decades of experience in analyzing the miners' victory.]

The Black Lung strike of West Virginia's miners illustrates the growing political consciousness of America's workers. It points again to the primary importance of the working class in struggles with the capitalist state.

Our working class has given many stirring examples of solidarity and fighting ability in struggles with ruthless employers for economic demands or for recognition of trade unions. But this strike has a special quality. It was a successful demonstration of workers' political power. Its effects are felt far and wide; and it gives workers confidence in their political future.

The Black Lung walkout was the first strike of its kind. It was purely political in character. Some other strikes have combined economic and political demands—with economic ones getting most attention. But West Virginia's miners had just one demand—a political one. They demanded passage of the State's first law to pay compensation to the victims of the coal dust plague that chokes men to death.

Forty thousand miners won this law from a reluctant legislature that always bowed to coal operators before. They won it with the help of a dramatic mass lobby that filled the Capitol rotunda and the galleries for the last two weeks of a three-week strike.

The miners also won with public support. They got this support because they were not just fighting for themselves. They were the vanguard of a national movement for health and safety today. . . .

[They had the support of] Dr. Buff, a distinguished heart specialist in Charleston, a scientist who devotes his knowledge and his enormous energy to the working people. He speaks at dozens of miners' meetings. He denounces the Rockefellers and other greedy coal barons. He voices his contempt for the industry's stooges in the legislature. . . .

Dr. Buff, I'm glad to say, doesn't stand alone. . . . Dr. Hawley Wells, one of Dr. Buff's colleagues, is an autopsy specialist from Morgantown. He is only 32, but he has examined the lungs of many hundreds of Black Lung victims. . . . Dr. Donald Rasmussen, the other Black Lung authority, is the young director of the Pulmonary Laboratory at Beckley, an important mine center. He is described by the Associated Press as "one of the world's few pneumoconiosis researchers." He has examined 3,000 miners in five years and he has evolved a series of tests to detect the dread killer when X–Rays show nothing. . . .

[T]he three doctors worked hand in hand with a group of rank-and-file miners in launching the Black Lung struggle. The three doctors formed the Physicians for Miners Health and Safety Committee. Rank-and-file miners and local unions established the West Virginia Black Lung Association. . . .

The Black Lung movement grew rapidly last winter. The doctors began speaking in local union halls where cold was kept out by pot-bellied stoves. The audience quickly expanded with big regional meetings, representing members of different local unions. The efforts of the international officers of the UMWA, led by Tony Boyle, to halt the rank-and-file drive meant nothing. . . .

The Charleston meeting got big coverage from press and television. Other meetings followed in regional centers. The miners were on the offensive. And several local unions began striking on Tuesday, February 18.

The strike started because Chairman J.E. Watson of the House Judiciary Committee had been sitting on the Black Lung bills for weeks. Watson smelled of coal. We heard miners ask him in the Capitol rotunda if he was a coal operator. The big, florid politician tried to escape. But the miners were around him. And he finally pleaded that his family wasn't in mining anymore. The family used to be in Consolidation Coal, he admitted. But it got out of the big company years ago, he insisted.

The miners received this denial with skeptical smiles.

The strike spread rapidly from mine to mine. Almost every pit in the southern fields of West Virginia was out by the weekend. And on Sunday the miners voted to march on the capitol building the next day. The vote was taken at a mass meeting of 1,500 men from many locals. They met in the mining town of Affinity near Beckley. And they applauded Dr. Buff to the echo when he said: "The legislature hasn't changed. They don't really care . . . because you're going to get it—you've got to get it." . . .

Pressure increased as miners in the northern fields of West Virginia walked out to the last man. And it was overwhelming after a mass meeting of thousands in Charleston's Municipal Auditorium on Wednesday, February 26. . . .

This meeting had more of a rank-and-file character than the big Charleston gathering in January. Many Black and white miners took the microphone to pledge solidarity after Dr. Buff and other main speakers concluded.

The *Daily World*— the only paper supporting the strike—got recognition at this meeting. Two thousand copies were given to miners as they came in. Many thanked the distributors and this writer. A young local leader held up our paper with its front-page strike headlines, as he addressed the meeting.

The strikers confronted Governor Arch Moore—a Republican—on the capitol steps after a two-mile parade from the meeting. The Governor was on the defensive. He had been elected with the help of the coal operators and the UMW heads. But now he was confronted with impatient and angry men. He begged them to consider him a friend. And he promised to call the legislature back into special session in July on the Black Lung issue if no bill was passed before the present session expired at Saturday midnight, March 8. . . .

[The coal operators themselves were frightened. The coal market was booming.] The "presumptive" clause came back—somewhat weaker than in the House version. And the Black Lung measure went through by a 34–2 vote, nine minutes before the midnight deadline on March 8.

The men did not go back to work until the Governor signed the bill on Tuesday, March 11. They made this decision at a huge meeting in Beckley on Sunday.

□ ———————————————————————————— □

RISE OF THE RANK AND FILE MOVEMENTS IN THE TRADE UNIONS

"The Rank and File Movements" by Jim West, *Political Affairs*, May, 1971

[*Throughout its years, as noted in Chapter I, the Communist Party centered its attention on the basic section of the working class.*

Jim West (b. 1914), a Party leader presently in Ohio, spent many years in industrial areas of the country. Here is a part of his report to the National Convention, March 13, 1971, in which he deals with the progress of the rank-and-file movements.]

Our Party alone, recognizing the full force of the laws of class struggle and placing reliance on the role of the rank-and-file and Left initiative in changing the labor movement and the relationship of forces in our country, took the initiatives which resulted in the historic National Rank and File Action Conference last June in Chicago. . . .

The rise of the rank-and-file movements goes far beyond the organized national center and its 17 state and local affiliates represented by the NCCTUAD [National Coordinating Committee for Trade Union Action and Democracy]. Many of these movements predate TUAD, such as the Ad Hoc Committee in steel, and some were important factors in bringing TUAD into being. . . .

Important rank-and-file movements with real muscle have emerged in a whole number of industries. Such is the case in the needle trades, in longshore, in locals of the auto union, especially in New York and New Jersey. Such is the case among the teachers where the rank-and-file movements have succeeded in knocking the anti-Communist clause out of the union constitution and where Shankerism is increasingly on the defensive and in many others too numerous to mention. In many of these situations, it is the Black caucuses which have taken the lead and paved the way for advance for all workers, as in the case of the national Black caucuses in the teachers' union, the steel union and others.

Let me single out some of the rank-and-file experiences.

The Miners for Democracy, a Western Pennsylvania rank-and-file movement which supported [Joseph A.] Yablonski, and took part in the National Rank and File Action Conference, has scored a tremendous victory in the election of officers in District 5 of the UMWA, the only district in which miners can elect their own officers at this time. It is already clear that while the election will be finally settled by the absentee ballots, the [Tony] Boyle machine has been given a smashing defeat. It is clear that the organized rank-and-file is a decisive force to be reckoned with and that things will never be the same in the Western Pennsylvania coal fields.

This victory is due to the courage, persistence and determination of the Miners for Democracy. It is also due to a correct policy and a resourceful struggle for that policy by the Coal Commission of the Party, led by Comrade Anton Krchmarek.

The Commission refused to allow the anti-Communism of a few leaders of Miners for Democracy to obscure the significance of a rank-and-file victory in District 5. It did all in its power to bring the fullest possible support to the rank-and-file slate. It took the initiative in mobilizing over 200 students and faculty members in a number of colleges to help the rank-and-file slate, including getting out campaign material and going into the remotest places to talk with coal miners and especially with pensioners. According to the leaders of Miners for Democracy, it was this activity by the students which was a prime reason for the victory. Here is a fine example of a labor–student alliance in action, one worthy of emulation in other labor struggles.

404

Because of this initiative and activity, the position now is much more favorable for overcoming the influence of anti-Communism if we consciously follow through. The Party's pamphlet, *Dig We Must Into the Coal Operators' Profits!* was a very important contribution to the miners' victory and a blow against anti-Communism. . . .

The fighting mood that exists among steelworkers is widely recognized. For example: the business magazine *American Machinist* writes that "the mood of the rank-and-file at this point appears to be this: If USW president I.W. Abel does not lead the workers in their quest for more money he will be brushed aside. . . ." (November 3, 1970).

The Abel leadership finds itself caught between the pressure of the rank-and-file for an all-out fight [for the Big Six Demands][5] and from the Nixon Administration to get the workers to accept an inadequate settlement without any real fight for the main demands.

The rank-and-file is not waiting for Abel to lead. It has been in motion for some time now, with one of the highest rates of unauthorized strikes of any industry in the country and with the steady rise in the number of rank-and-file movements.

The first among these is the Ad Hoc Committee of Concerned Steelworkers, a six-year old national Black caucus movement with over 3,000 organized supporters in the Midwest, East and deep South. The leadership of this movement is one of the main pillars of strength of TUAD, helping to build it wherever there is an Ad Hoc group.

The Ad Hoc Committee gave encouragement to and helped found a new national rank-and-file movement at the Chicago, June Conference, when 26 steelworkers came together and formed a provisional National Steelworkers Rank-and-File Committee. [In addition to the Big Six Demands], the program of this new committee . . . projects a concrete program for democratizing the union and for combatting racism. It makes clear its opposition to the war and exposes the role of the Nixon Administration, thus taking some first steps toward politicalizing the impending struggles.

This program has won the support of the Ad Hoc leaders nationally and in practically all localities. It has also won the support of an important steel local, the leaders of a Chicago local, the powerful rank-and-file caucus at Inland Steel and leaders of Black caucuses in Detroit and Youngstown. The latest word is that the leaders of another rank-and-file movement, based in the Youngstown-Warren-Western Pennsylvania areas and known as RAFT (Rank-and-File Team), have expressed their agreement with that program. . . .

What is developing in steel today is a widespread advance in understanding that you can't wage a successful struggle against the weak grievance set-up and bureaucratic procedures in the unions on a purely local level. More and more, it is recognized that the companies must be tackled on a company-wide scale; that the building of a powerful, effective, democratic union requires changes in structure and policies which can come about only through a concerted national effort. . . .

[I]t is the lesson which younger militant workers are now coming to learn. It is part of the heritage left to the American working class by William Z. Foster, who first laid down these principles in his plan for organizing the steel industry in 1919. It is the policy with which our Party and its general secretary, Gus Hall, are identified. And it is being relearned in a new way today.

The fight against racism in industry and in the labor movement is a central feature of work in the rank-and-file movements. These cannot win their objective without a conscious struggle against racism and for the full equality and dignity of Black, Chicano, Puerto Rican and American Indian workers, as well as a struggle for the rights of women. For their success depends on the building of ever stronger unity of the working class. . . .

The appeal issued by the national TUAD for the freedom of Angela Davis is a powerful, popular statement of labor's stake in this fight. . . .

One of the ideological hangups which hold back many of our white comrades from boldly and skillfully taking this fight into their shops and unions is a lack of confidence in the capacity of white workers to overcome racist influences. Many comrades are defeated before they start, so to speak. But this is in itself a Right opportunist capitulation to the racist ideology of the ruling class.

It is in order, therefore, to cite some examples which tend to prove that a new level of understanding is developing among white workers, that there is a new readiness to respond, that racism does not have to have unchallenged sway, that it is possible to defeat racism and advance to a new level of Black-white class unity.

Who would have believed a strike against racism? Not only that, but a strike lasting nine and a half months, in which the majority of strikers were white workers. Such a strike recently ended in complete victory in Peoria, Illinois, a typical small industrial town, at a plant of a few hundred workers organized in a UE local.

It began when the Black president of the local was insulted and physically assaulted by the supervisor in the course of an effort to solve a grievance. Defending himself against the attack, the Black worker laid the supervisor out. When the latter came to, he summarily fired the local president. Thereupon the whole shop walked out. . . . Before it was over, the community had been aroused and mobilized and the city council and the mayor had been forced to speak out against the company racism. Further, the main office, located in another state, had changed the local management and reinstated the Black local president with full back pay.

What is significant here? That the white majority saw company racism as a threat to their union, to their unity and power, to their right to elect officers of their own choice. . . .

This victory over racism has given these workers a new sense of strength and power, of unity, of class awareness, of awareness of racism as a divisive company tool. There were times when it looked as if the strike might be lost. They endured hardships and meager meals. It took a good deal of understanding and depth of conviction to stay out for nine and a half months. It was a great victory, the lessons of which these workers will never forget. And we may be assured that it was a good education for all working people in Peoria.

This is an example from the North. Here is another from the deep South. A new steel mill, under West German ownership, was built and opened in Georgetown, South Carolina. That state was deliberately picked because it is a "right-to-work" state. The work force is both Black and white. The United Steelworkers set out to organize it and succeeded in winning the bargaining election. But the company refused to negotiate a contract; in other words, it continued to refuse to recognize the union. A strike was called. State police and thugs were called in. A place to hold meetings became a problem. The white churches closed their doors to the strikers. The steel union organizers could not cope with the problem. Some white workers then proposed that the Southern Christian Leadership Conference be called upon for help. SCLC responded and sent in its labor director. He rallied the Black community. He talked with the Black ministers. The Black churches opened their doors to the strikers. White workers began to talk about joining the Black church. It was then that the white churches too, opened their doors to strike meetings. The strike was finally won, the union recognized, a contract negotiated. . . .

The Political Committee of the Party recognized that the time had come to fulfill the decision of the 19th Convention, as expressed in the report of Comrade Henry Winston, to go over fully to the policy of industrial concentration. It therefore established a Task Force, under the chairmanship of Comrade Gus Hall, whose mission it is to dig into the problems of overcoming resistance and difficulties in the way of working-class concentration, especially in the basic, trustified industries. . . .

The rank-and-file movement as a united front is not a coverup for hiding the role of the Communists; it is not a substitute for Communists; nor is it merely a group of Communists working under another name. None of these concepts has anything in common either with the united front or the role of Communists. No united front can long exist, let alone grow and become the prevailing influence in a union, without the role of the Communists, without their presence and without the fact of their presence, of their role becoming known to the other participants.

□ ──────────────────────────────────── □

THE SCIENCE OF LIBERATION

"A Talk to Teachers of Marxism" by James E. Jackson, *Political Affairs,* April 1974

[*James E. Jackson (b. 1914) is an outstanding Marxist-Leninist theoretician and national Party leader. He has participated in many ideological conferences in the United States and abroad. He was editor of* The Worker *and is head of the Educational Department of the Communist Party.*

The Teachers' Conference of the Center for Marxist Education was an outgrowth of lengthy discussions on teaching methods of Marxism-Leninism. It was held in early Spring in 1974, in New York City.]

Lenin is our model of the great teacher. Writing in praise of learning, he said: " . . . it is not enough to crush capitalism. We must take the entire culture that capitalism left behind and build socialism with it. We must take all its science, technology, knowledge and art. Without these we shall be unable to build communist society."

Here, Lenin is indicating a responsibility for one who would presume to teach the working people, the necessity not only to be a competent specialist in particular areas, but to have an approach toward enlarging the perimeter of one's general knowledge. Marxism is a frame, a tool, a guide to objective knowledge. It is not in itself a substitute for concrete contemporary as well as historical knowledge. And therefore the richness of the teaching process and the utilization of concepts grounded in the fundamental theory requires a wealth of illustrative material taken from life and from the various arts and sciences.

The input for teachers must be wide-ranging, full of the many-sided reflections of the variegated, multiformed reality of life. Otherwise, teaching will be a retreading of what is read in the text. But the textual concepts will come alive when they are richly illustrated from contemporary and moving reality. Therefore, all human knowledge is our heritage and our property, and we have to drink deeply of it as a continuous habit in order to enrich the ideas that we want to bring forward which deal with the primary concepts of our scientific theory.

Utilizing the science, the technology, the knowledge of art, "the great heritage" that Lenin referred to, requires a numerous cadre of revolutionary intellectuals, of working people of real creativity and broad learning who have been schooled in Marxism-Leninism and are committed to sharing this knowledge. The teacher, the working-class intellectual, is the conduit, the collator and organizer of this cultural and scientific heritage, and has the responsibility of processing it for dissemination to those who strive to change the world—to the working class in the first instance. The role of vanguard fighter, said Lenin, can be fulfilled "only by a party that is guided by the most advanced theory." And Marxist-Leninist theory, as a science, has to be studied with the same sense of discipline and responsibility that one would bring to the study of mathematics or any of the other scientific disciplines.

Marx and Engels, taking as their starting point a thorough study of the objective facts, formulated the conclusion that by the very course of capitalism's development the proletariat becomes a force destined "to accomplish a revolution in the capitalist mode of production and finally destroy classes." The historical importance of this role of the working class is determined, to cite Lenin's words, first of all "by its place in the system of social production, by its numerical strength, by its consciousness, organization and discipline." In this connection, the role of theory is to help to contribute to this process of creating, conditioning and qualifying the working class to fulfill its historic world-changing mission.

"The fundamental criterion by which classes are distinguished is the place they occupy in social production." Classes are defined in terms of "the relation in which they stand to the means of production," Lenin has taught us. The concept of the working class embraces a far broader dimension than merely the hired manual workers. It is more than those solely engaged in physical work. Long ago Karl Marx pointed out: "To work productively there is now no need to directly use one's hands. Already the cooperative nature of the process of labor itself invariably broadens the nature of productive labor and its courier the productive worker."

This is a most important concept, qualifying certain notions that are not necessarily Marxist-Leninist, which speak to the question of who are the workers and what is the working class. We confront in our time a galloping, scientific-technological revolution that is worldwide and characteristic of the age in which we live. The scientific and technological revolution finds its most favorable environment and socially progressive forms of manifesting itself in socialist society. But, nevertheless, it is also a factor of enormous significance in capitalist society. It unfolds under all social systems that prevail in human society today—both capitalist and socialist.

As a consequence of the scientific-technological revolution, new important changes are taking place in the structure of the working class. And these changes speak to the need for precision in defining what is the working class, and who are the workers. For the bourgeoisie is very much concerned with utilizing this moment of important changes brought about by the scientific and technological revolution to do two things. One is to diminish and put down the working class as the historic force for the transformation of society to the new and necessary stage of socialism and ultimately communism. Secondly, it strives to introduce a sectarian, quantitative definition of the working class in order to support the thesis that this class is no longer the relevant revolutionary force, as conceived of by Marx, capable of changing the world.

Is there a relative diminution in the size of the blue-collar strata of the working class? Data affirm this fact. Technological development in the productive process has shifted the proportions as between what we speak of as white-collar and blue-collar workers. The nature of labor as performed in this scientific-technical age may represent itself not in carrying enormous loads on one's back and developing callouses on one's hands. It may manifest itself in punching buttons on a console that moves huge and complicated production processes, on staggeringly lengthy assembly lines, which set in action programmed machining tools of infinitely complex character, etc.

Are these people workers? Of course they are. The very technological development of the production process enlarges the feeder category of the working force necessary to achieve its goals. Therefore we in turn must understand that the working class includes not only workers by hand but workers by brain. This category of the educated strata is an integral part of the working class. We need to perceive of and establish this because, as I said, one of the ideological pursuits of those who would denigrate the working class is to contend that the workers are a diminishing quantity, and that therefore the working class—even numerically speaking—has lost its strategic role, that it can neither take power nor aspire to power. But this technological and scientific revolutionary process is also further qualifying the working class to fulfill its historic political role. It is introducing, in a mass way and in depth, culture, science and organizational skills of a complicated character into the working class, and is thereby completing all of the objective conditions for the working class to produce its own intelligentsia, an intelligentsia of the workers themselves.

If in Marx's time one could speak of the necessity of the intellectual elements of the old classes, from among the sons and daughters of the bourgeoisie committed to the ideas of socialism, introducing socialist consciousness into the working class, we see that today there is already a working class whose perimeter has been expanded to embrace the technical and scientific categories of working people. The workers by brain are legitimately an integral part of the working class. They are related to the production process and the working class *per se.* They are not independent and antagonistic forces, although there is very often psychological lag in how they conceive of themselves. The working class, as Marx pointed out long ago, has many divisions in it: between the workers of lower and higher consciousness, between skilled and un-skilled. And it is riven by other divisions; foremost among them in our country . . . the exploitation by the bourgeoisie of the national and racial distinctions within the working class. But the logic of the relationship of the working class to the means of production, the consequences of the programming of the thought processes, the changes introduced in the position, viewpoint and behavior of that class by its objective place in the production process, will overcome and is overcoming these divisions.

While it is a departure from Marxism to *exclude* the technical and scientific workers and educated strata related to the production process from the working class, it is no less wrong from the standpoint of Marxist theory to *include* those strata whom Marx referred to as "the ruined bourgeoisie" and "the ruined proletariat," the *lumpenproletariat* who have fallen from the last rung of the social ladder, defeated by the long onslaught of the bourgeoisie, the dropouts of the social system as a whole, those who are beaten down. Such "theories," including those of the former Panther leader, Eldridge Cleaver, glorify the lumpen-proletariat and assign to it a special vanguard role in the revolutionary process. Cleaver popularized in the literary sense a concept that is widely attested to and theorized about in academic terms by Marcuse and others, who celebrate the victimized prisoners, who romanticize those whom Marx referred to as the "plebians of the city," those who have no stable status in the society. Such "theorists" confuse and equate general impoverishment, general deprivation and "vagabondage" with the work-ing class.

Marx and Lenin called for focus on the most advanced of the workers, on that section which has found the courage, discipline, the will, the capacity and strength to stand up against all the efforts of the bourgeoisie to accomplish their degradation on those who have confronted the class of the despoilers of humanity and exploiters of the toilers and stood up to the exploiters and held their status in society. This is where our focus is, this is why we speak of a concentration policy in respect to those strata of the working population who are related to the industrial process as the focal point for our energies: in order to deal with this basic body of the working class who have the greatest ability and who are situated objectively in the production process in such a way that that very process is conditioning them and preparing them to fulfill the role of gravedigger of imperialism.

The founders of scientific socialism, Marx and Engels, and the great organizing genius and theoretician of the revolutionary process which inexorably advances toward communism, V.I. Lenin, placed the importance of scientific theory at the highest level of concern for all who would be genuine revolutionaries. Marx was not yet 30 when he wrote, concerning this question of theory: "To approach the toiler without a strict scientific idea and a positive teaching is tantamount to engaging in the senseless and dishonest game of preacher, which supposes on the one hand, an inspired teacher, and on the other hand only jackasses listening to him with gaping mouths."

The teacher has to be more than a rhetorician. Rhetoric has its place in dramatizing a concept. Teaching also has its theater function. The teacher must keep people from sleeping and has to focus attention, but the attention-catching devices should be designed to focus on the idea and not on the teacher. The teacher isn't a performing puppet. *He has a responsibility for collating and putting in digestible form real data and real facts.* He is not just a poet, a balladeer, a troubadour, a preacher. Preaching has its place, poetry has its place, a teacher may utilize, on occasion, this or that art of the preacher and balladeer and poet, but he has a responsibility to the student to bring facts, to present them in a meaningful and digestible way.

A teacher should take care not to seek cheap fame by confounding and overwhelming his students with a string of profound-sounding but rarely used words and phrases. Strive to keep it simple: opt for "dents in the surface" rather than "adumbrations of the periphery." They mean the same, but the teacher on an ego trip wants his students to say in wonder: "Man, he's heavy!" when actually nobody knows what he's saying.

When you want to turn a bottle upside down, to shake it, say "shake the bottle," not "pronate and supernate." But some teachers thumb through Marxism—and I've seen some of the books—and they underline the most obtuse words, the words that no other teacher would use.

In bourgeois academic circles you find all kinds of ridiculous distortions of Marxist concepts. And every year there's some "in" word taken out of Marxism. A few years ago it was "alienation." Every ignoramus on every faculty was talking about "alienation," and, believe me, Marx wouldn't recognize what they were talking about.

When unfamiliar scientific and technical terms and concepts are necessary, and sometimes they are necessary, it's also important that the teacher take pains to define them, and illustrate them in terms that are already familiar. . . .

Part of the teaching process is to motivate students. And you cannot motivate them without establishing a certain identification with them as to where they're coming from and what their primary urgent aspirations are. To be able to inspire students is an art that has to be cultivated.

The role of teacher of the working class is a high calling and one should have the highest esteem for the title of teacher. The teacher must ever strive to extend his reach and capacity to fulfill this calling. In a certain sense the teacher prepares the productive strata who will change the world, and has a big input in determining how soon the promise date.

Finally, comrades, in the course of teaching, no matter how specialized a subject is, it is always necessary that the teacher intersperse his ideas and concepts, to weave into the subject the threads of the constantly changing realities of contemporary events and challenges. Because if there's a certain design to a teaching of a particular subject, the threads utilized must be validly related to life, and must be so understood and appreciated by all the students. Therefore, illustrations should not be obtuse, esoteric and unfamiliar, but should be illustrations that link the new ideas that you are expounding and presenting to the already familiar, and to the tempestuous movements of living reality.

We live in a confident time, when the main currents in social history are moving toward the fulfillment of socialism and the world revolutionary process is on the ascendant. At the same time one cannot brush under the rug such things as the tragic setback in Chile, and if one does not pose this terrible negative phenomenon one cannot verify the general trend. So the exceptions must be presented and explained. And they do not diminish or take away from the concrete proof of the general estimate.

So it is with the question of Solzhenitsyn. Fifty-two years of socialism and you've still got a Solzhenitsyn. How do you explain that? We must not shrink from this stubborn fact. But we must put the exception in its proper proportion and deal with it because revolutionary and social development is an uneven process. In Solzhenitsyn you have a tailist whose consciousness lags a whole era of time behind social development. He's still speaking in praise of the Czar. In another period, when the Revolution was hard pressed, and had no time for such foolishness, he would have been up against the wall. They wouldn't have bothered with him. It's affirmation of the triumph of democracy that the ravings of this pawn of bourgeois propagandists evokes no alarm in the Soviet Union.

So sometimes, by negative example, we explain the general and affirm the truth of the general.

The main thing in teaching, as has been pointed out here, is the knowledgeableness, the preparation of the teacher for his class. And teaching technique, as important as it is, and as creative as we must be to master the arts of easy and ready communication, involving all the processes of learning, involving all the styles and forms to do so, nevertheless does not substitute for content.

The primary appeal of the Marxist teacher lies in his preparation for delivering substantive content. You can't just command that people absorb. That is the art of the teacher: to find ways and means of transmitting ideas in the most effective and digestible form, that give pleasure while adding new dimensions of knowledge to students' understanding. Participatory teaching technique must contribute to that and must not be a cover for absence of content. It is but a form and it serves the objective of conveying content. But in certain circumstances it can, as has been indicated, turn into its opposite, become an obstacle to learning, obscuring content.

There are some things that don't lend themselves to popularization. Some things have to be studied in classic fashion and no matter how they are dramatized or illustrated the student is still going to have to burn some midnight oil to figure things out.

Therefore, the main thing is content. The basic thing in being a good teacher is to have been a good student of the subject being taught. The quality of the output is based on the quality and quantity of the input. You can't get around that. Preparation is key.

I once attended a Party school where we had an evaluation at which every student had to stand up and say what he had learned and what he had not learned. I said my problem was difficulty in expressing myself. "I know more about the subject but I can't get it out," I said. And so the teacher, Pop Mindel, a great Marxist teacher, asked me, "What's your name? What's your address?" I told him. "What's your telephone number?" I told him. He said, "You rattled all the answers off. You had no problem expressing yourself. Your problem is you don't know enough. When you know something you can express it. You know your name, so you don't stutter or have a problem formulating it." And that's usually the problem in communication. We take a headline of knowledge and try to stretch it into a book or into an hour's lecture presentation.

You can't keep pouring from a glass without refilling it. If you have a wealth of information, then you can present it, thimbleful or glassful at a time. You can put icing on it, color it with pretty colors, or put a cherry in it to make it palatable. Then the students will take it with pleasure. But you can't pour any of it from an empty glass.

And then in all our teaching we must always *stress fundamentals of Marxism-Leninism.* Just as any football coach will tell you, you can't overlearn the fundamentals. The basic positions must be taught. Then you can do all kinds of double and triple plays, all kinds of fancy work. But you *have to know the fundamentals.*

This is necessary especially when you have a heterogeneous class of students at different levels. Nobody can learn too much about the basics, about the fundamentals. For example, we can't be smug in our understanding of "Who is the working class?" and correspondingly, "What is a working class position?" For the working class, like every other reality, undergoes change.

Let me move to another thought which comes out of the discussion. . . . [W]e have to make an impact on the thinking of our students, to become crusaders to remove the wall of racism which divides and does such harm to the working class. I would suggest that in addition to starting from the standpoint of describing the misery that oppression and racism imposes upon Black people, we ought to also deal with the positive side of this problem, to approach it from the sunny side, so to speak, which sometimes is a far more effective teaching aid. One can often be more effective in teaching recognition and sensitivity to the need of whites to struggle for equality and freedom for Blacks by emphasizing how much Black and white have in common besides dealing with the question of the special double, triple oppression under which Blacks suffer.

One level, a limited level, is that attained when whites recognize that Blacks are victimized and doubly, specially oppressed. But it cannot be left on this level. Consciousness has to be raised to the level where Blacks are appreciated as a vital revolutionary and cultural force who have played and will play even more in the future a great progressive role in fulfilling social and political tasks of revolutionary change in our country. They come into the movement of social struggle and change, not just overly burdened and overly abused, but also *enlightened through their experience in struggle against this oppression.* And, against great odds,

415

they have also acquired and exercised considerable power and made considerable achievements.

Therefore, they are not a burden, they are not an object of charity that is added to the responsibilities of the white workers. They are a substantive, decisive part of the working class, first of all. And in a certain sense, and in certain areas, they are among its most *dynamic* components. They are a great tested, revolutionary allied force which brings strength, not added burdens, to the forces for social revolution in our country.

If approached from this angle, it would help simultaneously, while enlightening whites about the necessity for alliance, to move them to take up the struggle for Black liberation. Simultaneously this approach helps clarify and enlighten Blacks to build up their defenses against the perversion of their condition of oppression by the ideologies of separatism, of Black nationalism, and the influence of the bourgeoisie that such ideological currents reflect.

Blacks resent being seen only as victims, only as a burden, a sociological problem. Ninety percent of the time, Black people are preoccupied with the same things all people have in common. Black people share the same common living experiences, aspirations, life activities as whites. They have a great deal in common and they communicate through a common language across the color line. There is much common appreciation, much in common.

Blacks do not walk around under a special cloud, conceiving of themselves as some kind of sociological problem. They are people concerned with the problems and aspirations that people as a whole are concerned with. The strength that Blacks bring is well illustrated by the fact that the first worthy son of the American working class, who happens to be a Black man and son of a fighting people, Coleman Young, has become mayor of the fifth largest city in this country—the first time a trade unionist out of the *ranks* has become the mayor of a big city. This has enormous exemplary and challenging importance for the American labor movement. . . .

Thus a vision of the anti-monopoly, labor-based, people's coalition in governmental power is already present in embryo today in Detroit, the auto hub-city which is the heartland of the big industrial Midwest. Therefore, Blacks are a cultured and beautiful part of humanity, of our nation as a whole, and a vital sector of the working class who bring talent and strength to the common revolutionary cause.

This must be reflected in our teaching.

☐ ─── ☐

10.

THE PARTY RECORDS NEW ADVANCES

Furthering detente and disarmament, ending aggression and intervention in the affairs of other states, strengthening peaceful coexistence by increasing trade and developing other economic and cultural ties between the socialist and capitalist worlds, banishing the threat of nuclear war forever—these remain the central issues of our time.

These were among the key questions discussed in the report by the General Secretary, Gus Hall, to the 21st Convention of CPUSA in Chicago, June 26-30, 1975.

In the '50s and '60s, cold war incitement was aimed at aggravating problems in several socialist countries. Critical outbursts had occurred in several countries[1] reflecting dissatisfaction in the economic and political processes. The intrinsic democratic nature of the socialist states, however, made it possible to bring about a speedy correction. But the CIA persisted in attempts to foster counter-revolutionary actions. Their defeat helped prevent further deterioration in international relations. The mass media needed little encouragement to fan the anti–communist frenzy. In these circumstances disorientation took place in certain progressive circles. This also affected some members of the Communist Party.

The McCarthyite assault had previously taken its toll. While the Party was under severe attack, the Left in the trade unions and progressives generally also became victims. Violent attacks on the Black liberation movements increased, climaxed by the assassination of Dr. Martin Luther King, Jr.

The McCarran Act requiring the Party to supply a list of its members to the government was activated. (The Party never complied with this requirement.) The Party was under pressure from "left" and right tendencies in its leadership. Having been demoralized and disoriented by new problems in the socialist states, these forces were prepared for the liquidation of the Marxist-Leninist Party. They saw no future for it. But while the Party was prepared to discuss critical questions, it rejected political suicide unequivocally.

"Leftists" with their customary "revolutionary" phraseology pressed for the dissolution of the Party. They proposed that it be replaced by a nebulous amalgam which would create a new socialist formation. The ultra-left had lost the precarious foothold it had once attained among students and in middle class circles. The one thread common to all these tattered sects was their hostility to the Communist Party and the Soviet Union.

The right wing resurrected the old, anemic, political association concept, originated by Earl Browder in 1944 and overwhelmingly repudiated in 1945. They preferred a liberal propaganda sect flitting around the two capitalist parties.

Another one of their aims was the scuttling of international working-class solidarity, a fundamental principle throughout the Party's history. The intensified cold war atmosphere, combined with an increasing drive against the socialist states, provoked virulent anti-Sovietism. The hate chorus sought to make socialism itself suspect. The opportunist groups made their accommodation to this situation. The Right jumped on the anti-Soviet bandwagon.

The resoluteness of the Communist Party's support to internationalism is a brilliant page in its history. The initiative of Gus Hall

418

in leading the Party in defense of the Czechoslovak socialist revolution was in the finest tradition of international solidarity.[2]

The factional opposition continued intermittently for several years, although it did not halt the Party's activity (as the items in Chapters Eight, Nine and Ten testify). But the organization was affected, threatening the Party's very existence. Nevertheless, the "Left" and Right opposition was defeated. Some were expelled, while others withdrew from the organization.

The 21st Convention was a demonstration of the achievement of Party unity. It could now devote all its energies to mass activity, to strengthen the organization and increase the circulation of the Daily World. *The Party had reached a new plateau. Thus Gus Hall, in his convention report, characterized those who were "bewildered [because] only a few years ago some predicted [the Party] would die, would wither on the vine [but] most of the organizations they predicted would replace the Communist Party are now in shambles, and the one organization they predicted would die is now the most relevant, viable and growing organization on the left."* (The Crisis of US Capitalism and the Fight-Back, International Publishers, 1975). *This was no idle boast. It was the recognition that the Communist Party, a product of working-class development, cannot be destroyed.*

The improvements occurring in the Party were reflected in the composition of the delegations. It was no mere statistical factor. The Party began to attract young people to its ranks, and advance many to its leading bodies on every level. Arnold Becchetti, organization secretary, writing in Political Affairs *(August 1975) stressed this "was a youthful Convention [with] over half the delegates . . . 40 years of age or less." The attendance of Blacks, Puerto Ricans, Chicanos, Asians and Native Indian Americans was greater than before. The participation of nearly "20 per cent basic and industrial workers [and] some 42 per cent trade unionists" highlighted the Convention. These figures suggest what made it possible to place the Party on the ballot in several states in 1976.*

The huge US conglomerates, through their multinationals, penetrate every corner of the imperialist world. The assets of a single multinational frequently are larger than that of the gross national product of entire countries. Concentration is especially

419

heavy in the field of energy. According to the Columbia Journal of World Business, *US firms from 1961 to 1973 built or absorbed 5,476 plants abroad. Sixty-seven percent of foreign branches in capitalist countries and 60.6 percent in developing countries were US owned.*

Interfering in the affairs of other countries, creating tension, has become an instrument of foreign policy. The Central Intelligence Agency (CIA) serves as a vehicle plotting the overthrow of "antagonistic" governments. Chile was the most prominent and latest example of this policy. From Iran to Indonesia, from Nicaragua to Taiwan and from the Mediterranean to the Indian Ocean, our monopoly-dominated government did not and does not hesitate, if necessary, to use fascist blueprints to impose its domination.

But the age of imperialist rule by gunboat diplomacy is past. The oldest colonial empire—Portugal—was demolished. Fascist rulers in Spain and Greece were ousted. For the first time in half a century Europe is free from the fascist plague. The savage Shah of Iran has fled. The African continent, with the exception of its southern enclave, where racist fascism still rules, is now a region of independent states. In the Middle East the volatile atmosphere contradicts the Washington pretensions of a peaceful solution.

The monopolies reap phenomenal profits as inflation and unemployment grow. The report to the 21st Convention declared "the key link in the chain of life is the economic one." Unemployment in major industrial regions is at a double-digit level. Among youth, especially Black, the jobless rate hovers at 40 to 50 percent.

The Communist Party cooperated with Left forces, which led demonstrations in 35 cities on November 16, 1974. These were the first actions against unemployment and inflation initiated in the '70s. They contributed to the creation of the National Coalition to Fight Inflation and Unemployment (NCFIU) [now called the National Coalition for Economic Justice], a united-front movement in which Communists participate.

The rank and file organizations in the trade unions were a major casualty of McCarthyism. The militancy and initiative of these forces, essential to a vibrant trade union movement were stifled. Here again Communists working with the Left and progressives, as well as other independent forces, helped reconstitute this movement. A national center, Trade Unionists for Action and Democracy, was established; its publication is Labor Today. *The Coalition of Black Trade Unionists and organizations to protect women's rights in the trade unions were created. The Party's orientation is to help crystallize an alliance of Left and Center currents in the trade union movement, as the most effective instrument of struggle in the economic and political arena.*

The Communist Party enters its sixth decade with a proud record of achievement. It has withstood sharp attacks and defeated those who would destroy it. It was a part of and gave leadership in unprecedented struggles, helping to establish new bridgeheads for further advance.

To make any real progress today it is essential to curb the power of the huge monopolies which have merged with and control the state. State monopoly capitalism, seeking to shore up and save US capitalism in its advanced stage of crisis and decay, has devastating effects on every facet of our people's lives—living standards, human rights and dignity, all social progress, and world peace. The Party strives to create unity of "the working class and its allies to defend their interests against monopoly and to speed the creation of a new people's anti-monopoly political party. . . . It is impossible today to fight for democratic rights, for wage increases, or against racism, higher taxes and inflation, without confronting the power of the state monopoly galaxies."

Increasing numbers of the electorate, including prominent trade union leaders, are searching for ways to break out of monopoly's two-party grip. The Party has intensified its political activities, including the running of candidates on all levels, to help the people achieve an historic breakaway. Such a development will mark a giant radical, democratic leap for the majority of our people and open new roads toward a fundamental transformation of US society—toward socialism.

□ ————————————————————————— □

THE BLACK LIBERATION MOVEMENT

Strategy for a Black Agenda by Henry Winston,
International Publishers, 1973

[*The collapse of the imperialist system following World War II wrote*
finis *to its colonial domination over Africa. Imperialism through its
neocolonialist intervention nevertheless continues to be a threat to the
newly liberated countries of the continent.*

*During the same postwar period the Black liberation movement in the
United States reached new maturity. The spirited Freedom Movement
won wide support, attracting new adherents, nationwide.*

*The formation of the National Anti-Imperialist Movement in Soli-
darity with African Liberation (NAIMSAL), helped create ties between
anti-imperialist forces in the United States and those in Africa. Support
for the freedom of Angela Davis symbolized international solidarity
among the advanced forces on both continents.*

*It was during this vital period that many young Black men and women
began to study the classics of Marxism. Under these circumstances
pseudo-Marxists and various "leftist" groups introduced distorted and
diversionary concepts. Henry Winston takes up the struggle against these
misleading tendencies as being detrimental to the liberation movement.*

*In the chapter: "From Anti-Slavery to the Anti-Monopoly Strategy,"
he states the "aim of the anti-monopoly program, as advocated by the
Communist Party."*]

Now, over a hundred years after the Emancipation Proclamation of
January 1863, racism and oppression are more than ever essential to the
ruling class, as U.S. state monopoly capitalism enters a new and more
acute phase of the crisis and decline of capitalism. U.S. imperialism,
facing a world in which the forces of socialism and class and national
liberation are on the ascendancy and in which foreign imperialist powers
are challenging its domination, certainly can't do today what the slave
power was unable to do over 100 years ago—solve its problems through
aggression and expansion.

The monopolists are equally unable to solve their problems at home,
where they are not only imposing a wage freeze, but are also attempting
to impose a far more repressive racist freeze on Black liberation struggles
than that of the McCarthy period.

By perpetuating and intensifying racism, monopoly aims to stop the advance of the Black liberation movement, to destroy organized labor and suppress every struggle of the oppressed and exploited.

Monopoly capital, within today's context, aims to repeat the kind of assault on the people's rights that led to the betrayal of Reconstruction. Reaction of that period, through racism and violence, prepared the way for the Supreme Court to void the Civil Rights Act of 1875, whose passage had been won by the supporters of Reconstruction to solidify the gains they had made. Reaction's aim then was to push the country into a long era of segregation and semi-slavery.

Today state monopoly capitalism seeks to wipe out every trace of the struggles of the recent Civil Rights Decade. The increasing political repression, the attempted frameup of Angela Davis and other political prisoners, Nixon's racist nominations to the Supreme Court, are all part of monopoly's attempt to obliterate every advance made through Black and white struggle since Reconstruction was destroyed.

The betrayal of Reconstruction, it should be remembered, was the signal for a three-sided attack against the masses. The Old Slave Codes were replaced by the New Black Codes and the former chattel slaves were forced into semi-slavery, segregation and fascist oppression. At the same time, the escalation of the military plunder and massacre of the Indians was entering a climactic stage. And simultaneously, the courts that upheld the betrayal of Emancipation were declaring that workers, Black and white, did not have the right to organize. In other words, the courts had not only revived Chief Justice Roger B. Taney's pre-Civil War doctrine that the Black man "had no rights which the white man was bound to respect." They had also extended this into another phase of repression—that labor, whatever its color, had no rights that capital was bound to respect.

In 1875, when the robber barons were joining with the former slaveowners to prepare for the 1877 betrayal of Reconstruction, Judge Holden Owen, presiding over the trial of striking Pennsylvania miners, declared: "Any agreement, combination or confederation to increase the price of any vendible commodity, merchandise or anything else is a conspiracy under the laws of the U.S." Of course, this doctrine—like Nixon's wage "price" freeze—was applied only to labor, never to the capitalists' profits.

Because of the perpetuation of racism and the resulting division between the triply oppressed Black workers and the exploited white workers, it took more than 60 years of struggle against the bosses' government-supported violence to win the right to organize. Today, the rights of labor are once again under grave attack and labor's fate, as in the past, is inseparably bound up with that of the Black liberation movement.

The crisis of poverty and unemployment Black Americans now face, is, save for the almost total genocidal elimination of American Indians, without precedent for any segment of this country's population.

"The unemployment rate among Black workers in the ghetto now exceeds the general rate of unemployment of the entire nation during the depression of the 1930s," reported Herbert Hill, NAACP Labor Secretary, at the organization's 1971 National Convention.

"The rate of unemployment of Black workers in 25 major centers of urban non-white population concentration is now between 25 per cent and 40 per cent," stated Hill, "and the unemployment rate for Black youth will be in excess of 50 per cent by the middle of this summer. In 1933, the national unemployment rate was 24.9 per cent, the highest officially recorded unemployment in the history of the United States." Hill also pointed out that tens of thousands of Black workers are classified as employed but never have an income that could lift them above the poverty level.

Yet, stark as this statistical report is, it cannot possibly convey the disaster of racism, poverty and oppression affecting every aspect of the lives of Black Americans today. The end of the decade of civil rights struggles left the Black masses with a feeling of vast frustration; not only had their condition failed to improve; it had worsened.

This frustration was simultaneously experienced by many militant young fighters, Black and white, whose despair turned to disillusion with the preceding years of struggle. They were unable to differentiate the gains of the Civil Rights Decade—in terms of unity, militant mass action and consciousness—from the deepening crisis. They did not realize that under capitalism the most important fruit of struggle is the people's advance in unity and consciousness. In their frustration, they attacked the Civil Rights struggle itself, instead of seeing that it had created a bridge to the period ahead.

Thus, even before the hunger and frustration of Black masses led to the spontaneous outbursts in Watts, Detroit and Newark, Dr. Martin Luther King, Jr. encountered attacks not only from reaction but from segments of militant youth under the influence of sectarianism and pseudo-revolutionism.

While the open attacks from the latter were a relatively new development, King had long experienced pressure from the establishment liberals, the NAACP, the Urban League and others to limit mass struggle and to rely on the courts and "friends" within the two major parties. In this period—as the war in Vietnam continued and domestic conditions worsened—this pressure from the Right increased and was particularly aimed at preventing King from linking the Black liberation movement with the anti-war struggle.

At the same time, the frustrations of radical youth were intensified by the escalation of the Vietnam war in 1965—immediately after the new Civil Rights Act was passed. Many Black and white radicals, including Carmichael, Cleaver, Newton, Forman and Hayden, began to step up their attacks on the Civil Rights struggle. *They placed themselves in opposition to King, who was determined not to abandon, but to strengthen the forces of the Civil Rights Decade, to deepen and broaden them into a realignment that could carry the struggle against poverty and racist oppression to a new level.*

If King was not without error in coping with pressure from the Right, and later with that of the pseudo-radicals, his overall record was one of firm adherence to militant non-violent mass struggle. The maturing of his leadership, his recognition of the decisive role of the working class, his evolvement toward an anti-imperialist position, all of his steady and remarkable growth reflected his rejection of both the opportunist pressures to limit mass struggle and the super-revolutionary pressures to substitute the rhetoric of violence for the power of mass struggle.

King has been dead more than five years, but the attacks on his strategy and objectives continue from the Right and the pseudo-left. In fact, while Nixon is bent on destroying the advances of the Civil Rights Decade, it is ironic that the new "revolutionists" are so certain there is nothing worth saving from it! But Nixon recognizes—and fears—what the super-militants refuse to see; the Civil Rights Decade created the pre-conditions for the much higher level of struggle needed in the period ahead.

When King was assassinated in the spring of 1968, he was leading the strike of the predominantly Black sanitation workers of Memphis. His commitment to this courageous working-class struggle was a vibrant indication that in pressing for a new beginning in the strategy against racist oppression, poverty and war, he had come to a full realization of the meaning of his first major struggle, the Montgomery, Alabama bus boycott. This landmark battle was sparked by Mrs. Rosa Parks, a Black *working-class* woman, and carried on with courage and tenacity by primarily, Black working-class men and women. In the course of a decade of leadership of the liberation struggle, King came to understand that it was workers, more than any other stratum, who possess these qualities.

King realized that since these special qualities of workers had brought about the historic turning point in Montgomery, leading to the nation-wide involvement of many other sections of the population, including Black and white youth, in the struggle for equal rights, the new state—the struggle for jobs, for an end to poverty, racism and war—demanded a new strategy based on the working class, Black and white.

Although King's views were not identical with the Marxist conception of the role of the working class—which sees this class not only as the main social force but as the leader in the anti-monopoly struggle—he had come steadily closer to this outlook. *Moreover, it is especially meaningful that King moved in this direction at the time when Marcuse and others, with the assistance of the mass media, were making their greatest headway in promoting the idea among radical youth that the Marxist concept of the working class was outdated. . . .*

In Douglass' time, the strategy to break the slave power's control of Congress and the Federal Government was the pre-condition for the abolition of slavery. Today, the pre-condition for opening the path to the abolition of wage slavery and racist oppression through socialism is the strategy to defeat the threat of fascism and to break the monopolists' domination of Congress and the Federal Government.

"Whoever does not fight the reactionary measures of the bourgeoisie and the growth of fascism [in its] preparatory stages," stated Georgi Dimitrov, [before the Seventh World Congress of the Communist International on August 2, 1935], *"is not in a position to prevent the growth of fascism, but on the contrary, facilitates that victory."* (*United Front Against Fascism,* New Century Publishers, New York, 1950, p.9.)

The anti-coalition views of Carmichael, Forman, Boggs and others are nothing less than opposition to a united front against the "reactionary measures" with which monopoly prepares for its imposition of fascism.

However, regardless of the disruptive nature of the views of such Black radicals, it must be recognized that the main obstacle to Black and white unity against the common enemy is the influence of racism on white workers. And it is the primary responsibility of white revolutionaries to lead the fight against racist ideology and to mobilize white workers in the struggle against racism and in support of Black liberation as indispensable to the advance of their class interests.

The aim of monopoly is to force a reversal of every aspect of bourgeois democracy, limited as it is, in order to open the way for fascism. The aim of the anti-monopoly program, as advocated by the Communist Party, is to bring about a strategic breakthrough to a deeper and wider degree of

426

democracy, one that would powerfully accelerate the revolutionary process, opening the way to Black liberation and socialism.

Once this anti-monopoly strategy succeeds in breaking the control of state monopoly capital over Congress and the government, the forces exist, internally and internationally—in contrast to the anti-slavery period—that can prevent the betrayal of the struggle. There is such a perspective, and this is so, first of all, because the forces of class and national liberation, headed by the Soviet Union and the other socialist countries, have changed the world balance of power.

□ ——————————————————————————— □

THE ANGELA DAVIS CAMPAIGN

The Fight to Free Angela Davis,
Its Importance for the Working Class
by Charlene Mitchell, New Outlook Publishers, 1972

[*The acquittal of Angela Davis on June 4, 1972, twenty-one months after her arrest in a horrendous frame-up, was one of the outstanding events in the struggle for human rights in U.S. history. Angela Davis had been arrested on trumped-up charges of accomplice to murder and kidnapping on the spurious grounds that she had provided the guns for the tragic events which led to the fatal shooting of Jonathan Jackson, her close associate, two prisoners and the judge in a San Rafael, California courtroom. The charges carried the death penalty under California law.[3]*

The mass outcry in the country and internationally was initiated by the Communist Party. Instrumental in the campaign was the tireless and effective work of Franklin Alexander, Bettina Aptheker, Fania Jordan, Angela's sister, Sallye Davis, her mother, Charlene Mitchell, and the trial attorneys, Leo Branton, chief attorney, Doris Brin Walker, Margaret Burnham and Howard Moore, plus many others.

An important development following the campaign to free Angela Davis was the formation of the National Alliance Against Racist and Political Repression (NAARPR).

In six short years, the NAARPR has become an impressive national defense organization with branches all over the country. The Alliance continues the traditions of the International Labor Defense (1925-1946) and the Civil Rights Congress (1946-1956)[4] while at the same time it is much broader in scope. A new feature of the Alliance, both in leadership and membership, is the participation of a number of trade unions and the major representation of Chicano, Native American, Puerto Rican and Asian–American peoples.

A landmark case in the work of the Alliance has been the struggle around the Wilmington 10. A great national and international movement has arisen to win their vindication and freedom. As of now, only the courageous Rev. Ben Chavis, co-chairperson of the NAARPR, remains in prison.

A high point in the development of the campaign to free Angela Davis was a report by Central Committee member Charlene Mitchell (b. 1920) to the 20th Convention of the CPUSA held in New York in February, 1972. Mitchell was executive secretary of the National Committee to Free Angela Davis and is now executive secretary of the NAARPR.]

In the spring of 1969, at the time of the 19th Convention of our Party, we were discussing the increased repression in our country, the heightened attack on the leadership of radical organizations, especially Black organizations. Our convention sent a delegation to the demonstration in front of the New York State courthouse on behalf of the incarcerated Panther 21. The Panthers have since been acquitted in a people's victory, although these young men and women were denied any semblance of due process in almost two years of captivity, not to speak of the trumped-up charges that were the pretext for taking years out of their lives.

Little did we imagine that by the time of our 20th Convention our comrade, Angela Davis, would have spent more than 16 months in one jail cell after another on framed-up charges of murder, kidnapping and conspiracy, denied bail, and that it would be necessary to fight vigorously for even the most meager conveniences in detention.

Angela Davis is the object of a vicious, diabolical conspiracy. A conspiracy on the part of State and Federal governments. A conspiracy which involves directly the executive and judicial branches of government and their respective arms, the F.B.I. and the courts.

Communists have always known that capitalism, especially through its most reactionary spokesmen and leaders, is capable of unleashing everything at its disposal when its absolute rule appears to be threatened. Throughout the life of our Party, our comrades have been arrested, jailed, tried, convicted and imprisoned whenever the ruling class went on a reactionary right-wing path. The last such rampage was during the McCarthy period of the '50s, when the leadership of our Party was forced to spend a total of more than 100 years in prison. The conditions and events of that imprisonment resulted in the death of one comrade,

Robert Thompson, and the blinding of another, Henry Winston, now the National Chairman of our Party. Death, blindness and long years taken out of their lives and their leadership to our Party and our class on trumped-up charges under the infamous Smith Act!

We do not see the long punitive detention of comrade Angela as accidental. . . . Angela fights for an end to the racism that pollutes our entire country and is perpetuated by the ruling class and all its agents. She challenges their racist, imperialist aggression in Indochina and Southeast Asia, their role in the Middle East and their direct aid to the racist regimes in South Africa, Rhodesia and Portugal. Angela Davis struggles especially for the freedom of political prisoners and the ending of a prison system of which a major aim is to punish people on the basis of their color and their class, a prison system that attempts to dehumanize rather than rehabilitate, a prison system that intensifies the inherent racism of U.S. capitalism. Indeed, Angela challenges the very existence of the capitalist system which the rulers of our country hold so dear. . . .

In short, Angela Davis sat for months in a small windowless cell in Palo Alto, California, denied bail, because she is a Black woman and a Communist whose attempts to organize the exploited and oppressed were succeeding. That is why Angela Davis was deprived of her liberty and denied her constitutional and human rights. That is why she must be set free.

From October 13, 1971, the date of Angela's arrest, the sympathetic sentiment expressed itself immediately from California to New York. The groundswell of support has been unprecedented, especially in the Black community. Black people feared that Angela might be killed when the F.B.I., by placing her at the top of its "10 most wanted" list, issued what was tantamount to a license to any policeman or crazed racist to take her life. Black people know from their own history the lengths to which the racist ruling class will go to stop or set back the movement for freedom. Accordingly, Black people were among the first to see the frameup for what it is.

The Communist Party, prior to the arrest, had already assigned some of our foremost leading members to begin a movement to remove Angela from the F.B.I.'s "wanted" list and allow her to return to her community and her work. With Angela's arrest, these comrades, along with many non-Communists, brought into being the National United Committee to Free Angela Davis (NUCFAD). Franklin Alexander, then chairman of the Che-Lumumba Club of the Party in Los Angeles and member of the Southern California District Committee of the Party, along with Fania Davis Jordan (Angela's sister) who later joined the Communist Party, became the national coordinators of the committee. Within three months there were committees in most major cities throughout the nation. Demonstrations, meetings, rallies, events for fund-raising, obtaining resolutions and gathering petitions became the major work of thousands of people throughout the country. And Communists were the key organizers of this spontaneous sentiment for Angela's freedom.

The international support was almost immediate. Our general secretary, Comrade Gus Hall, held a press conference upon the heels of the arrest and telegrams and resolutions of protest went to Governors Rockefeller of New York and Reagan of California and to President Nixon demanding Angela's release. Telegrams and letters of support came in by the thousands from the socialist countries. Gatherings of peace, women's, trade union and educational organizations in the Soviet Union sent telegrams of protest. Angela Davis Committees were set up in many socialist countries. In the German Democratic Republic a card and letter writing campaign was launched that is unsurpassed. It is not unimportant to note that the people in the German Democratic Republic understand from first-hand experience the relationship between racism, anti-communism and repression.

The African National Congress and other organizations in many African countries joined the world protest. In European countries, including France, Denmark, Italy and Britain, Angela Davis Defense Committees were set up. Resolutions and protests began pouring in from India.

In Latin America, socialist Cuba took the lead in forming a committee to free Angela. Committees also came into being in Chile, Mexico and Venezuela.

Today, if you visit a horse farm in socialist Mongolia and enter the dwelling of any family, you will find a poster on the wall with a picture of Angela and the slogan "Free Angela."

In our own country the movement for Angela has become a nation-wide phenomenon. Many prominent individuals have publicly gone on record for Angela's freedom. They include Rev. Ralph D. Abernathy of the Southern Christian Leadership Conference; Charles Hayes of the Packinghouse Workers; Ossie Davis; Anne Braden, Southern Conference Educational Fund; David Livingston, Distributive Workers, District 65; elected officials including Ron Dellums, Mervyn Dymally, Jackie Vaughn, Coleman Young, Julian Bond, Sidney Von Luther and John Conyers. . . .

The support that Angela has won is so unprecedented that it was recorded by the Marin County, California, probation officer, who declared: "I also feel that since August 7, 1970, some significant things have happened that have a bearing on her case. She has received a great deal of support from numerous people in the country for her position. She is looked upon by a great number of people in this country as a leader for social reforms. There is, in my estimation, a commitment on Miss Davis' part to her family, attorneys and supporters who have given their time, skills and money to her case." . . .

Increasing numbers realize that there are many people in the jails and prisons throughout this country because of their political beliefs and their political activities. They are further realizing that many of the people who are in prisons have become rehabilitated in the fullest sense, that is, they are prisoners who have come to learn that their real enemy is capitalism and have decided on a course of political organizing as a means of obtaining redress of their grievances rather than returning to a life of petty crime.

Fleeta Drumgo and John Cluchette, the two remaining "Soledad Brothers" (George Jackson was brutally murdered by prison guards at San Quentin, August 21, 1971), now on trial in California, personify the injustice of the racist court system in the U.S. These two young men are guilty of no crime, yet are on trial for their lives. The case against them, contains not one iota of evidence. The prosecution has not been able to produce one single witness that can say he saw these two men kill a Soledad prison guard. Yet this is the crime of which they stand accused. These brothers have been framed. NUCFAD has correctly characterized their trial as a political trial. They are on trial because they were attempting to organize the prisoners in Soledad prison. [Fleeta Drumgo and John Cluchette have since been acquitted of this charge.]

Ruchell Magee has finally been successful in getting a new hearing on his original conviction. He has demanded the right to defend himself since public defenders have continually neglected to fight for his elementary rights. NUCFAD has sought to bring into the open the case of Ruchell Magee.

Indeed, the reality is that the fight to free Angela Davis becomes a struggle to free all political prisoners. . . .

Earlier we have spoken about support from numerous trade unions and organizations, yet there are only two trade union internationals that have spoken out, the American Federation of Teachers and the International Longshoremen's and Warehousemen's Union. It is of great importance that the World Federation of Trade Unions has endorsed the campaign for Angela's freedom. But where are the international unions whose main centers are in our own country? It becomes strikingly apparent that as of this moment the organized working class as a whole has not seen the relationship between racist repression and labor's own future. . . .

Unfortunately, as yet the working class as a whole has not seen the need to throw its organized weight into support of a sister trade unionist, Angela Davis.

It is true that the bourgeois ideology of racism has found acceptance by large numbers of white workers. It is also true that these workers can be won to understand that there are a great number of similarities between the designs of the Nixon Administration on the rights of all workers and the increasing withdrawal and denial of fundamental rights of all Black people, including Black workers. . . .

In short, Angela Davis represents not only a challenge to the racist, jingoist monopoly interests, but also a challenge to our Party and our class. Angela's freedom is directly linked to our ability to restore basic fundamental democratic rights. Moreover, her freedom opens the door to the extension of those rights to all who live in the United States. Though the white working class has been indoctrinated with the ideology of racism, it is far from correct to conclude that white workers cannot be won to the struggle to free Angela and other political prisoners. Indeed, the aforementioned union support through the leadership of Black trade unionists represents thousands of white trade unionists. The struggle to win white workers to fight racism not only must but can be won. This is a foremost task of white Communists.

NOTE: In an unprecedented victory, after a thirteen week trial, the jury declared Angela Davis innocent, on Sunday, June 4, 1972 at 12:30 p.m. This was hailed by the *Daily World* in a Special Issue on Tuesday, June 6, 1972.

□ ———————————————————————————————— □

THE STRUGGLE FOR JOBS

"Where Next in the Struggle for Jobs?" by Daniel Rubin, *Political Affairs*, October, 1975

[*Four months prior to the Party's twenty-first national convention (February 27, 1975), a national emergency meeting of Party leaders was convened where Gus Hall, in a critical report, stated that the work of the organization was insufficient to the requirements of the time. He out-*

lined a program *"to build a broad people's front in the struggle against the economic crisis." ("Build a People's Front Against the Economic Crisis!" by Gus Hall,* Political Affairs, *April 1975, p. 7.)*

The Party had already taken steps in helping to initiate demonstrations on November 16, 1974. This was a harbinger of the possibility of organizing greater mass action. An effective movement embracing different political views established a united front which took the shape of the National Coalition to Fight Inflation and Unemployment (NCFIU).

Daniel Rubin (b. 1931), a national Party leader, here gives his attention to the problems growing out of the economic crisis.]

[The] depression which began by official estimates in November 1973 . . . is now nearly two years old. As occurred during the Great Depression, it is likely to be of prolonged duration with some minor upturns in business activity during the course of it. But as Comrade Gus Hall, in his report to the 21st National Convention of the Communist Party, pointed out, we are dealing not only with the classical and inevitable business cycle of capitalism but also with the long-term phenomenon of the general crisis of capitalism, which is now in a new stage. The ability to mount a strong recovery, including with respect to employment levels, is much reduced by the generally weakened position of world capitalism and U.S. imperialism in particular and by imperialism's much sharper internal contradictions.

The outlook, therefore, for a very extended period, if not for the remaining life of capitalism, is for severe problems of mass unemployment, high rates of inflation and attempts by the ruling class to restore business activity at the expense of the masses. This would be done by . . . increasing exploitation and decreasing the working people's share of the national income by speedup, by undermining health and safety on the job, by drastic cuts in services, by maintaining an astronomical military budget and by shifting the actual tax burden even more onto the working people. . . .

Only a high level of organized, united, clear-sighted struggle by the working-class, Black and other specially oppressed peoples as a whole and middle strata, can defeat this program of the monopolies and protect the masses from the consequences of these objective processes of capitalism.

This crisis has caused massive suffering. The standard of living of the vast majority of the people is being driven down. According to official figures, the number of those living in poverty has increased by 1.3 million in 1974, to 24.3 million, while the real median income has decreased by 4 per cent compared to 1973. Two million have lost their job health plans and nearly a million have exhausted their unemployment benefits.

This, of course, does not tell the full story in human terms—the universal fear of poverty and starvation and insecurity among the masses. Among Black people unemployment is officially 13.7 per cent. Figures are similar among Chicanos, Puerto Ricans, Native American Indian and Asian-American peoples. Among youth a "jobless generation" is emerging, with rates among Black youth running as high as 65 per cent.[5] Women workers are also especially hard hit. There are growing numbers of instances of senior citizens, again especially Black seniors, who freeze to death because their utilities have been shut off or because of malnutrition. Vast areas of the cities, especially ghettos and barrios, look like the bombed-out cities of World War II. . . .

While the problems in New York City are the most acute, a substantial number of other cities are . . . similarly affected and the prospect is for an almost universal crisis development in the cities. This involves substantial cuts in the quantity and quality of education, health, cultural and recreational programs available and in garbage collection, street repair, mass transit, etc., but higher costs in fees or taxes for working people. Again we are dealing with problems of the living conditions of the masses which are long-term and will not go away of their own accord. . . .

The only real answers . . . are radical ones. Winning a radical program requires mass mobilization of the broadest sections of the people. Mobilization starts with projecting demands for the vital needs of the masses which they can identify as being in their interests.

Such a program of demands on the federal government includes 5-10 million jobs immediately in meaningful public works and service jobs at trade union wages for all the unemployed; a uniform national sytem of unemployment compensation providing coverage for every jobless worker including first time jobseekers, for the entire duration of unemployment at 75 per cent or more of normal wages. Also needed is amendment of the Wages and Hours Act to provide a shorter work week without reduction in pay—30 for 40 would provide millions more jobs at the expense of the big companies, not the workers. Removal of trade restrictions with the Soviet Union, Cuba and all other socialist countries would provide many more jobs. . . .

Most of the governmental budget comes from working people and is spent for the benefit of the monopolies. The biggest bonanza for monopoly and quite contrary to the interests of the masses is the hundred billion-plus military budget. Radically slashing it could provide funds for most of the needed programs.

434

By Ollie Harrington, *Daily World,* 1979

Closing tax loopholes for the big corporations and super-rich and other methods of radically shifting the burden of financing the federal budget can provide the necessary funds for the people's needs and still reduce deficit spending.

Deficit spending increases the amount of the people's tax money being funnelled by the budget to pay principal and interest to finance capitalists—who are the lenders. It also gives finance capital an ever greater hold on governmental spending and activity in general, as is demonstrated most clearly in the New York City budget crisis. With a different class orientation, it is possible at all levels, including the city one, to find alternatives to finance programs for the people without further deficit financing and with a substantial decrease of taxes on working people. . . .

The current mass movement for real solutions to the crisis is unprecedented, especially among workers. . . . Every major city in the country has seen some major labor rally or demonstration of the AFL-CIO and of many rank-and-file groups. Strike struggles, in numbers and duration, are exceptionally high. This is quite atypical of a depression, when workers are supposed to be on the defensive and afraid to strike for fear of loss of union and/or job. The April 26, [1975] Washington, D.C. action of 75,000 workers, sponsored by the Industrial Union Department, was a high point. There is a growth of rank-and-file union groups demanding more militant and class-conscious unionism. Some groups associated with Trade Unionists for Action and Democracy (TUAD) and the Coalition of Labor Union Women, have been active on these issues, as has been the Coalition of Black Trade Unionists (CBTU).

For a considerable period community–based actions, often with local labor participation, centered on inflation. These included food market picketing, meat boycotts, rent control fights and innumerable demonstrations, boycotts and lobbying efforts against increased utility rates. Last November 16 a broad coalition organized actions in 35 cities against inflation and unemployment. This coalition grew into the NCFIU which helped to stimulate the April 26 Washington action. It has held innumerable local actions, collected a couple of hundred thousand signatures on petitions, built local affiliates in more than 30 cities and organized a number of committees of the unemployed. The youth contingent of the NCFIU, in which Youth United for Jobs plays a major role, has brought out thousands of youth in a number of actions for jobs for youth—summer and otherwise. Women for Racial and Economic Equality has also been very active on these issues. . . .

Besides CBTU, the Urban League, the NAACP, Operation PUSH and to a lesser extent SCLC and a host of anti-poverty and other groups and many leading individuals in the Black community have been active on these issues, many in association with NCFIU. . . .

The fight for unity is an absolute necessity that needs ever more emphasis. It is complex. What disunites also must be considered. To call for unity based on a demand for full employment, while avoiding the special demands and needs of Black and other oppressed people cannot achieve unity. . . . It is a capitulation to the influence of ruling-class racism among masses. This combining of demands must be done with skill, so that white workers can see their stake in achieving unity on such a basis.

□ ——————————————————————————— □

BLACK CAUCUSES

Black Workers and the Class Struggle by Roscoe Proctor,
New Outlook Publishers, 1972

[*The Black Caucus movement in the trade unions took a great surge
forward in the late 1960s as Black workers brought the militancy of the
civil rights demonstrations into the shops. Here, encountering the racist
injustices which they had experienced in society at large, they organized
themselves into caucuses to advance their special demands.*

*The Black caucuses dovetailed with the developing rank-and-file
movement and strengthened working-class unity as well as the fighting
mood of the trade unions.*

*Roscoe Proctor (b. 1921), former legislative director, Oakland Divi-
sion of the International Longshoremen's and Warehousemen's Union,
Local 6, now national secretary of the Trade Union Department of the
Communist Party, discusses this trend in the labor movement.*]

Within the past generation, as a result of the civil rights movement,
migration to urban areas (North and South), changes in class composition, growth in trade union membership, increased Black awareness and
growing repression, an increased militancy can be registered among
Black people in the United States. This militancy finds expression,
among other forms, in a growing number of all-Black formations. These
have come into existence primarily to deal with and give leadership on
the problems of racism and on finding the path to eradicating our special
oppression.

These forms have sprung up in every area of life—in the community, in
the church, in Congress, in political parties, in police departments, in
campus Black studies programs, etc. But most important of all has been
the proliferation of independent Black formations within the trade union
movement. This is a positive development. The new level of struggle
conducted by these caucuses against speedup, bad working conditions
and increased repression in the plants is a struggle to raise the job
standards of all workers. Such caucuses are an integral part of the whole
rank-and-file upsurge and the sharpest attack on racism. This struggle
against racism is a struggle for the unity of the whole class.

There has also been an increased exposure of young Black people to
workingclass ideas, Marxist ideas. Some of these Black formations are
beginning to see the need to change the system itself as the ultimate

solution to Black oppression. This is new and highly significant for the advancement of the class struggle. This poses a serious question—the need for coordinating these all-Black forms within the context of the class struggle. . . .

While racist oppression is to a greater or lesser extent a common experience shared by all Black people and hence the struggle for complete equality unites all classes, it must be recognized that all of the major class divisions existing within the U.S. capitalist society are to be found among Black people. We as Black people have our own bourgeoisie, urban petty bourgeoisie and small farmers, plus our own workers—industrial and other. However, the significant fact about the class composition of Black people is that we are 94 per cent working class. More than 9 million Black people are now in the U.S. work force. We contribute a much larger proportion of the industrial proletariat than our proportion to the total work force. Black men and women working in basic industry totaled more than 2,700,000 in 1969.

An even more significant fact is that Black workers are located in the main at the heart of the production process: in the past 10 years Black operatives in basic industry increased by 600,000 and now total 2,004,000. In some industries we constitute the majority of all production workers. In others we constitute a majority in certain departments, especially where the work is hard, hot, heavy and dirty and where racism is more pronounced. Because of racism, we have been excluded from apprenticeship training and job upgrading programs. There are 250,000 Black steel workers and 300,000 Black UAW members. The majority of Local 10 of the ILWU on the West Coast—the biggest local in the longshore division—are Black, and 30,000 of the 116,000 longshoremen on the East Coast and Gulf ports are Black. The same proportions hold true for rubber, chemical, transportation and meatcutters as well as for many of the service industries, like hotel and restaurant, hospital, building service and government workers. . . .

Today Black caucuses are springing up in every major industry in the country. Like their historic predecessors, these movements are aimed mainly at the elimination of all forms of racial discrimination and oppression in the industries, the unions and the communities. What is new is that many of these caucuses reflect a deepening class consciousness among Black workers, and that many of their participants are open to or in some cases have already accepted the idea that fundamental, revolutionary change of the capitalist system is necessary for the achievement of total liberation for Black people. This is a highly significant development.

These new caucus movements fall into two main categories—those based in the shops and unions and those based in the communities. Most of the shop and union-based caucuses are made up of and led by rank-and-file workers, whose main concern is to change the racist policies and practices at the point of production and in the unions. There are also a number of caucuses made up exclusively of Black full-time union staffers, whose main interests are in the election of more Black workers to union offices at the International level, and in equal treatment for all Black staff members in regard to benefits, pensions, assignments, expenses, etc. . . .

A survey of many of these caucuses shows a wide variety of issues and demands being raised by them, including the right to strike, hiring of people who are unemployed or on welfare, reduction in the number of foremen and the amount of repression in the plants, no speed-up, elimination of tests in hiring or promotions which are unrelated to the skills required for the job, no discriminatory penalties and firings of Black workers, job training and upgrading programs for Black youth, equal job and promotion opportunities for all Black workers, a "say" by the unions in the introduction of any new, automated equipment into the plants. They are also raising such demands as the right to wear political pins on the job, such as Angela Davis buttons or Black liberation symbols. . . .

Many of these caucuses exist only at the local level, in one shop. Others are national formations, with chapters in many local areas. Among the industries in which caucuses exist are steel (four different caucuses, national in scope), auto (with caucuses in all of the Big Three), aircraft, foundries, telephone, longshore, transit, teachers, postal workers, building trades, etc. . . .

Today there is a need for a national Black workers' coordinating body. Its focus should be to coordinate efforts and activities of Black caucuses within the unions and to bring its experience, its strengths and its organization skills, as well as the strength of the entire labor movement, to the struggle being waged for equality and freedom within the Black community. With Black workers being the largest section of the Black community, the section that has the deepest roots in the organized sector of the trade union movement, we should, as Black workers, act as a bridge in uniting both of these movements, while at the same time combatting the evils and short-sightedness of racism that still exist within the trade union movement. The development of political class-consciousness among Black workers and the development of the Left trend within the labor movement is a decisive factor in the struggle for the advancement of the cause of all Black people and the elimination of our oppression.

□ ———————————————————————————————— □

INDIAN LIBERATION

"Wounded Knee and the Indian Future" by John Pittman, *Political Affairs*, July, 1973

[*A dramatic event in US Indian history was the 71-day occupation of the village of Wounded Knee in South Dakota by several score US Indians during February 27-May 8, 1973. Indian activities have proceeded beyond appeals to Washington. Their protests are being heard in the United Nations and by delegations to Europe, especially to socialist countries.*

John Pittman (b. 1906), a leading Afro-American Communist journalist and author with extensive national experience has also a wide knowledge in the international arena, which he contributes to an analysis of the new movement of the US Indian people.]

The 71-day occupation of the South Dakota hamlet of Wounded Knee by several score Native Americans, February 27-May 8, opened the year of 1973 with an exposure of monopoly greed and government perfidy in respect to the Indian peoples of the United States of North America. During the occupation there began another exposure of monopoly greed and duplicity of high government officials in respect to the laboring majority of the US population.... Wounded Knee brought into focus the 500 year-long conspiracy between government and private interests that has dispossessed the Indian peoples of 97 per cent of their land (1.9 billion acres), reduced them to chronic hunger and abysmal destitution, and today is continuing the theft of the remaining 3 per cent (55 million acres) and attempting to drive them into monopoly capital's reserve army of unemployed and underemployed labor....

In this sense, then, Wounded Knee signaled the urgent need of the U.S. laboring majority in their own self-interest to act in solidarity with the Indian peoples against the monopolies and their servile politicians. It challenged the sensitivity of the majority to sufferings inflicted on racially oppressed and exploited minorities. It pierced the virtually impenetrable miasma of racism and lies that has dehumanized Indians in the eyes of the majority and made them objects of hatred and ridicule, sometimes of pity, always of exploitation and violence. This was one of the stated objectives of the occupation's leaders. Obviously, they hoped their selfless action on the site of the mass grave of 300 of their unarmed ancestors, massacred by U.S. troops in December, 1890, would move the U.S. majority to support their demands in sufficient numbers to render unnecessary further Wounded Knees by the more than 300 tribes of Indian peoples.

The demands of the Wounded Knee Indians centered on the grievances of the 11,000–member Oglala Sioux tribe of the 2,500 square-mile Pine Ridge Reservation in South Dakota, second largest of the 265 federally-recognized land units reserved for Indians. The per capita annual income on this reservation, including welfare, is $850; the unemployment rate is 54 per cent in summer and 70 per cent in winter; and the pushout rate by the 12th grade in schools where 70 per cent of the teachers are white, is 81 per cent. . . .

Accordingly, the Wounded Knee spokesman demanded re-examination by the federal government of the status of treaties with the Oglala Sioux, and strict observance of the terms of the treaties in regard to the tribe's land and the obligation undertaken by the government to protect Indian lives and provide such services as health care, housing, employment, development and education. Other grievances expressed but subordinated to this main demand called for an end to "cultural genocide" in the schools and religious matters, for control of Indian education by the Indians themselves, for an end to the atrocities and brutalities inflicted on Indians by state police and vigilantes. . . .

With few exceptions, the monopoly-controlled U.S. information media suppressed the main demands or minimized their importance. Instead, the media gave maximum coverage to day-to-day events of the Indians' confrontation as the product of a "deep tribal split," the media and the government concealed its real character—that of a national liberation struggle by the Indians against the continuing plunder of the land and resources by private interests, with the aid of the federal government and its officials, and the default of the government on its commitments to provide protection and the public services for the Indians. Such a distortion of reality obviously conceals from non-Indian working people the connection of the Wounded Knee occupation to the struggle of the U.S. majority to defend their liberties and livelihood from attacks by the same monopolies and government officials.

Actually, to head off non-Indian support for Wounded Knee, some government officials and media organs and even [Richard] Wilson [tribal president] and his allies, resorted to crude outbursts of anti-communism. They tried to discredit the occupation leaders by depicting them as "outsiders," and as one white vigilante said, "Chicanos, Negroes, Russians and Cherokees . . . the American Communist movement." The Oglala Sioux, of course, knew the truth. More than a month before the occupation, after failing to impeach Wilson, three groups of the tribe—the Landowners, Treaty Council and Civil Rights Organization—had invited the American Indian Association (AIA) to help in dramatizing the tribe's grievances.

Although Wounded Knee projected the grievances and demands specifically of the Oglala Sioux, these were also generalizations of longstanding grievances and aspirations of the Indian peoples as a whole, who number approximately 850,000 by 1970 census count, including Alaska, but several times more if allowance is made of census under-counting and exclusion of many Chicanos and others of Indian descent. These grievances and demands go back to before the founding of the United States. "From the beginning," says the U.S. Senate Sub-committee on Indian Education in Appendix I of its Report, "Federal policy toward the Indian was based on the desire to dispossess him of his land. . . . Treaties, almost always signed under duress, were the window-dressing whereby we expropriated the Indian's land and pushed him back across the continent." From 1778 to 1871, through nearly 400 treaties and agreements "the Indian tribes ceded to the United States almost a billion acres. Although treaty provisions vary, in general, the Indians retained lands for their own use which were to be inalienable and tax exempt. The Federal government in turn agreed to provide public services such as education, medical care, technical and agricultural training." (Government Printing Office, Washington, D.C., 1969, pp. 142, 143.) . . .

When President Nixon on July 8, 1970, announced a new policy purporting to give the Indians self-determination, to continue acting as their trustee and protecting their land and resources, and ordered a restructuring of the Bureau of Indian Affairs (BIA), illusions arose that the Indians' grievances were at long last being heard. For several months certain new developments strengthened these illusions. Then came the awakening. Not only did the Nixon Administration fail to press Congress for adoption of enabling legislation to implement the promises, but other Nixon measures—revenue-sharing with the states, increasing military expenditures, policies fostering racial animosity among the white majority against the non-white minorities—in effect nullified the gesture of a new policy for the Indians and exposed its demagogic intent. . . .

[W]hen the BIA was transferred to Health, Education and Welfare, many Indians interpreted the move as a step toward reviving the old termination policy, abandoning them to the states, repudiating all obligations under treaties, and laying the groundwork for seizing the rest of their land. During 1970, more than 200,000 acres passed out of their hands. And under terms concluded as recently as 1971, the Indians of Alaska have been deprived of all but 10 million acres of the state's 375 million acres. . . .

Conditions of both reservation and urban Indians continue to deteriorate. "Life expectancy of a reservation Indian is 43 years; only 33 in Alaska and Arizona," writes William Meyer, whose Anglicized Cherokee name is Burning Bear. "Infant mortality is twice that of the rest of America. We have a 50 per cent high school dropout rate. . . . Jobs simply do not exist on the reservations. Unemployment may be normally as high as 75 per cent. . . . The yearly earnings of most reservation families fall far below the national level of poverty." (*Native Americans: The New Indian Resistance,* International Publishers, New York, 1971, pp. 43–44.) The approximately 400,000 Indians living in cities (by the 1970 census estimate but about six times that number according to Indian estimates) have found, for the most part, their change of residence has been from one area of poverty to another. In the conditions of growing automation and cybernation, of racist discrimination by both employers and trade unions, the untrained, unskilled Indian newcomers land on the bottom of the job ladder, receiving the lowest wages for the dirtiest, most onerous work, and living in the worst conditions of urban blight and official neglect. . . .

Confronted with these increasing threats to their lives and their lands, to their very survival, the Indian peoples have renewed and increased their resistance. Recent demonstrative actions and confrontations, of which Wounded Knee is an example, reflect this trend. Occupations of Alcatraz Island in San Francisco Bay, Ellis Island in New York Harbor, numerous offices of the BIA including the headquarters building in Washington, D.C., and abandoned U.S. military and other installations; demonstrations in Boston and Plymouth, Massachusetts, on anniversaries of the landing of the Pilgrims . . .; fish-ins on the Quillayute, Puyallup, Yakima, Green, Nisqually and Columbia Rivers and the Puget Sound waters of the Pacific Northwest;[6] the seizure of an area of Lassen National Forest and other territory claimed by the Pit River Indians of California; appeals for intervention in their behalf to the United Nations—these and other manifestations of their resistance during the last decade have broken through the conspiracy of the government and the media to forestall the U.S. majority's awareness and support of their just demands. None of these recent actions was more important, however, in presenting a carefully formulated and detailed program for the Indians' future than that of the convergence of Indian caravans in Washington, D.C. on the eve of the November 7, 1972, national elections.

The "Trail of Broken Treaties and Pan-American Native Quest for Justice," as its organizers called it, was, in the words of one of its two co-chairmen, Robert Burnette of the Rosebud Sioux, "the first national Indian effort we have ever made." The action and the "position paper," a manifesto of 20 demands, were planned and formulated by representatives of eight national Indian organizations and endorsed by four others. The first four–mile–long caravan arrived in Washington just before dawn on November 2 and was joined by other caravans before the Trail's mission ended November 8, after the country's first inhabitants had been cold-shouldered by the government, threatened with violence, and forced to prepare defenses in the BIA building against forcible eviction by massed federal police and troops.

Of the 20 demands presented to the government, 15 seek a redefinition of relations between the Indian peoples and government on federal, state and local levels, and propose the establishment of institutions in keeping with such relations according to a proposed timetable. The nub of these 15 demands is the assertion of the sovereignty of "Indian Tribes and Nations," and the insistence that "all Indian people in the United States shall be considered to be in treaty relations with the federal government governed by doctrines of such relationship." The remaining five demands call for restoration of the Indians' land base to 110 million acres, including 40 million acres in Alaska; protection of the Indians' religious freedom and cultural integrity; guarantees of the right of self-government and the establishment of means to implement that right; control by the Indian communities of governmental functions for health, housing, employment, economic development and education. . . .

[O]n January 9, the White House rejected the 20 proposals of the Trail of Broken Treaties. On May 31, the White House rejected the Wounded Knee demands, claiming in a letter to the traditional leaders of the Sioux that only Congress has the power to make basic changes in the government's relations with the Indian peoples.

From this it is evident that support of the non-Indian majority is essential for achieving a just and democratic solution of the problems of the Indian Peoples. In the coming struggle to forge this support, Marxism-Leninism offers tested and proven guide-lines. Especially topical and relevant are the appeals of Marx and Engels to the English working class

444

to cast off its own exploiters by joining the Irish struggle for emancipation from the same oppressors. So too were the anniversary observances last year of 50 years of the Union of Socialist Soviet Republics. Its successes in establishing equality both in law and in fact for the more than 100 nations and nationalities within its borders, and in developing relations of friendship and mutual cooperation among them, are a major source of its present power and prestige. These successes were fruits of the efforts of the Bolsheviks under the leadership of Lenin during their long struggle to win the Russian workers for the liberation of the nations and peoples oppressed by czarism. They are instructive especially in relation to the struggles of the peoples of the Soviet Northern and Central Asian territories; peoples whose conditions were similar to those of the Indian peoples of the U.S.A.

□ ──────────────────────────────── □

CHICANO PEOPLE: HISTORY OF OPPRESSION

Short History of Chicano Workers by Lorenzo Torres, Pamphlet, Reprint from *Political Affairs*, October-November 1973

[*The resolution of the CPUSA Twentieth Convention, says: "The Indian and Chicano people were stripped of their land, and this gigantic plunder laid the basis for the most advanced capitalist form of agricultural developments in Texas, California, Colorado and Arizona. Hundreds of thousands of Mexicans were brought across the borders, and together with Chicanos became the main source of labor in the mines, on the railroads, and later in steel, auto, the building trades and giant agricultural industry."* (Toward Chicano Liberation—the Communist Party Position, *New Outlook Publishers, 1972, p. 5.*)

Lorenzo Torres (b. 1927), a former leader of the copper miners, now chairman of the Party's Chicano Liberation Commission, outlines some major events in the struggles of Chicano workers.]

Chicanos are to be found in all categories of workers, but in their great majority they are to be found in the hardest, dirtiest and hottest jobs in modern industry, most often in unorganized shops. For Chicano workers job promotion has meant a long, hard-fought battle extending over all of their history.

Great-power chauvinism, racism, discrimination, terror and deportation have been the main weapons used by capitalism to block the advance of the Chicano workers. Historically, Chicanos have been among the last hired and first fired. All of these undemocratic and terrorist tactics are designed to keep the Chicano workers in the status of a source of cheap labor—of surplus labor in times of recession and readily available cheap labor in times of economic upsurge.

Many of the racist tactics developed against Black slaves and the genocidal tactics developed to eliminate the Indian population have been used also against Mexican and Chicano workers. The National Guard, vigilante groups, hangings, kidnappings, the police, the Immigration Service, court injunctions, peace bonds and all sorts of other devices—legal and illegal—have been used to keep the Chicano worker in his place, that is, at the lowest economic level. He has been confined to segregated towns where the company is the master—the law, the prosecutor and the jury. Oppression, segregation and super-exploitation have been the norm for all Chicano people. Yet through all of this they have struggled and survived. . . .

Perhaps one of the most interesting pieces of militant labor history is the story of the role of Chicano, Black and white rank-and-file workers in the Mine, Mill and Smelter Workers Union. This union, which was the successor of the Western Federation of Miners, did a magnificent job of organizing in the non-ferrous mining industry in the late thirties and early forties under the banner of the CIO.

But its success in organizing extended only to the unskilled and semi-skilled production workers. The skilled workers, Anglos for the most part, chose to remain in the craft unions. This resulted in the creation of a dozen small, powerless unions, and the burden for conducting any really effective negotiations thus fell upon the shoulders of the production workers. In the Southwest these were in the main Chicano miners and in the South they were mainly Black workers. Only in the East, Midwest and Northwest were there largely Anglo workers in the Union.

After World War II, came an upsurge of the anti-Communist drive. In 1947 the Taft–Hartley Act was passed with its Section 9H prohibiting Communists from holding union office. In 1949 Mine–Mill was thrown out of the CIO along with eleven other Left-led unions. An alliance was then formed to destroy Mine–Mill. The mining corporations, the United Steelworkers and the federal Justice Department joined in a well-financed, well-organized drive, based on anti-Communism, to destroy the union.

In order to hold its own, Mine–Mill had to consolidate its strength to meet the onslaught of raiding by the United Steelworkers, legal actions by the Justice Department and attacks by the corporations. In these struggles two organizational forms were adopted by the workers: 1) the formation of company-wide bargaining councils, and 2) the organization of a Black and Brown caucus to deal with area wage differentials and discrimination. (Neither form is now permitted within the United Steelworkers, with which Mine-Mill eventually merged.)

It was through these company-wide councils that the workers were able to render ineffective the 80-day "cooling-off" periods imposed under the Taft-Hartley Act to restrain unions from striking. The companies found that they could not tolerate the chill of non-producing workers. An interesting feature of these councils is that for the most part they were under Chicano leadership. . . .

From the foregoing we can reach certain conclusions which I hope will serve as guidelines for work, principally for trade union rank-and-file movements, Communists and other democratic forces who are concerned with developing a strong, class-conscious workingclass movement in the United States. . . .

Chicanos are a city people. Urbanization among them is practically as great as among the population as a whole. In addition, a very large part of the rural workers are machine operators—workers, not peasants.

In their largest numbers, Chicano workers are employed in manufacturing, construction and mining. They are mainly operatives, craftsmen and laborers. According to a *Business Week* report, in the western states they hold from 32 to 50 per cent of the jobs in basic industry.

Chicano workers are concentrated especially in underground mining. Some of these mines in Arizona and New Mexico operate with 85 per cent to nearly 100 per cent Chicano labor. In fact there are some places in which the only whites who go underground are supervisors or engineers.

The percentage of Chicano workers in basic industry is much higher than their percentage in the population as a whole. According to the census figures, in Texas 14.5 per cent of the population is Chicano, in Colorado 10.2 per cent, in New Mexico 34.6 per cent, in Arizona 16 per cent, and in California 13.5 per cent. To be sure, the census figures undercount the Chicano population, but not nearly enough to negate the basic pattern.

This indicates the basis for the stability of the Chicano population, since these jobs today are maintained through the operation of seniority clauses. It also explodes the jingoist picture of the "lazy Mexican."

Furthermore, it poses the demand for effective Chicano representation in the higher levels of leadership of the trade unions. There are at present no Chicano or Black executive board members in the United Steel-workers or in the California AFL-CIO setup. I know of only one Chicano (J. J. Rodriguez) who holds a statewide executive office. Though I have no precise knowledge with regard to other unions, the indications are that the situation is pretty much the same.

We must emphasize again that the high proportion of Chicano workers in basic industry means their predominance in the hottest, hardest, dirtiest and most unsafe jobs, just as is true of Black workers. Only economic need forces these workers to stick to the drudgery, speedup and unsafe conditions of these jobs. But the fact that they do so demonstrates something else. It lays bare the jingoist and racist character of the attacks on minority workers and welfare recipients by the Nixons and the Reagans, of their charges that minority group people do not want to work.

Our Party's decision to single out racism as the issue that cuts through all problems expresses a true Marxist-Leninist approach. Racism is a cancer in U.S. society that must be eliminated. It is the most divisive weapon of the ruling class. Our task is to unite all democratic forces— white, Black, Yellow, Red and Brown—against the oppression of the monopolies. The situation dictates it.

☐ ——————————————————————————— ☐

INTERNATIONAL SOLIDARITY WITH CHILE

End Fascist Terror and U.S. Imperialism in Chile
by Victor Perlo, New Outlook Publishers, 1974

[Immediately after the fascist coup in Chile which began on September 11, 1973, the Political Committee of the Communist Party USA declared that it was the solemn duty of the people of the United States "to protest and express solidarity with the people of Chile in every possible form." (Cited in World Magazine, *September 29, 1973.) The Party has actively participated in developing the Chile Solidarity Movement into a powerful nationwide force for human rights and democracy, in which an outstanding role has been played by the National Coordinating Center in Solidarity with Chile. Through the efforts of the world and U.S. movement, which includes trade unions, church groups, professional associations and other people's movements, many victims of fascist terror have been freed from Pinochet's torture chambers.*

448

The importance of international solidarity has been stressed by Luis Corvalan, General Secretary of the Communist Party of Chile, saved from death at the hands of the junta by the worldwide movement for his defense. In his report to the Plenary Session of the Central Committee of the Communist Party of Chile in August, 1977, he said: "Internationalism has acquired a new dimension for millions of Chileans. It is appreciated today better than yesterday and by more people as a material force of the greatest possible significance."

Noted Communist economist Victor Perlo describes the background and impact of the fascist coup.]

On September 11, 1973, the Chilean military launched a violent attack against the legal government of Chile. These putschists relied on modern armaments recently supplied by the United States—planes, tanks, helicopters and paratroop equipment. They also relied on secret CIA operatives. During the six weeks prior to the coup, 2,400 male tourists entered Chile from Miami, Washington, New York and Houston, despite the fact that regular tours were cancelled owing to the tense situation in Chile. It is standard procedure for CIA agents engaging in covert subversive activities to enter a country as "tourists." There is every reason to believe that these played important roles in the pre-coup sabotage operations as well as military and police actions during and after the coup.

By 1972, there were 2,200 U.S. citizens publicly reported as resident in Chile, mainly U.S. government employees. This is an unusual number for a country with which the U.S. government had cut off most relations. Their presence in these circumstances could only be for the purpose of hostile intrigues against President Allende. Included was a military mission which numbered 33 as of July 1, 1971. Such missions are critical for organizing coups.

Some Chilean officers took special military training in the United States from the U.S. Marines to prepare themselves for roles in the coup.

General Augusto Pinochet Ugarte, head man of the Junta, "visited the United States Southern Command in the Panama Canal Zone in 1965, 1968 and 1972, and toured the United States in 1968 as a guest of the U.S. Government."[7]

The Southern Command is the main center for U.S. imperialist intervention in Latin America. This 1972 Pinochet visit may well have been connected with the practical preparations for the coup.

An uprising of a small minority against the democratically elected Allende government would have been inconceivable and doomed to failure without such imperialist participation from the United States. The coup would never have been attempted without prolonged, painstaking efforts from the U.S. to stimulate it, help create the economic and political conditions for it and give it practical assistance.

Early on the morning of September 11, President Allende received news that a full coup d'etat had begun involving all branches of the armed forces against the legal government. Dr. Allende went immediately to the presidential palace, La Moneda, and personally took charge of its defense. It was clear that part of the guard force assigned to the palace had already yielded to the coup. Dr. Allende and about 40 guards loyal to the Popular Unity cause took up fighting positions within the palace, determined to defend to the last the constitutional authority vested in the Presidency. . . .

In 1971 the Allende Government, with the near-unanimous support of Congress, and strongly backed by the trade unions, nationalized the large copper mines. It also took over by purchase or intervention about half of the monopoly enterprises in Chile. It accelerated land reform and distributed the bulk of the large estates to peasant cooperatives. It raised living standards of the masses by raising wages of the lowest paid workers, cutting unemployment more than 50%, increasing industrial and agricultural production, providing medical aid and a sanitary water supply to the poor, providing a pint of milk daily to every child and building a record number of housing units. The gross national product increased 8.5% and personal consumption increased 12.9%, both in constant prices.

In 1971, before the counteroffensive of U.S. and Chilean reaction got into full gear, Chile registered the greatest one-year progress in its history.

The U.S. economic warfare damaged the Chilean economy, but failed to bring about economic collapse. Other countries offered credits: " . . . the most significant credits now come from the socialist countries, with the USSR replacing the United States as the largest lender to Chile . . . (in millions): USSR, $259; China, $55; Poland, $35; Bulgaria, $25; Hungary, $22; GDR, $20; Romania, $20; Czechoslovakia, $5; DPR Korea, $5."[8]

However, these credits were mainly for long-term development projects, and could not ease the immediate supply pinches imposed by U.S.-based economic warfare. However, the USSR also led in short-term credits for immediate necessities, with $109 million of these by November 1972. Included were at least $50 million in convertible currencies, which could be used to buy spare parts in capitalist countries.

There were also significant short-term credits from Argentina and Italy.

The supply of credits to Chile increased in 1973, as many West European and Latin American countries joined the socialist countries. Altogether several hundred million dollars additional was advanced. . . .

The USSR provided substantial technical assistance to Chile, notably at the mines, where Soviet specialists helped Chilean experts work out methods to increase production, following the departure of U.S. and some Chilean engineers. A Soviet-supplied prefab housing complex at Valparaiso was in operation and helping to ease the housing shortage. Soviet experts and supplies were helping to establish a modern fishing industry. In an interview early in May 1973, President Allende urged the *Pravda* special correspondent to convey to the Soviet government and people "our gratitude for the extensive support the Soviet Union has been giving us. The USSR's large scale economic, scientific, technical and cultural cooperation with Chile, the credits granted us on favorable terms, the all-around political support of Chile, particularly in our struggle against the international monopolies—all this is of vital importance to us."[9]

Copper production in the two largest mines exceeded the 1972 level in the first quarter of 1973, with rising copper prices on world markets. Despite all kinds of economic sabotage, overall economic activity was maintained at the 1972 level and industrial production increased slightly. This represented a remarkable recovery from the damaging truckowners lockout of October 1972. Talks were scheduled for a further rescheduling of foreign debts with European countries and the U.S.

The election of March 1973 showed a major gain for the Popular Unity coalition. It received 43.4% of the vote, as against 36.2% when Allende was elected in 1970, much to the surprise of Chilean and U.S. reactionaries.

It became clear that the Popular Unity government could not be defeated by hostile economic and political measures alone. Bernard Collier wrote in the *New York Times:* " . . . the election result was a clear sign to President Allende's political enemies that they could no longer count on the ballot box as a means of bringing him down."[10]

In the spring of 1972, Latin America was rife with rumors of a Chilean coup scheduled for September or October of that year. And indeed, in those months there was a series of disruptions engineered by reactionary forces. The most serious was the lockout by truckowners, who refused to drive or to let workers drive their vehicles for several weeks. Since almost all freight transport in Chile is by truck, this did serious damage to the economy and to the supply of goods to the population. A settlement was finally reached between the government and the truckowners, but it was clear even then that the real issues were not economic, but that the truckowners were serving the interests of those anxious to overthrow the Allende government. The 1972 September–October disruptions provided a "dry run" for the actual coup.

In November 1972, according to their own spokesman, a clique of fascist military officers began to work out detailed plans for the coup. They contacted the leaders of the truckowners, reactionary shopkeepers, and "key business men" to organize the stoppage of economic activity and massive political disruption in the immediate months before the coup. By May, when the coup plans became generally known, the workers began to organize armed defense detachments, to support the legitimate government. However, in the weeks before the coup, the fascist officers forced out of active command Gen. Carlos Prats Gonzalez, the army's commander-in-chief, and other loyal officers. Under the Arms Control Law they organized searches in factories and communities to seize the people's arms, and proceeded to establish control of road transit into and out of major cities. . . .

We do not yet know how many of the American "tourists" were directly engaged in the expert blowing up of power lines and railroad tracks and the dynamiting of workers' trucks.

But it is known that the fascist gang which organized the coup are the same individuals with whom the CIA and ITT representatives had maintained continuous contact. The strategy of the coup was exactly according to the instructions earlier voiced by the U.S. Ambassador to Chile, Nathaniel P. Davis. In a secret memorandum to the State Department, he said that Allende would not be overthrown unless public opposition became "so overwhelming and discontent so great, that military intervention is overwhelmingly invited."[11]

What he meant, of course, was the "overwhelming" discontent of the reactionary forces and the military. The majority of the Chilean people were not consulted. Shortly before the coup, one and a quarter million people, virtually half the population of the Santiago metropolitan area, carried out the largest demonstration in Chile's history in support of the legal government of Salvador Allende.

Only overwhelming military force, launched with the advantage of tactical surprise, could temporarily overcome the mass support of the Popular Unity regime. . . .

On the weekend before the coup, Ambassador Davis was recalled to Washington for consultations and sent back to Chile the day before the coup. U.S. Government spokesmen conceded that they had ample notice of the impending coup. State Department spokesman Paul J. Hare said, "No effort was made to contact the Allende Government about the coup rumors or to meet with military men to discourage them from carrying out the coup. The Administration resisted all efforts to persuade it to comment on the morality of the coup, in which a democratically elected government was overthrown. One official said that 'we will have to work with the generals and it makes no sense to issue some moral statment about democracy.'"[12]

The main response of Trotskyites, Maoists and all sorts of armchair "revolutionists" has been to blame Allende and the Popular Unity coalition for "permitting" the coup. They pretend, without looking at the available facts, that the Left coalition acted naively, with blind faith in the institutions of capitalist democracy and in a supposed "neutrality" of the Chilean armed forces.

Such arguments can divert honest people from understanding the nature of the imperialist enemies of Chilean independence and from recognizing the responsibilities of U.S. citizens to curb U.S. imperialism. The argument that the setback in Chile is the "fault" of the Popular Unity coalition gets the state-monopoly Watergate gang off the hook and fails to mobilize struggle against them in the United States.

Further, the argument is false. The leaders of the Allende Government and of the world Communist movement, were well aware of the dangers and difficulties. Chilean Communists knew from their own long experience of the frequent use of the military to break strikes, and, as in 1946, to expel Communists from the government. The ties of the Chilean military leaders to their counterparts in the Pentagon were also well known.

The Allende Government won the election and even increased its vote, on the basis of an economic and social program that would curb monopoly and in the process markedly improve the living conditions of the Chilean workers and peasants.

But the difficulties were many. The Popular Unity coalition controlled only the executive branch of the government. While it had the support of the Congress for such measures as nationalizing the copper mines and other large industries, it did not have a reliable majority in the Congress on many other measures that the economic warfare of imperialism made necessary and urgent. For example: during 1972 the Congress refused to vote the taxes necessary to finance needed government expenditures. The Congress passed an Arms Control Law that was used by the military for search-and-seize operations in working-class neighborhoods.

The judiciary in Chile is appointed for life. Most of its members had been appointed by previous reactionary governments and were subservient to the aims of the oligarchy and the military, not the Allende Government.

The executive branch of the government did not have the means to control the armed forces which are the principal instrument of the power of the state. The Allende government tried to neutralize the armed forces by improving the conditions of the soldiers and by relying on the patriotic elements in the officer corps, many of whom, as in other Latin American countries, had been influenced by anti-imperialist and Marxist ideology.

The main political effort was to win over a section of the middle class, especially those identified with the Christian Democrats, and to which the lower ranks of the officer corps were closely tied. The Popular Unity coalition was making gains in this effort, but before the tactic could fully succeed, the reactionaries struck. In fact, a number of observers have admitted that by 1976 the Popular Unity coalition would have won an unshakeable majority in Congress and would have moved rapidly forward on its program. Reaction needed the coup to prevent its certain defeat on the political and social fronts of struggle. In the process the leaders of the coup murdered those military leaders who had been won to accept the democratic will of the people.

The deep ties of the Popular Unity coalition with the struggles of the workers, peasants and other democratic strata in Chile had compelled a constitutional opening for an anti-monopoly government. As the danger of a coup developed, consistent efforts were made to organize workers into fighting detachments and to provide arms. But the Allende government never had a free hand in obtaining arms from overseas, or even from the Chilean military.

Thus, attempts to distribute domestic arms stockpiles to workers were only partly successful. Moreover, these small arms were no match for the planes, tanks and artillery supplied to the coup by the United States.

Even this short review of some of the obstacles that faced the Allende Government make its achievements stand out as remarkable and heroic accomplishments.

It has been said that the Popular Unity coalition made mistakes. In fact, there hasn't been a revolutionary movement in history that didn't make mistakes—this is hardly the issue. It is clear from writings of its spokesmen that the Popular Unity leadership will analyze their experiences and learn from them for the future. But that is their prerogative and responsibility. . . .

It is the special responsibility of all democratically minded people in the United States to curb the power of U.S. monopolies and conglomerates, abolish the CIA, and fully expose and punish the entire Watergate gang, including Richard Nixon. These measures will at the same time assist the Chilean people.

☐ ———————————————————————————————————— ☐

WOMEN'S LIBERATION

1. "Women's Rights and the Class Struggle"
by Alva Buxenbaum, *Political Affairs*, May 1973
2. "For a Class Approach to the Struggle for Women's
Equality" by Fern Winston,
***World Magazine*, January 4, 1975**

[*The past few years have seen the women's liberation movement come to the fore and achieve far-reaching prominence. The Communist Party of the USA right from its birth has fought for the equality of women. The Party was guided in this effort by the principle of Marxism-Leninism.*

At a time when the women's liberation movement has reached a new historical significance, it is well to note that as early as on the Second Anniversary of the Revolution, V.I. Lenin observed: "In the course of two years, Soviet power in one of the most backward countries of Europe did more to emancipate women and to make their status equal to that of the 'strong' sex than all the advanced, enlightened, 'democratic', republics of the world did in the course of 130 years." (V.I. Lenin, Collected Works, Vol. 30, Progress Publishers, Moscow, 1965.)

The Communist Party fights against the double yoke of oppression of U.S. working women in general and the triple yoke imposed upon Black, Chicano, Puerto Rican, Native-American and Asian-American women. It has emphasized the central role of the working women in the struggle for women's equality as well as their indispensability in the general class struggle.

Since its formation many women participated in the leadership of the Party. Among the pioneers who founded the Party were Ella Reeve Bloor, Anita Whitney, Margaret Prevey, Kate Sadler Greenhalgh, Hortense Allison, Sadie Van Veen, Jeanette Pearl, Rose Wortis, Margaret Krumbein, Rose Baron, Becky Buhay, Dora Lifshitz and Clara Bodian. Rose Pastor Stokes was the first national secretary of the Women's Commission, established in 1922.

They were followed by such exemplary women as Geraldine Lightfoot, widely known for her leadership in Chicago's South Side, Clara Colon, leader in defense activites during the 60s and Claudia Jones, a national leader in the Young Communist League and the Communist Party.

In the recent period, women in substantial numbers are in Party leadership in every level of activity. Two outstanding examples are Alva Buxenbaum (b. 1937), popular community leader who is secretary of the Economic and Social Rights Department of the CP and chairperson of its Women's Section, and Fern Winston (b. 1915), an active trade unionist and also a member of the Women's Section and National Council of the CP.]

1.

The "women's liberation" movement in the U.S. (as it is popularly called) has made a tremendous impact on large sections of the people of this country. It has been an important influence in changing attitudes and in raising the consciousness of women. Millions of women, including working-class women, now recognize to some degree the role of sex discrimination.

But the U.S. bourgeoisie has had long experience in taking advantage of weaknesses in workers' and people's movements. They have been able to use the divisions based on class and race between the "women's liberation" forces and broad sections of women. They have understood and utilized the problems stemming from the limited base of the "women's liberation" movement which is confined to petty-bourgeois and professional women and some very limited sections of white working-class women. They have understood the significance of this movement's failure to attract in any significant degree even the most advanced sections of Black, Puerto Rican, Chicano and Indian women—sections of the oppressed minorities that are in active struggle and whose participation is key to developing further any significant movement among working-class women, including white women. The women's liberation movement has failed to attract these women because it has failed to take up the questions of class oppression and racism, and instead has tended to pit the question of "women's liberation" against that of Black liberation. And this has had a devastating effect on that movement. First, some of its adherents began to raise issues that diverted them from the main problems of women, and they discussed questions and took actions that working-class women correctly considered frivolous. As they moved away from the basic questions of the working class, sex rather than class became for them the main basis of contradictions in society. Other sections of this movement are moving towards broader struggles and are beginning to form alliances with working-class women.

But the fight for women's equality in the United States did not begin with the "women's liberation" movement. Women, and especially working-class women, have been organized in struggle for a very long time. The history of the U.S. working-class movement is filled with the militant struggles of women. Working-class women were leaders in organizing the trade union movement.

Black women have been involved in massive numbers all over the country in struggles for Black liberation. They carried on these struggles in the churches, schools, courts and public facilities. They marched, picketed, sat down, boycotted and used every method of protest possible.

With an understanding and determination that comes from struggle, they began to see that the social system was the perpetrator of racism. Some began to conclude that the system had to be changed and many others saw that the question of job discrimination was more basic than the right to share public facilities equally. And so they carried their struggles into the shops and the trade unions themselves. Workers were influenced and trade unions began to feel the pressures to end discrimination in the unions against Black workers. The fact that 90 per cent of Black families in the U.S. are working class enabled masses of Black people to make the link between racism and the economic system. And from there other links were made as the demand became "Peace, Jobs and Freedom."

Women in the peace movement, many of whom had been influenced by or had participated in the civil rights movement, began to organize around the "Ban the Bomb" movement and later against the war in Indochina. Mass actions for peace grew to tremendous proportions and women played the leading role, even though they were not visible in the predominantly male top leadership. . . .

In the constant ebb and flow of these movements, particular groups of women began to recognize that they were allies of other groups of women. Consequently, women's political caucuses, trade union caucuses and women's departments in trade unions along with many other forms were organized by women themselves. Women organized as women, together with participation in the struggles for peace, Black liberation, welfare rights, health, education and child care. This stimulated a much broader and more far–reaching fight for women's equality. . . .

The U.S. Census Bureau reports that between 1960 and 1970 almost 12 million people were added to the work force and 65 per cent of these were women. It is currently estimated that women make up approximately 40 per cent of the total work force. Consequently, historic shifts are taking place in the lives of U.S. women. Economic necessity—the need for more than one wage earner in most working-class families—and rising social consciousness are moving women into the direct production processes in tremendous numbers. While women continue to hold a major and often predominant place in "traditional" women's occupations, in light and service industries, there is an increasingly significant move toward medium and heavy industry. . . .

Still the overwhelming majority of working women are unorganized, with women often making up the majority in some of the largest unorganized plants in the country. . . .

Black women have from the time of slavery been exploited and oppressed in unique ways under capitalism. Historically their families have been kept at the very bottom of the economic ladder. They have been forced to work in far greater proportion than have white women. They have been forced to accept the most menial, unrewarding, low-paid, generally unorganized jobs. Among the unorganized are millions of retail sales workers, office workers, agricultural workers and domestic workers. Most of them are women and a large proportion of these women are Black, Chicano and Puerto Rican women. Accordingly, Black women, for example, earn approximately one-half of what white women workers earn and one-fourth of what male workers earn. . . .

Yet Black women in the U.S. have proven themselves the most consistent and steady forces on picket lines, in actions for quality unbiased education, or in fighting for much-needed additional schools. They have given leadership in the fight for child care and rights of welfare mothers, and have demonstrated in many ways their opposition to the war in Vietnam. Add to this experience in struggle the fact that a large percentage of women going into industry are Black, and it is possible to understand why they are so important as a leading and conscious component of the working class. It clarifies, too, why corporate monopoly has singled out racism and male supremacy as its main ideological weapons of division among workers. And it is also clear why the Communist Party in the U.S. sees Black women as an important and essential force in the fight for women's equality and for working-class power. . . .

Monopoly goes to great lengths to conceal the fact that working-class housewives are in very large part unemployed workers. By forcing the family to depend primarily upon the husband's wages, monopoly perpetuates the myth that "woman's place is in the home." In that way it keeps most women out of the job market and avoids responsibility for the extra burdens placed on the worker's family and on the women in particular. Expenditures for child care, public education, health care, housing and other necessary social needs that should and can be public services, even under capitalism, are opposed and blocked because they don't produce profits. . . .

Since the beginning of private property the ideology of male supremacy has permeated every institution, every level of society. It is not an accident of nature, but a deliberate tool introduced and fostered to protect private property.

It is an ideology which stunts the growth not only of women but also men and of the family as a whole. Concepts of women as property, as sex objects, as weak and defenseless and often as emotionally delicate are all concepts that are part of capitalist ideology. Centuries of these ideas and variations on them have prevented men from seeing their own interest in the struggle for full equality of women.

It thus becomes easy for capitalism to discriminate against women—to keep them out of certain industries, out of the more skilled jobs and the professions, out of positions of leadership in trade unions and other organizations. It is an ideology that has been part of people's thinking for centuries and will not die easily. This backward notion seeps into the minds of all, even the most advanced of us. In the family under capitalism, it is a stumbling block to women's economic, political and social equality. It curtails the ability of women to participate in all the struggles for a better life. Many women don't have time to do so, with the worries of children and household on their minds. And those women who do participate in social movements do so—especially if they have children—at great expense. Yet there are thousands of active women, many of whom work; these are the women who are advancing and developing class consciousness. Special attention has to be given, especially in the case of working-class women, making it easier for them to be involved in struggles.

The working-class struggle for existence and survival, for emancipation from exploitation, requires a new outlook of cooperative, equal partnership in work, in struggle and in all relationships between men and women. Relationships of mutual respect and dignity in place of bourgeois competitiveness and disunity are developing.

The women's movement for equality and especially working-class women's movements, cannot be completely successful without new initiatives and sustained, conscious struggle by Communist men. A good starting point is to win the trade unions to organize the unorganized with special reference to women, to fight for elimination of the male–female wage differential and for child care. And it is most important to initiate a fight to make all jobs safe for both men and women. . . .

We see, too, the need to build, together with other forces, a women's organization which is led from the beginning by working-class women, an organization which reflects in its leadership the struggles of Black, Puerto Rican, Chicano and American Indian women in the United States.

As we struggle to implement this program we will also continue to advance the struggle for socialism which, in the long run, provides the real and lasting basis for full and equal rights for women.

2.

[The] understanding of the strategic importance of women as a crucial section of the working class determines the approach of Communists, and helps to shape our strategy and tactics in the fight for equal treatment of women on all levels. It is the foundation of our understanding of the necessity for working-class women to determine the direction of and become the decisive leadership in the struggle for women's equality. . . .

Although women are the majority in industries such as textile, garment, clerical and service industries, and are increasingly a force in basic industry, whatever the area, they earn less than men.

Women are the majority of the membership of 26 unions. A million women have joined unions since 1958, and have proven themselves to be among the most militant fighters and skilled organizers in many strike struggles. Despite this, of 34 million working women, only 4 million are organized into unions. It is not that women have ignored the trade union movement, but that the trade union movement has ignored women. A Kraft poll showed that 14% more women than men voted pro-union in California in 1969!

In 1970 only 8% of hospital and service industries were unionized; only 10% of sales workers and 15% of government workers. Office workers have just begun to be organized. Household workers, nearly all women and largely Black women, have struggled for years for a union without help from organized labor.

There is still not one woman on the AFL–CIO executive council. Women are only 7% of elected executive boards of unions in the U.S. and are rare in state and local labor councils. Trade unions have in the main failed to take up questions of special concern to women such as child care, maternity benefits, protective labor legislation.

Under the impact of the women's movement and the atmosphere it has helped to create, women workers began to organize into caucuses, then into regional conferences, which finally culminated in the founding convention last March in Chicago of the Coalition of Labor Union Women (CLUW). Surpassing all expectations, 3,200 women, representing 58 internationals, poured into Chicago from all parts of the country. Despite problems with some bureaucratic efforts to stifle rank-and-file expressions, many rank-and-file women, bringing with them the militancy, clarity and organizing skill learned in grassroots struggles for decent housing, peace, child care, welfare rights and the fight against racism, made their presence felt and made the fight against race and sex discrimination on the job, the right of women to leading positions in the unions, the fight to organize the 30 million unorganized women a part of the proceedings of the convention. . . .

The larger and better established organizations, such as the National Organization of Women, and the National Women's Political Caucus, [are] concentrating their efforts on winning ratification of the Equal Rights Amendment by the five states that have not yet done so.

The Equal Employment Opportunities Commission, in 1972, issued guidelines which required employers to extend laws enacted to protect the working conditions of women to men. This has not happened, however. In anticipation of the final ratification of the Equal Rights Amendment, many states have quietly enacted legislation eliminating protective laws. This means we are now faced with the job of legislative campaigns to re-enact these laws.

These conditions place before the movement for women's equality the need for an advanced women's organization, led by working women, an organization that would reflect in its leadership the most advanced struggles of Black, Puerto Rican, Chicano, Native American and Asian peoples.[13] Such an organization would base its actions on the concept that the possibility of winning struggles depends on the degree of unity forged in those struggles. It would understand that the degree of success in the fight against racism has been shown to be the determining factor in forging unity in all workers' and peoples' struggles in the U.S. In other words, the fight against racism must be given top priority in striving for the unity of all women. . . .

Such an organization would be of great help in guaranteeing the effectiveness of rank-and-file women directly from the shops, factories and offices; in influencing the struggles of the Coalition of Labor Union Women to achieve its stated goals of waging a battle against discrimination on the job, in the unions, for greater democracy in the unions and for organizing the unorganized.

□ ———————————————————————————————— □

PUERTO RICAN INDEPENDENCE

Puerto Rico's Goal: Self-Determination and Independence
by Grace Mora, published by *Voz Del Pueblo,* **1977**

[*Grace Mora (b. 1925) is President of the Puerto Rican Commission of the Communist Party and Director of* Voz del Pueblo.]

For the past 79 years, since the U.S. occupation, there has never been any real support for statehood. On the contrary, the organized forces have supported independence, in the main, and even those that do not take a position on the issue would not, under any circumstances, assimilate to the U.S. way of life. That is not to say that none would, but the majority—and I include a large percentage of the two million who have been forced to migrate to this country—would maintain their heritage. . . .

Very recently Gov. Romero Barcelo reaffirmed that Puerto Rican culture and language are not negotiable and that if Congress were not willing to grant statehood under those conditions, he would opt for independence. . . .

Ruben Berrios, president of the Puerto Rican Independence Party has said:

"Further, granting statehood to Puerto Rico will have to be implemented over widespread international opposition. Caribbean and Latin American nations can hardly be expected to applaud and forget when one of their own is swallowed by the colossus of the North. No one can foretell what exactly they would do when faced with such action. At the very least, it would certainly poison U.S.-Latin American relations for many decades." . . .

Puerto Rico is a captive market (the fifth largest in the world for U.S. exports) through what is called, in classic colonial economic theory, an assimilated tariff policy. The application of both U.S. tariffs and the offshore shipping laws now lock Puerto Rico into an expensive market with high maritime transportation costs. The savings to the Puerto Rican economy, if it had access to world market supplies, would be significant. Joining the Caribbean common market would also help in developing self-sufficiency.

The existence of extensive nickel and copper deposits in Puerto Rico, calculated at a value of at least $10 billion, would open up an additional avenue of production and self-reliant growth. Recent petroleum explorations demonstrate the very high possibility (according to the exploring company) of the existence of petroleum off the northern shore of the island. Only under independence could Puerto Rico be assured control over this resource, since according to federal law, states have sovereignty only to a three-mile limit, and by special concession to a 10-mile zone. The exact nature of the commonwealth's control is yet to be determined by the U.S. federal agencies or courts. . . .

Support for Puerto Rican independence becomes more and more visible each day in the U.S. Organizations are growing which wage a militant struggle and bring the colonial status of Puerto Rico before the U.S. public, especially in the past five or six years.

The U.S. Committee for Puerto Rican Decolonization, headed by Rev. David Garcia . . . is expected to embrace a broad section of the U.S. population, including legislators, churches and most especially trade unions. . . .

Many second generation Puerto Ricans like myself are very much concerned with conditions and the future of Puerto Rico. We maintain our language, our music, our customs and do our utmost to learn of our proud heritage, passing it on to our children and our children's children. We support independence and we will not submit to a bourgeois culture imposed by U.S. imperialism.

Movements for Puerto Rico's right as a nation, to self-determination and independence continue to grow. It is in harmony with the United Nations call for total elimination of colonialism. The UN Special Committee on Decolonization has consistently reaffirmed the "inalienable right of the people of Puerto Rico to self-determination and independence."

Self-determination and independence for Puerto Rico are also in line with the best traditions and self-interest of the people of the United States. Puerto Rico is a haven for low wages and for tax exemptions for U.S. corporations, which derive huge profits from the "run-away" shops established there. This undermines wages and union conditions in the United States.

Our own democratic rights are threatened by the use of Puerto Rico as a testing ground for reactionary social and economic programs. The dismantling of U.S. military bases, including nuclear facilities, is in the interest of peace for the Puerto Rican people, for the people of the U.S. and for the world.

As U.S. history demonstrates, the national aspirations of a people cannot be suppressed indefinitely. Stubborn rejection of this reality on the part of U.S. government has led to much misery for the people of the U.S. and for the peoples of Vietnam, Laos and Cambodia. . . .

Last January 6, Congressman Ronald Dellums (D–Cal) joined this movement with the introduction of H.R. 54: "To provide independence for Puerto Rico." In his speech introducing the resolution, Rep. Dellums explained the thrust of his stance:

"We do not want to debate what particular 'status' the Puerto Rican people support for their country. That is their choice. It is not the issue for us. For this government and, in particular, this Congress, what is at issue is the fact that no people can carry out their right to self-determination regarding their political future unless, and until, they are a free and sovereign nation, first. That is, Puerto Rico must be independent first, in order then to be able freely to choose what its relations with other countries, peoples and governments should be."

It is towards that end that Rep. Dellums introduced the joint resolution which said:

"That all powers and authority presently exercised by the three branches of the government of the United States, legislative, judicial and executive, and all its agencies and instrumentalities including the Armed Forces of the U.S., over the territory of Puerto Rico, are hereby relinquished and transferred unconditionally and without reservation to the people of Puerto Rico, in order to allow them to fully exercise their inalienable right to self-determination and independence, in accordance with their fully expressed will and desire."

It is time to put an end to the U.S. chauvinist and racist propaganda that Puerto Rico has to depend on the benevolence of Uncle Sam in order to survive. Puerto Rico is a Latin American nation, with a proud history, a rich culture and a beautiful language of its own, an island known as "La Perla de los Mares" (The Pearl of the Seas) and we intend to keep it that way. . . .

Imperialism has had its day; today and all the tomorrows belong to the people.

☐ ———————————————————————————— ☐

BRIEF SKETCH OF MARXIST YOUTH ORGANIZATIONS

**"Carrying the Baton Forward for Our Generation"
by James Steele.** *We Demand a Better Life for Our
Generation: Program Book, 4th National Convention,
Young Workers Liberation League,* **October 7-10, 1977**

[*The Young Workers League (YWL) was formed at a convention in May
1922. The previous month, an illegal convention created the Young
Communist League (YCL). The formation of the YWL gave legal status
to the Marxist youth movement.*

*Among the YCL leaders were many who were prominent in the Party
and working-class movements—Henry Winston, Gus Hall, Gil Green,
Bob Thompson, John Williamson, Claude Lightfoot, Pat Toohey,
Claudia Jones and Harry Gannes, to name a few. Among them were such
martyrs killed in the front lines of struggle as Joe York, Joe Bussell, Joe
Deblasio and Coleman Leny, murdered in the Ford Massacre and Curtis
Williams, a Black former Ford worker, who was clubbed and gassed, and
died of wounds later. Harry Simms, organizer of the National Miners
Union (NMU) and YCLer, was killed in a miners' struggle in Kentucky.*

*Hundreds of YCLers died in the fight against fascism in Spain and in
World War II. In the South, contributions were made by YCLers, among
them Ann Burlak and Sophie Melvin, in organizing textile workers in
Gastonia, and by Angelo Herndon and others in leading the unemployed
movement.*

*The YCL was disbanded in October 1943 and reorganized into the
American Youth for Democracy (AYD). Foster, in his* History of the
CPUSA, *characterizes the formation of the AYD under Browder's
influence:* " . . . not [as] an effort to find the basis for a broader Marxist
youth organization . . . but an attempt to wipe out Marxism-Leninism in
youth work. . . ."

*The Labor Youth League (LYL) (1948-56) came into existence during
one of the most difficult periods of American history. It was established
at the outset of the cold war and continued to be an active force among
youth during the period of repression, hysteria and arrests.*

*With the dissolution of the LYL, sporadic youth activities were carried
on in a number of localities by progressive and Communist Party youth.*

*Local progressive and socialist-oriented youth organizations began
slowly to develop. In New York City, Advance Youth Organization; in*

Philadelphia, the Socialist Youth Union; in San Francisco, the W.E.B. Du Bois Clubs. The magazine New Horizons *for youth was published in 1960. In 1964, the W.E.B. Du Bois Clubs of America was formed as a national organization at a conference in San Francisco. It published the* Insurgent.

By 1970, the need for a Marxist-Leninist youth organization was realized. A call to found such an organization was issued by the Du Bois Clubs, Communist Party youth clubs and independent youth groups. As a result of this move the Young Workers Liberation League (YWLL) was established. The YWLL continued the 59-year-old tradition in building a Marxist youth organization. Its publication is the Young Worker.

The Young Workers Liberation League held its fourth National Convention in New York City in October 1977. Below are parts of a feature article by James Steele (b. 1946), leading Communist and presently National Chairman of the YWLL, which appeared in its Convention Program Book.]

Like a Madison Avenue advertising firm coming up with rhymes for a television commercial, big business media—without shame or any sense of responsibility—have coined the phrase "jobless" and "excess baggage" generation to describe the wretched conditions of this country's youth. Big business and its media would also like to create the impression that the young generation of the latter 1970s is a "no–struggle" generation....

However, such an image that it is useless to struggle because "you can't beat city hall" or that today's youth is a "no–struggle" generation is a far cry from the truth. Just as yesterday when millions of youth refused to support and in fact militantly fought against the Vietnam war, today growing masses of the young generation are refusing to accept and are actively struggling against the blinded, jobless, racist, junkie, decadent, crime-ridden, neutron bomb/war-filled life monopoly capital is preparing them for and for them.

All across the United States young workers, unemployed youth, university and high school students—Black, Chicano, Puerto Rican, Asian, Native American Indian and white—are involved in struggle. From timber ranges of Maine to the great agricultural fields of California, from the docks of Seattle, San Francisco and Houston to the iron range of Minnesota, from the giant steel mills and auto plants of Chicago, Detroit and Cleveland to the deep mines of West Virginia, from the unemployment lines of New York and every other major city to the registration lines of every campus and classroom of every high school, young people are on the move. They are fighting mad and they are fighting back.

The Young Workers Liberation League has played a key role in the ever-mounting fightback of an ever-growing united youth movement. In the three years which have elapsed since our last national convention, the YWLL has added new achievements to its outstanding record as a leader and defender, an educator and mobilizer of the youth. The League's campaign for "Youth's Right to Earn, Learn and Live" has helped unite and give direction to the struggles of tens of thousands of youth and students. Three years ago we pointed out that unemployment was the main issue before the young generation and the main expression of the effects of racism on Black and other oppressed minority youth. Through our own special initiatives as well as by working with other youth organizations, especially the Youth Council of the National Coalition for Economic Justice, which brings together a broad range of youth and student organizations, we have helped bring the question of youth unemployment before the nation. . . .

The YWLL comes from a long line of democratic and revolutionary youth organizations and movements which distinguished themselves in their time by the ability to educate and lead masses of young people in struggle. The articles [in] this program book by Gil Green, former Chairman of the Young Communist League, which played an outstanding role in mobilizing the young generation of the 1930s and 1940s against the depression, racism and fascism, and for the building of the CIO; by Phil Bart, a leader of one of the first revolutionary youth organizations in this country's history—the Young Workers League; by Dr. James Jackson, himself a brilliant leader in the Southern Negro Youth Congress and now the National Education Director of the Communist Party, USA; and by Danny Rosenberg who recently returned from representing the YWLL in the Bureau of the World Federation of Democratic Youth; all attest to how deep the League's roots are. . . .

In a sense, we are accepting the baton of leadership from our predecessors. . . . We are proud that history has placed on our shoulder the responsibility of the education of young people to the facts of life of youth—struggle. We feel this way, we have this confidence because the YWLL in essence is a "mass school" where youth learn how to better struggle for the needs of their brothers and sisters, but is also a "classroom" in which attention is given to the individual, to stimulating character-building and creative personal development. In addition, the League's activities are fun. We think singing and dancing recreation and culture, friendship and doing things together are among the most important feature of being young.

And so the Fourth National Convention . . . express[es] the best of the

Young Workers Liberation League and the best of the young genera-tion—its multi-racial, multi-national unity, its militant international solidarity with our brothers and sisters of other lands struggling against imperialism, above all U.S. imperialism, the common foe of all youth. The Convention participants, like the League itself, are really like young construction workers. They are out to build a better life, a peaceful life, a productive and creative life out of the decay and parasitism of monopoly capitalism. They are confident that the future will be much, much brighter for youth than the present is. They know that victories today can lay the foundation for a development which brings a new life, a new society—socialism to their country in their lifetime.

□ ——————————————————————————— □

THE MIDDLE EAST CRISIS

Statement of the Communist Party, *Daily World,* January 24, 1978

[*The Middle East has been a tinder box whose eruption could effect not only the future peace in the region, but international relations. The Communist Party's concern and attention to this critical question is formulated in its statement, a part of which appears here.*]

Increasingly the Middle East is becoming an arena where the danger of war and possibly world war is ever present. The collusion between Arab and Zionist reaction, in the persons of Sadat and Begin, demonstrates that, contrary to those who would picture the source of the war danger as an "Arab–Israeli dispute," as a contention between states, the Middle East is a region where the class struggle and national liberation struggle hold center stage in the international arena. In this regard the recent meeting in Tripoli to form a front of anti-imperialist forces in the Arab world has great significance.

The Arab liberation movement, an important component of the world national liberation movement, confronts imperialism—US imperialism in its forefront—at a most critical point. The struggle for national independence, against colonialism and neocolonialism and for demo-cratic advance, is arrayed in the Middle East against imperialism seeking to maintain control over the extraction of petroleum, a most important energy resource and fundamental element of the world economy. Over 40 per cent of the return on US investment abroad comes from oil. The giant oil monopolies play a decisive role in the formation and execution of US imperialist foreign policy.

The most critical point of conflict today between the forces of national liberation and imperialism operating in the Middle East is in the area of Palestine and neighboring countries. The most important instrument of US imperialism in the area is Zionism and the power it wields as the dominant ideology and the holder of state power in Israel.

Over the past 30 years, the armies of the State of Israel have crossed the borders established in the 1947 United Nations partition of Palestine four times and occupied sizable territories belonging to nations and peoples living in the adjacent areas. That aggresion in combination with the betrayal of Arab reaction, makes for the major source of tension in the Middle East today and could lead again to war.

Israeli aggression is supported and promoted by US imperialism which benefits from perpetual tension and instability in the region and which sows division between Arab countries and continually strives to subvert, weaken and overthrow progressive regimes. This aggression flows directly from the ideology of Zionism and its program.

But the designation "Zionist" must never be confused with Jewish people. In Israel and throughout the world, Jewish people (as nearly all peoples) are characterized by separation into all economic classes and adhere to the political ideologies of those classes. Zionism is expansionist and proceeds on the premise of the denial of national rights of another people, and claims a divine blessing to seize the lands of others. Zionism is therefore racist and is recognized as such by the United Nations.

Within Israel, the main, most principled and consistent force against Zionism is the Communist Party of Israel (CPI), heroic fighter for peace and national liberation, opponent of racism and discrimination, vanguard of the Israeli working class, Jewish and Arab, and upholder of the interests of the Jewish and Arab peoples. The CPI fights for and organizes international support for the Arab minority in Israel who suffer second-class citizenship and cruel confiscation of ancestral lands. It does likewise for the majority of Israel's citizens—the "Sephardic" Jews who suffer discrimination and super-exploitation. Our Party, the Communist Party of the United States, is proud of its firm, long-standing fraternal relations with the CPI, which strengthen still more with each passing year.

The last elections in Israel, which showed a distinct and dangerous shift to the right with the election of the ultra-rightist and expansionist Likud government of Begin, heightens the danger of nuclear war in the

Middle East. It underscores again the necessity and responsibility of peace-loving forces in the United States to step up their efforts to force a reordering of priorities by the Carter Administration. It is more apparent now than ever that the main obstacle to reconvening the Geneva Conference—and thereby establishing a just peace in the Middle East— is Washington's political, economic and military support for the policies of the government of Israel—Labour or Likud—and for the collaborationist policies of Sadat and other Arab reactionaries. . . .

As part of its overall support for the liberation movement of the Arab peoples, the CPUSA supports self-determination and the national rights, including the right to a national state, of the Arab people of Palestine. We recognize without qualification the Palestine Liberation Organization as the sole legitimate representative of the Palestinian people. The national rights and self-determination for the Palestinian people, and recognition of the PLO are accepted by the vast majority of the nations of the world, and supported by the socialist community of nations, the Non-Aligned Movement, the United Nations, the Organization of Arab States, the World Peace Council, many governments in Western Europe and the Communist and Workers' parties of the world. . . .

Our Party recognizes the critical character of its role as a working-class party inside the USA confronting the forces of imperialism and campaigns to win our country to a policy of peace and non-interference in the affairs of the people of the Middle East. In our country a critical aspect of the work for peace and justice in the Middle East must be to win the mass of Jewish people—particularly workers—away from the influence of Zionism and for a program of peace, national liberation and justice.

Another crucial aspect of our work in the present period must be to intensify the struggle against anti-Arab chauvinism and racist attacks on Arab peoples, similarly as we conduct a struggle against anti-Semitism. This is a major factor even among some progressive circles and is a chief stumbling block toward expanding the movement for a just peace.

The CPUSA is committed to building and supporting activities in solidarity with peace, liberation and democratic movements in the Middle East and especially, at this time, with the Palestinian resistance movement. This must be a signal task for our entire Party and for the trade union, peace and other democratic movements.

□ ——————————————————————————————— □

ELECTIONS AND THE DEFENSE OF DEMOCRATIC RIGHTS

1. "The Successful California Signature Drive to Place the Hall-Tyner Ticket on the Ballot," speech by Jarvis Tyner, Los Angeles, September 11, 1976; 2. "1976 Elections: Mandate for People's Action" (Abridged Report to the Central Committee, CPUSA, November 19, 1976) by Gus Hall, *Political Affairs,* December 1976

[*The 1976 election campaign established a "political landmark" according to the estimate of the Party's Central Committee. Although it fulfilled legal requirements, some states denied the Party a place on the ballot. Yet ballot status was achieved in 19 states and the District of Columbia for the 1976 election. This compares favorably with 13 states in 1972 and two states in 1968. These gains registered a continuous struggle against restrictive election laws.*

Jarvis Tyner (b. 1941), now Chairman of the Communist Party of New York State, gives the reason for the Party's successes in the signature drive and response to its election program. Gus Hall takes up the current acute questions and projects a program which can help unite the people.]

1.

This meeting is a victory celebration not only for the Communist Party, but for democratic rights for the working people, youth and students of the state of California. The big industrial and agricultural monopolies and their two-party system tried to prevent an independent alternative from emerging in this state.

The ruling class did not want a Communist ticket. They knew the Communist Party would present a concrete program of struggle and expose Gerald Ford's Nixonism and Jimmy Carter's phony lesser-evil image as well as the carefully orchestrated notion that the people of California are giving mass support to Jerry Brown's program of austerity. Therefore, while mass pressure forced an amendment to the state election law, the big business politicians were confident that nearly 100,000 valid signatures would be more than anybody could collect.

But he who laughs last, laughs hardest. Just one week ago the Communist Party filed 149,000 signatures on petitions to put Gus Hall and myself on the ballot as independent candidates for President and Vice President.

Gus Hall and I were here in California at various times during the petition drive. At campaign rallies as well as through mass media we spoke directly to more than one and a half million Californians about things they had not heard from Carter or Ford, about issues relating to their day-to-day existence. We spoke about unemployment, about how they are going to feed their families, send their children to school, about the racist offensive and so forth. We spoke about the Communist Party election campaign and our program for cutting the military budget, creating jobs, ending racism and guaranteeing peace and security, and they listened. Nearly seventy trade unionists and community activists took out an ad in the *Los Angeles Times* supporting the Constitutional rights of the Communist Party and other independents to hold ballot status.

But the big job of collecting 150,000 signatures to guarantee a place on the ballot was done by hundreds of Party and Young Worker Liberation League members, supporters of the Party's democratic rights and others who wanted to see a serious discussion on the issues. We had sixty-one days in which to accomplish this task.

The big business politicians said it could not be done. They did not take us seriously at first. They thought our Party was too weak and that there was too much racism and anti-Communism among the masses. Could the Party which initiated and carried out the mass struggle which won the freedom for Angela Davis do it? Could the Party which, on September 1st, celebrated 57 years of overcoming every obstacle thrown in its path by the capitalists do it? Last Friday the question was answered. One hundred forty-nine thousand voters in California signed the petition for the right of our Party to be on the ballot.

The California petition campaign is one of the most brilliant pieces of mass work ever undertaken by our Party, a story of the dedication of the older generation combined with the vigor of youth. I would like to cite several examples of heroism and determination. One thinks of Jack Lutz, critically ill, who during periods of convalescence took his clipboard into the streets and filled petitions, saying that "putting Gus Hall and Jarvis Tyner on the ballot gives me new life." One thinks of other campaign workers, those in their seventies and eighties who collected more than a thousand signatures each. Many collected after working hours; others used their vacation time.

I would especially like to mention the role of the YWLL campaign workers who collected more than 2,500 signatures: Gary Redke who obtained 4,175 and Evelina Alarcon-Cruz, Chicano activist, who collected 218 in one day. This is the kind of effort that went into our

472

campaign to guarantee that voters across the state would have an alternative on November 22nd. In the process of collecting this tremendous number of signatures we helped to register approximately 5,000 voters, mainly Black, Chicano and youth who had been turned off by the two major party politicans. In two short months we did more for democratic rights in California than the two capitalist parties have done in two decades.

There is mass support for our rights and for the development of political independence which candidacy represents. The nearly 150,000 Californians who signed our petitions have made this clear in no uncertain terms.

My friends, these are critical times—times that demand clear thought and resolute action. Approaches that may have sufficed in the past are way out of step with the present. The success of the petition campaign should signal a new look at old problems.

It is more than a belief in democratic rights—it is interest in our policies and platform, a desire to find out about the Communist Party. And when you compare these attitudes with the poison spread during the McCarthy era as well as in the 1960s, you will conclude there is a new level of consciousness among large sections of the people. . . .

Today, the people of the U.S. face a serious challenge. Racism and the plight of the Black people and the other oppressed national minorities has gotten worse. This is attested to in the income gap between whites and the minorities which has become wider than it was in the 1960s. The minorities are being hit with the brunt of the mounting unemployment and inflation and cutbacks in social programs. Racism is not decreasing. It is becoming more widespread as witnessed in anti-busing riots and increased activities of the Ku Klux Klan and the Nazis.

Youth unemployment is worse now than in the 1960s. The monopolies are callously indifferent to a 60 per cent unemployment rate among Black, Chicano and Puerto Rican youth. In fact an entire generation faces the prospect of joblessness, increased drug addiction and a whole host of associated social evils.

We must see that dreaming of a New Deal coalition thru the Democratic Party will not do, nor can it be achieved. We must think and act resolutely in an independent direction. That means supporting and initiating independent candidates: working class, Black, Chicano, Puerto Rican and the unemployed; senior citizens, youth and women candidates should be encouraged. Independent electoral formations are needed locally. This is a part of the preparations for the building of a national anti-monopoly peoples' party.

The achievement of this goal requires that the most advanced and socially conscious voters support the Hall-Tyner ticket.

It is time for people to vote for what they need and want and not what they hope will be given. The people who voted for Nixon thought they had won—but we all lost.

Vote Communist! A vote for Hall and myself is a vote for democratic and social advance, for peace, equality and security.

2.

I believe we can all agree that our Party has conducted the most successful, most effective election campaign in history. Our achievements are extraordinary; the "centerpiece" has become a political landmark.

As we weigh our achievements and make our evaluation we must always keep in mind that our advances take place against a most powerful foe which concentrates its political and ideological guns, its organs of harassment, against our Party. No other party or organization faces the opposition we do.

In spite of this, we have overcome enormous obstacles. Many of the forces who have worked for ages to isolate us are themselves becoming isolated.

We have taken a historic step in creating a new political and ideological framework for tens of millions of our people. From now on they will view and weigh all developments within this new framework.

Tens of millions now see the Communist Party differently. We have a new status in the political spectrum. In their eyes we are now a valid, legitimate, legal, political party with a viewpoint that cannot be ignored. That, by itself, is a historic achievement. . . .

Before taking up some of the more general questions, let's clear up some questions concerning the votes for Communist candidates. Some problems have cropped up mainly because some comrades, in their enthusiasm, which is understandable, permitted their wishful thinking to soar to fanciful heights, without guidance from their knowledge of the political and ideological realities. As a momentary flight from reality this is permissible. But only if it is momentary. Of course we always expect a bigger vote. But it should be clear that our influence and the new and bigger hearing we get from millions does not automatically and immediately transfer itself into votes. Most of the seeds we plant do not come up in the first crop, the first season. The seeds we plant are perennials and are deep-rooted. . . .

In the final two weeks of the campaign a deliberate, well orchestrated campaign was conducted to make Carter appear the lesser evil. The propaganda campaign drove home the idea that each individual's vote was the one that would decide between these evils. In that sense the opinion polls have become an instrumental and influential element in the two-evil electoral process.

The extent and strength of influence of the lesser-evil approach on the Left and among more progressive voters is clear from the differences between the votes for the national Communist ticket and the votes for Communist candidates on the state and local levels. This has been a clear pattern in all of the elections for some time. The concept of "not wasting my vote" has a strong pull on the electorate. We have not yet replaced this with an acceptance and understanding of the significance of a protest vote. People who are with us, who support us, who actively campaigned for us, and even a few people in the Party did not vote for the Communist candidates. . . .

If we examine our vote within these political realities, we will be able to see the tremendous advances we have made. In general, we more than doubled our vote as compared to 1972. For ordinary politicians the only important factor is the number of votes they get. We must not make the mistake of measuring our electoral achievements the same way. Our most important achievements are political and ideological. Votes are important, but more important are the political and ideological advances.

There is no doubt that we are building a Communist constituency. We have reached the stage in this process where we must now take up seriously the task of electing Communists to office in city and state elections. This goal is within our reach in a number of cities.

Now some thoughts on the 1976 elections in general. . . .

Carter's shift in emphasis during the last two weeks of the campaign toward more promises on jobs, inflation, help to the elderly and aid to the urban centers made the lesser evil seem more real. The Carter people even picked up the slogan, "elect a worker to the White House," and the phrase, "the permanently unemployed."

Our campaign stressed that both Ford and Carter were candidates of Big Business. This was and is correct. As Carter's policies and programs unfold, this truth will dawn on millions. Now Ford is out and Carter is president, and we must now direct our attention to this new reality. This calls for a shift in tactical emphasis. . . .

We have to approach and influence people—the large section of the working class, the Black community, the Chicano and Puerto Rican communities—who voted for Carter in the hope that "he is different," that he will "respond," that he can be "influenced." We have to approach these sections of the voters with the understanding that they hope Carter can be influenced. And Carter's promises, no matter how vague, are the key to moving these people into struggle. No matter what Carter and the people around him or the George Meanys believe, and no matter whether people had illusions or not, the working class, the Black, Puerto Rican and Chicano people who in large numbers voted for Carter are now in a position of new political leverage, if they are organized to demand action on the promises.

The same applies to our approach to the people who did not vote, which is again a large section of the working class, the Black, Puerto Rican and Chicano communities, plus a larger section of the 18-30 age bracket. Our approach must be: "We understand your decision not to vote, but Carter is now the president, so that is where the pressure must now be directed. Now is the time to demand affirmative action. Boycotting the elections is one thing; abstaining from struggle is capitulation."

In fact, because of the nature of the Party's campaign . . . we must start from the premise that struggles and movements of the people will, to a large extent, determine what the Carter Administration and the Congress will do. We must not start with some preconceived notions and get frozen into being observers. . . .

Now some thoughts on the objective situation. . . .

In general, the Carter Administration will, of course, pursue an overall foreign policy of support for the U.S. banks and industrial corporations in their drive for profits in foreign lands. There will be some changes in tactics. I believe it is a fair assumption that at least the intent of the Carter Administration is outlined in Trilateral Commission reports. At the very center of that concept is aggressive use of the coordinated economic power of the industrialized imperialist nations, directed against the less industrialized and less developed countries, but in the first place against the socialist countries.

George Ball, a Wall Street biggie who is one of Carter's closest advisers, formulated this concept clearly: "We should not continue to . . . improve their industrial competence, or supply capital to develop their natural resources, unless they stop exploiting situations of local conflict, or, in their jargon, stop assisting wars of national liberation."

So it is clear, beside the basic irreconcilable contradiction between the two systems, one of the main roots of the anti-Sovietism of the U.S. is the Soviet Union's support of the national liberation movements. But this reality will continue. The basic contradiction will not disappear. And the Soviet Union will continue giving support to the national liberation movements. That is the reality the Carter Administration will have to adjust to.

Giving up support of the national liberation movements was the basic concession the Chinese leadership under Mao made to U.S. imperialism. This was clear in Angola and Chile. The bone in the throat of imperialism is that the other socialist countries have not followed in Mao's footsteps. The concept projected by the Trilateral Commission is to use the combined economic might of the imperialist countries as a carrot and a club. . . .

The most meaningful element on the world scene is that in spite of some setbacks and difficulties, the world revolutionary process is alive and well. It is one thing to deal with the world in books and campaign speeches, but in real life the Carter Administration will have to deal with the real world balance of forces.

In Africa, the Kissinger-imperialist ploys and timetables for retreat and the nature of the proposed interim governments in Rhodesia are not acceptable to the peoples and countries of Africa. The governments and movements of national liberation have their own timetable.

In the Middle East, the year of divisions and diversions brought on by the fighting in Lebanon seems to be coming to an end and with it the "breathing spell" it has provided for the forces of oil imperialism.

It has been a year of serious difficulties for the progressive movements in Chile, Brazil, Argentina, Uruguay and for the anti-imperialist movements in most of the countries of South America. Political mass murder has become the main weapon of reaction. But as elsewhere, there are growing new united movements that are laying the basis for a new people's offensive. The world-wide movements are forcing the fascist military junta to release some of the political prisoners in Chile.

The socialist countries are continuing on the path of stable growth. It is more realistic to base policies on the concept of the return of the glacial age than to think that economic pressures are going in any way to change the course of world socialism.

Many of the Carter foreign policy insiders are all spaced out about using the economic and ideological carrot. . . .

How to deal with these new hard world realities has brought to the surface a new split in the ranks of monopoly capital. The split surfaced with the reports of two separate groups, representing two opposite viewpoints on most questions—on detente, the arms race and trade.

The Pentagon military confrontation line was presented by a hastily called together outfit called the "Committee on the Present Danger." Most of the ultra-Right, cold war elements of monopoly capital are represented in this grouping.

The opposite point of view was presented by the U.S. United Nations Association. They take a more realistic position. This split could become a most significant factor in determining the course of the Carter Administration in foreign policy affairs. It is clear, the report of the U.S. United Nations Association provides powerful material for movements and actions in support of detente, for cuts in the military budget, including the drive for signatures on the new Stockholm Appeal. . . .

We must not start with any concept that foreign policy matters are frozen. We must always keep in mind that there is a gap between the designs and intentions of imperialism and what is realistically possible. And further, we can influence events to even widen that gap. The forces that moved the Nixon and Ford Administrations toward detente have become stronger.

Because of Ford's vetoes, and the campaigns of the Democratic candidates and the mass media, there are millions who believe that the economic crisis, the inflation and unemployment are the direct result of Ford's policies. Of course, this is one of the purposes of the two-party system: for the "outs" to divert the fire from the system of capitalism to the "ins." . . . The most fundamental factor influencing economic developments [however] is the ongoing process of deterioration and decay resulting in ever new levels of the general crisis. Carter will inherit a capitalism in crisis.

The economic booms are not what they used to be because capitalism has been depleting the traditional resources and reserves it could draw on. All past booms were fueled by some extraordinary new openings, including wars of aggression. But as it is with families, so it is with the capitalist structure, there is a basic flaw in all credit cards. There is always a date when you have to pay up. And as so many are finding out, if you don't pay, the credit flow stops. . . .

The extraordinary technological revolution of the last 25 years, including the production of automated equipment, has reached a point where it is not a new source for extraordinary expansion, thereby affecting capital expenditures and higher levels of unemployment. Without some extraordinary new avenues of expansion there is no way U.S. capitalism can fully use its present industrial production capacity, resulting in a sluggish building of new capacity. There are no extraordinary new openings on the world scene on the basis of superprofits. But with all of these new problems, monopoly capital has not given up on its drive for extraordinary profits. That sharpens the class contradiction.

This is the backdrop for the campaign of austerity for the people. On this both Ford and Carter agreed. This is also one of the ideas in the report of the Trilateral Commission. They are convinced this is one source that has not been depleted.

From the above, a number of conclusions follow:

1. The "pauses," the "lulls," the high unemployment, the inflation, are now features of economic booms.

2. It explains why it was that the economic issues became the main focal point of the presidential elections.

3. It is clear that the economic questions will remain on center stage for this period of time.

4. The economic issues will provide the key link in the struggles and pressures on the Carter Administration.

In a more extraordinary sense we face a new period, a new set of circumstances. The economic developments cast a new shadow over all questions.

The term "permanently unemployed" has a sharp, racist meaning. The home of the permanently unemployed is in the inner cities. To Black youth, to millions of Puerto Rican and Chicano youth, it means "dead-end." It is the label on the "excess baggage generation." . . .

We should be the only people in the U.S. who are not surprised at the economic developments of the past year, because we outlined their causes 19 months ago. While all the editorials and economic forecasters were talking about and forecasting big booms, we stated in our 21st convention in June 1975: "The present economic crisis has greatly aggravated all problems. When it abates it is going to leave behind it serious economic problems, including a higher level of unemployment. The standard of living will continue to decline; inflation is already taking on a new head of steam, and taxes and rents will continue upward. The present economic crisis is not over, but there are already factors building up that will lead to a new cyclical crisis. In a sense, at this stage of capitalist development the booms of the economic cycles will be 'boom-lets' and the busts will be more continuous. For capitalism, there are no periods of economic stabilization left. That is one of the new features of the new stage of the general crisis." (*The Crisis of U.S. Capitalism and the Fight-Back,* International Publishers, New York, 1975).

Each moment presents its own challenges. This moment is no exception. We cannot foresee all of the twists and turns, but the outlines are clear:

1. More than ever the responsibility of initiating struggles will fall on our shoulders.

2. More than ever the issues the people will respond to are the issues that are related to the crisis of everyday living, which start with the economic problems, but flow into all facets of life.

3. In addition to formulating programs and demands, the Party and people's organizations will have to become more involved with the concrete problems of the people, to serve the needs of individuals and/or specific groups.

There is one more area of mass work that we must take a new, hard look at. For a long time we have been talking about mass breakaways from the two-party system and the need to build a broad, meaningful alternative to the two old parties. Well, in its own way, such a shift is taking place now. Masses are breaking away by dropping out. We must give careful consideration to a number of developments.

There is an ongoing shift to the Left; the process of radicalization continues. We must consider the 80 per cent who did not participate in the primaries of the two old parties, and the 50 per cent of the eligible voters who did not vote on November 2. By and large they are the alienated, the disgusted, those turned off by the nature and role of the two parties. The *CBS–New York Times* poll indicated that 56 per cent of them are turned off by the two parties. I think the poll is correct. They are turned off by the two parties of capitalism, but they are not necessarily turned off by capitalism at this stage.

We have to weigh the close to one million McCarthy votes; votes he got without any real organization, or a clear, meaningful program of any kind. In fact, on many questions he was fuzzy and on some questions he had very wrong positions.

We have to weigh the meeting in Cincinnati of Black independents. This was a serious effort, a serious initiative to build a third party.

We have to weigh the experiences of CIPA (Committee for Independent Political Action) in the New York elections.

We have to weigh the votes for Amadeo Richardson, Herbert Aptheker and for the Communist candidates in Illinois, in Massachusetts, Rhode Island and all the other Communist candidates. The Communist candidates for state and city offices everywhere are getting a very substantial vote.

We have to evaluate the numerous newspaper and magazine articles, including in the *Amsterdam News,* which have advanced the concept of a new party. They are reflecting a growing support for political independence.

We have to evaluate the millions who voted for Carter with tongue-in-cheek; they are not wed to the Democratic Party. Many of them voted for Carter because there was no mass alternative. We have to assess the support the idea for a new, mass people's party received whenever it was raised in the campaign. The idea of a new, mass people's party is in the minds of millions. The time has come when we must stop just talking about it and take concrete steps. I am convinced there are forces who are ready and who expect us to take some initiatives in this direction. . . .

The biggest danger is that we will continue in our old way, as if the campaign had not taken place. The second danger is that we will assess the results, the effects of the campaign, based on the number of votes we received and make our plans accordingly. We can very easily dissipate what we gained in the last six months.

We must shift gears to see our Party as millions see us. They view the Party with great respect, as the most meaningful, serious and most viable force on the Left. We are not seen as "just one of the many groups on the Left–radical spectrum." For example, we are the only Left organization that is able to organize successful mass meetings. This in itself gives the Party a different image. During the elections all the other groups on the Left could do was to attend our meetings and they did. . . .

Comrade Tyner discussed at a Political Bureau meeting that the Party is in a period of transition, transition to becoming a mass party. That is absolutely true. The new challenges we face are related to this transition.

One of the first challenges the election campaign confronts us with is to continue to fight to speak to millions. We simply must not retreat into the old cocoons of isolation. . . .

The election campaign forces us to think through a number of questions. One of these is what I call political or ideological "stonewall-ing"—avoiding a discussion behind pat phrases and clichés. As the old saying goes, "It is not enough to be right." You can be right by stonewalling. But then people will not listen to what you say or read what you write. We must put an end to writing and talking for history, and put our emphasis on talking and writing in order to influence people. The only writing or talking that history will take note of is the kind that influences and moves people to make history. To recite facts and figures is not enough; it does not convince. It is necessary to argue and debate, to move people with logic from one point to another. To convince people you must be in the ballpark of their experience.

A good example of this is our best piece of campaign literature, the platform. This piece got the best reception. Yet, had we given it more thought, we would not have made "80 per cent reduction of the military budget" the first point of the platform. Why not? Because it is a point that raises some wrong questions in people's minds. Many people, when they see this, think, "could it possibly be that the Communists want to weaken the U.S. so it will be easy picking for the Soviet Union?" The first point of the program should have been on the economic questions, "putting our best foot forward." And the plank on the military budget should have included the concept of multilateral or bilateral reduction of arms. We don't propose that the U.S. unilaterally reduce armaments; it can be done through agreement of the U.S. and the Soviet Union. This is the only realistic approach. Why was it not put this way in the platform? We were not in the ballpark of the people's experience.

Another example—the charge that we are agents of a foreign power, or spies. That big lie has lost most of its effectiveness. Except for the ultra-Right and some people working in the mass media, we rarely hear this. But we face a leftover of that slander in the question: Is the CPUSA in any way dominated or influenced by the Communist Party of the Soviet Union? Of course, we answer by saying that we are not. But that is not enough. We have to reject the whole concept by adding: "We are not dominated and there are no parties who are trying to dominate us and we would reject such a thing as a matter of principle."

In answer to the charge of "Soviet aggression" we have to say, "The Russians have not come and they are not coming." Therefore our foreign policy has for fifty years been based on a fraud that has cost the taxpayer some two trillion dollars. There is no Soviet aggression because social-ism, by eliminating private profits, removes the motivation that leads to a policy of aggression. To avoid this explanation is stonewalling. We must also compare the two systems and explain why the U.S. does have an aggressive foreign policy. Much still has to be done not only in rejecting the charge, but in explaining why it is false. . . .

We have to explain that we are a force for democracy, that we are for the rule of the majority, that we would retain and adopt many features of this system. For example, there is an interesting reaction when you tell an audience that it was no accident that the Bill of Rights was not originally a part of the U.S. Constitution, but that it was adopted because the people would not accept the Constitution without it. The Bill of Rights is a part of the history and experience of the people, and has a very important revolutionary essence. The people would not accept a socialist constitution without a Bill of Rights. . . .

The same is true of our proposal for a new labor charter, a new basic labor law. There is a good response to it. It brings together a number of issues: the six hour day with the stipulation of no cut in pay; how to cut into unemployment, especially among the permanently unemployed sector; doing away with pay differentials because of region, age, sex or race. There is powerful support for this idea. We must find ways of transferring this into a movement for specific laws.

After this election campaign, even our weaknesses are not of the same kind as before. Our achievements and our weaknesses are related to the fact that our Party is in a period of transition; they are related to our becoming a mass Party in influence and size. We must find the solutions to our weaknesses within a forward thrust, not a return to the old days. . . .

We have planted some very important seeds, perennials with deep roots. Now we must reap the first harvest.

☐ ———————————————————————————— ☐

POSTSCRIPT

THE LOGIC OF NOBLE LIVES

[*The great ideals of communism have drawn thousands of intellectual giants from all fields into the ranks of the revolutionary working-class parties throughout the world. The sixty-year history of the Communist Party, USA is laced with such achievements as well. Two outstanding examples are Theodore Dreiser and W.E.B. Du Bois.*

Theodore Dreiser (1871–1945), great humanist and writer of "social daring," in a letter to W.Z. Foster, applied for Party membership in July, 1945. Several of Dreiser's novels are today literary classics.

On October 1, 1961, Dr. W.E.B. Du Bois (1868–1963), the father of the modern Black liberation movement, a pioneer organizer and inspirer of the independence struggles of the African peoples against colonialism, and an honored world figure in the cause of peace and friendship between the nations, applied for membership in the Communist Party, USA. A titan of our times, Du Bois' massive life-work in the social sciences and literature is an intellectual and cultural treasure for all humanity.]

Theodore Dreiser,
by Hugo Gellert

These historic years have deepened my conviction that widespread membership in the Communist movements will greatly strengthen the American people, together with the anti-fascist forces throughout the world, in completely stamping out fascism and achieving new heights of world democracy, economic progress and free culture. Belief in the greatness and dignity of man has been the guiding principle of my life and work. The logic of my life and work leads me therefore to apply for membership in the Communist Party.

Theodore Dreiser, July 1945

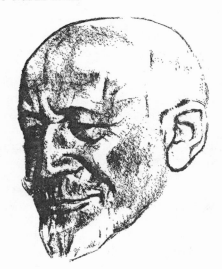

W.E.B. Du Bois,
by Hugo Gellert

To Gus Hall,
Communist Party of the U.S.A.
New York, New York.

On this first day of October, 1961, I am applying for admission to membership in the Communist Party of the United States. I have been long and slow in coming to this conclusion, but at last my mind is settled.

In college I heard the name of Karl Marx, but read none of his works, nor heard them explained. At the University of Berlin, I heard much of those thinkers who had definitively answered the theories of Marx, but again we did not study what Marx himself had said. Nevertheless, I attended meetings of the Socialist Party and considered myself a Socialist.

On my return to America, I taught and studied for sixteen years. I explored the theory of Socialism and studied the organized social life of American Negroes; but still I neither read or heard much of Marxism. Then I came to New York as an official of the new NAACP and editor of *The Crisis* Magazine. The NAACP was capitalist orientated and expected support from rich philanthropists.

But it had a strong Socialist element in its leadership in persons like Mary Ovington, William English Walling and Charles Edward Russell. Following their advice, I joined the Socialist Party in 1911. I knew then nothing of practical socialist politics and in the campaign of 1912, I found myself unwilling to vote the Socialist ticket, but advised Negroes to vote for Wilson. This was contrary to Socialist Party rules and consequently I resigned from the Socialist Party.

For the next twenty years I tried to develop a political way of life for myself and my people. I attacked the Democrats and Republicans for monopoly and disfranchisement of Negroes; I attacked the Socialists for trying to segregate Southern Negro members; I praised the racial attitudes of the Communists, but opposed their tactics in the case of the Scottsboro boys and their advocacy of a Negro state. At the same time I began to study Karl Marx and the Communists; I read *Das Kapital* and other Communist literature; I hailed the Russian Revolution of 1917, but was puzzled at the contradictory news from Russia.

Finally in 1926, I began a new effort: I visited Communist lands. I went to the Soviet Union in 1926, 1936, 1949 and 1959; I saw the nation develop. I visited East Germany, Czechoslovakia and Poland. I spent ten weeks in China, traveling all over the land. Then, this summer, I rested a month in Rumania.

I was early convinced that Socialism was an excellent way of life, but I thought it might be reached by various methods. For Russia I was convinced she had chosen the only way open to her at the time. I saw Scandinavia choosing a different method, half-way between Socialism and Capitalism. In the United States I saw Consumers Cooperation as a path from Capitalism to Socialism, while England, France and Germany developed in the same direction in their own way. After the depression and the Second World War, I was disillusioned. The Progressive movement in the United States failed. The Cold War started. Capitalism called Communism a crime.

Today I have reached a firm conclusion:

Capitalism cannot reform itself; it is doomed to self-destruction. No universal selfishness can bring social good to all.

Communism—the effort to give all men what they need and to ask of each the best they can contribute—this is the only way of human life. It is a difficult and hard end to reach—it has and will make mistakes, but today it marches triumphantly on in education and science, in home and food, with increased freedom of thought and deliverance from dogma. In the end Communism will triumph. I want to help to bring that day.

The path of the American Communist Party is clear: It will provide the United States with a real Third Party and thus restore democracy to this land. It will call for:

1. Public ownership of natural resources and of all capital.
2. Public control of transportation and communications.

3. Abolition of poverty and limitation of personal income.
4. No exploitation of labor.
5. Social medicine, with hospitalization and care of the old.
6. Free education for all.
7. Training for jobs and jobs for all.
8. Discipline for growth and reform.
9. Freedom under law.
10. No dogmatic religion.

These aims are not crimes. They are practiced increasingly over the world. No nation can call itself free which does not allow its citizens to work for these ends.

W. E. B. Du Bois

Dear Dr. Du Bois:

In reply to your letter of October 1st in which you made application for membership in the Communist Party of the United States allow me to relate the following:

I read it before our National Board on October 13th, where it was greeted with the highest enthusiasm and responded to with many heartfelt testimonials to the titanic labors which you have performed over a glorious span of 60 years of dedicated services and leadership in the cause of human progress, peace, science and culture.

Already in 1906 in your historic *Address to the Country of the Niagara Movement,* you had perceived the main line of development of our century, and wrote these prophetic words:

"The morning breaks over the hills. Courage, brothers! The battle for humanity is not lost or losing. The Slav is rising in his might, the yellow minions are testing liberty, the black Africans are writhing toward the light, and everywhere the laborer is opening the gates of Opportunity and Peace."

And so it has come, and is coming to pass. And knowledgeable people everywhere are mindful of the fact that your selfless labors and mighty works have been a powerful contribution to the dawn of our new epoch, the epoch of the final triumph of man over all manner of oppression, discrimination and exploitation.

You (the first Negro to receive the Doctor of Philosophy degree from Harvard University, in 1895) are the acknowledged Dean of American letters and most eminent living American scholar.

As editor, sociologist, historian, novelist, poet, publicist, lecturer, and organizer, you have made enduring contributions. Your life is a monumental example of achievement for all Americans.

For 50 years you have been a tireless champion of the national liberation of the African peoples and new Africa's wise counselor and "elder statesman."

For more than 60 years you have been the foremost philosopher, theoretician and practical organizer of the glorious Negro people's freedom struggle.

You have authored numerous books, each of which is a weapon against colonialism, racism, and imperialism, and for the victory of the cause of peace, freedom and the brotherhood of peoples.

You have raised your voice powerfully and incessantly against war machinations, for world peace and disarmament, for friendship with the socialist countries and co-existence between the two world social systems.

Your act of joining the Communist Party at this time not only expresses that recognition of the new world reality, of the great turn of the people of the world toward socialism for the solution of mankind's need for peace, brotherhood and well-being, but it constitutes an invitation and a challenge to men and women of science and culture, to creative thinkers of all countries, to the Negro masses and their outstanding leaders both here and abroad, to avail themselves of the social science of Marxism-Leninism and the fraternity of the Communist Parties to give new wings to their cause and their works.

You have chosen to join our Party precisely at the time when with brazen effrontery to the trends of the times, the most backward ultra-reactionary forces in our country's national life have temporarily dragooned the Supreme Court's majority into upholding the most flagrantly un-Constitutional thought-control laws—the McCarran Act and Smith Act, designed to muzzle free speech, ban freedom of association, persecute Communists and suppress our Party.

This is symbolic of the personal courage and heroic exercise of social responsibility which have characterized your service and leadership to the people's cause throughout your long life.

In joining the Communist Party, you have made that association which was clearly indicated by the very logic of your life.

Dear Dr. Du Bois, welcome into the membership of our Party! The title of Party Member is an honorable and worthy title worn with pride by the most dedicated and farseeing, the best sons and daughters of the workers and peoples of all lands in the first ranks of struggle for mankind's happy future.

With comradely greetings,
Gus Hall

APPENDIX

CONVENTIONS OF THE COMMUNIST PARTY, U.S.A.

[*This list gives the date and—in parenthesis—the number of each convention. The regular conventions of the Party were numbered only after the formation of the Workers Party in December 1921, although exceptions were made later for special conventions.*]

Communist Labor Party of America—August 31, 1919, Chicago
Communist Party of America—September 1, 1919, Chicago
United Communist Party of America—May 15, 1920, Bridgman, Mich.
Communist Party of America—July 1920, New York
United Communist Party of America—January 1921, Kingston, N.Y.
Communist Party of America—February 1921, Brooklyn, N.Y.
Communist Party of America (unified)—May 15, 1921, Woodstock, N.Y.
American Labor Alliance—July 1921, New York
Workers Party of America—December 24, 1921, New York (First)
Communist Party of America—August 17, 1922, Bridgman, Mich.
Workers Party of America—December 24, 1922, New York (Second)
Communist Party-Workers Party (merger)—April 7, 1923, New York
Workers Party of America—December 30, 1923, Chicago (Third)
Workers Party of America—July 10, 1924, Chicago (Nominating)
Workers (Communist) Party of America—August 21, 1925, Chicago (Fourth)
Workers (Communist) Party of America—August 31, 1927, New York (Fifth)
Workers (Communist) Party of America—May 25, 1928, New York (Nominating)
Workers (Communist) Party of America—March 1, 1929, New York (Sixth)
Communist Party of the U.S.A.—June 20, 1930, New York (Seventh)
Communist Party of the U.S.A.—May 29, 1932, Chicago (Nominating)
Communist Party of the U.S.A.—April 2, 1934, Cleveland (Eighth)
Communist Party of the U.S.A.—June 24, 1936, New York (Ninth)
Communist Party of the U.S.A.—May 27, 1938, New York (Tenth)

Communist Party of the U.S.A.—May 30, 1940, New York (Eleventh)
Communist Party of the U.S.A.—November 16, 1940, New York (Special)
Communist Political Association—May 20, 1944, New York (Twelfth)
Communist Party of the U.S.A.—July 26, 1945, New York (Thirteenth)
Communist Party of the U.S.A.—August 2, 1948, New York (Fourteenth)
Communist Party of the U.S.A.—December 28, 1950, New York (Fifteenth)
Communist Party of the U.S.A.—February 9, 1957, New York (Sixteenth)
Communist Party of the U.S.A.—December 10, 1959, New York (Seventeenth)
Communist Party of the U.S.A.—June 22, 1966, New York (Eighteenth)
Communist Party of the U.S.A.—July 4, 1968, New York (Nominating)
Communist Party of the U.S.A.—April 30, 1969, New York (Nineteenth)
Communist Party of the U.S.A.—February 18, 1972, New York (Twentieth)
Communist Party of the U.S.A.—June 27, 1975, Chicago (Twenty-First)
Communist Party, U.S.A.—August 22, 1979, Detroit (Twenty-Second)

NOTES

1. THE FIRST DECADE

1. An exposition on Trotskyism as a counter-revolutionary sect and its role from early days to the present, appears in a two-part article, "Trotskyism: 'Left-Wing' Voice of Reaction" by Hyman Lumer, *Political Affairs*, June and July, 1972.
2. Charles E. Ruthenberg in *The Liberator*, Feb. 1923.
3. Anthony Bimba, *History of the American Working Class*, p. 318.
4. *Labor Herald*, June 1923.
5. *Proceedings of the Third National Convention, Workers Party*, Dec. 1923, pp. 15–17.
6. The Conference for Progressive Political Action (CPPA) was organized by a number of conservative trade union leaders in 1922. At its height it represented some four million workers and farmers. It supported La Follette in 1924. Its strongest base was among the Railroad Brotherhoods.
7. Proceedings of the Second Convention, Workers Party, 1922, p. 19, *The Labor Herald*, Aug. 1923.
8. Nathan Fine, *Labor and Farmer Parties in the United States 1829–1928*, Rand School of Social Science, 1928.
9. *American Labor Year Book*, 1923–24, p. 158.
10. *Proceedings of the Third National Convention, Workers Party*, p. 21.
11. *The Liberator*, July 1924.
12. Later studies show that the Party was on the ballot in 14 states and received 38,080 votes.
13. Renaldo Cappellini was President of District 1, UMWA
14. Gertrude Haessler, who was editor of the Workers Correspondence columns of the *Daily Worker*, advised editors of shop papers not to publish "merely a shop newspaper with a purely trade union orientation." At the same time she cautioned against becoming abstract politically, "divorced from shop conditions." (*Shop Paper Manual*, Issued by Central Committee, CPUSA, 1930.)

2. THE GREAT DEPRESSION

1. *Organized Labor & the Black Worker, 1619–1973* by Philip S. Foner, N.Y., 1976, p. 188.
2. Cited in *A Documentary History of the Negro People in the United States*, Vol. III, p. 120, edited by Herbert Aptheker, Citadel Press, 1974.
3. By Act of Congress in 1924, Adjusted Service Certificates were issued to veterans of World War I averaging about $1,000 each. These certificates were to be redeemed by

the government at their face value in 1945. This came to be known as the Bonus. In 1932 the demand was for immediate full payment of the promised amount.

4. This is evidently a reference to the trial of Ned Cobb and other sharecroppers growing out of a confrontation with white sheriff's deputies in Tallapoosa County, Alabama, December 1932. Cobb was sentenced to 12 years in prison which he served in full.

3. CLASS STRUGGLE AND THE NEW DEAL

1. A brief account of the National Negro Congress is contained in items by its initiators, in *A Documentary History of the Negro People in the United States,* edited by Herbert Aptheker, with a Preface by William L. Patterson. (Citadel Press, Secaucus, N.J., 1974, Vol. III, pp. 211-235).
2. *The Working Woman* was the official organ of the Women's Department, CPUSA.
3. In 1953 Joseph P. Ryan was ousted as president of the International Longshoremen's Association and indicted for stealing union funds which he had earmarked "to fight Communism."
4. A valuable biography of Harold M. Ware was published in 1978 by the American Institute for Marxist Studies: *Harold M. Ware (1890-1935), Agricultural Pioneer, U.S.A. and U.S.S.R.* by Lem Harris.
5. The Seventh World Congress of the Communist International was held in Moscow in August 1935. The main report was delivered by its General Secretary, Georgi Dimitrov. It called for the greatest international unity against new fascist offensives and military aggression. (*The United Front—The Struggle Against Fascism and War* by Georgi Dimitrov, International Publishers, 1938).

   Dimitrov and two of his Bulgarian co-workers were arrested by the nazis in March 1933, and charged with instigating the fire which destroyed the Reichstag. In an epic trial Dimitrov defended himself in the nazi court room in a manner which aroused worldwide admiration. He exposed the fire as a nazi frameup. The judges were compelled to free him and his co-workers.

4. MASS INDUSTRIES ARE ORGANIZED

1. *The Peril of Fascism* by A.B. Magil and Henry Stevens, International Publishers, 1938.
2. *The United Front—The Struggle Against Fascism and War* by Georgi Dimitrov, International Publishers, 1938.
3. *Peace and War—United States Foreign Policy, 1931-1941,* United States Government Printing Office, Washington, 1943.
4. *The Cold War and Its Origins—1917-1950* by D.F. Fleming, Volume I, Doubleday & Company, 1961, p. 80.
5. *The Great Steel Strike and Its Lessons* by William Z. Foster, B.W. Huebsch, 1920.
6. *Steel and Metal Workers—It Takes a Fight to Win!* by Gus Hall, New Outlook Publishers, 1972.
7. Foster, *Op. cit.,* p. 209.
8. *Ibid.*
9. An important aspect of the victory in organizing steel was the higher percentage increase in wages given to those at the bottom of the wage scale. This particularly benefited Black and foreign-born workers. At the same time the Communist Party "exercised its influence to advance Blacks into positions of local union leadership." See: Edward Greer *"Racial Employment Discrimination in the Gary Works, 1906-1974,"* Gerald Erickson and Harold L. Schwartz (Eds.). *Social Class in the United States: Studies in Marxism,* Vol. 2, Marxist Educational Press (Minneapolis, 1977).
10. Issued respectively in August and October 1936 by Workers Library Publishers.

11. Travis was in charge of the Flint, Michigan, organizing campaign of the United Auto Workers Union and worked closely with Mortimer.
12. Federal unions were affiliated directly to the American Federation of Labor (AFL) in contrast to locals affiliated to international unions of the AFL.

5. THE GREAT ANTI-FASCIST WAR

1. The Voorhis Act (sponsored by Rep. Jerry Voorhis, a so-called liberal) was aimed at the CPUSA's affiliation with the Communist International (CI). Gus Hall comments: "The CPUSA disaffiliated from the CI some time before the International was discontinued. This 'disaffiliation' was not only because of anti-Communist laws. It was motivated by the deep-seated opportunistic Browder revisionist trends that had already set in. . . ." (*Imperialism Today,* International Publishers, 1972, pp. 321-22.) Despite moments of error, the Party has fought for and maintained a consistent policy of international working-class solidarity throughout the years.
2. An illuminating first-hand account of the roles of Roosevelt and Churchill in regard to the question of the Second Front can be found in Ivan Maisky, *Memoirs of a Soviet Ambassador,* Hutchinson, London, 1967, pp. 278-89.
3. *The Communist,* October 1939.
4. It is well known that the tide of war in Europe turned with the crushing defeat of the nazis at Stalingrad. The German commander, Marshal Von Paulus, surrendered there on January 31, 1943.

   But, as early as February 1942, a few months after the United States officially entered the war, the historic role of the Red Army was recognized in words of the highest praise by the ultra-conservative General Douglas MacArthur. An Associated Press dispatch on February 23, 1942, reported this statement by Gen. MacArthur: "The world situation at the present time indicates that the hopes of civilization rest upon the worthy banners of the courageous Russian Army. During my lifetime I have participated in a number of wars and have witnessed others, as well as studying in great detail the campaigns of outstanding leaders of the past. In none of these have I observed such effective resistance to the heaviest blows of a hitherto undefeated enemy, followed by a smashing counteroffensive which is driving that enemy back into his own land. The scale and grandeur of this effort marks it as the greatest military achievement of all time."
5. Earl Browder, the Party's General Secretary, was at this time in Atlanta Penitentiary following a conviction on a technical passport violation. (Harry Gannes, foreign affairs editor of the *Daily Worker,* and William Weiner, president of the International Workers Order, were among others indicted on similar charges. These prosecutions were evidently a retaliation by the government for the independent position taken by the Communists following the outbreak of World War II). Browder was pardoned by Roosevelt in 1942, a few months after the United States entered the war.
6. Following the abolition of slavery the 15th Amendment specifically guaranteed former slaves the right to vote. Subsequently the poll tax was devised as a principal instrument to deny freedmen the franchise. This was reinforced by widespread terror in which the Ku Klux Klan was a major instrument.

   The poll tax was finally abolished by Article XXIV of the Constitution, ratified on January 23, 1964.
7. On November 7, 1941, President Franklin Delano Roosevelt formally extended Lend-Lease aid to the Soviet Union.
8. After the death of New York City Councilman Peter V. Cacchione in November 1947, Si Gerson was named by the Party to fill the seat. However, the Tammany-controlled

Council refused by a split vote to seat him, despite the clear provisions of the City Charter.

Forced to run in a borough-wide race in 1948, Gerson received the endorsement of the American Labor Party and was therefore on the ballot on two lines—the CP and the ALP. He received about 150,000 votes, nearly 18,000 on the CP line and 132,00 on the ALP line. It was one of the biggest votes recorded for a Communist in the Party's history.

9. Hugh Quinn was an ultra-reactionary Queens Democratic Councilman who, in 1941, made an unsuccessful attempt to ban Cacchione from serving on the City Council.
10. Dorothy Cacchione is Pete Cacchione's widow.
11. See item p. 212.
12. Edouard Bernstein (1850-1932) was a German Social Democrat. After Engels' death in 1895 he became a revisionist of Marxism. Karl Legien (1861-1920), a Social-Democrat member of the Reichstag, opposed the German revolutionary uprising which overthrew the Kaiser in November 1918. A reactionary, class collaborationist labor leader, Samuel Gompers (1850-1924), was president of the American Federation of Labor (except in 1894), from its founding in 1886 until his death in 1924.
13. Some leaders were in the armed forces at this time.
14. In the South the liquidation of the Party extended even to the liquidation of the Communist Political Association.
15. The agreement reached at Teheran, Iran, in December 1943, among the Allied powers, represented by Roosevelt, Churchill and Stalin, was basically a military one. It established the date (June 6, 1944), place and strategy for the opening of the long-delayed second (western) front against the axis powers.

6. LABOR'S POSTWAR FIGHTBACK

1. It was not accidental that packinghouse workers pioneered in the struggle for Black and white unity. The 1918 organization drive was launched by Foster (who left to organize the steel campaign) and the strike was led by his associate, Jack Johnstone. They were leaders of the left and were later to make their contributions in the Communist Party.

   It was reported that the packing corporations aided by the police and the *Chicago Tribune* instigated the 1919 race riots. Jack Johnstone took the lead in organizing a rally of Black and white workers. A conservative observer wrote: "Black and white workers paraded through the Black belt on Sunday, July 6, and congregated in a playground near the yards.... 'It does me good ... to see such a checkerboard crowd,' said J.W. Johnstone of the SLC [Stockyards Labor Council] in welcoming the workers. 'You are standing shoulder to shoulder as men, regardless of whether your face is Black or white.'" (*Race Riot—Chicago in the Red Summer of 1919* by William M. Tuttle, Jr., Atheneum, 1974.)

2. Computed from data in U.S. Department of Commerce, *The National Income and Product Accounts of the United States, 1929-1965: Statistical Tables* (Washington, D.C.: U.S. Government Printing Office, n.d.), Tables 6.13, 6.1, 6.3.

3. During the 80th Congress (1947-1949) J. Parnell Thomas (R., N.J.) was chairman of the Un-American Committee. He was convicted of defrauding the government by padding his congressional payroll and sentenced to serve 6 to 18 months and fined $10,000. He was forced to resign his Congressional seat.

4. The noted military analyst P.M.S. Blackett says: "So, in truth, we conclude that the dropping of the atomic bombs was not so much the last military act of the Second World War, as the first act of the cold diplomatic war with Russia now in progress. The fact is however, that the realistic objectives in the field of *Macht-Politik,* so brilliantly achieved by the timing of the bomb, did not square with the advertised

objective of saving 'untold numbers' in the minds of many English and American people who knew, or suspected, some of the real facts." P.M.S. Blackett, *Military and Political Consequences of Atomic Energy* (London: Turnstile Press, 1948); cf. Herbert Aptheker, "Imperialism and the Bomb," *American Foreign Policy and the Cold War* (New Century Publishers, 1962).

5. D.F. Fleming, *The Cold War and its Origins 1917-1960,* Doubleday & Company, Inc., 1961.

6. Irving Potash was a founder of the Furriers Union. He was assaulted and jailed on numerous occasions for his militant leadership. As a member of the National Board of the CPUSA he was sentenced with the other Smith Act victims. Potash was highly respected internationally by Communist and trade union leaders.

   For a full account of gangster violence against the fur workers union and of the role of Irving Potash and Sam Burt in nailing the gangsters Lepke and Gurrah see Philip Foner, *The Fur and Leather Workers Union,* Nordan Press, Newark, N.J., 1950, Ch. 35-37.

7. Al Lannon was one of the thirteen Communist leaders convicted under the Smith Act in the Flynn Case in 1953. In sending him to prison, the government and the shipowners took their vengeance on a man who had dedicated his life to improving the conditions of maritime workers.

   In 1927 he was a member of the Sailor's Union of the Pacific. He then became a member of the International Seamans Union where the scrappy young sailor took the lead in bucking the do-nothing leadership. In the early thirties he helped form the left-wing Marine Workers Industrial Union.

   He was a leader in the maritime strikes of 1936 and 1937, and with the upsurge of the CIO he helped to form the militant National Maritime Union.

8. James Jackson was born in Richmond, Va., and spent his early years in activities in that state. He helped organize southern workers, and has made significant contributions to the study and understanding of the South.

   "In the spring of 1937 James Jackson and Columbus Alston, representing the CIO began to enroll tobacco workers in Richmond....

   "The pioneering efforts of the Richmond tobacco workers have had a profound effect upon Negroes in other industries." (*The Negro in Virginia,* by workers of the Writers' Program of the Works Projects Administration, State of Virginia, Hastings House Publishers, 1940.)

9. Theodore G. Bilbo was U.S. Senator from Mississippi from January 3, 1935 to August 23, 1947. A rabid white supremacist and lynchocrat, he gained notoriety as a fiery opponent of anti-lynching legislation and as proponent of deportation of millions of Blacks to Africa to maintain "racial purity."

10. Eugene "Bull" Connor, Birmingham Police Commissioner, was notorious for his extreme brutality in suppression of civil rights activities, especially for his use of police dogs.

11. A recent work on the 1948 elections noted that:

    "Communists were an important and influential part of the Progressive Party. That was so and there was no moral or ethical reason why it should not have been so. Communists should have the same rights of political participation as other Americans, and the fact that they did not during that dark age [of redbaiting, witch-hunting], should be a lasting source of shame, especially to those who called themselves liberals, yet contributed to their persecution." (Richard J. Walton, *Henry Wallace, Harry Truman and the Cold War,* Viking Press, 1976, p. 249.)

7. THE McCARTHY ERA

1. A United Press report from Tokyo of a Peking broadcast, February 22, 1953, acknowledged that US officers admitted the "set up of a cholera, yellow fever and typhus contamination belt in North Korea." Some of these officers later repudiated

their testimony. This is cited by Hershel D. Meyer in *The Last Illusion*. (Anvil-Atlas Publishers, 1954, p. 218.)

2. Henry Winston's speech was reported in the *Daily World*, June 21, 1978.
3. The US military was prepared again to use atomic weapons in Asia. This was made explicit by General MacArthur's reply to a question put to him at a Senate hearing:
"When MacArthur was pressing for the immediate bombing of China, Senator Wayne Morse asked him, 'Have you thought, General, what our casualty rate will be in Washington, D.C., in New York, or the other cities of the US if they put on atomic war, to say nothing of the American boys who are going to die in the air and sea?' MacArthur replied, 'All those risks, I repeat were inherent in the decision of the US to go into Korea.'" (*The New York Times*, May 6, 1951. Cited in Hershel D. Meyer, *The Last Illusion*, Anvil-Atlas Press, 1954.)
4. Upon a return from Europe in December 1953, Ernest T. Weir, Chairman of the National Steel Corporation, reported: "Europe generally sees no reason to fear Russian aggression now or in the near future." He found "a widely held opinion that the United States actually wanted a state of tension and fear to continue." [Footnote in original document.]
5. The Hon. George W. Crockett, Jr., was among a group of illustrious Black leaders who were prosecuted. He was later elected judge in the Recorder's Court of Detroit, Michigan.
6. Additional details on deportation of Asians are given in "A Brief History of US Asian Labor" by Karl G. Yoneda in *Political Affairs*, September 1976.
A chronic manifestation (not dealt with in the present excerpt) of "deportation terror" is the mass deportation of Chicano workers in the southwest—used as a means to disrupt organization drives and to promote sub-standard wages to the advantage of corporate agriculture.
7. William L. Patterson, in a foreword to the new (1971) edition of *We Charge Genocide*, declares it is "historically necessary . . . to return again to the UN" to consider the critical issue of genocidal practices against Blacks, Indian peoples, Chicanos and Asians. This significant document, presented to the international tribune in 1951, now includes in its demands the end of oppression of the Indian peoples and other minorities in the United States.
8. The reference is to the decision by the Supreme Court on May 17, 1954, in *Brown v. Board of Education* barring segregated public education. Characteristically, young Communists had always been active in fighting for this ruling—and remain active in seeking its implementation.

8. BLACK LIBERATION SPARKS THE SIXTIES

1. See *The New York City Teachers Union, 1916-1964* by Celia Zitron, Humanities Press, 1968.
2. *The Long Walk at San Francisco State* by Kay Boyle, Grove Press, 1970.
3. Ibid., pp. 51-52.
4. Weydemeyer (1818-1866), a German associate of Marx and Engels, emigrated to the United States in 1851 and was a pioneer American Communist. He served in the Civil War and was commissioned a brigadier general by President Lincoln. Sorge (1827-1906) emigrated in 1852 to the United States where he became the leader of the First International. (See also Karl Oberman, *Joseph Weydemeyer*, International Publishers, 1947.)
5. For a fuller discussion of the situation in eastern Europe in the latter half of the 1950s

see Herbert Aptheker, *The Truth About Hungary (Mainstream Publishers, 1957) and American Foreign Policy and the Cold War* (New Century, 1962). See also "Hungary in Travail" by Jessica Smith, in *New World Review,* December 1956, pp. 29–50.

6. *Declaration of the Twelve Communist and Workers Parties,* New Century Publishers, 1957.

7. After prolonged negotiations, and in an effort to alleviate the cold war, a Summit Meeting between President Dwight D. Eisenhower and Premier Nikita Khruschev was scheduled to take place in Paris on May 16, 1960. On May 1, a US espionage plane, a U2 piloted by Francis Gary Powers, flew deep into Soviet territory and was shot down. This US action created a serious crisis. Eisenhower refused to make an apology for the irresponsible action and the conference was not held.

Herbert Aptheker in *American Foreign Policy and the Cold War* (New Century Publishers, 1962), writes that "the United States boasts that it has been guilty of this vis-a-vis the USSR for at least 5 years—Representative Cannon of Missouri said it had been going on for fourteen years!—the victim of such boasts might very well view the procedure as highly provocative." (pp. 54-55)

8. "At the time of the Cuban crisis in October 1962, there were frequent references to the U.S. bases in Turkey with their Jupiter missiles, a part of the ring of bases that the U.S. has built around the Soviet Union." (*Labor Fact Book 16,* International Publishers, 1963).

9. VIETNAM AND THE PEACE UPSURGE

1. "Hard Hats and Hard Facts" by Gus Hall, New Outlook Publishers, New York, 1970.

2. International Association of Poets, Playwrights, Editors, Essayists, and Novelists.

3. Field secretary for the National Association for the Advancement of Colored People in Mississippi. He was murdered by racists on June 12, 1963.

4. Julian Bond is perhaps best known as a political activist in the State of Georgia.

5. The Big Six Demands of the National Steelworkers Rank-and-File for the 1971 wage contract were: 1) a substantive wage increase; 2) restoration of the cost of living escalator clause with no ceilings; 3) re-negotiation of the whole grievance procedure; 4) no change in work rules without approval of the union and workers involved; 5) additional job security; a six hour day, a five day week—30 hours of work at 40 hours pay; 6) reduction of the length of the contract from three to two years; if the present three year one is kept it should have an annual wage re-opener.

10. THE PARTY RECORDS NEW ADVANCES

1. *American Foreign Policy and the Cold War* by Herbert Aptheker, New Century Publishers, 1962. The author devotes a section to events in Hungary in 1956.

2. *Czechoslovakia at the Crossroads* by Gus Hall, New Outlook Publishers, 1968. This pamphlet is the product of an immediate reaction and decisive analysis of the crucial 1968 event which threatened a socialist state on Europe's western border.

3. See Bettina Aptheker, *The Morning Breaks* (New York, International Publishers, 1975) for an account of the Angela Davis case.

4. For an account of the formation of the Civil Rights Congress see William L. Patterson, *The Man Who Cried Genocide: An Autobiography* (New York, International Publishers, 1971), pp. 156–169.

5. "Amid America's prosperity, a depression is in progress. . . . The rate of joblessness among Black teenagers, climbing with little interruption through a quarter of a century, now is close to four in 10. . . . Official estimates of Black teenage unemployment, moreover, may seriously understate the situation. . . . It's widely agreed that so-called hidden unemployment—joblessness not picked up in surveys—is particularly prevalent among Black youths. The unemployment rate for Black teenagers is 'really

50%' or more, maintains Vernon E. Jordan, Jr., president of the National Urban League...." (Wall Street Journal, February 2, 1979).

6. For the C.P. position on Indian Liberation see: *Toward Peace, Freedom and Socialism.* Main Political Resolution, 21st National Convention, Communist Party, U.S.A., 1975, New Outlook Publishers, 1976, pp. 72-76.
7. *New York Times,* September 14, 1973.
8. Chile, *Facing the Blockade.*
9. *Pravda,* May 4, 1973.
10. *New York Times,* September 16, 1973.
11. *Washington Post,* March 28, 1972.
12. *New York Times,* September 14, 1973.
13. Women for Racial and Economic Equality was started in New York City in late 1974 as a local organization. It held its first convention as a national organization in September 1977 in Chicago.

INDEX

501

503

INDEX

I

Illinois 38, 44–46, 60, 141, 153–56, 187, 285, 286, 369, 406
Imada, Mary 385
Imperial Valley (California) 57, 87–91, 384–85
Independent Labor Party (Great Britain) 172
India 92, 193, 223, 295, 500
Indian Ocean 420
Indiana 149, 332
Indochina 223, 268, 274, 366–68, 429
Indonesia 223, 251, 420
Industrial Union Council, Greater N.Y. CIO 199
Industrial Workers of the World (IWW) 15, 34, 40
International Brigades 169
International Confederation of Free Trade Unions 240
International Conference of Negro Workers 57, 91–93
International Labor Defense (ILD) 72, 86–87, 87–91, 384–85, 427
International Ladies Garment Workers Union (ILGWU) 40–41, 98, 347
International Longshoremen's Association, AFL 114–15, 120
International Longshoremen's and Warehousemen's Union, (ILWU) 370, 379–80, 383, 431, 437
International Rubber Union 125
International Seamen's Union 114, 250, 497
International Workers Order (IWO) 55, 98, 110
Iowa 103, 126–31
Iran 238, 346, 420
Israel 365, 468–70
Italy 144, 166–71, 180, 184, 208, 225, 226, 273, 430
IUE (International Union of Electrical Workers) 239
Ivens, Joris 169

J

Jackson, Andrew 306
Jackson, Esther Cooper 254, 284
Jackson, George 431
Jackson, Harry 71
Jackson, James E. 99, 254, 267, 305, 329, 332, 408–16, 467, 497
Jackson, Jonathan 427
Jackson, Luther 245
Jackson, Judge Robert H. 295
Jacobs, Paul 359–62
Jamaica 57
Japan 144, 179–83, 225, 236–38, 250, 266, 275, 358
Japanese Workers Clubs 384–85
Japanese Labor Association 384
Jarama 170
Jarema, Stephen 211
Jefferson, Thomas 247, 283, 306
Jerome, V.J. 390
Johnson, Arnold 58
Johnson Beatrice 266

Johnson, Ed 367
Johnson, Hugh S. 181
Johnson, James 373–75
Johnson, Lyndon 363, 370
Johnson, Dr. Mordecai 254
Johnson, Tom 71
Johnston, James H. 245
Johnston, William H. 7
Johnstone, Jack 5, 147, 151, 496
Johnstown (Pa.) 153
Jones, Claudia 266, 287, 456, 465
Jordan, Fania Davis 427, 429
Jordan, Vernon E., Jr. 500
Jouhaux, Leon 136

K

Kansas City (Missouri) 84, 188
Kee, Salaria 170–71
Kehoe, Joseph 243
Kennan, George 229
Kennedy, John F. 309, 316, 356–58, 363
Kennedy, Joseph P. 142
Kennedy, Robert 264
Kent, Rockwell 390
Kentucky 54, 72, 465
Keynes, J.M. 351–52, 354
Khrushchev, Nikita 499
Killen, John O. 394
Kimoto, J. 384
King, Carol 290
King, Rev. Martin Luther, Jr. 317, 320–24, 364, 369–73, 418, 424–27
Kingston (N. Carolina) 285
Kissinger, Henry 477
Knowland, Senator William 367
Korea 223, 239, 263–67, 269, 271, 274, 283, 286, 288, 296, 299–301, 312, 318, 352, 490; Democratic Republic of 450
Krchmarek, Anton 404
Krumbein, Charles 6
Krumbein, Margaret 455
Krzycki, Leo 126, 155
Kuhn, Genne 401–3
Ku Klux Klan (KKK) 32, 83, 142, 162–64, 202, 285, 294, 473
Ky, Cao 375

L

Labor-Management Charter 220
Labor Research Association (LRA) 46, 103
Labor Youth League 266, 296, 465
Labor's Non-Partisan League (LNPL) 142, 143, 177
Laborers and Hodcarriers Union 399
La Follette, Robert M. 35, 36–39, 264, 278, 283
La Guardia, Fiorello 215
Lake Junalaska (N. Carolina) 298
Langer, Morris 241
Lanham, Henderson 286

512